CH00925673

Boston Studies in Philosophy, Religion and Public Life

Volume 9

Boston University Studies in Philosophy, Religion and Public Life is an interdisciplinary scholarly series which publishes seminal papers on topics of pressing and perennial interest at the intersection of philosophy, religion and public life. The series is especially interested in interdisciplinary work that illuminates questions of value, truth, reality and meaning, as well as topics in the relevant fields which have a particular intersection with public life (for example, philosophical and religious perspectives on contemporary issues in ethical and political philosophy). In addition, the series serves as a prominent forum for important academic work emerging within the specific sub-discipline of the philosophy of religion.

All books to be published in this Series will be fully peer-reviewed before final acceptance.

More information about this series at http://www.springer.com/series/8881

William R. Everdell

The Evangelical Counter-Enlightenment

From Ecstasy to Fundamentalism in Christianity, Judaism, and Islam in the 18th Century

Springer

William R. Everdell
History Teacher, Dean of Humanities
(emeritus) Saint Ann's School
Brooklyn, NY, USA

ISSN 2352-8206 ISSN 2352-8214 (electronic)
Boston Studies in Philosophy, Religion and Public Life
ISBN 978-3-030-69764-8 ISBN 978-3-030-69762-4 (eBook)
https://doi.org/10.1007/978-3-030-69762-4

This Springer imprint is published by the registered company Springer Nature Switzerland AG
The registered company address is: Gewerbestrasse 11, 6330 Cham, Switzerland

This book is for Barbara Everdell, the brilliantly empathetic 4th- and 5th-grade school administrator whom I worked with for 44 years, and who, I am lucky to say, still likes to hear me tell her what I'm doing. She has somehow gotten used to my contemplative scholarly silences, my intermittent absences from the present, and my extravagant concern about the thoughts and faiths and loves of people who died so long ago.

It is also for our four grandchildren: Will, Murphy, Lily, and Grace, who all write with verve but have yet to publish.

Preface

As a student in the 1960s, I was and have remained fascinated by the sudden rise of new convictions in Western culture, convictions then called "counter-cultural" that I have come, as a historian of culture, to understand in a larger sense, as "religious." This book began many years ago with one question: What is the best way to gain a humanist understanding of the startling similarity of convictions that Americans usually call "fundamentalist" in a host of fundamentally different religions, from the evangelical Protestant Christianity so common north and west of Jerusalem to the Salafist Islam (sometimes called "jihadist") that makes headlines east and south of it? I hope it will also show the results of having found so many more questions—questions that had at least to be approached, despite the well-known perennial disarray of so many proposed answers. Of these questions, in turn, the most important remained the question of what a religion ***is***.

It has seemed clear to me since I began that the best answers to all these questions would be historical, and not just because I'm a historian with a long-ago thesis comparing arch-reactionary Joseph de Maistre with his liberal contemporary Félicité de Lamennais, a historian who wrote his doctoral dissertation on arguments for Christianity in eighteenth-century France. The answers needed to be historical and even philosophical because they had to be based on the sort of rich knowledge of the extraordinary variety in human motivation and behavior that makes the historical record so particular and vivid. After many years of reading what the sciences have had to say about this disconcerting variety, and publishing two histories of ideas: one on republics ancient and modern, and another about early Modernism with chapters on Freud and Ramón y Cajal, I could find few helpful ways to approach these questions with Freud's psychology or Cajal's neurology, or any other science. Science aspires to universality—so far with reassuring success. A scientific "law" is a description of what "always" happens, anywhere, given certain preconditions, closely specifiable, of what *has* happened. That is why scientific laws relating to human behavior seem limited so far to measuring brain waves and locating neural regions with specific responses to very specific stimuli. Methods like psychoanalysis for linking conscious behavior to hard-to-define stimuli have so far proven to be unreliable. And efforts by neuroscientists since William James to demonstrate that we act before we think or feel have been frustrated.

After more than 40 years of teaching World History to high-school students, I have come to think that it is World History that provides what is most needed to evaluate human behavior—respect for its infinite possibility. When the net is cast wide enough, and a consistency in behavior is found across a multitude of cultures and subcultures, we are justified in identifying it as human. Whether or not we can account for it, we may call it, as the French sometimes do, a constant of the human spirit: not universally human but found somewhere in every human society.

This attenuated Enlightenment hope shaped this book, and I hope that readers will find it there. It begins and ends with a struggle to find answers to those general questions, but its armature is history, particularly biographies of remarkable and undeniably colorful contemporaries. They belong to many culture areas, including Arabia, Iraq, Eastern Europe, Western Europe, and New England, cultures not all linked mutually whose communication with each other has always been limited. My subjects began to come together for me when I realized that Nikolaus von Zinzendorf, Jonathan Edwards, John Wesley, Israel ben Eliezer, and Muḥammad ibn Abd al-Wahhab were near exact contemporaries. Self-conscious thinkers, writers, and leaders, their lives and works earn them today the title—or the charge—of "fundamentalist" opponents of the Enlightenment. And the Enlightenment is a term which, for those of us who are not Enlightenment scholars, has come to sum up intellectual commitments shared by Voltaire, Moses Mendelssohn, Hume, and Thomas Jefferson, with the possible addition of Muslims like Avicenna from nine centuries before.

I use the narrative form of linked profiles, which I used earlier to write *The First Moderns*, and which has its own pitfalls. As the critic Roger Shattuck, something of a non-fiction master, wrote, it is a bit of a postmodern technique to bring "apparently unrelated events and lives ... close in time and space" so that "the bare juxtaposition of elements gives the impression that the materials were simply there, and that, once conceived, the book assembled and wrote itself." Shattuck correctly labeled this style as montage, the quintessential production technique of the movies. Like E. L. Doctorow's novel *Ragtime* (and Kleist's 1810 novel *Michael Kohlhaas* on which it was modeled) it relies on a sort of ragtime of chronological coincidence, and a willingness, perhaps even a habit, on the part of the reader of filling in the transitions, explanations, and connections herself.

But that method can tempt your historical conscience. I fell back on interleaving explicit arguments with the biographies. The first of these arguments begins with the fact that Zinzendorf, Edwards, and the other contemporaries lived in an era we in the English-speaking West came to call "the Enlightenment" (and the French-speakers, *Lumières*, and the German speakers, *Aufklärung*). "Enlightenment" came to imply opposition to established religions and was famously defined by Immanuel Kant and friends in Berlin in 1784 as the salutary consequences, philosophical and educational, of the questioning of religious and state censorship. Because of that, "evangelical" leaders like Zinzendorf and Edwards have been taken to be in diametrical opposition, so diametrical an opposition that even good scholars (of

Western Christian culture, though less so of Jewish or Muslim) have entirely omitted the evangelicals from consideration. Instead, I contend, "evangelicals" can better be understood, not as the enemies of Enlightenment but as part of an intellectual movement that in the West was the Enlightenment's contemporary and that Isaiah Berlin called the Counter-Enlightenment. As my fellow scholar Graeme Garrard argues in *Counter-Enlightenments: From the eighteenth century to the present* (Routledge, 2006), we need to recognize the plurality of both Enlightenments and Counter-Enlightenments in Western culture. Thus, I argue here for us to risk clouding the concept by extending it to other cultures, to relax the cultural boundaries as well as the chronological. We need to recognize both Enlightenment and Counter-Enlightenment as terms that apply to movements that arise repeatedly in the history of thought.

My second argument is that this Counter-Enlightenment should be understood less as a wholesale rejection of the Enlightenment than as an amalgam of attempts to assimilate and transcend it, a "transmitter" and "bridge" as Steven Seidman argued in *Liberalism and the Origins of European Social Theory* (Blackwell, 1983), a "third way" as Christopher McIntosh put it in his book *The Rose Cross and the Age of Reason* (Brill, 1992). I consider this category an improvement on the "religious Enlightenment," scrupulously assembled by David Sorkin (*The Religious Enlightenment*. Princeton U.P. 2008) and William Bulman (*God in the Enlightenment*. Oxford U.P. 2016), even though it's a little less confined to the West. My contention is that the Counter-Enlightenment is a more comprehensive and comprehending way of dealing with the eighteenth-century founders of "fundamentalism" and "evangelicalism" not only in the West but in the cultures that are rooted in all three of the Abrahamic religions.

My third argument—philosophical rather than historical—is that to do such an analysis requires a definition of "religion" that recognizes (as the Western Counter-Enlightenment did) that the determinative trait of a religion is neither theology nor liturgy, but ethics. Human cultures and subcultures, and the individual humans who belong to them, inevitably try to assure themselves that their values, their commitments, their judgments of good and evil are correct. Religions, I argue, are best understood as the means by which humans seek that assurance that they can confidently distinguish good from evil, that they are right to value what they value. Such judgments can never be what we have come to call "scientific" because (as Isaiah Berlin argued, looking back on David Hume and Carl Becker) they have conflicting axioms that cannot be agreed on. They are judgments that challenge our accepted two-valued logic, and defy every attempt to make them universal.

Can those arguments be made successfully? I think so. Have they been? The reader must judge. The aim has been to add a little more order to an area of human knowledge which, unlike science, technology, engineering, and mathematics, seems to be short of that at present.

Brooklyn, NY, USA William R. Everdell

Acknowledgments

Coming so late to such old and mightily involving questions, I have many, many predecessors to acknowledge. It is my good fortune that so much ink and so many bytes have been shed on these interrelated topics; but I can hardly begin to thank my predecessors for their preparation of the field. I have tried to treat them, especially Isaiah Berlin and the intellectual historians, with the same respect they treated their own subjects, by using parenthetical dates in references which will reflect not only *what* their insights and discoveries were but exactly *when* they had them and when they first wrote them down. Modern intellectual historians of the caliber of Berlin (though with somewhat less range) are still at work, notably Frederick Beiser, W. R. Ward, Bernard McGinn, Mark Noll, Ann Thomson, Alexander Bevilacqua, Christopher de Bellaigue, Christopher Beckwith, Ahmad Dallal, Bernard Haykel, Natana Delong-Bas, John Voll, S. Frederick Starr, Marcia Hermansen, Christopher Beckwith, and David Biale and David Assaf together with their many collaborators on the massive *Hasidism: A New History*. Their work has been indispensable to me. So has the work of philosophers from William James to Charles Taylor and Daniel Dennett, anthropologists from Émile Durkheim to Ioan Lewis, and sociologists from Max Weber to Martin Marty, whose roster of virtuosos wrote the five fat volumes of his *Fundamentalism Project*. Most of those who are historians have done the exhaustive research in primary sources, especially in the languages other than French, German, and English, of which my command is not reliable, and have together made it possible for me to depend on them. I have allowed myself in most cases to adopt—even argue with—the interpretations they made of some of those primary sources, rather than contend in every case with the sources themselves.

I am even more grateful to those who know that their contribution to this project has not made its way to me via printed pages but across a classroom or a table, including my NYU dissertation adviser, the late Frank Manuel who wrote *The Eighteenth Century Confronts the Gods* (Harvard U.P. 1959), and other fellow scholars of the Western Enlightenment, who have done much to encourage a project like this that extends to non-Western cultures. Too many to name of my Saint Ann's School colleagues have done this, encouraging me as they did the students we shared. So have World historian Patrick Manning and the other scholar-teachers I served with on the Advanced Placement World History Test Development Committee. So have T.E.D. Braun, Ruth Necheles, Linda Merians, Jim May, Laura Kennelly, and many members of the several Societies for Eighteenth-Century Studies, the American (ASECS), the International (ISECS), and one of the regional (the East-Central American SECS or ECASECS), as well as the Eighteenth-Century Studies Group maintained by Columbia University for independent and non-Columbia scholars. I have had specific and valuable encouragement from Counter-Enlightenment specialists Darrin McMahon and Graeme Garrard ever since we were all brought together by Richard Lebrun at the French Revolution Bicentennial Congress in Paris in 1989, early in our careers, because of our common interest in the most thoroughgoing and unrelenting opponent of the Enlightenment—and of the Revolution—Joseph de Maistre.

Other face-to-face contributors include many of my inexhaustibly curious students over my 44 years at Saint Ann's School in Brooklyn. The younger ones have taught me more than they are so far willing to believe they have; but the older ones have begun to understand how much I owe them, for the questions they have asked and the insights they have shared that made me repeatedly rethink the history I thought I was introducing them to. They are now of all ages, from practicing philosopher Aeon Skoble to the bright, energetic, precociously scholarly, and occasionally bemused members of my twenty-first century electives in World History, like "Global History of Science" and "Dar al-Islam." Narrowing it severely down here, I would like to thank by name a few among those graduates I had the chance to learn from and teach, the ones who have gone on to write history themselves. Perhaps I can give a fillip here to their writing, short or long, published or performed: Ben Yarmolinsky '72, Bill Hogeland and Ann Hulbert '73, John Gartner '75, Professors Heather Williams '74, Elizabeth Wood '76, and Matthew Affron '81, Dan Bergner and John Pomfret '77, Andrew Kirtzman '78, Akiva Goldsman and Nancy Rommelman '79, Arthur Kroeber '80, Ann Midgette '82, Samantha Gillison '85, Dean Risa Goluboff and Professor Elizabeth Brannon '88, Alissa Quart '89, Professors Bernadette Meyler '91 and William Hurst '93, Meghan O'Rourke '93, Gena Oppenheim '96, Ben Adler '99, Sarah Coleman and Luke Reynolds '01, Rebecca O'Brien '02, John Ganz and Lena Dunham '04, Professors Jon Connolly and Billy Brewster, '04, Ingrid Norton '05, and Professor Eli Mandel '10. When Toby Berggruen '17 stops helping me vet my MSS and starts publishing his own, he will doubtlessly join them.

I am grateful as well to my Saint Paul's School classmate, Peter Neill, who left off writing novels to run the World Ocean Observatory. He generously read an earlier version of the manuscript and suggested large and salutary cuts, on the grounds that even a World History narrative is not liable to be dismissed simply because it is not encyclopedic. But neither Peter nor anyone else here mentioned is responsible for my mistakes or omissions.

Contents

Chapter 1
Introduction

Dialectic of Enlightenment: Ecstasy to Piety to Moralism

Abstract Revival in Jefferson's Virginia. Enlightenment and Isaiah Berlin's Counter-Enlightenment. Religion as Ecstatic Experience and Religion as Morality.

In the summer of 1776, as the Continental Congress was working its way toward a Declaration of Independence, there was a religious revival in Dinwiddie County, Virginia.

> In the summer at Boisseau's Chapel, during a sermon preached by that bold soldier of the cross, Thomas Rankin, such power descended that hundreds fell to the ground, and "the house seemed to shake with the presence of God." The building was filled to its utmost capacity, while hundreds stood without. "Look wherever we would," [...] says a writer, "we saw nothing but streaming eyes and faces bathed in tears, and heard nothing but groans and strong cries after God." In vain the preachers attempted either to sing, pray, or exhort. Every time their voices were silenced by the cries and groans around them. They could do nothing but sit in the pulpit and, filled with the divine presence, exclaim: "This is none other than the house of God; this is the gate of heaven!"[1]

It happened again in 1785.

> In the summer of the year, the glorious work of God broke out, on the banks of the James River, and from thence has spread almost over the state [of Virginia]. [2]

[1] An eyewitness account of Rankin's sermon on June 30, 1776, during a 1775–76 Methodist-led revival in Dinwiddie County, Virginia, a week before Independence was declared, in Annie Maria Barnes, *Scenes in Pioneer Methodism* (Nashville, TN: Publishing House of the Methodist Episcopal Church, South, 1890), pp 300–301.

[2] Rev. John Leland, *The Virginia Chronicle: with judicious and critical remarks, under XXIV heads*, (Fredericksburg, VA: Printed by T. Green, 1790, facsimile repr., Gale Group ECCO, n.d.), p34–35. John Leland (1754–1841), a Massachusetts-born Congregational, converted to Baptist and pastoring in Virginia, was one of the thinkers credited by Madison and Jefferson with the arguments against "an establishment of religion" that they used to disestablish the Protestant Episcopal Church of Virginia in 1786. Leland also favored abolishing slavery.

W. R. Everdell, *The Evangelical Counter-Enlightenment*, Boston Studies in Philosophy, Religion and Public Life 9,
https://doi.org/10.1007/978-3-030-69762-4_1

> … a great part of the congregation fall prostrate upon the floor or ground; many of whom entirely lose the use of their limbs for a season. Sometimes numbers are crying out at once, some of them in great distress, using such language as this, "God be merciful to me a sinner—Lord save me or I must perish—what shall I do to be saved? &c." others breaking out in such rapturous expressions as these; "bless the Lord, O my soul!—O sweet Jesus, how I love thee!—O sinners! Come, taste and see how good the Lord is! &c.[3]

And in 1787, near Petersburg, Virginia.

> The poor awakened sinners were wrestling with the Lord for mercy in every direction, some on their knees, others lying in the arms of their friends, and others stretched on the floor, not able to stand, and some were convulsed, with every limb as stiff as a stick. In the midst of this work several sleepers [support beams] of the house broke down at once, which made a very loud noise; and the floor sunk down considerably; but the people paid but little or no attention to it, and many of them knew nothing of it, for no one was hurt.[4]

And again in 1787, in Petersburg, as the Constitutional Convention was meeting in Philadelphia

> The whole company were affected, and numbers so wrought upon, that they fell down on their knees; and others dropped down on their faces, having the use of their limbs intirely suspended. Commonly, in these meetings, from one to ten were converted in a day. Saints were praising God aloud, and mourners crying for mercy as from the depth of hell; so that the noise of the people could be heard afar off. This induced numbers of people to come, so that in places where we used to have but twenty or thirty on a week day, now there will be a thousand, and sometimes more. […]
>
> All the Preachers' could do, was to go among the distressed, and encourage them. This likewise the old members did; Some lying as in the pangs of death, numbers as cold as clay, and as still as if dead; so that among six or seven thousand people, there were not many that had the proper use of their bodily power?, so as to take care of the rest; and to encourage the mourners. Hundreds of saints were so overcome with the power of God; that they fell down as in a swoon, and lay for twenty or thirty minutes, and some for an hour. During this time, they were happy beyond description; and when they came to themselves, it was with loud praises to God, and with tears, and speeches enough to break a rock, or melt the hardest heart.[5]

And on into the nineteenth century.

---

[3] Leland, *The Virginia Chronicle* (1790), facsimile, p34–35. Leland's own conversion was ecstatic only at its first manifestation, a "sound from the skies," in 1772. Thereafter, it mostly took the form of an argument inside Leland's own mind citing biblical passages on both sides and no other revelation. ("Events in the Life of John Leland Written by Himself," in *The Writings of the Late Elder John Leland, Including Some Events in His Life*, ed., L. F. Green, 1845, pp2–7 @ https://play.google.com/books/reader?id=bMAiAAAAMAAJ&hl=en&pg=GBS.PA14.w.1.3.0)

[4] A 1787 revival described in Jesse Lee, *A Short History of the Methodists in the United States of America*, Baltimore: Magill & Clime, 1810, p130–131, in John B. Boles, *The Great Revival: Beginnings of the Bible Belt* (1972), Lexington: KY: University Press of Kentucky, pb, 1996, p7; cf. Minton Thrift, *Memoir of the Rev. Jesse Lee with extracts from his journals*, NY: Bangs & Mason, 1823, repr., NY: Arno Press, 1969, p94–98.

[5] A 1787 revival described in R. (Richard) Garrettson, "An account of the Revival of the Work of God at Petersburg in Virginia," *Arminian Magazine* [London] 13(1790):301–302, 304. (Quoted in Ann Taves, *Fits, Trances, & Visions: Experiencing Religion and Explaining Experience from Wesley to James*, Princeton: Princeton University Press, 1999, p87n52).

> The minister condemned the wickedness of his hearers and portrayed Hell in vivid terms. Listeners felt guilty and were afraid; they wept, shouted, prayed, fell on the ground, shook in every joint, barked like dogs, and burst into a 'holy laugh'.[6]

> One man alerted the congregation to the devil's presence within the house and then began scuffling with an unseen antagonist as the rest of the company shouted encouragement: "Well done, Johnny! Gouge him, Johnny! Bite him, Johnny!" To even matters up, another of the brethren urged on the devil ("Fair play, there shall no man touch. Hurrah, Devil! I'll stand to your back!"). In due course, the fight spilled outdoors and the devil fled up into a tree, "whereupon his adversary began barking up the tree."[7]

Treeing the Devil,[8] falling as if slain, lying mute, jerking in ecstasy, laughing hysterically, spirit possession, trance, barking, witnessing, sharing visions, embracing fellow petitioners, all following on the confessing of seemingly ineradicable sinfulness, such behaviors are reported again and again by both supporters and skeptics who attended Baptist and Methodist services in late eighteenth-century Virginia. The services, which began with preachers' calls to conviction of sin and immediate repentance, would be called "camp" or "tent" meetings when they assembled outdoors, and sometimes even when they met indoors in meeting-houses. Sermons came thick and fast, often more than one at a time, and the sermons were sometimes chanted. In the slave society of Virginia, the congregations were often racially integrated, with some of the rituals and behaviors, especially chants, jerks and possession by the Spirit, recognizably West African.[9]

---

[6] George Eaton Simpson, *The Shango Cult in Trinidad* (Institute of Caribbean Studies, University of Puerto Rico, 1965), p109. This is a contemporary description of a nineteenth-century American revival, given by Simpson in order to compare it with African ritual. Simpson's description is quoted in Walter F. Pitts & Vincent L. Wimbush, *Old Ship of Zion: The Afro-Baptist Ritual in the African Diaspora* (NY: Oxford University Press, 1996), p44.

[7] James Potter Collins, *Autobiography of a Revolutionary Soldier* (1859; reprint, NY: Arno Press, 1979), p152–53, quoted in Christine Leigh Heyman, *Southern Cross: the Beginnings of the Bible Belt*, NY: Knopf, 1997, n33. James Taylor, *Autobiography of General James Taylor*, 3, DC, RLUC.

[8] "Treeing the Devil" is still recalled with affection by remaining partisans of the "old-time religion." In a self-published novel of 2010, one character muses: "Anyway this was way back. It's an old holiness thing. Treeing the Devil. Way extreme. Nowadays people around here don't like to be reminded of that because so many have become beholden to *Secular Humanistic* thinking." (Alexander Lawrence, *2nd Victory in Jesus*: Book 3 of *THE GOINS BRICOLAGE: A Saga of Tecumseh and Stonewall Counties in the State of Indiana*, iUniverse, 2010, p181).

[9] "Evangelical communities across the South were nurseries of an emerging biracial culture based on spiritual equality." —Jon F. Sensbach, *Rebecca's Revival: Creating Black Christianity in the Atlantic World* (Cambridge, MA: Harvard University Press, 2005), p75. The point has seemed somewhat overshadowed since Eugene Genovese (*Roll, Jordan, Roll: The World the Slaves Made*, New York: Pantheon, 1975) and Mechal Sobel (*The World They Made Together: Black and White Values in Eighteenth-Century Virginia*, Princeton, NJ: Princeton University Press, 1987) made it. The Yoruba "Shango" rite, described by a pioneering German anthropologist in 1913, suggests at least one of the sources of revival behavior: "Shango descends quite unexpectedly upon some man or woman dancer's head. The inspirationist rushes madly to the Banga, seizes an Ose-Shango, a beautifully carved club, or a Shere-Shango, that is, the holy rattle. This individual begins to caper before the others. The afflatus is patent. All agree in this: a being possessed by Shango or any other Orisha dances quite differently from ordinary folk. Such ecstatic behaviour certainly shows a state of feeling now almost completely foreign to us. […] Shango can possess several persons on one

Clearly, something was happening in the Commonwealth of Virginia in the late eighteenth century that was not the Constitutional Convention or even the American Revolution, something that still fits poorly with the way we like to narrate our American History. Genteel plantation Virginia, the Old Dominion of a virtuous and rational slaveowning aristocracy, was soon to provide the first, third, fourth and fifth presidents of the new United States; and the planters' world view, especially for Thomas Jefferson of Monticello near Charlottesville, was the Enlightenment. This was when to be "enlightened" was to be against tyranny—and against democracy—in politics, favorable to science, and deeply suspicious of what the enlightened English had begun to call religious "enthusiasm," and French *philosophes* like Voltaire called "fanaticism," or "superstition."[10] Indeed, the enlightened were suspicious of the religions themselves—any or all of them, but usually the one that they had been raised in.

In western Virginia, in the 1780s where plantations like Jefferson's were fewer and farther between, events unrolled that Jefferson would not hear about, and would have been unlikely to please him if he had. The revival, actually a series of boisterous, "enthusiastic" and quite democratic meetings in back country Virginia and further south, was preached by missionary ministers of recently founded radical Protestant Christian sects, Baptists and Methodists, and amateur preachers with no diplomas at all. It "convicted" and "saved" thousands, but, perhaps because its preachers had come out of New England's "Great Awakening" in the 1730s and

day, but not concurrently. And what in their frenzy these rapt enthusiasts may say passes for oracular truth." (Leo Frobenius, *The voice of Africa: being an account of the travels of the German Inner African Exploration Expedition in the years 1910–1912*, trans., Rudolf Blind, London: Hutchinson & Co., 1913, p213–14 @ https://archive.org/stream/voiceofafricabei01frobuoft/voiceofafricabei01frobuoft_djvu.txt). George Eaton Simpson, *Black Religions in the New World* (NY: Columbia University Press, 1978) summed up Simpson's many publications that have detailed how these African religious practices, including Shango, were carried to the Americas. Walter F. Pitts & Vincent L. Wimbush, *Old Ship of Zion: The Afro-Baptist Ritual in the African Diaspora* (NY: Oxford University Press, 1996) reviews what's known and adds more (more rhyme than reason), including the classic call-and-response pattern, and the Afro-Baptist breath groups ending in "*wo*!" or "*huh*!" for which the African precedents include Mandinka "breath groups" with nonsense end-syllables "*o*," "*wo*," and "*ye*," Benin "one-stroke recitation," Fulani chain-rhyme, and other West African rhythmic chants and nonce words that bespeak ecstasy and prefigure Pentecostal glossolalia. (pp 60–65) The classic general text on West-Africa-to-the-Americas elements of religion with a focus on the United States, is Albert Raboteau, *Slave Religion: The "Invisible Institution" in the American South* (rev. ed., NY: Oxford University Press, 2004). A strong recent report from this field of research is Jason R. Young's *Rituals of Resistance: African Atlantic Religion in Kongo and the Lowcountry South in the Era of Slavery* (Baton Rouge: Louisiana State University Press, 2011). Pitts and Wimbush's account, in which Simpson's description of the non-African-American revival above is quoted, is on page 44 of their *Old Ship of Zion*.

[10] One of the newest of many studies of the concept of "religious enthusiasm" in England is Lionel Laborie, *Enlightening Enthusiasm: Prophecy and religious experience in early eighteenth-century England* (Manchester, UK: Manchester University Press, 2015). A much older book, Wesley M. Gewehr's *The Great Awakening in Virginia, 1740–1790*, (Durham, NC: Duke University Press, 1930; reprint, LLC, June, 2011), seems to be the only book-length study there is on the "Great Awakening" in Jefferson's home state.

40s, and because its alumni would preach the "Second Great Awakening" when that burst forth in 1801 at Cane Ridge near Paris, Kentucky, the revivals in Virginia and the Carolinas that broke out in the 1760s and peaked in 1785–87 have never had a name of their own.

In 1785 Jefferson had just arrived in Paris, France, as Commissioner of the new American republic, replacing Benjamin Franklin. The slave Jefferson had inherited from his wife's family, 12-year-old Sally Hemings, was in Virginia taking care of the widower's youngest surviving white child, Polly. Sally would come to Paris with Polly in 1787, at the age of 14, when Jefferson was buying local vintages for his table and had begun entertaining France's liberal aristocrats as they talked about reforms. The reforms they discussed would be reflected in 1787 in the new U.S. Constitution, written in large part that year by Jefferson's political ally James Madison, which carefully omitted the words "slave," and "God" and allowed the constituent states to prevent slaves, women, children and men who lacked property from voting. As Jefferson left Paris in 1789, with his two white daughters and a pregnant black Sally, those same reforms would begin to be swept up and expanded in the French Revolution (which between 1792 and 1795 would disestablish the church, end slavery, and bring democracy to Europe by giving the vote to poor men).

Jefferson had been raised an Anglican in Virginia's unrevived established church, but he had become the principal author of the Virginia Statute of Religious Freedom, which disestablished the Episcopal Church when it finally passed the legislature in 1786. Baptists, who belonged to an unestablished Christian denomination, would quickly offer congratulations which Jefferson would graciously accept after he became president in 1801. Jefferson eventually put the Virginia Statute on his tombstone; but late in life he would perform a private surgical edit on the four Christian Gospels, cutting and pasting so that Jesus would not appear to have done any of those things that had so impressed the simple souls of his time and since. Out went the offer of God's grace, the resurrections, healings and other miracles that Jefferson's favorite Scottish philosopher, the Enlightenment *philosophe* David Hume, had so masterfully (and discreetly) proved to be unprovable.[11] Jefferson was a good enough politician to share this project with only a handful of enlightened friends. Revolutionary the Enlightenment could be, even to flirting (as Benjamin Franklin did) with letting propertyless men vote (the risky idea that was then called "democracy"); but the Enlightenment was never as collectively or as openly radical as some argue now, and never utopian.[12] It was not the *philosophes* who proved to be democratic and anti-deferential, but the evangelicals.

[11] David Hume, "On Miracles," Chapter 10 of *An Enquiry Concerning Human Understanding*. (1748).

[12] Jonathan Israel, *Radical Enlightenment: Philosophy and the Making of Modernity, 1650–1750* (NY: Oxford University Press, 2001). Israel's argument is massive and magisterial, but not, I think, appreciative enough of the restraint and caution of Franklin, Hume and other Enlightenment *philosophes*, not all of them "moderate," even in his final volume: *Enlightenment Contested: Philosophy, Modernity, and the Emancipation of Man 1670–1752* (NY: Oxford University Press, 2009). In all the immense erudition of Israel's work there seems little place for actual eighteenth-century debates about the nature and preconditions of religious experience, and no place at all for

They arose in the same century, but the Enlightenment and Evangelicalism (as we now agree to call them) are still thought of as immiscible, like oil and water. Psychologists today might describe these "revivals of religion" as unusual, even anomalous, but if they were, what is any popular music concert of today if not usual and nomalous. Enlightenment did not always mean in English what it means now, and for English-speaking Buddhists it still carries its earlier meaning of religious illumination.

So while Jefferson edged away from any truck with the supernatural, the Virginia revivals continued. Baptist missionary John Leland, who was born Congregational in New England, but converted to the Baptist faith by age 20, was never entirely comfortable with the wilder enthusiasm of the back country Baptists. He wrote of the 1785 revivals:

> At associations and great meetings, I have seen numbers of ministers and exhorters improving their gifts at the same time. Such a heavenly confusion among the preachers, and such a celestial discord among the people destroy all articulation, so that the understanding is not edified; but the awful echo sounding in the ears, and the objects in great distress, and great raptures before the eyes, raise great emotion in the heart. Some of the ministers rather oppose *this* work, others call it a little in question, and some fan it with all their might. Whether it be celestial or terrestrial, or a complication of both, it is observed by the candid, that more souls get first awakened at such meetings, than at any meetings whatever; who afterwards give clear rational accounts of a divine change of heart.[13]

Leland noticed that the "grace," "conviction," and "change of heart" seemed to come to some more than once, which was contrary to the doctrines of some Baptists:

> This exercise is not confined to the newly convicted and newly converted; but persons who have been professors a number of years, at such lively meetings, not only jump up, strike their hands together and shout aloud, but will embrace one another and fall to the floor.

"Embraces" raised his suspicions of the more extravagant behaviors which threatened "decency," but:

---

either Augustinianism or ecstasy. Jansenism, for example, is presented entirely in the context of the philosophical struggle between Cartesian and Aristotelian philosophy in *Radical Enlightenment* (pp19, 38–39); and Israel's hero Spinoza can never be called what the German Romantic writer Novalis called him, "a man drunk with God."

[13]Leland, *The Virginia Chronicle* (1790), facsimile, p 35. Leland was a stalwart of Jefferson's Republican political party, collaborating with him and Madison in disestablishing the Anglican church in Virginia, and, at Jefferson's invitation, preaching twice to Congress in January, 1802, two days after presenting him with a very big cheese. The 1,235 pound "Mammoth Cheese," made from the milk of "Republican cows" in Massachusetts, came on the day that Jefferson wrote his famous letter of January 1, 1802, to the Baptists in Danbury, Connecticut, about the "wall of separation" between church and state; but the more important gift to Jefferson was public recognition by a Protestant leader that the President might not be, as then charged, a deist enemy of religion. A recent article on the very political relation of Jefferson and Madison with the Virginia Baptists is Mark S. Scarberry, "John Leland and James Madison: Religious Influence on the Ratification of the Constitution and on the Proposal of the Bill of Rights," *Penn State Law Review*, Vol. 113:3, p738–40.

> I have never known the rules of decency to be broken so far, as for persons of both sexes, thus to embrace and fall at meetings.[14] It is not to be understood, that this exercise is seen in all parts of the state, at times, when God is working on the minds of the people; no, under the preaching of the same man, in different neighborhoods and counties, the same work, in substance, has different exterior effects.

He particularly appreciated harmony wherever it calmed the dissonance of revival. Music had not emerged earlier in New England when Congregational minister Jonathan Edwards first embraced the "Great Awakening," but Leland heard a lot more of it, much of it original, in Virginia.

> What Mr. *Jonathan Edwards* thought might be expedient in some future day, has been true in Virginia. Bands go singing to meeting, and singing home. At meeting, as soon as preaching is over, it is common to sing a number of spiritual songs; sometimes several songs are sounding at the same time, in different parts of the congregation. I have travelled through neighborhoods and counties at times of refreshing, and the spiritual songs in the fields, in the shops and houses, have made the heavens ring with melody over my head.[15]

Enthusiastic, or as we now say, "evangelical" Protestantism developed even further south than Virginia and North Carolina; and in South Carolina one historian has found evidence of something like revivals taking place in the 1670s.[16] Taking its West African elements along with it, it not only spread to the west, but doubled back east to where it had begun in New England. The untutored historian of the Methodist camp meeting at Oak Bluffs, on an island in Massachusetts, thought that such meetings had been brought to Massachusetts from beginnings

---

[14] *Ibid.* We don't know what Leland might have meant by breaches of "decency," but dancing was early prohibited by Baptists, and sex, drunkenness, undress and smoking were frowned on in public and at services—a beginning of moralism.

[15] *Ibid.*

[16] Thomas J. Little, *The Origins of Southern Evangelicalism: Religious Revivalism in the South Carolina Lowcountry, 1670–1760*, University of South Carolina Press, 2015. Among the many attempts made to bring as many of these revivals together as possible and to try to make general sense of them, range from the academic (Ellen Eslinger, *Citizens of Zion: The Social Origins of Camp Meeting Revivalism*, Knoxville: University of Tennessee Press, 1999), to the hagiographic (Kenneth O. Brown, *Holy Ground, Too: The Camp Meeting Family Tree*, Holiness Archives, 1997). "Evangelicals," as I hope to show, were and are not all Americans, or even all Westerners, least of all Protestant Christians. For the single most definitive study of the Protestant evangelicals everywhere in Western culture, we are all now indebted to W. R. (William Reginald) Ward's *The Protestant evangelical awakening* (Cambridge: Cambridge University Press, 2002), and for an introduction to a sizeable chunk of their world historical roots, *Early Evangelicalism: A Global Intellectual History, 1670–1789* (Cambridge: Cambridge University Press, September 25, 2006) by the same author. A more conventional interpretation than Ward's, with chronological scope and detail extended to the twentieth century, but sticking to only one of the West's languages, English, is the multivolume *A History of Evangelicalism: People, Movements and Ideas in the English-Speaking World*, (Downers Grove, IL: InterVarsity Press/IVP Academic, 2003–2017) by John Wolffe, David Bebbington, Geoffrey Treloar and Brian Stanley, which began in 2003 with Mark Noll's volume, *The Rise of Evangelicalism: The Age of Edwards, Whitefield and the Wesleys*. The best general introduction to the history of evangelicalism in the United States is now Frances Fitzgerald's *The Evangelicals: The Struggle to Shape America* (New York: Simon & Schuster, 2017), which builds on the work of almost all of evangelicalism's leading historians.

in early nineteenth-century Kentucky, but what seems to be the case is that they had been brought earlier to Kentucky from Virginia and to Virginia even earlier from Connecticut and Massachusetts—and the Carolinas.[17] Even staid Presbyterian Scotland began to shout, as its summertime open-air mass communion services that had begun in the seventeenth century became full-scale camp-meeting revivals by 1742, taking their cue from the New England "awakening" that they had earlier anticipated, and contributing in turn to the events in Virginia and later in the trans-Appalachian West.[18] Evangelical Christianity has been with us in America ever since.

We describe the behavior at those Virginia revivals as psychologically unusual now, emotionally expressive, products of direct experience, "spiritual" experience, and we still use the word "ecstasy," Greek for the state of being beside, or outside of oneself.[19] What these Americans thought at the time was that the grace of God could then and there enable conviction of sin, repentance and "change of heart" or "second birth" (salvation from eternal punishment after death), often through possession of the believer by the Holy Spirit, the third "person" of the Christian Trinity. Participants expected their soul's salvation, their body's healing, a revolution in their morals, the revival of Christianity, the equality of believers and the wholesale reform of human society coming either just before or just after the Second Coming of Jesus Christ (millennialism and apocalypticism). They welcomed what they thought of as the "revival" of the Christian religion, and of the evangelizing of its Gospels (*evangelia*) to the as yet unsaved. They rejected a paid, appointed clergy, refused submission to anyone but God, and set inspiration above both reason and education as a conduit for grace and a means to salvation.

[17]According to an 1858 account by a New England minister: "The practice of holding camp meetings was first introduced by the Presbyterians and Methodists, together, in the State of Kentucky, in the early part of the present century. It was soon after adopted by the latter denomination in the New England States." (Rev. Hebron Vincent, *A History of the Wesleyan Grove, Martha's Vineyard, Camp Meeting, from the First Meeting Held There In 1835, to that of 1858, Inclusive ; Interspersed With Touching Incidents And General Remarks*. Boston: Geo. C. Rand & Avery, 1858, p. xvii). Rev. Vincent was not what historians would want to call an authority, and he left out the New England preachers who had first revived Kentucky; but his timeline seems right otherwise. He described the original Oak Bluffs tent meeting of 1835 (almost exactly a century after Edwards had awakened Northampton, Massachusetts) as only a little less ecstatic. "The waving trees, the whispering breeze, the pathetic appeals, the earnest prayers, and the songs of praise, as well as the trembling of sinners under the Word, and the shining countenances of Christians lighted up with holy joy, all conspired to say " Surely the Lord is in this place." (Vincent, *A History of the Wesleyan Grove*, p20).

[18]Leigh Eric Schmidt, *Holy Fairs: Scottish Communions and American Revivals in the Early Modern Period*, (Princeton, NJ: Princeton University Press, 1989). Robert Burns, unmoved by holy fairs, immortalized one, rife with hypocrite preachers and young people drinking and hooking up, in a 1785 poem called "The Holy Fair" that is a masterpiece of popular anticlericalism. Still, to most of its participants the great "Work" of revival in Cambuslang, Scotland, in 1742, was no party.

[19]"Ekstasis" is the word used by Karen Armstrong in the most comprehensive of her books on religion, *The Battle for God* (NY: Knopf, 2000, pp xiv, 10 and *passim*) to introduce her sophisticated conception of pre-modern, pre-secular religious truth.

Do religions other than American Protestantism have such a tradition? Do others go in for spiritual possession, outspoken ecstasy and strenuous ritual? The answer of course is yes.[20] The camp meetings in 1780s Virginia were part of an evangelical surge that roiled Protestant Christianity over the whole European-American Atlantic world from the 1740s onward. The prayer of Hasidic Jews, beginning at the same time as the American Great Awakening, is a dance both individual and collective by which the unselfed "I" mystically joins the transcendant one. The Ṣufis of worldwide Islam prayed then (and still) in a chant form intended to bring on an ecstasy that will allow them to take leave of themselves and become one with God. Some Ṣufi "dervishes" slowly whirl, some howl, and other quieter Ṣufi *dhikr*s (prayer practices) are hardly less energetic. West African rituals on their own, with or without their influence on American revivalism, were outstanding examples of the ecstatic, both pagan and Islamic. And as we shall see, a group called "convulsionaries" carried the "jansenist" trend in European Catholicism from austerity to ecstasy.

Was this a worldwide religious revolution then? This book's view is less sweeping. It embraces all three Abrahamic religions, but focuses on only four religious movements within each one to try to describe similarities in the relationships between Hasidic Jews and militant messianic orthodox Jews, between Ṣufi Muslims and militant jihadist Waḥhabi Muslims, between "awakened" Protestant revivalist Christians and militant Protestant dispensational premillennialists, and between mystical or "convulsionary" and doctrinaire Catholic Christians. The objective is to see how they arose in history, and how their movements developed in the world, especially the Western and Atlantic worlds, but also in the South and East Asian worlds, into the extremes we wonder at today.[21]

Three of the movements—it may surprise some readers to know—can be said to have begun in the same generation, the one born at the turn of the seventeenth to the eighteenth century C.E. The four most eminent founders of each movement, Count Zinzendorf (b. 1700), the Ba'al Shem Tov (b. 1698), Jonathan Edwards (b. 1703), John Wesley (b. 1703), and Muhammad ibn ʿAbd al-Waḥhab (b. 1702/03), were in fact born within five years of each other. It was during the first half of what the West came to call its own Age of Enlightenment; but these movements stood so firmly against so many of the new ideas of the eighteenth century, that in our day they have earned classification under a new and different term, the "Counter-Enlightenment."

---

[20] To help me understand ecstasies in all three of the Abrahamic religions through the work of the subject's leading scholars, I have used a unique book that two of those scholars, Moshe Idel and Bernard McGinn, put together and titled *Mystical Union in Judaism, Christianity, and Islam: An Ecumenical Dialogue* (NY: Continuum, 1996). It is confined to the experience of "*unio mystica*" or mystical union with the divine, but that is most of what is meant by ecstatic experience.

[21] Volume 5 in the massive Fundamentalism Project of editors Martin Marty, R. Scott Appleby, and their team at the University of Chicago Press, *Fundamentalisms Comprehended* (1995), (University of Chicago Press, pb, 2004) makes a very serious stab at the comprehensive comparative study of fundamentalist, or what I would want to call "post-ecstatic evangelical" religious groups, including not only several kinds of Christianity and several kinds of Islam, but Judaism, Buddhism, Hinduism, Sikhism and even Marxism. The questions it raises are both usual and unusual, and all are useful.

Israel Ben Eliezer (1698–1760), the first of the five to be born, belongs in this company because he was the founder of the strain of Judaism that we call Hasidic. As a poor peddler in indigenous medicines and magic, he migrated in 1740 to Międzybóż, a village on the vast estate of a nobleman in Polish Galicia. The large and prudent Jewish minority community that he joined there was tolerated by its Catholic landlord and thus wary of exuberance, but within a few years Ben Eliezer had had ecstatic visions of God, and the community had taken him up as its religious leader, giving him the title of Ba'al Shem Tov, or Master of the [Holy] Name.

Nikolaus Ludwig von Zinzendorf (1700–1760) was an evangelical Protestant Christian, one of the first, at least insofar as our term "evangelical" can be applied in the mid-eightneenth century. He was also a Count of the Holy Roman Empire, heir to a title and a large estate in the old state of central Germany called Saxony. In 1721, he heard of a group of Protestant refugees from the Catholic province of the Empire called Moravia (now in the Czech Republic), just south of his estate. He invited the refugees to settle on the manor he had just acquired from his grandmother, and within weeks Count Zinzendorf had become their religious leader, arranging for their adoption of his Lutheran Pietist faith and a revival of the former Bohemian Unitas Fratrum (United Brethren). He was also their feudal lord, and built them into a utopian community that was egalitarian (though not so egalitarian when it came to him), which soon undertook a worldwide evangelical mission that reached east to the borders of Russia and west to the Americas (including Honduras and Pennsylvania). It became known as the Bohemian Brethren, or the Moravians, after the province the refugees had come from.

Jonathan Edwards (1703–1758), who shows up in so many American history and literature courses, was the Congregational minister in colonial Massachusetts whose own "conversion," as he called it, and efforts to revive the faith of his congregation resulted in what American historians would later call the Great Awakening. The account he wrote of his success in inspiring conversion among the young men and women of his frontier parish in Northampton was sent to London in 1736 and had an immediate effect there; but in English North America the effect was galvanic. It propagated not only among Congregational Church members (the descendants of the English Puritan radicals) but among American Protestant Christians in general, whether or not they were Congregational, and it became the founding event of what Americans now call "evangelical" Protestantism.

John Wesley (1703–1791), the founder of Methodism, began as a priest in the unawakened (un-woke?) Church of England, the established Protestant state church that Edwards's ancestors had rejected. Wesley learned how to conduct missions from the Moravians, and later, when his ecstatic conversion came (rather quietly) in 1738, it came at a Moravian service. Methodism soon became independent of the Church of England, and a worldwide movement. It pioneered in England, and later brought to North America (with Wesley's friend George Whitefield), the ritual methods together called "revival," which had evolved to invite ecstatic conversion among all classes. With the expansion of the British Empire in the nineteenth century, it would reach as far as southern Africa and east Asia and remain, at 60–80 million adherents, one of the largest Protestant denominations of Christianity. Christianity itself, in all its forms, is now the religion of an estimated 2.42 billion of the world's people, or more adherents than any other organized religion, including Islam.

As for Muhammad ibn ʿAbd al-Waḥhab (1702/03–1787), he was the founder of a strain of Islam he called the *muwahḥidun* (*ahl al-tawhid* or People of the Singleness of God). Its enemies soon came to call it Waḥhabiya (Wahhabism), and it is now the state religion of Saudi Arabia. ʿAbd al-Waḥhab's opportunity for ecstatic experience came in the 1730s when he encountered Ṣufi teachings after his studies in Medina, but whatever his experience was, it seems to have been unconvincing or incomplete. It helped turn him into a non-practicing enemy of Sufism and of every other form of Islam besides Sunni and Hanbali orthodoxy. Returning to his hometown, ʿAbd al-Waḥhab bound his teaching of the Sunnah, or tradition, strictly by the Hanbali interpretation of Islamic law, *shariah*, and restricted even more by a refusal to tolerate any popular practices that smacked of idolatry or association of others with the one God, Allah. This included any ecstatic or mystic self-identification with Allah, and any veneration of the tombs of dead heroes and heroines of Islam, whom Westerners called "saints."

The alliance ʿAbd al-Waḥhab made in 1744 between his family and the family of a local Emir, Muhammad ibn Saʿud, provided ʿAbd al-Waḥhab and his heirs with some direction of the policies of Emir ibn Saʿud and his heirs, and the dyarchy made war to the knife with surrounding Muslim heretics. In 1801, the son of the first Saudi imam ibn ʿAbd al-Waḥhab, and the grandson of his Emir ibn Saʿud used the *muwahḥidun* army to attack Karbala, Iraq, destroying the tomb there of Hussein, the grandson of the Prophet Muhammad and the founder of what had since become Shiʿah Islam. In 1803–1805 they used it to capture Mecca and Medina and destroy the tombs there of the Prophet himself and members of his family. In Muhammad ibn ʿAbd al-Waḥhab, unlike in the other three, we find the cycle of ecstasy to piety (εὐσέβεια or *eusebeia* in pagan Greece), to moralism and dogmatism in a single life.

With these founders and others as examples, "evangelical religion" can be defined historically across all the Abrahamic faiths using the four features that David Bebbington proposed to characterize only one form of one of those faiths, evangelical Christianity: a set of values and practices that includes (1) the inerrancy of a scripture, (2) the centrality of divine mercy (for Christians, this would mean the sacrifice and atonement of Jesus), (3) a commitment to spreading the faith (evangelizing), and primarily (4) an expectation that a believer will experience personal inspiration direct from the "divine" and the "transcendant," an inspiration which, according to believers, will produce "amendment of life" or "conversion" of the soul and its will.[22] In all three Abrahamic religions the ecstatic inspiration, called "an access of grace" in Christianity, *devekut* (rapture leading to vision) in Judaism, and in Islam, *wajd* or *hal* (ecstatic feeling) leading to *wasilah* (means to inspiration)

---

[22] David W. Bebbington, *Evangelicalism in Modern Britain: A History from the 1730s to the 1980s*, NY/London: Unwin Hyman, 1989, pp. 1–19 for the "Bebbington quadrilateral" defining the term "evangelicals."

enabling *waqfat* or *fanâ* (the passing away of the self) and *baqa* (being in God),[23] is thought of as both a source and as a human response to that source, which is conceived as a single god, the one to whom English speakers give the name of God, Arabic speakers Allah, and Hebrew speakers Elohim or (when permitted) Yahveh.

Evangelical religion, thus defined, is the subject of this book. It has had its own history, though usually confined to one Abrahamic religion and to one language at a time. Christian evangelicalism has a particularly voluminous historiography, but Ṣufi Islam has one, too, and Hasidic Judaism is not far behind. Indeed, I am indebted to much of it and grateful.[24]

But the contention here is larger than separate historiographies: that the historical developments of all three of these evangelical strains in the religious monotheisms of the modern world have been parallel. They all begin in a form of mysticism, the ecstatic experience of a particular grace and consciousness of the presence of the divine—a single god. They all proceed from there to a militant commitment to consequent moral judgments of good and evil, losing in the process the piety, the "blessed assurance," guaranteed at first by that ecstatic experience. They end paradoxically far from ecstasy in a fundamentalist approach to scripture, a moralism that insists on the letter of law[25]—and in many cases they find a millennialist belief that the end of the world (and the world's total divine renewal) can be brought about by an exclusion—even an extermination—of the mortal opposition.

Our focus is on a history of the founding figures and of some of their predecessors and successors, the most passionate and ecstatic—and the most dogmatic and legalistic—representatives of the three religions. This history is an extended, and intentionally colorful one of a long and particularly significant train of events that should prove, among other things, that whatever the truth of their doctrine might be, the hopes of both the tolerant and the intolerant that "religion" might finally become extinct are not only vain but self-contradictory.

Meanwhile, the ecstatic experience, which in itself and independent of doctrine we may call the experience of grace, is clearly to be found not only in eighteenth-century Virginia, but everywhere in Western culture, and in virtually every other culture. It's been argued that the phenomenon is entirely independent of religions,

---

[23] R. A. Nicholson, *The Mystics of Islam*, 1914, repr., Arkana Books, 1989; World Wisdom, 2002, p. 43. Idries Shah, *Oriental Magic*, Arkana Books, 1993, p. 70. Both sources are based on ʿAbd al-Karīm ibn Hūzān Abū al-Qāsim al-Qushayrī al-Naysābūrī, *Al-Qushayri's Epistle on Sufism* (MS ca. 1045 CE, trans., Alexander Knysh, Garnet Publishing, 2007). Note that "The Enlightenment" in the Western European sense is usually translated in Arabic as التنوير, *al tanwir*, which, though it recalls a root for "lighting," usually denotes "education," and, as in Western languages, that is not the same as the "enlightenment" that comes from ecstasies.

[24] I should point out here that without the research into the primary sources done by these predecessors, especially those whose command of Arabic or Hebrew is not as rudimentary as mine, but who have published their work in English, French or German, this history could not have been written.

[25] This dialectic of "piety" and "moralism" in religious expression may have appeared first in Joseph Haroutunian's classic history, *Piety versus Moralism: The Passing of the New England Theology* (NY: Henry Holt, 1932), but it remains valid and can be extended, I think, to religions other than American Protestantism.

unless simple erotic ecstasy, or the common reaction of mere humans to catastrophic social change or cultural despair is uniformly to be labeled religious.

Even more interesting to the historian is the fact that the experience becomes more "popular" in some times and places than it does in others. Thus we can see it flare up in the early eighteenth century in Christianity—Catholic as well as Protestant—and with the same urgency at the same time in Judaism and Islam. That remarkable co-incidence is why this book asks license to wander across religious, denominational and doctrinal boundaries—not to mention temporal and geographical ones—in the examination of multiple instances of this single experience, possibly one of the more common experiences of humankind—despite the many names it has been given and the difficulty of repeating it—and to wander without differentiating between the genuine and the illusory, excluding the fraudulent only when and where it can clearly be determined to be fraudulent. This author's own culture (and historical training) makes it easiest to find it in the Abrahamic monotheisms; but he thinks he can discern the same sequence of related experiences in Hinduism, Buddhism, and even Confucianism, as well as classic paganism, shamanism, and traditional and local cults on all continents. Something like it can be seen in the Longhouse Religion preached by Handsome Lake among the embattled Iroquois in the 1790s, the Shawnee visions of Tecumseh's brother The Prophet, or the Ghost Dance prophesied by Wovoka among the equally embattled Paiute a century later.

To demonstrate, we have only to range Shubal Stearns, the New England Baptist who became the first revival evangelist in Virginia, against his Virginia contemporary, Thomas Jefferson. Or Voltaire, Franklin, Hume, Moses Mendelssohn, Kant, and others whom students of the eighteenth century put in the foreground of the West's Enlightenment, against their very different contemporaries, well known to them but backgrounded and (except for Rousseau) rarely mentioned in scholarly papers. Voltaire's brother Armand Arouet was a convert to an enthusiastic sect of Catholics called "Jansénistes," and believed that the miraculous cures and ecstatic prophesies of the jansenist "convulsionaries" heralded the return of Christ. At the same time, in the same France, the proscribed Protestants were exfoliating a similar sect, the Camisards, whom the English (notably Shaftesbury) ironically called the "French Prophets" when they crossed the Channel and tried to convert England. The eminently reasonable Deist Ben Franklin was induced by a *fortissimo* revival sermon from his visiting English friend the Reverend George Whitefield, to contribute to that evangelical Church-of-England minister's program for new churches in the American south and mass conversions in the American west. In the Scotland of David Hume and Adam Smith, Presbyterian ministers devised the first outdoor mass communion services, an early model in the rise of outdoor revivals in both England and America.[26]

In Saxony, where Moses Mendelssohn became a leader of the Jewish Enlightenment, Count Zinzendorf had established the pioneering Protestant evangelical community of the Moravian United Brethren. North of Saxony, the parents

[26] Schmidt, *Holy Fairs* (1989), 2nd ed., pb, Grand Rapids, MI: Eerdmans, 2001.

of Immanuel Kant had shared ecstatic prayer in their Pietist Lutheran conventicles, and well south of Saxony, in a small town in Galicia, Rabbi Israel ben Eliezer, the Ba'al Shem Tov, was trembling before the Torah as he talked to God, turning his encounter with the mysticism and magic of Kabbalah into a new kind of ecstatic religious understanding and practice in Judaism which would come to be called Hasidic.

In the very large world of Dar al-Islam, "science" had retreated in the 12th and 13th centuries after triumphing in the 9th and 10th.[27] At the same time Ṣufi mystics, who had arisen in the eighth century, never stopped dancing in ecstasy, and Ṣufi sages, who had long denied the universality of reason, preserved an alternative vision. By a curious backward route, they also initiated a transmission in the 18th century to the likes of Muhammad ibn ʿAbd al-Waḥhab of Arabia, Shah Waliullah of Delhi, and the Mahdis of Afghanistan, Somalia, Sumatra and the Sudan, with Ibrahima Sori, Karamoko Alfa Barry and Uthman Dan Fodio, of a new level of conviction which an eighteenth-century French *philosophe* would unhesitatingly have called "fanatisme"—the state of being possessed by a god—but which was, as we shall see, built on a disillusioned post-Ṣufi rejection of precisely that concept of possession.

The European and American world in that same eighteenth century was the era of the Enlightenment: of Newton's predictable cosmos, Voltaire's cool rationalism, Franklin's practical science, Jefferson's deism, Moses Mendelssohn's bounded Judaism (*ḥaskalah*, the ancestor of what we now call "Reform"), Diderot's ethical experimentalism, Bentham's utility calculus, Madison's disinterested or interest-balancing constitutionalism, the unmanageable "invisible hand" of Adam Smith, the Unitarianism of Boston's Reverend Charles Chauncy and English chemist Joseph Priestley, even Hume's ever-incomplete induction and Kant's self-limiting epistemology. This was the century of the *philosophes*, the era when the English word "Enlightenment," the French word *Lumières* (lights), the Spanish word *Illuminismo* (illumination), the Russian просвещение, (*Prosveshcheniye*, education by illumination), and the German word *Aufklärung* (illumination/clarification) ceased to mean a religious inner light or subjective inspiration and came to mean instead the cool and common, outer, objective sort of light—the daylight of reason—combined with a prudent silence about shadows beyond its reach. It very much resembles the common sense which Descartes—himself an intense dreamer—mocked in the ironic opening sentence of his *Discourse on Method*, as "the most evenly distributed of all intellectual qualities, because everyone thinks he has enough of it, and even the most acquisitive seem never to want more of it than they have."

We can recognize in Descartes' *bon sens* (common sense) a healthy share of what the nineteenth century would call the scientific attitude, or simply, "science."

[27] An interesting recent historical study describes how methods of interpretation, sanctified as "Enlightenment" approaches were not first applied to Arabic or Islamic texts by Muslims, but by Europeans. It leaves out what might be called a Muslim Enlightenment featuring the scientific and philosophical work done by Muslims in the 8th-10th centuries: Alexander Bevilacqua, *The Republic of Arabic Letters: Islam and the European Enlightenment*, Cambridge, MA: Harvard University Press, 2018.

Nature was cast by Newton's Enlightenment disciples as the source of reliable knowledge, gained by repeatable experiments, which revealed ever more precisely measurable material qualities, whose relations could be described mathematically. It was physics, clearly distinguished at last from metaphysics. The belief that two plus two was invariably equal to four seemed unlikely to let you down, or meet with an unanswerable argument. Knowledge of what the Enlightenment saw as "religion" could not be acquired like mathematics. It had already badly failed to prove its universality in the sixteenth-century European Wars of Religion, and it was not in the same category of reliability. Descartes had unobtrusively bracketed it away in his 1637 *Discourse on Method*. A generation later, Newton had turned as much as he could of it into cosmology. A century later Voltaire simply made a standing joke of theology—and three centuries after Voltaire, the brilliant Bertrand Russell was still smiling.

The Enlightenment as a movement agreed on a suspicion of all known "revealed" religions, especially those with theologies, from Hinduism and Islam to Judaism and Christianity, and of all religious organizations, whether church or *shul* or *ulama* and *ummah*.[28] The Enlightenment was anticlerical (priests were considered unnecessary or detrimental to religion), "antinomian" (anti-law in the sense that laws about human conduct were understood not as a supernatural but a natural creation, or possibly a human one), and anti-liturgical (ritual was thought to be not only atavistic or primitive but irrelevant to both belief and ethics). The only membership organization for whose rituals Enlightened Westerners seemed able to set aside their suspicion was the Freemasons, an international brotherhood (and in the radical Netherlands, a brother-and-sisterhood) which was devoted to deism's single creator God (a secret which it kept from all outsiders) and which preached ethical universalism and human equality (albeit from the topmost ranks of a complicated co-optive hierarchy of its own).

Morals were important to Enlightenment thinking, of course, and so was society. Indeed, most Enlightenment thinkers dreamed that without religion to complicate things, it could make morals as universal as mathematics. Most Enlightenment thinkers were confident that what they identified as "religion" (God and the supernatural)

---

[28] Christopher de Bellaigue, *The Islamic Enlightenment*, has recently argued that the Enlightenment was not a Western invention but a global human trend. To do this he uses the history of Islam—and not in the 800s with the likes of Avicenna, but in the 1800s, with the likes of Muhammad Ali of Egypt, a time when the Enlightenment pretty clearly came to Dar al-Islam from Europe. De Bellaigue writes that his "is the first … written in English, for the general reader, that documents Islam's transformation," and "argues that an Islamic Enlightenment did indeed take place, under the influence of the West, but finding its own form." By "Enlightenment" he means the term that "evokes the defeat of dogma by proven knowledge, the demotion of the clergy from their position as arbiters of society and the relegation of religion to the private sphere. It denotes the ascendancy of democratic principles and the emergence of the individual to challenge the collective to which he or she belongs." And he adds the even more contentious proposition (contentious since Hume and Herder) that "These ideas are transferable across all systems of belief," meaning that Enlightenment is universal, as characteristic of human societies as religion is. (de Bellaigue, *The Islamic Enlightenment: The Struggle Between Faith and Reason, 1798 to Modern Times*, NY: Liveright (Kindle Edition), 2017, p. xxiv).

could be separated from both. In the seventeenth century Spinoza had simply identified Nature with God, and derived *Ethics* (his 1677 title) from that.[29] Enlightenment deists, however, imagined the relationship between a person and God to be as distant and impersonal as it was possible to conceive; because a god whose major role was to create and maintain the universe must surely have bigger and better things to consider than any one among the many millions of human lives lived or yet to be lived on one of God knows how many habitable planets. A similar change in a child's faith in Santa Claus comes with her growing appreciation of the engineering difficulties the saint must encounter in delivering gifts to millions of earth's children in one night. A few eighteenth-century Enlightenment atheists like David Hume, Denis Diderot and the Baron d'Holbach took the small step that remained and argued that such a distant relationship with God was a relationship with nothing, with no one at all.

In short, so many Western thinkers—especially Americans—have so loved the Enlightenment, that they have chipped away what were the companions of its own time and exhibited it as a monolith. But, as Enlightenment scholars have objected in vain, a monolith is something the Western Enlightenment never was.[30] Its prophets and scientists, preachers and encyclopedists, enthusiasts and rationalists, Romantics and Augustans, evangelicals and deists, Shakers and Unitarians, *ḥasidim* and

[29] Spinoza, famously labeled an atheist Jew, is a key figure in the Enlightenment, as Jonathan Israel's great work on the radical Enlightenment reminds us, but also in the changeover from what we call the Enlightenment to the Counter-Enlightenment. In 1783–85, the Enlightenment's great German Jewish exemplar, Moses Mendelssohn, got into a pamphlet war about Spinoza with his friend, the Counter-Enlightenment's Friedrich Heinrich Jacobi. Neither was as appreciative of Spinoza as Herder and many other Counter-Enlightenment figures became somewhat later, but in his pamphlet Jacobi argued for faith and revelation over reason and Mendelssohn the contrary.

[30] Enlightenment specialists of the past two generations have done a lot to make this clear, but education in the humanities for non-specialists, perhaps especially in America, has yet to be updated in the twenty-first century. In an earlier book, *Christian Apologetics in France: The Roots of Romantic Religion, 1750–1801*. (Lewiston, NY: Edwin Mellen Press, 1989), I found no difficulty recognizing many commitments characteristic of the Enlightenment in Christian clerics. Jesuits in particular adopted empiricism in what they thought of as theological nonessentials like natural philosophy (science), which is not why Voltaire attacked them or why the Pope expelled their Society. Recent studies which have gone deeper, destabilized the "monolith," and found similar ideological diversity, begin with Jeffrey D. Burson's "Towards a New Comparative History of European Enlightenments: The Problem of Enlightenment Theology in France and the Study of Eighteenth-century Europe," *Intellectual History Review* 18:2(July, 2008), p173–187; and David Sorkin's *The Religious Enlightenment: Protestants, Jews, and Catholics from London to Vienna*. (Princeton, NJ: Princeton University Press, 2008). Sorkin notably includes the French abbé Lamourette whose apologias for Catholic Christianity in the 1780s abandoned the seventeenth-century norm (natural religion first, followed by prophecies authenticated by miracles proving revealed religion) for an epistemology based on acknowledgement of finitude, "sentiment" as a source of truth, and a "heart" religion that resembles seventeenth-century Protestant Pietism. The French philosophic party found it ridiculous. Sorkin finds it "Enlightened." But Lamourette's view, explicitly respectful of Rousseau's, as I found writing *Christian Apologetics in France*, is actually a better example of the Counter-Enlightenment than can be found in Bonald or Joseph de Maistre.

maskilim,[31] were all contemporaries, like the Ṣufis, the Salafin and the scientists in the enlightened Islamic tenth century, and again in the more Salafist 18th. Dissent from Enlightenment showed up the moment the word began to be used, some of it from within the movement itself.

As for the ecstatic experiences exhibited by those people in Virginia (and by the Ḥasidim and the Ṣufis) and deemed by them to have joined them to the divine, it is more common in the world's historical record than most American historians expect. Educated converts may never have been a majority even at earlier times and in societies that approve of conversion more than ours does. The big data may not be in yet, but it seems that a solid majority of western intellectuals since the Enlightenment has failed to report any personal experiences of grace, and many of them have proceeded on the assumption that most such experiences must be either illusory, drug-induced or delusional, even psychotic.[32] Or worse, un-modern. Or simply fraudulent, following what Montaigne, a skeptical Christian, wrote in the middle of his religion's civil wars in the sixteenth century, "I find no quality so easy to counterfeit as religious devotion."[33] The record does indeed show that religious ecstasy and its immediate results are alarmingly easy to fake or enact and not impossible for companions to evoke, or the self to induce. Not all accounts and not even most of them, however, can be dismissed this way. Ecstasy happens, often involuntarily, and so does religious commitment and moral change.

Christians have called the fruits of ecstasy "grace," "conversion," "sanctification," "gifts of the Spirit" or even "baptism of fire"; and most evangelical or charismatic

[31] Introducing in 2017, the first comprehensive history of Hasidism in English—the third in any language since Shmuel Abba Horodezky's in 1922 and Simon Dubnow's, 90-year old classic in Hebrew, (*Toldot ha-ḥasidut*, 3v, Tel Aviv, 1930–1932, also published in German), David Biale and his team of seven authors cleared the historiography by asserting a premise much like that of this book: "We are accustomed to think of the Enlightenment and its critique of religion as representing modernity, while seeing movements of religious revival as reactionary, throwbacks to an earlier age.

"Yet the story of modernity is more complex. As we now know, the trajectory of history did not lead in a straight line from religion to secularism, 'darkness' to 'light': religion is as much a part of the modern world as it was of the medieval. As much as religion typically claims to stand for tradition, even the most seemingly 'orthodox' or 'fundamentalist' forms of religion in the modern world are themselves products of their age. Just as secularism was incubated in the womb of religion, so religion since the eighteenth century is a product of its interaction with secularism." (David Biale, David Assaf, Benjamin Brown, Uriel Gellman, Samuel Heilman, Moshe Rosman, Gadi Sagiv, Marcin Wodziński, and Arthur Green, *Hasidism: A New History*, Princeton, NJ: Princeton University Press. 2017, Kindle Edition, p. 1)

[32] Any list of such minority intellectuals under mainstream suspicion must begin with Blaise Pascal, the great seventeenth-century mathematician, an Augustinian Catholic and a Jansenist. His brief, written account of his ecstatic vision of the divine was found at his death, sewn into his coat. Notable exceptions in the nineteenth century include both Tolstoy and Dostoevsky, and in the twentieth century C. S. Lewis and the Inklings, the painter Georges Rouault, the philosopher Simone Weill, James Baldwin (until he loudly recanted), and Paul Ricœur the epistemologist of faith versus suspicion himself.

[33] "Je ne trouve aucune qualité si aysee à contrefaire, que la devotion, si on n'y conforme les moeurs et la vie : son essence est abstruse et occulte, les apparences faciles et pompeuses." Michel de Montaigne, "Du repentir (On repentance)," *Essays* III:2.

congregations disqualify from the pastoral-intellectual life anyone who has not had the experience. On the contrary, for anyone aspiring today to a Western intellectual profession, even a specifically American one, a conversion experience can easily be a disqualification.[34] This mutual prejudice has everything to do with the experience itself, and hardly anything to do with doctrine. Neither the possibility of fraud, nor the prejudice of a few, nor a psychological or sociological "explanation" is a condition sufficient to argue that the experience of most of those Virginian Baptists was not "real," or that the behavior that ensued was not honest and right from the point of view either of the participants or of the God whose existence and concern they so passionately affirmed.

Liberal thought was once patient, even indulgent with religion, perhaps because liberalism was ascendant enough to be generous, or perhaps because many liberals nursed a hope that religion was on a natural course to extinction, like slavery or aristocracy, that they could afford to be smug. According to Bertrand Russell, "Religion is something left over from the infancy of our intelligence; it will fade away as we adopt reason and science as our guidelines."[35] Atheists in particular have insisted that religion is a disorder that must somehow be fixed if the world is to survive or move "into broad, sunlit uplands," as Churchill, describing his country as a defender of "Christian Civilization," put it during the 1940 air Battle of Britain. Indeed, a democratic majority of my own history students has held over many years that the best thing to do with religion would be to get rid of it.

My response has been to try to show my students that, like communism, neither democracy nor capitalism nor modernization is likely to provide this outcome, or anything like it. What the students recommend now was taken up quite a long time ago by Paul-Henri Thiry, the Baron d'Holbach, who led a salon in Enlightenment

---

[34] A few "mainstream" religious denominations ordinarily disdain ecstasy and rapture, like Reform Judaism, Unitarian Protestantism and Sunni Islam. The protestant Church of England, together with its offspring the U.S. Episcopal Church in which this writer was confirmed, has long expressed pride in its determination to show as little "enthusiasm" as possible: In the year that the Glorious Revolution put Protestants William and Mary on the English throne in place of Catholic James II, a book appeared by one William Wharton titled *The Enthusiasm of the Church of Rome ...* . Wharton's attack on enthusiasts, Catholic ones in particular, exulted that:

"It has been the peculiar happiness of the Church of England to create a right sense of Religion and Piety in all her Communicants, and secure to them the practice of a rational Devotion. She makes no pretensions to private Inspirations, and extraordinary Illuminations of the Holy Ghost; and all her Children are more apt to deride, than admire the follies of the Enthusiasts.... Not so the Church of Rome, ... (Wharton, *The Enthusiasm of the Church of Rome demonstrated in some observations upon the life of Ignatius Loyola*, London, 1688, p. 16, in Keitt, "Religious Enthusiasm, the Spanish Inquisition, and the Disenchantment of the World" *Jnl of the History of Ideas* 65:2(April, 2004) p231).

Nevertheless, there were evangelicals in the Church of England, notably the "Clapham Sect," whom some now call "pre-Victorians," and that there were enough of them in the British elite, even in Parliament, to lead the British opponents of slavery and win parliamentary abolition of the slave trade.

[35] This sentiment is repeatedly attributed to Bertrand Russell, but the Bertrand Russell Society has yet to track down a source for it in Russell's writings.

Paris which regularly referred to all religions as "the sacred disease" (the Greek name for epileptic seizures that the great ancient Greek physician Hippocrates had rejected).[36] They hoped a cure could be found, or that religion, particularly the Jansenist "convulsionaries" who had writhed and prophesied in Paris a decade or so before d'Holbach's salon, could be fought like smallpox, with educational inoculation;[37] but events since d'Holbach's eighteenth century have offered more than enough proof to convince a historian that the "sacred disease" is not, in fact, curable. David Hume, the consummate Enlightenment *philosophe* who came to d'Holbach's salon in 1762 and was no partisan of theism, avoided that risky line of argument by distinguishing an undefined "true religion" from two ecstatic "false" ones, "Superstition and Enthusiasm," in a 1741 *Essay* of that name.[38] And the very Enlightened Earl of Shaftesbury had already written in 1707, "even atheism is not exempt from it [enthusiasm]. For, as some have well remarked, there have been Enthusiastical atheists."[39]

---

[36] One of d'Holbach's many polemical writings was, indeed, *La Contagion sacrée, ou Histoire naturelle de la superstition* [*The Sacred Contagion: A Natural History of Superstition*] ("Londres" [London], 1768). The Baron's many books were usually published like this one, anonymously and, actually or purportedly, in cities like London or Amsterdam that were not subject to the French Catholic state censorship.

[37] Alan Charles Kors, *D'Holbach's Coterie: An Enlightenment in Paris* (Princeton, NJ: Princeton University Press, 1976) is still the best introduction to the *coterie Holbachique*, its international reach, and its take on Enlightenment.

[38] Of the two "false religions," Hume distinguished "superstition" as the one that appeals to the fearful or melancholic person. By contrast, Hume writes, a healthy, well-endowed and willful person will have a more positive imagination and tend to the other "false religion" that he called (as had Shaftesbury) "enthusiasm." ("True religion" is neither, but both corrupt it.) Living in Scotland and France, Hume saw both Methodists and Jansenists arise in his time, and memorably describes the onset of enthusiasm in these bold imaginers: "Every thing mortal and perishable vanishes as unworthy of attention. And a full range is given to the fancy in the invisible regions or world of spirits, where the soul is at liberty to indulge itself in every imagination, which may best suit its present taste and disposition. Hence arise raptures, transports, and surprising flights of fancy; and confidence and presumption still encreasing, these raptures, being altogether unaccountable, and seeming quite beyond the reach of our ordinary faculties, are attributed to the immediate inspiration of that Divine Being, who is the object of devotion. In a little time, the inspired person comes to regard himself as a distinguished favourite of the Divinity; and when this frenzy once takes place, which is the summit of enthusiasm, every whimsy is consecrated: Human reason, and even morality are rejected as fallacious guides: And the fanatic madman delivers himself over, blindly, and without reserve, to the supposed illapses of the spirit, and to inspiration from above. Hope, pride, presumption, a warm imagination, together with ignorance, are, therefore, the true sources of ENTHUSIASM." (Hume, "Of Superstition and Enthusiasm," in *Essays Moral and Political*, Edinburgh: A. Kincaid 1741, pp141–143).

[39] "there have been *Enthusiastical atheists*. Nor can divine inspiration, by its outward marks, be easily distinguished from it. For inspiration is a real feeling of the Divine Presence, and enthusiasm *a false one*. But the Passion they raise is much alike." —Anthony Ashley Cooper, 3rd Earl of Shaftesbury, "A Letter Concerning Enthusiasm" (Sep, 1707) *Characteristics of Men, Manners, Opinions, Times* (1st edition, 1708), London: Grant Richards, 1900, vol. 1, Sec. 7, p. 37. Shaftesbury's opinions circulated widely and were often reprinted. The *OED* quotes this one from the 1737 edition (*Characteristicks*, §7:1737, I, 53). The edition John Adams used was the 5th

Confucians follow a religion which lacks most of these "religious" commitments, and this may be because, despite postulating a universe that endorses a morality, it has no formulable theology. Perhaps if we do as Confucius advised Tzu-lu and the ruler of Wei and get the words right, explanations will follow.

> If names be not correct, language is not in accordance with the truth of things. If language be not in accordance with the truth of things, affairs cannot be carried on to success.[40]

The new Western Enlightenment had many opponents who were orthodox, and some who were evangelical, but it also acquired enemies who were neither. In the twentieth century, Humanities scholars here in the West fielded three new terms to try to comprehend the Enlightenment's discontents without including the evangelicals. Conventional wisdom among these scholars had been that the Enlightenment was succeeded after the French Revolution by the culture of Romanticism. Romantics like Keats and Poe, Schiller and Victor Hugo were thought of as supplanting Alexander Pope, Jane Austen, Kant and Voltaire, as Beethoven supplanted Bach, and Goya's *Dreams of Reason Produce Monsters* supplanted Velazquez. Romanticism stood for the rehabilitation of emotion, of magic, mystery, the irrational and the ineffable, the infinite undefinable over the finite and measurable. Feelings were to be expressed rather than bridled or tamed or moderated, or even justified. The disordered and sublime was more evocative, and likely to be truer, than the ordered and beautiful. And whether or not demons existed, religion was no longer the adversary, as Romantic literary icons like Chateaubriand tried to argue in 1801 in *The Genius of Christianity*, and Madame de Staël in 1810 in *On Germany*.[41]

Nevertheless, the scholars did not really try to apply the term "Romanticism," since it seemed to require confinement to the period 1790–1830 (or for the French, 1830–1850), *after* the Enlightenment, appropriate for a reaction but not for a coeval. The brilliant historian of ideas Isaiah Berlin used the term at the beginning of his career, but not after he became Sir Isaiah in the middle of it. The term "Pre-Romanticism," conceived primarily for European literatures between 1750 and 1800, was championed in the 1920s by pioneering professors of Comparative Literature like Paul Van Tieghem in France, but it failed signally to persuade professors of

---

(Birmingham, 1773). Shaftesbury's disparagement of "enthusiasm" was early, but as we shall see, it was a holding action that ended in the Counter-Enlightenment.

[40] Kong Fuzi [Confucius], *Xunzi* [*Analects*] Book XIII, verse 3, tr. Legge.

[41] François René de Chateaubriand, *Le génie du christianisme, ou beautés de la religion chrétienne*, 5v, Paris: Migneret, 1801–02. Madame de Staël (Germaine de Staël-Holstein), *De l'Allemagne*, Paris: Nicolle, 1810 (edition destroyed by order of Napoleon), reprinted, London: John Murray, 1813. Staël's verdict on Enlightenment empiricism, inspired by her appreciation of Kant, was: "Dogmatic disbelief, which is to say that which places in doubt all that which can't be proved by our sensations, is the source of the great irony of man towards himself: all moral degradation stems from that." (*De l'Allemagne*, Part 3, Chapter 4, translated by Claudia Moscovici @ https://literaturesalon.wordpress.com/2010/09/08/madame-de-stael-the-ultimate-philosophe-and-salonniere/).

English literature.[42] The third and last rubric was "Counter-Enlightenment,"[43] first inscribed in dictionaries by Isaiah Berlin through his article by that name in the *Dictionary of the History of Ideas* (1973).[44] There, Berlin summed up the better

[42] Paul Van Tieghem, *Le Préromantisme, Etudes d'histoire littéraire européenne*, 3v, Paris: Alcan, 1924, 1930, 1947. Marshall Brown's *Preromanticism* (Stanford, CA: Stanford University Press, 1998) did bring the term back recently with a wonderfully perceptive and seriously philosophic thematic approach to seventeent- and eighteenth-century English literature, but he made no attempt to apply it to any other Western literature. Both the oldest effort to gather the literatures of the entire world under a single set of categories (H. M. Posnett, *Comparative Literature*, London: Kegan Paul, Trench / NY: D. Appleton (International Scientific Series v50), 1886), and the most recent (David Damrosch, *How to Read World Literature*, Wiley-Blackwell, 2009; 2nd ed., 2017) do not offer much help in analyzing the categories that relate to religion.

[43] The term is not, of course, contemporary with the movement, though it does seem to have first appeared as the German *Gegenaufklärung* in the *Deutsche Monatsschrift* for November, 1790. James Schmidt describes finding, forgetting, relocating, losing, and recovering this 1790 reference in his blog *Persistent Enlightenment*: "Robert Wokler, J.G.A. Pocock, and the Hunt for an Eighteenth-Century Usage of 'Counter-Enlightenment'" @ https://persistentenlightenment.com/2016/10/12/robbie-wokler-j-g-a-pocock-and-the-hunt-for-an-eighteenth-century-usage-of-counter-enlightenment/.

[44] Isaiah Berlin came to own the term "Counter-Enlightenment," but so far as I can determine from Henry Hardy's editing of his published legacy, he did not use it much before his article, "The Counter-Enlightenment," in the *Dictionary of the History of Ideas* (NY: Scribner's, 1973, vol. 2, pp100–112), preferring before 1970 to think of its elements under the rubric of Romanticism (cf. Berlin, *The Roots of Romanticism* (MS 1965), ed., Henry Hardy, Princeton, NJ: Princeton University Press, 1999, pb, 2001). The term "Enlightenment" is itself a retronym, but "Counter-Enlightenment," is even more so, coming more than a century and a half after the fact. "Counter-Enlightenment" was probably introduced into anglophone criticism long after the Enlightenment (but before Berlin) by William Barrett in a 1949 article in *Partisan Review*. Barrett wrote: "Mr. [Lionel] Trilling indicates what might be described as the Counter-Enlightenment in the figures of Pascal, Blake, Burke and Wordsworth. I agree that the movement of the Counter-Enlightenment is a very deep and significant one in modern thought ..." His roster included Rousseau, Nietzsche (though Nietzsche called Pascal's work a "suicide of reason"), and extended on to as recent a thinker as Heidegger. (William Barrett, "Art, Aristocracy, and Reason," *Partisan Review* 16:6(1949), as quoted by Schmidt @ https://persistentenlightenment.com/2014/01/20/countere5/). The term was probably suggested by the English word "Counter-Reformation" (*OED*, 1840) and augmented by "Counter-Renaissance," invented by Hiram Haydn in his *The Counter-Renaissance* (New York, 1950). It was used by E. V. Walter ("Power, Civilization and the Psychology of Conscience," *American Political Science Review*, 53:3(September, 1959), p. 654), and by the Americanist Leo Marx in "American Studies—A Defense of an Unscientific Method" (1967, p. 1) as well as in his 1968 review of Frank Manuel's *A Portrait of Isaac Newton*, and was applied to Rousseau in my 1971 doctoral dissertation, published as *Christian Apologetics in France, 1750–1801* (Lewiston, NY: Edwin Mellen Press, 1987), pp. 87–92. In 1982 David Berman began reporting encounters with counter-enlightenment in eighteenth-century Ireland (Berman, "Enlightenment and counter-enlightenment in Irish philosophy and the culmination and causation of Irish philosophy," *Archiv für Geschichte der Philosophie* 64(1982), p148–165, 257–279) In 1989 Christopher McIntosh titled his detailed Oxford dissertation on Rosicrucianism in the eighteenth century as "The Rosicrucian Revival and the German Counter-Enlightenment" but he rebalanced it with Enlightenment in the book he made of the dissertation, *The Rose Cross and the Age of Reason* (Leiden: Brill, 1992; 2nd ed., Albany, NY: State University of New York Press, 2011). By 1998 C. D. A. Leighton had begun to find Counter-Enlightenment in certain trends in Anglicanism. The Counter-Enlightenment has since been extended with great effect by Darrin McMahon in "The Counter-Enlightenment and the Low Life of Literature in Pre-Revolutionary France," *Past &*

half of his ongoing life's work on the intellectual history of powerful, anti- and ante-Enlightenment philosophers like Vico, Hamann, Herder, Fichte, Hegel, and Schelling, German except for Vico, bound together with German literary and religious scholars the philosophers knew, like the Schlegel brothers, the pivotal theologian Friedrich Schleiermacher, and canonical German imaginative writers (labeled "Storm and Stress," "Early Romantic" and "Romantic") who often moved in the same circles, like Tieck, Hölderlin, Novalis (Friedrich von Hardenberg), Schiller, and even Goethe.[45]

To these Berlin added post-French Revolution conservatives and religio-political reactionaries from all over Europe, like Hamann, Möser, Maistre, Bonald,

---

Present, 159(May, 1998), p. 77–112, and in his *Enemies of the Enlightenment: The French Counter-Enlightenment and the Making of Modernity* (NY: Oxford University Press, 2001). Important contributions have also come from James Schmidt ("What Enlightenment Project?" Tenth International Congress on the Enlightenment, Dublin, July 25–31, 1999), from Didier Masseau (*Les ennemis des philosophes: l'antiphilosophie au temps des Lumières*, Paris: Albin Michel, 2000), from Graeme Garrard (*Rousseau's Counter-Enlightenment: A Republican Critique of the Philosophes*, Albany, NY: State University of New York Press, 2003, and *Counter-Enlightenments: From the eighteenth century to the present*. London/New York: Routledge, 2005), from Mark Lilla, ("What Is Counter-Enlightenment?" in Joseph Mali & Robert Wokler, eds. *Isaiah Berlin's Counter-Enlightenment, Transactions of the American Philosophical Society*, 93:5(2003), pp1–12) and from Robert Wokler who included his own 2000 address in the book he edited in 2003 with Joseph Mali (*Isaiah Berlin's Counter-Enlightenment*) with essays by Lilla, Mali, McMahon, and Garrard, as well as by Roger Hausheer, Frederick Beiser, Lionel Gossman, John E. Toews and Michael Confino. More recent scholarly reaction has begun to call it an un-historical category, like "Pre-romanticism," or a myth, as Robert E. Norton did in his "The Myth of the Counter-Enlightenment" (*Journal of the History of Ideas*, 68:4(October, 2007), p635–658); but the master Enlightenment historian, Jonathan Israel, has continued to use the term without apology, even about Rousseau. (Jonathan Israel, "Rousseau, Diderot, and the 'Radical Enlightenment': A Reply to Helena Rosenblatt and Joanna Stalnaker," *Journal of the History of Ideas* 77:4(Oct, 2016), p649–677).

[45] Giambattista Vico (1668–1744), Johann Gottfried Herder (1744–1803), Johann Gottlieb Fichte (1762–1814), Georg Wilhelm Friedrich Hegel (1770–1831), and Friedrich Schelling (1775–1854) are known to students of Philosophy but still hardly known (even the celebrated Hegel) to students of Literature. Johann Georg Hamann (1730–1788) whose sudden conversion from Deism to a Pietist and Biblical Lutheranism came in 1758, remains neglected by anglophone readers, even after Isaiah Berlin and Frederick Beiser (*The Fate of Reason: German Philosophy from Kant to Fichte*, Cambridge, MA: Harvard University Press, 1987) demonstrated his importance. Friedrich Schleiermacher (1768–1834) is still conventionally compartmentalized as a theologian. The Schlegel brothers August (1767–1845) and Friedrich (1772–1829), Ludwig Tieck (1773–1853), Friedrich Hölderlin (1770–1843), and "Novalis" (Friedrich von Hardenberg, 1772–1801) remain on few non-German syllabi. Friedrich Schiller (1759–1805) and Johann Wolfgang von Goethe (1749–1832) are, of course, two colossal icons of German literature in a multitude of its forms, including poetry, plays, history and philosophy. That polyvalence helps keep them on the "Romantic" roster, despite their later insistence on their own "Classicism." Isaiah Berlin began his long study of what he came to call the Counter-Enlightenment with a study of many of these figures, his 1965 Mellon Lectures, published as *The Roots of Romanticism*. (ed., Henry Hardy, Princeton, NJ: Princeton University Press, 1999, pb, 2001), and despite deep and intelligent criticism, it has not been discredited. Cf. H. G. Callaway, Review of Berlin, *The Roots of Romanticism*, ResearchGate, January, 2003, Online @ https://www.researchgate.net/publication/317845465_Review_of_Berlin_The_Roots_of_Romanticism.

Gentz, Görres, Adam Müller, Edmund Burke, and the English poet Samuel Taylor Coleridge.[46] All of these men lived and wrote as the 18th century turned to the 19th and criticized the Enlightenment for four major faults, its distrust of passion and enthusiasm, its insistence on the epistemological independence and pre-eminence of "reason," its evasion of infinites, its insistence, in the name of universalism, on often arid generalizations that purged more particular truths, its philosophical antipathy to revealed religion, its hostility to received ideas and values, and what they saw as the failure of its faith-free universalism. Berlin's "Counter-Enlightenment," shows every sign of surviving and I will use it here, opening it as boldly as possible to other, quite different religious and cultural traditions.[47] Rolling out an up-to-date category should stimulate understanding, though it may not guarantee it.

The Counter-Enlightenment arose only a little later than evangelicalism in the Abrahamics, in the same eighteenth century. Up to now it has been confined to an intellectual movement in the Christian West. Berlin, the preeminent intellectual historian of the Counter-Enlightenment, located its origins in Germany, but Berlin hardly admitted that evangelicals of any kind might have preceded or helped to shape what he first called "Romanticism," writing, "We do not regard the Hebrew prophets or Savonarola or even Methodist preachers as particularly Romantic."[48] Berlin did however place German Pietists, including the proto-evangelical Zinzendorf, among those "Roots of Romanticism,"[49] and he was right. Nearly all of those German thinkers, including Hamann, Tieck, Hölderlin, Schiller and Schleiermacher, had been raised in the pre-evangelical "heart" religion of Lutheran Pietism. Novalis, whose

[46] Contemporaries Joseph de Maistre (1753–1821) and Louis de Bonald (1754–1840) became the two polemical leading lights of the reactionary Right in the French Restoration. Justus Möser (1720–1794), Friedrich von Gentz (1764–1832), Joseph Görres (1776–1848), and Adam Müller (1779–1829) played much the same role for German-speaking Europe. Burke and Coleridge played leading parts in English conservatism, though not in American until much later. Berlin did not miss much, but he did leave out the Romantic poet Robert Southey, friend of Coleridge, who wrote an admiring biography of John Wesley: *The Life of Wesley and the Rise of Methodism.* (2v. 1820; London: Longman, Brown, Green, and Longmans, 1846 @ https://archive.org/details/lifewesleyandri01soutgoog/page/n406/mode/2up). Berlin also missed Emmanuel Swedenborg (1668–1772), the Swedish Enlightenment mining engineer and mineralogist who regularly reported visions of Heaven and Hell; but Swedenborg had no political position and perhaps that omission was deliberate. John Wesley himself read Swedenborg, but wrote of his visions in Enlightenment register in his *Journal* in 1770: "one might as easily swallow the stories of 'Tom Thumb'." Nevertheless, among Swedenborg's appreciative Counter-Enlightenment readers was Wesley's conservative biographer Robert Southey, and among his most enthusiastic was an anticlerical pro-revolutionary artist who signed with the Swedenborgian New Jerusalem Church in London as a sympathizer in 1789, left it when it expelled its radicals, but reflected Swedenborg's visionary influence for the rest of his life—William Blake.

[47] I tried to corral Jean-Jacques Rousseau with the term Counter-Enlightenment in my *Christian Apologetics in France, 1750–1801* (1971, repr., Lewiston, NY: Edwin Mellen Press, 1987), pp 87–92.

[48] Berlin, *The Roots of Romanticism* (MS 1965), ed., Henry Hardy, Princeton, NJ: Princeton University Press, 1999, pb, 2001, p. 23.

[49] Berlin, *The Roots of Romanticism*, chapter 3, p. 43.

father was close to Moravians, gave Zinzendorf high praise.[50] In any case, it was Berlin who first made the point that no matter what you called it, the movement's core was the idea that the individual and particular is truer than the universal, that feeling can be better than thinking, that expressing or indulging the "passions" was far better than bridling them.

Instead of reason, Counter-Enlightenment thinking made "passion" and "commitment" valuable in themselves, even in those who were committed passionately to what most people in their own culture might condemn as "wrong" or even "evil," like Karl Moor, the outlaw of Schiller's play, *The Robbers* (1781). As the Counter-Enlightenment began to change minds in each Western country, "enthusiasm" rather abruptly became a desirable reaction instead of an unmannerly excess;[51] "rational," "interest," and "measured" became suspect qualities; "artificial" switched from complimentary to disparaging, and "ecstasy" returned from ancient Greek to name a madness that was "divine," or, to use a Romantic, Counter-Enlightenment term, "sublime."[52] It was a positively Nietzschean transvaluation of values before Nietzsche had been born.

---

[50] "only rarely does a sturdy, eternal spark of life leap forth and a small community comes together… So it was with Zinzendorf, Jacob Böhme, and several others." Novalis, *Christendom or Europe* (MS, 1799), in Novalis, *Philosophical Writings*, ed. & trans., Margaret Mahony Stoljar, Albany, NY: State University of New York Press, 1997, p. 142. Martin Dyck's *Novalis and Mathematics* (Assen, Netherlands: Royal VanGorcum, 1959) reminds us that Novalis's positive view of "heart" religion went along with an advanced appreciation of the mathematical infinite, and included the fragment "Reine Mathematik ist Religion"—"Pure mathematics is religion." Nor was this attitude confined to German Romantics. Madame de Staël, a contemporary who was French, but Swiss by origin, learned about the Moravians when she was writing her extraordinary book on German culture, and she included an admiring chapter on them. (Staël, *De l'allemagne*, 1810, 1813, Part 4, Chapter 3). William Law, the nonjuring Anglican minister who in 1728 published the oft reprinted *A Serious Call to a Devout and Holy Life* (likewise a call to an English pietist Protestantism), later fell very hard for Jacob Böhme and made a big effort to bring Behmenism into the English mainstream. His influence had become such that he might have succeeded if his correspondent John Wesley had not rejected it.

[51] The topic of enthusiasm, the word and its Romantic reversing of field, is time-honored among scholars of English literature, the latest study being Lionel Laborie's irenic revision of the quarrel, *Enlightening Enthusiasm: Prophecy and religious experience in early eighteenth-century England* (Manchester, UK: Manchester University Press, 2015). Another, more literary study was slyly titled by its author, Shaun Irlam, *Elations: The Poetics of Enthusiasm in Eighteenth-Century Britain* (Stanford, CA: Stanford University Press, 1999). The checkered career of "enthusiasm" in the eighteenth century was earlier traced by Michael Heyd in his *"Be Sober and Reasonable" The Critique of Enthusiasm in the Seventeenth and Early Eighteenth Centuries* (Leiden: E. J. Brill, 1995). In German, the word often closest to "enthusiasm" is *Schwärmerei*, and a good historian's look at that is Anthony J. La Vopa's "The Philosopher and the 'Schwärmer': On the Career of a German Epithet from Luther to Kant," in Lawrence E. Klein & Anthony J. La Vopa, eds. *Enthusiasm and Enlightenment in Europe, 1650–1850*, 1998 (also published in *Huntington Library Quarterly*, vol. 60(1997): 1–2, pp. 85–115).

[52] That classic Enlightenment thinkers, including Adam Smith, considered the "interests," rational, long-term and material, to be a salutary check to the unruly "passions" was nicely demonstrated by Albert O. Hirschman in his classic intellectual history, *The Passions and the Interests* (Princeton, NJ: Princeton University Press, 1976), a book perhaps too deeply appreciated by liberal econo-

A second more philosophical idea flowed partly from the rehabilitation of passion: the idea that because values and ethics were human-made, so entirely human-created that different cultures could not be compared on a single scale of values. They were lacking a common measure, incommensurable like rational and irrational numbers. Philosophical "universalism," the view that human knowledge or any of its branches can be reduced to a single set of principles, simply could not be applied to ethics. Since the irreducible individual was more to be trusted than the mass, and the anecdote more than the generalization, a universal ethics was a chimera. Counter-Enlightenment thinkers followed Hamann and Herder in giving up on both religious and moral universalism. With Christian evangelicals religion dictated morals, and similarly with Muslims and Jews, but religion got shakier in the eighteenth century and it was certainty that lost its universality.

Not to be Draconian in distinguishing one constellation of ideas from another, we should credit that insight about the impossibility of ethical universalism to the Enlightenment *philosophes* themselves. Denis Diderot used the time he could spare from editing the *Encyclopedia*, to write unpublished books that laid an axe to ethical universalism.[53] The Enlightenment's most thoroughgoing skeptic, David Hume, pointed out in his first book in 1739 that a value is not intrinsic to the object valued but is instead attached to the object by human beings, following both their many emotions and their rational consciousness with all their conflicts and contradictions:

> Since morals, therefore, have an influence on the actions and affections, it follows, that they cannot be deriv'd from reason; and that because reason alone, as we have already prov'd, can never have any such influence. Morals excite passions, and produce or prevent actions. Reason of itself is utterly impotent in this particular. The rules of morality, therefore, are not conclusions of our reason.[54]

The Enlightenment's paragon, Immanuel Kant, did his best to take on Hume on this point and to make ethics and religion both reasonable. One of his arguments, the one that concludes with the "categorical imperative," is found convincing by many

mists. The Romantics of the Counter-Enlightenment reversed the valuation—and a more recent generation of economists have won Nobels by rediscovering the "irrational" springs of human behavior.

[53] The materialist attack on moral universalism by Diderot (1713–1784) is found in his fictional Tahitian dialogue, *Supplément au voyage de Bougainville*, published 12 years after his death in 1796, and in his dialogue *Rameau's Nephew*, which was not published until 1805—translated into German by Goethe.

[54] [David Hume], *Treatise of Human Nature*, London, 1739, Book 3: Of Morals, Part 1: Of Virtue and Vice in General, Section 1: Moral Distinctions not deriv'd from Reason, T 457. Hume's priority in this matter, and subsequent evaluations of his contribution, are discussed by Ronald J. Glossop, "The Nature of Hume's Ethics," *Philosophy and Phenomenological Research* 27(1967), pp527–536, especially page 533. A thorough review of Hume's attempt to recast the meaning of religion is a chapter in J. Samuel Preus, ed., *Explaining Religion: Criticism and Theory from Bodin to Freud* (New Haven: Yale University Press, 1987), an outstanding history of the ideas of religion in the West from Bodin in the late sixteenth century to Freud in the early 20th. Preus, however, does not go into this Humean demolition of "reasonable" ethics.

today, but later philosophers, beginning with Kant's neighbor and correspondent Hamann, have not all agreed that religion can be got around so easily.

Evangelical Christianity, the revival Christianity of eighteenth-century back-country Virginia, thrived on Counter-Enlightenment attitudes. The rehabilitation of passion and commitment, and the discrediting of ethical universalism suited them well, even though most of those original German Romantics drew back from evangelical religious affiliation. And we will find similar insights coming along with ecstatic experience not only in revivalist Protestantism, but also in Hasidic Judaism and Ṣufi Islam.

After evangelical religious revival, moreover, what happens next—less dramatically, of course—is the cooling off. The initial ecstasies, prove hard to repeat (at least before the availability of mind-altering drugs), often difficult to maintain, onerous to pass on, almost impossible to inherit. Like that related phenomenon dubbed *charisma* by Max Weber, enthusiasm can hardly survive being institutionalized. As enthusiasm's first English historian, Ronald Knox, wrote more than fifty years ago: "Always the first fervours evaporate; prophecy dies out, and the charismatic is merged in the institutional. 'The high that proved too high, the heroic for earth too hard'—it is a fugal subject that runs through the centuries."[55]

Indeed, time and again, in all kinds of religions, historians can see the second and third generations of evangelical movements pass—or as the evangelicals say, sink—into a state where ecstasy or even fervent faith becomes more rare. For the enthusiastic few, it can be poignant, even tragic. For the rest it will be a return to that desirable postwar state for which conservative U.S. president Warren Harding coined the word "normalcy."

Jewish kabbalists called the normal הלכה—*halakha*—rabbinic law, custom and tradition,[56] or *nigleh*—the non-esoteric, communicable by any old person to a younger. The *Mithnagdim*, eighteenth-century rabbis and their followers who opposed the Ḥasidim on the meaning of kabbalah, called it by a name which people today translate with the Greek word "Orthodox." Ḥasidim faulted it, calling it *shelo lishmah* (unspiritual) or even "joyless." They compared such religious duties to the forlorn remains of God's kabbalistic *zimzum* or "withdrawal" from the created world.

In Islam, the poetry of the Prophet's ecstasies in the *Qur'an*, and the stories of the Prophet, the *ahadith*, as reported by his first followers, the Salafin, were sublimated into law, *shariah* and its four main schools. This is the Sunnah, or tradition, of the Sunni mainstream of Islam. Shiʿa Islam, beginning as Shiʿatu Ali, the Party of Ali, differed over the caliphate of Ali and his descendants, but derived a similar shariʿah. Ṣufi Muslims followed shariʿah from both Shiʿa and Sunni, but were wary of a narrowly judicial Islam which one of the earliest Ṣufis called a "sleep," and one of the

[55] Ronald Knox, *Enthusiasm: A Chapter in the History of Religion, with Special Reference to the Seventeenth and Eighteenth Centuries* (1950), NY: Oxford University Press Galaxy pb, 1961, p1 (Knox's quotation is from Robert Browning's poem, "Abt Vogler").

[56] The Hebrew word is also transliterated as Halacha and Halachah.

latest called hypocritical.[57] More often they called it one form or another of selfishness, the egotism that prevented what they strove for—union with the divine. It was the opposite of *ḥal* (ecstatic state); it was the inability to act;[58] it was non-being, literal unreality, disunion with the real, which was Allah.

American Calvinists called the retreat from inspiration "backsliding," "ignorance," "indifference," "dullness," "dryness," "coldness," "declension," "spiritual sluggishness"[59] and "inanition." "Literalism" and "lip service" came to stand in for "inspiration," and what we now call immediacy and spontaneity. As one nineteenth-century history described it among the Baptists of Boston in 1740, "a torpid community [in a] long and heavy slumber [sunk in] a cold, cadaverous formalism"[60]

And as some will remember, a generation of 1960's activists in the West called it "the 1980s."

In the words of Irshad Manji, a gay left-wing activist, but faithful Muslim woman who was educated among Protestant fundamentalists in Georgia, and has earned her living in Canada as a comedian: "The crucial equilibrium between past and future steadily degenerated into a defensive preoccupation with the past—and, in particular, into a fixation on the founding moment. I call it *fundamentalism*."[61] The distinguished historian of jihad in Muslim India, Ayesha Jalal, calls fundamentalism the result of a "rationalization of the mythical."[62] I would like to call it a failed rationalization of the mystical. This is the counterintuitive process by which "enlightenment," meaning exceptional intellectual illumination or spiritual vision, became the enemy of "The Enlightenment," meaning the improvement of material, mental and social life by the means and attitudes of science.

We should caution ourselves that it is always possible that the "rise" which some historians of Western religion see in religious expression during the eighteenth

---

[57] "a sleep" (Rabi'a al-'Adawiya #30, in Michael A. Sells & Ernst, eds. *Early Islamic Mysticism*, NY: Paulist Press (Classics of Western Spirituality), 1996, p 163. A historian heard the same complaint more recently in Pakistan: "Those hypocrites! They sit there reading their law books and arguing about how long their beards should be, and fail to listen to the true message of the prophet." (recorded in Pakistan by William Dalrymple, "The Muslims in the Middle," *New York Times*, 16Aug, 2011). Both of the Ṣufis quoted above were women.

[58] Abu ʿAbd Allah al-Ḥarith al-Muḥasibi (d. 243/857), *The Book on the Observance of the Rights of God* (*kitab ar-riy'aya li ḥuquq Allah*), in Sells & Ernst, eds. *Early Islamic Mysticism*, p173.

[59] Charles Grandison Finney, *Lectures on Revivals of Religion by Charles Grandison Finney*, ed., William G. McLoughlin (Cambridge, MA: Belknap Press of Harvard University Press, 1960), Lecture 1.

[60] David Benedict, *General History of the Baptist Denomination in America* (NY: Sheldon, Lamport & Blakeman, 1855), p391–393, in H. Leon McBeth, ed., *A Sourcebook for Baptist Heritage* (Nashville, TN; Broadman Press, 2004), 7:1, p143.

[61] Irshad Manji, *The Trouble With Islam: A Muslim's Call for Reform in Her Faith* (NY: St. Martin's, 2004, since retitled *The Trouble With Islam Today*). Irshad Manji was born in Uganda to an Indian father and an Egyptian mother, graduated high school in the U.S. state of Georgia, and in presenting herself as neither Waḥhabi nor Ṣufi, Sunni nor Shiʿa, may represent an alternative future for Islam.

[62] Ayesha Jalal, *Partisans of Allah: Jihad in South Asia*, Cambridge, MA: Harvard University Press, 2008, p. 105.

century is only an effect of a change in perspective. Such an argument would contend that behavior seen as ordinary in previous eras, like mysticism, inspiration and transcendental experience, was made to seem extraordinary in an age whose leading thinkers were "secularized," so suspicious of unusual feelings and uncomfortable with theology and with infinities in general, that they shifted the meaning of "enlightenment" from grace to reason, and gave the pejorative name "enthusiasm" to attitudes and behaviors which their militant rationalism condemned. Our eighteenth-century enthusiasts, in their turn, may have been simply conservatives, anxious to hold on the faith of their fathers—or at least to the behaviors of their parents. Over against all religions, there is always irony at work, the irony, if no other, of time and space.[63]

Historians must treat religion as if it exists, whether or not gods exist, and also as if almost everyone exhibits it. The life of religion, like the life of Oliver Wendell Holmes's Common Law, has not been logic, much less doctrine; it has been experience. Historians study what humans do, and historians are obliged, I think, to approach religion as a ground of human action, and of human ethics—a general, and by definition the fundamental—ground. My object here is to give an account of at least some of these experiences; accounting *for* them may not be possible. The philosophical key to any account I can give is that the historical record—a record of experience—tells us that experiences that are ecstatic, like "second birth," or "mystic union" are the most insistent guarantors of ethical principles and ethical behavior, of choices of values, and of judgments of good and evil—judgments which are never "scientific" and cannot be. Ecstatic experiences, however, are not only unusual, they cannot be reliably repeated, even when people want to repeat them. Because they are so hard to replicate (at least without chemical help), the sciences have so far been unable to assimilate them, and even the faiths in which they have arisen have sometimes found them abnormal and suspicious.

Some will be irritated by a study centered on religious behavior instead of doctrine and belief, while others, like readers of *Varieties of Religious Experience* (1902),

[63] Martin Marty, the magisterial historian of Western religion, who began publishing his four-volume *Modern American Religion*, with a volume subtitled *The Irony of It All* in 1986, introduced it with a chapter called "Modern Religion and Irony" taking his cue not only from the 1960s theoreticians of literary irony but from Reinhold Niebuhr's *The Irony of American History* (NY: Scribner's, 1952) as seen by Richard Reinitz's *Irony and Consciousness: American Historiography and Reinhold Niebuhr's Vision* (Lewisburg, PA, Bucknell University Press, 1980). Marty's ironic take on twentieth-century American religion includes not only the normal irony implicit in the historical perspective and the inevitable mismatch of former hopes with outcomes, but another irony implicit in attitudes to religion, something Reinitz, who called himself a member of "Atheists for Niebuhr," dubbed "humane irony," or ironic distance combined with sympathy. Marty quotes Niebuhr's characterization of God as "a divine judge who laughs at human pretensions without being hostile to human aspirations." (Marty, *Modern American Religion*, v1, *The Irony of It All*, Chicago: University of Chicago Press, 1986, p6). Nevertheless, the paradox implied by irony in religion remains outstanding. There is no way of rising above beliefs by rising above belief itself. Nor is an inability to rise above one's own belief a proof that one's belief is true. This vein in ethical epistemology, which might be labeled "counter-empirical," can be found as far back in the history of philosophy as the 1883 *Prolegomena to Ethics* of T. H. Green (1836–1882).

by O. W. Holmes's contemporary William James, will merely be unimpressed. It is timely history nevertheless. There has been a lot of writing published in the U.S. and Europe about religious matters in the past decade; and the atheists not only seem louder than usual, but considerably more irked by the theists than they have been in the past.[64] On the other side, "fundamentalists" (legalists and scripturalists) profess a goal of dictating federal law and policy and evangelical Protestant fundamentalists now and then claim to control branches of the U.S. government.

Major philosopher Jürgen Habermas summed up the situation in one of his essays not long ago: "Two countervailing trends mark the intellectual tenor of our age—the spread of naturalistic worldviews and religious orthodoxies."[65] Salafi Muslims (who seek to emulate Islam's first generation of believers—the Salafin) expect no less of their own lawmakers, believing as they do that their law is from God. The members of religious minorities complain either of oppression by other religious minorities or marginalization by religious majorities. Sects of Islam, the world's second largest religion, are at daggers drawn, sometimes even in relatively tolerant Indonesia, and those of the very smallest Abrahamic faith, Judaism, cannot even agree on what to wear. Terrorism is used by several Abrahamic sects as a weapon against the others, just as it has been by sects of such non-Abrahamic religions as Hinduism and atheist materialism; and here and there fear argues for the use of the same tactic, even among Ṣufis, secularists, "mainstream" Christians and Buddhists. The only peaceful news seems to be that Catholic and Protestant Christians have mostly left off killing each other, even in Ireland.

So are these coincidences in three rich religious traditions significant? Can we say that something happened in the eighteenth century to the religious experience of the Abrahamic world? To the psychological potentialities of Westerners? Or would we then risk affirming that there was "a mighty work of God" in Nejd and Medina in Arabia, Geneva in Switzerland, the Cévennes and Paris in France, Cambuslang, Scotland, the Staffordshire potteries in England, Międzybóż in Galicia, Herrnhut in Saxony, or in Northampton, Massachusetts and the Appalachian foothills of Virginia, in the eighteenth century—and why not then in the 1740s in Futa Jallon in West Africa, Delhi in North India, or in 1969 in Woodstock, New York? I frame no such hypothesis here, and only continue to hope that human history can make some sense of human events.

To the repeated historicizing of transcendent experiences, the discipline of History must be a key. What follows is a history composed of instances of this

---

[64] Atheists are not entirely agreed on either a catechism or an ethic, but since Stalin's death, they have rarely done violence to one another and the philosophically minded among them do publish together. Christopher Hitchens, Richard Dawkins, Sam Harris, and Daniel Dennett, earned the title of the "four horsemen of atheism" after their lively conversation in 2007 was filmed and went viral. It was published in 2019, after Hitchens died, as *The Four Horsemen: The Conversation That Sparked an Atheist Revolution* (NY: Random House, 2019), with new essays by Dawkins, Harris, Dennett, and the very funny Stephen Fry.

[65] Jürgen Habermas, *Between Naturalism and Religion: Philosophical Essays*, trans., Ciaran Cronin, Cambridge, UK: Polity, 2008, "Introduction" p. 1.

model: ecstasy, explained not always in religious terms, producing moral conversion with enormous social consequences, and followed by the effort to perpetuate the moral conversion without reliably repeating the ecstatic experience. This large particular case of the phenomenon can be summarized in Western terms as the clash of a thesis, Enlightenment, and an antithesis, Enthusiasm (with synthesis one or the other or indefinitely delayed). It is a history of some highly consequential changes rung on one of the constants of the human spirit.

Bibliography

Abrahams, Roger D., and John F. Szwed, eds. 1983. *After Africa: Extracts from British Travel Accounts and Journals of the Seventeenth, Eighteenth and Nineteenth Centuries Concerning the Slaves, their Manners and Customs in the British West Indies*. New Haven, CT: Yale University Press.

Abbey, Charles J. 1896. *The English Church in the Eighteenth Century*. new ed. London, New York, and Bombay: Longmans, Green, and Co.. Ch 3: "The Deists" @ https://biblehub.com/library/abbeythe_english_church_in_the_eighteenth_century/chapter_iii_the_deists.htm; Ch 7: "Enthusiasm" @ https://biblehub.com/library/abbey/the_english_church_in_the_eighteenth_century/chapter_vii_enthusiasm.htm; Ch 9: "The Evangelical Revival" @ https://biblehub.com/library/abbey/the_english_church_in_the_eighteenth_century/chapter_ix_the_evangelical_revival.htm.

Abrams, M.H. 1971. *Natural Supernaturalism*, 1973. New York: W.W. Norton.

Academy of Humanism Staff ed. 1994. *Challenges to the Enlightenment: In Defense of Reason and Science*. Amherst, NY: Prometheus Books.

Adams, David J. 2000. Un ouvrage anti-philosophique inconnu. *Recherches sur Diderot et sur l'Encyclopédie* 29: 178–182.

Adams, Geoffrey. 1991. *The Huguenots and French Opinion, 1685-1787: The Enlightenment Debate on Toleration*. Waterloo, ON: Wilfred Laurier University Press.

Adams, Leonard. 2017. *Coyer and the Enlightenment*. Oxford: Voltaire Foundation.

al-Qushayrī (ʿAbd al-Karīm ibn Hūzān Abū al-Qāsim al-Qushayrī al-Naysābūrī). *Al-Qushayri's Epistle on Sufism*. (MS ca. 1045 CE), Translated by Alexander Knysh, Garnet Publishing, (2007).

Albertan-Coppola, Silviane. *Recherches sur la littérature apologétique catholique en France de 1730 à 1770*. thèse de doctorat, 3ème cycle, Paris-Sorbonne IV (1981).

———. Pensée apologétique et Pensée des Lumières. In *Transactions of the Seventh International Congress on the Enlightenment, Budapest, 26 July – 2 August, 1987. Studies on Voltaire and the Eighteenth Century*, 1989. Oxford: Voltaire Foundation.

———. 1988. L'Apologétique catholique française à l'âge des lumières. *Revue de l'Histoire des Religions* ccv2: 151–180.

———. 1990. La faute à Diderot? *Recherches sur Diderot et sur l'Encyclopédie* 8 (1): 29–49.

———. *L'Apologétique (1670-1740): sauvetage et naufrage de la théologie*. University de Genève, Institut d'histoire de la Réformation, 1990. Actes, Geneva, 1991.

———. 1996a. Apologistes et clandestins au siècle des Lumières. In *Tendances actuelles dans la recherche sur les clandestins à l'âge classique. Actes de la journée d'étude de Créteil du 12 avril 1996, textes réunis et publiés par Geneviève Artigas-Menant & Antony Mac Kenna, in La Lettre clandestine #5*, 267–278. Paris: Presses de l'University de Paris-Sorbonne.

———. 1996b. Les préjugés légitimes de Chaumeix ou l'*Encyclopédie* sous la loupe d'un apologiste. *Recherches sur Diderot et sur l'Encyclopédie* 20: 149–158.

———. 1996c. Apologistes et clandestins au siècle des Lumières. In *Tendances actuelles dans la recherche sur les clandestins à l'âge classique, Actes de la journée d'étude de Créteil du 12 avril 1996, textes réunis et publiés par Geneviève Artigas-Menant & Antony Mac Kenna. in La Lettre clandestine #5*, 267–278. Paris: Presses de l'University de Paris-Sorbonne.

———. Les réfutations catholiques du *Dictionnaire philosophique*. In Ulla Kölving & Christiane Mervaud, eds. *Voltaire et ses combats. Actes du Congrès international d'Oxford-Paris 1994* (1994). Oxford, Voltaire Foundation, 1997a, vol. 2, pp. 785-797.

———. 1997b. Apologétique. In *Dictionnaire européen des Lumières*. Paris: PUF.

———. 2010. *Des Monts-Jura à Versailles, le parcours d'un apologiste du XVIIIe siècle: l'abbé Nicolas-Sylvestre Bergier*. Paris: Champion.

Allan, David. 2005. Opposing enlightenment: Reverend Charles Peters's reading of the *Natural History of Religion. Eighteenth-Century Studies* 38 (2): 301–321.

Almond, Philip C. 2009. *Heaven and Hell in Enlightenment England*. Cambridge: Cambridge University Press.

Alpert, M. 1997. The French enlightenment and the jews: an essay by Abbé Grégoire. *Patterns of Prejudice* 31: 31–41.

Altmann, Alexander. 1973. *Moses Mendelssohn: A Biographical Study*. University of Alabama Press.

Amend, Anne. Le système de l'enthousiasme d'après Mme de Staël. In: dans Kurt Kloocke ed. *le Groupe de Coppet et l'Europe. 1789–1830. Actes du Ve Colloque de Coppet, 8-10 juillet 1993.* Lausanne: Institut Benjamin Constant, 1994, p. 269-290.

Ameriks, Karl. 2000. *The Cambridge Companion to German Idealism*. Cambridge: Cambridge University Press.

Anchor, R. 1967. *The Enlightenment Tradition*. Berkeley: University of California Press.

Andrew, Edward G. 2001a. *Conscience and Its Critics: Protestant Conscience, Enlightenment Reason, and Modern Subjectivity*. Toronto: University of Toronto Press.

Appiah, Kwame Anthony. 2014. *Lines of Descent*. Cambridge, MA: Harvard University Press. (on Herder).

———. Dialectics of Enlightenment, rvw of Justin Smith, *Irrationality*. In: *New York Review of Books*, 9th May 2019.

Andrew, Edward G. 2001b. *Conscience and Its Critics: Protestant Conscience, Enlightenment Reason, and Modern Subjectivity*. Toronto: University of Toronto Press.

Arico, Santo L. 1999. Satire in the Abbé Coyer's *Ridiculous Admonitions. Romance Notes* 39 (2): 215–222.

Armenteros, Carolina. 2011. *The French Idea of History: Joseph de Maistre and His Heirs, 1794–1854*. Ithaca, NY: Cornell University Press.

———. 2007. From human nature to normal humanity: Joseph de Maistre, Rousseau, and the Origins of Moral Statistics. *Journal of the History of Ideas* 68 (1): 107–130.

Armenteros, Carolina, and Richard A. Lebrun. 2011a. Introduction. In *Joseph de Maistre and the legacy of Enlightenment. [articles presented at "Reappraisals, Reconsidération", the Fifth International Colloquium on Joseph de Maistre, held at Jesus College, Cambridge, on 4 and 5 December 2008]*, ed. Armenteros, 8–13. Oxford: Voltaire Foundation.

———, eds. 2011b. *Joseph de Maistre and his European Readers. From Friedrich von Gentz to Isaiah Berlin*. [Conference articles]. Leiden, Boston: Brill.

Armogathe, Jean-Robert. 1999. À propos de Nicolas Sylvestre Bergier. In *Etre matérialiste à l'Âge des Lumières. Mélanges offerts à Roland Desné*, ed. dans Beatrice Fink and Gerhardt Stenger. Paris: Presses universitaires de France.

———. 1973. *Le Quiétisme*. Paris: Presses Universiataires de France.

Armstrong, Karen. 2000. *The Battle for God*. New York: Knopf.

Arnold, Gottfried. *Historie und Beschreibung der mystischen Theologie oder geheimen Gottesgelehrtheit wie auch alten und neuen Mysticorum*. Frankfurt (1703).

Asani, Ali S. 2002. *Ecstasy and Enlightenment: The Ismaili Devotional Literature of South Asia*. London: I.B. Tauris. Reviewed by Zawahir Moir, *Journal of Islamic Studies* 15:3(September 2004), pp. 357-359 http://www3.oup.co.uk/islamj/hdb/Volume_15/Issue_03/eth309.sgm.abs.html.

Atmaja, Dwi S., Mark Woodward, and Richard C. Martin. 1997. *Defenders of Reason In Islam: Mu'tazililism From Medieval School To Modern Symbol: An Exploration of Fundamentalism in Islam from the Ninth Century to the Present*. London: Oneworld Academic.
Attfield, Robin. 2004. Rousseau, Clarke, Butler and critiques of Deism. *British Journal for the History of Philosophy* 12 (3): 429–443.
Aulard, Alphonse. 1892. *Le Culte de la Raison et le Culte de l'Etre Suprême*. Paris.
Baertschi, Bernard. 1991. L'athéisme de Diderot. *Revue Philosophique de Louvain* 89: 4.
Bain, A. 1882. *James Mill: A Biography*. New York: Henry Holt and Company.
Baker, Keith M. On the problem of the ideological origins of the French revolution. In *Inventing the French Revolution*, ed. K.M. Baker, 1990. Cambridge: Cambridge University Press.
Baker, K.M., and P.H. Reill, eds. 2001. *What's Left of Enlightenment? A Postmodern Question*. Stanford: Stanford University Press.
Balcou, J. 1975. *Fréron contre les philosophes*. Geneva: Droz.
———. 1973. *Le dossier Fréron*. Geneva: Droz.
Baldi, M.L., and Andrew Michael Ramsay. 1989. Ciclicita e progreso nell'antica teologia alle soglie dell'illuminismo. *Rivista di storia della filosofia* 44 (2): 443–476.
Bandelier, André. 1997. Lire une correspondance: Georges-Louis Liomin, pasteur, à Jean-Henri-Samuel Formey, secrétaire de l'Académie de Berlin. In *C'est la faute à Voltaire, c'est la faute à Rousseau. Recueil anniversaire pour Jean-Daniel Candaux*, ed. dans Roger Durand, 131s. Geneva: Droz.
Barbeau, Jeffrey W., ed. 2018. *Religion in Romantic England: An Anthology of Primary Sources*. Waco, TX: Baylor University Press.
Barnes, Annie Maria. 1890. *Scenes in Pioneer Methodism*. Nashville, TN: Publishing House of the Methodist Episcopal Church, South.
Barnett, Christopher B. 2016. *Kierkegaard, Pietism and Holiness*. New York: Routledge.
Barnett, S.J. 1999. *Idol Temples and Crafty Priests: The Origins of Enlightenment Anticlericalism*. London: Macmillan.
———. 2003. *The Enlightenment and Religion: The Myths of Modernity*. Manchester, UK/New York: Manchester University Press. New York: Oxford University Press, 2013.
Barrett, William. 1949. Art, aristocracy, and reason. *Partisan Review* 16: 6. (early use of the English term "Counter-Enlightenment").
Barth, J., and S.J. Robert. 2004. *Romanticism and Transcendence: Wordsworth, Coleridge, and the Religious Imagination*. Columbia: University of Missouri Press.
Bassiri, Nima. 2013. The brain and the unconscious soul in eighteenth-century nervous physiology: Robert Whytt's *Sensorium Commune*. *Journal of the History of Ideas* 74 (3): 425–448.
Bates, David. 2000. The Mystery of truth: Louis Claude de Saint-Martin's Enlightened Mysticism. *Journal of the History of Ideas* 61 (4): 635–655.
Bayle, Pierre. 1970. *Projet et Fragments d'un Dictionnaire critique. 1692*. Geneva: Slatkine Reprints.
———. 1710. *An Historical and Critical Dictionary*. London: C. Harper et al.
———. *The Dictionary Historical and Critical of Mr. Peter Bayle*. 2v, London: Knapton, 1734–1738.
———. 1969. *Dictionnaire historique et critique. [1st ed. 2v, 1695–97] Réimpression de la cinquième édition, Amsterdam 1740, revue, corrigée et augmentée de remarques critiques, avec la vie de l'auteur par M. Des Maizeaux. 4v*. Geneva: Slatkine reprints.
———. 1991. *Historical and Critical Dictionary: Selections*. Translated by Richard H. Popkin. (1965). Indianapolis: Hackett.
———. Pierre Bayle, pour une histoire critique de la philosophie. Choix d'articles philosophiques du Dictionnaire historique et critique. Ed. Jean-Michel Gros with Jacques Chomarat. Paris: Honoré Champion, coll. "La vie des huguenots," #16, (2001).
Bebbington, David W. Evangelical Christianity and the Enlightenment. in Eden & Wells (1991).
———. 1989. *Evangelicalism in Modern Britain: A History from the 1730s to the 1980s*. New York/London: Unwin Hyman.

Bebbington, David, Mark Noll, John Wolffe, Geoffrey Treloar & Brian Stanley. *A History of Evangelicalism: People, Movements and Ideas in the English-Speaking World*. 5v, Downers Grove, IL: InterVarsity Press/IVP Academic, 2003–2017.
Becker, Carl L. 1932. *The Heavenly City of the Eighteenth-Century Philosophers*. New Haven, CT: Yale University Press. pb 1959.
Becker, George. 1991. Pietism's confrontation with enlightenment rationalism: an examination of the relation between Ascetic Protestantism and Science. *Journal for the Scientific Study of Religion* 30: 140.
Becker-Cantarino, Barbara. 2004. *German Literature of the Eighteenth Century: The Enlightenment and Sensibility*. Rochester, NY: Camden House/Boydell & Brewer.
Beebe, Gayle D. 1999. *The Interpretive Role of the Religious Community in Friedrich Schleiermacher and Josiah Royce: Heavenly Bonds*. Lewiston, NY: Edwin Mellen Press.
Beik, Paul. 1956. *The French Revolution Seen from the Right: Social Theories in Motion, 1789–1799*. Philadelphia: American Philosophical Society.
Beilin, Lewis. *The Thorn: Pascal and the French Critics of the Pensées, 1623–1777*. 2v, PhD diss't, University of Chicago, (1997).
Beiser, Frederick C. 1993. *Enlightenment, Revolution, and Romanticism: The Genesis of Modern German Political Thought, 1790–1800*. Cambridge: Harvard University Press.
———. 1993. *The Fate of Reason: German Philosophy from Kant to Fichte*. incl. "The Attack of the Lockeans.", reprint 1993. Cambridge, MA: Harvard University Press.
———. Berlin and the German Counter-Enlightenment. in Joseph Mali & Robert Wokler, eds. *Isaiah Berlin's Counter-Enlightenment, Transactions of the American Philosophical Society* 93(5)(2003), pp. 105-116.
———. 2006. *The Romantic Imperative: The Concept of Early German Romanticism*. Cambridge, MA: Harvard University Press.
———. 2008. *German Idealism: The Struggle Against Subjectivism, 1781–1801*. Cambridge, MA: Harvard University Press.
———., ed. 1996. *The Early Political Writings of the German Romantics*. Cambridge, MA: Harvard University Press.
de Bellaigue, Christopher. 2017. *The Islamic Enlightenment: The Struggle Between Faith and Reason, 1798 to Modern Times, New York*. Liveright: Kindle ed.
Benedict, David. 1855. *General History of the Baptist Denomination in America*. New York: Sheldon, Lamport & Blakeman.
Bennett, Joshua. A History of 'Rationalism' in Victorian Britain, *Modern Intellectual History* 15:1(2018), pp. 63-91.
Bentley, G.E., Jr. 2001. *The Stranger from Paradise: A Biography of William Blake*. New Haven, CT: Yale University Press.
Berenson, Edward. 1988. A New Religion of the Left: Christianity and Social Radicalism in France, 1815-1848. In *The French Revolution and the Transformation of Modern Political Culture. v3, The Transformation of Political Culture, 1789–1848*. Oxford: Pergamon Press.
Bergier, Nicholas-Sylvestre. 1999. *Le déisme réfuté par lui-même: ou Examen, en forme de Lettres, des Principes d'incrédulité répandus dans les divers Ouvrages de M. Rousseau. (Paris, 1765)*. Paris: Vrin.
Berkvens-Stevelinck, Christiane. 1997. Cénacles libertins ou premières loges? Les débuts de la franc-maçonnerie hollandaise. *Dix-huitième siècle* 29.
Berlin, Isaiah. 1990. "Joseph de Maistre and the Origins of Fascism" (MSS 1940s; lecture, Princeton University, 1962). In *The Crooked Timber of Humanity: Chapters in the Hitory of Ideas*, ed. Henry Hardy. London: John Murray. Princeton, NJ: Princeton University Press, 2nd ed. 2013, pp. 95–177.
———. 1969. Political ideas in the Twentieth Century (1949). In *Four Essays on Liberty*. New York: Oxford University Press.
———. *Political Ideas in the Romantic Age: Their Rise and Influence on Modern Thought*. (Flexner Lectures, 1952, with revisions to 1959) ed. Henry Hardy, Princeton, NJ: Princeton University Press, 2006, pb, 2008.

———. *Freedom and its Betrayal: Six Enemies of Human Liberty.* (BBC lectures, 1952: Helvétius, Rousseau, Fichte, Hegel, Saint-Simon & Maistre) ed. Henry Hardy, Princeton, NJ: Princeton University Press, 2003. (Review by Joshua L. Cherniss in *History of European Ideas* 31:4(2005), p. 514).

———. 1969. Historical inevitability (Comte Trust Lecture, 1953). In *Four Essays on Liberty.* New York: Oxford University Press.

———. "The Philosophers of the Enlightenment," Introduction to Berlin, ed. *The Age of Enlightenment: The Eighteenth-Century Philosophers.* New York: New American Library, pb, 1956.

———. 1969. "John Stuart Mill and the Ends of Life" (1959). In *Four Essays on Liberty.* New York: Oxford University Press.

———. 2000. "Vico" (1960). In *Three Critics of the Enlightenment: Vico, Hamann, Herder*, ed. Henry Hardy. Princeton, NJ: Princeton University Press.

———. 2000, pb, 2013. "The Purpose of Philosophy," (1962). In *The Power of Ideas*, ed. Henry Hardy, 29–42. Princeton, NJ: Princeton University Press.

———. "Liberty," (1962) in *The Power of Ideas.* ed. Henry Hardy, Princeton, NJ: Princeton University Press, 2000, pb, 2013, pp. 134–138.

———. "Herder and the Enlightenment" (lecture, 1964) in *Three Critics of the Enlightenment: Vico, Hamann, Herder.* ed. Henry Hardy. Princeton, NJ: Princeton University Press, 2000.

———. *The Magus of the North: J. G. Hamann and the Origins of Modern Irrationalism.* (1965) in *Three Critics of the Enlightenment: Vico, Hamann, Herder.* ed. Henry Hardy, Princeton, NJ: Princeton University Press, 2000.

———. *The Roots of Romanticism.* ("Sources of Romantic Thought" Mellon Lectures, 1965) ed. Henry Hardy, Princeton, NJ: Princeton University Press, 1999, pb, 2001, 2nd ed. 2013.

———. "The Essence of European Romanticism," (1967) in *The Power of Ideas*, ed. Henry Hardy, Princeton, NJ: Princeton University Press, 2000, pb, 2013, pp. 243-248.

———. 1969. *Four Essays on Liberty.* New York: Oxford University Press.

———. *Against the Current: Essays in the History of Ideas.* ed. Henry Hardy. Oxford, 1970; 2nd ed. Princeton, NJ: Princeton University Press, 2013.

———. "The Counter-Enlightenment," *Dictionary of the History of Ideas.* New York: Scribner's, 1973, v2, pp. 100–112 (Vico, Rousseau, Hamann → Maistre, Bonald) repr. in: Berlin, *Against the Current: Essays in the History of Ideas.* ed. Henry Hardy. Oxford, 1970; 2nd ed. Princeton, NJ: Princeton University Press, 2013, pp. 243–248.

———. "The Apotheosis of the Romantic Will," (1975) in *The Crooked Timber of Humanity: Chapters in the Hitory of Ideas.* ed. Henry Hardy. London: John Murray 1990; Princeton, NJ: Princeton University Press, 2nd ed. 2013, pp. 219-252.

———. *Vico and Herder.* (1976) in *Three Critics of the Enlightenment: Vico, Hamann, Herder.* ed. Henry Hardy. Princeton, NJ: Princeton University Press, 2000.

———. *Russian Thinkers.* (1978) ed. Henry Hardy, New York: Penguin, 2008.

———. *Concepts and Categories: Philosophical Essays.* (1978) ed. Henry Hardy, Princeton, NJ: Princeton University Press, 2nd ed. 2013.

———. *Against the Current: Essays in the History of Ideas.* (1979) ed. Henry Hardy, 2nd ed. New York: Penguin, 2008.

———. "Alleged Relativism in Eighteenth-Century European Thought," (1980) in *The Crooked Timber of Humanity: Chapters in the Hitory of Ideas.* ed. Henry Hardy. London: John Murray 1990; 2nd ed. Princeton, NJ: Princeton University Press, 2013, pp. 73-75.

———. "Reply to Hans Aarsleff," *London Review of Books* 20:3(5–18 Nov. 1981): 7–8.

———. "The Pursuit of the Ideal: The Revolt Against the Myth of an Ideal World," (1988) in *The Crooked Timber of Humanity: Chapters in the Hitory of Ideas*, ed. Henry Hardy. London: John Murray 1990; 2nd ed. Princeton, NJ: Princeton University Press, 2013, pp. 1–20.

———. *The Crooked Timber of Humanity: Chapters in the Hitory of Ideas.* ed. Henry Hardy. London: John Murray 1990; 2nd ed. Princeton, NJ: Princeton University Press, 2013.

———. "My Intellectual Path", (1998) in *The Power of Ideas*. ed. Henry Hardy, Princeton, NJ: Princeton University Press, pb, 2013, pp. 1–28.
———. *The Proper Study of Mankind: An Anthology of Essays*. ed. Henry Hardy & Roger Hausheer, New York: Farrar, Straus and Giroux, 1998; 2nd ed. New York: Vintage, 2013 (including "Herder").
———. *Three Critics of the Enlightenment: Vico, Hamann, Herder*. (1960, 1965, 1976) ed. Henry Hardy, Princeton, NJ: Princeton University Press, 2000.
Berman, David. "Enlightenment and counter-enlightenment in Irish philosophy and the culmination and causation of Irish philosophy," *Archiv für Geschichte der Philosophie* 64(1982), pp. 148–165, 257–279.
Berman, David, and Patricia O'Riordan, eds. 2001. *The Irish Enlightenment and Counter-Enlightenment*. Bristol, UK: Thoemmes.
Bernet, Jacques. «Les limites de la déchristianisation de l'an II éclairées par le retour au culte de l'an III: l'exemple du district de Compiègne,» *Annales historiques de la Révolution française*, 312, avril-juin 1998, p. 285-300.
———. «Un morceau choisi de la théologie politique "constitutionelle": le discours de l'abbé Jacques-Michel Coupe à l'assemblée d'élection des curés du district de Noyon, 15 mai 1791,» *Annales historiques de la Révolution française*, 312, avril-juin 1998, pp. 327–330.
Besse, Guy. 1996. Une lettre du chanoine Bergier (1774). *Dix-huitième siècle* 28: 259–266.
Betts, C. J. *Early Deism in France: From the So-Called 'Deistes' of Lyon (1564) to Voltaire's* ***'Lettres philosophiques'*** *(1734)*. The Hague/Boston: Martinus Nijhoff, 1984.
———. "Constructing utilitarianism: Montesquieu on suttee in ***Lettres Persanes***," *French Studies*, 51:1(janvier 1997), 19–29.
Bevilacqua, Alexander. 2018. *The Republic of Arabic Letters: Islam and the European Enlightenment*. Cambridge, MA: Belknap Press of Harvard University Press.
Beyreuther, FS Erich. *Zinzendorf und Pierre Bayle, ein Beitrag zur Frage des Verhältnisses Zinzendorfs zur Aufklärung*. Hamburg: L. Appel, 1955.
———. "Die Paradoxien des Glaubens: Zinzendorfs Verhältnis zu Pierre Bayle und zur Aufklärung," in *Studien zur Theologie Zinzendorfs*. Neukirchen-Uluym, 1962.
Bianchi, Serge. «La "bataille du calendrier" ou la décade contre le dimanche. Nouvelles approches pour la réception du calendrier républicain en milieu rural,» *Annales historiques de la Révolution française*, 312, avril-juin 1998, pp. 245–264.
Biale, David, David Assaf, Benjamin Brown, Uriel Gellman, Samuel Heilman, Moshe Rosman, Gadi Sagiv, Marcin Wodziński, and Arthur Green. 2017. *Hasidism: A New History*. Princeton, NJ: Princeton University Press. Kindle Edition.
Birken, Lawrence. *Hitler as Philosophe: Remnants of the Enlightenment in National Socialism*. 1995.
Black, J., and Roy Porter, eds. 1996. *Dictionary of Eighteenth-Century History with Documents*. London: Penguin.
Bloch, Olivier. 1982. *Le matérialisme du 18e siècle et la littérature clandestine*. Paris: Vrin.
Bloch, R. Howard. 1994. *God's Plagiarist: Being an Account of the Fabulous Industry and Irregular Commerce of the Abbé Migne*. Chicago: University of Chicago Press.
Bödeker, Hans Erich & Ulrich Herrmann, eds. *Über den Prozeß der Aufklärung in Deutschland. im 18. Jahrhundert. Personen, Institutionen u. Medien*. Göttingen: Veröff. des Max-Planck-Inst. für Geschichte 85, 1987, pp. 39–52.
Boer, Roland. 2011. *On Marxism and Theology. II: Criticism of Religion*. (Brill, 2009) pb. Chicago, IL: Haymarket Books.
Bogue, D. & Bennett, J. *The History of Dissenters, From The Revolution To The Year 1808*. 4v, London: Bogue and Bennett, 1809–1812. (Swedenborgian Church, v4, pp. 126–145).
Bokobza, Kahan Michèle. 2000. *Libertinage et folie dans le roman du 18e siècle*. Louvain: Peeters.
Boles, John B. 1996. *The Great Revival: Beginnings of the Bible Belt (1972)*. Lexington, KY: University Press of Kentucky.

Bollacher, Martin. "Wilhelm Abraham Teller Ein Aufklärer der Theologie," in Hans Erich Bödeker & Ulrich Herrmann, eds. *Über den Prozeß der Aufklärung in Deutschland. im 18. Jahrhundert. Personen, Institutionen u. Medien*. Göttingen: Veröff. des Max-Planck-Inst. für Geschichte 85, 1987, pp. 39–52.

Boller, Paul F. Jr. *George Washington and Religion*. Dallas, 1963.

Bonald, Louis-Gabriel-Ambroise, Vicomte de. Démonstration philosophique du principe constitutif de la Société-Méditations politiques tirées de l'Évangile. (1830) Paris: Hachette, 2016; Wentworth Press, 2018.

Bongie, Laurence L. 2000. *David Hume: Prophet of the Counterrevolution*. Indianapolis, IN: Liberty Fund.

Boor, Friedrich de. "Erfahrung gegen Vernunft. Das Bekehrungserlebnis A. H. Franckes als Grundlage für den Kampf des Hallischen Pietismus gegen die Aufklärung," in FS Martin Schmidt. *Der Pietismus in Gestalten und Wirkungen*. ed. Heinrich Bornkamm, F. Heyer & A. Schindler, Bielefeld, 1975.

Bost, Hubert. "La superstition pire que l'athéisme ? Quelques réactions aux paradoxes de Bayle dans l'Europe protestante au XVIIIe siècle", *le Spectateur européen. The European Spectator*. 3(2002), pp. 17–45.

Bots, J. A. Hans, ed. *Critique, savoir et érudition à la veille des Lumières/Critical Spirit, Wisdom and Erudition on the Eve of the Enlightenment: Le/The* **Dictionaire historique et critique** *de/ of Pierre Bayle (1647–1706)*. Amsterdam et Maarssen: APA-Holland University Press, coll. "Studies of the Pierre Bayle Institute, Nijmegen/Études de l'Institut Pierre Bayle, Nimègue," 28, 2001.

Botting, Eileen Hunt, ed. 2006. *The End of Enlightenment?* Thousand Oaks, CA: Sage. (*American Behavioral Scientist* 49:5(January, 2006)).

Bouchardy, Jean-Jacques. *Pierre Bayle, la nature et la "nature des choses"*. Paris: Honoré Champion, coll. "La vie des Huguenots," #14, 2001.

Boulad-Ayoub, Josiane. «'Le moyen le plus sur...' ou les partis pris de Condorcet, president du premier Comité révolutionniare d'instruction publique» dans Anne-Marie Chouillet et Pierre Crepel, eds. *Condorcet. Homme des Lumières et de la Révolution*. Fontenay-aux-roses: ENS éditions, coll. «Theoria», 1997.

———. 1992. 'La Nature, la raison, l'expérience…' ou la réfutation du matérialisme dans l'apologétique chrétienne des Lumières. *Dialogue* 31: 1.

Bourel, Dominique. 2006. Y a-t-il des Lumières juives ou qu'est-ce que la Haskalah? *SVEC* 12: 113–123.

Bourignon, Antoinette. *An admirable Treatise of Solid Virtue*. (Amsterdam: Henry Wetstein, [1693]) London, 1699. Edited and abridged by John Wesley in *A Christian Library* #36. Bristol: Felix Farley, 1749–1755.

———. *Toutes Les Oeuvres De Mlle. Antoinette Bourignon: Contenues En Dix-Neuf Volumes*. [Vol. 18] *Le Nouveau Ciel Et la Nouvelle Terre: Contenant Des Merveilles inouïes, jamais vûes ni declarées de personne*. ed. Pierre Poiret. Amsterdam: Arentz, 1679.

Bousquet, Jacques, ed. 1972. *Le 18e siècle romantique*. Paris: Hean-Jacques Pauvert.

Boutin, Pierre. 1998. La philosophie naturelle comme enjeu institutionnel: l'opposition de l'Église catholique à la franc-maçonnerie. *Dix-huitième siècle* 30: 397–411.

Bowie, Andrew. "Kant and Schleiermacher," *Kant, Romanticism and the Origins Of Modernity*. conf. University of Warwick, UK, 4 July, 2000.

Bowman, F.P. 1980. *Le discours sur l'éloquence sacrée à l'époque romantique: Rhétorique, apologétique, herméneutique (1777–1851)*. Geneva: Droz.

Boyer d'Argens. *la Philosophie du bon sens ou Réflexions philosophiques sur l'incertitude des connaissances humaines, à l'usage des cavaliers et du beau sexe*. Édition établie et présentée par Guillaume Pigeard de Gurbert. Paris: Honoré Champion, coll. "Libre pensée et littérature clandestine," #11, 2002.

Bozeman, Theodore Dwight. 1977. *Protestants in an Age of Science: The Baconian Ideal and Ante-bellum American Religious Thought*. Chapel Hill, NC: University of North Carolina Press. ("beatification of Bacon").

Bradley, James E. & Dale van Kley. "Religion and politics in enlightenment Europe" @ https://www.researchgate.net/publication/37710073_Religion_and_politics_in_enlightenment_Europe/link/551032cb0cf2a7335e84a506/download. 2002.
Bradley, Owen. 1999. *A Modern Maistre: The Social and Political Thought of Joseph de Maistre*. Lincoln and London: University of Nebraska Press.
———. 2001. Maistre's theory of sacrifice. In *Joseph de Maistre's Life, Thought and Influence, Selected Studies. Montréal & Kingston*, ed. Richard A. Lebrun, 65–83. London, Ithaca: McGill-Queen's University Press.
Branch, Lori. 2006. *Rituals of Spontaneity: Sentiment and Secularism from Free Prayer to Wordsworth*. Waco, TX: Baylor University Press.
———. rvw of "Anthony Ashley Cooper, Third Earl of Shaftesbury, *ASKÉMATA [Exercises]*, Vol. 2.6 of *The Shaftesbury Standard Edition: Complete Works, Correspondence and Posthumous Writings*," *Eighteenth-Century Studies* 46:2(Winter, 2013), pp. 223–238.
Brantley, Richard E. 1984. *Locke, Wesley and the Method of English Romanticism*. Gainesville, FL: University Press of Florida.
———. 1975. *Wordsworth's "Natural Methodism"*. New Haven, CT: Yale University Press.
———. "Johnson's Wesleyan Connection," Eighteenth-Century Studies 10:2(Winter 1976–77), pp. 143-168.
———. 1987. Charles Wesley's experimental art. *Eighteenth Century Life* 11: 1–11.
———. 1990. The Common Ground of Wesley and Edwards. *Harvard Theological Review* 83: 271–303.
Braun, T.E.D. 1972. *Un ennemi de Voltaire: Le Franc de Pompignan—sa vie, ses oeuvres, les rapports avec Voltaire*. Geneva: Droz.
———. 1997. La Présentation positive du déisme dans les oeuvres de fiction [de Voltaire]. In *Voltaire et ses combats*, ed. Ulla Kölving and Christian Mervaud. Oxford: Voltaire Foundation.
———. "Rousseau and Le Franc de Pompignan on Reforming the Theater," in *Pensée Libre* 6(1997).
Brekke, Luke. "Heretics in the Pulpit, Inquisitors in the Pews: The Long Reformation and the Scottish Enlightenment," *Eighteenth-Century Studies* 44:1(Fall, 2010), pp. 79–98.
Breuer, Mordechai & Michael Graetz. *Tradition and Enlightenment 1600-1780*. Translated by William Templer. v1 of Meyer & Brenner, eds. *German-Jewish History in Modern Times*. Study of the Leo Baeck Institute. New York: Columbia University Press, 1996.
Brewer, Daniel. 1997. Political Culture and Literary History: La Harpe's *Lycée*. *Modern Language Quarterly* 58 (2): 1–22.
Brockliss, Laurence. 2002. *Calvet's Web: Enlightenment and the Republic of Letters in Eighteenth-Century France*. Oxford: Oxford University Press.
Brodin, Pierre. "Les Quakers américains et la France au dix-huitième siècle," *French Review* (1976).
Bronner, Stephen Eric. "Interpreting the Enlightenment: Metaphysics, Critique, and Politics," *Logos* 3:3(Summer 2004) @ www.logosjournal.com/bronner_enlightenment.pdf.
Brown, Kenneth O. *Holy Ground, Too: The Camp Meeting Family Tree*, Holiness Archives, 1997.
Brown, Marshall. 1998. *Preromanticism*. Stanford, CA: Stanford University Press.
Brown, Stewart J. & Timothy Tackett. eds. *The Cambridge History of Christianity*. Volume 7, *Enlightenment, Reawakening and Revolution* 1660–1815. Cambridge: Cambridge University Press, 2014.
Brye, Bernard de. 1985. *Un Evêque d'ancien régime à l'épreuve de la Révolution: Le Cardinal A.L.H. de la Fare (1752–1829)*. Paris: Publications de la Sorbonne.
Buchan, James. 2004. *Crowded With Genius: The Scottish Enlightenment, Edinburgh's Moment of the Mind*. New York: HarperCollins.
Buckley, Thomas E.S.J. 1995. After Disestablishment: Thomas Jefferson's Wall of Separation in Antebellum Virginia. *Journal of Southern History* 61: 445–480.
Buckley, Thomas E. 1977. *SJ. Church and State in Revolutionary Virginia*. Charlottesville: University of Virginia Press.
Buffat, Marc. "Voltaire selon Faguet, ou l'irréligion de Voltaire," *Cahiers Voltaire*, 1(2002).

Bullock, Steven C. 1996. *Revolutionary Brotherhood: Freemasonry and the Transformation of the American Social Order, 1730-1840.* Chapel Hill: University of North Carolina Press.

Bulman, William J. 2015. *Anglican Enlightenment: Orientalism, Religion and Politics in England and its Empire, 1648–1715.* Cambridge: Cambridge University Press.

———. 2018. Secularist Sacerdotalism in the Anglican Enlightenment, c. 1660–1730. In *Let There Be Enlightenment: The Religious and Mystical Sources of Rationality*, ed. Dan Edelstein and Anton Matytsin. Baltimore: Johns Hopkins University Press.

———. 2016. Enlightenment for the culture wars. In *God in the Enlightenment*, ed. William J. Bulman and Robert G. Ingram, 1–41. Oxford: Oxford University Press.

Bulman, William, and Robert G. Ingram. 2016. *God in the Enlightenment.* New York: Oxford University Press.

Bultmann, Rudolf. 2019. *History and Eschatology: The Presence of Eternity.* Waco, TX: Baylor University Press.

Bunge, Mario. Counter-enlightenment in contemporary social studies. In *Academy of Humanism Staff ed. Challenges to the Enlightenment: In Defense of Reason and Science*, 1994. Amherst, NY: Prometheus Books.

van Bunge, Wiep. 1995. Balthasar Bekker on Daniel: an early enlightenment critique of millenarianism. *History of European Ideas* 21 (5): 659–673.

Burns, R. Arthur. 2002. Christian missions and the enlightenment (review). *The Catholic Historical Review* 88 (2): 370–372.

Burson, Jeffrey D. 2008. Towards a new comparative history of European enlightenments: the problem of enlightenment theology in France and the study of eighteenth-century Europe. *Intellectual History Review* 18 (2): 173–187.

———. *The Rise and Fall of Theological Enlightenment, Jean-Martin de Prades and Religious Polarization in Eighteenth-Century France.* University of Notre Dame Press, 2010.

Butler, Joseph. *The Works of Joseph Butler.* ed. William E. Gladstone (1896), 3v, Bristol, UK: Thoemmes Press, 1995.

———. *The Analogy of Religion, Natural and Revealed, to the Constitution and Course of Nature. To Which are Added, Two Brief Dissertations: Of Personal Identity, Of the Nature of Virtue.* (1736) Palala Press, Kindle ed. 2016.

———. 2017. In *Fifteen Sermons and Other Writings on Ethics*, ed. David McNaughton. Oxford: Oxford University Press (British Moral Philosophers).

Butterfield, Lyman Henry. "Elder John Leland, Jeffersonian Itinerant," 62 *Proc. Of The Am. Antiquarian Soc'y* 155, 156-57 (1952), reprinted in *Colonial Baptists and Southern Revivals: An Original Anthology* (1980). By an associate editor of the first five volumes of *The Papers of Thomas Jefferson.*

Byrne, J. 1996. *Glory, Jest and Riddle: Religious Thought in the Enlightenment.* London: SCM Press.

Cahen, Raphaël, *Friedrich Gentz, 1764–1832: Penseur post-Lumières et acteur du renouveau de l'ordre européen au temps des révolutions* (Pariser Historische Studien #108). Boston: Oldenbourg De Gruyter, 2017.

Callaway, H.G. Review of Isaiah Berlin. *The Roots of Romanticism.* (The A. W. Mellon Lectures in the Fine Arts, 1965), edited by Henry Hardy. Princeton, NJ: Princeton University Press, 1999. ResearchGate, January, 2003, online @ https://www.researchgate.net/publication/317845465_Review_of_Berlin_The_Roots_of_Romanticism. (Critical but hardly dismissive.)

Carspecken, Phil Francis. 2003. Ocularcentrism, phonocentrism and the counter enlightenment problematic: clarifying contested Terrain in our Schools of Education. *Teachers College Record* 105 (6): 978.

Cascardi, Anthony J. 1986. *The Bounds of Reason: Cervantes, Dostoevsky, Flaubert.* New York: Columbia University Press.

———. 1999. Cambridge University Press (Literature, Culture, Theory #30). In *Consequences of Enlightenment.* New York.

Cassara, Ernest. 1975. *The Enlightenment in America.* New York: Twayne (World Leaders Series, #50).

Cassirer, Ernst. 1951. *The Philosophy of the Enlightenment 1932*. Princeton, NJ: Princeton University Press. Boston: Beacon Press, 1962.

Cave, Christophe. 2000. Le rire des anti-philosophes. *Dix-huitième siècle* 32: 227–239.

Cazzaniga, G.M. 1998. "The religion of modern man: The age of Enlightenment and the birth of freemasonry" [in Italian]. *Belfagor* 53 (5): 513–524.

Chai, Leon. 1990. *The Romantic Foundations of the American Renaissance*. Ithaca, NY: Cornell University Press.

———. 1998. *Jonathan Edwards and the Limits of Enlightenment Philosophy*. New York: Oxford University Press.

Chakrabarty, Dipesh. "Radical Histories and [the] Question of Enlightenment Rationalism: Some Recent Critiques of Subaltern Studies," in *Economic and Political Weekly* (8 Apr, 1995), pp. 751–9, 752–3.

Champion, Justin. 2000. *Écrasez l'infâme*: clever clerics and the politics of knowledge? *British Journal for the History of Philosophy* 8 (1): 149–158.

———. 1992. *The Pillars of Priestcraft Shaken*. Cambridge: Cambridge University Press.

Chandler, James. 2011. Edgeworth and the Lunar enlightenment. *Eighteenth-Century Studies* 45 (1): 87–104.

Mita, Choudhury, and Daniel J. Watkins. 2019. *Belief and Politics in Enlightenment France: Essays in Honor of Dale K. Van Kley*. New York: Oxford University Press (Oxford University Studies in The Enlightenment).

Charles, Sébastien. "L'immatérialisme en terre ennemie: la pensée berkeleyenne dans le matérialisme des Lumières," *Lumen. Travaux choisis de la Société canadienne d'étude du dix-huitième siècle. Selected Proceedings from the Canadian Society for Eighteenth- Century Studies*, XX, 2001, pp. 49–69.

Chartier, Roger. *The Cultural Origins of the French Revolution*. Translated by Lydia G. Cochrane. Durham: Duke University Press, 1989; 1991. (Enlightenment defined by Counter-Enlightenment)

Chateaubriand, François René de. *Le génie du christianisme, ou beautés de la religion chrétienne*, 5v, Paris: Migneret, 1801–02.

Cherniss, Joshua L. Book Review: Isaiah Berlin, *Freedom and its Betrayal*. (London: Chatto and Windus, 2002); *The Proper Study of Mankind*. (London: Pimlico, pb, 1998; New York: Farrar, Straus and Giroux, 1998). in *History of European Ideas* 31:4(2005), pp. 512–517.

Chevallier, Marjolaine. 1994. *Pierre Poiret (1646–1719): du protestantisme à la mystique*. Paris: Labor et Fides.

Chouillet, Anne-Marie, ed. 1993. *Les ennemis de Diderot. actes du colloque organisé par la Société Diderot*. Paris: Klincksieck.

Chubilleau, E., and E. Puisais, eds. 2000. *Les athéismes philosophiques*. Paris: Kimé.

Clark, J.C.D. 1986. *Revolution and Rebellion: State and Society in England in the Seventeenth and Eighteenth Centuries*. Cambridge: Cambridge University Press.

———. 1993. *The Language of Liberty, 1660–1832: Political Discourse and Social Dynamics in the Anglo-American World*. Cambridge: Cambridge University Press.

———. 1995. *Samuel Johnson: Literature, Religion, and English Cultural Politics from the Restoration to Romanticism*. Cambridge: Cambridge University Press.

———. 2000. *English Society 1660–1832: Religion, Ideology and Politics During the Ancien Regime*. 2nd revised ed. Cambridge: Cambridge University Press.

Clarke, Samuel. *The Works of Samuel Clarke*. ed. Benjamin Hoadly (1738), 4v, Bristol, UK: Thoemmes Press, 2002. (Including the sermons attempting to reconstruct religion and ethics on the basis of Newtonian science).

Cohen, I. Bernard, et al., eds. 1990. *Puritanism and the Rise of Modern Science: The Merton Thesis*. New Brunswick: Rutgers University Press.

Coleman, Charly J. "The Value of Dispossession: Rethinking Discourses of Selfhood in Eighteenth-Century France," *Modern Intellectual History* 2:3(Nov 2005), pp. 299–326. (Fénelon, Rousseau, Saint-Martin, and a "discourse of dispossession" or Christian and republican self-sacrifice).

Colie, Rosalie L. 2009. *Light and Enlightenment*. Cambridge: Cambridge University Press. (Dutch Arminians and Cambridge Platonists).
Collins, James Potter. *Autobiography of a Revolutionary Soldier*. (1859) reprint, New York: Arno Press, 1979.
Commager, Henry Steele. 1977. *The Empire of Reason: How Europe Imagined and America Realized the Enlightenment*. Garden City, New York: Doubleday Anchor.
Compagnon, A. 2005. *Les Antimodernes: de Joseph de Maistre à Roland Barthes*. Paris.
Confino, Michael, Isaiah Berlin, Alexander Herzen, Russia's Elusive Counter-Enlightenment. in Joseph Mali & Robert Wokler, eds. *Isaiah Berlin's Counter-Enlightenment. Transactions of the American Philosophical Society* 93:5(2003), pp. 177–192.
Confucius [Kong Fuzi], *Xunzi* [*Analects*], Translated by James Legge. Bilingual edition. 中州古籍出版社, 2016.
Conklin, Carli N. 2020. *The Pursuit of Happiness in the Foundng Era: An Intellectual History*. Columbia, MO: University of Missouri Press.
Conlon, Pierre M. *Le Siècle des Lumières. Bibliographie chronologique*. 3v. (to 1736). Geneva: Droz, 1981–1985.
Constant, Benjamin. *Œuvres*. ed. Alfred Roulin. Paris: Gallimard/Pléiade, 1957.
———. 1998. *Œuvres complètes. I, Écrits de jeunesse (1774-1799)*. Tübingen: Max Niemeyer Verlag.
———. 1999. *De la religion considérée dans sa source, ses formes et ses développements (MS, 1824-1830) Texte intégral présenté pat Tzvetan Todorov et Étienne Hofmann*. Arles: Actes Sud.
———. *De la religion, considérée dans sa source, ses formes et ses développements*. Tome II (1825) Ed. Pierre Deguise with Kurt Kloocke. Tübingen: Max Niemeyer Verlag, coll. "Oeuvres complètes", série "Oeuvres" #18, 1999.
———. Discours au Tribunat. De la possibilité d'une constitution républicaine dans un grand pays *(1799–1803)*. Ed. Kurt Kloocke with. Tübingen, Max Niemeyer Verlag, coll. "Oeuvres complètes", série "Oeuvres", #4, 2005.
———. *Florestan. De l'esprit de conquête et de l'usurpation. Réflexions sur les constitutions (1813–1814)*. Ed. María Luisa Sánchez-Mejía with Béatrice Fink. Tübingen, Max Niemeyer Verlag, coll. "Oeuvres complètes", série "Oeuvres", #8, 2 vol. 2005.
———. *Principes de politique et autres écrits (juin 1814–juillet 1815). Liberté de la presse. Responsabilité des ministres. Mémoires de Juliette. Acte additionnel. Etc.* Eds. Olivier Devaux & Kurt Kloocke. Tübingen, Max Niemeyer Verlag, coll. "Oeuvres complètes", série "Oeuvres", #9, 2 v, 2001.
Cooper, Anthony Ashley, 3rd Earl of Shaftesbury (1671-1713). *The Shaftesbury Standard Edition: Complete Works, Correspondence and Posthumous Writings*. Stuttgart-Bad Cannstatt: frommann-holzboog Verlag, 1981-2020+
———. *ASKÉMATA* [*Exercises*]. Edited, translated and annotated by Wolfram Benda, Christine Jackson-Holzberg, Patrick Müller and Friedrich A. Uehlein. Vol. 2.6 of *The Shaftesbury Standard Edition: Complete Works, Correspondence and Posthumous Writings*. Stuttgart-Bad Cannstatt: frommann-holzboog Verlag, 2011.
———. A Letter Concerning Enthusiasm (Sep, 1707), *Characteristics of Men, Manners, Opinions, Times*. (1711, 2nd ed. 1714), v1. London: Grant Richards, 1900.
Copeland, Clare, and Jan Machielsen, eds. 2013. *Angels of Light? Sanctity and the Discernment of Spirits in the Early Modern Period*. Leiden: E. J. Brill.
Corrigan, John. 1991. *The Prism of Piety: Catholick Congregational Clergy at the Beginning of the Enlightenment*. New York: Oxford University Press.
Cosmos, Georgia. 2005. *Huguenot Prophecy and Clandestine Worship in the Eighteenth Century: 'The Sacred Theatre of the Cévennes'*. Aldershot and Burlington, VT: Ashgate.
Coudert, Allison, and Richard H. Popkin, eds. 1999. *Leibniz, Mysticism and Religion*. Kluwer Academic Publishers.
Cragg, G. R. *The Church and the Age of Reason, 1648–1789*. Penguin, 1970.

Creed, John Martin, Boys Smith, and John Sandwith. 2013. *Religious Thought in the Eighteenth Century*. (Illustrated from Writers of the Period). Cambridge: Cambridge University Press.
Crisp, Roger. "Hume and utility as a moral property," Conference by the British Society for the History of Philosophy in collaboration with The Department of Philosophy, University of Edinburgh, The Mind Association, and The Foundation for Intellectual History, University of Edinburgh, 18–19th September 2002.
Crouter, Richard. 2008. *Friedrich Schleiermacher: Between Enlightenment and Romanticism*. Cambridge: Cambridge University Press.
Cunliffe, C., ed. 1992. *Joseph Butler's Moral and Religious Thought: Tercentenary Essays*. Oxford: Clarendon Press.
Cunningham, Andrew, and Michael Jardine, eds. 2009. *Romanticism and the Sciences*. Cambridge: Cambridge University Press. pb, May 13.
Cunningham, Andrew. 2001. A reply to Peter Dear's Religion Science and Natural Philosophy, thoughts on Cunningham's thesis. *Studies in History and Philosophy of Science* 32A (2): 387–393.
Curran, Mark. 2012. *Atheism, Religion and Enlightenment in Pre-revolutionary Europe*. London: Boydell & Brewer Ltd.
Cushing, Max Pearson. *Baron d'Holbach*. (1914) Project Gutenberg EBook #5621, May, 2004, posted July 4, 2002 @ https://archive.org/stream/barondholbachast05621gut/7bdho10.txt.
Daily, D. 1999. *Enlightenment Deism: The Foremost Threat to Christianity*. Philadelphia: Dorrance.
Dainat, H., & W. Voßkamp, eds. *Aufklärungsforschung in Deutschland*. Heidelberg 1999. (with chapters by Rosenberg and Schönert on the Enlightenment).
Dalrymple, William. "The Muslims in the middle," *New York Times*, 16Aug, 2011
Damrosch, David. *How to read world literature*, Wiley-Blackwell, 2nd ed., 2017.
Darcel, Jean-Louis. "Les Années d'apprentissage d'un contre-révolutionnaire: Joseph de Maistre à Lausanne, 1793–1797," *Revue des études maistriennes*, No. 10 (1986–87): 7–135.
———. 1977. Joseph de Maistre et la Révolution française. *Revue des études maistriennes* 3: 29–43.
———. 1980. Des Pénitents noirs à la franc-maçonnerie: aux sources de la sensibilité maistriennes. *Revue des études maistriennes* 5–6: 69–95.
———. 1985. Les bibliothèques de Joseph de Maistre, 1768–1821. *Revue des études maistriennes* 9: 5–118.
———. 1981. Registres de la correspondance de Joseph de Maistre. *Revue des études maistriennes* 7: 9–266.
———. 2001. Les chemins de l'exil, 1792–1817. *Revue des études maistriennes* 13: 35–48.
———. "The Apprentice Years of a Counter-Revolutionary: Joseph de Maistre in Lausanne, 1793-1797," dans Richard A. Lebrun ed. *Joseph de Maistre's Life, Thought and Influence. Selected Studies*. Montréal & Kingston, London, Ithaca, NY, McGill-Queen's University Press, 2001, pp. 32–46.
———. 2001. Les chemins de l'exil, 1792-1817. *Revue des études maistriennes* 13: 35–48.
———. 2001. Joseph de Maistre and the House of Savoy: some aspects of his career. In *Joseph de Maistre's Life, Thought and Influence. Selected Studies*, ed. dans Richard A. Lebrun, 47–61. Montréal & Kingston, London, Ithaca, NY: McGill-Queen's University Press.
———. 2001. Joseph de Maistre, New mentor of the prince: unveiling the mysteries of political science. In *Joseph de Maistre's Life, Thought and Influence. Selected Studies*, ed. dans Richard A. Lebrun, 120–130. Montréal & Kingston, London, Ithaca, NY: McGill-Queen's University Press.
———. 2001. The roads of exile, 1792–1817. In *Joseph de Maistre's Life, Thought and Influence. Selected Studies*, ed. Richard A. Lebrun, 15–31. Montréal & Kingston, London, Ithaca, NY: McGill-Queen's University Press.
Darnton, Robert. 1985. Readers Respond to Rousseau. In *The Great Cat Massacre*. New York: Vintage.

———. 1968. *Mesmerism and the End of the Enlightenment in France*. Cambridge, MA, New York: Schocken. 1970. (notes convulsionaries and jansenists).
———. 1993. La lecture rousseauiste et un lecteur “ordinaire” au XVIIIe siècle. In *Pratiques de la lecture*, ed. dans Roger Chartier. Paris: Payot.
———. 1993. La lecture rousseauiste et un lecteur ‘ordinaire’ au XVIIIe siècle. In *Pratiques de la lecture*, ed. dans Roger Chartier, 161–199. Paris: Payot, coll. “Petite bibliothèque Payot,”. 167.
———. 1971. The high enlightenment and the low-life of literature in pre-revolutionary France. *Past and Present* 51.
———. 1979. *The Business of Enlightenment: A Publishing History of the Encyclopédie, 1775–1800*. Cambridge, MA: Harvard University Press.
———. 1971. In search of the enlightenment: recent attempts to create a social history of ideas. *J Mod Hist* 43: 113–132.
Dart, Gregory. 1999. *Rousseau, Robespierre and English Romanticism*. New York: Cambridge University Press.
Davie, Donald. 1982. *Dissentient Voice: Enlightenment and Christian Dissent: The Ward-Phillips Lectures for 1980 with some Related Pieces*. Notre Dame, IN: University of Notre Dame Press.
Dauber, Jeremy Asher. 2004. *Antonio's Devils: Writers of the Jewish Enlightenment and the Birth of Modern Hebrew and Yiddish Literature*. Stanford, CA: Stanford University Press.
De Dijn, Annelien. “From the Enlightenment to the Terror: New Genealogies,” rvw essay on Dan Edelstein, *The Terror of Natural Right: Republicanism, the Cult of Nature, and the French Revolution*. (Chicago: UCP, 2009); Dan Edelstein, *The Enlightenment: A Genealogy*. (Chicago: UCP, 2010), *Modern Intellectual History* 10:1(April, 2013), pp. 153–162.
Dear, Peter. 2001. Religion, science and natural philosophy, thoughts on Cunningham's thesis. *Stud Hist Philos Sci* 32A (2): 377–386.
Deism, French. Article électronique, *The Internet Encyclopedia of Philosophy*. 1996. @ http://www.utm.edu/research/iep/d/deismfre.htm.
Delon, Michel, ed. 1997. *Dictionnaire européen des Lumières*. Paris: Presses universitaires de France.
Dendle, Peter, ed. 1999. Hume's *dialogues* and *paradise lost*. *Journal of the History of Ideas* 60 (2): 257–276.
Dennett, Daniel. 2006. *Breaking the Spell: Religion as a Natural Phenomenon*. New York: Viking. (Reviews by H. Allen Orr, *The New Yorker*, 3 Apr 06, pp. 80–83; Leon Wiseltier, *New York Times Book Review*, 19Feb06).
Dermenghem, Emile. 1946. *Joseph de Maistre mystique: ses rapports avec le martinisme, l'illuminisme et la franc-maçonnerie, l'influence du doctrines mystiques et occultes sur sa pensée religieuse*. Paris: La Colombe.
Dickens, A.G., and John Tonkin. 1985. *The Reformation in Historical Thought*. Cambridge, MA: Harvard University Press.
Dickey, Laurence. 1987. *Hegel: Religion, Economics, and the Politics of Spirit, 1770–1807*. New York: Cambridge University Press.
Diderot, Denis (1713–1784). *Supplément au voyage de Bougainville: ou dialogue entre A et B sur l'inconvénient d'attacher des idées morales à certaines actions physiques qui n'en comportent pas*. (1796) Diderot Publishing, 2017.
———. *'Rameau's Nephew'—'Le Neveu De Rameau': A Multi-Media Bilingual Edition*. Edited by Marian Hobson. Translated by Caroline Warman & Kate E. Tunstall. Music Director Pascal Duc. Open Book, Kindle ed. 2016. (1st published as *Rameaus Neffe* tr. Goethe, 1805)
Dieckmann, H., ed. 1948. *«Les Philosophe». Texts and interpretation*. Saint-Louis, MO: Washington University Studies.
Djaït, Hichem. *L'Europe et l'Islam*. Paris, 1978.
Domenech, Jacques. 1990. *“Sade contre les Lumières,” Actes du Séminaire «Lumières et Révolution françaises». 16-25/II/89*. Cairo: Centre d'études françaises.
———. “*La Nouvelle Héloïse*, parangon des romans épistolaires anti-philosophiques,” *Études Jean-Jacques Rousseau*, #5, *La Nouvelle Héloïse aujourd'hui*, 1992.

———. Les antiphilosophes ennemis de Voltaire. In: Ulla Kölving & Christiane Mervaud, eds. *Voltaire et ses combats. Actes du Congrès international d'Oxford-Paris (septembre 1994).* Oxford, Voltaire Foundation, 1997, v2, pp. 761–777.

———. 1997. Anti-Lumières. In *Dictionnaire des Lumières européennes*. Paris: PUF.

Donakowski, Conrad L. "Bavaria Sancta Meets Raison d'État: Liturgy and Ritual as Mass Medium for the Enlightenment in Bavaria," in Ian Germani et Robin Swales (ed.) *Symbols, Myths & Images of the French Revolution*. Regina: The Canadian Plains Research Center, University of Regina, 1998.

Doyle, William. 1994. *Jansenism, Catholic Resistance to Authority from the Reformation to the French Revolution. A Global-Historical Interpretation.* Cambridge: Cambridge University Press. New York: St. Martin's, 2001.

Drury, John, ed. 1989. *Critics of the Bible, 1724–1873*. New York: Cambridge University Press.

Dubnow, Simon. *Toldot ha-ḥasidut*. [*History of Hasidism in the Period of its Rise and Growth*]. 3v, Tel Aviv, 1930–1932.

Duff, David. 2005. *Shelley and the Revolutionary Sublime*. New York: Cambridge University Press.

Dumarsais, César Chesneau (1676–1756). *Examen de la religion, ou Doutes sur la religion dont on cherche l'éclairsissement de bonne foi*. (London, 1767) ed. Gianluca Mori. Oxford: Voltaire Foundation, 1999.

Dupré, Louis. 2004. *The Enlightenment & the Intellectual Foundations of Modern Culture*. New Haven, CT: Yale University Press.

Dyck, Martin. 1959. *Novalis and Mathematics*. Assen, Netherlands: Royal VanGorcum.

Eagleton, Terry. "The Enlightenment Is Dead! Long Live the Enlightenment," rvw of Louis Dupré, *The Enlightenment. Harper's Magazine*, March, 2005, pp. 91–95.

Earman, John. 2003. *Hume's Abject Failure: The Argument Against Miracles*. Oxford: Oxford University Press.

Edelstein, Dan. 2009. *The Terror of Natural Right: Republicanism, the Cult of Nature, and the French Revolution*. Chicago: University of Chicago Press.

———. 2010. *The Enlightenment: A Genealogy*. Chicago: University of Chicago Press.

Edelstein, Don, and Anton Matytsin, eds. 2018. *Let There Be Enlightenment: The Religious and Mystical Sources of Rationality*. Baltimore: Johns Hopkins University Press.

Eick, David. "Defining the Catholic Enlightenment: The *Dictionnaire de Trévoux*," American Society for Eighteenth-Century Studies 31st Annual Meeting, University of Pennsylvania, April 14, 2000.

Einboden, Jeffrey. 2014. *Islam And Romanticism: Muslim Currents From Goethe To Emerson*. London: Oneworld Academic.

Eliot, S. & B. Stern, eds. *The Age of Enlightenment: An Anthology of Eighteenth-Century Texts*. Oxford, 1979.

Ellenzweig, Sarah. 2008. *The Fringes of Belief: English Literature, Ancient Heresy, and the Politics of Freethinking, 1660–1760*. Stanford, CA: Stanford University Press. (Rochester, Blount, Behn, Fontenelle, Swift, Pope).

Elmarsafy, Ziad. 2009. *The Enlightenment Qur'an: The Politics of Translation and the Construction of Islam*. New York: Oxford University Press.

Emerson, Ralph Waldo. 1983. "Swedenborg; Or, The Mystic" (*Representative Men*. III, 1850) in Emerson, *Essays and Lectures*. *Library of America*: 661–689.

Emerson, Roger L. 1987. Latitudinarianism and the English Deists. In *Deism, Masonry, and the Enlightenment*, ed. J.A. Leo Lemay, 19–48. Newark: University of Delaware Press.

English, John C. 1989. John Wesley and the English enlightenment: an 'Appeal to Men of Reason and Religion'. *Studies on Voltaire and the Eighteenth Century* 263: 400–403.

Epstein, Klaus. 1973. *Die Ursprünge des Konservativismus in Deutschland. Der Ausgangspunkt: Die Herausforderung durch die Französische Revolution 1770–1806*. Berlin: Propyläen-Verlag.

Eshet, Dan. 2001. Rereading Priestley: science at the intersection of theology and politics. *History of Science* 39 (2): 127–159.

Eslinger, Ellen. 1999. *Citizens of Zion: The Social Origins of Camp Meeting Revivalism*. Knoxville: University of Tennessee Press.

Everdell, William R. 1975. The Rosières movement, 1766–1789, a Clerical Precursor of the Revolutionary Cults. *French Historical Studies*: 23–36.

———. 1989. *Christian Apologetics in France, 1750–1801. (New York University diss't, 1971)*. Lewiston, NY: Edwin Mellen Press.

Fairchild, Hoxie Neale. 1939. *Religious Trends in English Poetry, v1, 1700-1740, Protestantism and the Cult of Sentiment*. New York: Columbia University Press.

Faivre, Antoine. 1980. Joseph de Maistre et l'illuminisme: rapports avec Willermoz. *Revue des études maistriennes* 5–6: 125–132.

———. *Mystiques, Théosophes et Illuminés au Siècle des Lumières*. Hildesheim, 1976.

Feiner, Shmuel. 2004. *The Jewish Enlightenment. Translated by Chaya Naor*. Philadelphia: University of Pennsylvania Press.

———. 2010. *Moses Mendelssohn: Sage of Modernity (2005)*. Translated by Anthony Berris. New Haven, CT: Yale University Press.

Feingold, "Patrons and professors: the origins and motives for the Endowment of University Chairs, in Particular the Laudian Professorship of Arabic," chap. 6 of *The 'Arabick' Interest of the Natural Philosophers in Seventeenth-Century England*. ed. G. A. Russell. Leiden, 1994.

Feingold, Mordechai. 1997. Oriental studies. In *Chap. 8 of The History of the University of Oxford. vol. 4, Seventeenth-Century Oxford*, ed. Nicholas Tyacke. Oxford: Oxford University Press.

Fenn, R.A. 1987. *James Mill's Political Thought*. New York: Garland Publishing.

Fenves, Peter D. "Afterword" to Werner Hamacher. *Two Studies of Friedrich Hölderlin*. Translated by Julia Ng. Stanford, CA: Stanford University Press (Meridian: Crossing Aesthetics), 2020.

———. "The Scale of Enthusiasm," in Lawrence E. Klein & Anthony J. La Vopa. *Enthusiasm and Enlightenment in Europe, 1650–1850*. 1998 (also published in *Huntington Library Quarterly*, vol. 60 (1997): 1–2, pp. 117–152.

———. 2003. *Late Kant: Towards Another Law of the Earth. 1960*. New York: Routledge.

Ferngren, Gary B., ed. 2002. *Science and Religion: A Historical Introduction*. Baltimore, MD: Johns Hopkins University Press.

———., ed. 2000. *The History of Science and Religion in the Western Tradition: An Encyclopedia. (Garland Reference Library of the Humanities)*. New York: Garland.

Feroli, Teresa. Review of Clement Hawes. *Mania and Literary Style: The Rhetoric of Enthusiasm from the Ranters to Christopher Smart. Criticism*, 40:2(1998), 311–313.

Ferrone, V. 1999. L'illuminismo italiano e la rivoluzione napoletana del '99. *Studi Storici* 40 (4): 993–1008.

Ferry, Luc. «La naissance de la pensée contre-révolutionnaire en Allemagne: Jacobi et Gentz,» dans Sylvain Simard ed. *la Révolution française au Canada français. Actes du colloque tenu à l'Université d'Ottawa du 15 au 17 novembre 1989*. Ottawa, Presses de l'Université d'Ottawa, Actexpress, 1991, p. 379–396.

———. 1996. *l'Homme Dieu ou le sens de la vie*. Paris: Grasset. (Rousseau and Secularism).

Fichte, Johann Gottlieb. *Attempt at a Critique of All Revelation* (*Versuch einer Kritik aller Offenbarung*. 1792), ed. Allen Wood & tr. Garrett Green. Cambridge: Cambridge University Press, 2010 @ http://privatewww.essex.ac.uk/~wmartin/FichteDeductionofReligion2.pdf.

———. *Essai d'une critique de toute révélation* (*Versuch einer Kritik aller Offenbarung*. 1792), ed. & tr. J.C. Goddard. Paris: Vrin, 2000.

Fieser, James, ed. *Early Responses to Hume*. v5&6, *Early Responses to Hume's Writings on Religion*. 2nd ed. revised, Bristol, UK: Thoemmes Press, 2005.

Fink, Beatrice, and Gerhardt Stenger, eds. 1999. *Etre matérialiste à l'Âge des Lumières. Mélanges offerts à Roland Desné*. Paris: Presses universitaires de France.

Finney, Charles Grandison. 1960. In *Lectures on Revivals of Religion by Charles Grandison Finney*, ed. William G. McLoughlin. Cambridge, MA: Belknap Press of Harvard University Press.

Fischer, Kevin. *Converse in the Spirit: William Blake, Jacob Boehme, and the Creative Spirit*. Fairleigh Dickinson University Press, 2004.

Fitzgerald, Frances. 2017. *The Evangelicals: The Struggle to Shape America.* New York: Simon & Schuster.

Fix, Andrew C. 1991. *Prophecy and Reason: The Dutch Collegians in the Early Enlightenment.* Princeton, NJ: Princeton University Press.

Fleming, Patrick C. "The Rise of the Moral Tale: Children's Literature, the Novel, and The Governess," *Eighteenth-Century Studies* 46:4(Summer, 2013), pp. 464–478.

Foley, Adam. 2017. Miltonic Sublimity and the Crisis of Wolffianism before Kant. *Journal of the History of Ideas* 78 (1): 51–72.

Forbes, A.M. "Ultimate Reality and Ethical Meaning: Theological Utilitarianism in 18th-Century England," *Ultimate Reality and Meaning*, 18:2(June 1995): 119–38.

Forbes, Robert. "The Evangelical Enlightenment" Society for the History of the American Republic conference, 1997.

Force, James E., and Richard Henry Popkin, eds. 1999. *Newton and Religion: Context, Nature, and Influence.* Kluwer Academic Publishers.

Forstman, Jack. *A Romantic Triangle: Schleiermacher and Early German Romanticism.* Missoula, MT: 1977.

Freud, H. H. «Palissot and les philosophes», *Diderot Studies*, n°10, 1967.

Frobenius, Leo. *The voice of Africa: being an account of the travels of the German Inner African Exploration Expedition in the years 1910-1912*, trans., Rudolf Blind, London: Hutchinson & Co., 1913.

Fulford, Tim, ed. 2002. *Romanticism and Millenarianism.* New York: St. Martin's/Palgrave.

Funkenstein, Amos. 1986. *Theology and the Scientific Imagination.* Princeton, NJ: Princeton University Press.

Garcia, Humberto. 2012. *Islam and the English Enlightenment, 1670–1840.* Baltimore: Johns Hopkins University Press.

Gardner, Sebastian. 1999. *Routledge Philosophy Guidebook to Kant and the Critique of Pure Reason.* New York: Routledge.

Garnett, J. 1992. Bishop Butler and the Zeitgeist. In *Joseph Butler's Moral and Religious Thought: Tercentenary Essays*, ed. C. Cunliffe. Oxford: Clarendon Press.

Garrard, Graeme. 1966. Joseph de Maistre's Civilization and its Discontents. *Journal of the History of Ideas*: 429–446.

———. 1994. Rousseau, Maistre, and the counter-enlightenment. *History of Political Thought* 15 (1): 97–120.

———. 1997. The Counter-Enlightenment Liberalism of Isaiah Berlin. *Journal of Political Ideologies* 2 (3): 281–291.

———. "Isaiah Berlin's Joseph de Maistre," in *The Counter-Enlightenment and Its Legacy: A Symposium in Memory of Sir Isaiah Berlin.* University of Tel Aviv, January, 2000.

———. *The Counter-Enlightenment: From Rousseau to Rorty.* New York, 2001.

———. 2001. Joseph de Maistre and Carl Schmitt. In *Joseph de Maistre's Life, Thought and Influence. Selected Studies*, ed. dans Richard A. Lebrun, 220–238. Montréal & Kingston, London, Ithaca, NY: McGill-Queen's University Press.

———. 2003. *Rousseau's Counter-Enlightenment: A Republican Critique of the Philosophes. Albany.* New York: State University of New York Press.

———. "Isaiah Berlin's Joseph de Maistre," in Joseph Mali & Robert Wokler, eds. *Isaiah Berlin's Counter-Enlightenment, Transactions of the American Philosophical Society*, 93:5(2003), pp.117–132.

———. 2005. *Counter-Enlightenments: From the eighteenth century to the present. (Routledge Studies in Social and Political Thought)*, 2006. London/New York: Routledge.

———. 2006. The enlightenment and its enemies. *American Behavioral Scientist* 49 (5).

———. 2007. Strange Reversals: Isaiah Berlin's enlightenment and counter-enlightenment. In *The One and the Many: Reading Isaiah Berlin*, ed. R. Wokler and G. Crowder. New York: Prometheus Books.

———. 2011. The war against the enlightenment. *European Journal of Political Theory* 10: 277–286.

Garrett, Clarke. 1975. *Respectable Folly: Millenarians and the French Revolution in France and England.* Baltimore, MD: Johns Hopkins University Press.

———. 1987. *Spirit Possession and Popular Religion: From the Camisards to the Shakers.* Baltimore, MD: Johns Hopkins University Press. 1998.

———. 1998. *Origins of the Shakers: From the Old World to the New World.* Baltimore, MD: Johns Hopkins University Press.

Garrettson, R[ichard]. "An account of the Revival of the Work of God at Petersburg in Virginia," *Arminian Magazine* [London] 13(1790):301–302, 304.

Garrioch, David. 1996. *The Formation of the Parisian Bourgeoisie, 1690-1830. Part One: "The Jansenist Years".* Cambridge, MA: Harvard University Press.

———. 2002. *The Making of Revolutionary Paris.* Berkeley: University of California Press.

Gascoigne, John. 1989. *Cambridge in the Age of the Enlightenment: Science, Religion and Politics from the Restoration to the French Revolution.* Cambridge: Cambridge University Press.

———. 1994. *Joseph Banks and the English Enlightenment: Useful Knowledge and Polite Culture.* Cambridge: Cambridge University Press.

———. 2010. *Science, Philosophy and Religion in the Age of Enlightenment: British and Global Contexts.* New York: Ashgate.

Gaskin, John. "Recent replies to Hume's demolition of the design argument," Conference run under the British Society for the History of Philosophy in collaboration with The Department of Philosophy, University of Edinburgh, The Mind Association, and The Foundation for Intellectual History, University of Edinburgh, 18-19th, September 2002.

Gaustad, Edwin S. *Faith of the Founders: Religion and the New Nation, 1776–1826.* Foreword by Randall Balmer, Waco, TX: Baylor University Press, September, 2011.

Gay, Peter. 1995. *The Enlightenment: An Interpretation,* v1. In *The Rise of Modern Paganism (1966).* New York: Vintage.

———. 1969. *The Enlightenment: An Interpretation,* v2. In *The Science of Freedom (1969).* New York: W. W. Norton.

Genovese, Eugene. 1975. *Roll, Jordan, Roll: The World the Slaves Made.* New York: Pantheon.

Gerrish, B.A. 1984. *A Prince of the Church: Schleiermacher and the Beginnings of Modern Theology.* Philadelphia, PA: Fortress Press.

Gewehr, Wesley M. 2011. *The Great Awakening in Virginia, 1740–1790.* Durham, NC: Duke University Press, 1930; reprint, LLC.

Gibbs, F.W. 1967. *Joseph Priestley: Revolutions of the Eighteenth Century.* New York: Doubleday.

Gierl, Martin. *Pietismus und Aufklärung.* Vandenhoeck & Ruprecht (Gebundene Ausgabe), 1997.

Gill, Frederick C. 1954. *The Romantic Movement and Methodism: A Study of English Romanticism and the Evangelical Revival (1937).* London: Epworth Press (E. C. Barton).

Gill, Stephen. 1989. *William Wordsworth: A Life.* Oxford: Clarendon Press/Oxford University Press.

Gimenez, Raphaël. 1992. *L'Espace de la douleur chez Loaisel de Tréogate, 1752–1812.* Paris: Minard.

Giri, Bed Prasad. 1998. *Postmodernism as counter-enlightenment: Habermas's critique of postmodernity revisited.* University of Virginia.

Gjesdal, Kristin. "Hermeneutics, Individuality and Tradition: Schleiermacher's Idea of *Bildung* in the Landscpe of Hegelian Thought," 92-109, in Nassar, ed. *The Relevance of Romanticism: Essays in German Romantic Philosophy.* Oxford University Press, 2014.

Glaudes, Pierre. *Joseph de Maistre et les figures de l'histoire: Trois essais sur un précurseur du romantisme français. Cahier Romantique* No 2, Clermont-Ferrand 1997.

Glossop, Ronald J. 1967. The nature of Hume's ethics. *Philosophy and Phenomenological Research* 27: 527–536.

Goddard, Jean-Christophe. "Le Dieu de Fichte et le Dieu de Rousseau," *Fichte und die Aufklärung/ Fichte e l'illuminismo,* conference, Bologna, 11 aprile 2003.

Godechot, Jacques. 1971. *The Counter-Revolution: Doctrine and Action, 1789–1804*. New York: Howard Fertig.
Goetz, Rose. "Trois idéologues devant le phénomène religieux: Volney, Destutt de Tracy, Daunou," *Studies on Voltaire and the Eighteenth Century*, 2(2000).
Goldstein, Jan E. 2010. *Hysteria Complicated by Ecstasy: The Case of Nanette Leroux*. Princeton, NJ: Princeton University Press.
———. 2005. *The Post-Revolutionary Self: Politics and Psyche in France, 1750–1850*. Cambridge, MA: Harvard University Press.
———. "Enthusiasm or Imagination? Eighteenth-Century Smear Words in Comparative National Context," in Klein, Lawrence E. & Anthony J. La Vopa. *Enthusiasm and Enlightenment in Europe, 1650–1850*. 1998 (also published in *Huntington Library Quarterly*, vol. 60(1997): 1–2, pp. 29–49.
Gonzaga, Mary, Sr. 1920. *"The mysticism of Johann Joseph von Görres [1776–1848] as a reaction against rationalism," Diss't*. Washington, DC: Catholic University of America.
Goodman, Dena. 1994. *The Republic of Letters. A Cultural History of the French Enlightenment*. Ithaca and London: Cornell University Press. Revised edition, 1996.
Goring, Paul. 2005. *The Rhetoric of Sensibility in Eighteenth-Century Culture*. New York: Cambridge University Press.
Gossman, Lionel. "Benjamin Constant on Liberty and Love" in Joseph Mali & Robert Wokler, eds. *Isaiah Berlin's Counter-Enlightenment, Transactions of the American Philosophical Society*, 93:5(2003).
Gottlieb, Susannah Young-Ah. "Two Versions of Voltaire: W. H. Auden and the Dialectic of Enlightenment," PMLA 120:2(March, 2005), pp. 388–403.
Goyau, Georges. 1921. *La Pensée religieuse de Joseph de Maistre d'après des documents inédites*. Paris: Perrin.
Gozzi, Carlo. *The Tale of the Green Bird*. (Venice: Sant'Angelo Theater, 19 Jan, 1765) in Gozzi. *Five Tales for the Theatre*. Translated by Albert Bermel; Ted Emery. Chicago: University of Chicago Press, 1989. (satirizing the *philosophes*' utilitarian ethics).
Gordon, Daniel. 2001. On the supposed obsolescence of the French enlightenment. In *Postmodernism and the Enlightenment: New Perspectives in Eighteenth-Century French Intellectual History*, ed. Daniel Gordon. New York: Routledge.
Gray, John. 1995. *Enlightenment's Wake: Politics and Culture at the Close of the Modern Age*. London/New York: Routledge.
Green, T.H. 1884. *(1836–1882) Prolegomena to Ethics*. Oxford: Clarendon Press.
Greene, Robert. 1981. Whichcote, Wilkins, 'Ingenuity,' and the reasonableness of Christianity. *Journal of the History of Ideas* 42 (2): 227–252.
———. 1997. Instinct of nature: natural law, synderesis, and the moral sense. *Journal of the History of Ideas* 58 (2): 173–198.
Greig, Martin. 1993. The reasonableness of Christianity: Gilbert Burnet and the Trinitarian Controversy of the 1690s. *Journal of Ecclesiastical History* 44 (4): 631–651.
Grell, Ole Peter. 2000. In *Toleration in Enlightenment Europe*, ed. Roy Porter. New York: Cambridge University Press.
Grenby, M.O. 1998. The anti-Jacobin Novel: British fiction, British conservatism, and the revolution in France. *History* 83 (271): 445–471.
———. 2001. *The Anti-Jacobin Novel: British Conservatism and the French Revolution*. New York: Cambridge University Press.
Gretchanaïa, Elena. 2000. Un brouillon de *Valérie* de Mme de Krüdener dans les archives de Moscou. *Dix-huitième siècle* 32: 343–350.
Griefer, Elisha. 1961. Joseph de Maistre and the reaction against the eighteenth century. *American Political Science Review* 15: 591–598.
Grodzins, Dean. 2014. *American Heretic: Theodore Parker and Transcendentalism*. Chapel Hill: University of North Carolina Press.

Gross, Paul R., Norman Levitt, and Martin W. Lewis, eds. 1996. *The Flight from Science and Reason, Annals of the New York Academy of Sciences*. Vol. 775. New York: New York Academy of Sciences.

Grote, Simon. 2017. Pietist Aisthēsis, Moral education, and the beginnings of aesthetic theory. In *Ch 2 of The Emergence of Modern Aesthetic Theory: Religion and Morality in Enlightenment Germany and Scotland*. Cambridge: Cambridge University Press.

Guénot, Hervé. «Palissot de Montenoy un "ennemi" de Diderot et des philosophes» *Recherches sur Diderot et sur l'Encyclopédie*, 1 Oct, 1986, pp. 59–63.

———. *Le Personnage du philosophe au théâtre entre 1750 et 1772*. Thèse, 2 vol. University de Paris-III, UER de littérature française, 1982.

Gunny, Ahmad. 1996. *Images of Islam in Eighteenth-Century Writings*. London: Grey Seal.

Gunter, W. Stephen. 1989. *The Limits of "Love Divine": John Wesley's Response to Antinomianism and Enthusiasm*. Nashville: Kingswood Books.

Gura, Philip F. 2007. *American Transcendentalism: A History*. New York: Hill & Wang. pb, 2008.

Guyon-Lecoq, Camille. 1996. *La vertu des passions, esthétique et morale de la tragédie lyrique (1673–1733)*. Paris: Université de Paris-IV-Sorbonne, thèse de doctorat, 3 vol. Dir.: Jean Dagen.

Haakonssen, Knud, ed. 1994. *Enlightenment and Religion: Rational Dissent in Eighteenth-Century Britain*, 1996. Cambridge: Cambridge University Press.

Haas, John W., Jr. 1994. Eighteenth century evangelical responses to science: John Wesley's Enduring Legacy. *Science and Christian Belief* 6: 83–100.

Habermas, Jürgen. 2008. *Between Naturalism and Religion: Philosophical Essays, Translated by Ciaran Cronin*. Cambridge, UK: Polity.

Hall, Mark David. 2013. The religious beliefs of America's founders: reason, revelation, and revolution. *Journal of American History* 99: 1226–1227.

Hamann, Johann Georg (1730-1788). *Sämtliche Werke*, ed. Joseph Nadler, Vienna, 1949-57.

———. *Writings on Philosophy and Language* (Cambridge Texts in the History of Philosophy). Translated and Edited by Kenneth Haynes. Cambridge University Press, 2007.

Hamilton, Alastair. *William Bedwell, the Arabist, 1563–1632*. Published for the Sir Thomas Browne Institute by E.J. Brill/Leiden University Press, 1985.

———. 1999. Western attitudes to Islam in the enlightenment. *Middle Eastern Lectures 3*: 69–85.

Hammer, Stephanie. The first Fin-de-Siècle: Retheorizing Sentimentality, Storm and Stress, Pre-Romanticism, and the Late Enlightenment," Western Society for Eighteenth-Century Studies, Conference, California State University, San Bernardino, 19-21 February 1999.

———. *The Sublime Crime: Fascination, Failure, and Form in Literature of the Enlightenment*. Southern Illinois University Press, 1994.

———. 2001. *Schiller's Wound: The Theater of Trauma from Crisis to Commodity*. Wayne State University Press.

Hampsher-Monk, Iain. 2018. The spirits of Edmund Burke. *Modern Intellectual History* 15 (3): 865–877.

Hampton, Alexander J.B. 2019. *Romanticism and the Re-Invention of Modern Religion: The Reconciliation of German Idealism and Platonic Realism*. Cambridge: Cambridge University Press.

Hardenberg, Georg Philipp Friedrich Freiherr von. Novalis: Philosophical Writings. trans. and ed. Margaret Mahoney Stoljar, Albany: State University of New York Press, 1997.

Harding, Anthony John. 2003. *Coleridge and the Inspired Word*. Toronto: McGill-Queens University Press.

Hardy, Henry, ed. 1999. *Isaiah Berlin's The Roots of Romanticism: The A.W. Mellon Lectures in the Fine Arts*. Princeton, NJ: Princeton University Press.

Haroutunian, Joseph. 1932. *Piety versus Moralism: The Passing of the New England Theology*. New York, Henry Holt: pb. New York: Harper Torchbooks, 1970.

Harris, James. "David Hume, Calvinist," Conference run under the British Society for the History of Philosophy in collaboration with The Department of Philosophy, University of Edinburgh,

The Mind Association, and The Foundation for Intellectual History, University of Edinburgh, 18–19th September, 2002.
Harris, Sam. 2004. *The End of Faith: Religion, Terror, and the Future of Reason*. New York: Norton.
———. 2006. *Letter to a Christian Nation*. New York: Random House. (militantly antireligious).
Harrison, Peter. 1990. *"Religion" and the Religious in the English Enlightenment*. Cambridge: Cambridge University Press.
———. 1999. Prophecy, Early Modern Apologetics, and Hume's Argument Against Miracles. *Journal of the History of Ideas* 60 (2): 241–256.
———. 2011. Experimental Religion and Experimental Science in Early Modern England. *Intellectual History Review* 21 (4): 413–434.
Hartmann, Pierre. "Éducation et aliénation dans *Les Égarements du coeur et de l'esprit*", *Revue d'histoire littéraire de la France*, 96:1(janvier-février 1996), p. 71-97.
Hatch, Nathan O., and S. Harry. 1988. *Stout, Eds, Jonathan Edwards and the American Experience*. Oxford: Oxford University Press.
Hausheer, Roger. "Enlightening the Enlightenment" in Joseph Mali & Robert Wokler, eds. *Isaiah Berlin's Counter-Enlightenment, Transactions of the American Philosophical Society*, 93:5(2003), pp. 33–50.
Havens, George R. 1965. *The Age of Ideas: From Reaction to Revolution in Eighteenth-Century France (1955)*. New York: Free Press.
Hawes, Clement, ed. 1999. *Christopher Smart and the Enlightenment*. New York: St. Martin's Press.
———. 1996. *Mania and Literary Style: The Rhetoric of Enthusiasm from the Ranters to Christopher Smart*. New York: Cambridge University Press. (Ranters, Quakers & Diggers; Swift, Smart).
Hayden, Hiram. 1950. *The Counter-Renaissance*. New York: Scribner.
Hazard, Paul. *La crise de la conscience européenne (1680–1715)*. (Paris: Boivin, 1935) Paris: Arthème Fayard, 1961.
Hedley, Douglas. *Coleridge, Philosophy and Religion: Aids to Reflection and the Mirror of the Spirit*. Cambridge: Cambridge University Press, January 2009.
Hegel, Georg Wilhelm Friedrich (1770–1831). *Lectures on the Philosophy of Religion: One-Volume Edition, The Lectures of 1827* (Hegel Lectures) Edited and Abridged by Peter C. Hodgson. Translated by Robert F. Brown, Peter C. Hodgson & J. Michael Stewart. Oxford: Clarendon Press, 2006.
———. *The Phenomenology of Spirit* [*Phänomenologie des Geistes*, 1807]. Translated and Edited by Terry Pinkard. Cambridge: Cambridge University Press (Cambridge Hegel Translations), 2017. Kindle Edition.
———. *Lectures on the Philosophy of History*. Translated by Ruben Alvarado. WordBridge Publishing, 2011.
Henderson, G. D. *Mystics of the North-East, including: I. Letters of James Keith, M.D., and others to Lord Deskford. II. Correspondence between Dr. George Garden and James Cunningham*. Aberdeen, Printed for the Third Spalding Club, 1934. (Episcopalians in early 18thc Scotland reading Fénelon, via Jeanne Guyon).
Henderson, G., and D. Chevalier. 1952. *Ramsey*. Edinburgh/London: Nelson.
Hentsch, Thierry. 1988. *L'Orient imaginaire: La vision politique occidentale de l'est méditerranéen*. Paris: Editions de Minuit.
Herder, Johann Gottfried (1744–1803). *Werke in zehn Bänden*. 10v, Deutscher Klassiker Verlag, 1985–98.
———. "This Too a Philosophy History for the Formation of Humanity" in *Philosophical Writings*. Translated and Edited by Michael N. Forster. Cambridge: Cambridge University Press, 2002.
Herrero, Javier. Los Origines del pensamiento reaccionario español. (1971) Zaragoza: Prensas de la Universidad de Zaragoza, 2020. ("movimiento antiillustrado").
Herrick, James A. 1997. *The Radical Rhetoric of the English Deists: The Discourse of Skepticism, 1680-1750*. Columbia: University of South Carolina Press.

Heyd, Michael. 1981. The reaction to enthusiasm in the seventeenth century: towards an integrative approach. *Journal of Modern History* 53: 258–280.

———. 1982. *Between Orthodoxy and the Enlightenment: Jean-Robert Chouet and the Introduction of Cartesian Science in the Academy of Geneva*. The Hague: Nijhoff.

———. "The Reaction to Enthusiasm in the 17th century: from antistructure to structure," in *Religion* 15(1985), 279–289.

———. 1995. *"Be Sober and Reasonable": The Critique of Enthusiasm in the Seventeenth and Eighteenth Centuries, Brill's Studies in Intellectual History*. Vol. 63. Brill: Leiden.

Heydt, Colin. 2017. The problem of natural religion in Smith's moral thought. *Journal of the History of Ideas* 78 (1): 73–94.

Heyman, Christine Leigh. 1997. *Southern Cross: The Beginnings of the Bible Belt*. New York: Knopf.

Hibbs, Thomas S. 2017. *Wagering on an Ironic God: Pascal on Faith and Philosophy*, 2018. Waco, TX: Baylor University Press.

Himmelfarb, Gertrude. 2004. *The Roads to Modernity: The British, French, and American Enlightenments*. New York: Knopf. pb Vintage, 2005.

———. 1995. *The De-Moralization of Society: From Victorian Virtues to Modern Values*. New York: Knopf.

———. *Past and Present: The Challenges of Modernity, from the Pre-Victorians to the Postmodernists*. (Encounter Classics) Encounter Books, 2017.

Hirschman, Albert O. 1976. *The Passions and the Interests*. Princeton, NJ: Princeton University Press.

Hitchens, Christopher, Richard Dawkins, Sam Harris, and Daniel Dennett. 2019. *The Four Horsemen: The Conversation [2007] That Sparked an Atheist Revolution*. New York: Random House.

Hobhouse, Stephen. '*Fides et ratio*', the book which introduced Jacob Boehme to William Law. *The Journal of Theological Studies* 37, London, 1936, pp. 350-368.

Hofmann, Étienne. 2002. Histoire, politique et religion: essai d'articulation de trois composantes de l'oeuvre et de la pensée de Benjamin Constant. *Historical Reflexions/Réflexions Historiques* 28 (3): 397–418.

Holbach, Paul-Henri Thiry, Baron d'. *La Contagion sacrée, ou Histoire naturelle de la superstition [The Sacred Contagion: A Natural History of Superstition]*. "Londres" [London], 1768.

Hölderlin, Friedrich (1770–1843). *Hyperion*. (1797, 1799). Translated by Ross Benjamin. Brooklyn, NY: Archipelago Books, 2008.

Holt, P.M. 1973. *Studies in the History of the Near East*, 3–63. London: Routledge. (On English scholarly achievements in Arabic studies).

Horkheimer, Max, and Theodor Adorno. 2002. *Dialectic of Enlightenment (Cultural Memory in the Present). (1947) tr. Edmund Jephcott*. Stanford, CA: Stanford University Press.

Howells, Robin. 1995. Rousseau and voltaire: a literary comparison of two *Professions de foi*. *French Studies* 49 (4): 397–409.

Hoyles, John. "Nature and Enthusiasm," *The Edges of Augustanism*. Springer International Archives of the History of Ideas Archives internationales d'Histoire des Idees (ARCH, volume 53), pp. 123-132. (that for Law religious enthusiasm or divine illumination is natural and reason unnatural.).

Hulliung, Mark. 1994. *The Autocritique of Enlightenment: Rousseau and the Philosophes*. Cambridge: Harvard University Press.

Hume, David. 1985. In *Essays, Moral, Political and Literary*, ed. Eugene F. Miller. Indianapolis, IN: Liberty Classics.

———. *The Complete Works of David Hume: An Enquiry Concerning Human Understanding, A Treatise of Human Nature, The History of England, The Natural History of Religion, Essays, Personal Correspondence*. Kindle ed. 2020.

Hunt, Lynn, Margaret C. Jacob, and Wijnand Mijnhardt. 2010. *The Book That Changed Europe: Picart and Barnard's Religious Ceremonies and Customs of All the Peoples of the World. (1723–1737)*. Cambridge, MA: Belknap Press of Harvard University Press.

Hunter, Ian. 2006. *Rival Enlightenments: Civil and Metaphysical Philosophy in Early Modern Germany*. Cambridge: Cambridge University Press.

Hunter, J. Paul. 1990. *Before Novels: The Cultural Contexts of Eighteenth-Century English Fiction*. New York: Norton.

Hunter, Michael, and David Wooton, eds. 1992. *Atheism from the Reformation to the Enlightenment*. Oxford: Clarendon Press.

Hurlbutt, Robert. 1965. *Hume, Newton, and the Design Argument*. Lincoln: University of Nebraska Press.

Hutcheson, Francis. 1999. *On the Nature and Conduct of the Passions. (1748)*. Manchester, UK: Clinamen Press.

Hutin, Serge. 1960. *Les Disciples anglais de Jacob Boehme au 17e et 18e siècles*. Paris: Denoël.

Hyland, P., O. Gomez & F. Greensides, eds. *The Enlightenment: A Sourcebook and Reader*. London, 2003.

Ida, Hisashi, *Genèse d'une morale matérialiste: les passions et le contrôle de soi chez Diderot*. Paris: Honoré Champion, coll. "Les dix-huitièmes siècles," 53, 2001.

Idel, Moshe, and Bernard McGinn, eds. 1996. *Mystical Union in Judaism, Christianity, and Islam: An Ecumenical Dialogue*. New York: Continuum.

Irlam, Shaun. 1999. *Elations: The Poetics of Enthusiasm in Eighteenth-Century Britain*. Stanford, CA: Stanford University Press.

Israel, Jonathan. 2001. *Radical Enlightenment: Philosophy and the Making of Modernity, 1650-1750*. New York: Oxford University Press. pb, 2002.

———. 2006. Enlightenment! Which Enlightenment? *Journal of the History of Ideas* 67 (3).

———. 2006. *Enlightenment Contested: Philosophy, Modernity, and the Emancipation of Man 1670–1752*. New York: Oxford University Press. 2009.

———. *A Revolution of the Mind: Radical Enlightenment and the Intellectual Origins of Modern Democracy*. New York: Oxford University Press, 2008; pb Princeton, NJ: Princeton University Press, 2011.

———. 2013. *Democratic Enlightenment: Philosophy, Revolution, and Human Rights, 1750-1790*. New York: Oxford University Press.

———. "Tolerance and Intolerance in the Writings of the French *Antiphilosophes*," in John Christian Laursen & María José Villaverde, eds. *Paradoxes of Religious Toleration in Early Modern Political Thought*. Lexington Books, 2012.

———. 2016. Rousseau, Diderot, and the 'Radical Enlightenment': a reply to Helena Rosenblatt and Joanna Stalnaker. *Journal of the History of Ideas* 77 (4): 649–677.

Jacob, Margaret. 1981. *The Radical Enlightenment: Pantheists, Freemasons and Republicans*. London: Allen & Unwin.

———. 2001. *The Enlightenment: A Brief History with Documents*. Boston: St. Martin's/Bedford.

———. "The Nature of Early Eighteenth-Century Religious Radicalism," in *Republic of Letters: A Journal for the Study of Knowledge, Politics, and the Arts* I:1(May 1, 2009 @ http://rofl.stanford.edu/node/42.

Jacobs, Helmut C. & Gisela Schlüter, eds. *Beiträge zur Begriffsgeschichte der italienischen Aufklärung im europäischen Kontext*. Francfort/Berlin/Berne/Bruxelles/New York/Oxford/Vienne: Peter Lang, coll. "Europäische Aufklärung in Literatur und Sprache," 12, 2000.

Jacques-Chaquin, Nicole. «La passion des sciences interdites: curiosité et démonologie (XVe-XVIIIe siècles),» in Nicole Jacques-Chaquin et Sophie Houdard ed. *Curiosité et libido sciendi, de la Renaissance aux Lumières*. v1, Fontenay-aux Roses: ÉNS Éditions, ÉNS Fontenay-Saint Cloud, 1999.

Jacques-Lefèvre, Nicole. *Louis-Claude de Saint-Martin, le Philosophe inconnu (1743–1803). Un illuministe au Siècle des Lumières*. Paris: Éditions Dervy, « Bibliothèque de l'hermétisme », 2003.

Jalliet, Aline. 1994. Loaisel de Tréogate, romancier féministe? *Dix-huitième siècle* 26: 475–485.

Japaridze, Tamar. *The Kantian Subject: Sensus Communis, Mimesis, Work of Mourning*. State University of New York Press, 1999.

Jaquier, Claire. *l'Erreur des désirs. Romans sensibles au XVIIIe siècle*. Lausanne: Payot, coll. "Études et documents littéraires," 1998.

Jalal, Ayesha. 2008. *Partisans of Allah: Jihad in South Asia*. Cambridge, MA: Harvard University Press.

Jay, Martin. 2006. *Songs of Experience: Modern American and European Variations on a Universal Theme*. Berkeley: University of California Press. (Schleiermacher distinguished from Kant in the history of epistemology).

Jennings, Jeremy. "The Debate about Luxury in Eighteenth- and Nineteenth-Century French Political Thought," *Journal of the History of Ideas* 68:1(2007), p79-106.

Jesse, Horst. 2003. *Friedrich Daniel Ernst Schleiermacher: Der Kirchenvater des 19.* Frieling: *Jahrhunderts*.

Johnson, David. 1999. *Hume, Holism, and Miracles*. Ithaca, NY: Cornell University Press.

Johnson, George. 1995. *Fire in the Mind: Science, Faith, and the Search for Order*. New York: Knopf.

Johnson, W.R. 2001. *Lucretius and the Modern World*. Duckworth: Herndon, VA.

Joling-van der Sar, Gerda Joke. "The Spiritual Side of Samuel Richardson: Mysticism, Behmenism and Millenarianism in an Eighteenth-Century English Novelist," PhD Diss't, Universiteit van Leiden, 27 Nov 2003. PDF @ http://home.hccnet.nl/j.t.joling/The%20Spiritual%20Side%20of%20Samuel%20Richardson%20a4.pdf.

Jordan, W. K. *The Development of Religious Toleration in England*. 3v. New York: Peter Smith repr. 1965.

Juranville, Françoise. «Un roman d'apprentissage au XVIIIe siècle: écriture et gai savoir dans *Les Égarements du coeur et de l'esprit*,» *Revue d'histoire littéraire de la France*, 96:1(janvier-février 1996), pp. 98–110.

Kahan, Michèle Bokobza. "Ethos in Testimony: The Case of Carré de Montgeron, a Jansenist and a Convulsionary in the Century of Enlightenment," *Eighteenth-Century Studies* 43:4(Summer, 2010), p419-433.

Kail, Peter. "'The Naturalism of David Hume': Kemp-Smith Revisited," Conference run under the British Society for the History of Philosophy in collaboration with The Department of Philosophy, University of Edinburgh, The Mind Association, and The Foundation for Intellectual History, University of Edinburgh, 18-19th, September 2002.

Kant, Immanuel. *Groundwork of the Metaphysic of Morals*. (1785) Translated by Mary Gregor, Jens Timmerman. Cambridge: Cambridge University Press (Texts in the History of Philosophy), 1998, 2nd ed. 2012.

———. *Critique of Practical Reason*. (1788) Translated by Mary Gregor. Cambridge: Cambridge University Press (Texts in the History of Philosophy), 1997, 2nd ed. 2015.

———. *Religion within the Boundaries of Mere Reason*. (1792-93) ed. Allan Wood & George Di Giovanni. Cambridge: Cambridge University Press (Texts in the History of Philosophy), 1999; 2nd ed. 2018.

Karsenti, Bruno. "Préface" to Durkheim. *Sociologie et philosophie*. Paris: Quadrige, 2014.

Katz, Steven T., ed. 1978. *Mysticism and Philosophical Analysis*. Oxford: Oxford University Press.

———., ed. 1983. *Mysticism and Religious Traditions*. Oxford: Oxford University Press.

Keitt, Andrew. 2004. Religious Enthusiasm, the Spanish Inquisition, and the disenchantment of the world. *Journal of the History of Ideas* 65 (2): 231–250.

Keller, Mary. 2001. *The Hammer and the Flute: Women, Power, and Spirit Possession*. Baltimore, MD: Johns Hopkins University Press. (spirit possession neither madness nor imposture).

Kenshur, Oscar. "Doubt, Certainty, Faith, and Ideology," in Paul R. Gross, Norman Levitt & Martin W. Lewis, eds. *The Flight from Science and Reason, Annals of the New York Academy of Sciences* v. 775 (New York: New York Academy of Sciences, 1996), pp. 526–536.

Kenshur, Oskar. "The Politics of Civic Religion in Dryden and Gibbon" 8Oct88: Midwestern American Society for Eighteenth-Century Studies, Notre Dame, Indiana.

Ketcham, Ralph. "James Madison and Religion—a New Hypothesis," in Robert Alley, ed. *James Madison on Religious Liberty*. Prometheus Books, 1985.

Keymer, Tom. 2004. *Richardson's 'Clarissa' and the Eighteenth-Century Reader*. New York: Cambridge University Press.

Kirscher, Roger. 2000. Les néologues autour de Friedrich Nicolai et de sa revue *Allgemeine Deutsche Bibliothek* (1765-1792). Une volonté de réforme théologique 'éclairée'. *Dix-huitième siècle* 32: 445–456.

Klauber, Martin I. 1990. Reason, revelation, and cartesianism: Louis Tronchin and enlightened orthodoxy in late seventeenth-century Geneva. *Church History* 59: 326–339.

———. 1994. *Between Reformed Scholasticism and Pan-Protestantism: Jean-Alphonse Turretin (1671-1737) and Enlightened Orthodoxy at the Academy of Geneva*. London/Toronto: Associated University Presses.

Klein, Lawrence E. & Anthony J. La Vopa, ed. *Enthusiasm and Enlightenment in Europe, 1650-1850*. Henry E. Huntington Library and Art Gallery, 1998 (also published in *Huntington Library Quarterly*, vol. 60(1997):1-2. Essays by Klein, La Vopa, Peter Fenves, Jan Goldstein, Jon Mee, J. G. A. Pocock, and Mary D. Sheriff).

Klein, Lawrence E. "Sociability, Solitude and Enthusiasm." in Klein & La Vopa, eds. *Enthusiasm and Enlightenment in Europe, 1650-1850*, 1998 (also published in *Huntington Library Quarterly*, vol. 60(1997): 1-2, pp153-177).

———. 1994. *Shaftesbury and the Culture of Politeness: Moral Discourse and Cultural Politics in Early Eighteenth-Century England*. Cambridge: Cambridge University Press.

Kleingeld, Pauline. 2011. *Kant and Cosmopolitanism: The Philosophical Ideal of World Citizenship*. Cambridge: Cambridge University Press, Kindle ed.

Klemme, Heiner F. *Reception of the Scottish Enlightenment in Germany: Six Significant Translations 1755-1782*. Thoemmes Continuum; Facsimile edition, 2000.

Klinck, David. *The French Counterrevolutionary Theorist Louis de Bonald (1754-1840)*. New York, Peter Lang (Studies in European History, v18), 1997.

Knox, Ronald. *Enthusiasm: A Chapter in the History of Religion, with Special Reference to the Seventeenth and Eighteenth Centuries* (1950), New York: Oxford University Press Galaxy pb, 1961.

Knox-Shaw, Peter. 2004. *Jane Austen and the Enlightenment*. New York: Cambridge University Press.

Knudsen, Jonathan B. 1986. *Justus Möser [1720–1794] and the German Enlightenment*. New York: Cambridge University Press.

Koch, G. Adolf. *Religion of the American Enlightenment*. New York: Thomas Y. Crowell, Apollo pb, 1968, repr. of *Republican Religion: The American Revolution and the Cult of Reason*. New York, 1933.

Koeninger, Frieda. "Putting the Inquisition on Trial: The Case of fray Juan Francisco Ramirez," American Society for Eighteenth-Century Studies 31st Annual Meeting, University of Pennsylvania, April 14, 2000.

Kontler, László. 2001. 'Mahometan Christianity': Islam and the English Deists. In *Frontiers of Faith: Religious Exchange and the Constitution of Religious Identities 1400-1750*, ed. Eszter Andor and István György Tóth. Budapest/New York: Central European University Press.

Kooy, Michael John. 2000. Aesthetics and Education: Coleridge, Kant, Schiller. In *Kant, Romanticism and the Origins Of Modernity, conf. University of Warwick, UK, 4 July*.

Koretsky, Deanna P. "Sarah Wesley, British Methodism, and the Feminist Question, Again," *Eighteenth-Century Studies* 46:2(Winter, 2013), pp. 223-238. (Charles Wesley's daughter as a forgotten early and counter-enlightenment feminist).

Kors, Alan Charles. 1976. *D'Holbach's Coterie: An Enlightenment in Paris*. Princeton, NJ: Princeton University Press.

Kors, Alan C. ed. *Encyclopedia of the Enlightenment*. 4 vols, Oxford, 2003.

Kors, Alan Charles, and Paul J. Korshin, eds. 1987. *Anticipations of the Enlightenment in England, France, and Germany*. Philadelphia: University of Pennsylvania Press.

Koselleck, Reinhard. *Critique and Crises: Enlightenment and the Pathogenesis of Modern Society*. (*Kritik und Krise*. 1959) tr. Cambridge, MA: MIT Press, 1998.

Kramer, Fritz W. 1985. Empathy— Reflections on the history of ethnology in Pre-Fascist Germany: Herder, Creuzer, Bastian, Bachofen, and Frobenius. *Dialectical Anthropology (Historical Archive)* v9 (1–4): p337–p347.

Kramer, Martin. 1996. Fundamentalist Islam at Large: The Drive for Power. *Middle East Quarterly*: 37–49.

Kramnick, Isaac. ed. *The Portable Enlightenment Reader*. London, 1995.

Krell, David Farrell. 1998. *Contagion, Sexuality, Disease and Death in German Idealism and Romanticism*. Bloomington: Indiana University Press.

Kuzniar, Alice. Philosophic Chiliasm: generating the future or delaying the end? *Eighteenth Century Studies*, 19(1985–86), 1-20.

La Mettrie, Julien Offray de. *Œuvres philosophiques*. ed. F. Markovits, 2 vols. Paris: Fayard, 1987.

La Vopa, Anthony J. 2017. *The Labor of the Mind: Intellect and Gender in Enlightenment Cultures*. Philadelphia: University of Pennsylvania Press.

La Vopa, Anthony J. 2009. A New Intellectual History? Jonathan Israel's Enlightenment. *Historical Journal* 52 (/3): 717–738.

La Vopa, Anthony J. 2001. *Fichte: The Self and the Calling of Philosophy, 1762–1799*. New York: Cambridge University Press.

———. "The Philosopher and the "Schwärmer": On the Career of a German Epithet from Luther to Kant," in Klein, Lawrence E. & Anthony J. La Vopa, *Enthusiasm and Enlightenment in Europe, 1650-1850*. 1998 (also published in *Huntington Library Quarterly*, vol. 60(1997): 1-2, pp. 85-115).

La Vopa, Anthony J. 1988. *Grace, Talent, and Merit: Poor Students, Clerical Careers, and Professional Ideology in Eighteenth-Century Germany*. New York: Cambridge University Press.

Labio, Catherine. 2004. *Origins and the Enlightenment: Aesthetic Epistemology from Descartes to Kant*. Ithaca, NY: Cornell University Press.

Laborie, Lionel. 2015. *Enlightening Enthusiasm: Prophecy and Religious Experience in Early Eighteenth-Century England*. Manchester, UK: Manchester University Press.

———. rvw of "Jordan Rosenberg, Critical Enthusiasm: Capital Accumulation and the Transformation of Religious Passion," *Eighteenth-Century Studies* 46:2(Winter, 2013), 311–313.

Labrousse, Élisabeth. 1996. *Pierre Bayle, hétérodoxie et rigorisme*. Paris: Albin Michel.

———. 1985. *Essai sur la Révocation de l'Édit de Nantes: Une foi, une loi, un roi?* Geneva: Labor et Fidès. Paris: Payot, 1990.

Lafage, Franck. 1998. *Le Comte Joseph de Maistre (1753-1821): Itinéraire intellectuel d'un théologien de la politique*. Paris: L'Harmattan. (Maistre as a "theologian of politics").

Laforge, François. 1997. Les curés de Troyes et le combat contre l'impiété. *Recherches sur Diderot et sur l'Encyclopédie*: 143–147.

Lamennais, Hugues-Félicité Robert de (1782-1854). *Paroles d'un croyant*. Paris: May, 1834 (Brussels, 1838 @ https://ia800203.us.archive.org/16/items/parolesduncroya00daogoog/parolesduncroya00daogoog.pdf).

———. *Œuvres completes*. 10v, Paris: Paul Daubré & Cailleux, 1836–1837 @ https://archive.org/details/oeuvrescomplte08lameuoft.

———. *Essai sur l'indifférence en matière de religion*. 3v, Paris; Tournachon-Molin et H. Seguin, 1817-1823.

———. *De la religion considérée dans ses rapports avec l'ordre civil et politique* (1825–1826) in *Œuvres completes*. v7, Paris: Paul Daubré & Cailleux, 1836-37 @ https://archive.org/details/bub_gb_E0os6wjfTk0C.

Lamennais, Hugues-Félicité Robert de. 1838. *Le Livre du people*. Paris: Delloye/Lecou.

Lamennais, Hugues-Félicité Robert de. *Esquisse d'une philosophie*. 4v, Paris: Pagnerre, 1840-46.

Lamennais, Lacordaire & Montalembert, eds. *L'Avenir* (I:1, 16 Oct, 1830).

Landmann, M. 1976. Critiques of reason from Weber to Bloch. *Telos* 29: 187–198.

Lange, Friedrich Albert. 1905. *Geschichte des Materialismus und Kritik seiner Bedeutung in der Gegenwart*. Leipzig: Reclam.

Lapointe, Linda & Marie Claude Mirandette. «Le sentimentalisme contre-révolutionnaire dans l'iconographie de la Révolution française,» dans *Iconographie et image de la Révolution fran-*

çaise. Actes du colloque tenu dans le cadre du 57e Congrès de l'ACFAS les 15 et 16 mai 1989 à l'Université du Québec à Montréal organisé par Claudette Hould et James Leith. Montréal, Association canadienne- française pour l'avancement des sciences, coll. "Les cahiers scientifiques," 72, 1990, p. 160–180.

Larkin, Edward T. "Bishop Johann Michael Sailer: Enlightener and Enlightenment Critic," American Society for Eighteenth-Century Studies 31st Annual Meeting, University of Pennsylvania, April 14, 2000. (Sailer a Catholic Enlightenment Jesuit).

Lassere, Pierre. *le Romantisme français. Essai sur la révolution dans les sentiments et dans les idées au XIXe siècle.* (Paris, 1907) Reprint: Genève: Slatkine, 2000. (esp. Rousseau).

Laursen, John Christian. "Télémaque manqué: Reverdil at Court in Copenhagen," dans *Reconceptualizing Nature, Science, and Aesthetics: Contribution à une nouvelle approche des Lumières helvétiques.* Geneva: Éditions Slatkine, coll. "Travaux sur la Suisse des Lumières," 1, 1998.

———. Ed. *Histories of Heresy in Early Modern Europe: For, Against, and Beyond Persecution and Toleration.* Springer, 2002.

Lauvergnat-Gagnière. *Lucien de Samosate et le Lucianisme en France au XVIe siècle, Athéisme et polémique.* Geneva: Droz, 1988.

Law, William (1686–1761). *The Works of the Reverend William Law.* re-ed. Hildesheim/New York: Georg Olms Verlag, 1974.

———. *A Serious Call to a Devout and Holy Life.* (London: William Innys, 1729) in *The Complete Works of WILLIAM LAW* (17v in 1) www.ClassicChristianeBooks.com, Kindle Edition.

Lawrence, Alexander. *2nd Victory in Jesus*: Book 3 of *THE GOINS BRICOLAGE: A Saga of Tecumseh and Stonewall Counties in the State of Indiana*, iUniverse, 2010.

Lawrence, Bruce. *Defenders of God: The Fundamentalist Revolt Against the Modern Age.* Columbia, SC: University of South Carolina Press, 1989, 2nd ed. 1995.

Le Guillou, Louis. "Joseph de Maistre et Lamennais, 1820–1821," *Revue des études maistriennes*, No. 8 (1983): 85–100.

Lears, Jackson. "Keeping It Real," rvw of Jay, *Songs of Experience.* in *The Nation*, 282:23(12 Jun 2006).

Lebrun, Richard A. 2001. *Joseph de Maistre's Life, Thought, and Influence: Selected Studies.* Montréal: McGill-Queen's University Press.

———. "Joseph de Maistre and Edmund Burke: A Comparison," dans Richard A. Lebrun ed. *Joseph de Maistre's Life, Thought and Influence. Selected Studies*, Montréal & Kingston, London, Ithaca, NY, McGill-Queen's University Press, 2001.

———. 2001. Joseph de Maistre dans le monde anglophone. *Revue des études maistriennes* 13: 91–108.

———. Joseph de Maistre in the Anglophone World. In dans Richard A. Lebrun ed. *Joseph de Maistre's Life, Thought and Influence. Selected Studies.* Montréal & Kingston, London, Ithaca, NY, McGill-Queen's University Press, 2001, pp. 271–289.

———. 1972. Joseph de Maistre and Rousseau. *Studies on Voltaire and the Eighteenth Century* 88: 881–898.

———. 1988. *Joseph de Maistre: An Intellectual Militant.* Kingston and Montreal: McGill-Queen's University Press.

———. Joseph de Maistre: how catholic a reaction? Canadian Catholic Historical Association *Study Sessions*, 1967.

———. 1985. Les lectures de Joseph de Maistre d'après ses registres inédits. *Revue des études maistriennes* 9: 126–194.

———. "The 'Satanic' Revolution: Joseph de Maistre's 'Religious' Judgment of the French Revolution," *Proceedings of the Annual Meeting of the Western Society for French History*, 16 (1989):234–40.

———. *Throne and Altar; The Political and Religious Thought of Joseph de Maistre*, Ottawa: University of Ottawa Press 1965.

———., ed. 2001. *Joseph de Maistre's Life, Thought, and Influence: Selected Studies*. Kingston and Montreal: McGill-Queen's University Press.

———. ed. & tr. *Maistre Studies*. Lanham, MD: University Press of America 1988. (Thirteen articles from the *Revue des études maistriennes*).

Lebrun, Richard & Carolina Armenteros. 'Introduction', in: Armenteros & Lebrun eds. *Joseph de Maistre and the legacy of Enlightenment* (Oxford 2011) 8–13.

———. eds. *Joseph de Maistre and his European Readers. From Friedrich von Gentz to Isaiah Berlin*. Leiden & Boston, 2011.

Leduc, Jean. "Les Sources de l'athéisme et de l'immoralisme du marquis de Sade," *Studies on Voltaire and the Eighteenth Century* 68(1969).

Lee, Jesse. 1810. *A Short History of the Methodists in the United States of America*. Baltimore: Magill & Clime.

Lehmann, Hartmut. "Vorüberlegungen zu einer Sozialgeschichte des Pietismus im 17./18. Jahrhundert," in *Pietismus und Neuzeit*, 21(1995), pp. 69–83.

Lehmann, Hartmut, Heinz Schilling & H.-J. Schrader, eds. *Jansenismus, Quietismus, Pietismus*. Göttingen, 1977, 2002.

Lehner, Ulrich L. "Catholic Theology and Enlightenment (1670-1815)" in *The Oxford Handbook of Catholic Theology*. Eds. Lewis Ayres and Medi-Ann Volpe. Oxford: Oxford University Press 2015; Theology Faculty Research and Publications e-Publications@Marquette, 1-1-2015.

———. 2016. *The Catholic Enlightenment: The Forgotten History of a Global Movement*. Oxford: Oxford University Press.

Leibniz, Gottfried Wilhelm (1646–1715). *Unvorgreffliches Bedencken über eine Schrifft genandt* **Kurze Vorstellung**. MSS, 1697, 1698.

———. *Dissertation on Predestination and Grace*. [*De praedestinatione et gratia dissertatione*. MS, c1701-1706]. Translated and Edited by Michael J. Murray. New Haven, CT: Yale University Press, 2011.

———. *Theodicy* (*Essais de Théodicée*, 1709) Edited by Austin Farrar. Translated by E.M. Huggard, Open Court, 1985; Project Gutenberg, 2005 @ https://www.gutenberg.org/files/17147/17147-h/17147-h.htm.

Leighton, C. D. A. "Scottish Jacobitism, Episcopacy, and Counter-Enlightenment," *History of European Ideas* 35:1(March, 2009), pp. 1-10.

Leighton, C.D.A. 1998. The Nonjurors and the counter enlightenment: some illustration. *Journal of Religious History* 22 (3): 270–286.

———. 1998. William Law, Behmenism and counter-enlightenment. *Harvard Theological Review* 91 (3): 301–320.

———. 1999. Hutchinsonianism: a counter-enlightenment reform movement. *Journal of Religious History* 23 (2): 168–184. (17).

———. 2000. Knowledge of divine things: a study of Hutchinsonianism. *History of European Ideas* 26 (3–4): 159–176.

———. 2000. Antichrist's revolution: some Anglican apocalypticists in the age of the French wars. *Journal of Religious History* 24 (2): 138–141.

———. 2009. Scottish Jacobitism, episcopacy, and counter-enlightenment. *History of European Ideas* 35 (1): 1–10.

Leithart, Peter J. 2014. *Gratitude: An Intellectual History*. Waco, TX: Baylor University Press. 2018. (Grace in a way).

Leland, John (English Anglican). *Leland's Deistical Writers*. (1807), 2v, Bristol, UK: Thoemmes Press, 2003.

——— (New England Baptist), *The Writings of the Late Elder* John Leland, *Including Some Events in His Life*, ed. L. F. Greene, New York, 1845.

———. *The Virginia Chronicle: with judicious and critical remarks, under XXIV heads*, Fredericksburg, VA: Printed by T. Green, 1790, facsimile repr. Gale Group ECCO, n.d., pp. 34–35.

LeMay, J. Leo, ed. 1988. *Deism, Masonry, and the Enlightenment: Essays honoring Alfred Owen Aldridge*. Cranbury, NJ: University of Delaware Press.
Lenci, Mauro. "The Sleep of Reason: Anti-Enlightenment Political Thought, *c*.1700-*c*.2000," IHR seminars: History of Political Ideas, London, 23Nov05.
Lerner, Ralph. 1994. *Revolutions Revisited: Two Faces of the Politics of Enlightenment*. Chapel Hill: University of North Carolina Press.
———. 2000. *Maimonides' Empire of Light: Popular Enlightenment in an Age of Belief.* Chicago: University of Chicago Press.
Lessing, Gotthold Ephraim. *Laokoön*. (1767) Translated by Edward Allen McCormick. Baltimore: Johns Hopkins University Press, 1984.
Lestition, Steven. 2007. Countering, transposing, or negating the enlightenment: a response to Robert Norton. *Journal of the History of Ideas* 68 (4): 659–681.
Leventhal, Herbert. 1976. *In the Shadow of the Enlightenment: Occultism and Renaissance Science in Eighteenth-Century America*. New York: New York University Press.
Levin, David, ed. 1963. *The Puritan in the Enlightenment: Franklin and Edwards*. Chicago: Rand McNally (Berkeley Series in American History).
Lewis, Jayne Elizabeth. 2017. *Religion in Enlightenment England: An Anthology of Primary Sources*. Waco, TX: Baylor University Press.
Lichtheim, George. "Rousseau and De Maistre," *New Statesman*, 16 September 1966, 398-399.
Liedman, Sven-Eric, ed. *The Postmodernist Critique of the Project of Enlightenment*. Amsterdam, 1997.
Liggio, Leonard. "Eighteenth Century: The Counter-Enlightenment," (on Benjamin Constant's concept of liberty) in Edward B. McLean, Ed. An Uncertain Legacy: *Essays on the Pursuit of Liberty*. Wilmington, Del: Intercollegiate Studies Institute, 1997.
Lilla, Mark. "What Is Counter-Enlightenment?" in Joseph Mali & Robert Wokler, eds. *Isaiah Berlin's Counter-Enlightenment, Transactions of the American Philosophical Society*, 93:5(2003), pp. 1–12.
———. 2007. *The Stillborn God: Religion, Politics and the Modern West*. New York: Knopf. (from lectures delivered at Oxford University in 2003).
Lindberg, David C., and L. Ronald. 1986. *Numbers, eds. God and Nature: Historical Essays on the Encounter Between Christianity and Science*. Berkeley: University of California Press.
———. 2004. *Numbers, eds. When Science and Christianity Meet*. Chicago: University of Chicago Press.
Linker, Damon. 2000. From Kant to schelling: counter-enlightenment in the name of reason. *Rev Metaphys* 54 (2).
Little, Thomas J. *The Origins of Southern Evangelicalism:* Religious Revivalism in the South Carolina Lowcountry, 1670–1760, University of South Carolina Press, 2015.
Livingston, David N. D. G.. Hart & Mark Noll, eds. *Evangelicals and Science in Historical Perspective*. New York: Oxford University Press, 1998.
Lok, Matthijs. 2014. Vijanden van de Verlichting. Antiverlichting en Verlichting in de Europese intellectuele geschiedenis, [Enemies of the Enlightenment. Counter-Enlightenment and Enlightenment in European Intellectual History]. *Tijdshrift voor Geschiedenis* 127 (2): 211–228.
Lomonaco, Fabrizio. "Jean Barbeyrac et le 'pyrrhonisme historique' dans la *Bibliothèque raisonnée des ouvrages des savants de l'Europe*," dans Jens Häseler & Antony McKenna ed. *la Vie intellectuelle aux Refuges protestants. Actes de la Table ronde de Münster du 25 juillet 1995*. Paris: Honoré Champion éditeur, coll. "Vie des Huguenots," 5, 1999, pp. 253–267.
Longenecker, Stephen L. 2002. *Shenandoah Religion: Outsiders and the Mainstream, 1716–1865*. Waco, TX: Baylor University Press.
Lotterie, Florence & Darrin M. McMahon, eds. *Les lumières européennes dans leur relation avec les autres grandes cultures et religions du XVIIIe siècle*. Paris: Honoré Champion, coll. "Études internationales sur le dix- huitième siècle," 5, 2001, 2002.

Lough, J. The literary underground revisited. *Studies on Voltaire and the Eighteenth Century* 329, 1995.
Low, Lisa. 1995. Anthony. In *Milton, the metaphysicals, and romanticism*, ed. John Harding. New York: Cambridge University Press.
Lubac, Henri de. La postérité spirituelle de Joachim de Flore. v, *De Joachim à Schelling*. Paris: Lethielleux, 1979.
Lund, Roger D., ed. 1995. *The Margins of Orthodoxy: Heterodox Writing and Cultural Response, 1660–1750*. New York: Cambridge University Press.
MacIntosh, Terence. 2015. Pietists, Jurists, and the early enlightenment critique of private confession in Lutheran Germany. *Modern Intellectual History* 12 (3): 627–656.
Mack, Phyllis. 1993. *Visionary Women: Ecstatic Prophecy in Seventeenth-Century England*. Berkeley: University of California Press.
———. Die Prophetin als Mutter: Antoinette Bourignon. In: Hartmut Lehmann & A. C. Trepp, eds. *Im* Zeichen der Krise. Im Europa des *17. Jahrhunderts*. Göttingen, 1999.
Mali, Joseph & Robert Wokler, eds. *Isaiah Berlin's Counter-Enlightenment*. in *Transactions of the American Philosophical Society*, 93:5(2003). (Essays by Mali, Wokler, Mark Lilla, Roger Hausheer, Darrin McMahon, Frederick Beiser, Graeme Garrard, Lionel Gossman, John E. Toews and Michael Confino).
Mali, Joseph. "Berlin, Vico, and the Principles of Humanity," in Mali & Wokler, eds. *Isaiah Berlin's Counter-Enlightenment, Transactions of the American Philosophical Society*, 93:5(2003), 51-90.
Maloy, J.S. 2017. Bodin's readers and radical democracy in early New England. *Journal of the History of Ideas* 78 (1): 1–26.
Manji, Irshad. 2004. *The Trouble With Islam: A Muslim's Call for Reform in Her Faith*. New York: St. Martin's. (new edition retitled *The Trouble With Islam Today*).
Manuel, Frank E. 1959. *The Eighteenth Century Confronts the Gods*. Cambridge, MA: Harvard University Press. pb, Atheneum, 1967.
———. 1992. *The Broken Staff: Judaism Through Christian Eyes*. Cambridge, MA: Harvard University Press.
Mapp, Alf, Jr. 2003. *The Faiths of Our Fathers: What the Founders Really Believed*. Lanham, MD: Rowman & Littlefield.
Marso, L.J. 1998. The Stories of Citizens: Rousseau, Montesquieu, and de Staël Challenge Enlightenment Reason. *Polity* 30 (3): 435s.
Martin, Jean-Clément. 1998. *Contre-Révolution, Révolution et Nation en France 1789–1799*. Paris: Seuil.
Martus, Steffen. 2015. *Aufklärung: Das deutsche 18. Jahrhundert: Ein Epochenbild*. Berlin: Rowohlt.
Marty, Martin, and R. Scott Appleby, eds. 1995. *Fundamentalisms Comprehended. (Fundamentalism Project, v.5)*. Chicago: University of Chicago Press. pb, 2004.
———, eds. 1986. *Modern American Religion, v1, The Irony of It All*. Chicago: University of Chicago Press.
Marx, Leo. "American Studies—A Defense of an Unscientific Method" (1967) @ http://xroads.virginia.edu/~DRBR/marx2.html. ("romantic counter-Enlightenment").
Masseau, Didier. *Les Ennemis des philosophes. L'antiphilosophie au temps des Lumières*. Paris: Albin Michel, 2000; Paris: Honoré Champion, 2001. (incl. «Le théâtre antiphilosophique»).
———. «La marquise de La Ferté-Imbault, reine antiphilosophe des Lanturelus», dans Pierre Popovic et Érik Vigneault ed. les Dérèglements de l'art. Formes *et procédures de l'illégitimité culturelle en France (1715-1914)*. Montréal, Presses de l'Université de Montréal, 2000, p. 35–50.
———. 1994. *L'Invention de l'intellectuel dans l'Europe du XVIIIe siècle*. Paris: PUF.
Mathieson, W. L. *The Awakening of Scotland*. (1910) Chapter 5 "The Noontide of Moderatism" @ https://electricscotland.com/history/awakening/chapter05.htm.

Matthews, Bruce. F. W. J. Schelling's Berlin Lectures*: The Grounding of Positive Philosophy*, State University of New York Press, 2007.

———. 2011. *Schelling's Organic Form of Philosophy: Life as a Schema of Freedom*. State University of New York Press.

———. "The New Mythology: Romanticism between Religion and Humanism," pp. 202–220, in Nassar, ed. *The Relevance of Romanticism: Essays in German Romantic Philosophy*. Oxford University Press, 2014.

———. "Schelling: a brief biographical sketch of the Odysseus of German Idealism," in *The Palgrave Handbook to German Idealism*. Palgrave, 2014.

———. Existence as the inverted idea, or the transcendance of ecstatic immanence. lecture on Schelling @ Humboldt University, 2014.

Matthews, Michael R. "Mario Bunge and the Enlightenment Project in Science Education" in *Mario Bunge: A Centenary Festschrift*. Springer, 2019, pp. 645-682.

Matysin, Anton. 2016. Reason and utility in French religious apologetics. In *God in the Enlightenment*, ed. William J. Bulman and Robert Ingram, 63–82. Oxford: Oxford University Press.

———. 2016. *The Specter of Skepticism in the Age of Enlightenment*. Baltimore: Johns Hopkins University Press.

May, Henry F. 1991. *The Divided Heart: Essays on Protestantism and the Enlightenment in America*. Oxford: New York.

Matysin, Anton. 1976. *The Enlightenment in America*. New York: Oxford University Press.

McBeth, H. Leon, ed. 2004. *A Sourcebook for Baptist Heritage*. Nashville, TN: Broadman Press.

McCalman, Iain. 2003. *The Last Alchemist: Count Cagliostro, Master of Magic in the Age of Reason*. New York: HarperCollins.

———. 1988. *Radical Underworld: Prophets, Revolutionaries and Pornographers in London, 1795-1840*. Cambridge: Cambridge University Press.

McCardle, Arthur W. 1986. *Friedrich Schiller and Swabian Pietism*. New York: Peter Lang.

McDowell, Paula. 2002. Enlightenment enthusiasms and the spectacular failure of the Philadelphian Society. *Eighteenth-Century Studies* 35 (4): 515–533.

McGann, Jerome. 1983. *The Romantic Ideology: A Critical Investigation*. Chicago: University of Chicago Press. (critique of M. H. Abrams on Classic and Romantic).

McGinn, Bernard. *Presence of God: a History of Western Christian Mysticism*. v6, Part 1, *Mysticism in the Reformation (1500-1650)*. Herder & Herder, 2017, pb, 2017.

———. *Presence of God: a History of Western Christian Mysticism*. v6, Part 2, *Mysticism in the Golden Age of Spain (1500-1650)*. Herder & Herder, pb 2019.

———. *Presence of God: a History of Western Christian Mysticism*. v6 Part 3, *The Persistence of Mysticism in Catholic Europe: France, Italy, and Germany 1500-1675*. Herder & Herder, 2020.

McGinn, Bernard, and Moshe Idel, eds. 1996. *Mystical Union in Judaism, Christianity, and Islam: An Ecumenical Dialogue*. New York: Continuum.

McGuiness, P., A. Harrison, and R. Kearney, eds. 1997. *John Toland's Christianity Not Mysterious: Texts, Associated Works and Critical Essays*. Dublin: Lilliput Press.

McGuiness, P. 1997. *Christianity not mysterious* and the enlightenment. In *John Toland's Christianity not Mysterious: Texts, Associated Works and Critical Essays*, ed. P. McGuiness, A. Harrison, and R. Kearney. Dublin: Lilliput Press.

McIntosh, Christopher. "The Rosicrucian Revival and the German Counter-Enlightenment" diss't, Oxford, 1989.

———. *The Rose Cross and the Age of Reason*. Leiden: Brill, 1992; 2nd ed. Albany, New York: State University of New York Press, 2011.

McKenna, Anthony. 1990. Sur l'hérésie dans la littérature clandestine. *Dix-huitième siècle* 22: 301–313.

———. 2006. La préparation de l'*Anti-Pascal*: le rôle de Fontenelle. *SVEC* 10: 327–337.

McLemee, Scott. 1998. Under the influence: the long shadow of Emanuel Swedenborg. *Lingua Franca*: 59–61.

McMahon, Darrin M. Enemies of the Enlightenment: Anti-Philosophes and the Birth of the French Far Right, 1778-1830," New Haven, Yale University diss't, 1997.
———. The counter-enlightenment and the low life of literature in pre-revolutionary France. *Past & Present*, 159(1998), 77-112.
———. "The Counter-Enlightenment and the Origins of French Conservatism," Columbia University 18thC Studies Group, Faculty House, 21 Jan 1999.
———. 2001. *Enemies of the Enlightenment: The French Counter-Enlightenment and the Making of Modernity*. New York: Oxford University Press.
———. "Seeing the Century of Lights as a Time of Darkness: The Catholic Counter-Enlightenment in Europe and the Americas," in Lotterie & McMahon, eds. *Les lumières européennes dans leur relation avec les autres grandes cultures et religions du XVIIIe siècle*. Paris: 2001.
———. "Narratives of Dystopia in the French Revolution: Enlightenment and Counter-Enlightenment, the *Isle des philosophes* of the Abbé Balthazard," in Weber and Lay, eds. *Fragments of Revolution* YPS 101(2002).
———. "The Real Counter-Enlightenment: The Case of France," in Joseph Mali & Robert Wokler, eds. *Isaiah Berlin's Counter-Enlightenment, Transactions of the American Philosophical Society*, 93:5(2003), pp91-104.
McManners, John. 1985. *Death and the Enlightenment: Changing Attitudes to Death among Christians and Unbelievers in Eighteenth-Century France*. New York: Oxford University Press.
———. *Church and Society in Eighteenth-Century France*. v1, *The Clerical Establishment and its Social Ramifications*. New York: Oxford University Press (Oxford History of the Christian Church), 1998, 1999.
———. *Church and Society in Eighteenth-Century France*. v2, *The Religion of the People and the Politics of Religion*. New York: Oxford University Press (Oxford History of the Christian Church), 1998.
———. 1977. The Church and the Revolution. In *Lectures on European History, 1789-1914: Men, Machines and Freedom (1966)*. Oxford: Basil Blackwell.
Mee, Jon J. 1993. *Dangerous Enthusiasm: William Blake and the Culture of Radicalism in the 1790s*. New York: Oxford University Press.
———. 1996. Apocalypse and ambivalence: The politics of millenarianism in the 1790s. *South Atlantic Quarterly* 95 (3): 671–698.
———. "Anxieties of Enthusiasm: Coleridge, Prophecy, and Popular Politics in the 1790s," in Klein, Lawrence E. & Anthony J. La Vopa. *Enthusiasm and Enlightenment in Europe, 1650-1850*. 1998 (also published in *Huntington Library Quarterly*, vol. 60(1997): 1-2, pp. 179-203).
———. 2011. *Conversable Worlds: Literature, Contention, and Community 1762 to 1830*. Oxford: Oxford University Press.
———. *Print, Publicity, and Popular Radicalism in the 1790s: The Laurel of Liberty*. (Cambridge Studies in Romanticism) Cambridge: Cambridge University Press, 2018.
Méheust, Bertrand. 1999. *Somnambulisme et médiumité: v1, Le Défi du magnétisme; v2, Le Choc des sciences psychiques*. Le Plessis-Robinson: Institut Synthélabo.
Mell, Don, Theodore E. Braun, and Lucia Palmer, eds. 1988. *Man, God and Nature in the Enlightenment*. East Lansing, MI: Colleagues Press.
Melton, J. Van Horn. 2001. *The Rise of the Public Sphere in Enlightenment Europe*. Cambridge, Cambridge University Press.
Melzer, Arthur M. 1996. The origin of the counter-enlightenment: Rousseau and the New Religion of Sincerity. *American Political Science Review* 90 (2): 344–360.
Meslier, Jean. *Œuvres complètes*. ed. J. Deprun & R. Desné, 3 vols. Paris: Anthropos, 1970–1972.
Meyer, Michael A. & Michael Brenner, eds. *German-Jewish History in Modern Times*. v1, *Tradition and Enlightenment 1600-1780*. by Mordechai Breuer and Michael Graetz. Translated by William Templer, Study of the Leo Baeck Institute. New York: Columbia University Press, 1996.

Michalson, Gordon E. 1999. *Kant and the Problem of God.* Blackwell.
Michon, Hélène. 2006. Voltaire, lecteur de Pascal ou la question du langage équivoque. *SVEC* 10: 349–359.
Midelfort, H., and C. Erik. 2005. *Exorcism and Enlightenment: Johann Joseph Gassner and the Demons of Eighteenth-Century Germany*. New Haven, CT: Yale University Press.
Mills, Frederick V., Sr. 1978. *Bishops by Ballot: An Eighteenth-Century Ecclesiastical Revolution*. New York: Oxford University Press.
Miltchyna, Vera. "Joseph de Maistre's Works in Russia: A Look at their Reception," dans Richard A. Lebrun ed. *Joseph de Maistre's Life, Thought and Influence. Selected Studies*, Montréal & Kingston, London, Ithaca, NY, NY, McGill-Queen's University Press, 2001, 241–270.
———. 2001. Oeuvres de Joseph de Maistre en Russie: aperçu de la réception. *Revue des études maistriennes* 13: 63–89.
Minois, Georges. 1998. *Histoire de l'athéisme: les incroyants dans le monde occidental des origines à nos jours*. Paris: Fayard.
———. 2003. *History of Suicide: Voluntary Death in Western Culture*. Baltimore, MD: Johns Hopkins University Press.
Monglond, André. *le Préromantisme français*. (Grenoble, 1930) Reprint: Genève: Slatkine Reprints, 2000.
Monod, Albert. *De Pascal à Chateaubriand: Les défenseurs français du christianisme de 1670 à 1802*. (Paris: Alcan, 1915); reprint Wentworth Press, 2019.
Montmasson, J.M. 1928. *L'Idée de Providence d'après Joseph de Maistre*. Lyon: Vitte. (the central idea of Maistre's *Les Soirées de Saint-Pétersbourg*).
Mori, Gianluca. 2000. Jean Meslier, stratonicien *redivivus*. In *Materia actuosa... Mélanges en l'honneur d'Olivier Bloch. Paris*, ed. M. Benitez, A. McKenna, G. Paganini, and J. Salem. Slatkine: Champion/ Genève.
———. Bayle, Saint-Evremond, and Fideism: A Reply to Thomas M. Lennon. *Journal of the History of Ideas* 65:2(2004) 323–334.
Mornet, Daniel. *le Romantisme en France au XVIIIe siècle*. (Paris, 1912) Reprint: Genève: Slatkine Reprints, 2000.
———. *le Sentiment de la nature en France, de J.-J. Rousseau à Bernardin de Saint-Pierre. Essai sur les rapports de la littérature et des moeurs*. (Paris, 1907) Reprint: Genève: Slatkine Reprints, 2000.
———. *Les Origines intellectuelles de la Révolution Française, 1715-1787*. (1933) 6th ed. Paris: Armand Colin, 1967.
Mounsey, Chris. *Christopher Smart: Clown of God*. Bucknell University Press (Bucknell Studies in Eighteenth-Century Literature and Culture), 2001.
Moureau, François. "L'esprit et la lettre de la censure chez Malesherbes: l'abbé Foucher, Estève et la chasse aux athées," dans Roger Durand ed. *C'est la faute à Voltaire, c'est la faute à Rousseau. Recueil anniversaire pour Jean-Daniel Candaux*. Geneva: Droz, 1997, p. 101s.
Mornet, Daniel. "À l'origine du texte: le manuscrit inconnu des *Difficultés sur la religion*," *Revue d'histoire littéraire de la France*, 92, 1, janvier-février 1992, pp. 92-104.
Müller, Adam (1779–1829). *Adam von Müller's gesammelte schriften*. Munich: Georg Franz, 1839.
Nadon, Christopher, ed. 2013. *Enlightenment and Secularism: Essays on the Mobilization of Reason*. Lanham, MD: Lexington Books (Rowman & Littlefield).
Nahon, Michelle. 2017. *Martinès de Pasqually. Un énigmatique franc-maçon théurge du XVIIIe siècle, fondateur de l'ordre des Élus Coëns. Édition revue et complétée. Préface de Jean-Claude Drouin*. Postface de Roger Dachez, Paris: Dervy.
Nakhimovsky, Isaac. 2003. The Enlightened Epicureanism of Jacques Abbadie: *L'Art de se connoître soi-même* and the morality of self interest. *History of European Ideas* 29: 1–14.
Nassar, Dalia, ed. 2014. *The Relevance of Romanticism: Essays in German Romantic Philosophy*. Oxford University Press.
Neaimi, Sadek, ed. 2003. *L'Islam au siècle des Lumières: Image de la civilisation islamique chez les philosophes français du XVIIIe siècle*. Paris: L'Harmattan.

Newport, Kenneth G. C. & Crawford Gribben. eds. *Expecting the End: Millennialism in Social and Historical Context.* Baylor University Press, November 2006.
Nicholls, Angus. "Goethe, Romanticism and the Anglo-American Critical Tradition," *Romanticism on the Net* 28(November, 2002).
Nicholls, D. 1995. *God and Government in an "Age of Reason"*. London: Routledge.
Nicholson, R. A. *The Mystics of Islam.* (1914) reprint, Arkana Books, 1989; World Wisdom, 2002.
Nicolson, Marjorie H. 1959. *Mountain Gloom and Mountain Glory: The Development of the Aesthetic of the Infinite.* Ithaca, NY: Cornell University Press.
Niebuhr, Reinhold. *The Irony of American History.* (1952) in *Reinhold Niebuhr's Major Works on Religion and Politics.* Ed. Elisabeth Sifton, Library of America, 2015, pp. 459–589
Noggle, James. "Literary Taste as Counter-Enlightenment in Hume's *History of England*" *SEL Studies in English Literature 1500–1900* 44:3(Summer 2004), 617–638.
Noll, Mark. 1989. *A[llan]. Princeton and the Republic, 1768-1822: The Search for a Christian Enlightenment in the Era of Samuel Stanhope Smith.* Princeton, NJ: Princeton University Press.
———. 2003. *A[llan]. The Rise of Evangelicalism: The Age of Edwards, Whitefield and the Wesleys.* Downers Grove, IL: InterVarsity Press/IVP Academic.
Norton, David. 1993. *A History of the Bible as Literature. v2, From 1700 to the Present Day.* New York: Cambridge University Press.
Norton, Robert E. The Myth of the counter-enlightenment. *J Hist Ideas*, 68:4(2007), 635-658.
———. "Johann Gottfried Herder: Selected Early Works, 1764-1767, Addresses, Essays, and Drafts, Fragments on Recent German Literature," Book review, *The Review of Metaphysics* 48:4(June 1, 1995), 895-898.
———. 1995. *The Beautiful Soul: Aesthetic Morality in the Eighteenth Century.* Ithaca, NY: Cornell University Press.
"Novalis" (Georg Philipp Friedrich Freiherr von Hardenberg). *Historische-Kritische Ausgabe - Novalis Schriften.* eds. Richard Samuel, Hans-Joachim Mähl & Gerhard Schulz, 6v, Stuttgart: Verlag W. Kohlhammer, 1960–2006.
———. *Philosophical Writings.* Translated and Edited by Margaret Mahony Stoljar. Albany: State University of New York Press, 1997.
———. *Fragmente und Studien; Die Christenheit oder Europa.* ed. Carl Paschek, Stuttgart: Reclam, 1984, 1996.
———. *Fichte Studies.* ed. Jane Kneller. Cambridge: Cambridge University Press Texts in the History of Philosophy, 2000.
Nusseibeh, Sari. 2017. *The Story of Reason in Islam.* Stanford, CA: Stanford University Press.
Oberg, Barbara B., and Harry S. Stout, eds. 1993. *Benjamin Franklin, Jonathan Edwards, and the Representation of American Culture.* Oxford: Oxford University Press.
O'Cathesaigh, Sean. "Enlightenment and the Inner Light," dans Jens Häseler & Antony McKenna ed. *la Vie intellectuelle aux Refuges protestants.* Actes de la Table ronde de Münster du 25 juillet 1995. Paris: Honoré Champion éditeur, coll. "Vie des Huguenots," 5, 1999, p. 173–184.
O'Keefe, Cyril B. "Contemporary Reactions to the Enlightenment (1728-1762): A Study of Three Critical Journals, the Jesuit *Journal de Trévoux*, the Jansenist *Nouvelles Ecclésiastiques*, and the Secular *Journal Des Savants*" Thesis University of Toronto, 1974.
O'Meara, Thomas, *Romantic Idealism and Roman Catholicism.* (Schleiermacher) —Elias Bongmba, H-AMREL, 14 Jan 2002.
Ortiz-Oses, A. Religion between Enlightenment and romanticism. [in Spanish]. *Pensiamento,* 53:205 (January-April 1997), 127-234.
Osler, M. J. "Mixing Metaphors: Science and Religion or Natural Philosophy and Theology in Early Modern Europe," *History of Science*, 36:1:111(mars 1998), p. 91-113.
Outler, Albert C. "Pietism and Enlightenment: Alternatives to Tradition." In *Christian Spirituality III.* edited by Louis Dupre and Don Saliers, 240–56. New York: Crossroad, 1989.
Outram, Dorinda. 1995. *The Enlightenment.* Cambridge: Cambridge University Press.
IV Owen, John M., and J. Judd Owen. 2010. *Religion, the Enlightenment, and the New Global Order.* New York: Columbia University Press (Columbia Series on Religion and Politics). 2011.

Packham, Catherine. "Animal economy and political economy, Hume and Adam Smith" Conference run under the British Society for the History of Philosophy in collaboration with The Department of Philosophy, University of Edinburgh, The Mind Association, and The Foundation for Intellectual History, University of Edinburgh, 18-19th September 2002.

———. "Cicero's Ears, or Eloquence in the Age of Politeness, Oratory, Moderation, and the Sublime in Enlightenment Scotland," *Eighteenth-Century Studies* 46:4(Summer, 2013), pp. 499-512.

Paine, Thomas. "Origin of Freemasonry," *The Complete Writings of Thomas Paine*. ed. Philip Foner. New York: The Citadel Press, 1969, II: 830–841.

———. *Collected Writings: Common Sense / The Crisis / Rights of Man/The Age of Reason / Pamphlets, Articles, and Letters*. ed. Eric Foner, Library of America, 1995.

Palissot de Montenoy, Charles. 1975. (1730–1814). *Les Philosophes*. (1778). In *Exeter*, ed. Thomas J. Barling. University Press.

——— *Mémoires pour servir à l'histoire de notre littérature, depuis François premier jusqu'à nos jours*, 2v, 1771; Genève: Moutard, 1779.

Palissot de Montenoy, *Questions importantes sur quelques opinions religieuses*. Paris: Hautbout l'Ainé, L'An VI (1797/1798).

Palmer, Robert R. 1939. *Catholics and Unbelievers in Eighteenth-Century France*. Princeton, NJ: Princeton University Press.

Pappas, John Nicholas. *Berthier's Journal de Trévoux and the Philosophes*. v3-4, Geneva, 1957.

Patouillet, Louis. *Dictionnaire des livres Jansénistes ou qui favorisent le Jansénisme*. 4v, Anvers, 1752.

Pečar, Andreas, and Damien Tricorne. 2015. *Falsche Freunde: War die Aufklärung wirklich die Geburtsstunde der Moderne?* Campus: Frankfurt-am-Main.

Phillips, D.Z., and Timothy Tessin, eds. 1999. *Religion and Hume's Legacy*. New York: Palgrave.

Picard, Bernard & Jean Frederic Bernard. *Cérémonies et coutumes religieuses de tous les peuples du monde representées par des figures dessinées de la main de Bernard Picard: avec une explication historique, & quelques dissertations curieuses*. 7 vols. (folio), Amsterdam: J.F. Bernard, 1723-1737; 9 vols. (folio), Amsterdam: J. F. Bernard, 1723-1743.

———. *Religious Ceremonies and Customs of All the Peoples of the World*. 7v, London, 1733-1739 (Dutch, 1726-1738; German, 1746).

Terry, Pinkard. 2001. *Hegel: A Biography*. New York: Cambridge University Press.

Pinker, Steven, *Enlightenment Now: The Case for Reason, Science, Humanism, and Progress*, 2018.

Pinson, Koppel S. 1934. *Pietism as a Factor in the Rise of German Nationalism*. New York: Columbia University Press.

Pintard, René, *Le Libertinage érudit dans la première moitié du XVIIe siècle*. (Paris 1943) Geneva: Slatkine, 1983. (La Mothe Le Vayer, Gassendi, Guy Patin).

Pitts, Walter F., and Vincent L. Wimbush. 1996. *Old Ship of Zion: The Afro-Baptist Ritual in the African Diaspora*. NY: Oxford University Press.

Plantinga, Alvin, and Nicholas Wolterstorff, eds. 1984. *Faith and Rationality*. South Bend, IN: University of Notre Dame Press.

Platon, Mircea. 2017. *Touchstones of Truth: The Antiphilosophes Enlightenment of J.-B.-L. Gresset, L.-M. Deschamps, and S.-N.-H. Linguet (1735-1794)*. Iaşi: Timpul.

———. 2011. Newtonian Science, Commercial Republicanism, and the Cult of Great Men in La Beaumelle's *Pensées* (1752). *History of Political Economy* 43 (3).

Plongeron, Bernard. 1973. *Théologie et politique au siècle des Lumières (1770-1820)*. Geneva: Droz.

Pocock, J. G. A. "Superstition and Enthusiasm in Gibbon's History of Religion" in E-CL, n.s. 8(1982), 83–94.

———. "Enthusiasm, the Antiself of Enlightenment," in Klein & La Vopa, eds. *Enthusiasm and Enlightenment in Europe, 1650-1850*. Henry E. Huntington Library and Art Gallery, 1998, p7-28; and in *Huntington Library Quarterly*, 60(1998).

Pocock, J.G., and A. Virtue. 1989. *Commerce, and History: Essays on Political Thought and History, Chiefly in the Eighteenth-Century England*. Berkeley, CA: University of California Press.

Pocock, J.G.A. 1999. *Barbarism and Religion. v1, The Enlightenments of Edward Gibbon.* New York: Cambridge University Press.

———. 1999. *Barbarism and Religion. v2, Narratives of Civil Government.* New York: Cambridge University Press.

Pocock, J. G. A. “Enlightenment and counter-enlightenment, revolution and counter-revolution; a eurosceptical enquiry,” *History of Political Thought*, 20:1(1999), pp. 125-139(15).

Pollock, Benjamin. "Franz Rosenzweig", *The Stanford Encyclopedia of Philosophy* (Spring 2019 Edition), Edward N. Zalta (ed.), https://plato.stanford.edu/archives/spr2019/entries/rosenzweig/.

Pomeau, René. 1956. *La religion de Voltaire*. Paris: Nizet.

Popkin, Jeremy D. 2005. Back From the Grave: Marc Fumaroli’s Chateaubriand. *Modern Intellectual History* 2 (3): 419–431.

Popkin, Richard H. 1988. *Millenarianism and Messianism in English Literature and Thought, 1650-1800.* New York & Leiden: E.J. Brill.

———. 1993. Sources of knowledge of sextus Empiricus in Hume’s time. *Journal of the History of Ideas* 54 (1): 137–141.

———. ed. *Millenarianism and Messianism in Early Modern Europe and America.* 4v, Dordrecht: Kluwer Academic Publishers, 2001. Vol. 1: *Jewish Messianism in the Early Modern World.* ed. Matt Goldish & Richard H. Popkin. Vol. 2: *Catholic Millenarianism: From Savonarola to the Abbé Grégoire*. ed. Karl A. Kottman. Vol. 3: *The Millenarian Turn: Millenarian Contexts of Science, Politics, and Everyday Anglo-American Life in the Seventeenth and Eighteenth Century.* ed. James E. Force & Richard H. Popkin. Vol. 4: *Continental Millenarians: Protestants, Catholics, Heretics*, ed. John Christian Laursen & Richard H. Popkin.

Porret, Michel. “Magiciens, ‘devineresses’ ou imposteurs? La répression des ‘superstitions’ au XVIIIe siècle: l’exemple genevois,” dans Benoît Garnot ed. *la Petite Délinquance du Moyen Âge à l’époque contemporaine*. Dijon: Éditions universitaire de Dijon, coll. “Publicationss de l’Université de Bourgogne,” XC. “Série du Centre d’études historiques,” 8, (n.d.) p. 455-464.

Porset, Charles. 1998. *Hiram Sans-Culotte? Franc-maçonnerie, Lumières et Révolution. Trente ans d’études et de recherches*. Paris: Éditions Honoré Champion.

Porset, Charles, and Cécile Revauger. 1998. *Franc-maçonnerie et religion dans l’Europe des Lumières*. Paris: Éditions Honoré Champion.

Porter, David. “China and the Critique of Religious Intolerance in Eighteenth-Century France,” version électronique d’une communication destinée au congrès de l’American Society for Eighteenth-Century Studies de 1999. http://www.richmond.edu/~jhayes/conference/porter.html.

Porter, Roy. *Enlightenment Britain and the Creation of the Modern World.* London: Penguin, 2000; 2nd ed. London, 2001.

———. 2001. *The Creation of the Modern World: The Untold Story of the British Enlightenment.* New York: Penguin.

———. 2005. *Flesh in the Age of Reason: How the Enlightenment Transformed the Way We See our Bodies and Souls*. London.

———, ed. 2003. *Cambridge History of Science. v4, Eighteenth Century*. New York: Cambridge University Press.

Porter, Roy, and Mikulis Teich, eds. 1981. *Enlightenment in National Context.* Cambridge: Cambridge University Press.

Posnett, H. M. Comparative Literature. London: Kegan Paul, Trench/NY: D. Appleton (International Scientific Series v50), 1886.

Pranchère, Jean-Yves. 1992. L’Autorité contre les Lumières: la philosophie de Joseph de Maistre. In *Université de Rouen doctoral thesis*.

———. 1992. *Qu’est-ce que la royauté? Joseph de Maistre*. Paris: Vrin.

———. “Joseph de Maistre's Catholic Philosophy of Authority,” dans Richard A. Lebrun ed. *Joseph de Maistre's Life, Thought and Influence. Selected Studies*. Montréal & Kingston, London, Ithaca, NY, McGill-Queen's University Press, 2001, p. 131-150.

———. 1996. La persistance de la pensée maistrienne. *Revue des études maistriennes* 12: 205–239.

———. "The Persistence of Maistrian Thought," dans Richard A. Lebrun ed. *Joseph de Maistre's Life, Thought and Influence. Selected Studies*. Montréal & Kingston, London, Ithaca, NY, McGill-Queen's University Press, 2001, p. 290-325.

———. "The Social Bond according to the Catholic Counter-Revolution: Maistre and Bonald," dans Richard A. Lebrun ed. *Joseph de Maistre's Life, Thought and Influence. Selected Studies*. Montréal & Kingston, London, Ithaca, NY, McGill-Queen's University Press, 2001, p. 190-219.

———. "Une philosophie de l'autorité: Joseph de Maistre," *Transversalités: revue de l'Institut catholique de Paris*, 70, avril-juin 1999, p. 71-92.

Preus, J. Samuel, ed. 1987. *Explaining Religion: Criticism and Theory from Bodin to Freud*. New Haven: Yale University Press.

Price, J.V. 1995. *ed. The History of British Deism. 8v*. London: Routledge.

Prickett, Stephen. 2008. *Romanticism and Religion: The Tradition of Coleridge and Wordsworth in the Victorian Church*. Cambridge: Cambridge University Press.

———. 1996. *Origins of Narrative: The Romantic Appropriation of the Bible*. New York: Cambridge University Press.

Prince, Michael. 1996. *Philosophical Dialogue in the British Enlightenment: Theology, Aesthetics and the Novel*. Cambridge: Cambridge University Press.

Printy, Michael. 2013. The determination of man: Johann Joachim spalding and the protestant enlightenment. *Journal of the History of Ideas* 74 (2): 189–212.

Prunier, Clotilde. 1996. *Catholiques, presbytériens et enjeux de l'instruction dans les Highlands d'Écosse au dix-huitième siècle*. Grenoble: Université Stendhal, thèse de doctorat.

———. "Les catholiques en Écosse au XVIIIe siècle," dans Pierre Morére ed. *Écosse des Lumières: le XVIIIe siècle autrement*. Grenoble, 1997, p. 105-149.

Raboteau, Albert. *Slave Religion: The "Invisible Institution" in the American South* (1978), rev. ed., NY: Oxford University Press, 2004.

Rack, Henry D. 1993. *Reasonable Enthusiast: John Wesley and the Rise of British Methodism*. Nashville: Abingdon Press.

Radest, Howard B. 1990. *The Devil and Secular Humanism; the Children of the Enlightenment*. New York: Praeger.

Ramsay, Chevalier Andrew Michael. *les Principes philosophiques de la religion naturelle et révélée dévoilés selon le mode géométrique*. (1748-49) Traduction, introduction, notes et index par Georges Lamoine. Geneva: Slatkine, coll. "L'âge des lumières" #18, 2002.

———. *Discours prononcé à la réception des francs-maçons par le chevalier André-Michael de Ramsay*. (1737) Édition de Georges Lamoine. Toulouse: Éditions SNES, 1999.

———. *les Voyages de Cyrus. Avec un discours sur la mythologie*. (1727) Édition critique établie par Georges Lamoine. Geneva: Slatkine, coll. "L'âge des lumières," #17, 2002.

Randall, John Herman, Jr. *The Role of Knowledge in Western Religion*. (1955-56). Boston: Starr King Press, 1958.

Reardon, Bernard M.G. 1985. *Religion in the Age of Romanticism: Studies in Early Nineteenth-Century Thought*. Cambridge, MA: Cambridge University Press.

Rebotton, Jean. 1978. Lamartine et la famille Maistre. *Revue des études maistriennes* 4: 91–139.

———. 1977. Nouveau aperçus sur l'éducation et l'attitude religieuse du jeune Maistre. *Revue des études maistriennes* 3: 5–23.

Redwood, John. 1996. *Reason, Ridicule and Religion: The Age of Enlightenment in England 1660-1750. Cambridge, MA: Harvard University Press, 1976; 2nd ed*. London: Thames & Hudson.

Reed, T.J. 2015. *Light in Germany: Scenes from an Unknown Enlightenment*. Chicago: University of Chicago Press.

Reedy, W. Jay. "The Traditionalist Critique of Individualism in Post-Revolutionary France: The Case of Louis de Bonald" *History of Political Thought* 16:1(Spring, 1995) p49-75.

———. "Maistre's Twin? Louis de Bonald and the Counter-Enlightenment," dans Richard A. Lebrun ed. *Joseph de Maistre's Life, Thought and Influence. Selected Studies*. Montréal & Kingston, London, Ithaca, NY, McGill-Queen's University Press, 2001, p. 173-189.

Reid-Maroney, Nina. 2001. *Philadelphia's Enightenment, 1740-1800: Kingdom of Christ, Empire of Reason*. Westport, CT: Greenwood Press.

Reinitz, Richard. 1980. *Irony and Consciousness: American Historiography and Reinhold Niebuhr's Vision*. Lewisburg, PA: Bucknell University Press.

Rescher, Nicholas. 1999. *Kant and the Reach of Reason: Studies in Kant's Theory of Rational Systematization*. Cambridge: Cambridge University Press.

Rétat, Pierre. 1971. *Le* ***Dictionnaire*** *de Bayle et la lutte philosophique au XVIIIe siècle*. Paris: Société d'Edition 'les Belles Lettres'.

Rex, W. 1985. *Essays on Pierre Bayle and Religious Controversy*. The Hague: M. Nijhoff.

Richardot, Anne. 1998. *Point de lendemain*: le crépuscule du libertinage. *Studies on Voltaire and the Eighteenth Century* 358: 247–256.

———. «Un philosophe au purgatoire des Lumières: Démocrite», *XVIIIe Siècle*, 2000, p. 197-212.

Richardson, Samuel. *Pamela, ou La vertu récompensée*. [1747-48], traduit de l'Anglois (translation traditionally attributed to Prévost) à Amsterdam, et se trouve à Paris, Rue et Hôtel Serpente, 1784.

Richardson. *Lettres Angloises, Ou* Histoire *de Miss Clarisse Harlove*. Tome Second, A Dresde: Walther, 1751. Traduction de Prévost (Cf. 1777 and 1784).

Ridley, Jasper. *The Freemasons: A History of the World's Most Powerful Secret Society*. Arcade, 2002.

Riquet, Michel. "Joseph de Maistre et le Père Barruel," *Revue des études maistriennes*, No. 5-6 (1980): 283-95.

Rivers, Isabel. "Religion and Literature" in Richetti, ed. *Cambridge History of Eighteenth Century Literature*. p. 467.

———. 1991. *Reason, Grace, and Sentiment: A Study of the Language of Religion and Ethics in England, 1660-1780. vol I, Whichcote to Wesley*. Cambridge: Cambridge University Press.

———. *Reason, Grace and Sentiment: A Study of the Language of Religion and Ethics in England, 1660-1780*. vol V, *Shaftesbury to Hume*. Cambridge: Cambridge University Press, 2000.

———. *Vanity Fair and the Celestial City: Dissenting, Methodist, and Evangelical Literary Culture in England 1720-1800*. Abridged - Annotated Edition, Oxford: Oxford University Press, 2018.

———. 2009. Review essay: writing the history of early evangelicalism. *History of European Ideas* 35 (1): 105–111.

Rix, Robert. (n.d.) "William Blake and the Radical Swedenborgians," (@ http://esoteric.msu.edu/VolumeV/Blake.htm).

Roe, Nicholas. *Wordsworth and Coleridge: The Radical Years*. (1988) Oxford University Press; 2nd ed., 2019.

Robertson, J. "The Case for the Enlightenment", in: J. Robertson, *The Case for the Enlightenment: Scotland and Naples 1680-1760*. Cambridge 2007, pp. 1-52.

Robertson, Ritchie. "The Enlightenment in New Focus," *Modern Intellectual History* 15:3 (2018), pp849-863 (Rvws of Steffen Martus, *Aufklärung: Das deutsche 18. Jahrhundert: Ein Epochenbild* (Berlin: Rowohlt, 2015), T. J. Reed, *Light in Germany: Scenes from an Unknown Enlightenment* (Chicago: University of Chicago Press, 2015, and Andreas Pečar & Damien Tricorne, *Falsche Freunde: War die Aufklärung wirklich die Geburtsstunde der Moderne?* Frankfurt-am-Main: Campus, 2015.

Roche, D. 1998. *France in the Enlightenment (1993)*. Cambridge, MA: Harvard University Press.

Rodinson, Maxime. *La fascination de l'Islam*. (Poches Sciences, 1980) Paris: La Découverte Kindle ed. 2013.

Rosa, Susan. "Seventeenth-Century Catholic Polemic and the Rise of Cultural Rationalism: An Example from the Empire" *Journal of the History of Ideas* 57:1(1996) 87.

Rosa, Susan & Dale Van Kley. "Religion and the Historical Discipline: A Reply to Mack Holt and Henry Heller," *French Historical Studies* 21:4(Fall, 1998), 611-629

Rosenberg, Jordana. *Critical Enthusiasm: Capital Accumulation and the Transformation of Religious Passion*. Oxford: Oxford University Press, 2011. Rvw by Lionel Laborie in *Eighteenth-Century Studies* 46:2(2013), 311–312.

Rosenblatt, Helena. "Re-evaluating Benjamin Constant's liberalism: industrialism, Saint-Simonianism and the Restoration Years," *History of European Ideas* 30:1(2004), 23-37.

———. "The Language of Genevan Calvinism in the Eighteenth Century," dans *Reconceptualizing Nature, Science, and Aesthetics: Contribution à une nouvelle approche des Lumières helvétiques*. Geneva: Éditions Slatkine, coll. "Travaux sur la Suisse des Lumières," 1, 1998.

———. "Why Constant? A Critical Overview of the Constant Revival," *Modern Intellectual History* I:3(November, 2004), pp. 359-385.

———. "Rousseau, the 'Traditionalist', *Journal of the History of Ideas* 77:4(2016), 627–635.

Roussin, Philippe, ed. 1998. *Critique et affaires de blasphème à l'époque des Lumières*. Paris: Honoré Champion.

Rubiés, Joan-Pau. 2019. *"The Jesuits and the Enlightenment," Oxford Handbook of the Jesuits*. Oxford: Oxford University Press.

Ruderman, David B. 2000. *Jewish Enlightenment in an English Key: Anglo-Jewry's Construction of Modern Jewish Thought*. Princeton, NJ: Princeton University Press.

Ruffin, J. Rixey. *A Paradise of Reason: William Bentley and Enlightenment Christianity in the Early Republic*. New York: Oxford University Press, 2008. Rvw by Jonathan M. Yeager in *Eighteenth-Century Studies* 44:4(Summer, 2011), pp. 547-548.

Russo, Elena. 2006. *Styles of Enlightenment: Taste, Politics, and Authorship in Eighteenth-Century France*. Baltimore: Johns Hopkins University Press.

Ryan, Robert M. *The Romantic Reformation: Religious Politics in English Literature, 1789–1824*. New York: Cambridge University Press, 1997, 2000, 2004.

Saisselin, Rémy G. 1970. *The Rules of Reason and the Ruses of the Heart: A philosophical dictionary of classical French criticism, critics, and aesthetic issues*. Cleveland, OH: The Press of Case Western Reserve University.

Salaün, Franck. 1996. *l'Ordre des moeurs. Essai sur la place du matérialisme dans la société française du XVIIIe siècle*. Paris: Kimé. Avec une retranscription de la "Lettre au R.P. Berthier sur le matérialisme" (1759).

Salem, Jean. 2006. Thèmes épicuriens dans *les Égarements du coeur et de l'esprit* de Crébillon. *SVEC* 12: 141–153.

Sanford, Charles B. 1987. *The Religious Life of Thomas Jefferson. (American Sceptics -- The Enlightenment Generation) pb*. Charlottesville: University of Virginia Press.

Saul, John Ralston. 1985. *Voltaire's Bastards: The Dictatorship of Reason in the West*. New York, Free Press: (pb Vintage, 1992).

Scarberry, Mark S., John Leland, and James Madison. Religious influence on the ratification of the constitution and on the proposal of the bill of rights. *Penn State Law Review* 113, 3: 738–740.

Schama, Simon. 2017. *The Story of the Jews: Volume 2, Belonging: 1492-1900*. New York: Ecco.

Schelling, Friedrich (1775–1854). *The Schelling Reader*. Edited by Benjamin Berger & Daniel Whistler. New York: Bloomsbury Academic, 2020.

Schering, Ernst. "Pietismus und die Renaissance der Mystik. Pierre Poiret als Interpret und Wegbereiter der romanischen Mystik in Deutschland," in Dietrich Meter, ed. *Pietismus-Herrentum-Erweckungs-bewegung*. Cologne, 1982.

Schiller, Friedrich (1759–1805). *On the Aesthetic Education of Man* [*Über die ästhetische Erziehung des Menschen in einer Reihe von Briefen*, 1795] Translated by Reginald Snell. Mineola, NY: Dover, 2004.

Schlegel, August Wilhelm (1767–1845). *Sämmtliche Werke*. Leipzig: Weidmann'sche Buchhandlung, 1847, Kindle ed.

Schlegel, Friedrich (1772–1829) & Dorothea. *Ästhetische & Politische Werke* (*Versuch über den Begriff des Republikanismus*, *Über das Studium der Griechischen Poesie*, *Georg Forster*, *Über*

Lessing, Über Goethes Meister, Gespräch über die Poesie, Über die Unverständlichkeit). E-artnow, Kindle ed. 2017.

Schleiermacher, Friedrich. *On Religion: Speeches to Its Cultured Despisers* [*Über die Religion.* 1799]. Translated by John Oman. New York: Harper Torchbook, 1958; ed. Richard Crouter. Cambridge: Cambridge University Press (Texts in the History of Philosophy), 1991.

———. *Der christliche Glaube nach den Grundsätzen der evangelischen Kirche in Zusammenhange dargestellt* [*The Christian Faith*]. (1821, 2nd ed. greatly altered, 1830–1831) Gotha: Friedrich Andreas Perthes, 1889 (A.k.a. *Glaubenslehre*).

———. *Theology of Schleiermacher: A Condensed Presentation of His Chief Work. "The Christian Faith"* Translated and abridged by George Cross. (University of Chicago Press, 1911) Grand Rapids, MI: Christian Classics Ethereal Library (CCEL) @ https://www.ccel.org/ccel/c/cross_g/theology/cache/theology.pdf).

———. *Hermeneutics and Criticism And Other Writings.* ed. Andrew Bowie. Cambridge: Cambridge University P. Texts in the History of Philosophy, 1999.

———. *Lectures on Philosophical Ethics.* Translated by Louise Adey Huish. Edited by Robert B. Louden. Cambridge: Cambridge University Press (Texts in the History of Philosophy), 2002.

Schluter, G. 1994. L'orthodoxie, la hétérodoxie, et les origines de la tolérance: Voltaire et l'émancipation politique des Huguenots. *Neohelicon* 21 (1): 341–358.

Schmidt, Alexander. "Scholarship, Morals and Government: Jean-Henri-Samuel Formey's and Johann Gottfried Herder's Responses to Rousseau's *First Discourse*," *Modern Intellectual History* 9:2(2012), pp. 249-274. [Formey. "Examen philosophique"; Herder. "Vom Einfluß der Regierung auf die Wissenschaften"; Rousseau. "Discours des Arts et Sciences"].

Schmidt, Heinrich Julian (1818–1886). Erstes Buch - "Leibniz und der Pietismus, 1681-1719" & Zweites Buch – "Der Rationalismus, 1719-1750: 1735-1739, Der Pietismus: Zinzendorf, Moser, Edelmann, Haller" in *Geschichte des geistigen Lebens in Deutschland von Leibniz bis auf Lessings Tod 1681-1781.* v1, Leipzig: Wilhelm Grunow, 1862. (These were retitled "Die Kopfzeit" and "Nachkommer des Pietismus' (1733-1748)—Zinsendorf, Haller, Moser" in the posthumous *Geschichte der deutschen Literatur von Leibniz bis auf unsere Zeit* [History of German Literature from Leibniz to the Present]. 4v, 1886-1896].

Schmidt, James. "Aufklärung, Gegenaufklärung, Dialektik der Aufklärung", in J. Schmidt (ed.), *Aufklärung und Gegenaufklärung in der europäischen Literatur, Philosophie und Politik von der Antike bis zur Gegenwart.* Darmstadt 1989, pp. 1-33.

———. "Aufklärung. "Introduction: What is Enlightenment? A Question, its Context, and Some Consequences," in: J. Schmidt ed. *What is Enlightenment? Eighteenth-century Answers and Twentieth-Century Questions.* Berkeley and Los Angeles: University of California Press, 1996, pp. 1–45.

———. "Aufklärung. "What Enlightenment Project?" *10th International Conference on the Enlightenment.* Dublin, July 25-31, 1999, repr. *Political Theory* 28:6(2000), 734-757.

———. (n.d.) "Aufklärung. "Robert Wokler, J.G.A. Pocock, and the Hunt for an Eighteenth-Century Usage of 'Counter-Enlightenment'" Persistent Enlightenment blog @ https://persistentenlightenment.com/2016/10/12/robbie-wokler-j-g-a-pocock-and-the-hunt-for-an-eighteenth-century-usage-of-counter-enlightenment/.

———. "Aufklärung. "Inventing the Enlightenment: Anti-Jacobins, British Hegelians and the Oxford English Dictionary," *Journal of the History of Ideas* 64:3(2003), pp. 421–43.

———. "Aufklärung. "Mediation, Genealogy, and (the) Enlightenment," rvws of Siskin & Warner, eds. *This is Enlightenment.* and Edelstein, *The Enlightenment: A Genealogy. Eighteenth-Century Studies* 45:1 (Fall, 2011), pp127-139.

———, ed. 1996. *What is Enlightenment? Eighteenth-Century Answers and Twentieth-Century Questions.* Berkeley: University of California Press.

Schmidt, Leigh Eric. 2000. *Hearing Things: Religion, Illusion, and the American Enlightenment.* Cambridge, MA: Harvard University Press. pb 2002.

———. *Holy Fairs: Scottish Communions and American Revivals in the Early Modern Period,* Princeton, NJ: Princeton University Press, 1989, 2nd ed., pb, Grand Rapids, MI: Eerdmans, 2001.

Schnegg, Brigitte. Looking back to the future: designs for an ideal society in the swiss enlightenment. in Joy Charnley & Malcolm Pender ed. *Visions of Utopia in Switzerland*. Francfort/Berlin/Berne/Bruxelles/New York/Oxford/Vienne: Peter Lang, coll. "Occasional Papers in Swiss Studies," 3, 2000.

Schofield, Robert E. 2004. *The Enlightenment of Joseph Priestley: A Study of His Life and Work from 1733 to 1773*. University Park, PA: Penn State University Press.

———. John Wesley and Science in 18th Century England. *Isis* 44 (1953): 331–40.

Schreiner, Susan. *Are You Alone Wise? The Search for Certainty in the Early Modern Era*. New York: Oxford University Press (Oxford Studies in Historical Theology), 28 December 2010, pb, 2012.

Schwartz, Hillel. 1980. *The French Prophets: The History of a Millenarian Group in Eighteenth-Century England*. Berkeley: University of California Press.

———. 1978. *Knaves, Fools, Madmen, and that Subtile Effluvium: A Study of the Opposition to the French Prophets in England, 1706-1710*. Gainsville, Fl: University Presses of Florida.

Segal, R. A. "Hume's *Natural History of Religion* and the Beginning of the Social Scientific Study of Religion," *Religion*, 24, 3 (1994): 225-34.

Segala, Marco. Électricité animale, magnétisme animal, galvanisme universel: A la recherche de l'identité entre l'homme et la nature/Animal electricity, animal magnetism, universal galvanism: In search of universal harmony between man and nature," *Revue d'Histoire des Sciences* 54:1(2001), pp. 71-84.

Seguin, Maria Susana. *Science et religion dans la pensée française du XVIIIe siècle: le mythe du déluge universel*. Paris: Éditions Honoré Champion, coll. Les dix-huitièmes siècles 52, 2001.

Seidman, Steven. 1984. *Liberalism and the Origins of European Social Theory*. Berkeley: University of California Press.

Seillière, Ernest. *Le Mal romantique - Essai sur l'impérialisme irrationnel*. (Paris: Plon, 1908) Reprint, Forgotten Books, 2018.

———. 1911. *Les Mystiques du néo-romantisme, évolution contemporaine de l'appétit mystique*. Paris: Plon.

———. *Les éducateurs mystiques de l'âme moderne: Madame Guyon et Fénelon, précurseurs de Rousseau*. 1918.

———. 1919. *Les étapes du mysticisme passionnel: De Saint Preux à Manfred*. Paris: Renaissance du livre.

Seillière, Ernest, Joseph de Maistre Rousseau, *Comptes rendues des séances de l'Academie des Sciences Morales et Politiques*, 194(1920): 321–363.

Seillière, Ernest. 1929. *Romanticism. [Le Romantisme, 1925] Translated by Cargill Sprietsma*. New York: Columbia University Press.

———. *Le Romantisme et la religion: essais sur le mysticisme chétien et le mysticisme naturiste*. Paris: Nouvelle Revue Critique, 1932.

———. *Léon Bloy, psychologie d'un mystique*. Paris: Nouvelle Revue Critique, 1936.

Sells, Michael A. Sells & Ernst, eds. *Early Islamic Mysticism*, NY: Paulist Press (Classics of Western Spirituality), 1996.

Semple, Robert A. *History of the Rise and Progress of Baptists in Virginia*. Richmond, VA: John O'Lynch, 1810. (revised ed, ed. Rev. Beale, Richmond: Pitt and Dickinson, 1894).

Sensbach, Jon F. 2005. *Rebecca's Revival: Creating Black Christianity in the Atlantic World*. Cambridge, MA: Harvard University Press.

Shaftesbury, Anthony Ashley Cooper, 3rd Earl of (1671-1713). "A Letter Concerning Enthusiasm" (Sep, 1707) in *Characteristics of Men, Manners, Opinions, Times*. v1, London: Grant Richards, 1900.

———. *The Shaftesbury Standard Edition: Complete Works, Correspondence and Posthumous Writings*, Stuttgart-Bad Cannstatt: Frommann-Holzboog, -2018ff.

Shah, Idries. *Oriental Magic*, Arkana Books, 1993.

Shaw, Jane. 2006. *Miracles in Enlightenment England*. New Haven, CT: Yale University Press.

Shea, Louisa. 2009. *The Cynic Enlightenment: Diogenes in the Salon*. Baltimore: Johns Hopkins University Press.

Shea, William M., and Peter A. Huff, eds. 1995. *Knowledge and Belief in America: Enlightenment Traditions and Modern Religious Thought*. Cambridge: Cambridge University Press. 2003.

Sheehan, Jonathan. 2003. Enlightenment, religion, and the enigma of secularization. *American Historical Review* 108 (4): 1061–1080.

———. When was disenchantment? History and the secular age, *Varieties of Secularism in a Secular Age*. ed. Craig Calhoun, Michael Warner, and Jonathan Van Antwerpen. Cambridge, MA: Harvard University Press, 2010.

———. 2016. Suffering Job: Christianity Beyond Metaphysics. In *God in the Enlightenment*, ed. William Bulman and Robert G. Ingram. Oxford: Oxford University Press.

———. 2015. *with Dror Wahrman. Invisible Hands: Self-Organization and the Eighteenth Century*. Chicago: University of Chicago Press.

Sher, Richard B. 1985. *Church and University in the Scottish Enlightenment: The Moderate Literati of Edinburgh*. Princeton, NJ: Princeton University Press.

Sheriff, Mary D. "Passionate Spectators: On Enthusiasm, Nymphomania, and the Imagined Tableau ," in Klein, Lawrence E. & Anthony J. La Vopa, *Enthusiasm and Enlightenment in Europe, 1650-1850*. 1998 (also published in *Huntington Library Quarterly*, vol. 60(1997): 1–2, pp. 51-83).

———. 2008. *Moved by Love: Inspired Artists and Deviant Women in Eighteenth-Century France*. Chicago: University of Chicago Press.

Siedentop, Larry Alan. "The Limits of the Enlightenment: A Study of Conservative Political Thought in Early Nineteenth-century France with Special Reference to Maine de Biran and Joseph de Maistre," Oxford University D Phil thesis 1966.

Simpson, George Eaton. *The Shango Cult in Trinidad*. Institute of Caribbean Studies, University of Puerto Rico, 1965.

———. *The Shango Cult in Nigeria and Trinidad*. St. Augustine, U.W.I., Faculty of Social Sciences, 1971.

Siskin, Clifford. 2010. In *This is Enlightenment*, ed. William Warner. Chicago: University of Chicago Press.

Smith, Adam. *Theory of the Moral Sentiments*. (1759) ed. Knud Haakonssen. Cambridge: Cambridge University Press Texts in the History of Philosophy, 2002, online 2012.

Smith, John H. "Friedrich Schlegel's Romantic Calculus: Reflections on the Mathematical Infinite around 1800," pp. 239-257, in Nassar, ed. *The Relevance of Romanticism: Essays in German Romantic Philosophy*. Oxford University Press, 2014.

Smith, Justin E.H. 2019. *Irrationality: A History of the Dark Side of Reason*. Princeton, NJ: Princeton University Press.

Smith, Preserved. 1962. *The Enlightenment (1934)*. New York: Collier Books.

Sobel, Mechal. 1987. *The World They Made Together: Black and White Values in Eighteenth-Century Virginia*. Princeton, NJ: Princeton University Press.

Socher, Abraham P. *The Radical Enlightenment of Solomon Maimon: Judaism, Heresy, and Philosophy*. Stanford, CA: Stanford University Press (Stanford Studies in Jewish History and Culture), 2006.

Soltner, Jean-Louis. 1980. Le Christianisme de Joseph de Maistre. *Revue des études maistriennes* 5–6: 97–110.

Sorkin, David. 2008. *The Religious Enlightenment: Protestants, Jews, and Catholics from London to Vienna. (Jews, Christians, and Muslims from the Ancient to the Modern World #42)*. Princeton, NJ: Princeton University Press.

Southey, Robert. *Letters from England: by Don Manuel Alvarez Espriella. Translated from the Spanish*. (1807) Edited by Jack Simmons. London: Cresset Press, 1951.

———. *The Life of Wesley and the Rise of Methodism*. (2v. 1820; London: Longman, Brown, Green, and Longmans, 1846 @ https://archive.org/details/lifewesleyandri01soutgoog/page/n406/mode/2up).

Spector, Sheila. "Kabbalistic Sources—Blake and His Critics," *Blake: An Illustrated Quarterly* 67 (ie 17:3) Winter 1983-84).
Sposito, Frank Andreas. "A Political Theory of Romanticism: Aesthetic Criticism and Common Sense in Counter-Enlightenment Thought," Ph.D. dissertation. University of California, San Diego: 1995.
Spencer, Mark G. *Hume and Eighteenth-Century America: The Reception of Hume's Political Thought in America, 1740-1830*. Rochester. New York: University of Rochester Press/Boydell & Brewer, 2004.
Spink, J. *French Free Thought From Gassendi to Voltaire*. (1960) Bloomsbury Academic, 2014.
Staël, Madame de (Germaine de Staël-Holstein). *De l'Allemagne*, Paris: Nicolle, 1810. reprinted, London: John Murray, 1813.
——— (n.d.) (Germaine de Staël-Holstein). On Germany. [*De l'Allemagne*]. Translated by Claudia Moscovici @ https://literaturesalon.wordpress.com/2010/09/08/madame-de-stael-the-ultimate-philosophe-and-salonniere/).
Stalnaker, Joanna. 2016. Jonathan Israel in dialogue. *Journal of the History of Ideas* 77 (4): 637–648.
Stanley, Brian. ed. *Christian Missions and the Enlightenment*. Routledge, 2015.
Starr, S. Frederick. *Lost Enlightenment: Central Asia's Golden Age from the Arab Conquest to Tamerlane*. Princeton, NJ: Princeton University Press, 2013, Kindle ed.
Stein, Stephen J., ed. *Jonathan Edwards's Writings; Text, Context, Interpretation*. Bloomington: Indiana University Press, 1996. Rvw by Amy Plantinga Pauw in *Journal of the History of the Behavioral Sciences* 34:3(Summer, 1998) p338.
Stephen, Leslie. *History of English Thought in the Eighteenth Century*. (1876, 3rd ed. 1902), 2v. New York: Harcourt, Brace & World/Harbinger pb, 1962.
Sternhell, Zeev. 2006. *Anti-Lumières: Du XVIIIe siècle à la guerre froide*. Paris: Fayard.
———. 2009. *The Anti-Enlightenment Tradition, tr. David Maisel*. New Haven, CT: Yale University Press.
Strickland, Lloyd. *Proofs of God in Early Modern Europe: An Anthology*. Waco, TX: Baylor University Press, 2018.
Stromberg, Roland N. 1954. *Religious Liberalism in Eighteenth-Century England*. London: Oxford University Press.
Stuke, H. "Aufklärung", in: O. Brunner, W. Conze & R. Koselleck, eds. *Geschichtliche Grundbegriffe: Historisches Lexikon zur politisch-sozialen Sprache in Deutschland*. vol. I, Stuttgart, 1972, pp. 243–342.
Sullivan, Robert E. 1982. *John Toland and the Deist Controversy. A Study in Adaptations*. Cambridge, MA: Harvard University Press.
Sullivan, Robert. Rethinking christianity in enlightened Europe. *Eighteenth-Century Studies*, 34:2(hiver 2001), 298–309.
Sullivan, Robert E. *John Toland and the Deist Controversy: A Study in Adaptations*. Cambridge, MA, 1982.
Sutcliffe, Adam. 2004. Cambridge University Press. In *Judaism and enlightenment*. New York: pb 2005.
Swedenborg, *Spiritual Diary*, 1747-1765, 5v, MS posthumously published by General Church of the New Jerusalem, new ed. 2013. Kindle ed.
Sweet, Paul R. 1970. *Friedrich von Gentz: Defender of the Old Order*. CT: Greenwood Press.
Swift, Jonathan. *Sermons*. in Herbert Davis, ed. *The Prose Works of Jonathan Swift*. v9, *Irish Tracts and Sermons*. Oxford: Basil Blackwell, 1948.
Switzer, R., ed. 1970. *Chateaubriand: Actes du Congrés de Wisconsin (1968)*. Geneva: Droz.
Tabaki, Anna. 1991. Les dominantes idéologiques et esthétiques du discours théâtral au temps des Lumières en Grèce. *Revue des études sud-est européennes, 29* 1–2: 39–50.
———. "La réception du théâtre de Voltaire dans le Sud-Est de l'Europe (première moitié du XIXe siècle)," dans Ulla Kölving et Christiane Mervaud ed. *Voltaire et ses combats*. Oxford: Voltaire Foundation, 1997, vol. II, p. 1539-1549.

Tackett, Timothy. 1986. *Religion, Revolution, and Regional Culture in 18th Century France: The Ecclesiastical Oath of 1791*. Princeton, NJ: Princeton University Press.

———. 2001. Interpreting the Terror. *French Historical Studies* 24 (4): 569–578. (10).

Tafel, Rudolph L. 1869. Swedenborg and Freemasonry. *New Jerusalem Messenger*: 26–67.

Tallis, R. 1997. *Enemies of Hope: A Critique of Contemporary Pessimism: Irrationalism, Anti-Humanism and Counter-Enlightenment*. Basingstoke: Macmillan. Reprint. London: Macmillan, 1999.

Tarantino, Giovanni. "The books and times of Anthony Collins (1676–1729), free-thinker, radical reader and independent Whig," in Ariel Hessayon & David Finnegan, eds. *Varieties of Seventeenth- and Early Eighteenth-Century English Radicalism in Context*. New York: Routledge, 2011.

Taves, Ann. 1999. *Fits, Trances, & Visions: Experiencing Religion and Explaining Experience from Wesley to James*. Princeton: Princeton University Press.

Taylor, James. *Autobiography of General James Taylor*. 3, DC, RLUC.

Taylor, John Tinnon. *Early Opposition to the English Novel: The Popular Reaction from 1760 to 1830*. (1943) Edited by Aleks Matza. Kindle ed. 2014.

Thomas, Keith. 1971. *Religion and the Decline of Magic*. New York: Scribner's.

Thomas, W. 1979. *The Philosophic Radicals: Nine Studies in Theory and Practice, 1817-1841*. Oxford: Oxford University Press.

Thompson, E.P. 1993. *Witness against the Beast: William Blake and the Moral Law*. Foreword by Christopher Hill. New York: Cambridge University Press.

Thomson, Ann. 2008. *Bodies of Thought: Science, Religion, and the Soul in the Early Enlightenment*. New York: Oxford University Press.

———. "Les Lumières et le monde islamique," in *Les Lumières et la solidarité internationale*. ed. Michel Baridon. Dijon, 1997, 101–111.

———. "Religious heterodoxy and political radicalism in late 17th and early 18th-century England." *Républicanisme anglais et idée de tolérance*. Confluences XVII. Université de Paris X-Nanterre, 2000. 129–47.

———. 2000. *"Matérialisme et mortalisme". Materia actuosa, Antiquité, âge classique, Lumières. Mélanges en l'honneur d'Olivier Bloch*, 409–426. *Paris*: H. Champion.

———. "Mechanistic Materialism vs Vitalistic Materialism?" M. Saad, ed. *Materialism and Vitalism*. La Lettre de la Maison française d'Oxford 14 (2001): 22-36.

———. "Pantheism." *Oxford Encyclopedia of the Enlightenment*. New York: Oxford University Press, 2002.

Thrift, Minton. *Memoir of the Rev. Jesse Lee with extracts from his journals*, NY: Bangs & Mason, 1823, repr. NY: Arno Press, 1969.

Thurston, Benjamin. "Joseph de Maistre's Theory of Language: Language and Revolution," dans Richard A. Lebrun ed. *Joseph de Maistre's Life, Thought and Influence. Selected Studies*. Montréal & Kingston, London, Ithaca, NY, McGill-Queen's University Press, 2001, pp. 105-119.

Thouard, Denis. 2006. Qu'est-ce que les Lumières pour le premier romantisme? *SVEC* 12: 197–212.

Thun, Nils. *The Behmenists and the Philadelphians: A Contribution to the Study of English Mysticism in the 17th and 18th Centuries*. Uppsala, 1948.

Todorov, Tzvetan. 2009. *In Defence of Enlightenment*. Translated by Gila Walker. London: Atlantic Books.

Toews, John E. Berlin's Marx: Enlightenment, Counter-Enlightenment, and the Historical Construction of Cultural Identities" in Joseph Mali & Robert Wokler, eds. *Isaiah Berlin's Counter-Enlightenment, Transactions of the American Philosophical Society*, 93:5(2003), pp 163-176.

Toland, John. 1997. In *Christianity Not Mysterious (1696-97)*, ed. Philip McGuinness, Alan Harrison, and Richard Kearney. Dublin: Lilliput Press.

———. 1704. *Letters to Serena*. London.

Tonneau, Olivier. 2006. 'Ah ! Si vous pouviez lire au fond de mon coeur' Diderot et le mythe de l'intériorité. *SVEC* 12: 291–298.
Toomer, G.J. 1995. *Eastern Wisedome and Learning: The Study of Arabic in Seventeenth-Century England.* Oxford: Oxford University Press.
Torrey, Norman L. *Voltaire and the English Deists.* (1930) Literary Licensing, LLC, 2013.
Touitou, Béatrice. *Baculard d'Arnaud.* Paris/Rome, Memini, coll. "Bibliographica. Bibliographie des écrivains français," v9, 1997.
Trapnell, William H. 1996. Can a coherent doctrine be extracted from Thomas Woolston's writings? Thoughts on spiritual transfiguration, Deism, and Christian mysticism from the age of enlightenment [in French]. *Revue de l'histoire des religions* 213 (3): 321–344.
Triomphe, Robert. 1968. *Joseph de Maistre: Etude sur la vie et sur la doctrine d'un matérialiste mystique.* Geneva: Droz.
Trouille, Mary Seidman. *Sexual Politics in the Enlightenment: Women Writers Read Rousseau.* State University of New York Press, 1997.
Tsapina, Olga. "Orthodox Enlightenment: Oxymoron or Historical Reality," American Society for Eighteenth-Century Studies 31st Annual Meeting, University of Pennsylvania, April 14, 2000.
Tulloch, John. 1872. *Rational Theology: Christian Philosophy in England in the Seventeenth Century.* Vol. 2. Blackwood: Edinburgh/London.
Tumbleson, Raymond D. 1996. 'Reason and Religion': The Science of Anglicanism. *Journal of the History of Ideas* 57 (1): 131.
Turner, Jack. 2011. John Locke, Christian Mission, and Colonial America. *Modern Intellectual History* 8 (2): 267–297. ("The roots of toleration in the modern West were partly evangelical.").
Turner, James. 1985. *Without God, Without Creed: The Origins of Unbelief in America. Baltimore, MD: Johns Hopkins University Press.* 1988.
Ullmann-Margalit, Edna & Avishai Margalit, eds. *Isaiah Berlin: A Celebration.* Chicago: University of Chicago Press, 1991. (Includes: Michael Ignatieff, Leon Wieseltier, Ronald Dworkin, Stephen Spender, Joseph Brodsky, G. A. Cohen, et al.).
Unger, Rudolf. *Hamann und die Aufklärung.* Jena, 1911.
Uphaus, Robert W. & Gretchen M. Foster, eds. *The Other Eighteenth Century: English Women of Letters 1660-1800.* Michigan State University Press, 1999.
Van Der Lugt, Maria. 2017. The body of Mahomet: Pierre Bayle on War, Sex, and Islam. *Journal of the History of Ideas* 78 (1): 27–50.
Van Tieghem, Paul. *Le Préromantisme, Etudes d'histoire littéraire européenne.* 3v. Paris, 1924, 1930, 1947.
Venturi, Franco. 1971. *Utopia and Reform in the Enlightenment. (the 1969 G. M. Trevelyan lectures at Cambridge University).* Cambridge: Cambridge University Press.
———. 1972. *Italy and the Enlightenment: Studies in a Cosmopolitan Century.* New York: New York University Press.
———. *Settecento Riformatore.* (5v, Turin: Einaudi, 1969-91) v1, *Da Muratori a Beccaria, 1730-1764.* Milan: Mondadori (I classici della storia), 2012.
———. *The End of the Old Regime in Europe, 1768-1776: The First Crisis.* (v3 of *Settecento Riformatore*) tr. R. Burr Litchfield, Princeton University Press, 1989.
Vico, Giambattista (Giovan Battista) (1668–1740). *The New Science of Giambattista Vico* [*Principi di Scienza Nuova*, 1725, 1730, 1744], Translated by Thomas G. Bergin and Max H. Fisch. Ithaca, NY: Cornell University Press, 2nd ed. 1968.
Viguerie, Jean de. "La Vendée et les Lumières: Les Origines Intellectuelles de l'Extermination," in *La Vendée dans l'Histoire: Actes du Colloque.* Paris: Perrin, 1994, pp. 36-51.
Vincent, Rev. Hebron. *A History of the Wesleyan Grove, Martha's Vineyard, Camp Meeting, from the First Meeting Held There In 1835, to that of 1858, Inclusive ; Interspersed With Touching Incidents And General Remarks.* Boston: Geo. C. Rand & Avery, 1858.
Vincent, K. Steven. 2004. Benjamin Constant, the French revolution, and the problem of modern character. *History of European Ideas* 30 (1): 5–21.

Venturi, Franco. "Benjamin Constant, the French Revolution, and the Origins of French Romantic Liberalism," in *French Historical Studies* 23:4(2000), 607-637 (on "enthusiasm"s rehabilitation, p 628-632).
Vissière, Isabelle & Jean-Louis, eds. *Lettres édifiantes et curieuses des jésuites de l'Inde au dix-huitième siècle*. Saint-Étienne: Publications de l'Université de Saint-Étienne, coll. "Lire le dix-huitième siècle," 2000.
Vyverberg, Henry. 1958. *Historical Pessimism in the French Enlightenment*. Cambridge, MA: Harvard University Press.
Wacker, Grant. 2018. *Augustus H. Strong and the Dilemma of Historical Consciousness*. Waco, TX: Baylor University Press.
Wade, Ira O. 1971. *The Intellectual Origins of the French Enlightenment*. Princeton, NJ: Princeton University Press.
———. 1977. *The Structure and Form of the French Enlightenment. v1, Esprit Philosophique*. Princeton, NJ: Princeton University Press.
———. *The «Philosophe» in the French Drama of the Eighteenth Century*. (Paris: Presses universitaires de France, 1926) Princeton, NJ: Princeton University Press, 1965.
Wainwright, William J. *Reason and the Heart: A prolegomenon to a critique of passional reason*. Ithaca, New York: Cornell University Press, 1995 (Jonathan Edwards)
Waldron, Jeremy. 2002. *God, Locke, and Equality: Christian Foundations in Locke's Political Thought*. New York: Cambridge University Press.
Walker, Mack. 1981. *Johann Jakob Moser and the Holy Roman Empire of the German Nation*. Chapel Hill, NC: University of North Carolina Press.
Walter, E.V. 1959. Power, civilization and the psychology of conscience. *American Political Science Review* 53 (3): 654.
Wallace, Miriam L., ed. *Enlightening Romanticism, Romancing the Enlightenment: British Novels from 1750 to 1832* (2009) London: Routledge, 2016.
Walzer, Arthur E. *George Campbell Rhetoric in the Age of Enlightenment*. State University of New York Press (Suny Series in Rhetoric in the Modern Era), 2003.
Ward, W[illiam] R[eginald]. *Early Victorian Methodism*. 1976.
———. 1991. *The Protestant Evangelical Awakening*, 2002. Cambridge: Cambridge University Press.
———. 1992. *The Protestant Evangelical Revival*. New York: Cambridge University Press.
———. "German Pietism, 1670-1750," *Journal of Ecclesiastical History*, 44(1993). p479-505. (bibliographical survey).
———. 1999. *Christianity Under the Ancien Régime, 1648–1789*. Cambridge: Cambridge University Press.
———. 2006. *Early Evangelicalism: A Global Intellectual History, 1670-1789*. Cambridge: Cambridge University Press.
———. "Mysticism and Revival: The Case of Gerhard Tersteegen," in FS John Walsh, *Revival and Religion since 1700*. ed. Jane Garnett and Colin Matthew. London, 1993.
Ward, Patricia A. *Experimental Theology in America: Madame Guyon, Fénelon, and Their Readers*. Waco, TX: Baylor University Press, September 2009.
Waring, E. Graham, ed. 1967. *Deism and Natural Religion: A Source Book*. New York: Frederick Ungar.
Watts, Isaac. 1999. *Selected Works of Isaac Watts. ed. Andrew Pyle, 8v*. Bristol, UK: Thoemmes Press.
Weil, Françoise. "Les livres persécutés en France de 1720 à 1770," *la Lettre clandestine*. No. 6 Paris: Presses de l'Université de Paris-Sorbonne, 1997.
Wells, Colin. 2002. *The Devil and Doctor Dwight: Satire and Theology in the Early American Republic*. Chapel Hill: University of North Carolina Press.
Westfall, Richard S. 1973. *Science and Religion in Seventeenth-Century England*. Ann Arbor, MI: University of Michigan Press.
Wharton, William. *The Enthusiasm of the Church of Rome demonstrated in some observations upon the life of Ignatius Loyola*, London, 1688.

White, Daniel E. 2010. *Early Romanticism and Religious Dissent*. Cambridge: Cambridge University Press.

Williams, Raymond. 1958. *Culture and Society 1780-1950*. London: Chatto & Windus. (socialist nostalgia for the values of the Welsh Baptist chapel).

———. 1961. *The Long Revolution*. London: Chatto & Windus. (socialist nostalgia for the values of the Welsh Baptist chapel).

Williamson, George S. 2004. *The Longing for Myth in Germany: Religion and Aesthetic Culture from Romanticism to Nietzsche*. Chicago: University of Chicago Press.

Williamson, Karina. 1979. Smart's *Principia*: Science and Anti-Science in *Jubilate Agno*. *Review of English Studies* 30 (120): 409–422.

Wilson, Ellen Gibson. 1990. *Thomas Clarkson: A Biography*. New York: St. Martin's.

Wilson, Lindsay. 1993. *Women and Medicine in the French Enlightenment*. Baltimore, MD: Johns Hopkins University Press.

Winnett, A.R. 1974. *Peter Browne, Provost, Bishop, Metaphysician*. London: S.P.C.K.

Winship, Michael P. 1995. *Seers of God: Puritan Providentialism in the Restoration and Early Enlightenment*. Baltimore: Johns Hopkins University Press.

Wokler, Robert. "Isaiah Berlin's Enlightenment and Counter-Enlightenment," public lecture at the Central European University, Budapest, 27 March 2000. (initially prepared for the Oxford Political Thought Conference and a symposium held in Tel Aviv on 'Isaiah Berlin's Counter-Enlightenment' in January 2000 @ www.ceu.hu/jewishstudies/pdf/02_wokler.pdf.

———. "Isaiah Berlin's Enlightenment and Counter-Enlightenment" in Joseph Mali & Robert Wokler, eds. *Isaiah Berlin's Counter-Enlightenment, Transactions of the American Philosophical Society*, 93:5(2003), 13-32.

———. *Rousseau, the Age of Enlightenment, and Their Legacies*. Edited by Bryan Garsten. Princeton, NJ: Princeton University Press, 2012.

Wokler, Robert & Joseph Mali eds. *Isaiah Berlin's Counter-Enlightenment, Transactions of the American Philosophical Society*, 93:5(2003). Essays by Wokler, Mali, Mark Lilla, Roger Hausheer, Darrin McMahon, Frederick Beiser, Graeme Garrard, Lionel Gossman, John E. Toews and Michael Confino.

Wokler, Robert & G. Crowder eds. *The One and the Many: Reading Isaiah Berlin*. Amherst, New York: Prometheus Books, 2007.

Walter, E. V. "Power, Civilization and the Psychology of Conscience," *American Political Science Review*, 53:3(1959), p. 654),

Wolfe, Charles T. "Les vrais-faux jumeaux du matérialisme et de l'athéisme. Prolégomènes à une étude comparative.," *La question de l'athéisme au XVIIe siècle*, Colloque du CNRS (Centre National de la Recherche Scientifique), CHPM (Centre d'Histoire de la Philosophie Moderne). Paris: June 15, 2001.

Wolin, Richard. 2004. *The Seduction of Unreason: The Intellectual Romance with Fascism from Nietzsche to Postmodernism*. Princeton, NJ: Princeton University Press. ("affinities between the Counter-Enlightenment and postmodernism.").

———. 2016. Introduction to the Symposium on Jonathan Israel's *Democratic Enlightenment*. *Journal of the History of Ideas* 77 (4): 615–626.

Wood, A. Skevington. 1992. *Revelation and Reason: Wesleyan Responses to Eighteenth-Century Rationalism*. Bulkington: The Wesley Fellowship.

Worden, Barbara S. "The Emotional Evangelical: Blake and Wesley." *Wesleyan Theological Journal* 18, no. 2 (Fall 1983): 67-79.

Wood, Gordon. 1987. Ideology and the Origins of a Liberal America. *William and Mary Quarterly, 3rd ser.* 44: 628–640.

———. 1980. Evangelical America and Early Mormonism. *New York History* 61: 359–386.

Wood, Paul, ed. 2004. *Science and Dissent in England, 1688-1945*. Burlington, VT: Ashgate.

Yoder, Diane. (n.d.) "Satisfying the Head as Well as the Heart: James Marsh, Samuel Taylor Coleridge and the American Transcendentalist Movement" M. A. Thesis in Theology and Literature, Antioch College PDF @ https://www.academia.edu/6424934/Satisfying_the_

Head_as_Well_as_the_Heart. Chapter 2 @ https://archive.vcu.edu/english/engweb/transcendentalism/roots/marsh.html

Yolton, J. R. Porter, P. Rogers & B. Stafford, eds. *The Blackwell Companion to the Enlightenment.* Oxford, 1991.

Yong, Amos. 2004. The Holy Spirit and the World Religions: On the Christian Discernment of Spirit(s) 'After' Buddhism. *Buddhist-Christian Studies* 24: 191–207.

Young, B. W. *Religion and Enlightenment in Eighteenth-Century England: Theological Debate from Locke to Burke.* Oxford: Clarendon Press, 12 March, 1998.

———. 'See *Mystery* to *Mathematics* Fly!': Pope's *Dunciad* and the Critique of Religious Rationalism. *Eighteenth-Century Studies* 26(1992–93), 435-448.

Young, B.W. 1994. The Soul-Sleeping System:' Politics and Heresy in Eighteenth-Century England. *Journal of Ecclesiastical History* 45: 64–81.

Young, Edward. Night Thoughts (1744), ed. Stephen Cornford, Cambridge: Cambridge University Press, 2008.

———. *Night Thoughts or the Complaint and the Consolation* (1797), ill. William Blake. eds. Robert Essick & Jenijoy La Belle. New York: Dover, 1975.

Young, Jason R. 2011. *Rituals of Resistance: African Atlantic Religion in Kongo and the Lowcountry South in the Era of Slavery.* Baton Rouge: Louisiana State University Press.

Zammito, John. Reconstructing German Idealism and Romanticism: Historicism and Presentism. *Modern Intellectual History* I:3(November, 2004), 427-438.

Zande, Johan van der. "Thespis For and Against: Sulzer and Rousseau on Theater and Politics," dans *Reconceptualizing Nature, Science, and Aesthetics: Contribution à une nouvelle approche des Lumières helvétiques.* Geneva: Éditions Slatkine, coll. "Travaux sur la Suisse des Lumières," 1, 1998.

Zaretsky, Rob. 2001. *Frail Happiness: An Essay on Rousseau.* University Park, PA: Penn State University Press.

Zaretsky, Rob, and J. Scott. 2007. *So Great a Noise: Jean-Jacques Rousseau, David Hume and the Limits of Human Understanding.* New Haven, CT: Yale University Press.

Zauner, Ursula. *Das Menschenbild und die Erziehungstheorien der französischen Materialisten im 18. Jahrundert.* Francfort, Berlin, Berne, New York, Paris et Vienne: Peter Lang, coll. "Europäische Hochschulschriften: Reihe 13, Französische Sprache und Literatur," 235, 1998.

Ziolkowski, Theodore. 2003. *Clio the Romantic Muse: Historicizing the Faculties in Germany.* Ithaca, New York: Cornell University Press.

Žižek, Slavoj, Clayton Crockett, and Creston Davis, eds. 2011. *Hegel and the Infinite: Religion, Politics, and Dialectic.* New York: Columbia University Press.

Chapter 2
The Crucible of the Counter-Enlightenment I

Abstract Zinzendorf and the Moravians.

> Slowly, slowly we are learning that the eighteenth century was more than an age of reason. Religious thinkers and believers did not simply evaporate under the brilliant illumination of the self-anointed representatives of Enlightenment; instead they often sturdily resisted the trivializing voices of advanced criticism and crackling anticlericalism.[1]
>
> The 18th century was in many ways the great age of self-invention, when people were able to refashion themselves, like quicksilver, over and over again.[2]

On the last day of January, 1739, Nicolaus Ludwig, Count of Zinzendorf and Herrnhut in Upper Lusatia, in the German Kingdom of Saxony, landed at Christiansfort, the one-horse port city of Saint Thomas, in the Danish Virgin Islands, and immediately set about to find the Moravian mission, which he had sent off seven years before, after meeting Anton, a freed African slave, at the court of the King of Denmark in 1732. His mission: to bring the grace of God to the sugar-and-slave islands of the West Indies. Zinzendorf was the chief executive of the newly revived Bohemian Brethren, or Moravian church, whose remnants he had recently settled on his baronial lands in Herrnhut (Lord's Shelter), and of the Moravians' mission to the West Indies. The mission now consisted, after seven years, of a minister named Frederick Martin, his local assistant Matthias and Matthias's wife Rebecca Freundlich (Figs. 2.1 and 2.2).

All three evangelists turned out to be in town—in jail in fact, in the fort that gave Christiansfort its name. Their crime: refusing to take oaths. The official pastor of St. Thomas, a Dutch Lutheran, after trying and failing to stop them from baptizing African slaves, had trumped up a charge of theft against them. Not only had Martin and Matthias Freundlich refused to give evidence under oath (the evidence in question was in their own favor, but Moravianism forbade oath-taking), Freundlich had

[1] H. C. Erik Midelfort, *Exorcism and Enlightenment: Johann Joseph Gassner and the Demons of Eighteenth-Century Germany*, New Haven: Yale U.P., 2005, p2.

[2] Charles McGrath, Review of Rodney Bolt, *The Librettist of Venice: The Remarkable Life of Lorenzo Da Ponte, Mozart's Poet, Casanova's Friend, and Italian Opera's Impresario in America*, in *New York Times*, 21 July, 2006, p. B32.

W. R. Everdell, *The Evangelical Counter-Enlightenment*, Boston Studies in Philosophy, Religion and Public Life 9,
https://doi.org/10.1007/978-3-030-69762-4_2

Fig. 2.1 Nikolaus Ludwig, Graf von Zinzendorf und Pottendorf (1700–1760) portrait by Balthasar Denner—18. Apr 2005 upload to de.wikipedia by de:Benutzer:Joachim T., Public Domain, https://commons.wikimedia.org/w/index.php?curid=826213

also refused to remarry his wife in the Lutheran rite, because, he claimed, they had already been married in a Moravian rite by the Reverend Martin after his arrival in 1737. Freundlich's wife Rebecca was in jail, too, having likewise helped Martin to baptize slaves and likewise refused to remarry her husband. As Rebecca Freundlich, she was now a full-fledged and indispensable member of the mission, preaching grace and salvation to the island's blacks, a task made easier for her by the fact that she was not only black herself, a mulatto servant in one of the great plantation houses, but also free, a freed descendant of Africans.

As noblemen will, Zinzendorf went right to the top and protested to Herr Moth, the island's governor. The three prisoners were released immediately and for the next two weeks the evangelical Count went around the island with them, preaching to the 800 or so black Christians there and restoring order, as he understood it, to the Moravian community. Since the first missionaries in 1732, the Moravian "pedagogy of conversion" had included the equality of believers (women included) in multiracial communities, with rituals to reinforce it that ran from decision-making by vote, or by lot, to dormitory living, highly organized choral singing, the kiss of peace, the laying on of hands and the washing of each other's feet. Missionaries visited slaves in their cabins, shared their food and clothing, greeted them like friends with a warm handshake, and sat and talked with them "as if they were … equals."[3] The planters watched this with both irritation and fear, remembering the briefly successful slave revolt of 1733 on the neighboring island of St. John. Zinzendorf busied himself and set up four districts of church administration, each to be divided into the now standard Moravian "choirs" of small bands who sang together, grouped as unmarried men, unmarried women, married men and married women. He appointed the "elders, helpers, overseers, advisors, distributors of alms"[4] and all the other administrative offices he had developed for a full-fledged Moravian establishment, egalitarian but minutely organized, since the refugee church had settled on his estates in 1722.

In a later century, such an initiative would suggest preparations for political independence, reform or even democracy and insurrection, and in 1739 most whites in an American slave enclave like St. Thomas probably saw it that way. Not Zinzendorf. On the 15th of February, the day before he left, the Count gave a farewell sermon in Dutch to a congregation of some 300 slaves and freedmen—a sermon which made it very clear that the equality Zinzendorf meant for the slaves of St. Thomas was either only for the church community or definitely not of this world. Speaking at the house of the liberal slaveowning planter Carstens in the town now called Charlotte Amalie, Zinzendorf peremptorily explained that their freedom was evangelical, not

[3] Sylvia R. Frey & Betty Wood, *Come Shouting to Zion: African American Protestantism in the American South and British Caribbean to 1830*, Chapel Hill: U. of North Carolina Press, 1998, p83–84, quotation on p84. The Methodists would copy much of this.

[4] John R. Weinlick, *Count Zinzendorf: The Story of His Life and Leadership in the Renewed Moravian Church*, Abingdon Press, 1956; Bethlehem, PA: Moravian Church in America, pb, 1989, p145–46. Weinlick depends on the source of all sources for Zinzendorf, comprehensive but tendentious, which is the earliest biography by Zinzendorf's disciple, friend and successor. The Moravian Bishop August Spangenberg, whose *Leben des Herrn Nicolaus Ludwig, Grafen und Herrn von Zinzendorf und Pottendorf, beschrieben von August Gottlieb Spangenberg*: in 8 Theilen, 1772–1775, now exists in a new edition (8 Bände in 4 Bänden, NY: Olms, (Gebundene Ausgabe - 1. January 1971)) and in an abridged English translation as *The Life of N. L. Count Zinzendorf, Translated [in an Abridged Form] from the German, by S. Jackson*, London: Holdsworth, 1838. The long labors of Erich Beyreuther have dominated Zinzendorf scholarship, and include an indispensable short biography, *Nikolaus Ludwig Graf von Zinzendorf Selbstzeugnissen und Bilddokumente: Eine Biographie* (3rd edition, Basel: Brunnen Verlag Giessen, 2000). A more recent popular biography of Zinzendorf by Eika Geiger, *Nikolaus Ludwig Graf von Zinzendorf: Seine Lebensgeschichte* (Hänssler Verlag, 1999), adds little.

juridical, freedom from sin instead of from slavery.[5] To slavery, in fact, Zinzendorf gives one of the era's standard endorsements as God's curse on the children of Ham.

> God has punished the first Negroes with slavery. The blessed state of your souls does not make your bodies accordingly free, but it does remove all evil thoughts, deceit, laziness, faithlessness, and everything that makes your condition of slavery burdensome. For our Lord Jesus was himself a laborer for as long as he stayed in the world.[6]

The next day the Count set off for Amsterdam and home, buying one of the slaves of St. Thomas and freeing him to return for missionary training at Herrnhut. He stopped en route at the other Danish sugar islands of St. John and St. Croix, and the Dutch island of St. Eustatius, where he wrote another of his hundreds of hymns, "The Saviour's Blood and Righteousness," and where he met a Portuguese Jew named DaCosta, for whom he paid passage and gave up his stateroom so that DaCosta and his wife could go to Amsterdam. To Zinzendorf's surprise, DaCosta, though entirely grateful, declined to convert to Moravian Christianity. The Count was undaunted by this and began a mission to the Jews as soon as he got back to Europe.[7]

Popping in and out became Zinzendorf's mode of operation. The walkabout is evangelical in the first, older sense of the term, the sense in which the Christian priority is to preach the Gospel ("*evangelium*") to the uninitiated everywhere with the ambition of bringing grace to every corner of the world and baptizing everyone in it. But Zinzendorf was also evangelical in the sense that would become dominant in his lifetime; he expected grace, and expected it to be personally experienced. Repeatedly. To Zinzendorf himself grace may not have come suddenly; but to him and to many others it seemed that it had come on the 13th of August, 1727, to the entire community of 300-odd refugees that had settled five years before near his chateau at Herrnhut on his estates in Saxony.

The refugees were Protestants from Moravia, the eastern part of the Kingdom of Bohemia (now the Czech Republic), a branch of Protestant Christianity that had appeared before Luther was born, and had, in fact, been one of the larger influences on him. One of these proto-Protestants, Jan Hus of Bohemia/Moravia, still a Czech national hero, had been executed for heresy in 1415, a century before Luther's *95 Theses*.[8] Hus's ideas had survived him, and his successors, variously known as Hussites, Ultraquists, Taborites or Böhmische Brüder (Bohemian Brethren), had carried on Hussite doctrines and practices under intermittent persecution. They were religious radicals. Most rejected infant baptism, purgatory, saint-veneration,

[5] Weinlick, p145–46.

[6] Translated into Creole by Mingo, English translation in Jon F. Sensbach, *Rebecca's Revival: Creating Black Christianity in the Atlantic World*, Cambridge, MA: Harvard U.P., 2005, p142.

[7] Weinlick, *Count Zinzendorf*, 1989, p146–47; Klaus-Gunther Wesseling, "Die Herrnhuter Judenmission betreibt Samuel Lieberkühn" (s.d.); Wesseling, "Zinzendorf," *Biographisch-Bibliographisches Kirchenlexikon*, vol. XIV (1998), p509–547 @ www.bautz.de/bbkl/z/zinzendorf_n_l.shtml.

[8] Hus's English counterpart was John Wycliffe, the founder of the egalitarian Lollard heresy in England.

relic-worship, oath-taking, transformation of the communion bread and wine, the old fasts and feasts of the Catholic calendar. They required their clergy to do without a salary, compete in preaching with laymen, and to preach in the language of the country instead of in Latin. Most importantly, they believed, human beings could not save themselves or be saved by priests or ritual. They believed that they were fundamentally helpless without the grace of God—helpless even to believe.

The Taborite wing of the Hussite movement, which claimed enough grace to do without bishops and reject capital punishment, had been annihilated militarily in 1434. After defeat its elements had gone to ground and adopted complete nonviolence and community of property. In 1457, meeting in a village on the manor of Lititz in Bohemia, Taborites had formed a church of their own, and in 1467 established a line of their own clergy by securing a laying-on-of-hands from a priest who belonged to the Waldensians, a renegade sect that was even older than the Hussites.[9] By the sixteenth century, precisely in the decisive years of the Reformation, the main Hussite branch, Unitas Fratrum (in English, the Unity of Brethren, Bohemian Brethren or Brethren of the Law of Christ) had become the third largest church of Bohemia and Moravia; but unlike the radicals, it had accepted the necessity of violent self-defense. The Unity of Brethren constructed church buildings and relieved their clergy of the obligation to live in the poverty typical of Jesus's apostles. Their leading thinker, Lukas of Prague (c.1460–1528), had produced a uniform songbook in 1505, then a uniform liturgy, then a "beginners' catechism. Tolerated *de facto* by state-established Catholicism, they had drawn nearer and nearer to the doctrines and practices, not of the Lutheran churches which were now rising, but to the Catholic church of Rome. Lukas in fact had written a letter to Luther in which he defended the celibacy of the priests, and the "holy Number Seven" of sacraments. (Luther had already married a nun and reduced the seven sacraments to three.) In 1575 the Unity of Brethren had finally drawn up its own written creed, the *Confessio Bohemia*, in Latin rather than Czech, which condemned the adult baptism they had practiced uniformly up to 1535. On the basis of this Bohemian Confession of Faith there had followed in the same year a reunion of the Brethren with the other branches of the Hussite church, except for a few loyal and stubborn believers who were derided as "fanatics" and "legalists."

Persecution of the Hussites had ended in 1609, when the Brethren was registered under the Kingdom of Bohemia's new Toleration Act and was accepted by the state as a Christian denomination. Nine years without persecution followed (a brief episode in the long and spectacularly intolerant history of eastern Europe) which ended with the Thirty Years War, the last great European "religious" war. Not so surprisingly this religious war began as an attack on the Kingdom of Bohemia. Indeed, by the end of the first three years of war (1618–1621), the Empire's Catholic reconquest had expelled all the Protestants from the Kingdom, and the Bohemian Brethren's one remaining bishop, John Amos Comenius, had led most of the group into exile.

[9] Dr. Hans Grimm, "Tradition and History of the Early Churches of Christ In Central Europe," (1962+) Translated by Dr. H. L. Schug @ http://www.netbiblestudy.net/history/new_page_7.htm.

A full century after the crushing of Protestantism in Bohemia and neighboring Moravia, some three hundred survivors of the Brethren migrated north across the Moravian border into the Imperial (and still Protestant) province of Saxony. In 1722 these exiles found shelter on the Saxon manor of Graf von Zinzendorf, a Lutheran, devout and Pietist, in search of a vocation, and a German landlord in need of workers. Five years after that, their new community of Herrnhut was swept by the "spiritual awakening," remembered by the renewed Moravian Church as the date of its founding (Fig. 2.2).

Fig. 2.2 Nikolaus Ludwig, Graf von Zinzendorf und Pottendorf (1700–1760) in a scholar's coif. Copper engraving "Gemeinfrei" at http://www.zeno.org/Literatur/M/Zinzendorf,+Nikolaus+Ludwig+von

The prelude to the Moravian awakening was more political than religious. In the five years since its arrival, the small community of exiles had begun to show divisions. On May 12, 1727, Zinzendorf had confronted them with a three-hour sermon, and assumed formal leadership of the congregation by presenting it with the *Manorial Injunctions and Prohibitions*,[10] a thick civil law code composed of 41 separate statutes that he had written for them in his capacity as their landlord and feudal superior. Each parishioner then came up and agreed to the code by clasping Count Zinzendorf's hand, after which twelve elders, chosen for spirituality, were elected—the first four by lottery—to govern the entire community, and the congregation began to be subdivided into bands called "classes" and singing "choirs."[11] The noble and the highly educated were specifically excluded from eldership (except, of course, for Zinzendorf himself).

On June 15, the Herrnhut congregation met again to sign the *Manorial Injunctions* a second time for good measure, and Zinzendorf, who had clearly not been idle the past month, offered them a new document, a religious covenant, this time with 42 points, the *Brotherly Union and Compact of the Brethren from Bohemia and Moravia and Others, Binding Them to Walk According to the Apostolic Rule*.[12] Agreed to and signed that day by the Herrnhuter, this *Brüderlicher Verein und Willkür* became the founding act by which the Bohemian Unity of Brethren of the fifteenth century became the "Evangelical Unity of Brethren" "Herrnhuters" and "Renewed Moravians" of the eighteenth.[13] Zinzendorf, already the congregation's protector, assistant pastor and catechist, was named *Vorsteher* or *Ordinarius*, an ecclesiastical title which went beyond the usual noble power to appoint a minister to a parish and might reasonably be translated as CEO.

More than a month passed, and then, on August 5th Zinzendorf joined fourteen of his Moravian Brethren in an extraordinary nightlong prayer session, and on the 10th, the pastor of the manorial congregation at nearby Berthelsdorf, Johann

[10] *Herrschaftliche Gebote und Verbote* [Manorial Injunctions and Prohibitions], in Hans-Christoph Hahn & Hellmut Reichel, with Kai Dose ... et al., eds., *Zinzendorf und die Herrnhuter Brüder: Quellen zur Geschichte der Brüder-Ünität von 1722 bis 1760*, Hamburg: F. Wittig, 1977, p70–75.

[11] Saxony was full of music, most of it in Lutheran churches. In 1727, in Leipzig, Saxony, Johann Sebastian Bach was in his fourth year training the choir and composing and performing a Lutheran church cantata a week, at the Thomaskirche. Pietists thought Bach's music too complex and attention-getting, which is one of the reasons he had limited his stay as organist in Mühlhausen to one year, 1707–08.

[12] Or "*Brotherly Union and Agreement* of the Brethren from Bohemia and Moravia and Others, Binding Them to Walk According to the Apostolic Rule," in Emilie Griffin & Peter C. Erb, eds., *The Pietists: Selected Writings*, Mahwah, NJ: Paulist Press, 2006; San Francisco, CA: HarperSanFrancisco, 2006, p155–163. German original in Hahn & Reichel, eds., 1977, p75–80.

[13] Evangelische Brüder-Unität or Herrnhuter Brüdergemeine. Weinlick, p. 74.

Andreas Rothe, a Pietist Lutheran whom the Count had appointed to the living in 1722, had a public conversion experience, complete with a sudden prostration, in the middle of a service at Herrnhut.

> Pastor Rothe was so overcome by God's nearness during an afternoon service at Herrnhut, that he threw himself on the ground during prayer and called to God with words of repentance as he had never done before. The congregation was moved to tears and continued until midnight, praising God and singing.[14]

The day after, August 11, Berthelsdorf's Pastor Rothe invited the Herrnhuters to a joint "love feast" with his congregation at Berthelsdorf on the 13th. (The "love feast," or αγαπη in Gospel Greek, was a highly informal communion meal, a mass in the manner of the earliest Christians, which was then becoming a characteristic rite for Pietists and other incipient evangelicals.) Pastor Rothe began the day at Herrnhut with an invitational sermon to the Herrnhut congregation, after which everyone walked the mile to Berthelsdorf, where, on Wednesday evening, the 13th of August, the love feast duly took place, harmonized with choral singing, uniting the newly covenanted Unity of Brethren with the neighboring village congregations of Berthelsdorf and Hennersdorf. Pastor Johan Süss of Hennersdorf gave the canonical absolution from sin, and consecrated the bread and the wine, with Rothe joining the congregation. Prayers were said for the wayward Herrnhuter Brothers, Melchior Nitschmann and Christian David, then on mission in Sorau, Hungary. (Nitschmann and David, it later transpired, had gone repentant to a missionary in Sorau that same morning to retract David's earlier schismatic views, and had been moved to fall to their knees in prayer.) The event was celebrated by Renewed Moravianism almost immediately as its birthday. For Zinzendorf, who probably presided benignly as Ordinarius, and for many others then and since, August 13, 1727, was this community's "Pentecost,"[15] the event by which the Moravians became the vessel of God's grace and vanguard of the new evangelical movement in Protestant Christianity—and of the Counter-Enlightenment in the West.

Almost immediately there was a new-style conversion. An eleven-year old Herrnhut girl, Susannah Kühnel, who had been overheard by the neighboring Liebich children, seeking grace and "the salvation of her soul with strong crying and tears," became so absorbed in prayer for three days following the epochal love feast that she neglected to eat. Finally, on August 17th, "having passed through a severe spiritual struggle," Susannah came to her father and announced, "Now I am become a child of God; now I know how my mother felt and feels."[16] Susannah, of course, became a leader of the "great revival" among the Moravians of Herrnhut, and the date of her conversion would be remembered with an annual Children's Festival,

---

[14] GLIMPSES, #37(1998).

[15] Spangenberg, *Leben Zinzendorfs*, v3, p436, cited by Stoeffler; Weinlick, p78–79.

[16] This is Jacob Liebich's account, given many years later, as quoted in Joseph Edmund Hutton, *History of the Moravian Church*, Book III—*The Rule of the Germans*, Ch 2, "The Fight for the Gospel, Or, Moravians and Rationalists, 1775–1800" @ http://www.everydaycounselor.com/hutton/iii2.htm.

including special children's religious rites that went on annually for over forty years.[17] Though Enlightenment thinking might characterize such conversions as childish superstition, and twentieth-century minds suspect child abuse, this evangelical tradition by which the unformed and the uninformed were most apt to experience grace, had a long history by 1727, buttressed by a scriptural warrant from the Psalms, "Out of the mouths of babes and sucklings hast thou ordained strength,"[18] a verse which has continued to assure the children and the ignorant among evangelicals that, when it comes to grace, they may be especially favored by God.

Finally, on August 12, 1729, Zinzendorf presented yet another constitutional document to his Herrnhuter dependents, the *Notariats-Instrument*, whereby 83 Herrnhuter men of 47 families, the lord of the manor (Zinzendorf), the German pastor (Rothe), the Bohemian pastor of Grosshennersdorf, and the justice of Berthelsdorf, already a legal community with a town meeting, a church council, a communal court, and elders, agreed to the membership requirements for the congregation. Members were to be called "Brethren" and "Sisters" (with the names "Bohemian" and "Moravian" disowned as sectarian) and they prudently claimed loyalty to the Augsburg Confession of the Lutheran faith.[19] Nevertheless, the first of its seven conditions for membership was "conversion" (second birth), the sixth was that the grace which inspired such a conversion could not be inherited, and the seventh was that spiritual truth was more important than life.[20] Ratified on 27 September, it was the third and last document formalizing the Herrnhut experiment.[21] Zinzendorf had created—or taken advantage of—an intentional community based on immediate accesses of grace, harking back to the earliest days of the Reformation. He had done it not only with shared enthusiasm and ecstasy, but equally by handing down law. Despite the central place of music in Moravian ritual, the consequences of these two—ecstasy and law—would not always be in harmony.

Count Nicolaus Ludwig (1700–1760), Graf und Herr von Zinzendorf und Pottendorf, Disciple or Ordinary of the Unity of Brethren/Renewed Moravian Church is surely one of the most unexpected characters of the eighteenth century. He had been born in the last year of the previous century, on the 26th of May, in Dresden, the capital of Saxony. Six weeks later, his father had died, and he had been eventually raised in Dresden, but not by his mother. Doing the honors for the infant Count was his mother's mother, Henrietta von Gerstorff (or Gersdorf) of the manor of Grosshennersdorf, a woman of abundant, though unconventional piety. Her faith,

[17] The children's rites, but not the Festival, were abandoned by the decision of the Moravian annual meeting, or synod, of 1769.

[18] *Psalm* 8:2, quoted by Jesus in *Matthew* 21:16. We shall find a love of simplicity—and simpletons—in Hasidic Judaism as well.

[19] Zinzendorf reportedly said of this: "I should certainly have been no friend to Luther if I had let this opportunity slip of uniting the brethren with us." (in Spangenberg, *Leben Zinzendorfs*, tr., Jackson, p82, in Weinlick, p82).

[20] Weinlick, p82.

[21] Weinlick, p81.

in fact, was Pietism, a renewed Lutheranism, and she had gone so far as to enlist the aged Pietist leader, Philipp Jakob Spener, as the baby's godfather.[22]

Zinzendorf had no sudden conversion and never remembered his own life in the Pietist terms of struggle (*Busskampf*) and breakthrough (*Durchbruch*). Grace to him, as to Augustine, was pretty well irresistible, nor did he think there was much one could do by oneself that would bring it on. It had come to him from his grandmother's nurture, a "continual affective response" rather than the once-for-all conversion favored by Pietists,[23] and though centered theologically on Christ's redemption, never excluded the basic Biblical faith.[24] As a child Zinzendorf had been pious to the point of what must have been priggishness. When he finally got around to getting ordained as a minister by the Lutherans in 1734, he explained to those who examined him for the post:

> I was but ten years old when I began to direct my companions to Jesus, as their Redeemer. My deficiency in knowledge was compensated by sincerity. Now I am thirty-four; and though I have made various experiences; yet in the main my mind has undergone no change. My zeal has not cooled. I reserve to myself liberty of conscience; it agrees with my internal call to the ministry. Yet, I am not a free thinker. I love and honor the [established] church, and shall frequently seek her counsels. I will continue as heretofore, to win souls for my precious Saviour, to gather his sheep, bid guests, and hire servants for him. More especially I shall continue, if the Lord please, to devote myself to the service of that congregation whose servant I became in 1727. Agreeably to her orders, under her protection, enjoying her care, and influenced by her spirit, I shall go to distant nations, who are ignorant of Jesus and of redemption in his blood [...][25]

According to one biographer, he "could not fit" the conversion pattern of struggle-breakthrough to his own experience. Even if he could have done so, he objected to ascribing uniformity to God's ways of dealing with individuals."[26] Grace could come to anyone at any time in any one of a thousand ways; his job, he thought, was to open the possibilities to as many people as he could. That, of course, was the double commitment by which self-described "evangelicals" recognize each other today: individual and irresistible grace, and spreading the word about it.

At the normally enthusiastic age of fifteen, Zinzendorf and two fellow-students had founded a society hopefully called the Order of the Grain of Mustard Seed with the grand goal of propagating Christianity in the world (Pietist and Protestant Christianity, of course). Within a month of Herrnhut's great inspiration of August, 1727, the members of the little congregation of survivors and exiles were undertaking a vast program of missions, ecumenically first to other Christians and then to non-Christians. Zinzendorf had probably first heard about "missionaries" when he was ten, and enrolled in the illustrious Pietist school of August Hermann Francke.

---

[22] Stoeffler, p133; Stoeffler, ed., p125.

[23] Zinzendorf, *London Sermons* (1753) cited in Stoeffler, p144.

[24] Zinzendorf, *London Sermons* (1753) cited in Stoeffler, p145.

[25] Zinzendorf, statement to examiners for ministry at Tübingen, 17 December, 1734, in Weinlick, p119–120.

[26] Weinlick, p113.

Francke had sent two Pietist missionaries out in 1706, four years before Zinzendorf's arrival, one to the Danish East Indies, the other to the Malabar Coast of India. The great seventeenth-century rationalist Leibniz had argued for Christian expansion in *Novissima Linica*, one of his uncountable learned papers.

But this was small potatoes. Not since the Jesuits in the sixteenth century had Christianity been seriously spread by missionaries, and Protestant Christianity had hardly been spread at all.[27] All its travels had been not to challenge persecution, but to escape it, a Protestant habit changed by the Moravians in a way that is with us still. At the end of September, 1727, a pair of Herrnhuters Gottlieb Wried and Andrew Beyer, were on their way around politically divided Germany, from Lichtenstein to Bavaria, with Beyer going on to Teschen in Silesia. At Jena's Pietist-inspired university, the two missionaries contacted professors Buddeus and Spangenberg, together with their students. Theology Professor August Gottlieb Spangenberg not only became a convert but emerged later as the movement's leading scholar and historian, and one of his Jena students, Peter Böhler, would one day put no less a personage than John Wesley on the road to evangelical conversion. At the same time Brothers Christian David and David Nitschmann (one of dozens of Moravian Nitschmanns and a future bishop) left Hungary for Austria, and another Brother took their place. Still other Brothers set off for Switzerland and the German states of Württemberg, the Palatinate and Pomerania on the Baltic Sea.[28] Three more left central Europe to go to England in an effort to enlist the Church of England's Society for the Propagation of Christian Knowledge. Another went to Stockholm to inspire the Swedish Lutherans, and two more to Reval and Riga to do the same for the Estonians and Latvians in Russia.

There were laws and treaties to make such missions difficult, a legacy of the patchwork peace that had finally stanched the overwhelming bloodshed of the Reformation; but they did not stop the Herrnhuters. Two Brethren, Melchior Nitschmann and George Schmidt, went back to the long-ago birthplace of the movement, Moravia, only to be thrown into prison for preaching heterodoxy. Nitschmann died in the Moravian jail in 1729, but when Schmidt got out alive after six years he immediately set out on a mission to West Africa.[29] In February, 1728, missionaries' letters were read aloud to the homebodies in Herrnhut from some 100 distant places, including Turkey, Ethiopia, Lapland, Greenland and Siberia; subsequent repeats of the ceremony resulted in a custom of Saturday service each month for mission reports. The eighteenth century in world history is often characterized as the age of the Atlantic trade basin; and the Moravian project demonstrates that the Counter-Enlightenment was as keen to spread out around that basin as the Enlightenment was. By 1736, there were Moravian missions among the rebel French Huguenots in the Cévennes, three Moravian missionaries in Dutch Suriname and Berbice

---

[27] Kenneth Scott Latourette, *A History of the Expansion of Christianity*, Vol. 3: *Three Centuries of Advance AD 1500-AD 1800*, New York: Harper, 1939, p42.

[28] Weinlick, p88.

[29] Weinlick, p88.

(Guyana) in South America, and the indispensable Spangenberg himself had sailed to North America, where he and his mission got to Savannah, Georgia, in 1735 (with fellow passengers John and Charles Wesley), only two years after its founding. Spangenberg's mission, kicked out by Georgia, founded Nazareth, Bethlehem, and Emmaus, Pennsylvania, in the 1740s. By 1737, black and white Moravians were preaching in Elmina in West Africa, Cape Colony in South Africa, and among the slaves of South Carolina. In 1739 they reached Ceylon and Algeria; in 1740 the Mahican Indians of New York; in 1754, Jamaica.[30] In the 1750s Spangenberg, now a bishop and Zinzendorf's most important deputy, returned with a mission which founded Moravian communities in North Carolina. The effort was at least as ambitious and nearly as global as the Jesuit missions to the east two centuries before, except that the Moravians were offering ecstatic experience instead of a rite or a doctrine, not baptism but grace, not the Trinity but second birth.

That same year, Zinzendorf began his own astonishing career as a Brethren missionary, hoping to make his new syncretic Christianity universal. He was already a traveler in religion. In 1719, at age 19, he had gone to Paris to investigate a possible rapprochement between the augustinian Catholicism called Jansenism, then under state sanction in France, and his own augustinian Lutheran Pietism. He had had a long conversation with six jansenist clerics, two priests, two bishops and two Cardinals, including Noailles who had officially appealed against the anti-Jansenist sanction in 1717, 1718 and the year they met. Though there had been some agreement about grace, no one was converted.[31] Now, in November, 1727, Zinzendorf set off from Herrnhut to complete the conversion of Prince Christian Ernest of the small German state of Saalfeld, stopping in Jena, where he coached the new converts left behind by Wried and Beyer, and in three other towns, Rudelstadt, Bayreuth and Coburg.[32] The next year he went to both Pietist universities, Jena and Halle, and the next he was patching up quarrels in other German Moravian communities. By 1731 he was on a mission to Denmark (agreed to after a drawing of lots by his Herrnhut congregation), and it was on this errand that he met Count Laurwig of Copenhagen and his body servant "Anton" (Anthony Ulrich), a baptized African Christian from the Danish West Indies and brother of Anna who was still enslaved there. Zinzendorf brought Anton back to Herrnhut to call for missions to the West Indies sugar islands (a call that, as we have seen, was answered). Two years later in 1733 Zinzendorf was preaching in Stralsund, Sweden. In 1735, having finally taken time to be ordained a Lutheran minister, he paid second visits to Lutheran Denmark and Sweden, and then in a chilly November, a few days before the birth of his ninth, and fifth surviving, child, he began what he called a "witness journey," on foot and servantless in ordinary clothes, through south Germany and Switzerland, including Bayreuth, Zürich and Nuremberg.

[30] Weinlick, p213.

[31] Weinlick, p45; Beyreuther, *Eine Biographie*, pp. 35–40; Stoeffler p? Stoeffler puts the Noailles meeting in 1720.

[32] Weinlick, p89.

Banished in 1736 from his home state of Saxony for deviating from the doctrine of the established Lutheran church, holding unauthorized conventicles and enticing peasants away from the lands of other Counts, Zinzendorf set out from Herrnhut at midnight on the fifteenth of February on a journey to the Netherlands, catching up with his wife, his daughter Benigna and twelve others on the road, and visiting Jena on the way.[33] In Amsterdam, he arranged to settle Moravians at Herrendyk which would be, with the neighboring congregation of Zeist, the mother congregation of Moravianism in Holland for over two centuries, and a base for missions to Greenland, Abyssinia (Ethiopia), the Americas, the Near East, and the doubtlessly exasperated Jews of Amsterdam.[34] In 1736 he was all over Germany again at the head of what he called his Pilgrim Congregation, founding a new headquarters congregation, called Herrnhaag (Lord's Place), outside of Saxony in Wetterau (Wetteravia) and preaching in the old imperial capital of Frankfurt-am-Main. In Frankfurt, Moravians would impute grace to many, including the mother of the poet Goethe, and Susannah von Klettenberg, the model for the "beautiful soul" of Goethe's early bestseller, the pioneering sentimental novel, *Wilhelm Meister*.[35]

In 1737, Zinzendorf founded a society of the saved in London which would gain a charter from the Church of England, and help initiate the Methodist evangelical movement by inspiring George Whitefield and the Wesley brothers. That winter, now an ordained bishop, the Count was in Prussia, where, having been refused the pulpits of the Calvinist state church, he was preaching in rented quarters to crowds that spilled onto the streets of Berlin. Back home in Herrnhut by the summer of 1738, his exile from Saxony temporarily rescinded, he was in time to greet the just-converted Methodist apostle, John Wesley. The following December, he sailed from Amsterdam on that flying inspection tour of the Danish West Indies with which this chapter began.

With Moravian missions in America flourishing, Zinzendorf went west again in 1741, accepting the vote of his Moravian annual synod that he go to Pennsylvania, and resigning as bishop in order to carry out the commission. He remained for more than a year, in the ineffective incognito of an untitled gentleman, celebrating love feasts on the wild frontier in the new Moravian settlements like Nazareth and Bethlehem, amateurishly bushwacking into the wilderness to baptize Indians, and holding conference after conference of American clergymen in an all but fruitless attempt to bring the already bewildering array of Christian denominations in America under Moravian primacy in his increasingly capacious tent.

Not long after his return from western Pennsylvania in 1743, Zinzendorf was in the West's far east, Poland and Latvia. For the next fifteen years of his life, though he never again traveled so far away, he was almost constantly on the move, trying to administer two mother congregations, Herrnhut and Herrnhaag, in two different

[33] Weinlick, p126.

[34] Weinlick, p126–27.

[35] Weinlick, p134. Goethe never became a member himself, but he would be a frequent visitor to this congregation.

German states, together with a far-flung network of other congregations and missions stretching from St. Petersburg to the Cape of Good Hope, Greenland to Suriname, as he trolled for conversions from members of all religions (including Dutch Jews and French Catholics), sought alliances between Moravianism and every other form of Protestantism, and attempted to secure toleration for Moravians under the laws of as many western nations as he could.

Nor did he ever stop building new communities. In 1753 Spangenberg, the evangelizer of Savannah who was now a Moravian bishop, signed the papers in London for the purchase by Zinzendorf's Herrnhuter governing board of nearly 100,000 acres in western North Carolina, to which Bishop Spangenberg gave the name Wachovia in honor of another of Zinzendorf's estates, Die Wachau in Saxony's Wach valley. Moravians from Pennsylvania, Germany, the West Indies and Maine came to Wachovia to found congregational communities there whose secularized descendants still dot the map of the Winston-Salem tobacco country: Bethabara (1753), Bethania (1759), Friedberg (Peace Mountain, in German), Friedland (Peace Land), Hope and Salem (1780).[36] They were racially integrated. Wachovia's habit of blowing conch shells to rouse the congregation for meetings or alarms was learned from Africans in the West Indies.[37] In 1742, the newly settled Moravian settlement of Bethlehem decided to hire non-Moravian black slaves from the West Indies as hired hands for Nazareth, Gnadenthal and themselves; but to pay them wages and to allow them, if they received grace, the citizenship of church membership.[38] Rebecca Freundlich of the Danish West Indies lived to join the Unmarried Women's Choir at Herrnhaag itself and, after marrying again and being ordained a deaconess, the Married Women's Choir in 1745. Following that she went with her new husband on a mission to his native West Africa, where she ended her very Moravian life.

A year later in 1754, a preaching mission at Warwick, Pennsylvania, colonized from Bethlehem, began its life as a permanent Moravian congregation under the new name of Lititz, after a village 100 miles east of Prague near the border of Moravia and Silesia which Bohemian Brethren exiles had settled before Herrnhut.[39] Moravians also settled Graceham, Maryland, Schoenbrunn and Gnadenhutten ("Grace Houses"), Ohio, and Hope, New Jersey. In 1799 the Moravian Society for the Propagation of the Faith Among the Heathen met in Salem, North Carolina, to consider a mission to convert the Cherokee Nation, and within two years they began

[36] Gardiner, p7; Sensbach, p47.

[37] Sensbach, p55.

[38] "And should we be compelled to keep hired hands, it would be preferable to buy negroes from Saint Thomas and employ them as regular servants who would receive wages…" (Hamilton, ed., *Bethlehem Diary*, I, 1742–1744, p105–106, in Sensbach, p52–53) How commerce moved in on Moravian religious community is described in detail in Katherine Carté Engel's *Religion and Profit: Moravians in Early America* (Philadelphia: U. of Pennsylvania Press, 2009).

[39] Weinlick, p213.

building the Springplace Mission in northwestern Georgia to serve as the project's headquarters and home community.[40] And that was just in North America.

As the movement grew, so did criticism and opposition. Opposition, of which there was plenty, confused Zinzendorf; but his typical reaction to it was more curiosity than dismissal, and he was not the sort of doctrinaire who insisted on words rather than experience. He seems to have believed that his highly Christocentric theology and experiential liturgy, his focus on grace, was or would become the linchpin of a reunion of all Protestant—indeed, perhaps all Christian—denominations. When his own Lutherans, both orthodox and Pietists, and others, beginning as soon as "the middle of the year 1728" objected to the novelty of a noble in charge of a religion, to his apparently open relations with Catholics[41] and to his outsized zeal, Zinzendorf changed nothing. When separatist and radical allies of the likes of John Conrad Dippel, John Frederick Rock and Caspar Schwenkfeld, were bothered by his promotion of unordained laypeople to the posts of missionary, service leader and church administrator,[42] he did not exactly ignore them but he again changed nothing.

Zinzendorf did, however, acknowledge one serious mistake and reverse one of his largest initiatives, the one recorded by him as the "Sifting Period" and by history as the "blood and wounds" episode, an overindulgence in metaphor that nearly cost the Count his movement. It began, he once asserted, in 1734.

> Since that year 1734 the propitiatory sacrifice of Jesus became our special and only testimony, our universal remedy against all evil in teaching and practice, and remains so to eternity.[43]

That year Zinzendorf had yet another moment of feeling and wrote yet another of his hundreds of hymns for the Moravian choirs.[44]

> Jesus, our glorious head and chief,
> Sweet object of our heart's belief!
> O let us in thy nail prints see
> Our pardon and election free.[45]

The "nail prints" were, of course, the wounds of the Passion, or redemptive suffering of Jesus during the Crucifixion—the Crucifixion being the basic means of grace for the Renewed Moravians as it has been for so many other kinds of Christians. Zinzendorf began recommending prayers, songs and rites to his entire community which not only emphasized but personalized the wounds and the blood, equating them with freely available saving grace. One early historian of Moravianism

---

[40] Rowena McClinton, ed., *The Moravian Springplace Mission to the Cherokees*, Volume 1, 1805–1813, U. of Nebraska Press.

[41] Weinlick, p104. He never did send his letter to Pope Benedict XIII.

[42] Weinlick, p102.

[43] in Jacob Wilhelm Verbeek, *Des Grafen von Zinzendorf, Leben und Character*, p142, in Weinlick, p115. Weinlick himself (p198–205) and Stoeffler (p151) put the stronger focus on 1740.

[44] Weinlick, p116, 198.

[45] in Weinlick, p116.

attributed the new metaphorical line to what Zinzendorf had learned from the luxuriant variety of religions in the wilds of Pennsylvania: that the grace to believe and to be forgiven for one's sins, plus the further grace to live on without sinning (this was beginning to be called "sanctification") could not and must not be attributed to anything in Christianity beyond that redemptive suffering on the cross.[46]

To some extent Zinzendorf's new focus picked up on a long medieval tradition of devotion to the Passion. To imagine bloody holes in Jesus' palms and feet, a bleeding scalp under the crown of thorns, or the slashes made on his back by the scourge or in his side by the spear of the Roman guards had been a central theme in medieval art that continued, especially in Germany, well into the sixteenth century. (And of course, the appeal of the brutality has been perennial, as witnessed by Mel Gibson's 2004 movie, *The Passion of the Christ.*) A twelfth-century Limoges sermon pictured a dove flying into Christ's side wound, and the thirteenth century had produced St. Bernard's hymn, "O sacred head sore wounded." (Bernard's Cistercian order had a devotion identifying the side wound as the site of Eve's extraction and likening it to a birth canal.) There were also the passion plays, and the Incarnation cults of the 13th and 14th centuries, rediscovered by Caroline Bynum.[47] In the fourteenth century the English solitary anchoress Julian of Norwich (c1342–1414) had even counted 660,000 wounds in the crucified Christ (the thorns and scourge-ends mostly); but the fact is that, despite the medieval focus on the Passion it was unusual, even in the Middle Ages to see the Passion as a ticket to heaven. Grünewald's famous painting of it, on the altarpiece at Isenheim, was intended to provide the suffering inmates of a hospital for the dying with a sense that Jesus knew and had shared their pain, lest they give up the hope of salvation.

In any case, the less exuberant eighteenth century was not imagining anywhere near this much blood. It seems to have had appeal for the American Indians, but Zinzendorf's verbal metaphors struck the culture of his contemporaries in Enlightenment Europe as extravagant, much as the images in Mel Gibson's film would strike audiences two centuries later. Zinzendorf himself described his saved Moravians as "little blood worms in the sea of grace."[48] Eldress Anna Nitschmann wrote, "It is well with me in Jesus' side hole."[49] She had already written in a circular letter to believers, "Like a poor little worm, I desire to withdraw myself into his

[46] David Cranz (1723–1777), *The Ancient & Modern History of the Brethren* [*Alte und Neue Brüder-Historie oder kurz gefaßte Geschichte der Evangelischen Brüder-Unität in den älteren Zeiten und insonderheit in dem gegenwärtigen Jahrhundert*, Barby, 1771], Transl. Into English with Notes By Benjamin la Trobe, London: W. & A. Strahan, 1780, p368, quoted in Weinlick, p203).

[47] Caroline Bynum's pioneering study, *Holy Feast and Holy Fast: The Religious Significance of Food to Medieval Women* (The New Historicism: Studies in Cultural Poetics, 1, Berkeley: U. of California Press, pb, January 7, 1988) mentions the Incarnation cults. Her *The Resurrection of the Body in Western Christianity, 200–1336*, (NY: Columbia U.P., 1995) is also of interest on this point. *Wonderful Blood: Theology and Practice in Late Medieval Northern Germany and Beyond* (Philadelphia: U. of Pennsylvania Press, 2007), her newest book, is even more relevant, a study of devotions based on the blood of Christ in a German and European context.

[48] Zinzendorf, 1742, in Weinlick, p199.

[49] Anna Nitschmann, 1742, in Weinlick, p199.

wounds and nailprints [...]"[50] A year or so later, Zinzendorf formed the Order of the Little Fools, encouraged to behave like children since God had revealed himself "not to the wise and prudent, but to babes." Members addressed the Count and Countess as "Papa" and "Mama" or "Little Papa" and "Little Mama" and addressed Christ as "Brother Lambkin."[51] When the Little Fools spoke of themselves as "little doves flying about in the atmosphere of the cross," it might seem merely sentimental to us, not to say tacky; but when they called themselves:

> "little bees who suck on the wounds of Christ, who feel at home in the side hole and crawl in deep,"
> "little fish swimming in the bed of blood"
> "bloodthirsty beasts"
> "blood leeches"
> "wound worms"
> "side-hole hearts"[52]

there was clearly a move into a very different range of metaphor.

The bloody side-wound soon became everything from the cup of communion wine-blood to the gate of heaven, or more spectacularly, from a place for the Moravian believer to imagine settling in and making himself at home, to the birth canal of the New Birth. To a twentieth-century mind it can smack of the psychotic, though it clearly was not. In fact, it is not sadomasochism, but rather sentimentalism, something that was to become more familiar after artistic and literary Romanticism had opened the nineteenth century.[53] To an educated eighteenth-

---

[50] Anna Nitschmann, 1740, in Weinlick, p199.

[51] In his later history of the Moravians, Bishop Spangenberg, no friend of the "Little Fools" and other theological novelties, described it thus: "He made a particular covenant with the brethren and sisters who were the most like him, which had reference solely to a simple and childlike deportment. They agreed to expect every blessing from the love of Jesus, believingly adhere to his word, filially cast all care upon him, and heartily rejoice in him." (in Weinlick, p199).

[52] Translation quoted in Weinlick, p199–200. It is not, I think, accidental that certain cantatas of Bach come to mind, like "Mein Herz schwimmt im Blut," which translates as "My heart swims in blood."

[53] The English hymn "Rock of Ages" (1776), by an Anglican turned Calvinist named Augustus Toplady, envisions God in much the same way.

> Rock of Ages, cleft for me,
> Let me hide myself in Thee;
> Let the water and the blood,
> From Thy wounded side which flowed,
> Be of sin the double cure
> Save from wrath; and make me pure.
> Not the labor of my hands
> Can fulfill Thy law's demands;
> Could my zeal no respite know,
> Could my tears forever flow,
> All for sin could not atone;
> Thou must save, and Thou alone.

century mind, both religious and "philosophic," the blood-and-wounds theology was inappropriate, possibly bizarre, and (to those to whom heresy still meant something) vaguely heretical.

That did not daunt Count Zinzendorf, at least not yet. In 1744 he visited Gnadenberg (Grace Mountain) and composed *The Litany of the Life, Suffering and Wounds of Our Lord Jesus Christ*, prayers and responses on the blood and wounds, which included a not very successful effort to connect the growing cult with the venerable Christian communion through which a worshiper drinks blood that points to resurrection.[54] Three years later, in 1747, he gave thirty-four sermons on his litany at Herrnhaag which compared the Trinity to a family with the Holy Spirit as Mother, and envisioned the Church as the "visible wound-church," born from Christ's side wound, and thus the daughter-in-law of the Father and Mother, complete with sexual terminology. One distracted theologian characterized this trope as "undue exaltation of marriage as the symbol of the marriage between Christ and the soul of the believer." Zinzendorf's twelfth supplement (1748) to the now voluminous Moravian hymnbook became notorious for blood-and-wounds imagery. At Herrnhaag especially, Moravian simplicity yielded to biblical scenes decorating chapels, "tableaux and transparencies" to illustrate the suffering on the cross, and a multiplication of festivals to as many as forty a year, including the birthdays of Zinzendorf and members of his family.[55] Prostration before the communion table, rather than mere kneeling, became a reinforced ritual.[56]

What Zinzendorf and his defenders called the "Sifting Period" of Moravian theology[57] came to a head in 1748 when the Count appointed his son, Christian Renatus (the middle name is Latin for "born again") to the pastoral leadership of the mother congregation now at Herrnhaag. It would come to an end in 1750 when he fired him. Fast-rising Christian Renatus, leader at 17 of a Single Brethren choir, ordained an Elder and appointed pastor at 21, went head over heels for blood and wounds during his brief tenure, and made Herrnhaag its most important source. Most affected was probably the newest of the mission congregations at distant Bethlehem, Pennsylvania.[58] Least affected was the original congregation at Herrnhut. Soon the trend alienated other Moravian congregations in Sweden, the Baltic states, and Tübingen, Germany, and non-Moravian Protestants began preaching and publishing critical pamphlets.[59] Zinzendorf himself heard criticism from several of his closest

---

[54] Weinlick, p200.

[55] Weinlick, p200.

[56] Craig Atwood, "Understanding Zinzendorf's Blood and Wounds Theology," American Historical Association, Seattle, January, 2005; *Journal of Moravian History* 1(Fall 2006) pp. 31–47.

[57] Weinlick, p198–205.

[58] Weinlick, p201–02.

[59] Weinlick, p201–02. Attacks included Johann Philipp Fresnius (1705–1761), *Tried and True Reports of Things Herrnhutian, 1747–51*, 1747. (Stoeffler, p?); 1749?, ??, *Serious Objections to the Pernicious Doctrine of the Moravians and Methodists*, 1749 (Weinlick, p214);??, *A Kindly and Friendly Letter to the People Called Moravians in Derbyshire, by a curate whose church has emptied to Moravianism*, 1749 (Weinlick, p214); "A Lover of the Light" [John Wesley], *Contents of a*

followers, older Moravian leaders like Peter Böhler, Christian David, John Watteville, the elder whom Christian Renatus had replaced at Herrnhaag; but as yet the Count wasn't listening.[60] In November, 1748, Zinzendorf's right-hand man in North America, August Spangenberg, resigned to protest the assignment of Bishop named Camerhof as his assistant in 1747, bringing blood and wounds with him from Herrnhaag When the economy of Bethlehem, Pennsylvania, was nearly wrecked by another bishop named Nitschmann, who had led the Third Sea Congregation to America, 120 strong from Wetterau (Herrnhaag).[61] Spangenberg retired and returned to Europe.

> I myself was much displeased with him [Zinzendorf] at the time, and he no less with me, because he knew my sentiments; and this went so far, on both sides, that it could not remain concealed from the church, though we both loved each other dearly.[62]

Zinzendorf only began to lose confidence in the new direction when he visited London in December, 1748, and heard more criticism, this time from a Herrnhuter elder with a title, Karl von Peistel.[63] A couple of months later on 10 February, 1749, convinced at last, Zinzendorf wrote a letter to all the Moravian congregations in which, pope-like, he ordered a retreat from blood-and-wounds, and advised his son Christian Renatus to step down as pastor of Herrnhaag and come to him in London. He suppressed the Twelfth Supplement to *Hymns*, and sent Bishops David Nitschmann and Leonard Dober to inspect the churches in continental Europe.[64] In November, when Watteville and Spangenberg returned from America, Zinzendorf sent them to join Bishops Nitschmann and Dober in their inspection tour to root Herrnhaag's theological influence out of the churches.[65] He did not give up on his once-only version of ecstasy as conversion; but eventually, with some reluctance, he began purging his own writings of "excesses."

According to the Moravians' eighteenth-century historian, David Cranz, Zinzendorf's detour into blood-and-wounds was caused by his insistence that grace

---

Folio History, 1749 (against Zinzendorf, *Acta Fratrum Unitatis in Anglia*, calling Moravians heretics and deceivers and criticizing "blood and wounds" imagery) (Weinlick, p213). Weinlick collects (pp214–215) several publications from a minor pamphlet war waged four years after Zinzendorf's 1749 change of course: Henry Rimius, *A Candid Narrative of the Rise and Progress of the Herrnhuters*, 1753 (first published in German, by a former Prussian royal councillor living in London, who would follow it with four more polemics.);??, *A Short Answer to Mr. Rimius' Long Uncandid Narrative*, 1753?; Andrew Frey, *The True and Authentic Account of Andrew Frey*, 1753 (first published in German, by a former Moravian confessing the worst of the Sifting Period); Zinzendorf, *The Ordinary of the Brethren's Churches: Short and Peremptory Remarks on the Way and Manner wherein he has been hitherto Treated in Controversies*, 1753?; Zinzendorf, *The Plain Case of the Representatives of the Unitas Fratrum*, 1753?; Zinzendorf, *An Exposition, or True State of the Matters objected in England to the People known by the name of Unitas Fratrum*, 1753?

[60] Weinlick, p203.

[61] Weinlick, p201.

[62] Spangenberg in Weinlick, p204.

[63] Weinlick, p196.

[64] Weinlick, p204.

[65] Weinlick, p204.

came only once to each Christian, and that it could only enable one action—belief that Christ's suffering had saved your soul. The ability to avoid sin after finding faith, called "sanctification" by later evangelicals, was not, in Zinzendorf's view, an additional benefit of God's grace. Ministers who preached sanctification, including many he had met in America, were, in his opinion, dividing Christianity, and their reeducation could only be accomplished if they were confronted with the crucifixion.

> The ordinary had, during his abode among the various sects in Pennsylvania, acquired a further insight, than he had before into the emptiness and pernicious tendencies of all the methods of sanctification, which are not, solely and alone deduced from the merits of Jesus. On his return to Europe, [...he...] labored against it in his discourses and hymns, endeavouring fully to enthrone the merits and wounds of Jesus; and showing that not only the forgiveness of sins and salvation were to be deduced from thence, but that the cleansing from sin, and our true sanctification and preservation, flowed solely from this fountain.[66]

Zinzendorf himself, however, blamed not so much his own theological ideas, or his own ecstasies, as the undisciplined use that others in the larger church had made of them.

> The test we have gone through has been brief but fearful. I probably occasioned it by giving utterance to an idea which I have never been able to lay aside, and which I still hold, namely, that in order to enjoy all the blessings purchased by the death of Jesus, we must become children in the bottom of our hearts. I have been powerfully impressed by this idea, and have sought to inculcate it in my brethren. It found acceptance and was immediately carried into effect. But what was at first a small circle of men, who really had the spirit of children, soon grew into a large society and in a few years greatly degenerated.[67]

Some, including Zinzendorf's American biographer, John R. Weinlick, suggest that blood-and-wounds was essentially a style of religious expression characteristic of the Pietism of Zinzendorf's childhood and similar predecessors.

> The Moravians were not alone in their offense of good taste[?]. The age in which they lived produced the Berleberg Bible with its strange symbolical interpretations of the Scriptures. Older contemporaries of the Brethren, like Rock, Dippel, and Hochmann, had brought to the Pietism of southwestern Germany an extremely mystical emphasis [...] in Switzerland there was a piety with a sentimental terminology introduced by Lutz early in the century. The use of endearing diminutives in connection with religious matters was a weakness of Pietism in general. Both the French and German literature of the time reeked with sentimentality. Herrnhaag's location made it especially vulnerable to the spirit of the age.[68]

Perhaps location is indeed what tells, or language, or even date. In November, 1749, the Mennonites[69] of Gelderland in the Netherlands, who had nothing in

---

[66] David Cranz, *The Ancient & Modern History of the Brethren*, Transl. la Trobe, 1780, p368, in Weinlick, p203.

[67] Zinzendorf, quoted in Bovet, *Le Comte de Zinzendorf*, tr., John Gill, *The Banished Count*, p251, in Weinlick, p205.

[68] Weinlick, p202?

[69] Mennonites are a grace-seeking, nonviolent, Anabaptist (anti-infant-baptism) Protestant Christian sect founded by a Dutchman, Menno Simons (1496–1561) in the 1540s, and well represented among the Pennsylvania "Dutch" (*deutsch*, or German) today.

common with the Moravians except Protestantism, were described as going into regular ecstasies in their private prayer meetings.

> They would sigh, groan, and bawl. They made the strangest contortions, and wrung their hands with violence. A cold sweat overspread their faces. They were dying with drought and could hardly drink. They breathed with difficulty; their whole body was convulsed. They were exactly in the situation of a person afflicted with the falling sickness, for they could neither walk nor support themselves. [They would exclaim] "Alas what shall I do? Ah, give me Jesus; I want Jesus."[70]

But the English establishment, who had stopped producing religious revolutionaries in the seventeenth century, and acquired their new reputation for robust common sense and equanimity in the 18th, thought the Moravians shameful. In 1754, a Bishop of the protestant Church of England, obviously an Enlightened sort, published a short book on how bad things were with the Moravians:

> The filthy dreamers have been so evidently detected, their immoralities and impieties so manifested unto all men that their shame is sufficiently conspicuous, and no serious and good person, no sincere Christian especially can look upon them in a favorable light.[71]

In the imagination's group portrait of the Enlightenment, behind his better-known contemporaries Voltaire, Dr. Johnson, Kant and Benjamin Franklin, and behind even the bishops of established churches, Zinzendorf might appear as the obscure but amiable long-haired and wigless eccentric in the twelfth row, near the praying poet Christopher "Kit" Smart, the noble physicist Emilie du Châtelet, the literary penitent Sor Juana Inés de la Cruz, the transvestite Chevalier d'Eon, Swedenborg the visionary, Mesmer the animal magnetist and perhaps Cagliostro the magician. Eighteenth-century studies in anglo-american universities never touch him, and the fact that the eighteenth century was the fountainhead of Christian (as well as Judaic and Islamic) evangelicalism only makes those professors more wary. Perhaps the closest they come to naturalizing Zinzendorf is in the debate among literature professors about where to put the visionary poet William Blake, a debate whose outcome inevitably turns on just how crazy you may think Blake was, or how safe you may feel in sweeping him over the threshold from the eighteenth century when he was born into the "Romantic" nineteenth century when he died. Since Zinzendorf died forty years before the nineteenth century began, he can no more be dressed in Romantic motley than explained away as a conventionally pious Victorian. Like Blake, Zinzendorf must remain in the eighteenth century and tangle with the liberals, *philosophes*, deists, atheists, skeptics and rationalists who set the tone for the Enlightenment as it has been handed down to us.

In fact, Zinzendorf has many traits in common with Blake; and if he reported fewer of his visions, he wrote just as much poetry, most of it in the form of songs and hymns for religious services. Zinzendorf was, in fact, the only known theologian who was also a missionary to Caribbean slaves and North American Indians, the founder and administrator of a new church and a Count of the Holy Roman

[70] Stinstra, *Essay on Fanaticism*, 1774, in Knox, *Enthusiasm*, p389.

[71] Bishop of Exeter, *The Moravians Compared and Detected*, 1754, quoted in Weinlick, p214.

Empire. The church he founded produced leaders in its turn, men and women Zinzendorf had undertaken to train, and they taught one of the most eminent Protestant theologians of the nineteenth century (Schleiermacher), one of the most original eighteenth-century German philosophers (Herder), the greatest German writer of any century (Goethe) and of course the greatest revival preachers of the age as well as a good many of the founders of the subsequent evangelical movements in Protestant Christianity, including Methodism.

In 1757, at the urging, he said, of his board, Zinzendorf secretly married one of his traveling mission companions, Anna Nitschmann (the "little worm in Jesus' side-hole"), in Disciple House, Berthelsdorf, though it was only a year after his first wife had died and only a week after the close of the customary mourning period. Erdmuth, who had borne Zinzendorf his twelve children, had often taken over some of his administrative duties in the Moravian movement. She had also been, like the Count, a titled noble, while Anna was only a peasant's daughter and past childbearing at 42. Nevertheless, "Papa" Zinzendorf was anxious to return to his place in Herrnhut's Married People's Choir.[72] All present were told to keep the wedding secret because of the way Zinzendorf's mother, still alive, still pious, but still very much a titled noble, might react.[73] Thus did the Count's metamorphosis from Tory landed aristocrat to radical religious leader complete itself, and when he died three years later in 1760 he was laid out in a priest's surplice.[74] In the middle of the skeptics' Enlightenment, he had become the prototype and originator of the new evangelical age in the West.

Bibliography

Aalen, Leiv. 1966. *Den junge zinzendorfs teologie [Die Theologie des jungen Zinzendorf]*. Berlin/Hamburg: Lutherisches Verlagshaus. Arbeiten zur Geschichte und Theologie des Luthertums, vol. 16.

Addison, W.G. 1935. *The Renewed Church of the United Brethren, 1722–1930*. London: SPCK. www.english.umd.edu/englfac/WPeterson/ELR/full-bibliography/ rvw by E.W.W. in *English Historical Review* 50 (1935): p368–69.

Aland, Kurt. 1943. *Spener-Studien* (*Arbeiten zur Kirchengeschichte*, vol. 28 and *Arbeiten zur Geschichte des Pietismus*, vol. 1), Berlin: W. de Gruyter.

Appel, Helmut. 1964. *Phillipp Jacob Spener, Vater des Pietismus*. Berlin: Evangelische Verlaganstalt.

Atwood, Craig. 2004. *Community of the Cross: Moravian Piety in Colonial Bethlehem* (Max Kade Research Institute). University Park, PA: Penn State University Press.

[72] Weinlick, p226.

[73] Weinlick, p227.

[74] The Brotherhood is still extant and still global. Its administrative history since Zinzendorf is nicely digested in Dietrich Meyer, *Zinzendorf und die Herrnhuter Brüdergemeine: 1700–2000*, Göttingen: Vandenhoeck & Ruprecht, 2009.

Barthold, Friedrich Wilhelm (1799–1858). 1968. Die Erweckten in protestantische Deutschland wahrend des Ausgangs des 17. und der ersten Halfte des 18. Jahrhunderts. Darmstadt: Wissenschaftliche Buchgesellschaft.

Bauch, Hermann. 1974. *Die Lehre von Wirken des Heiligen Geistes im Fruhpietismus: Studien zur Pneumatologie und Eschatologie von Campegius Vitringa, Philipp Jacob Spener und Johann Albrecht Bengel* (Diss't, Mainz, 1967), Hamburg-Bergstedt: H. Reich.

Bauer, Bruno. 1849. *Einfluss des englischen Quakerthums auf die deutscher Kultur*. Berlin.

Bauman, Clarence. 1990. *The Spiritual Legacy of Hans Denck*. Including the German text as established by G. Baring & W. Fellmann. New York: E.J. Brill.

Becker, George. 1991. Pietism's confrontation with enlightenment rationalism: An examination of the relation between ascetic protestantism and science. *Journal for the Scientific Study of Religion* 30: 140.

Becker-Cantarino, Barbara. 2004. *German Literature of the Eighteenth Century: The Enlightenment and Sensibility*. Rochester: Camden House/Boydell & Brewer.

Bengel, Johann Albrecht. 1751. *Abriß der sogenannten Brüdergemeine…*

Beyreuther, F.S. Erich. 1955. *Zinzendorf und Pierre Bayle, ein Beitrag zur Frage des Verhältnisses Zinzendorfs zur Aufklärung*. Hamburg: L. Appel.

———. 1957. *Die junge Zinzendorf*. Marburg am der Lahn: Verlag der Francke-Buchhandlung.

———. 1961. *Zinzendorf und die Christenheit, 1732–1760*. Marburg an der Lahn: Verlag der Francke Buchhandlung.

———. 1962. Die Paradoxien des Glaubens: Zinzendorfs Verhältnis zu Pierre Bayle und zur Aufklärung. In *Studien zur Theologie Zinzendorfs*. Neukirchen-Uluym.

———. 1965. *Nikolaus Ludwig von Zinzendorf in Selbstzeugnisse und Bilddokumenten*. Reinbek Bei Hamburg: Rowohlt.

———. ed. 1976. *Antizinzendorfiana aus der Anfangszeit 1729–1735*. Nachdr. d. Ausg. Breslau. 1729 u. Frankfort a. M. 1743. Hildesheim, New York: Olms.

———. 1978. *Geschichte des Pietismus*. Stuttgart.

———. 1982a. *August Hermann Francke, 1663–1727. Zeuge des lebendigen Gottes*, Marburg-an-der-Lahn, 1956. Cologne.

———. 1982b. *Pietismus-Herrnhutertum-Erweckungsbewegung*. Cologne.

———. 2000. *Nikolaus Ludwig Graf von Zinzendorf Selbstzeugnissen und Bilddokumente: Eine Biographie*. Basel: Brunnen Verlag Giessen.

———. ed. *Nikolaus Ludwig von Zinzendorf. Materialien und Dokumente*. Reihe 2. *Nikolaus Ludwig Graf von Zinzendorf. Leben und Werk in Quellen und Darstellungen*, vol. 14.

Bintz, Helmut. 1979. *Nikolaus-Ludwig Graf von Zinzendorf: Dichter der christlichen Gemeinde*. Stuttgart: Quell.

Bishop, John J. 1969. Review of William J. Murtagh. Moravian architecture and town planning. *The Journal of the Society of Architectural Historians* 28 (4): 299–300. http://links.jstor.org/sici?sici=0037-9808%28196912%2928%3A4%3C299%3AMAATP%3E2.0.CO%3B2-P.

Blackwell, Jeannine. 1995. Gedoppelter Lebenslauf der Pietistinnen: autobiographische Schriften der Wiedergeburt. In *Geschriebenes Leben: Autobiographik von Frauen*, ed. M. Holdenried, 49–60. Berlin: E Schmidt.

Blanning, T.C.W., and Peter Wende. 2002. *Reform in Great Britain and Germany, 1750–1850*.

Blaufuss, Dietrich, ed. 1986. *Pietismus-Forschungen zu Phillip Jacob Spener und zum spritualistisch-radikalpietistischen Umfeld*. Frankfurt-am-Main/New York: Peter Lang.

Boehme/Böhme/Behmen, Jakob (1575–1624). 1978. *The Way to Christ* [*Weg zu Christo*]: ("On True Repentance, I. 1622 & II. 1623" "On True Resignation (*Gelassenheit*?). 1622" "On the Supersensual Life. 1622" "On Holy Prayer. 1624" "The Precious Gate. 1620" "Consolation Treatise on the Four Humors. 1624" "On the New Birth. 1622" and "The Conversation Between an *Enlightened* and *Unenlightened* Soul" 1624). Trans. by John Sparrow. London, 1648. 1st English publication of what will become *The Way to Christ* (ed. Gichtel, 1682; Trans. by Peter C. Erb. Mahwah, NJ: Paulist Press).

Bovet, Félix. 1865. *Le comte de Zinzendorf.* 3e éd. rev. et augm. Paris: Librairie Française et étrangère.

Bowman, Carl F. 1995. *Brethren Society: The Cultural Transformation of a "Peculiar People".* Baltimore, MD: Johns Hopkins University Press.

Braw, C. 1986. *Bücher im Staube: Die Theologie Johann Arndts in ihren Verhältnis zur Mystik.* New York: E.J. Brill.

Brecht, Martin. 1995. Das Aufkommen der neuen Frömmigkeitsbewegung in Deutschland. In *Die Geschichte des Pietismus*, ed. M. Brecht and K. Deppermann, vol. 1. Göttingen: Vandenhoeck und Ruprecht.

Brecht, Martin, Klaus Deppermann, and Ulrich Gäbler. 1993. *Geschichte des Pietismus.* 4 vols., vol. 1, *Der Pietismus vom siebzehnten bis zum frühen achtzehnten Jahrhundert.* Göttingen: Vandenhoeck & Ruprecht (Gebundene Ausgabe).

———. 1995. *Geschichte des Pietismus.* 4 vols., vol. 2, *Der Pietismus im achtzehnten Jahrhundert.* Göttingen: Vandenhoeck & Ruprecht (Gebundene Ausgabe)

Brethren Encyclopedia. 1983–1984. 3 vols., Brethren Encyclopedia Inc.

Brumbaugh, Martin G. 1899. *History of the German Baptist Brethren.* Brethren Publishing House. Reprint 1961.

Bruns, Hans. 1937. *Ein Reformator nach der Reformation.* Marburg: *Leben und Wirken Philipp Jakob Speners.*

Bunke, Ernst. 1939. *A.H. Francke, der Mann des Glaubens und der Liebe.* Giessen/Basel.

Calvin, John. 1548. *Commentary on Galatians* @ http://www.ccel.org/c/calvin/comment3/comm_vol41/htm/iii.ii.htm.

———. 1557. *Commentary on the Psalms.* In Calvin, *Opera Omnia, Corpus Reformatorum.* eds. G. Baum, E. Cunitz, and E. Reuss, vol. 31. Brunswick: C. Schwetschke, 1863–1900.

Canstein, Carl Hildebrand von. 1741. *Ausführliche Beschreibung der Lebensgeschichte... des seligen Herrn D. Philipp Jakob Speners.* In *Speners kleine geistliche Schriften.* ed. J.A. Steinmetz, 2 vols., Magdeburg.

Carl, Johann Samuel. 1730/33. *Geistliche Fama: mittheilend einige neuere Nachrichten von göttlichen Erweckungen, Wegen, Führungen u. Gerichten*, vol. 1, 1730/33, vol. 5, 1743.

Chakrabarti, Pratik, and Mark Harrison. 2003. The Moravian connection: missionary networks and medico-botanical knowledge in late-eighteenth-century India. *Transmission and Understanding in the Sciences in Europe, 1730–1870.* conf. Maison Française, Oxford, 30–31 May 2003.

Clarke, Wendy Whitman. 2004. Time capsule: The 18th-century village of Old Salem, North Carolina, endures as a lovingly restored urban oasis. *Smithsonian*, May 2004, 98–99.

Comenius, John Amos (Jan Komensky). 1660. *Ecclesia Slavonica historiola.* Amsterdam.

———. 1702. *Historia fratrum Bohemorum.* ed. Buddeus, Halle.

———. 1982. *Grosse Didaktik.* ed. Andreas Fitner, Stuttgart: Kiepenheuer.

Cranz, David (1723–1777). 1973a. *Alte und Neue Brüder-Historie oder kurz gefaßte Geschichte der Evangelischen Brüder-Unität in den älteren Zeiten und insonderheit in dem gegenwärtigen Jahrhundert.* Barby, 1771. In *Nikolaus Ludwig von Zinzendorf. Materialien und Dokumente.* Reihe 2, Bd. XI, Hildesheim-New York.

——— (1723–1777). 1973b. *The Ancient & Modern History of the Brethren* [*Alte und Neue Brüder-Historie oder kurz gefaßte Geschichte der Evangelischen Brüder-Unität in den älteren Zeiten und insonderheit in dem gegenwärtigen Jahrhundert.* Barby, 1771], Trans. into English with Notes by Benjamin la Trobe. London: W. & A. Strahan, 1780. In *Nikolaus Ludwig von Zinzendorf. Materialien und Dokumente.* Reihe 2, Bd. XI, Hildesheim-New York.

Crowner, David, and Gerald Christianson, eds. 2003. *The Spirituality of the German Awakening.* Mahwah, NJ: Paulist Press.

David, Zdeněk V. 2014. The views of Hus and Utraquism in the Bohemian catholic enlightenment. In *XIth Symposium on the Bohemian Reformation and Religious Practice*, Prague, 18–20 June 2014.

de Boor, Friedrich. 1975. Erfahrung gegen Vernunft. Das Bekehrungserlebnis A.H. Franckes als Grundlage für den Kampf des Hallischen Pietismus gegen die Aufklärung. In *Der Pietismus*

in Gestalten und Wirkungen. ed. F.S. Martin Schmidt, Heinrich Bornkamm, F. Heyer, and A. Schindler. Bielefeld.
Deghaye, P. 1969. *La Doctrine esotérique de Zinzendorf, 1700–1760*. Paris.
Deppermann, Klaus. 1961. *Der hallesche Pietismus und der Preussische Staat unter Friedrich III*. Göttingen: Vandenhoeck & Ruprecht.
Driver, Cecil. 1946. *Tory Radical: The Life of Richard Oastler [1789–1861]*. Oxford: Oxford University Press. (Oastler was educated in England by Moravians 1798–1806).
Durnbaugh, Donald. 1967. *The Brethren in Colonial America (1700–1783)*. Elgin, IL: Brethren Press.
———. 1992. *Brethren Beginnings*. Brethren Encyclopedia Inc.
———. 1997. *Fruit of the Vine: A History of the Brethren, 1708–1995*. Elgin, IL: Brethren Press.
Ehwalt, J.G. 1756. *Die alte und neue Lehre der böhmischen Brüder*. Danzig: Schuster.
Erb, Peter, ed. 1983. *The Pietists*. Mahwah, NJ: Paulist Press.
Erbe, Helmuth. 1929. *Bethlehem, Pa: Eine kommunistische Herrnhuter Kolonie des 18. Jahrhunderts*. Herrnhut: Winter.
Fogleman, Aaron Spencer. 2015. *Two Troubled Souls: An Eighteenth-Century Couple's Spiritual Journey in the Atlantic World*. Chapel Hill: University of North Carolina Press.
Francke, August Hermann. 1727. *Pietas Hallensis. An Historical Narration* [...]. Edinburgh.
———. 1962. *August Hermann Franckes Schrift über eine Reform des Erziehungs- und Bildungswesens als Ausgangspunkt einer geistlichen und sozialen Neuordnung der Evangelischen Kirche des 18. Jahrhunderts: der Grosse Aufsatz*. (1704) Mit einer quellenkundlichen Einführung. Hrsg. v. Otto Podczeck. Berlin. Akademie.
———. 1983. "On Christian Perfection," and "Autobiography,". In *The Pietists*, ed. Peter Erb. Mahwah, NJ: Paulist Press.
Frauer, Hans-Dieter. 2009. *Das schwäbische Paradies: Geschichten zur Geschichte—Pietismus in Württemberg*. Francke-Buchhandlung.
Freeman, Arthur J. 1999. *An Ecumenical Theology of the Heart: The Theology of Count Nicholas Ludwig von Zinzendorf*. Moravian Church in America.
Friesen, Abraham. 1998. Present at the inception: Menno Simons: Beginnings of Dutch anabaptism. *The Mennonite Quarterly Review* 72 (3): 351.
Gawthorp, Richard L. 1993. *Pietism and the Making of Eighteenth-Century Prussia*. New York: Cambridge University Press.
Geiger, Erika. 1999. *Nikolaus Ludwig Graf von Zinzendorf: Seine Lebensgeschichte*. Holsgerlingen: Hänssler Verlag.
Gembicki, Dieter. 2002. Voltaire et Zinzendorf à Genève : une rencontre manquée entre Lumières et piétisme? *Dix-huitième siècle* 34: 108. Numéro spécial: *Christianisme et Lumières*. ed. Coppola, pp 465–478.
Gerrish, B.A. 1984. *A Prince of the Church: Schleiermacher and the Beginnings of Modern Theology*. Philadelphia, PA: Fortress Press.
Gierl, Martin. 1997. *Pietismus und Aufklärung*. Vandenhoeck & Ruprecht (Gebundene Ausgabe): Göttingen.
Gindely, A. 1861. *Quellen zur Geschichte der böhmischen Brüder*. Vienna.
Gleixner, Ulrike, ed. *Texte zur Geschichte des Pietismus: Beate Hahn Paulus*, Die Talheimer Wochenbücher 1817–1829. Vol. 5, 2007. Göttingen: Vandenhoeck & Ruprecht (Gebundene Ausgabe).
Goldschmidt, Stephen. 2001. *Johann Konrad Dippel (1673–1734), Seine radikalpietistische Theologie und ihre Entstehung*. Göttingen.
Gollin, G.L.. 1967. Moravians in Two Worlds: A Study of Changing Communities.
Greschat, Martin. 1972. Zur neueren Pietismusforschung. Ein Literaturbericht. *Jahrbuch des Vereins für Westfälische Kirchengeschichte* 65: 220–268.
———. ed. 1977. *Zur neueren Pietismusforschung*. Wege der Forschung, vol. 440, Darmstadt, *Jahrbuch des Vereins für Westfälische Kirchengeschichte* 65 (1972), 220–268.

Griffin, Emilie, and Peter C. Erb, eds. 2006. *The Pietists: Selected Writings (1983)*. San Francisco: HarperSanFrancisco.

Grünberg, Paul. 1893–1906. *Philipp Jakob Spener*. 3 vols., Göttingen.

Hahn, Hans-Christoph, Hellmut Reichel, with Kai Dose et al. eds. 1977. *Zinzendorf und die Herrnhuter Brüder: Quellen zur Geschichte der Brüder-Ünität von 1722 bis 1760*. Hamburg: F. Wittig.

Hahn, Hans Christoph, Dietrich Meyer, et al., eds. 1987. *Bibliographisches Handbuch zur Zinzendorf*. Düsseldorf: C. Blech (Yale Divinity School).

Hamilton, J. Taylor. 1900. *A History of the Moravian Church: The Unitas Fratrum or the Unity of the Brethren During the Eighteenth and Nineteenth Centuries*. Bethlehem, PA: Times Publishing Company, Printers. Reprint, CreateSpace Independent Publishing Platform, 2017.

Hamilton, Kenneth Gardiner. 1940. John Ettwein and the Moravian Church During the Revolutionary Period, Diss't. Columbia University in *Transactions of the Moravian Historical Society* 12(3–4): 85–429, Bethlehem, PA: Times Publishing Co. 1940; Woodbridge, CT: Research Publications, 1983.

Hamilton, Kenneth G. ed. and Trans. 1971. *Bethlehem Diary, I, 1742–1744*. Bethlehem, PA.

Havens, Mary B. 1990. *Zinzendorf and the Augsburg Confession: An ecumenical Vision?* Atlanta: Emory University Press.

Heppe, H.L.J.. 1875. *Geschichte der quietistischen Mystik der katholischen Kirche*. Berlin. Reprint Hildesheim/New York: Olms, 1978.

———.. 1879. *Geschichte des Pietismus und der Mystik in der Reformirten Kirche, namentlich der Niederlande*. Leiden, new ed. Hamburg Severus-Verlag, 2011.

Hoffmann, Barbara. 1978. *Radikalpietismus um 1700: Der Streit um das Recht auf eine neue Gesellschaft*. Frankfurt am Main/New York: Campus Verlag, 1998.

Hostetler, John A. 1980. *Amish Society*. 4th ed. Baltimore: Johns Hopkins University Press, 1993.

———., ed. 1992. *Amish Roots: A Treasury of History, Wisdom, and Lore*. Baltimore: Johns Hopkins University Press.

———. 1997. *Hutterite Society*. Baltimore: Johns Hopkins University Press.

Hutton, Joseph Edmund. 1922. *A History of Moravian Missions*. London: Moravian Publication Office, Kindle ed.

Hutton, James (1715–1795). 2011. *Memoirs of James Hutton: Comprising the Annals of His Life and Connection with the United Brethren*. (1856) ed. Daniel Benham. Nabu Press.

Hutton, Joseph Edmund. 2018. *A History of the Moravian Church*. (1909) repr. Franklin Classics, Kindle ed.

Hynson, Leon O. 1979. John Wesley and the "Unitas Fratrum": A theological analysis. *Methodist History* 18: 26–60.

———. 1994. Wesley's 'Thoughts Upon Slavery': A declaration of human rights. *Methodist History* 33 (1): 46–57.

Jesse, Horst. 2003. *Friedrich Daniel Ernst Schleiermacher: Der Kirchenvater des 19. Jahrhunderts*. Frieling.

Jung, Martin H. 2005. *Pietismus*. Frankfurt: Fischer.

Kelpius, Johannes. 1951. *Johannes Kelpius: A Method of Prayer* (1700c). Trans. Christopher Witt, Philadelphia, 1761. ed. E.G. Alderfer. New York: Harper.

Kim, Moon-Kee. 1994. Das Kirchenverstandnis Phillip Jacob Speners, ThD Diss't, Augustana HS, Neuendettelsau (microfiche, Library of Congress).

Kinkel, Gary Steven. 1988. Count Zinzendorf's doctrine of the Holy Spirit as Mother. Diss't, University of Iowa.

———. 1990. The big chill: The theological disagreement which separated John Wesley and Count Zinzendorf. *Unitas fratrum* 27–28: 89–112.

Klien, Walter Conrad. 1942. *Johann Conrad Beissel: Mystic and Martinet, 1690–1768*. Philadelphia: University of Pennsylvania Press.

Knorr von Rosenroth, Christian. 1951. *The Kabbalah Unveiled*. Trans. by Samuel Liddell MacGregor Mathers. London: Routledge & Kegan Paul.

———. 1999. *Kabbala Denudata*. (5v, 1677–1684) 2v, Heidelberg: Olms.

Koecher, J.C. 1741. *Die drey letzten und vornehmsten Glaubensbekenntnisse der böhmischen Brüder*. Leipzig.

Kupisch, Karl. 1953. *Vom Pietismus zum Kommunismus*. Berlin: Lettner.

Langton, Edward. 1956. *History of the Moravian Church*. London: Allen & Unwin.

Lewis, Arthur James. 1962. *Zinzendorf, The Ecumenical Pioneer: A Study in the Moravian Contribution to Christian Mission and Unity*. Philadelphia: Westminster Press/London: SCM Press.

Lindberg, Carter, ed. 2008. *The Pietist Theologians: An Introduction to Theology in the Seventeenth and Eighteenth Centuries*. New York: John Wiley.

Linde, Jan Marinus van der. 1956. *Het visioen van Hernhut en het apostolaat der Moravische Broeders in Suriname, 1735–1863*. Paramaribo: C. Kersten.

MacIntosh, Terence. 2015. Pietists, Jurists, and the early enlightenment critique of private confession in Lutheran Germany. *Modern Intellectual History* 12 (3): 627–656.

Marissen, Michael. 2016. *Bach & God*. New York: Oxford University Press.

Maser, Peter. 1990. *Hans Ernst von Kottwitz: Studien zur Erweckungsbewegung des frühen 19. Jahrhunderts in Schlesien und Berlin*. Göttingen: Vandenhoeck & Ruprecht.

McCardle, Arthur W. 1986. *Friedrich Schiller and Swabian Pietism*. New York: Peter Lang.

Meyer, Henry Herman. 1928. *Child Nature and Nurture: According to Nicolaus Ludwig von Zinzendorf*. Chicago: Abingdon Press.

Meyer, Mathias. 1992. *Feuerbach und Zinzendorf: Lutherus redivivus und die Selbstauflösung der Religionskritik*. Hildesheim: Olms.

Meyer, Dietrich. 2000. *Zinzendorf und die Herrnhuter Brüdergemeine, 1700–2000*. Göttingen: Vandenhoek & Ruprecht, 2009.

Meyer, Gerhard, and Erich Beyreuther, eds. 1975. *Erster (& Zweiter) Sammelband über Zinzendorf.*, 2 vols. Olms: Hildesheim/New York.

Mezezers, Valdis. 1975. *The Hernhuterian Pietism in the Baltic, and Its Outreach into America and Elsewhere in the World*. North Quincy, MA: Christopher Publishing House.

Midelfort, H., and C. Erik. 2005. *Exorcism and Enlightenment: Johann Joseph Gassner and the Demons of Eighteenth-Century Germany*. (Terry Lecture Series) New Haven, CT: Yale University Press.

Modrow, Irina. 1992. Der radikale Pietismus…. *Frühneuzeit-Info* 3 (2): 29–39.

———. 1994. *Dienstgemeine des Herrn Nikolaus-Ludwig von Zinzendorf*. Hildesheim/New York: Olms.

Moravian Church. 1978. *Kleines Brüdergesangbuch: Hirten-Lieder von Bethlehem*. Nachdr. d. Ausg. London, 1754; Hildesheim/New York: Olms, in *Nikolaus Ludwig von Zinzendorf, Materialen und Dokumente*. Reihe 4, vol. 5.

Mühlenberg, Heinrich Melchior. 1942–58. *The Journals of Henry Melchior Muhlenberg*. ed. and Trans. Theodore G. Tappert, and John W. Doberstein, 3 vols. Philadelphia: Mühlenberg Press.

———. 1986. *Die Korrespondenz Heinrich Melchior Muhlenbergs aus der Anfangszeit des deutschen Luthertums in Nordamerika*. ed. Kurt Aland. Berlin.

———. 2002. *Die Korrespondenz Heinrich Melchior Mühlenbergs aus der Anfangszeit des deutschen Luthertums in Nordamerika/1777–1787*: Bd V (*Texte Zur Geschichte Des Pietismus*). ed. Beate Köster, Karl-Otto Stohmidel, Volker Depkat & Kurt Aland. Berlin: de Gruyter.

Nagler, A.W. 1918. *Pietism and Methodism: OR The Significance of German Pietism in the Origin and Early Development of Methodism*. Nashville: Publishing House, Methodist Church South @ https://archive.org/stream/pietismmethodism00nagl/pietismmethodism00nagl_djvu.txt.

Newman, A. 1993. The death of Judaism in German protestant thought from Luther to Hegel. *Journal of the American Academy of Religion* 61 (3): 485–504.

Noth, Isabella. 2005. *Ekstatischer Pietismus, Die Inspirationsgemeinden und ihre Prophetin Ursula Meyer 1682–1743*. Vandenhoeck & Ruprecht (Gebundene Ausgabe): Göttingen.

"Novalis" (Georg Philipp Friedrich Freiherr von Hardenberg). 1960–2006. *Historische-Kritische Ausgabe—Novalis Schriften*. (HKA) eds. Richard Samuel, Hans-Joachim Mähl, and Gerhard Schulz, 6 vols. Stuttgart: Verlag W. Kohlhammer.

———. 1984, 1996. *Fragmente und Studien; Die Christenheit oder Europa*. ed. Carl Paschek. Stuttgart: Reclam.

———. 1997. *Philosophical Writings*. Trans. and ed. by Margaret Mahony Stoljar. Albany: State University of New York Press.

———. 2000. *Fichte Studies*. ed. Jane Kneller. Cambridge: Cambridge University Press Texts in the History of Philosophy.

O'Neill, Tim. 1993. The erotic freemasonry of Count Nicholas von Zinzendorf. In *Secret and Suppressed: Banned Ideas & Hidden History*, ed. Jim Keath. Portland: Feral House.

Oetinger, Friedrich Christoph (1702–1782). 1759. *Reden nach dem allgemeinen Wahrheitsgefühl*. ebd. (beide Samml. als Weinsberger Predigtbuch, n.A., Leonberg 1848) (Pietist sermons by the "Magus of the South").

Offen, Karl, and Terry Rugeley. 2014. *The Awakening Coast: An Anthology of Moravian Writings from Mosquitia and Eastern Nicaragua, 1849–1899*. Lincoln: University of Nebraska Press.

Pelikan, Jaroslav. 1973. Pietism. In *Dictionary of the History of Ideas*. New York: Scribner's.

Peschke, Erhard. 1969. *August Hermann Francke. Werke in Auswahl*. East Berlin.

Peucker, Paul. 1993. 'Godts Wonderen met Zyne Kerke': Isaac le Long (1683–1762) en de Herrnhutters. *De Achttiende Eeuw* 25 (2): 151–185.

Pfister, Oskar (1873–1956). 1910. *Die Frömmigkeit des Grafen Ludwig von Zinzendorf: eine psychoanalytische Studie*. Leipzig: F. Deuticke, *Schriften zur angewandten Seelenkunde*; Heft 8 ("Blood-and-wounds").

Pietismus und Neuzeit. 1995. Göttingen: Vandenhoeck und Ruprecht, vol. 21.

Pleijel, Hilding. 1935. *Der schwedische Pietismus in seinen Beziehungen zu Deutschland: Eine kirchengeschichtliche Untersuchung*. Lund.

Podmore, Colin. 1998. *The Moravian Church in England, 1728–1760*. New York: Oxford University Press.

Pond, Enoch (1791–1882). 1851. Memoir of Count Zinzendorf: Comprising a Succinct History of the Church of the United Brethren from its Renewal at Herrnhut to the Death of its Illustrious Patron. 2nd ed.. Boston: Massachusetts Sabbath School Society.

Reichel, Levin Theodor. 1888. *The Early History of the Church of the United Brethren (Unitas Fratrum) Commonly Called Moravians: In North America, A. D. 1734–1748*. Reprint, HardPress Publishing, 2013.

Reichel, Jörn. 1969. *Dichtungstheorie und Sprache bei Zinzendorf; der 12. Anhang zum Herrnhuter Gesangbuch*. Bad Homburg: v. d. H. Gehlen.

Rengstorf, Karl H. 1994. Die deutschen Pietisten und ihr Bild des Judentums. In *Begegnung von Deutschen und Juden*, ed. J. Katz and K.H. Rengstorf. Tübingen: Niemeyer.

Renkewitz, Heinz. 1969. *Hochmann von Hochenau (1670–1721). Quellenstudien zur Geschichte des Pietismus*. Witten.

Rimius, Heinrich (d. 1759). 1754. *The History of the Moravians: From Their First Settlement at Herrnhaag in the County of Budingen, Down to the Present Time, with a View Chiefly to Their Political Intrigues/Collected from the Public Acts of Budingen, and from Other Authentic Vouchers, All Along Accompanied with the Necessary Illustrations and Remarks. The Whole Intended to Give the World Some Knowledge of the Extraordinary System of the Moravians, and to Shew How It May Affect Both the Religious and Civil Interests of the State*. Trans. from the German. London: Printed for J. Robinson.

Ritschl, Albrecht. 1880–1886. *Geschichte des Pietismus*. 3 vols., Bonn: Marcus, repr. Berlin, 1966.

Ritter, Abraham. 1857. *History of the Moravian Church in Philadelphia*. Philadelphia: Hayes & Zell.

Robson, D.W. 1997. Anticipating the Brethren: The Reverend Charles Nisbet Critiques the French revolution. *Pennsylvania Magazine of History and Biography* 121 (4): 303–328.

Rosen-Prest, Viviane 2002. *l'Historiographie des huguenots en Prusse au temps des Lumières entre mémoire, histoire et légende: Jean Pierre Erman et Pierre Chrétien Frédéric Reclam.* ***Mémoires pour servir à l'histoire des réfugiés françois dans les États du roi (1782–1799).*** Paris: Honoré Champion, coll. "La vie des huguenots," 23.

Rousseau, Jean-Jacques. 2002. *De la Suisse suivi du Journal (septembre 1764) de J.C. von Zinzendorf.* Paris: Honoré Champion, coll. "L'âge des Lumières," 20. Édition critique par Frédéric S. Eigeldinger. (Karl Johann Christian, Graf von Zinzendorf, 1739–1813).

Salomon, Gustav. ed. 1879. *Bibliotheca Gersdorfio-Zinzendorfiana: Verzeichniss der Bibliotheken der verstorbenen Herren Grafen Friedrich Caspar von Gersdorf, Grafen Ludwig von Zinzendorf, Gründer der Brüdergemeinde zu Herrnhut, Herrn von Schrautenbach, sowie der Herren Syndiken D. Nitschmann und Fr. Köber: I. Abtheilung, Theologie und Neben-Wissenschaften, welche am 7. Januar 1880 und folgende Tage … durch Gustav Salomon … gegen Baare Zahlung versteigert werden.* Dresden: Thomass.

Sappington, Roger. 1976. *Brethren in the New Nation.* Brethren Press, 1785–1865.

Schmidt, Heinrich Julian (1818–1886). 1886–1896. *Geschichte des geistigen Lebens in Deutschland von Leibniz bis auf Lessings Tod.* 1861–1863 [History of German Literature from Leibniz to the Present. posthumously revised as *Geschichte der deutschen Literatur von Leibniz bis auf unsere Zeit.* 4 vols.

Schmidt, Martin. 1975. *Der Pietismus in Gestalten und Wirkungen. Martin Schmidt zum 65. Geburtstag.* ed. Heinrich Bornkamm, F. Heyer, and A. Schindler. Bielefeld.

———. 2008. *Pietismus* (1983), 3rd ed. Kohlhammer Verlag.

Schrautenbach, Ludwig Carl Freiherr von (1724–1783). 1851. *Der Graf von Zinzendorf und die Brüdergemeine seiner Zeit.* ed. Friedrich Wilhelm Kölbing, intr. Gerhard Meyer, repr. d. Ausg. Gnadau, Menz, u. Leipzig: Kummer. Reprint, Hildesheim/New York: G. Olms, 1972.

Scougal, Henry. 1677. *The Life of God in the Soul of Man.* Grand Rapids, MI: Christian Classics Ethereal Library. Accessed 14 October 2003.

Sensbach, Jon F. 1998. *A Separate Canaan: The Making of an Afro-Moravian World in North Carolina, 1763–1840.* Chapel Hill: University of North Carolina Press.

———. 2005. *Rebecca's Revival: Creating Black Christianity in the Atlantic World.* Cambridge, MA: Harvard University Press, pb 2006.

Simons, Menno. 1871. *Complete Works of Menno Simons.* Trans. by John Funk. Reprint, Pathway Pub., 1983.

Sommer, Elisabeth. 1994. A different kind of freedom? Order and discipline among the Moravian Brethren in Germany and Salem, North Carolina, 1771–1801. *Church History* 63 (2): 221–234.

———. 1998. Gambling with God: The use of the lot by the Moravian Brethren in the eighteenth century. *Journal of the History of Ideas* 59 (2): 267–286.

———. 2000. *Serving Two Masters: Moravian Brethren in Germany and North Carolina, 1727–1801.* Lexington: University Press of Kentucky.

Spangenberg, August Gottlieb. 1838. *The Life of Nicholas Lewis Count Zinsendorf.* Trans. from the German, by S. Jackson. Abridged. London: S. Holdsworth.

———. 1971a. *Leben des Herrn Nicholas Ludwig von Zinzendorf.* 3 vols., 1772–75; repr. Hildesheim/New York: Olms.

———. 1971b. *Leben des Herrn Nicolaus Ludwig Grafen und Herrn von Zinzendorf und Pottendorf.* 8 Bände in 4 Bänden (Gebundene Ausgabe). New York: Olms.

Spener, Phillip Jacob. 1700–02. *Theologische Bedencken.* 4 vols. Halle.

———. 1711. *Letzte Theologische Bedencken.* 2 vols. Halle.

———. 1716. *Erbauliche Evangelisch- und Epistolische Sonntags-Andachten.* Frankfurt.

———(1635–1705). 1830. *Das geistliche Priestertum aus gottlichem Wort kurzlich beschrieben…* ed. J Wilke, Berlin: L. Oehmigke.

———. 1964, 2002. *Pia Desideria* (fall, 1675, 1678). Trans. Theodore G. Tappert. Eugene, OR: Wipf and Stock.

Steele, Richard B. 1995. John Wesley's synthesis of the revival practices of Jonathan Edwards, George Whitefield, Nicholas von Zinzendorf. *Wesleyan Theological Journal* 30 (1): 154–172.

Stephens, W.P. 1988. Wesley and the Moravians. In *John Wesley: Contemporary Perspectives*, ed. John Stacey, 23–36. London: Epworth.
Stoeffler, F. Ernest. 1971. *The Rise of Evangelical Pietism*. 1965, 2nd ed.
———. 1973. *German Pietism During the Eighteenth Century*, Studies in the History of Religion. Vol. 24. E. J. Brill: Leiden.
———. 1976a. Tradition and renewal in the ecclesiology of John Wesley. In *Traditio—Krisis—Renovatio aus theologischer Sicht*, ed. B. Jaspert and R. Mohr, 298–316. Marburg: Elwert.
———. 1976b. Pietism, the Wesleys and Methodist beginnings in America. In *Continental Pietism and Early American Christianity*, ed. F. Ernest Stoeffler, 184–221. Grand Rapids, MI: Wm. B. Eerdmans.
———, ed. 1976c. *Continental Pietism and Early American Christianity*. Eerdmans: Grand Rapids, MI.
———. 1986. Religious roots of the early Moravian and Methodist movements. *Methodist History* 24 (3): 132–140.
Stoudt, J.J. 1940. Count Zinzendorf and the Pennsylvania congregation of god and the spirit. *Church History* 9: 366–438.
Strom, Jonathan. 2002. Problems and promises of Pietism research. *Church History* 71 (3): 536–554.
Swensson, Eric. Reception of the Doctrine of Justification Among German Lutheran Pietists. www.holytrinitynewrochelle.org/yourti89645.html. 6 February 05.
Tappert, Theodore G. 1964, 2002. "Introduction" to Spener, *Pia Desideria*. Trans. Tappert. Eugene, OR: Wipf and Stock.
Tauler, Johannes. 1985. *Sermons*. Trans. Maria Shrady. Mahwah, NJ: Paulist Press.
Tersteegen, Gerhard. 1784–85. *Auserlesene Lebensbeschreibungen heiliger Seelen*. 3 vols., 3rd ed. Essen.
———. 1979. *Geistliche Reden*. I, ed. A. Löschhorn and W. Zeller. Göttingen.
Thompson, H.P. 1951. *Into All Lands: A History of the Society for the Propagation of the Gospel in Foreign Parts, 1701–1950*. London.
Thorp, Daniel B. 1989. *The Moravian Community in Colonial North Carolina: Pluralism on the Southern Frontier*. Knoxville: University of Tennessee Press.
Tipton, Baird. 1975. How can the religious experience of the past be recovered? The examples of Puritanism and Pietism. *Journal of the American Academy of Religion* 43 (4): 695–707.
Towlson, Clifford W. 1957. *Moravian and Methodist: Relationships and Influences in the Eighteenth Century*. London: Epworth Press.
Urner, Hans. 1952. *Der Pietismus*. Gladbeck: Heilmann.
Verbeek, Jacob Wilhelm. 1845. *Des Grafen von Zinzendorf, Leben und Character*. Gnadau: H.L. Menz.
Waite, Gary K. 1990. *David Joris and Dutch Anabaptism, 1524–1543*. Waterloo, ON: Wilfred Laurier University Press.
Walch, Johann Georg. 1747. *Theologisches Bedencken von der Beschaffenheit der herrnhutischen Secte*. Frankfurt: Leonrad Buchner.
Wallmann, Johannes. 1970. *Philipp Jakob Spener und die Anfänge des Pietismus*. Tübingen.
———. 1990. *Der Pietismus*. Göttingen: Vandenhoeck und Ruprecht.
———. 2005. *Der Pietismus: Ein Handbuch*. Uni-Taschenbücher
Ward, William Reginald. 1991, 1992. *The Protestant Evangelical Awakening*. Cambridge: Cambridge University Press
———. 1993a. German Pietism, 1670–1750. *Journal of Ecclesiastical History* 44: 479–505. (bibliographical survey).
———. 1993b. Mysticism and revival: The case of Gerhard Tersteegen. In F.S. John Walsh. *Revival and Religion since 1700*, ed. Jane Garnett and Colin Matthew. London.
———. 1999. *Christianity Under the Ancien Régime, 1648–1789*. Cambridge: Cambridge University Press.

———. 2006. *Early Evangelicalism: A Global Intellectual History, 1670–1789*. Cambridge: Cambridge University Press.

Watzlawick, Helmut. 1997. Un été pluvieux dans la vie du comte de Zinzendorf. In *C'est la faute à Voltaire, c'est la faute à Rousseau. Recueil anniversaire pour Jean-Daniel Candaux*, ed. dans Roger Durand, 141s. Geneva: Droz.

Weber, Max. 1930. *The Protestant Ethic and the Spirit of Capitalism* (1904–05). London.

Weigelt, Horst. 1965. *Pietismus Studien*. Stuttgart.

———. 2001. *Geschichte des Pietismus in Bayern*. Göttingen: Vandenhoeck & Ruprecht.

Weinlick, John R. 1989. *Count Zinzendorf: The Story of His Life and Leadership in the Renewed Moravian Church*. Abingdon Press, 1956; Bethlehem, PA: Moravian Church in America.

Wellenreuther, Hermann. 1972. *Glaube und Politik in Pennsylvania, 1681–1776*. Cologne.

Wettach, Theodor. 1971. *Kirche bei Zinzendorf*. Wuppertal: Brockhaus.

Wheeler, Rachel. *Moravian Mission to the Mahicans*. Seattle: American Historical Association, January 05.

Winkler, Johann Peter Siegmund (1702–1786). *Des Herrn Grafen Ludwig von Zinzendorf etc. Unternehmungen in Religions-Sachen ause eigener Erfahrung und schrifftlichen Documenten* [microform]. Leipzig: bey Johann Christian Langenheim, 1740.

Wintermeyer, Rolf. 1994. L'autobiographie piétiste, remède, rite d'initiation ou œuvre littéraire. In *Littérature et civilisation à l'agrégation d'allemand*, 85–121.

Wolf, Stephanie G. 1976. *Urban Village: Population, Community, and Family Structure in Germantown, Pennsylvania, 1683–1800*. Princeton, NJ: Princeton University Press.

Zimmerman, Matthias. 2002. *Der Einfluß des Pietismus auf die deutsche Literatursprache im 18. Jahrhundert - mit einer Analyse zweier Texte von N.L. Graf v. Zinzendorf und F.G. Klopstock*. Grin e-Bucher.

Zimmermann, Matthias. 2007. *Der Einfluß des Pietismus auf die deutsche Literatursprache im 18. Jahrhundert - mit einer Analyse zweier Texte von N.L. Graf v. Zinzendorf und F.G. Klopstock*. Grin Verlag, Oktober.

Zinzendorf, Nicolaus Ludwig. 1740. *Herrn Graf Ludwigs von Zinzendorf Anstalten und Lehrsätze aus gewessen Urkunden gezogen, und in ihrem Wiederspruch gegen die augspurgische Confession und übrigen symbolischen Bücher* [microform]. Leipzig: bey Johann Christian Langenheim.

———. 1751. *Maxims, Theological Ideas and Sentences, out of the Present Ordinary of the Brethren's Churches: His Dissertations and Discourses from the Years 1738–1747*. Extracted by J. Gambold. London: J. Beecroft.

———. 1845. *Geistliche Gedichte des Grafen von Zinzendorf*. Stuttgart: J. G. Cotta'schen Verlag. (Microform, Albany State University Library).

———. 1962. Schriften des jüngeren Zinzendorf von Nikolaus Ludwig von Zinzendorf. In *Hauptschriften*, vol. 1. Hildesheim: Olms.

———. 1962–1963. *Hauptschriften in sechs Bänden*. Hildesheim: G. Olms.

———. 1963. Londoner Reden. In *Hauptschriften*, vol. 5. Hildesheim: G. Olms.

———. 1964–1966. Büdingische Sammlungen. In *Zinzendorf, Ergängzungsbände zu den Hauptschriften*, ed. E. Beyreuther and G. Meyer. Hildesheim: Olms.

Zinzendorf, Nicolaus Ludwig Graf von. 1964–1985. In *Ergängzungsbände zu den Hauptschriften*, ed. Erich Beyreuther and Gerhard Meyer. Hildesheim: Olms.

Zinzendorf, Nicolaus Ludwig. 1965, 1976. *Antizinzendorfiana aus der Anfangszeit 1729–1735*. Nachdr. d. Ausg. Breslau, 1729; Frankfort a. M. 1743, ed. Erich Beyreuther and Gerhard Meyer. Hildesheim/New York: Olms. *Nikolaus Ludwig von Zinzendorf, Materialien und Dokumente*. Reihe 2, *Nikolaus Ludwig Graf von Zinzendorf, Leben und Werk in Quellen und Darstellungen*, vol. 14. The first work is by "ein Liebhaber der reinen Gottseligkeit." The second work was published by the Akademische Buchdruckerei Societatis Jesu under the title: *Unpartheyische Nachricht von … der so genannten Schefferianer und Zinzendorffianer …*.

———. 1965–76. *Nikolaus Ludwig von Zinzendorf, Materialien und Dokumente*. Reihe 2, Nikolaus Ludwig Graf von Zinzendorf. *Leben und Werk in Quellen und Darstellungen*. Hildesheim/New York: Olms.

———. 1979. In *Texte zur Mission mit e. Einf. in d. Missionstheologie Zinzendorfs*, ed. Helmut Bintz. Hamburg: Wittig.

———. 1984. In *Correspondance with Ludwig Friedrich zu Castell-Remlingen (Franken)*, ed. Horst Weigelt. Neustadt a. d. Aisch: Degener.

———. 1998. *Zinzendorf: Nine Public Lectures on Important Subjects in Religion Preached in Fetter Lane Chapel in London in the Year 1746*. Trans. and ed. by George W. Forell, Iowa City: University of Iowa Press, 1973; Eugene, OR: Wipf and Stock

Zorb, E.H. 1957. Count Zinzendorf: As the 18th-century ecumenist. *Ecumenical Review* 9: 419–428.

Chapter 3
Christian Antecedents

Abstract Zinzendorf's Christian Antecedents: Spener's Pietist Protestantism, Lutheran Protestantism. Luther's conversion, Augustine's, and Paul's. Paul and his Corinthians, Greek ecstasies. From Paul forward to Augustine, Calvin, and Jonathan Edwards.

It should now be easier to see Zinzendorf as the leader of an *avant-garde*, rather than the eccentric pioneer of a retreat to the past. Nevertheless, it is perfectly clear that ecstasy was not discovered in the eighteenth century. Neither were its ensuing, and (as we might say) "life-changing" consequences for piety (eusebeia or εὐσέβεια in Greek, pietas and in fact religio in Latin). Nor were its subsequent sacralization of rituals (thrēskeia or θρησκεία), of morals, laws, dogmas and priests, And it was hardly confined to Protestant Christianity, nor indeed to any particular religion, theist or not. The founders of all three Abrahamic religions, Abraham, Moses, Jesus and Muhammad, are all reported as having been beside or outside of themselves as they received what theologians call "revelation" from the One god. Muhammad, in fact, reported his experience himself in the *Qu'ran*. And all three Abrahamic religions developed ecstatic counter-enlightenments and counter-pious moralisms in the wake of uncertain returns of ecstasy. We pause here to run the clock backward, then forward again, to see a pattern in Christianity that runs much deeper than the eighteenth-century Enlightenment.

Zinzendorf, of course, was a Christian, indeed a Lutheran Protestant Christian, whose religious beliefs had been presented to him through the sort of Protestantism that was a strong undercurrent in seventeenth-century Germany, a religion of piety rather than prescription (moralist or legalist), a religion often characterized as "heart" rather than head, which historians have come to call "Pietism." Zinzendorf's mother, in fact, had appointed the "father" of Pietism, Philipp Jakob Spener (1635–1705), as the godfather of the young nobleman.

Zinzendorf was also a Saxon and Pietism was a relatively new trend in the mainstream Protestant Christianity that was the state religion of Luther's home state of

W. R. Everdell, *The Evangelical Counter-Enlightenment*, Boston Studies in Philosophy, Religion and Public Life 9,
https://doi.org/10.1007/978-3-030-69762-4_3

Saxony.[1] It had been launched mostly by teachers and graduates of the Lutheran universities of Jena and Halle, beginning in the later 1600s, after the great German disaster of the Thirty Years War—the war that drove what became Zinzendorf's Moravians out of Bohemia (and Descartes to his doubts). Its German precedents include post-Reformation cosmos mystics like Jakob Boehme, pre-Reformation mystics like Meister Eckhart, Johann Tauler and Heinrich Suso, the medieval sisterhood of the Beguines, and particularly the dedicated but un-ecstatic Brethren of the Common Life, founded in the Netherlands in 1375.

Indifferent to the clerical hierarchy, post-Reformation Pietism was suspicious of doctrinal Lutheran orthodoxy and even on occasion hostile to it. Johann Arndt's 1605 book, known in English as *True Christianity*, a founding document of Lutheran Pietism, centers on heartfelt experience rather than the application of doctrine.[2] It was reprinted through a century and a half: 95 editions by 1740, including 6 in Latin, 5 in English, 4 in Dutch, 3 each in Danish Swedish and French, two in Czech, and 1 each in Russian and Icelandic. In 1675, Philipp Spener wrote a long preface to a new edition of Arndt's 1615 sermon collection which, under the title *Pious Wishes*, became a founding document on its own that was fundamental to Spener's godson, Zinzendorf, and to his teachers.[3] Spener praised worship in *ecclesiolae in ecclesia* (little churches within the church), or "conventicles" (to use the contemporary British term for unlicensed home churches and outdoor prayer meetings), often without benefit of clergy.

Spener also insisted on what Pietists got in the habit of calling *Religion des Herzens* or "religion of the heart." Pietists preferred to feel the presence of divinity rather than that of an appointed minister, putting generosity of spirit ahead of

[1] Pietism may be said to have begun in the late Renaissance, but historians did not really name it until the nineteenth century. The most extensive study was made by Albrecht Ritschl in the 1880s and has become interpretively outdated (Ritschl, *Geschichte des Pietismus*, 3v, Bonn: Marcus, 1880-1886). Pietists are not all German. F. Ernest Stoeffler moved his scope to both sides of the Atlantic in several books, notably *German Pietism During the Eighteenth Century*. (Brill, 1973) and *The Rise of Evangelical Pietism*. (Brill, 1965). Norbert Schmidt, Heinrich Bornkamm, Frank Lüdke, Horst Weigel and especially Martin Schmidt have added much the subject. Martin Brecht led the production of a German successor to Ritschl (Martin Brecht & Klaus Depperman, eds. *Geschichte des Pietismus*. 4v. Vandenhoeck & Ruprecht, 1995) An excellent summary of Pietism is part of Eric Swensson's article, "Reception of the Doctrine of Justification among German Lutheran Pietists" @ www.holytrinitynewrochelle.org/yourti89645.html, 6Feb05.

[2] Johann Arndt (1555-1621), *Vier* [later, *Sechs*] *Bücher vom wahren Christentum*. (1st ed. Braunschweig, 1605), Translated by Peter Erb as *True Christianity*. (Mahwah, NJ: Paulist Press (Classics of Western Spirituality), 1979.

[3] Spener's classic text is: Philipp Jakob Spener, *Pia Desideria* [*Pious wishes, or Heartfelt Desire / for a God-pleasing Reform / of the true Evangelical Church, / Together with Several Simple Christian Proposals / Looking Toward this End*] (German, 1675, Latin 1678), tr. Theodore G. Tappert, Eugene, OR: Wipf and Stock, 1964, 2002. Cf. J. Wallmann, "Reflexionen und Bemerkungen zur Frömmigkeitskrise des 17. Jahrhunderts," in *Krisen des 17. Jahrhunderts. Interdisziplinäre Perspektiven*, ed., M. Jakubowski-Tiessen, Göttingen: Vandenhoek & Ruprecht, 1999, p25-42; and W[illiam] R[eginald] Ward's culminating and now definitive work on the origins of evangelical Christianity, *Early Evangelicalism: A Global Intellectual History, 1670-1789*. (Cambridge: Cambridge University Press, 2006), pp 7-8.

calculations of interest—faith, in a sense, before good works. The grace of God which Luther thought had saved him, Pietists agreed, was a presence that must be waited on rather than called upon. Pietists, however, did not think grace was entirely irresistible when it came. They referred to the necessary repentance as a struggle (*Busskampf*), a little like the Muslim "greater *jihad*," followed by a breakthrough (*Durchbruch*); and they were wary lest thought and prayer become too deliberate—less spontaneous than raw emotion. Pietists did not bark, gyrate or fall senseless, but they did show what others recognized (and the Enlightenment stigmatized) as "enthusiasm," feelings no less extravagant for being quietly expressed. Pietists have long been acknowledged as the most obvious of the immediate precursors of Western evangelicalism.

The Lutheran Protestantism that Pietism sprang from is conventionally called the first of the Protestant denominations. It was founded by Martin Luther in the early 1500s, soon after he discovered a revolutionary consequence in a sentence of the Epistle, or letter, that Saint Paul had written to the earliest Christian community in Rome back in the first century. The sentence, "The just shall live by faith," was in Latin in Luther's Bible, and at first had puzzled this recently appointed Professor of Bible at the new University of Wittenberg. Luther was also a monk in the Augustinian order who made all of the confessions of sin that the liturgy prescribed, and many, many more besides, but was tormented, despite his confessions (or more accurately because of them) by his inability to believe in the promised forgiveness, or in his own salvation. He could get no assurance that he was among the subset of humankind's innumerable sinners who would be saved from eternal punishment—or had been saved already—by what he called the *gratia*, or grace of God. What Luther rather suddenly concluded was that the meaning of "The just shall live by faith" was that the "works" prescribed by his Catholic Church—especially confession and penance, but even the mass—were of no real consequence. That if you believed that God could or would save you, you were saved, made "just" or justified, precisely because you believed it. For Luther it was much more of an intellectual insight than an ecstatic revelation,[4] but what Luther made of that sentence of Paul's generated ecstasies all over Christian Europe and soon changed half of Christendom in the Protestant Reformation.

To make what he had made of Paul, Luther had used the writings of the patron saint of his monastic order, Augustine, the North African bishop of the late and newly christianized Roman Empire more than a thousand years before Luther. It was Augustine who had made the freely offered "grace" of God a concept essential to Christianity. He had done so before his own ecstatic conversion in the course of wrestling with the two-god religion of Manichæism, and, after his conversion, with the humanist Christianity of the English monk, Pelagius. And Augustine had done it in large part through his reading of what Paul had written some three centuries before.

[4]Though the insight was, in fact, accompanied by the relief of Luther's chronic constipation. Luther describes the "Tower Experience" in *Luther's Works*, v34, p. 337.

The surviving *Epistles* of Paul had found their first great critical reader in Saint Augustine, who knew enough Greek to read the *Epistles* and the rest of the New Testament, but who wrote only in Latin.[5] In fact, Augustine's own conversion experience had begun, by his own account, with a Neoplatonic vision of the ladder of being as it rose from the finite and material to the infinite and utterly immaterial.[6] Then in response to the disembodied voice of a child, overheard in a Milanese garden, repeatedly saying "take up and read," he obeyed, and took up his own book of Paul's *Epistles*, and opened it to a passage in *Romans* (13:13–14) on the desires of the flesh.[7] Augustine, who had long been wrestling with his delight in sex, food and drink, finally found the "will" to give those up. His baptism followed, and the conversion was sealed later during an increasingly elevated conversation with his dying mother at Ostia, by the ultimate in ecstatic *visiones* of an infinite that "transcended" their minds.[8] Paul's conversion was not from Judaism, like Paul's, and not from any of the current Roman paganisms, but from Manichæism, a religion lately arisen in the eastern end of the declining Roman Empire that conceived of not one god, or many, but rather two—two gods, one good and the other evil.[9]

Augustine's conversion to monotheist Catholic Christianity was more intellectual, and less visionary, than Paul's; but the results of this conversion for human responsibility were so enormous that Augustine has been called Christianity's third founder.

It began with Augustine's first post-conversion work, *De spiritu et littera* (*On the Spirit and the Letter*, 394–95 C.E.) where he wrote that what Saint Paul had meant by the justice (*justitia*) of God in *Romans* or *Galatians* was neither an attribute of God, nor the activity of God in condemning and punishing sinners, but an activity

---

[5] Peter Brown's biography of Augustine (*Augustine of Hippo*, Berkeley: U. of California Press, 1967, revised edition, Berkeley, 2000) has superseded all others in English. In a review of Sarah Ruden's new translation of Augustine's late fourth century Latin autobiography, *Confessions* (New York: Modern Library, 2017), Brown took the opportunity to restate his view of Augustine and update it slightly (Brown, "Dialogue With God," *New York Review of Books* 45:16(October 20, 2017), pp45-46.

[6] Augustine, *Confessions*, Book 7, Chapter XVII:23. "And thus with the flash of a trembling glance, it arrived at that which is. And I saw thy invisibility [*invisibilia tua*] understood by means of the things that are made." Augustine's formula for the experience was "withdrawing his thoughts from experience"—*visio*. Translator Albert Outler unhesitatingly labels it to invoke the late Greek platonist, Plotinus, a "Plotinian ecstasy" (Outler, tr., Augustine, *Confessions*, 1955, note 214 @ https://en.wikisource.org/wiki/The_Confessions_of_Saint_Augustine_(Outler).

[7] Augustine, *Confessions*, Book 8, Chapter XII:29. Here, Augustine makes claim to a revelation, but not to an ecstatic alienation of mind or faculties.

[8] Augustine, *Confessions*, Book 9, Chapter X:23-25. Augustine's word for their ecstasy was again *visio*, or *rapiare*.

[9] Augustine's conversion unleashed in him an avalanche of attacks on Manichæism. A short list of those that survive includes *Concerning Two Souls, Against the Manichæans* [*De Duabus Animabus Contra Manichæos*] CE 391; *Against the Epistle of Manichæus Called Fundamental* [*Contra Epistolam Manichæi Quam Vocant Fundamentum*] CE 397; and *Reply to Faustus the Manichæan* [*Contra Faustum Manichæum*] CE 400. Book 5 of his *Confessions* is replete with it.

of God by which he took charge of sinners and made them just again.[10] With a small sideswipe against another commentator, Augustine's book opened an epic argument with Pelagius, a monk from Britain on the collapsing Roman frontier, who was also a reader of Paul. Theirs was a knock-down, drag-out about the great paradox in all monotheistic religions, the reason for evil. Pelagius wrote and preached that human beings were, if not good, at least good enough to master their own faults, or sins, or to regret them and ask for forgiveness and improved behavior. Stephen Sondheim updated Pelagius lyrically in *West Side Story* in 1958:

THE JETS: We ain't no delinquents,

We're misunderstood.
Deep down inside us there is good!
ACTION: There is good!
THE JETS: There is good, there is good,
There is untapped good!
Like inside, the worst of us is good!

Newly converted to faith in a god, *Deus*, who was both single and good, and a cosmos which could not have two or more moral meanings but only one, Augustine, could not agree. If he had not yet summoned the "will" to change his life, it must be that he had not yet experienced (he thought) divine intervention by the One God. For Paul and Augustine human beings are "fallen" and incapable of doing good without access (προσαγωγή) to charis (χάρις) divine help or grace.[11] In the answering Augustinian lyric of Stephen Sondheim:

BABY JOHN: It ain't just a question of misunderstood;
Deep down inside him, he's no good!
ACTION: I'm no good!
ALL: We're no good, we're no good, we're no earthly good,
Like the best of us is no damn good.[12]

No human had the power to overcome his own sin, Augustine concluded—"sin" usually summed up for Christians by Jesus as a failure to love God and one's neighbor. Overcoming sin required χάρις (*charis*), the gracious and gratuitous help of

[10] "The righteousness of God [is…] not that whereby He is Himself righteous [and thus justly punishes sinners], but that with which He endows man when He justifies the ungodly." (translated in *Basic Writings of Saint Augustine*, ed. Whitney Oates, New York: Random House, 1948, v1, p471). The Latin original is "*Iustitia* […] Dei non qua Deus iustus est, sed qua induit hominem, cum iustificat impium." (Augustine, "De Spiritu et Littera Liber Unus," Cap. 9, in Aurelii Augustini, *Opera Omnia*, editio latina @ http://www.augustinus.it/latino/spirito_lettera/index.htm, Pl.4. - editio latina

[11] The *loci classici* for this in Paul's Greek are *Ephesians* 2:18, *Ephesians* 3:12, and *Romans* 5:2.

[12] Stephen Sondheim, "Gee, Officer Krupke," *West Side Story*, Act 2, Sc. 2, 1958. The idea is perennial, especially in the once Augustinian United States. At college in the 1950s, Joan Didion felt she was living in a "fallen" world: "I suppose I am talking about just that: the ambiguity of belonging to a generation distrustful of political highs, the historical irrelevancy of growing up convinced that the heart of darkness lay not in some error of social organization but in man's own blood. If man was bound to err, then any social organization was bound to be in error." —Joan Didion, "A Generation Not for Barricades," *Life Magazine*, 5 June, 1970, p26.

God himself, experienced by the believer. Augustine found this doctrine in Paul's *Epistle to the Romans* (as an Augustinian monk named Martin Luther did a millennium later); but Augustine followed it up with a solution to what theologians call the "problem of evil," the paradox that if there was only one all-powerful god, the evil in the world of which a singular God was the creator, must logically have been put there by God. Raised a pagan in the long mantic twilight of the Roman Empire, Augustine had for a while believed with the Manichæans that there were two gods, one good and one evil, which makes the paradox somewhat easier to resolve; but for a monotheist, the "problem of evil" is so intractable that the American poet Archibald MacLeish turned it into an aphorism: "If God is God, he is not good; if God is good, he is not God."[13]

Augustine's solution, if it is a solution, was to assert that love and freedom imply each other. No one can love who is not free to do so, he argued, so if humans were created to love, they must have been created free to love—and, by the same token, free *not* to love. Thus evil must have come into the world via the free will of man and woman, not the acts of God. No small victory for human liberty, this argument is still reflected in Western legal traditions, all of which begin with the assumption that transgressions are committed by free, and therefore responsible, individuals. Only the χάρις or grace of God, extended to and experienced by an individual, can overcome such freedom and provide the possibility of love to those who choose against it. No doubt there are children of authoritarian parents of every religion and irreligion who would be grateful if they had a belief like that of grace passed on to them.

Augustine had found most of this by extrapolating from the Letters or *Epistles* of a sainted Apostle of Jesus who had never met him in the flesh. The sainthood of Saul of Tarsus, the Jew whom Christians call Saint Paul, has been inferred by Christians from his tireless preaching of Jesus's divinity all over the Roman Empire, and from the letters that he wrote to the Empire's nascent Christian communities that have survived to this day and were written before the Gospel accounts of Jesus own preaching were written down. Paul's letters called on non-Jews to join such communities, making the religion potentially universal, and Paul himself into Christianity's second founder.

There is a bright light in the heavens, reports Chap. 9 of the New Testament book, *Acts of the Apostles*, and Saul of Tarsus, a Roman citizen and an official of the synagogue, on his way to Damascus to root out the heretic "Christians" there, is abruptly thrown to the ground. Suddenly blinded, he hears a voice: "Saul, Saul, why are you persecuting me?" "Who are you, Lord?" says Saul. "I am Jesus," answers the voice, and Saul, who was born in a town far from Jerusalem and has never seen Jesus before his execution, believes him. Jesus then orders Saul to proceed to Damascus to learn what to do with the rest of his life. After three days fasting in the city, Saul, a Jew, recovers his sight and becomes Paul, the most indefatigable, the

[13]MacLeish coined this in his 1958 play, *J.B.*, based on the Biblical book of *Job*, (New York: Houghton Mifflin Harcourt, 1959)

most influential, and by nearly all accounts the most consequential of all the early Christian evangelists.[14]

It is an arresting story of ecstatic conversion, perhaps the most important in the history of Christianity, since whether or not we trust as history the stories Luke tells in his *Acts of the Apostles*, it remains true for historians that it was Paul, more than anyone else, who deliberately opened the Christian movement to the millions in the Roman Empire who were not Jews like himself.[15] Paul's conversion also became a model for future conversions to Christianity. *Acts* set it down more than a generation after the event; but Paul had already written his own account sometime between 48 and 51 A.D., in the first chapter of his *Epistle to the Galatians*. *Galatians*, which is probably either the first or second of Paul's seven authentic letters (*Epistolae*) to the new Christian communities springing up around the Empire of the Caesars, describes an experience somewhat less spectacular, but equally sudden and seemingly supernatural:

> But when he who had set me apart before I was born, and *had called me through his grace* [*charitos*, or generosity, in Paul's Greek] was pleased to *reveal his Son to me*, in order that I might preach him among the Gentiles, I did not confer with flesh and blood.[16]

Later, in the second of the two Epistles that Paul wrote to reprove and calm the over-ecstatic Christians at Corinth, the apostle described, in the third person, a vision which most commentators think must have been his own. Paul protests humility, but he offers proof that he (if it was he) had been truly *raptus*—taken out of himself—that day.

> I must boast; there is nothing to be gained by it, but I will go on to visions and revelations of the Lord. I know a man in Christ who fourteen years ago was *caught up to the third heaven—whether in body or out of the body I do not know*, God knows. And I know that this man was *caught up into Paradise—whether in body or out of the body I do not know*, God

---

[14] The story is told no less than three times in Luke's *New Testament* Book of the *Acts of the Apostles*: *Acts* 9:1-22, *Acts* 22:6-21, and *Acts* 26:9-22 (King James version).

[15] The extraordinary far-reaching consequences of that story for history are starkly summed up by no less than Friedrich Nietzsche, a Greek philologist and pastor's son: "That the ship of Christianity threw overboard a good deal of its Jewish ballast, that it went, and was able to go, among the pagans—that was due to this one man...." (Nietzsche, *The Dawn* (*Morgenröte*, 1881) in *The Portable Nietzsche*, Translated and Edited by Walter Kaufmann. New York: Viking Press, 1954, p76-77.) George Bernard Shaw's view was wittier but if anything more negative: "it was Paul who converted the religion that had raised one man above sin and death into a religion that delivered millions of men so completely into their dominion that their own common nature became a horror to them, and the religious life became a denial of life" (Shaw, "Preface" to *Androcles and the Lion*, New York: Brentano's, 1916). Apothegms aside, Paul's conversion, his career and their consequences have filled many volumes, but they can be found summarized with heroic brevity by Garry Wills in his *What Paul Meant* (New York: Viking Penguin, 2006).

[16] St. Paul, *Galatians* 1:15-16 (King James version. The original Greek is οτε δε ευδοκησεν ο θεοσ ο αφορισας με εκ κοιλιας μητρος μου και καλεσας δια της **χαριτος** αυτου αποκαλυψαι τον υιον αυτου εν εμοι ινα ευαγγελιζωμαι αυτον εν τοις εθνεσιν ευθεως ου προσανεθεμην σαρκι και αιματι)

> knows—and he *heard things that cannot be told, which man may not utter*. On behalf of this man I will boast, but on my own behalf I will not boast, except of my weaknesse.[17]

It probably helped Paul with the Corinthians to be able to refer to his own conversionary rapture, because, as both of his letters to them make abundantly clear, most of the Christians in Corinth were as beside themselves as Paul had been that once. They were trembling and falling in prayer, prophesying (14:1–5), both men and women (14:34), ranting in unknown languages (14:23), healing by miracles, "discerning spirits," indulging in unregulated diets and unorthodox sex (Chap. 5, verse 1 mentions mother-son incest), a whole ecstatic gamut. Paul had to tell them, in the most famous paragraph in all his writings, that no matter how exciting all these various gifts might be, the greatest by far of "gifts of the spirit" was simply love, disinterested, selfless love of neighbor, *agape* (ἀγάπη in Paul's Greek) and in Latin, *caritas*—a derivative of the Greek χάρις (caris) or grace—which English has shrunk to "charity." This, the most poetic of all the verses of Paul, suggests that he may not have hated himself nearly as much as Shaw and Nietzsche would one day charge:

> If I speak with the tongues of men and of angels, and have not charity, I am become as a sounding brass or a tinkling cymbal. And if I should have prophecy and should know all mysteries and all knowledge, and if I should have all faith, so that I could remove mountains, and have not charity [ἀγάπην], I am nothing. And though I bestow all my goods to feed the poor, and though I give my body to be burned, and have not charity, it profiteth me nothing.[18]

Clearly Paul had taken his ecstatic vision as a revelation by the God of Israel intended to change his life and his ethics, and he did that. It was not, however, altogether in the Torah—the Law—that he found those ethics, but in the stories of Jesus. Moreover, once he had undertaken to change his life according to this new dispensation, he adopted the duty to proselytize it, including tasks like showing the Corinthians which of their antinomian ecstasies the new law would permit or discourage.

Although no account of Paul's ecstatic conversion can inspire much trust in post-Enlightenment minds,[19] it remains a fact that in Paul's own time, about 35 A.D.,

[17] St. Paul, 2 *Corinthians* 12:1-5 (King James version)

[18] St. Paul, 1 *Corinthians* 13:2-3 (King James version) Paul's word for selfless love, αγαπε (*agape*, is traditionally rendered *caritas* in the Latin Bible, and "charity" in the King James, which is not etymologically related to *agape*; but, tellingly, it is related to Paul's word for grace—χαρις/ *charis*). Modern English translations render *agape* simply as "love." One may add that whether Paul himself was very loving or lovable remains in question. The admittedly unfriendly Nietzsche described Paul as "a very tortured, very pitiful, very unpleasant man, unpleasant even to himself." (Nietzsche, *The Dawn* (*Morgenröte*, 1881) tr. Kaufmann in *The Portable Nietzsche*, p77.)

[19] The important book by philosopher Alain Badiou, *Saint Paul: La fondation de l'universalisme* (Paris: PUF, 1997; 2nd ed., 2002), shows a remarkable understanding of "grace," even in Greek, despite Badiou's declared Marxist atheism. Grace continues to fascinate even its doubters. Another French writer, Pierre Michon, recently conjured the sword-swinging Irish saint Columba on horseback, such that "God, King of this world and the next, can count on his sword to persuade the disciples of the monk Pelagius, who deny Grace, that Grace is devastating and can be weighed in

accounts of experiences like his were common. The first one described in *Acts of the Apostles* is the well-known "Pentecost" during which the bereft disciples of the crucified Jesus find themselves suddenly preaching to the multicultural crowd in Jerusalem for the Passover in languages these disciples had never learned to speak, and attributing the phenomenon to the "coming of the Holy Spirit."

Paul wrote in Greek, and used the Greek vocabulary for religious experience already developed by Greek pagans who came long before him, found in the writings of the historian Herodotus, the physician Hippocrates, and Plato. It was still being used by those who came after him, like Plutarch the historian and moralist, Lucian the satirist, and the Neoplatonic philosophers like Plotinus. The Greek, and later the Roman world had long known of such experiences. The words in ancient Greek and Latin that describe them are legion (as Jesus numbered the demons that possess the lunatic in the gospel of Mark). Prominent among them are εκστασιος (*ekstasios*, ecstasy, being outside oneself), ενθουσιασμος (*enthousiasmos*, enthusiasm, possession by a god), and μυστικοσ (*mystikos*, mystic, initiated into the μυστηρια—mysteries—of the goddess Demeter at Eleusis, and thus, able to communicate immediately with the gods). Such experiences lead to γνοσις (*gnosis*, esoteric knowledge of the divine) and, too often, δεσιδαιμονια (*desidaimonia*, irrational fear of gods).

In Latin the states of mind are *fanaticus* (possessed by a god), *inspiratus* (inspired, having breathed in a god's spirit), *superstitio* (standing over in awe), *raptus* (enraptured, taken away from, or out of oneself) from *rapiare*. The resulting phenomena were *visiones*, visions. Such words still give away the game.[20] All have been used since their origins to describe a strain of religious belief which assumes that the relationship between divinity and a believer can sometimes be not only immediate and personal, but involve a sort of division, alienation or abnegation of self. The experience is accompanied by powerful feelings and evokes and often indeed glories in religious devotion or behavior which is unconventional, often visible, vocal, public, socially inappropriate, and physical. This religion falls into trances, but also sings, shouts, dances, laughs uncontrollably, speaks in tongues, shakes and

iron." (Pierre Michon, "Tristesse de Columbkill," tr. Ann Jefferson, "Columbkill's Sadness," in *Winter Mythologies and Abbots*, New Haven: Yale U.P., 2014). And Brooklyn poet Marianne Moore wrote: . . . . . To explain grace requires / a curious hand. If that which is at all were not forever, / why would those who graced the spires / with animals and gathered there to rest, on cold luxurious / low stone seats—a monk and monk and monk—between the thus / ingenious roof-supports, have slaved to confuse / grace with a kindly manner, time in which to pay a debt, / the cure for sins ... (Moore, "Pangolin" in *The Complete Poems of Marianne Moore*, New York: Macmillan/Viking, 1967) And Bono (Paul David Hewson), the born-again Irish Anglican bandleader of U2, put it with no second thoughts in 2005: "along comes this idea called Grace to upend all that 'as you reap, so you will sow' stuff. Grace defies reason and logic. Love interrupts, if you like, the consequences of your actions." (*Bono: In Conversation with Michka Assayas*, Riverhead Books, 2005, reposted @ www.teilhard.com)

[20] The absence of some words can make the same story more precise. *Insanus*, *furibundus*, *studiosus*, and *acer*, were Latin words for extreme emotion, but not for being beside oneself. Only *phrenīticus*, a loan word from Greek that meant delirious, could sometimes mean both.

trembles, raises the roof—and offends, embarrasses and inspires the suspicion and scorn of those who don't. Not to mention their offers of therapy.

The experience of grace was not the only experience that Christians had in the Dark Ages after Augustine, and in the Middle Ages, the Renaissance and the Reformation, and since, that would qualify as mystical. What we now think of as the fundamental "mystical" experience, that of self-abnegating, self-overwhelming union with the divine, continued in every subsequent Christian century. Christian mystics in Europe came in all of Europe's languages, and (unlike priests) in all of its genders. They were sometimes made saints, but more often denominated heretics and suppressed. Many were jailed and quite a few were burned—except in England, which burned witches as enthusiastically as other states, but almost never burned mystics.

Among the mystics who were canonized as saints were the great radical Saint Francis of Assisi (1182–1226) and the Franciscan who wrote Saint Francis's official biography, Saint Bonaventure (1221–1274). Bonaventure, though influential in the politics of the Church and sober and scholarly in most of his theological writings,[21] was an ecstatic after office hours. The story was told of Thomas Aquinas (once a classmate of Bonaventure at the University of Paris) visiting Bonaventure's cell while Bonaventure was writing his definitive life of Saint Francis and finding the biographer in an ecstasy. Aquinas is said to have left him alone with the comment, "Let us leave a saint to work for a saint."

Germans more often got burned, though some escaped judgment. Mechthild of Magdeburg (1212–1299) was among those who managed to avoid both canonization and condemnation, at least in their lifetimes. Mechthild wrote most of the mystical tract, *The Flowing Light of the Godhead*, a work that was known to Dante and influenced his *Paradiso*. Though a woman of some privilege, she joined Magdeburg's local Beguines, an uncloistered association of unmarried, usually well-off women, who took no vows, were controlled by no order, lived separately in the cottages of a "beguinage," and did charitable work.[22] After several years at this new kind of monastery, she joined one of the old-fashioned ones in 1268, becoming a Benedictine nun, to which she may have been led by the visions she had experienced and written about in *The Flowing Light*, when she was still a Beguine.

"Meister" Eckhart, the Dominican Johannes Eckhart (c1260-c1328), was accused of associating with the heretic Beghards, investigated for heresy, and tried by a Bishop's court; but a conviction never issued. Pope John XXII, to whom Eckhart

---

[21] An exception was Bonaventure's book, *Itinerarium Mentis in Deum* (The Journey of the Mind to God), which influenced later mystics like Heinrich (Henry) Suso.

[22] And intellectual work as well. Mechthild's big book, *The Flowing Light of the Godhead*, about the annihilation of the individual soul in God, contains this piece of worldly wisdom: "Foolishness is satisfied with itself alone; wisdom can never learn enough." Her original phrasing ("Dú trumpheit behaget ir selbe alleine, dú wisheit kan niemer volleleren.") reminds us that in medieval German "Trumpheit" meant "foolishness," and "Trump" meant "fool." —Mechthild of Magdeburg, *Das fließende Licht der Gottheit*. (ed., Hans Neumann, 2 volumes, Munich: Artemis, 1990, book 4, chap 4, 1:117.7-8), quoted by Bernard McGinn in his *Presence of God*, v3, *The Flowering of Mysticism*. (New York: Crossroad Herder, 1998), Preface p. xi.

had appealed, did put out a bull condemning seventeen mystical propositions from Eckhart's sermons and his *Book of Divine Comfort*—but Eckhart had died the year before the bull.[23] Eckhart's German Dominican disciples Johannes Tauler (c1300–1361) and Suso (Heinrich Seuse, 1295–1366) shared his state of mind and ran into the same suspicions, when together with other Eckhart followers of all classes and both sexes they founded a group called the Friends of God (John 15:14 & James 2:23), which popularized mysticism along the Rhine (Switzerland, Bavaria, the Rhineland, and the Netherlands). These pre-Quaker Friends did not disparage learning in the fashion of evangelical Protestants later; but the Friends of God did place critical reason well below their experience—which they were convinced was experience of the divine. Tauler's own mysticism was explicitly anti-rational. As he wrote in his second Sermon for Ascension Day:

> The third type of captivity is that of natural reason. This is the downfall of many, because they spoil everything which should be born in the spirit—be it doctrine or truth of whatever kind—by lowering it to the level of their reasoning powers.[24]

The main way for heretical thinkers to avoid trouble was to acknowledge and approve of the Church's priesthood with its sacramental monopoly, but that was hard for mystics, who felt they could lose the sinful self and reach the divine without passing through mass and penance. It was that possibility that would make Luther's sudden grasp of "justification," not by works but "by faith," such a revolutionary one in 1517.

A French woman, Marguerite Porete, wrote a much-read heretical manuscript, *The Mirror of the Simple Souls Who Are Annihilated and Remain Only in Will and Desire of Love*,[25] which remains to describe her vision of seven spiritual stages through which any soul should pass, as hers had, to reach "annihilation" in perfect union with the divine. The manuscript was anonymous, but she was tried and burnt at the stake in 1310 in a cruel prelude to the Church Council held by Pope Clement V at Vienne in 1311, a Council which condemned so many of the contemporary (and anticlerical) mystical movements, including the Beguines, the Beghards and the antinomian Brethren of the Free Spirit, or Joachimites, with whom Porete was

[23] One of Eckhardt's Latin sermons is on 1 Corinthians 15:1-10 ("By God's grace I am what I am."). It tries to define "grace." (Eckhart, *Sermons*, #XXV for 11th Sunday after Trinity. @ https://biblehub.com/sermons/auth/eckhart/outward_and_inward_morality.htm)

[24] Johannes Tauler, "Ascendens Christus in altum, captivam duxit captivitatem," in Tauler, *Sermons*, tr., Maria Shrady (Mahwah, NJ: Paulist Press, 1985), p70. The influence of Dominican Johannes Tauler (c1300-1361) was enhanced by book wrongly attributed to him, *Theologica Germanica*, 1516-18, which was edited by Luther and became a source for John Wesley. Luther made a marginal note in ca. 1516 on Tauler's Christmas sermon, referring to Augustine. The sermon ends: "Cherish this deep silence within, nourish it frequently, so that it may become a habit, and by becoming a habit, a mighty possession. For what seems quite impossible to an unpracticed person becomes easy to a practiced one. It is a habit which creates skill." (Tauler, "Puer natus est," in Shrady, tr., *Sermons*, p40)

[25] Marguerite Porete, *The Mirror of Simple Souls*, tr., Ellen L. Babinsky, (Mahwah, NJ: Paulist Press, 1993). The original French title is *Le Mirouer des simples âmes anienties et qui seulement demeurent en vouloir et désir d'amour.*

accused of associating. The Brethren of the Free Spirit were branded as heretics for reporting visions, and their fate was later visited on the Waldensians, the Hussites and the English Lollards, but the main heresy that got all of these condemned was their failure to acknowledge as a matter of law the monopoly of the Church on dispensing the "means of salvation," the tools to get to Heaven. That failure was a proto-Protestant heresy that would later put Martin Luther under the same ban. The Council of Vienne in 1311 expelled from the faith any who might teach that sinlessness could be attained by ordinary people during their mortal lives. (This doctrine was named "perfectionism" when it was adopted by John Wesley's Methodists in the eighteenth century, but it is not a doctrine that an organization like the medieval Church, diligently providing what most believed to be the sole means to escape eternal punishment, could safely allow to spread.)

Mystics abounded in High Middle Ages Christianity, especially in England; and English mystics seem never either to have offended an Inquisition or been officially canonized as saints. Four of them, Richard Rolle, Julian of Norwich, Walter Hilton, and the author of *The Cloude of Unknowyng*, all wrote powerfully of their personal experience of the divine, attained in stages through meditation, and the sublimation of the self.

Rolle (1290–1349), a priest educated at the Sorbonne and Oxford, wrote *Incendium Amoris* [*The Fire of Love*]. He had had his first mystical experience two years and eight months after leaving the clerical elite to become an English hermit. Julian of Norwich was remarkable for having been the first woman who ever wrote a book in English. She had only one ecstatic vision, on a single day and night in May, 1373, but it came in 16 separate episodes, and she wrote about it on three separate occasions. The final document, *Revelations of Divine Love* [*in Sixteen Shewinges*] (1393) written after she became a solitary anchoress, remains a classic of the mystical discovery of union with the divine.

> For I saw truly that [...] our soul is so fully oned to God of His own Goodness that between God and our soul may be right nought.
>
> And to this understanding was the soul led by love and drawn by might in every Shewing[26]

The *Scale,* or *Ladder*, *of Perfection*, written by the English Augustinian mystic Walter Hilton (c1345–1396), elaborates more stages of mystical gnosis, and *The Cloude of Unknowyng*, written in about 1375 by an unknown parish clergyman (who also produced a free translation of the *Mystical Theology* by Pseudo-Dionysius the Areopagite) is salted with colloquial warnings against self-created visions and dubious psychological explanations.

> For whoever hears or reads about all this, and thinks that it is fundamentally an activity of the mind, and proceeds then to work it out along these lines, is on quite the wrong track. He manufactures an experience that is neither spiritual nor physical.[27]

---

[26] Julian of Norwich, *Revelations of Divine Love*. (New York: Penguin, 1998), Chapter 46.

[27] The Cloud of Unknowing, tr., Clifton Wolters, New York: Penguin Classics, 1961, p57

Both the *Scale* and the *Cloud*, however, make clear that the goal of meditation is to lose the self. The believer's finite self seems, in a thoroughly non-rational experience, to fade away in a merger with the infinite—and unknowable—Being. The experience is a gift of grace, undeserved, but a gift one must nevertheless strive for. It is not offered to everybody, but no one seems to be excluded.

> So pay great attention to this marvelous work of grace within your soul. It is always a sudden impulse and comes without warning, springing up to God like some spark from the fire.

> For though we through the grace of God can know fully about all other matters, and think about them—... yet of God may no man think. [...] By love he can be caught and held, but by thinking never [...] Strike that thick cloud of unknowing with the sharp dart of longing love, and on no account whatever think of giving up.[28]

This sort of Enlightenment would come to seem quite un-English by the time of John Locke, but not in the fourteenth century.

All accounts of mysticism were challenged in the twentieth century by Freud's unconscious, and may change in the 21st, due not only to a widespread moral revaluation of selfishness and the spread of chemical stimulants to ecstasy, but also to the rising tide of neuroscience and its new ability to detect the taking of action before any decision to take action comes to mind. As Sam Harris puts it, "Free will is an illusion. Our wills are simply not of our own making. Thoughts and intentions emerge from background causes of which we are unaware and over which we exert no conscious control." If the neuroscience turns out right, it may become difficult to continue behaving as free, loving or responsible.[29] But William James may have made more sense when he turned freedom into an act of faith: "My first act of free will shall be to believe in free will." Or Isaac Bashevis Singer when he said, "We must believe in free will; we have no choice."[30]

---

[28] Ibid., p59, 60. A. C. Spearing's newer translation of the same passage is quoted in the *Wikipedia* article on "*The Cloud of Unknowing*." "For He can well be loved, but he cannot be thought. By love he can be grasped and held, but by thought, neither grasped nor held. And therefore, though it may be good at times to think specifically of the kindness and excellence of God, and though this may be a light and a part of contemplation, all the same, in the work of contemplation itself, it must be cast down and covered with a cloud of forgetting. And *you must step above it* stoutly but deftly, with a devout and delightful stirring of love, and struggle to pierce that darkness above you; and beat on that thick cloud of unknowing with a sharp dart of longing love, and do not give up, whatever happens. (The Cloud of Unknowing and other works, Translated by Elizabeth Spearing, New York: Penguin Classics. 2001. My italics.)

[29] Sam Harris, *Free Will*, New York: Free Press, 2012, Chapter 1. The science, which began in the 1980s with experiments by Benjamin Libet and others, can be found presented in detail in Daniel Wegner, *The Illusion of Conscious Will* (Cambridge, MA: MIT Press, 2002)

[30] William James, *Diary*, entry for April 30, 1870, in Ralph Barton Perry, *The Thought and Character of William James* (Boston, Little, Brown, 1936) vol.1, p.323. The idea appears in James, "The Will to Believe," though not as an aphorism. (James, "The Will to Believe: An Address to the Philosophical Clubs of Yale and Brown Universities" (April & May, 1896), in James, *Writings 1878-1899*. (Library of America, 1992), pp. 457-479. Isaac Bashevis Singer (1902-1991) repeated his own aphorism in several interviews ("Isaac Singer's Promised City," *City Journal* (Summer 1997).

For Augustinian Christians such advice would not have come amiss. The same would be true for many believing Jews and Muslims, especially the Ash'arites and Ṣufis among the Muslims, and the Kabbalist Jews.

Again, in the thought of the converted Augustine, grace was a free, unearned and unwilled gift from God to humans, unwilled because no human could strive for it without God, unearned because no human deserved it, free because no human (except Jesus) could offer anything in return. Pelagius, Augustine thought, was wrong to suggest that humans could ask for grace on their own rather than having it bestowed on them; wrong to contend that Jesus's sacrifice had made it possible for any human to find her or his own way to salvation, or, in other words, to have the grace necessary to ask for grace.

And in the sixteenth century in Christian Europe, Augustine's legacy reached Calvin. John Calvin's experience, like Luther's, was fundamentally intellectual rather than ecstatic, without the personal confrontation with divinity that Paul and Augustine had reported, and for him, the analysis of Augustine was even more starkly binary. His rediscovery of the Augustinian doctrine of grace led to the grim conclusion that only a few (the "elect" or the chosen), would be saved.

John Calvin—Jean Cauvin—was a Frenchman from the western province of Picardy. Like other emerging Protestants, he went into exile in Switzerland after the King of France proscribed the emerging Reformation in 1534. Guillaume Farel, who had left earlier, found Calvin there and pressed him into service to reform the city-republic of Geneva. By the time Calvin had published his own commentary on Paul's *Epistle to the Galatians* in 1548,[31] he had become the preeminent leader of the clergy of the Reformed Church of Geneva and people would soon call him the "Protestant Pope."

On his own conversion, Calvin wrote no more than a sentence or two in a preface to his *Commentary on the Psalms* published years later in 1557. Around 1530, Calvin would recall, "Providence [was] turning my bridle."[32] The conversion seems to have taken place during the five years between 1528 and 1533, after Calvin transferred from the humanities to law school at his father's command, and began to suffer the migraines and indigestion he would have for the rest of his life. He describes no physical seizure like Paul's and not even a sudden intellectual illumination like Luther's. But he emerged in 1533 an intense, ever-smoldering firebrand, who would spend the rest of his life in the work of formulating and spreading his faith.

[31] "[Paul] pursues this subject to the end of the *second* Chapter, *Galatians* 2, when he proceeds to argue the doctrine, that we are justified in the sight of God by Free Grace, and not by the Works of the Law. His argument is this: If Ceremonies have not the power of bestowing Justification, the observation of them is therefore unnecessary. We must remark, however, that he does not confine himself entirely to Ceremonies, but argues generally about Works, otherwise the whole discussion would be trifling." —Calvin, *Commentary on Galatians* (1548), tr., ?, @ http://www.ccel.org/c/calvin/comment3/comm_vol41/htm/iii.ii.htm

[32] Calvin, *Commentary on the Psalms* (1557), "Preface," in Calvin, *Opera Omnia, Corpus Reformatorum*, eds., G. Baum, E. Cunitz, and E. Reuss, Brunswick: C. Schwetschke, 1863-1900, vol. 31, col. 24.

Their different characters experienced different after-effects of conversion. Where Luther was plumpish and ate with even greater relish after his discovery of justification by faith, Calvin was lean. Dyspeptic and headache-ridden, he ate one frugal meal a day and slept little. The rest of his time was spent in reading, writing and meetings. The estimate is three to four three-hour sermons a week, three lectures on theology a week, and a meeting with a Genevan church or government council twice a week. With only a little less regularity, he wrote to about 300 correspondents and produced enough books and pamphlets to fill sixty double-column folio volumes.

Geneva when Calvin arrived in the 1530s was a free, self-governing city-republic which spoke French and had yet to join the Swiss Confederation. Calvin took over its church and Geneva reacted by throwing him out. He returned, and they took him back. Geneva under Calvin's ascendancy became the international headquarters of a form of Protestantism that came to be called "Calvinism"; but the sixteenth- and seventeenth-century Genevans called it "Reformed," as did the French, Germans and Dutch, while Scots called it "Presbyterian," and the English and New Englanders called it "Puritan" and "Congregational." Calvin did not choose all its doctrines, but he did reduce them to plain French prose in his summary of "reformed" theology, *The Institutes of the Christian Religion*.

First published in French in 1534, and burnt in Latin by the censor in Paris in 1544, *The Institutes* belongs with *Das Kapital* and *The Origin of Species* as one of the most influential books ever written in the West. Humanist in its exhaustive classical scholarship, lawyerly in the inexorability of its arguments, *The Institutes* was perhaps most deeply original in the asceticism of its style. It made something of a revolution in French literature; today Calvin's French contemporary Rabelais, exuberant and forgiving, cannot be read without commentary, while the implacable Calvin is often as clear as Hemingway—and more humorless.

Calvin's *Institutes* says very little about conversion, and hardly anything about "heart religion" or piety. Nevertheless it was Calvin's *Institutes*, that became the second Bible for those who preached conversion; and it does say a good deal about grace, especially about its limited availability. Luther had found exuberant release from guilt by unpacking a particular verse, *Romans* 1:17, "The just shall live by faith," concluding that if you believed that you were saved—then you *were* saved (and God's grace had made you believe it). Calvin reduced Luther's plenitude to precision, together with all of Paul; but he kept adding to the logical implications. Man, said ancient judeo-christian doctrine, was an inveterate sinner—"fallen" with Adam in Eden and "utterly depraved" as the English wrote. "The best of us is no damn good," as Stephen Sondheim would put it. God would therefore never find a human being who was inherently worthy of redemption—except Jesus, of course.

And God (according to this primordial Christian doctrine) had nevertheless redeemed the human species from punishment by undergoing crucifixion in the person of Jesus. On the other hand, asserted Calvin, if ordinary persons are depraved, that depravity must make them incapable of believing that that Crucifixion had redeemed them from punishment. Therefore, if they did believe it, they must have had help from God to believe it. Since God was omnipotent, but resolved to preserve human free will, it must not be that God would help anyone to believe; but since God was just, he must find it necessary to damn everyone for the unbelief that resulted from their helplessness. Logic further required, according to Calvin, that since God, however just, was also merciful in redeeming guilty mankind, he would freely give the capacity to believe. But, being just, he must give it only to some, who would be saved, and not to others, who would be damned. Further, since God, being timelessly omniscient, must know everything that had happened and that would happen, he would know whether each and every human was ultimately saved or damned before he or she was even born. Such is Calvinist doctrine in a nutshell. It helps explain why Zinzendorf was a Lutheran and not, like his evangelical contemporaries George Whitefield and Jonathan Edwards, a Calvinist.

Calvinism has also, famously since Max Weber pointed it out in 1905, fostered the "Protestant ethic" of hard work, saving and capital accumulation.[33] This was because so many Calvinists, uncertain of their election, came to believe that God's way of gracefully letting them know that they were bound for Heaven rather than Hell was to grant them steady habits and worldly success with or without a sudden infusion of the Holy Spirit. Not for nothing did the New England state of Connecticut, with its state-established Puritan Congregational Church, call itself for more than a century the "Land of Steady Habits." The only problem with this was the law's regularity closed in on the essentially antinomian spirit of ecstatic faith. Accesses of grace became rare, and the dynamism due to the assurance of the first generations of Calvinists began to slack off.[34]

Meanwhile a small minority of inward-looking believers introduced ecstasy into Protestant Christianity. Ecstatics were set loose by the Reformation, in spite of predestination, and many of the proliferating Protestant sects in the sixteenth century were antinomian. The Anabaptists (believing baptism was for believers after, and not before, receipt of grace) got a start in a private home in Zurich, Switzerland, when Conrad Grebel baptized George Cajacob whom friends called "Blaurock" (Blue-Blouse). Blue-Blouse then baptized everybody else in the house, and they decided to separate true and truly baptized believers from all other Christians. Harassed the following week in their hometown, they began wandering through Switzerland making converts until they were arrested and condemned to prison by

---

[33] Weber's book was first published in 1904-05 in two issues of the journal, *Archiv für Sozialwissenschaft und Sozialpolitik*. The translation by Talcott Parsons known in U.S. colleges, *The Protestant Ethic and the Spirit of Capitalism*, was published in London in 1930.

[34] The *Institutes* also had a great deal to say about church organization, a new, less parochial, less ostentatious, more effective and more egalitarian form of church organization. Geneva under Calvin became the general headquarters of a militant, federal and republican form of Protestant church government (called "presbyterian" in English) that was so aptly organized by Calvin for missionary export that it was able to move in and take over against violent state opposition not only in Geneva, but in parts of north Germany, a good part of France and England, half the Netherlands and the whole of Scotland, not to mention Massachusetts and Connecticut, providing a model for revolutionary organizations from the Calvinist Puritans who beheaded King Charles I in 1649 down to the Russian Bolsheviks and the Algerian FLN.

Zurich officials led by Zwingli, the leader of the new Swiss Protestantism.[35] After Grebel's visit to nearby Sankt Gallen, the Protestant pastor there, Johannes Kessler, described Anabaptist converts meeting in the fields and "dying": groaning, sweating, twisting their fingers, crumpling to the ground and writhing, seemingly following St. Paul's saying, "I die daily." An unsympathetic observer, Kessler also wrote of them sitting motionless until moved to an action by the Spirit, cutting off their hair, babbling like children, and tearing up their Bibles or burning them in bonfires, seemingly following St. Paul's saying, "the letter killeth but the spirit giveth life." Kessler also reports an antinomian approach to the former Catholic sacrament of marriage involving an alfresco exchange of rings, followed by the new couple tearing off their clothes and fornicating in the fields.[36] (It sounds quite Corinthian, or perhaps 1960s; but it serves in any case to undermine the old canard that all religious ecstasy is only an outlet for sublimated sex.)

Grebel's group was an example for two other radically unorthodox Protestant groups, who were to find safety from orthodox persecution only in the New World, the Hutterites from Tyrol and the Mennonites from Switzerland, none of whom supported revivals.[37] It was sects like these that served George Fox as precedents when he assembled the Religious Society of Friends, or Quakers, in 1640s England.

Protestants in England also produced, like the German Lutherans, a version of Pietism, the "heart" religion that went beyond orthodox doctrines of grace to the experience itself, often including the traditional mystic loss of "self." "Heart" thinkers included Puritan Dissenters like Richard Baxter and Anglicans from Henry Scougal to William Law.[38] Perhaps the best known is John Bunyan, the tinker whose account of his own conversion (with frequent backslides) in *Grace Abounding to the Chief of Sinners*, was written while he was in prison for religious dissent, and published in 1666. Bunyan was a gifted writer and conversion led him to become a

---

[35] Jörg Cajacob "Blaurock", *Reminiscences*. (1525) Translated in Denis R. Janz, ed. *A Reformation Reader: Primary Texts With Introductions* (Minneapolis: Fortress Press, 1999), pp. 168-70 @ http://www.gjlts.com/Church%20History/Reformation%20History/blaurockreminiscences.pdf..

[36] Johannes Kessler, *Sabbata* (ed. Emil Egli & Rudolf Schoch. St. Gallen: Fehr'sche Buchhandlung, 1902), pp. 185-197.

[37] Otto Friedrich. *The End of the World: A History*. New York: Fromm International, pb 1986, p. 150.

[38] Their writing includes Richard Baxter (1615-1691), *Call to the Unconverted to Turn and Live*. 1658 (Grand Rapids, MI: Christian Classics Ethereal Library, accessed 2020-12-2), and Henry Scougal (1650-1678), *The Life of God in the Soul of Man*, 1677 (Grand Rapids, MI: Christian Classics Ethereal Library, accessed 2003-10-14). Baxter's and Scougal's books were instrumental in the conversion of George Whitefield. Many of those non-German Pietists are studied in Charles E. Hambrick-Stowe's survey, *The Practice of Piety: Puritan Devotional Disciplines in Seventeenth-Century New England*. (Chapel Hill: U. of North Carolina Press, 1982) in the works of F. Ernest Stoeffler: *The Rise of Evangelical Pietism* (1965) (Eugene, OR: Wipf & Stock, 2007), *German Pietism During the Eighteenth Century* (E. J. Brill, 1973), in the collection Stoeffler edited, *Continental Pietism and Early American Christianity*. (Grand Rapids, MI: Eerdmans, 1976), and in W. R. Ward's masterpieces, *The Protestant Evangelical Awakening*. (Cambridge: Cambridge University Press, 1991, 1998) and *Early Evangelicalism: A Global Intellectual History, 1670-1789*. (Cambridge: Cambridge University Press, 2006).

preacher, moving beyond Puritanism to the new Anabaptist or "Baptist" denomination.[39]

And there was at least one intellectual reaction to the irresistible grace and enslaved will of Augustinian Protestants. A sort of renewed Pelagianism, it coalesced in the sixteenth-century United Provinces of the Netherlands as they began fighting their long war of independence against the Spanish crown, and the Pelagian resister was Jacobus Arminius (Jakob Hermanszoon,1560–1609) a pastor of the Calvinist Dutch Reformed Church and professor in Amsterdam. Arminius had begun looking into Paul's *Epistle to the Romans* in 1591 and raising Augustinian questions about whether it justified Calvinist predestination. Arminius came slowly to the conclusion that God had given everyone the grace necessary to believe, and thus that God might not have 100% of the agency when humans were looking to be saved. In 1604 Arminius questioned predestination in a public controversy and by 1608 he was arguing his position before the Supreme Court of the United Provinces.

By 1619, ten years after his death, his views had become an –ism, Arminianism, officially condemned by the Dutch national Reformed Church at the Synod of Dort, and Arminians were being accused of being traitorous agents of King Philip of Spain. The government of the province of Holland, which had tried to protect the Arminians, fell, and the republic's chief executive was seized, tried and executed. Arminianism nevertheless survived and continued to challenge Calvinist orthodoxy for more than two centuries—as long as that orthodoxy continued to be understood.[40] Nor should it escape notice that both the eighteenth-century Enlightenment in general, and its Counter-Enlightenment dissenter, Jean-Jacques Rousseau, would

---

[39] John Bunyan, *Grace Abounding To The Chief Of Sinners In A Faithful Account Of The Life And Death Of John Bunyan, Or, A Brief Relation Of The Exceeding Mercy Of God In Christ To Him, / Namely In His Taking Him Out Of The Dunghill, And Converting Him To The Faith Of His Blessed Son Jesus Christ. / Here Is Also Particularly Shewed, What Sight Of, And What Troubles He Had For Sin; And Also, What Various Temptations He Hath Met With, And How God Hath Carried Him Through Them.* (1666) in John Stachniewski & Anita Pacheco, eds. ***Grace Abounding**: with Other Spiritual Autobiographies.* (New York: Oxford University Press, 1998). Bunyan's allegorical narrative of conversion, *The Pilgrim's Progress*, was one of the most popular books in English literature.

[40] The Augustine-Pelagius argument has never really ended, and will be seen to return with a vengeance in the evangelical counter-enlightenment. For the first two centuries of the argument's history the best study may be the Patristic Monograph by Rebecca Harden Weaver, *Divine Grace and Human Agency: A Study of the Semi-Pelagian Controversy* (Macon, GA: Mercer University Press, 1996, 1998). In the seventeenth century Arminius became a sort of Pelagius *redivivus* as he and his followers, called Remonstrants, challenged the Augustinianism of Calvin; and the debate went on with Arminian John Wesley in the eighteenth century, crypto-Arminian Charles Grandison Finney in the 19th, and Billy Graham in the 20th. After translating St. Augustine's *Anti-Pelagian Writings*, in 1887 for Philip Schaff, ed., *Select Library of the Nicene and Post-Nicene Fathers of the Christian Church* (New York: The Christian Literature Company, 1887), American Theology Professor Benjamin Breckinridge Warfield (1851–1921) an anti-Arminian Presbyterian, went on to write "Augustine and the Pelagian Controversy" (Christian Literature Company, 1887) a Calvinist account of the argument which is still cited. And in Anthony Burgess's 1962 novel, *The Wanting Seed* (New York: Norton), the Augustine-Pelagius argument provides a frame for grand stages in world history.

be Arminian/Pelagian in their view of human nature, believing that humans were naturally good and that only badly structured social institutions (including established religions) could corrupt them.

Jonathan Edwards, in the far West of English America, Northampton, Massachusetts, would oppose both Arminians and Anabaptists. He descended from Puritans and Dissenters who had approved of Augustinian grace and of Pietist experience and practice. The son and grandson of Congregational ministers, Edwards trained as a minister himself at Connecticut's new Congregational college—Yale.

And Edwards would be Calvinist through and through. He would believe that man was fallen, and believe in a grace that could save an elect through piety; but he would also believe in ecstasy—that one might receive grace through a personal ecstatic experience, a change of heart. Indeed he would also believe and preach that whole communities could receive it at once through many near-simultaneous individual ecstatic experiences. These communal ecstasies would be brought on by an eloquence of conviction invoking the presence of God, even, and perhaps especially, in faraway New England.

Bibliography

Acheson, R.J. 2016. *Radical Puritans in England, 1550-1660*. Routledge.

Achinstein, Sharon. 2003. *Literature and Dissent in Milton's England*. New York: Cambridge University Press.

Agamben, Giorgio. 2005. *The Time That Remains: A Commentary on the* ***Letter to the Romans***. Translated by Patricia Dailey. Stanford, CA: Stanford University Press (Meridian: Crossing Aesthetics).

Alderfer, ed. 1951. *Johannes Kelpius: A Method of Prayer*. New York: Harper.

Almond, Philip C. 1993. Henry More and the Apocalypse. *Journal of the History of Ideas* 54 (2): 189.

———. 1994. *Heaven and Hell in Enlightenment England*. New York: Cambridge University Press.

Anderson, Marvin W. 1987. *Evangelical Foundations: Religion in English, 1378-1685*. New York: Peter Lang. (American University Studies, Series 7, v33). Rvw by Donald Dean Smeeton, *Sixteenth-Century Studies* 20:2(Summer, 1989), p304.

Anderson, Virginia DeJohn. 1991. *New England's Generation: The Great Migration and the Formation of Society and Culture in the Seventeenth Century*. Cambridge: Cambridge University Press.

Annesley, Samuel, Thomas Case, and Nathaniel Vincent. 1981. *Puritan Sermons, 1659-1689, Being the Morning Exercises at Cripplegate, St. Giles in the Fields, and in Southwark by Seventy-Five Ministers of the Gospel in or Near London*. Vol. 6, 1682–1844. Wheaton, Illinois: Richard Owen Roberts.

Armogathe, Jean-Robert. 1985. *Croire en liberté: L'Eglise catholique et la révocation de l'Edit de Nantes*. Paris: O.E.I.L./Histoire pb.

———. 2005. *L'Antéchrist à l'âge classique: Exégèse et politique*. Paris: Mille et une nuits, pb.

Armstrong, Brian. 1969. *Calvinism and the Amyraut Heresy: Protestant Scholasticism and Humanism in Seventeenth-Century France*. Madison: University of Wisconsin Press.

Arnold, Brian J. 2018. *Justification in the Second Century*. Waco, TX: Baylor University Press. (on grace)

Arnold, Gottfried. 1699-1700. *Unparteyische Kirchen- und Ketzer-Historie*. Frankfurt.

———. 1701. *Das Leben der Gläubigen*. Halle.
———. 1703. *Historie und Beschreibung der mystischen Theologie oder geheimen Gottesgelehrtheit wie auch alten und neuen Mysticorum*. Frankfurt.
Arthur, Anthony. 1999. *The Tailor-King: The Rise and Fall of the Anabaptist Kingdom of Münster*. New York: St. Martin's.
Astell, Mary, and John Norris. 2005. In *Letters Concerning the Love of God*, ed. E. Derek Taylor and Melvyn New, vol. 1695. Burlington, VT: Ashgate.
Aston, Margaret. 1984. *Lollards and Reformers: Images and Literacy in Late Medieval Religion*. Ronceverte, WV, UK: Hambledon Press.
———. 1992. *Faith and Fire: Popular and Unpopular Religion, 1350-1600*. Rio Grande, OH: Hambledon Press.
d'Aubigné, Agrippa. 1981–1985. In *Histoire universelle*, ed. André Thierry, vol. 3. Geneva: Droz.
Atkinson, Geoffroy, and Abraham C. Keller. 1970. *Prelude to the Enlightenment: French Literature, 1690-1740*. Seattle, WA: University of Washington Press.
Audisio, Gabriel. 1999. *The Waldensian Dissent: Persecution and Survival. c. 1170-c. 1570*. Translated by Claire Davison. New York: Cambridge University Press.
Augustine (Aurelius Augustinus, Saint). 1955. *Confessions and Enchiridion*. Translated by Albert Outler. Philadelphia: Westminster Press. https://en.wikisource.org/wiki/The_Confessions_of_Saint_Augustine_(Outler).
———. 1948. In *Basic Writings of Saint Augustine*, ed. Whitney Oates. Random House: New York.
———. n.d. *Opera Omnia*. editio latina. http://www.augustinus.it/latino/spirito_lettera/index.htm, Pl.4. - editio latina.
———. 2003. In *Augustine's Commentary on* ***Galatians****: Introduction, Text, Translation, and Notes*, ed. Eric Plumer, 6. New York: Oxford University Press.
Backus, Irena. (Geneva)2000. *Reformation Readings of the* ***Apocalypse****: Geneva, Zurich, and Wittenberg*, 21. New York: Oxford University Press.
Badiou, Alain. *Saint Paul: The Foundation of Universalism*. Translated by Ray Brassier. Stanford, CA: Stanford University Press (Cultural Memory in the Present), 2003. (*Saint-Paul: la fondation de l'universalisme*. Paris: PUF, 1997).
Bailey, Margaret Lewis. 2015. *Milton and Jakob Boehme: A Study of German Mysticism in Seventeenth-Century England*. Vol. 1914). Reprint. Palala Press.
Bailey, Michael D. 2008. Concern over Superstition in Late Medieval Europe. *The Religion of Fools? Superstition Past and Present; Past & Present* 199 (Supplement 3): 115–133. http://past.oxfordjournals.org/content/vol199/suppl_3/index.dtl?etoc.
Bainton, Roland. 2008. *Christian Attitudes Toward War And Peace A Historical Survey And Critical Reevaluation*. (Abingdon Press, 1960) Reprint. Eugene OR: Wipf & Stock.
———. *Women of the Reformation: In Germany and Italy*. Minneapolis: Augsburg Fortress, 1971, pb 2007.
———. *Women of the Reformation: In Germany. Women of the Reformation: In France and England*. Minneapolis: Augsburg Fortress, 1973, pb 2007.
———. *Women of the Reformation: In Germany. Women of the Reformation: In France. Women of the Reformation: From Spain to Scandinavia*. Minneapolis: Augsburg Fortress, 1977, pb 2007.
Ball, B.W.A. 1975. *A Great Expectation. Eschatological Thought in English Protestantism to 1660*. New York: Brill.
Balmer, Randall. 1989. *A Perfect Babel of Confusion: Dutch Religion and English Culture in the Middle Colonies*. New York: Oxford University Press.
———. 1999. *Blessed Assurance: A History of Evangelicalism in America*. Boston: Beacon Press.
Bangs, Carl. 1998. *Arminius: A Study in the Dutch Reformation*. Vol. 1985. Wipf & Stock: Eugene, OR.
Barbour, Reid. 2001. *Literature and Religious Culture in Seventeenth-Century England*. New York: Cambridge University Press.
Barnes, Robin Bruce. 1987. *Prophecy and Gnosis: Apocalypticism in the Wake of the Lutheran Reformation*. Stanford, CA: Stanford University Press.

Barton, Carlin A. 1989.Martyrological Motifs in Judaism and Early Christianity. *AHA*, SF,
Baskerville, Stephen. 1993. *Not Peace But a Sword: The Political Theory of the English Revolution.* New York: Routledge.
Battis, Emery. 1962. *Saints and Sectaries: Anne Hutchinson and the Antinomian Controversy in the Massachusetts Bay Colony.* Chapel Hill, NC: University of North Carolina Press.
Bauch, Hermann. *Die Lehre von Wirken des Heiligen Geistes im Fruhpietismus: Studien zur Pneumatologie und Eschatologie von Campegius Vitringa, Philipp Jacob Spener und Johann Albrecht Bengel.* (Diss't, Mainz, 1967), Hamburg-Bergstedt: H. Reich, 1974.
Bauckham, Richard. *Tudor Apocalypse*, Abingdon, 1978.
Bauer, Bruno. *Einfluss des englischen Quakerthums auf die deutscher Kultur.* Berlin, 1849.
Bauman, Clarence. 1990. *The Spiritual Legacy of Hans Denck.* Including the German text as established by G. Baring & W. Fellmann. New York: E.J. Brill.
Baxter, Richard (1615-1691). *Call to the Unconverted to Turn and Live.* (1658) Christian Classics Ethereal Library. https://www.ccel.org/ccel/baxter/unconverted.html.
Baylor, Michael G., ed. 1991. *The Radical Reformation.* Cambridge: Cambridge University Press.
Beck, J., ed. 1979. *Le Concile de Basle (1434): Les origines du théâtre réformiste et partisan en France.* New York: Brill.
BeDuhn, Jason David. 2000. *The Manichaean Body In Discipline and Ritual.* Baltimore, MD: Johns Hopkins University Press.
Beeke, Joel R. 1995. *Assurance of Faith: Calvin, English Puritanism, and the Dutch Second Reformation.* 2nd ed. New York: Peter Lang (American University Studies, Series 7, Theology & Religion, 89). [c.1600-1760].
Benedict, Philip. 2002. *Christ's Churches Purely Reformed: A Social History of Calvinism.* New Haven, CT: Yale University Press.
Benedict, P. 1991. *The Huguenot Population of France, 1600-1685: The Demographic Fate and Customs of a Religious Minority. Transactions of the American Philosophical Society, v81, pt 5, 1991.* Philadelphia: American Philosophical Society.
Bennett, Joan S. 1989. *Reviving Liberty: Radical Christian Humanism in Milton's Great Poems.* Cambridge, MA: Harvard University Press.
Benoist, Elie. 1693–1695. *Histoire de l'Edit de Nantes et sa revocation.* 5v, Delft.
Bercovich, Sacvan. 1993. *The Office of* ***The Scarlet Letter***. Baltimore: Johns Hopkins University Press.
———. 1975. *The Puritan Origins of the American Self.* New Haven, CT: Yale University Press.
Berman, Harold J. 2004. *Law and Revolution. II, The Impact of the Protestant Reformations on the Western Legal Tradition.* Cambridge, MA: Harvard University Press.
Bernard, P. 1987. *Explication de l'Edict de Nantes [microform]: par les autres edicts de pacification, déclarations & arrests de réglement.* Zug [Switzerland]: IDC.
Bernstein, A.E. 1978. *Pierre d'Ailly and the Blanchard Affair. University and Chancellor of Paris at the beginning of the Great Schism.* New York, Brill.
Bernstein, Alan E. 2017. *Hell and Its Rivals: Death and Retribution among Christians, Jews, and Muslims in the Early Middle Ages.* Ithaca, NY: Cornell University Press.
Betteridge, Thomas. 1999. *Tudor Histories of the English Reformations, 1530-83. St Andrews Studies in Reformation History.* Brookfield, Vermont and Aldershot, Hants: Ashgate Publishing.
Betts, C., and J. Early. 1984. *Deism in France: From the So-Called 'Deistes' of Lyon (1564) to Voltaire's* ***'Lettres philosophiques'*** *(1734).* The Hague/Boston: Martinus Nijhoff.
Biller, Peter. 2006. Goodbye to Waldensianism? *Past and Present* 192: 3–33.
Birnstiel, Eckart. 2001. avec la collaboration de Chrystel Bernat. ed. *la Diaspora des huguenots. Les réfugiés protestants de France et leur dispersion dans le monde (XVIe-XVIIIe siècles).* Paris: Honoré Champion, coll. La vie des huguenots, 17.
Blackwell, Jeannine. 1995. Gedoppelter Lebenslauf der Pietistinnen: autobiographische Schriften der Wiedergeburt. In *Geschriebenes Leben: Autobiographik von Frauen*, ed. Holdenried, 49–60. Berlin: E Schmidt.
Blau, Joseph Leon. *The Christian Interpretation of the Cabala in the Renaissance* (1944).

"Blaurock" (Jörg Cajacob). 1999. *Reminiscences*. (1525) Translated in Denis R. Janz. *A Reformation Reader: Primary Texts With Introductions*. Minneapolis: Fortress Press, pp. 168-70. http://www.gjlts.com/Church%20History/Reformation%20History/blaurockreminiscences.pdf.
Blumhofer, Edith L., and Mark A. Noll, eds. 2006. *Singing the Lord's Song in a Strange Land: Hymnody in the History of North American Protestantism*. University of Alabama Press, 2004. Rvw by Robin A. Leaver. *J Am Acad Relig* 74: 262–266. http://jaar.oxfordjournals.org/cgi/content/full/74/1/262?etoc.
de Boer, Wietse. 2001. *The Conquest of the Soul: Confesson, Discipline, and Public Order in Counter-Reformation Milan*. Boston: Brill.
Boehme/Böhme/Behmen, Jakob (1575-1624). *The Way to Christ* [*Weg zu Christo*]: ("On True Repentance, I, 1622 & II, 1623" "On True Resignation (*Gelassenheit*?), 1622" "On the Supersensual Life, 1622" "On Holy Prayer, 1624" "The Precious Gate, 1620" "Consolation Treatise on the Four Humors, 1624" "On the New Birth, 1622" and "The Conversation Between an **Enlightened** and **Unenlightened** Soul" 1624). Translated by John Sparrow, London, 1648. *The Way to Christ*. Translated by Peter C. Erb. (Mahwah, NJ: Paulist Press, 1978).
Bohatec, J. *Calvin und das Recht* (1934). repr. 199?.
Bono (Paul David Hewson). *Bono: In Conversation with Michka Assayas*. Riverhead Books, 2005. reposted. www.teilhard.com.
Bornkamm, Heinrich, F. Heyer, and A. Schindler, eds. 1975. *Der Pietismus in Gestalten und Wirkungen. Martin Schmidt zum 65. Geburtstag*. Bielefeld.
Bosco, Ronald A., ed. 1978. *The Puritan Sermon in America, 1630-1750*. Scholar's Facsimiles.
Bourne, Russell. 1990. *The Red King's Rebellion: Racial Politics in New England 1675-1678*. New York: Atheneum; pb, Oxford University Press, 1991.
Bouwsma, William J. 1987. *John Calvin, a Sixteenth Century Portrait*. Oxford: New York.
Bowd, Stephen. 2008. 'Honeyed Flies' and 'Sugared Rats': Witchcraft, Heresy, and Superstition in the Bresciano, 1454-1535. *The Religion of Fools? Superstition Past and Present; Past & Present* 199 (Supplement 3): 134–156. http://past.oxfordjournals.org/content/vol199/suppl_3/index.dtl?etoc.
Bowden, Hugh. 2008. Before Superstition and After: Theophrastus and Plutarch on *Deisidaimonia*. *The Religion of Fools? Superstition Past and Present; Past & Present* 199 (Supplement 3): 56–71. http://past.oxfordjournals.org/content/vol199/suppl_3/index.dtl?etoc.
Boyer, Paul, and Stephen Nissenbaum. 1974. *Salem Possessed: The Social Origins of Witchcraft*. Cambridge, MA: Harvard University Press.
Bozeman, Theodore Dwight. 2004. *The Precisianist Strain: Disciplinary Religion and Antinomian Backlash in Puritanism to 1638*. Chapel Hill: University of North Carolina Press.
———. 2014. *To Live Ancient Lives: The Primitivist Dimension in Puritanism*. Vol. 1988. Chapel Hill, NC: University of North Carolina Press.
Brachlow, Stephen. 1988. *The Communion of Saints: Radical Puritan and Separatist Ecclesiology 1570-1625*. New York: Oxford University Press.
Brecht, Martin. 1985. *Martin Luther*. (1981) 3v. Translated by James Schaaf. Fortress Press.
Brecht, Martin, and Klaus Depperman, eds. 1993. *Der Pietismus vom siebzehnten bis zum fruhen achtzehnten Jahrhundert. (Geschichte des Pietismus. 1)*. Vandenhoeck & Ruprecht: Göttingen.
———, eds. 1995. *Der Pietismus im achtzehnten Jahrhundert. (Geschichte des Pietismus. 2)*. Vandenhoeck & Ruprecht: Göttingen.
Breen, Louise A. 2001. *Transgressing the Bounds: Subversive Enterprises among the Puritan Elite in Massachusetts, 1630-1692*. Oxford/New York: Oxford University Press.
Bremer, Francis J. 2003. *John Winthrop: America's Forgotten Founding Father*. New York: Oxford University Press.
Brock, P. June 1994. Dilemmas of a Socinian Pacifist in 17th-Century Poland. *Church History* 63 (2): 190–200.
Brown, Dale. 1996. *Understanding Pietism*. (1978) revised edition, Evangel Pub House.
Brown, Peter. *Augustine of Hippo*. Berkeley: University of California Press, 1967, revised edition, Berkeley, 2000.

———. 2017. *"Dialogue With God," New York Review of Books 45:16(October 20, 2017), pp45-46. Review of Sarah Ruden's new translation of Augustine. Confessions.* New York: Modern Library.

Brown, Stewart J., and Timothy Tackett, eds. 2014. *The Cambridge History of Christianity. Volume 7, Enlightenment, Reawakening and Revolution 1660-1815.* Cambridge: Cambridge University Press.

Bubenheimer, Ulrich. 1989. *Thomas Müntzer: Herkunft und Bildung: Studien und Texte.* Leiden: E.J. Brill.

Bunyan, John. *Grace Abounding To The Chief Of Sinners In A Faithful Account Of The Life And Death Of John Bunyan, Or, A Brief Relation Of The Exceeding Mercy Of God In Christ To Him, / Namely In His Taking Him Out Of The Dunghill, And Converting Him To The Faith Of His Blessed Son Jesus Christ. / Here Is Also Particularly Shewed, What Sight Of, And What Troubles He Had For Sin; And Also, What Various Temptations He Hath Met With, And How God Hath Carried Him Through Them.* 1666. Project Gutenberg. https://www.gutenberg.org/files/654/654-h/654-h.htm.

———. ***Grace Abounding****: with Other Spiritual Autobiographies*. ed. John Stachniewski & Anita Pacheco. New York: Oxford University Press, 1998, '*A Relation of the Imprisonment of Mr John Bunyan*', '*Confessions*' by Richard Norwood, '*A Short History of the Life of John Crook*', '*The Lost Sheep Found*' by Lawrence Clarkson, '*The Narrative of the Persecution of Agnes Beaumont*', Appendix: "Radical and Nonconformist Groups in Seventeenth-century England".

Burgess, Anthony. 1962. *The Wanting Seed. (novel).* New York: W. W. Norton.

Burridge, Kenelm. 1969. *New Heaven, New Earth: A Study of Millenarian Activities.* Oxford: Basil Blackwell.

Burtchaell, James Tunstead. 1992. *From Synagogue to Church: Public Services and Offices in the Earliest Christian Communities.* New York: Cambridge University Press.

Bush, Michael. 1996. *The Pilgrimage of Grace: A Study of the Rebel Armies of October 1536.* Manchester: Manchester University Press.

Büsser, F. 1985. *Wurzeln der Reformation in Zürich. Zum 500 Geburtstag des Reformators Huldrych Zwingli.* New York: Brill.

Butler, Jonathan M. 1983. *The Huguenots in America: A Refugee People in New World Society,* 1992. Cambridge, MA: Harvard University Press.

———. 1991. Historiographical Heresy: Catholicism as a Model for American Religious History. In *Belief in History: Innovative Approaches to European and American Religion*, ed. Thomas Kselman, 286–309. Notre Dame, IN: University of Notre Dame Press.

Butler, Martin. 1984. *Theatre and crisis, 1632-1642.* Cambridge: Cambridge University Press.

Cadoux, Cecil John. 2011. *The Early Christian Attitude to War: A Contribution to the History of Christian Ethics.* (1919). Kindle ed.

Caldwell, Patricia. 1983. *The Puritan Conversion Narrative: The Beginnings of American Expression.* New York: Cambridge University Press.

Calvin, Jean. 1992. *Commentarii in Pauli Epistolas ad Galatas, ad Ephesios, ad Philippenses, ad Colossenses (1548) in Ioannis Calvini Opera omnia. Series 2, Opera exegetica Veteris et Novi Testamenti. v16, ed. H. Feld.* Geneva: Droz.

———. 1965. *The Epistle of Paul the Apostle to the Galatians* (1548). ed. T. H. L. Parker; Grand Rapids, MI: Eerdmans, and later reprints.

———. n.d. *Commentary on Galatians* (1548). http://www.ccel.org/c/calvin/comment3/comm_vol41/htm/iii.ii.htm.

———. 1997. *Sermons on Galatians.* Translated from French by K. Childress. Banner of Truth Trust: Edinburgh.

———. 1863-1900. In *"Preface" to Commentary on the Psalms. (1557). in Calvin. Opera Omnia, Corpus Reformatorum*, ed. G. Baum, E. Cunitz, and E. Reuss, vol. 31. Brunswick: C. Schwetschke.

Campbell, Douglas. 2009. *The Deliverance of God: An Apocalyptic Rereading of Justification in Paul.* Grand Rapids, MI: Eerdmans.

Capp, Bernard S. 1972. *The Fifth Monarchy Men*. London.
Caricchio, Mario. 2011. News from the New Jerusalem: Giles Calvert and the radical experience. In *Varieties of Seventeenth- and Early Eighteenth-Century English Radicalism in Context*, ed. Hessayon and Finnegan. London: Ashgate.
Cary, Phillip. 2008a. *Inner Grace: Augustine in the Traditions of Plato and Paul*. New York: Oxford University Press.
———. 2008b. *Outward Signs: The Powerlessness of External Things in Augustine's Thought*. New York: Oxford University Press.
Chastel, André. 1953. L'Antéchrist à la Renaissance. In *Cristianesimo e ragion di stato: L'Umanesimo e il demoniaco nell'arte*, ed. Enrico Castelli. Rome.
Chatellier, Louis. 1989. *The Europe of the Devout: The Catholic Reformation and the Formation of a New Society*. New York: Cambridge University Press.
Christian, William A. 1988. *Local Religion in Sixteenth-Century Spain*. Princeton, NJ: Princeton University Press.
Chu, Jonathan M. 1985. *Neighbors, Friends, or Madmen: The Puritan Adjustment to Quakerism in Seventeenth-Century Massachusetts Bay*. Westport, CT: Greenwood Press.
Clancy, T.H. 1975–1976. Papist-Protestant-Puritan: English religious taxonomy 1565-1665. *Recusant History* 13.
Claydon, Tony. 1996. *William III and the Godly Revolution*. Cambridge: Cambridge University Press.
Cloud of Unknowing, The. Translated by Clifton Wolters. New York: Penguin Classics, 1961.
Cloud of Unknowing, The. *and Other Works*. New York: Penguin Classics, new ed. 2001 Introduction and notes by A. C. Spearing. Translated by Elizabeth Spearing. New York: Penguin Classics) new ed. 2001.
Cohn, Norman. 1994. *Cosmos, Chaos and the World to Come: The Ancient Roots of Apocalyptic Faith*. New Haven, CT: Yale University Press.
———. 1957. *The Pursuit of the Millennium: Revolutionary Messianism in Medieval and Reformation Europe and Its Bearing on Modern Totalitarian Movements*. 2nd ed. New York: Harper Torchbooks, 1961; London, 1970.
Cohn-Sherbok, Dan. 2006. *The Politics of Apocalypse: The History and Influence of Christian Zionism*. Oxford, UK: Oneworld.
Collinson, Patrick. 1988. *The Birthpangs of Protestant England: Religious and Cultural Change in the Sixteenth and Seventeenth Centuries*. New York: St. Martin's.
———. 1983. *Godly People: Essays on English Protestantism and Puritanism*. Ronceverte, WV, UK: Hambledon Press.
———. 2004. *The Reformation*. New York: Modern Library.
de Paris, Colloque. 1985. *La Révocation de l'Edit de Nantes et le protestantisme français en 1685: actes du colloque de Paris (15-19 octobre 1985)*. réunis par Roger Zuber et Laurent Theis. *Paris: au siège de la Société*: 1986.
Como, David. "The Kingdom of England, the Kingdom of Christ, and the Kingdom of Traske: The Persistence of Radical Puritanism in Early Stuart England," American Historical Association, New York City, 5Jan97.
Cooper, Frederick. 1996. "Race, Ideology, and the Perils of Comparative History" review of Frederickson, *Black Liberation*, and Campbell, *Songs of Zion*, 1995. *American Historical Review* 101 (4): 1122–1138.
Cooper, Kate. 1999. *The Virgin and the Bride: Idealized Womanhood in Late Antiquity*. Cambridge, MA: Harvard University Press.
Cooper, Stephen Andrew. 2005. *Marius Victorinus' Commentary on* ***Galatians***. New York: Oxford University Press.
Cope, Esther S. 1993. *Handmaid of the Holy Spirit: Dame Eleanor Davies, Never Soe Mad a Ladie*. Ann Arbor: University of Michigan Press.
Copeland, Clare, and Jan Machielsen. 2013. *Angels of Light? Sanctity and the Discernment of Spirits in the Early Modern Period*. Leiden: E. J. Brill.

Cottret, B.J. 1992a. *The Huguenots in England: Immigration and Settlement, 1640-1700.* New York: Cambridge University Press.

———. 1996. Les pères et la religion du Père: les oeuvres d'un mémorialiste protestante, Jacques Fontaine (1658-1728). *Études théologiques et religieuses* 71 (4): 511–522.

Cottret, Bernard. 1999. *Calvin. Lattès, 1995.* Paris: Payot.

———. 1992b. *Cromwell.* Paris: Fayard.

Court, Antoine. 2002. *Histoire des troubles des Cévennes.* Montpellier: Presses du Languedoc. Présentation par Otto Selles. Antoine Court, pasteur et historien: l'histoire des camisards et la lutte pour la liberté religieuse. p. 13–32.

Cowan, Ian B. 1982. *The Scottish Reformation: Church and Society in Sixteenth-Century Scotland.* New York: St. Martin's Press.

Cowan, Ian B., and Duncan Shaw, eds. 1983. *The Renaissance and Reformation in Scotland: Essays in Honor of Gordon Donaldson.* Edinburgh: Scottish Academic Press.

Cowing, Cedric B. 1995. *The Saving Remnant: Religion and the Settling of New England.* Urbana, IL: University of Illinois Press.

Cramer, Peter. 1993. *Baptism and Change in the Early Middle Ages, c.200-c.1150.* New York: Cambridge University Press.

Cressy, David. 1987. *Coming Over: Migration and Communication between Europe and New England in the Seventeenth Century.* New York: Cambridge University Press.

———. 1997. *Birth, Marriage and Death: Ritual, Religion, and the Life-Cycle in Tudor and Stuart England.* New York: Oxford University Press.

Cross, F.L., and E.A. Livingstone. 1997. *The Oxford Dictionary of the Christian Church.* Oxford: Oxford University Press.

Crouzel, Henri. 1989. *Origen: The Life and Thought of the First Great Theologian.* Translated by A. S. Worrall. New York: HarperCollins.

Crouzet, Denis. 1990. *Les Guerriers de Dieu: La Violence au temps des troubles de religion.* Vol. 2. Seyssel.

Cunningham, Andrew, and Ole Peter Grell. 2001. *The Four Horsemen of the Apocalypse: War, Famine, Disease and Gospel in Reformation Europe.* Cambridge: Cambridge University Press.

Dan, Joseph, ed. 1997. *The Christian Kabbalah.* Cambridge, MA: Harvard College Library.

Daniell, David. 1996. *William Tyndale: A Biography.* New Haven, CT: Yale University Press.

Davidson, Peter, ed. 1998. *Poetry and Revolution: An Anthology of British and Irish Verse, 1625-1660.* Oxford: Clarendon. Review by Jack Craze. Celtic Rhymers and English Cavaliers. *Times Literary Supplement*, 5001 (February 5, 1999): 25].

Davis, J.C. 1986. *Fear, Myth and History: The Ranters and their History, 1649-1984.* Cambridge: Cambridge University Press. (contending Ranters never existed).

Davis, Natalie Z. 1987. *Fiction in the Archives: Pardon Tales and Their Tellers in Sixteenth Century France.* Stanford, CA: Stanford University Press.

Dayfoot, Arthur Charles. 1998. *The Shaping of the West Indian Church, 1492-1962.* Gainesville: University of Florida Press.

Dedieu, J. 1920. *Le rôle politique des Protestants français de 1685 à 1715.* Paris: Bloud & Gay.

Delbanco, Andrew. 1989. *The Puritan Ordeal.* Cambridge, MA: Harvard University Press.

Demos, John. 1970. *A Little Commonwealth: Family Life in the Plymouth Colony.* New York: Oxford University Press.

———. 1982. *Entertaining Satan: Witchcraft and the Culture of Early New England.* New York: Oxford University Press.

Dickens, A.G. 1982. *Lollards and Protestants in the Diocese of York, 1509-1538. London, 1959.* Ronceverte, WV, UK: Hambledon Press.

Didion, Joan. 1970. A Generation Not for Barricades. In *Life Magazine. 5 June.*

Dix-Septième Siècle. 194 (janvier-mars) special section on the Bible in the 17th century (Protestant, Catholic, and Libertine).

Dodd, C.H. 1957. *The Meaning of Paul for Today.* London/Swarthmore, PA: 1920, rev, ed.

Dodds, E.R. 1965. *Pagan and Christian in an Age of Anxiety: Some Aspects of Religious Experience from Marcus Aurelius to Constantine (The Wiles Lectures, 1963)*. Cambridge: Cambridge University Press.

———. 2004. *Pagan. The Greeks and the Irrational (Sather Classical Lectures #25, 1949-50)*. Berkeley: University of California Press.

Dodge, Guy Howard. 1947. *The Political Theory of the Huguenots of the Dispersion, with special reference to the thought and influence of Pierre Jurieu*. New York: Columbia University Press.

Dolan, Jay P. 1985. *The American Catholic Experience: A History from Colonial Times to the Present, Garden City*. New York: Doubledaey(?).

Le Dompnier, B. 1985. *Venin de l'hérésie: Image du protestantisme et combat catholique au XVIIe siècle*. Paris: Editions du Centurion.

Dryerre, J. Meldrum. 2013. *Heroes and Heroines of the Scottish Covenanters*. John Ritchie Ltd., Kindle ed.

Ducasse, André. 1989. *La guerre des Camisards: La résistance huguenote sous Louis XIV. (1962)*. Paris: Hachette.

Duffy, Eamon. 1993. *The Stripping of the Altars: Traditional Religion in England, c. 1400-c. 1580*. New Haven, CT: Yale University Press.

———. 2001. *The Voices of Morebath: Reformation and Rebellion in an English Village*. New Haven, CT: Yale University Press.

Duke, Alastair. 1990. *Reformation and Revolt in the Low Countries*. Ronceverte, WV, UK: Hambledon Press.

Duvernoy, Jean. 1994. *Cathares, Vaudois et Béguins: Dissidents du pays d'oc*. Toulouse: Privat.

Eckhart von Hochheim (c1260-1328). 1981. *Meister Eckhart: The Essential Sermons, Commentaries, Treatises and Defense*. (Classics of Western Spirituality) Translated by Edmund Colledge. Mahwah, NJ: Paulist Press.

——— (c1260-1328). n.d. *Sermon* #XXV for 11th Sunday after Trinity. https://biblehub.com/sermons/auth/eckhart/outward_and_inward_morality.htm.

Ehrman, Bart. 2004. *Lost Christianities: The Battles for Scripture and the Faiths We Never Knew*. New York: Oxford University Press.

———. 2007. *Misquoting Jesus: The Story Behind Who Changed the Bible and Why*. New York: HarperOne Reprint.

Eire, Carlos M.N. 1986. *War Against the Idols: The Reformation of Worship from Erasmus to Calvin*. Cambridge: Cambridge University Press.

Elwood, Christopher. 1998. *The Body Broken: The Calvinist Doctrine of the Eucharist and the Symbolization of Power in Sixteenth-Century France*. New York: Oxford University Press.

Emmerson, Richard K., and Bernard McGinn, eds. 1993. *The Apocalypse in the Middle Ages*. Ithaca, NY: Cornell University Press.

Englander, David, Diana Norman, Rosemary O'Day, and W.R. Owens, eds. 1989. *Culture and Belief in Europe, 1450-1600: An Anthology of Primary Sources*. New York: Blackwell.

Erasmus, Desiderius. 1984. *Paraphrases on Romans and Galatians (1535) ed. Robert D. Sider; Translated by J. B. Payne et al. Collected Works. 42*. Toronto: University of Toronto Press.

———. 1535. *Des. Erasmi Roterodami In Novum Testamentum annotations*. Basiliae: Froben.

———. 1993. In *Erasmus' annotations on the New Testament: Galatians to the Apocalypse: facsimile of the final Latin text with all earlier variants. (1535)*, ed. Anne Reeve; Intro by M.A. Screech; SHCT 52;. Leiden: E. J. Brill.

Erb, Peter. 1983. *The Pietists*. Mahwah, NJ: Paulist Press.

Erikson, Erik. 1958. *Young Man Luther: A Study in Psychoanalysis and History*. New York: W.W. Norton. (psychology of religion).

Estes, James Martin. 1983. *Christian Magistrate and State Church: The Reforming Career of Johannes Brenz*. Toronto.

Fairbairn, Donald. 2003. *Grace and Christology in the Early Church*. New York: Oxford University Press.

Faurey, Joseph. *L'Édit de Nantes et la question de la tolérance*. 1929.

Fernández-Armesto, Felipe. 2000. "Real Zeal," review of Tracy, *Europe's Reformations*. In *New York Times Book Review*, 28.
Fernández-Armesto, Felipe, and Derek Wilson. 1997. *Reformations: A Radical Interpretation of Christianity and the World (1500-2000)*. New York: Scribner.
Fincham, Kenneth. 1993. *The Early Stuart Church, 1603-1642*. Stanford, CA: Stanford University Press.
Fisher, Linford D. J., Stanley Lemons & Lucas Mason-Brown. 2014. *Decoding Roger Williams: The Lost Essay of Rhode Island's Founding Father*. Waco, TX: Baylor University Press.
Fitzgerald, Allan D.O.S.A., ed. 1999. *Augustine Through the Ages: An Encyclopedia*. Grand Rapids, MI: Eerdmans.
Flasch, Kurt. *D'Averroes à Maître Eckhart: Les sources arabes de la mystique allemande*. Conférences Pierre Abelard. Paris: Vrin, 03/2008.
Flinker, Noam. 2011. The poetics of biblical prophecy: Abiezer Coppe's late converted midrash. In *Varieties of Seventeenth- and Early Eighteenth-Century English Radicalism in Context*, ed. Hessayon and Finnegan. London: Ashgate.
Flint, Valerie I.J. 1992. *The Imaginative World of Christopher Columbus*. Princeton.
Fontana, Benedetto. 1999. Love of Country and Love of God: The Political Uses of Religion in Machiavelli. *Journal of the History of Ideas* 60 (4): 639–658.
Fortson, Dante. 2017. *Pre-Slavery Christianity: It Was Never The White Man's Religion*. Amazon Kindle.
Foster, Stephen. 1991. *The Long Argument: English Puritanism and the Shaping of New England Culture, 1570-1700*. Chapel Hill: University of North Carolina Press.
Foster, Walter R. 1958. *Bishop and Presbytery: The Church of Scotland, 1661-1688*. London.
Fox, George. 1879. In *Selections from the Epistles of George Fox*, ed. Samuel Tuke. Cambridge, MA.
———. 1948. In *George Fox's "Book of Miracles"*, ed. Henry J. Cadbury. Cambridge.
Franklin, Don O. 1994. J.S. Bach and Pietism. *Pietisten* 7 (1) http://pietisten.org/viii/1/bach.html.
Fraser, Antonia. 1996. *Faith and Treason: The Story of the Gunpowder Plot*. New York: Doubleday.
Freeman, Charles. 2004. *The Closing of the Western Mind: The Rise of Faith and the Fall of Reason*. New York: Knopf. (Augustine et al.).
Freyburger, G.M.L. 1986. *Les Sectes religieuses en Grèce et à Rome*. Paris: Les Belles-Lettres.
Friedman, Jerome. 1987. *Blasphemy, Immorality, and Anarchy: The Ranters and the English Revolution*. Athens: Ohio University Press.
Friedrich, Otto. 1986. *The End of the World: A History*. New York: Fromm International.
Friesen, Abraham. 1990. *Thomas Muentzer; a Destroyer of the Godless: The Making of a Sixteenth-Century Religious Revolutionary*. Berkeley: University of California Press.
Friesen, Steven J. 2001. *Imperial Cults and the* ***Apocalypse of John****: Reading Revelation in the Ruins*. New York: Oxford University Press.
Frith, Katherine R. 1979. *The Apocalyptic Tradition in Reformation Britain, 1530-1645*. New York: Oxford University Press.
Fuhr, Andreas. 1985. *Machiavelli und Savonarola*. Frankfurt: *Politische Rationalität und politische Prophetie*.
Fulbrook, Mary. 1983. *Piety and Politics: Religion and the Rise of Absolutism in England, Württemberg, and Prussia*. New York.
Fulton, Rachel. 2003. *From Judgment to Passion: Devotion to Christ and the Virgin Mary, 800-1200*. New York: Columbia University Press.
Gadoffre, Gilbert. 1997. *La Révolution Culturelle dans la France des Humanistes: Guillaume Budé et François I*. Geneva: Droz.
Gager, John G. 2000. *Reinventing Paul*. New York: Oxford University Press.
Garrison, Janine. 1985. *L'Édit de Nantes et sa Révocation: Histoire d'une intolérance*. Paris: Editions du Seuil.
Geerken, John H. 1999. Machiavelli's Moses and Renaissance Politics. *Journal of the History of Ideas* 60 (4): 579–595.

Gerson, Jean. 1978. In *De jurisdictione spirituali et temporali*, ed. G.H.M. Posthumus Meyjes. New York: Brill.

Ghosh, P. 2003. Max Weber's idea of 'Puritanism': a case study in the empirical construction of the Protestant ethic. *History of European Ideas* 29 (2): 183–222.

Gildrie, Richard P. 1975. *Salem, Massachusetts, 1626-1682: A Covenant Community*. Charlottesville: University of Virginia Press.

Gilman, Ernest B. 1986. *Iconoclasm and Poetry in the English Reformation: Down Went Dagon*. Chicago: University of Chicago Press.

Godbeer, Richard. 1992. *The Devil's Dominion: Magic and Religion in Early New England*. New York: Cambridge University Press.

———. 2002. *Sexual Revolution in Early America*. Baltimore, MD: Johns Hopkins University Press.

Goertz, Hans-Jurgen. 1996. *The Anabaptists*. New York: Routledge.

Golden, Richard M. 1981. *The Godly Rebellion: Parisian Curés and the Religious Fronde, 1652-1662*. Chapel Hill, NC: University of North Carolina Press.

Goldmann, Lucien. 1959. *Le Dieu caché: Etude sur la vision tragique dans les Pensées de Pascal et dans le theatre de Racine*. Paris: Gallimard.

Gordon, Richard. 2008. Superstitio, Superstition and Religious Repression in the Late Roman Republic and Principate (100 BCE-300 CE). *The Religion of Fools? Superstition Past and Present; Past & Present* 199 (Supplement 3): 72–94. http://past.oxfordjournals.org/content/vol199/suppl_3/index.dtl?etoc.

Gouhier, Henri. 1954. La Crise de la théologie au temps de Descartes. *Revue de Théologie et de Philosophie, 3e sér* IV: 19–54.

———. 1924. *La pensée religieuse de Descartes*. Paris: Vrin.

Grafton, Anthony. 2004a. *Conversion in Late Antiquity and Middle Ages*. Rochester/New York: Boydell & Brewer.

———. 2004b. *Conversion: Old Worlds and New*. Rochester/New York: Boydell & Brewer.

———. Style and Substance in a Conversation with Angels: The Case of Trithemius. *Conversations with Angels*, 9-10 September, 2005, interdisciplinary conference at CRASSH, Cambridge. http://www.crassh.cam.ac.uk/events/2004-5/angels.html>.

Grafton, Anthony, and Joanna Weinberg. 2011. *"I have always loved the holy tongue": Isaac Casaubon, the Jews, and a Forgotten Chapter in Renaissance Scholarship*. Cambridge, MA: Belknap Press of Harvard University Press.

Grant, Michael. 2000. *Saint Paul (1976)*. London: Phoenix Press pb.

Graves, Michael P. 2009. *Preaching the Inward Light: Early Quaker Rhetoric*. Waco, TX: Baylor University Press.

Greaves, Richard L. 1986. *Deliver Us from Evil: The Radical Underground in Britain, 1660-1663*. New York: Oxford University Press.

———. 1992. *John Bunyan and English Nonconformity*. Rio Grande, OH: Hambledon Press.

Green, Steven K. 2015. *Inventing a Christian America: The Myth of the Religious Founding*. 1st ed. New York: Oxford University Press.

Gunn, Giles B. 1979. *The interpretation of otherness: literature, religion, and the American imagination*. New York: Oxford University Press.

Gura, Philip F. 1984. *A Glimpse of Sion's Glory: Puritan Radicalism in New England, 1620-1660*. Middletown, CT: Wesleyan University Press.

Guthrie, W.K. 1966. *Orpheus and Greek Religion: A Study of the Orphic Movement*. New York: W. W. Norton, repr.

Gwynn, Robin D. 1985. *Huguenot Heritage: The History and Contribution of the Huguenots in Britain*. New York: Routledge.

Haase, E. 1959. *Einführung in die Literatur des Refuge: der Beitrag der französischen Protestanten zur Entwicklung analytischer Denkformen am Ende des 17. Jahrhunderts*. Berlin: Duncker & Humbolt.

Hagen, Kenneth. 1990. *Augustine, the Harvest, and Theology (1300-1500): Essays dedicated to Heiko Augustinus Oberman*. New York: E.J. Brill.

Hall, David D. 1989. *Worlds of Wonder, Days of Judgment: Popular Religious Belief in Early New England*. New York.

———. 1972. *The Faithful Shepherd: A History of the New England Ministry in the Seventeenth Century*. Chapel Hill: University of North Carolina Press, Omohundro Institute.

———., ed. 1968. *The Antinomian Controversy 1636-1638: A Documentary History*. Middletown, CT: Wesleyan University Press; 2nd ed. Durham, NC: Duke University Press, 1990.

———., ed. 1991. *Witch-Hunting in Seventeenth-Century New England: A Documentary History 1638-1692*. Boston: Northeastern University Press; 2nd ed. Duke University Press, 2005.

Hall, David D., et al., eds. 1984. *Saints and Revolutionaries: Essays on Early American History*. New York.

Hambrick-Stowe, Charles E. 1982. *The Practice of Piety: Puritan Devotional Disciplines in Seventeenth-Century New England*. Chapel Hill: University of North Carolina Press.

Hamilton, Alastair. 1981. *The Family of Love*. Cambridge: James Clarke.

Hamilton, Donna B., and Richard Strier, eds. 1996. *Religion, Literature, and Politics in Post-Reformation England, 1540-1688*. New York: Cambridge University Press.

Hammond, prof. Gerald (English, UniversityManchester). In the Belly of the Whale: the Rise and Fall of Religious Language in the Early Modern Period. Conf. on *The Nature Of Religious Language*, Roehampton Institute, London, 11-12 Feb 1995.

Hampton, Stephen. 2008. *Anti-Arminians: The Anglican Reformed Tradition from Charles II to George I*. (Oxford Theology and Religion Monographs) New York: Oxford University Press.

Hancock, Ralph C. 1989. *Calvin and the Foundations of Modern Politics*. Ithaca, NY: Cornell University Press.

Hanlon, Gregory. 1993. *Confession and Community in Seventeenth-Century France: Catholic and Protestant Co-existence in Aquitaine*. Philadelphia: University of Pennsylvania Press.

Hansen, Chadwick. 1969. *Witchcraft at Salem*. New York: George Braziller; New American Library-Mentor, 1970.

Harley, David N. 1993. Medical Metaphors in English Moral Theology, 1560-1660. *Journal of the History of Medicine and Allied Sciences*. 48 (4): 396–435.

Harline, Craig, and Eddy Put. 2000. *A Bishop's Tale: Mathias Hovius Among His Flock in Seventeenth-Century Flanders*. New Haven, CT: Yale University Press, pb.

Harris, Sam. 2012. *Free Will*. New York: Free Press.

Harris, Tim, Paul Seaward, and Mark Goldie, eds. 1990. *The Politics of Religion in Restoration England*. Cambridge, MA: Blackwell.

Harrison, Jane. 1903. *Prolegomena to the Study of Greek Religion*, 1991. Princeton, NJ: Princeton University Press.

———. 2003. *Epilegomena to the Study of Greek Religion*. (Cambridge, 1921) and *Themis: a Study of the Social Origins of Greek Religion*. (Cambridge, 1912, 2nd rev. edition, Cambridge, 1927) Kessinger Publications.

Häseler, Jens. 1997. 'Liberté de pensée'. Éléments d'histoire et rayonnement d'un concept. In *la Philosophie clandestine à l'Âge classique. Actes du colloque de l'Université Jean Monnet Saint-Étienne du 29 septembre au 2 octobre 1993 organisé par Antony McKenna*, ed. dans Antony McKenna and Alain Mothu, 495–507. Paris & Oxford: Universitas & Voltaire Foundation.

———. Réfugiés français à Berlin lecteurs de manuscrits clandestins. dans Guido Canziani, avec la collaboration de Marialuisa Baldi & Gianni Paganini. ed. *Filosofia e religione nella letteratura clandestina. Secoli XVII e XVIII*. Francoangeli, p. 373-385.

Häseler, Jens, and Antony McKenna, eds. 1999. *la Vie intellectuelle aux refuges protestants. Actes de la Table ronde de Münster du 25 juillet*. Vol. 5. Paris: Éditions Honoré Champion, coll. "La vie des Huguenots.

———, eds. 2002. *la Vie intellectuelle aux refuges protestants II. Huguenots traducteurs. Actes de la Table ronde de Dublin, juillet 1999*. Vol. 20. Geneva: Slatkine, coll. "La vie des huguenots,".

Hayden, J. Michael, and Malcom R. Greenshields. 1993. The Clergy of Early Seventeenth-Century France: Self-Perception and Society's Perception. *French Historical Studies* 18 (1).

Haydon, C.J. Walsh, and S. Taylor, eds. 1993. *The Church of England c. 1689-c. 1833*. Cambridge: Cambridge University Press.
Hayes, T. Wilson. 1979. *Winstanley the Digger: A Literary Analysis of Radical Ideas in the English Revolution*. Cambridge, MA: Harvard University Press.
Hefner, Robert, ed. 1993. *Conversion to Christianity: Historical and Anthropological Perspectives on a Great Transformation*. Berkeley: University of California Press.
Heimert, Alan, and Andrew Delbanco, eds. 1985. *The Puritans in America: A Narrative Anthology*. Cambridge, MA: Harvard University Press.
Hellemo, G. 1989. *Adventus Domini: Eschatological Thought in 4th-Century Apses and Catecheses*. New York: E.J. Brill.
Heller, Henri. *Iron and Blood: Civil Wars in Sixteenth-Century France*. Montreal, 1991.
Heller, Henry. 1996. Putting History Back into the Religious Wars: A Reply to Mack P. Holt. *French Historical Studies* 19: 853–861.
Helm, Paul. 2004. *John Calvin's Ideas*. New York: Oxford University Press.
Henry, Nathaniel H. 1988. *The True Wayfaring Christian: Studies in Milton's Puritanism*. New York: Peter Lang.
Hessayon, Ariel, and David Finnegan. 2011. Introduction: reappraising early modern radicals and radicalism. In *Varieties of Seventeenth- and Early Eighteenth-Century English Radicalism in Context*, ed. Hessayon and Finnegan. London: Ashgate.
Hill, Christopher. 1964. *Society and Puritanism in Pre-Revolutionary England*. New York: Schocken Books.
———. 1965. *Intellectual Origins of the English Revolution. (Ford Lectures, 1962)*, 1980. New York: Oxford University Press.
———. 1969. Plebeian Irreligion in Seventeenth-Century England. In *Studien über die Revolution*, ed. Manfred Kossok. Berlin.
———. 1984. *The Experience of Defeat: Milton and Some Contemporaries*. New York: Viking.
———. 1988a. *The Experience of Defeat: Milton. A Tinker and a Poor Man: John Bunyan and his Church, 1628-1688*. New York: Knopf.
———. 1988b. *A Turbulent, Seditious and Factious People: John Bunyan and his Church*. Oxford: Clarendon Press.
———. 1990a. *Antichrist in Seventeenth-Century England*. New York: Verso.
———. 1990b. *A Nation of Change and Novelty: Politics, Religion and Literature in Seventeenth-Century England*. New York: Routledge.
———. 1997. *Intellectual Origins of the English Revolution, Revisited*. New York: Oxford University Press.
Hillerbrand, Hans J., ed. 1988. *Radical Tendencies in the Reformation: Divergent Perspectives*. Kirksville, MO: Sixteenth Century Journal.
———., ed. 1995. *The Oxford Encyclopedia of the Reformation. 4v*. New York: Oxford University Press.
Hilton, R.H., and T.H. Aston, eds. 1988. *The English Rising of 1381*. New York: Cambridge University Press.
Hoffmann, George. 2002. Anatomy of the Mass: Montaigne's 'Cannibals'. *PMLA* 117 (2): 207–221.
Hoklotubbe, T. Christopher. 2017. *Civilized Piety: The Rhetoric of Pietas in the Pastoral Epistles and the Roman Empire*. Waco, TX: Baylor University Press.
Holston, James. 1986. *A Rational Millennium: Puritan Utopias of Seventeenth-Century England and America*. New York: Oxford University Press.
Holt, Mack P. 1993. Putting Religion Back into the Wars of Religion. *French Historical Studies* 18 (2): 524–551.
———. 1995. *The French Wars of Religion 1562-1629*. Cambridge.
———. 1996. Religion, Historical Method, and Historical Forces: A Rejoinder. *French Historical Studies* 19: 863–873.

Höpfl, Harro, ed. 1991. *Luther and Calvin on Secular Authority*. Cambridge: Cambridge University Press.

Horst, I.B., ed. 1986. *The Dutch Dissenters. A critical companion to their history and ideas. With a bibliographical survey of recent research pertaining to the early Reformation in the Netherlands*. E.J. Brill: Leiden.

Howells, R.J. 1983. *Pierre Jurieu: Antinomian Radical*. Durham: University of Durham.

Hsia, Ronnie Po-Chia. 1989. *Social Discipline in the Reformation: Central Europe, 1550-1750*. New York: Routledge.

———. 1984. *Society and Religion in Münster, 1535-1618*. New Haven, CT: Yale University Press.

———, ed. 2014. *The Cambridge History of Christianity. Volume 6. Reform and Expansion 1500–1660*. Cambridge: Cambridge University Press.

Hudson, Anne. 1985. *Lollards and Their Books*. Ronceverte, WV, UK: Hambledon Press.

Hudson, D. Dennis. 2000. *Protestant Origins in India: Tamil Evangelical Christians, 1706-1835*. Grand Rapids, MI: Eerdmans.

Hughes, Ann. 1997. *Print Culture, Religious Radicalism and Heresiography in the English Revolution*. New York City: American Historical Association.

———. 2004. ***Gangraena*** *and the Struggle for the English Revolution*. New York: Oxford University Press.

Hunter, Michael, and David Wooton. 1992. *Atheism from the Reformation to the Enlightenment*. Oxford: Clarendon Press.

Hutton, Sarah. 2011. A radical review of the Cambridge Platonists. In *Varieties of Seventeenth- and Early Eighteenth-Century English Radicalism in Context*, ed. Hessayon and Finnegan. London: Ashgate.

Hynes, Sandra. 2011. Mapping friendship and dissent: the letters from joseph Boyse to Ralph Thoresby, 1680-1710. In *Varieties of Seventeenth- and Early Eighteenth-Century English Radicalism in Context*, ed. Hessayon and Finnegan. London: Ashgate.

Inge, William Ralph (1860-1954) *Christian Mysticism*. (Bampton Lectures, Oxford University 1899) Methuen, 1899.

Ingle, H. Larry. 1996. *First Among Friends: George Fox and the Creation of Quakerism*. New York: Oxford University Press.

James, Frank A. 1998a. *Peter Martyr Vermigli and Predestination: The Augustinian Inheritance of an Italian Reformer*. New York: Oxford University Press.

James, Susan. 1998b. *Passion and Action: The Emotions in Seventeenth-Century Philosophy*. Oxford: Clarendon. (Descartes, Malebranche, Hobbes, Spinoza; Pascal, Locke, Hume).

James, William. The Will to Believe: An Address to the Philosophical Clubs of Yale and Brown Universities. April & May 1896. *The New World*, Volume 5 (1896), pp. 327–347; and in James, *Writings 1878-1899*. (Library of America, 1992), pp. 457–479.

Janssens-Knorsch, Uta. 1999. French Protestants and Private Societies. In *la Vie intellectuelle aux Refuges protestants. Actes de la Table ronde de Münster du 25 juillet 1995*, ed. dans Jens Häseler and Antony McKenna, vol. 5, 99–110. Paris: Champion, coll. "Vie des Huguenots.

Johnston, Warren. 2011. Radical revelation? Apocalyptic ideas in late 17th-century England. In *Varieties of Seventeenth- and Early Eighteenth-Century English Radicalism in Context*, ed. Hessayon and Finnegan. London: Ashgate.

Jones, Rufus M. 1959. *Spiritual Reformers in the Sixteenth and Seventeenth Centuries (1914)*. Boston: Beacon pb.

Jonge, Henk Jan de. *De bestudering van het Nieuwe Testemant aan de Noordnederlandse universiteiten en het Remonstrants Seminarie van 1575 tot 1700*, 1980. North Holland: Amsterdam.

Julian of Norwich. 1998. *Revelations of Divine Love*. Translated by Elizabeth Spearing. Introduction and notes by A. C. Spearing. New York: Penguin.

Jurdjevic, Mark. 2004. Prophets and Politicians: Marsilio Ficino, Savonarola and the Valori Family. *Past & Present* 183 (1): 41–77.

Kagan, Richard L. 1991. *Lucrecia's Dreams: Politics and Prophecy in Sixteenth-Century Spain*. Berkeley: University of California Press.

Kaphagawani, Didier Njirayamanda. 1999. *Leibniz on Freedom and Determinism in Relation to Aquinas and Molina*. Ashgate.
Kappler, Émile. 2002. *Bibliographie critique de l'oeuvre imprimée de Pierre Jurieu (1637-1713)*. Vol. 19. Geneva: Slatkine, coll. "La vie des huguenots,".
Karlsen, Carol F. 1987. *The Devil in the Shape of a Woman: Witchcraft in Colonial New England*. New York: W. W. Norton; Vintage, 1989.
Katchen, Aaron. 1964. *Christian Hebraists and Dutch Rabbis: Seventeenth Century Apologetics and the Study of Maimonides' "Mishnah Torah"*. Harvard University Center for Jewish Studies, London & Cambridge, MA: Harvard University Press.
Kautsky, Karl. 1908. *Der Ursprung des Christentums: Eine historische Untersuchung [Foundations of Christianity]*. Sutttgart: J.H.W. Dietz.
Keayne, Robert. 1964. *The* ***Apologia*** *of Robert Keayne: The Self-Portrait of a Puritan Merchant. ed*. New York: Bernard Bailyn.
Keeble, N.H. 1987. *The Literary Culture of Nonconformity in Later Seventeenth-Century England*. Leicester University Press; Athens, GA: University of Georgia Press, 1987.
Kibbey, Ann. 1986. *The Interpretation of Material Shapes in Puritanism: A Study of Rhetoric, Prejudice and Violence*. New York: Cambridge University Press.
Kienzle, Beverly Mayne, and Pamela J. Walker, eds. 1998. *Women Preachers and Prophets Through the Two Millennia of Christianity*. Berkeley: University of California Press.
King, John N. 1982. *English Reformation Literature: The Tudor Origins of the Protestant Tradition*. Princeton, NJ: Princeton University Press.
Kingdon, Robert M. 1967. *Geneva and the Consolidation of the French Protestant Movement, 1564-1572*. Geneva: Droz.
———. 1995. *Adultery and Divorce in Calvin's Geneva*. Cambridge, MA: Harvard University Press.
Kittelson, J.M. 1975. *Wolfgang Capito: From Humanist to Reformer*. New York: E.J. Brill.
Klaasen, W. 1978. *Michael Gaismair: Revolutionary and Reformer*. New York: E.J. Brill.
Knight, Janice. 1995. *Orthodoxies in Massachusetts: Rereading American Puritanism*. Cambridge: Harvard University Press.
Knoppers, Laura. The Antichrist, the Babilon, the great dragon': Monstrous Representations of Oliver Cromwell. *Monstrous Bodies / Political Monstrosities in the Early Modern Period: A Symposium*. Pennsylvania State University 10-11 Nov, 2000.
Knott, John R., Jr. 1980. *The Sword of the Spirit: Puritan Responses to the Bible*. Chicago: University of Chicago Press.
Krausmüller, Dirk. 2004. Killing at god's command: Niketas Byzantios' polemic against Islam and the Christian tradition of divinely sanctioned murder. *Al-Masaq: Islam and the Medieval Mediterranean* 16 (1): 163–176.
Krey, Philip D. 1992. Nicholas of Lyra: Apocalyptic Commentator, Historian and Critic. *Franciscan Studies* 52: p53–p89.
Kroll, Richard, Richard Ashcraft, and Perez Zagorin, eds. 1992. *Philosophy, Science and Religion in England, 1640-1700*. Cambridge: Cambridge University Press.
Kugel, James L. 2017. *The Great Shift: Encountering God in Biblical Times*. New York: Houghton Mifflin Harcourt.
Kupperman, Karen Ordahl. 1994. *Providence Island, 1630-1641: The Other Puritan Colony*. New York: Cambridge University Press.
Labrousse, Élisabeth. 1964. *Pierre Bayle. v1, Du pays de Foix à la cité d'Erasme*. The Hague: Springer.
———. 1985. *Essai sur la Révocation de l'Édit de Nantes: Une foi, une loi, un roi?* Geneva: Labor et Fidès; Paris: Payot, 1990.
———. 1996a. *Conscience et conviction: Études sur le XVIIe siècle*. Paris/Oxford: Voltaire Foundation.
———. 1996b. *Pierre Bayle, hétérodoxie et rigorisme*. Paris: Albin Michel.
Lake, P. 1988. *Anglicans and Puritans? Presbyterianism and English Conformist Thought, Whitgift to Hooker*. Winchester, MA: Unwin Hyman.

Lake, Peter. Measure for Measure, Anti-Puritanism, and 'Order' in Early Stuart England. Annual CUNY Shakespeare conference "'Of Government the Properties to Unfold': Shakespeare's *Measure for Measure* in Context," April 23, 1999.

Lamont, William. 1996. *Puritanism and Historical Controversy*. Toronto: McGill-Queen's University Press (Studies in the History of Religion).

La Mothe Le Vayer. n.d. *Œuvres de François de La Mothe Le Vayer, Conseiller d'Estat Ordinaire*. 15+v. Paris, 1669ff.

Lang, August. 1941. *Puritanismus und Pietismus. Studien, zu ihrer Entwicklung*. Neukirchen.

Laplanche, François. 1965. *Orthodoxie et Prédication: l'oeuvre d'Amyraut et la querelle de la grace universelle*. Paris: Presses Universitaires de France.

———. *L'Evidence du Dieu chrétien: Religion, culture et société dans l'apologétique protestante de la France classique (1576-1670)*. Paris 1983.

———. 1986. *L'Écriture, le Sacre et l'Histoire: Érudits et politiques protestants devant la Bible en France au XVIIe siècle*. Amsterdam-Maarsen: APA-Holland University Press.

LaPlante, Eve. 2004. *American Jezebel: The Uncommon Life of Anne Hutchinson, the Woman Who Defied the Puritans*. San Francisco: HarperSanFrancisco.

Leites, Edmund. 1988. *Conscience and Casuistry in Early Modern Europe*. New York: Cambridge University Press.

———. 1986. *The Puritan Conscience and Modern Sexuality*. New Haven, CT: Yale University Press.

Leithart, Peter J.. 2014. *Gratitude: An Intellectual History*. Waco, TX: Baylor University Press; June, 2018. (Grace in a way).

Lemons, J. 2019. *Stanley. Retracing Baptists in Rhode Island: Identity, Formation, and History*. Waco, TX: Baylor University Press.

Lepore, Jill. 1998. *The Name of War: King Philip's War and the Origins of American Identity*. New York: Knopf.

La, Salle, and Jean-Baptiste de. 2001. *l'Expérience de Dieu avec Jean-Baptiste de La Salle*, 144. Montréal: Fides, coll. "L'expérience de Dieu,".

Laurence, Anne. 1990. *W.R. Owens & Stuart Sim. eds. John Bunyan and his England, 1628-1688*. Rio Grande, OH: Hambledon Press.

Lauriol, Claude. 1999. Un huguenot homme de lettres: La Beaumelle. In *la Vie intellectuelle aux Refuges protestants. Actes de la Table ronde de Münster du 25 juillet 1995*, ed. dans Jens Häseler and Antony McKenna, vol. 5, 339–350. Paris: Champion, coll. "Vie des Huguenots,".

Laursen, John Christian. 1998. Télémaque manqué: Reverdil at Court in Copenhagen. In *Reconceptualizing Nature, Science, and Aesthetics: Contribution à une nouvelle approche des Lumières helvétiques*, vol. 1. Geneva: Éditions Slatkine, coll. "Travaux sur la Suisse des Lumières,".

———, ed. 1995. *New Essays on the Political Thought of the Huguenots of the Refuge*. Leiden/New York: E.J. Brill.

———, ed. 2002. *Histories of Heresy in Early Modern Europe: For, Against, and Beyond Persecution and Toleration*. Palgrave/Macmillan.

Laursen, John Christian, and Cyrus Masroori. 1999. Liars and Unbelief in the Forgotten Utopia: Denis Veiras' *History of the Sevarambians* at the Roots of Modernity. In *la Vie intellectuelle aux Refuges protestants. Actes de la Table ronde de Münster du 25 juillet 1995*, ed. dans Jens Häseler and Antony McKenna, vol. 5, 185–202. Paris: Champion. coll. "Vie des Huguenots,".

Laursen, John Christian, Cary J. Nedermann, and Ian Hunter, eds. 2005. *Heresy in Transition: Transforming Ideas of Heresy in Medieval and Early Modern Europe (Catholic Christendom, 1300–1700)*. London: Ashgate, Kindle ed.

Laursen, John Christian & María José Villaverde. eds. 2012. *Paradoxes of Religious Toleration in Early Modern Political Thought*. Lexington Books.

Lerner, and Mahdi, eds. 1963. *Medieval Political Philosophy: A Sourcebook*. New York: Free Press of Glencoe.

Lerner, Robert E. 1972. *The Heresy of the Free Spirit in the Later Middle Ages*, 1992. Notre Dame, IN: University of Notre Dame Press.
———. 1987a. Millennialism. In *Dictionary of the Middle Ages*, ed. Joseph R. Strayer, vol. 8, p384–p388. New York.
———. 1987b. Millennialism. In *Encyclopedia of Apocalypticism*, ed. Bernard McGinn, vol. 2, 326–360. New York.
Lesnick, Daniel R. 1988. *Preaching in Medieval Florence: The Social World of Franciscan and Dominican Spirituality*. Athens, GA: University of Georgia Press.
Lewalski, Barbara Kiefer. 1979. *Protestant Poetics and the Seventeenth Century Religious Lyric*. Princeton, NJ: Princeton University Press.
Ligou, Daniel. 1968. *Le Protestantisme en France de 1598 à 1715*. Paris: Société d'édition d'enseignement supérieure.
Little, David. 1984. *Religion, Order, and Law: A Study in Pre-Revolutionary England (1969)*. Chicago: University of Chicago Press.
Liu, Tai. 1986. *Puritan London: A Study of Religion and Society in the City Parishes*. Cranbury, NJ: University of Delaware Press.
Lloyd, Arnold. 1950. *Quaker Social History, 1660-1738*. London.
Locher, G.W. 1981. *Zwingli's Thought. New perspectives*. New York: Brill.
Loewenstein, David. 2001. *Representing Revolution in Milton and his Contemporaries: Religion, Politics, and Polemics in Radical Puritanism*. New York: Cambridge University Press.
Longfellow, Erica. 2004. *Women and Religious Writing in Early Modern England*. New York: Cambridge University Press.
Lubac, Henri de. 1979. *La postérité spirituelle de Joachim de Flore. v De Joachim à Schelling*. Paris: Lethielleux.
Lockridge, Kenneth A. 1970. *A New England Town: The First Hundred Years*. New York: W. W. Norton.
Lovejoy, David S. 1985. *Religious Enthusiasm in the New World*. Cambridge, MA: Harvard University Press.
Lucas, Paul R. 1976. *Valley of Discord: Church and Society along the Connecticut River, 1636-1725*. Hanover, NH: University Press of New England.
Lüdke, Frank, and Norbert Schmidt, eds. 2017. *Pietismus - Neupietismus - Evangelikalismus: Identitätskonstruktionen im erwecklichen Protestantismus*. LIT Verlag.
Lyotard, Jean François. 2000. *The Confession ofAugustine*. Stanford, CA: Stanford University Press.
Macfarlane, Alan. 1971. *Witchcraft in Tudor and Stuart England: A Regional and Comparative Study*. New York.
———. 1978. *The Origins of English Individualism: The Family, Property and Social Transition*. Oxford.
Mack, Phyllis. 1993. *Visionary Women: Ecstatic Prophecy in Seventeenth-Century England*. Berkeley: University of California Press.
———. 1999. Die Prophetin als Mutter: Antoinette Bourignon. In *Im Zeichen der Krise. Im Europa des 17. Jahrhunderts*, ed. Hartmut Lehmann and A.C. Trepp. Göttingen.
MacCulloch, Diarmaid. 1996. *Thomas Cranmer: A Life*. New Haven, CT: Yale University Press.
MacDonald, Michael. 1981. *Mystical Bedlam: Madness, Anxiety, and Healing in Seventeenth-Century England*. New York.
MacLeish, Archibald. 1959. *J.B. (premiere, Yale University Theatre, 23 April, 1958)*. New York: Houghton Mifflin Harcourt.
MacMullen, Ramsay. 1997. *Christianity and Paganism in the Fourth to Seventh Centuries*. New Haven, CT: Yale University Press.
Magdelaine, Michelle. 1985. *Le refuge huguenot*. Paris: A. Colin.
Mandrou, Robert, et al. 1977. *Histoire des protestants en France*. Toulouse: Privat.
Marius, Richard. 1999. *Martin Luther: The Christian Between God and Death*. Cambridge, MA: Harvard University Press.

Markschies, Christoph. 2015. *Christian Theology and Its Institutions in the Early Roman Empire: Prolegomena to a History of Early Christian Theology*. Translated by Wayne Coppins. Waco, TX: Baylor University Press.
Marshall, Cynthia. 1991. *Last Things and Last Plays: Shakespearean Eschatology*. Carbondale, IL: Southern Illinois University Press.
Martin, J.W. 1989. *Religious Radicals in Tudor England*. Ronceverte, WV, UK: Hambledon Press.
McDowell, Nicholas. 2011. The beauty of holiness and the poetics of Antinomianism: Richard Crashaw, John Saltmarsh and the language of religious radicalism in the 1640s. In *Varieties of Seventeenth- and Early Eighteenth-Century English Radicalism in Context*, ed. Hessayon and Finnegan. London: Ashgate.
———. 2003. *The English Radical Imagination: Culture, Religion, and Revolution, 1630-1660*. New York: Oxford University Press.
McGee, J. Sears. 1976. *The Godly Man in Stuart England: Anglicans, Puritans, and the Two Tables*. New Haven, CT: Yale University Press.
McGinn, Bernard. 1978. Angel Pope and Papal Antichrist. *Church History* 47: p155–p173.
———. 1994a. 'Pastor Angelicus': Apocalyptic Myth and Political Hope in the Fourteenth Century. In *Apocalypticism in the Western Tradition*, 221–251. Aldershot.
———. 1994b. *Presence of God: A History of Western Christian Mysticism. v1, The Foundations of Mysticism: Origins to the Fifth Century*. Herder & Herder, repr.
———. 1996. *Presence of God: A History of Western Christian Mysticism. v2, The Growth of Mysticism: Gregory the Great Through the 12th Century*. Herder & Herder, repr.
———. 1998. *Presence of God: A History of Western Christian Mysticism. v2,. Presence of God: A History of Western Christian Mysticism. v3, The Flowering of Mysticism: Men and Women in the New Mysticism: 1200-1350*. Herder & Herder, repr.
———. 2005. *Presence of God: A History of Western Christian Mysticism. v4, The Harvest of Mysticism in Medieval Germany*. Herder & Herder, repr.
———. 2017a. *Presence of God: A History of Western Christian Mysticism. v4. Presence of God: A History of Western Christian Mysticism. v5, The Varieties of Vernacular Mysticism (1350-1550)*. Herder & Herder, repr.
———. 2017b. *Presence of God: A History of Western Christian Mysticism. v4. Presence of God: A History of Western Christian Mysticism. v6, Part 1, Mysticism in the Reformation (1500-1650)*. Herder & Herder, April 1, 2017.
———. 2019. *Presence of God: A History of Western Christian Mysticism. v4. Presence of God: A History of Western Christian Mysticism. v6, Part 2, Mysticism in the Golden Age of Spain (1500-1650)*. Herder & Herder.
———. 2020. *Presence of God: A History of Western Christian Mysticism. v4. Presence of God: A History of Western Christian Mysticism. v6 Part 3, The Persistence of Mysticism in Catholic Europe: France, Italy, and Germany 1500-1675*. Herder & Herder. *Presence of God: A History of Western Christian Mysticism*.
McGrath, Alister E. 2012. *Reformation Thought: An Introduction. (1988)*. 4th ed. Wiley-Blackwell.
———. *The Intellectual Origins of the European Reformation*. Cambridge, MA: Blackwell, 2nd ed. 2003.
———. 1990. *A Life of John Calvin: A Study in the Shaping of Western Culture*. Cambridge, MA: Blackwell.
McKee, Elsie Anne. 1990. *Diakonia in the Classical Reformed Tradition and Today*. Grand Rapids, MI: Eerdmans.
McKibbens, Thomas R., ed. 2017. *Baptists in Early North America—First Baptist Church*. Vol. IV. Boston, MA: Mercer University Press.
McKim, Donald K. 1988. *Ramism in William Perkins' Theology*. New York: Peter Lang.
Mechthild of Magdeburg (c.1207—c.1282-94). 1990. In *Das fliessende Licht der Gottheit (MS, 6 books, 1260-1282)*, Translated by Henry of Nördlingen from Middle Low into Middle High German, ed. Hans Neumann, vol. 2. Munich: Artemis.

Menocal, María Rosa. 2001. *The Ornament of the World: How Muslims, Jews, and Christians Created a Culture of Tolerance in Medieval Spain*. New York: Little, Brown.

Mentzer, Raymond A., Jr. 1994. *Blood and Belief: Family Survival and Confessional Identity among the Provincial Huguenot Nobility*. West Lafayette, Indiana: Purdue University Press.

———. 2000. Morals and Moral Regulation in Protestant France. *Journal of Interdisciplinary History* 31 (1): 1s.

Mercier-Faivre, Anne-Marie. 1998. Le rêve des origines: du protestantisme à la franc-maçonnerie. In *dans Franc-maçonnerie et religion dans l'Europe des Lumières*, 57–76. Paris: Champion.

———. 1997. Les traités sur la tolérance: Voltaire et les protestants français, une confrontation. *Studies on Voltaire and the Eighteenth Century*: p613–p630.

———. Les protestants français du XVIIIe siècle à la recherche d'une identité. dans *Le roi, le protestant et la république*. Cêtre, 1995, p. 35-47.

———. 1999. *Un Supplément à l'Encyclopédie, le Monde primitif de Court de Gébelin*. Paris: Honoré Champion/Slatkine.

Metaxas, Eric. 2017. *Martin Luther: The Man Who Rediscovered God And Changed the World*. New York: Viking.

Michon, Pierre. "Tristesse de Columbkill," tr. Ann Jefferson, "Columbkill's Sadness". In *Winter Mythologies and Abbots*, 2014. New Haven: Yale University Press.

Middlekauff, Robert. 1999. *The Mathers: Three Generations of Puritan Intellectuals, 1696-1728*. Berkeley: University of California Press.

Milbank, John, Slavoj Žižek & Creston Davis, *Paul's New Moment: Continental Philosophy and the Future of Christian Theology*, 2010.

Mills, Kenneth, and Anthony Grafton, eds. 2004a. *Conversion in Late Antiquity and the Early Middle Ages: Seeing and Believing*. Rochester, New York: University of Rochester Press.

———, eds. 2004b. *Conversion: Old Worlds and New*. Rochester/New York: University of Rochester Press.

Milton, Anthony. 1994. *Catholic and Reformed: The Roman and Protestant Churches in English Protestant Thought, 1600-1640*. New York: Cambridge University Press.

Milton, John. 1973. In *Christian Doctrine [De Doctrina Christiana. MS found 1823]. Vol. VI, Complete Prose Works of John Milton*, ed. Maurice Kelley. Translated by John Carey. New Haven: Yale University Press.

Minnich, Nelson H. Concepts of Reform Proposed at the Fifth Lateran Council. *Fifth Lateran Council (1512-1517)*. London, 1993, 163-254.

Labriola, Albert C., and John W. Smeltz. 2002. *The Mirror of Salvation [Speculum Humanae Salvationis. MS 1309-1324] tr.* Ithaca, NY: Duquesne University Press (Studies in the Humanities.

Mithridates, Flavius. 1963. *[Samuel ben Nissim Bulfarag]*: *Sermo de Passione Domini* (1481). Chaim Wirszubski ed. The Israel Academy of Sciences and Humanities (Jewish convert to Christianity, familiar with Arabic, who translated Kabbala and taught Pico Aramaic).

Molinos, Miguel. 1688. *The Spiritual Guide, which Disentangles the Soul, and brings it by the inward Way to the getting of perfect Contemplation, and the Rich Treasure of Internal Peace. Also the substance of several letters sent from Italy concerning the Quietists*. (Venice, 1685), English translation, London, Reprint University Microfilms. https://www.adamford.com/molinos/src/s-guide-20071210.pdf.

Monter, E. William. 1999. *Judging the French Reformation: Heresy Trials by Sixteenth-Century Parlements*. Cambridge, MA: Harvard University Press.

Moore, Marianne. 1967. *The Complete Poems of Marianne Moore*. New York: Macmillan/Viking.

Morgan, Edmund S. 1975. *American Slavery, American Freedom: The Ordeal of Colonial Virginia*. New York.

———. 1963. *Visible Saints: The History of a Puritan Idea*. Ithaca, NY: Cornell University Press.

———.. "Back to Basics," *New York Review of Books* 47:12(20Jul00), p47-49.

———. 1958. *The Puritan Dilemma: The Story of John Winthrop (1958)*. Boston: Little, Brown.

———. 1966. *The Puritan Family: Religion and Domestic Relations in Seventeenth-Century New England. (1944), new ed.* New York: Harper Torchbooks.
Morgan, John. 1985. *Godly Learning: Puritan Attitudes Towards Reason, Learning, and Education, 1560-1640.* New York: Cambridge University Press.
Morrill, John. 1991. *ed. The National Covenant in its British Context, 1638-51.* New York: Edinburgh University Press.
Mours, S. 1967. *Le protestantisme en France au XVIIe siècle.* Paris: Librarie Protestante.
Muchembled, Robert. 1985. *Popular Culture and Elite Culture in France, 1400-1750.* Translated by Lydia Cochrane. Baton Rouge: LSU Press.
Mudroch, Vaclav. 1979. In *The Wyclyf Tradition*, ed. A.C. Reeves. Athens: Ohio University Press.
Muller, Richard A. 1999. *The Unaccommodated Calvin: Studies in the Foundation of a Theological Tradition.* New York: Oxford University Press.
Murdock, Graeme. 2000. *Calvinism on the Frontier 1600-1660: International Calvinism and the Reformed Church in Hungary and Transylvania.* New York: Oxford University Press.
Murphy-O'Connor, Jerome O.P. 1996. *Paul: A Critical Life.* New York: Oxford University Press.
———. 2004. *Paul: His Story.* New York: Oxford University Press.
Murray, Gilbert (1866-1957), *Five Stages of Greek Religion: Studies Based on a Course of Lectures Delivered in April 1912 at Columbia University*, 1935.
Nederman, Cary J. 2013. 2012 Arthur O. Lovejoy Lecture: Civil Religion—Metaphysical, Not Political: Nature, Faith, and the Communal Order in European Thought, c.1150-c.1550. *Journal of the History of Ideas* 74 (1): 1–22.
Neele, Adriaan C. 2019. *Before Jonathan Edwards: Sources of New England Theology.* New York: Oxford University Press.
Netanyahu, Benjamin. 2001. *The Origins of the Inquisition in Fifteenth-Century Spain.* 2nd ed. New York: New York Review Books.
Newcomb, B.H. 1995. The English Puritan Clergy's Acceptance of Political Parties, 1570-1700. *Journal of Religious History* 19 (1): 43–61.
Niccoli, Ottavia. 1990. *Prophesy and People in Renaissance Italy.* Cochrane, Princeton: Translated by Lydia G.
Nicolson, Adam. 2003. *God's Secretaries: The Making of the King James Bible.* New York: HarperCollins.
Nietzsche, Friedrich. 1954. *The Portable Nietzsche. Translated and Edited by Walter Kaufmann.* New York: Viking Press.
Nock, Arthur Darby. 2019. *Conversion: The Old and the New in Religion from Alexander the Great to Augustine of Hippo (1933) Waco.* TX: Baylor University Press.
Norton, Mary Beth. 2002. *In the Devil's Snare: The Salem Witchcraft Crisis of 1692.* New York: Knopf.
Nuttall, Geoffrey F., Roger Thomas, H. Lismer Short & R. D. Whitehorn. *The Beginnings of Nonconformity.* (Hibbert Lectures 1962) London: Clarke, 1964, PDF. https://www.unitarian.org.uk/sites/default/files/1964_Begginnings_Of_Nonconformity.pdf.
Oakley, Francis. 1964. *The Political Thought of Pierre d'Ailly: The Voluntarist Tradition.* New Haven, CT: Yale University Press.
———. 1984a. *Natural law, conciliarism, and consent in the late Middle Ages: studies in ecclesiastical and intellectual history.* London.
———. 1984b. *Omnipotence, Covenant and Order: An Excursion in the History of Ideas from Abelard to Leibniz.* Ithaca, NY: Cornell University Press.
———. 1994. Constance, Basel and the Two Pisas: The Conciliarist Legacy in Sixteenth and Seventeenth Century England. *Annuarium Historiae Conciliorum* 1: 26.
———. 1997. Locke, Natural Law and God—Again. *History of Political Thought* 18 (4): 624–651.
———. 1998a. The Absolute and Ordained Power of God in Sixteenth- and Seventeenth-Century Theology. *Journal of the History of Ideas* 59 (3): 437–462.

———. 1998b. The Absolute and Ordained Power of God and King in the Sixteenth and Seventeenth Centuries: Philosophy, Science, Politics, and Law. *Journal of the History of Ideas* 59 (4): 669–690.

———. 1999. Bronze-Age Conciliarism: Edmond Richer's Encounters with Cajetan and Bellarmine. *History of Political Thought* 20 (1): 65–86.

Oberman, Heiko A. 1992. *The Dawn of the Reformation: Essays in Late Medieval and Early Reformation Thought*. Grand Rapids, MI: Eerdmans.

———.. 1989. *Luther: Man between God and the Devil*. Translated by Eileen Walliser-Schwartzbut. New Haven, CT: Yale University Press, 1990, 2006.

———. 1991. *& Frank A. James III. eds. Via Augustini: Augustine in the Later Middle Ages, Renaissance and Reformation*. New York & Leiden: E.J. Brill.

O'Cathesaigh, Sean. 1999. "Enlightenment and the Inner Light," dans Jens Häseler & Antony McKenna. ed. *la Vie intellectuelle aux Refuges protestants. Actes de la Table ronde de Münster du 25 juillet 1995*. Paris: Champion, coll. "Vie des Huguenots," 5, p. 173-184.

Odile, Martin. 1986. *La conversion protestante à Lyon (1659-1687)*. Geneva: Librairie Droz.

Oort, J. van. 1991. *Jerusalem and Babylon: A Study into Augustine's* ***City of God*** *and the Sources of His Doctrine of the Two Cities*. New York: E.J. Brill.

O'Shea, Stephen. 2000. *The Perfect Heresy: The Revolutionary Life and Death of the Medieval Cathars*. New Haven, CT: Yale University Press, pb.

Osler, M.J. 1998. Mixing Metaphors: Science and Religion or Natural Philosophy and Theology in Early Modern Europe. *History of Science* 36 (1:111): 91–113.

Ozment, S.E. 1969. *Homo spiritualis. A comparative study of the anthropology of Johannes Tauler, Jean Gerson and Martin Luther (1509-1516) in the context of their theological thought*. New York: Brill.

Packull, Werner O. 1996. *Hutterite Beginnings: Communitarian Experiments during the Reformation*. Baltimore: Johns Hopkins University Press.

Page, Sophie. Speaking with Spirits: The Medieval Quest for Celestial Knowledge and Elevation. *Conversations with Angels*, 9-10 September, 2005, interdisciplinary conference at CRASSH, Cambridge. http://www.crassh.cam.ac.uk/events/2004-5/angels.html.

Pagels, Elaine. 1995. *The Origin of Satan*. New York: Random House.

———. 2003. *Beyond Belief: The Secret Gospel of Thomas*. New York: Random House.

Pannier, J.L. 1911. *Église reformée de Paris sous Henri IV: rapports de l'église et de l'état, , vie publique et privée des protestants, leur part dans l'histoire de la capitale, le mouvement des idées, les arts, la société, le commerce*. Paris: H. Champion.

———. 1922. *Église reformée de Paris sous Louis XIII (1610-1621): rapports de l'église et de l'état, , vie publique et privée des protestants, leur part dans l'histoire de la capitale, le mouvement des idées, les arts, la société*. Istra: Strasbourg.

Papàsogli, Benedetto. 1991. *Il "Fondo del cuore": Figure dello spaziuo interiore nel Seicento francese*. Pisa: Libreria Goliardica.

Parente, J.A. 1987. *Religious drama and humanist tradition*. New York: Brill.

La Parker, D. 1980. *Rochelle and the French Monarchy: Confict and Order in Seventeenth-Century France*. London: Royal Historical Society.

Parker, Kenneth L. 1986a. *The English Sabbath: A Study of Doctrine and Practice from the Reformation to the Civil War*. Cambridge: Cambridge University Press.

Parker, T.H.L., ed. 2001. *[Calvin's] Commentaries on* ***Romans****, 1532-1542*. T&T Clark.

———., ed. 1986b. *Calvin's New Testament Commentaries*. (1971) Reprint. Louisville, KY: Westminster John Knox Press.

Parnham, D. 2001. Politics Spun Out of Theology and Prophecy: Sir Henry Vane on the Spiritual Environment of Public Power. *History of Political Thought* 22 (1): 53–83.

Parrinder, Geoffrey. 1998. *A Concise Encyclopedia of Christianity*. Oxford: Oneworld.

———. 1995. *Mysticism in the World's Religions*. Oneworld: Oxford, UK.

Parry, G.J.R. 1987. *A Protestant Vision: William Harrison and the Reformation of Elizabethan England*. New York: Cambridge University Press.

Partee, Charles. 1977. *Calvin and Classical Philosophy*. (Brill, 1974). Louisville, KY: Westminster John Knox Press.
Pascoe, L.B. 1973. *Jean Gerson, Principles of Church reform*. New York: Brill.
Patrides, C.A., and Joseph A. Wittreich, eds. 1984. *The Apocalypse in English Renaissance Thought and Literature*. Ithaca, NY: Cornell University Press.
Patterson, Lloyd. 1967. *God and History in Early Christian Thought*. London.
Pelagius. 1922–1931. *Pelagius' Exposition of Thirteen Epistles of St. Paul*. (before 410 AD), ed. A. Souter; TS 9.1-3; Cambridge: Cambridge University Press, vol. 2, pp. 306–43.
———. *Pelagius's Commentary on St Paul's Epistle to the Romans*. (before 410 AD), ed. & tr. T. de Bruyn; OECS; Oxford: University Press (Oxford Early Christian Studies), 1993.
Pelikan, Jaroslav. 1999. *Jesus Through the Centuries: His Place in the History of Culture*. New Haven, CT: Yale University Press.
———. 1973–1990. *The Christian Tradition: A History of the Development of Doctrine*. Vol. 5. Chicago: University of Chicago Press.
Perry, Ralph Barton. 1944. *Puritanism and Democracy*. New York: Vanguard Press; New York: Harper Torchbooks, 1964.
———. 1936. *The Thought and Character of William James*. Boston: Little, Brown.
Peschke, Erhard. 1969. *August Hermann Francke*. East Berlin: *Werke in Auswahl*.
Pettegree, Andrew. 1992. *The Early Reformation in Europe*. New York: Cambridge University Press.
Pettegree, Andrew, Alastair Duke, and Gillian Lewis, eds. 1994. *Calvinism in Europe, 1540-1620*. New York: Cambridge University Press.
Pettit, Norman. *The Heart Prepared: Grace and Conversion in Puritan Spiritual Life*. New Haven: Yale University Press, 1966; Middletown, CT: Wesleyan University Press, 1989. (neo-Arminian American "preparationists" vs. "voluntarists.").
Philbrick, Nathaniel. 2006. *Mayflower*. New York: Viking Penguin, 2007.
Pidoux, Pierre. 1962. *Le Psautier huguenot du XVIe siècle*. v1, *Les Mélodies*. v2, *Documents et bibliographie*. Basel.
Pintard, René. 1983. *Le Libertinage érudit dans la première moitié du XVIIe siècle. Paris, 1943*. Slatkine reprint: Genève/Paris.
Pleijel, Hilding. 1935. *Der schwedische Pietismus in seinen Beziehungen zu Deutschland: Eine kirchengeschichtliche Untersuchung*. Lund.
Plumer, Eric. 2003. *Augustine's Commentary on* ***Galatians****: Introduction, Text, Translation, and Notes*. New York: Oxford University Press.
Poiret Naudé, Pierre (1646-1719). 1687. *La Paix de bonnes âmes dans tous les Parties du Christianisme sur les Matières de Religion* … Amsterdam.
Poiret Naudé. 1687. *L'Oeconomie divine ou système universel et démontré des oeuvres et des desseins de Dieu envers les hommes*. 7v, Amsterdam.
———. 1713. *The Divine Economy* … (*L'Oeconomie divine*, 1687) tr. 6v, London.
———. 1691. *La Théologie de l'Amour, ou la vie et les oeuvres de Sainte Cathérine de Gênes*. Cologne.
———. 1679. *Mémoire touchant la vie de Mlle. A. Bourignon*.
Poiret, Pierre. ed. *Oeuvres*. (of Antoinette Bourignon), (19v, Amsterdam, 1679), Translated and Edited by George Garden, 9v, London, 1696–1708.
Polizzotto, Lorenzo. 1994. *The Elect Nation: The Savonarolan Movement in Florence, 1494-1545*. Oxford: Clarendon.
Poole, Kirsten. 2000. *Radical Religion from Shakespeare to Milton: Figures of Nonconformity in Early Modern*. Cambridge: Cambridge University Press.
Pope, Robert G. 1969. *The Half-Way Covenant: Church Membership in Puritan New England*. Princeton, NJ: Princeton University Press.
———. 1969-1970. New England versus the New England Mind: The Myth of Declension. *Journal of Social History* 3: 95–108.

Popkin, Richard H. 1988. *Millenarianism and Messianism in English Literature and Thought, 1650-1800*. New York & Leiden: E.J. Brill.

———. 1987. *Isaac La Peyrère (1596-1676): His Life, Work and Influence*. New York & Leiden: E.J. Brill.

———. ed. *Millenarianism and Messianism in Early Modern Europe and America*. 4v, Dordrecht: Kluwer Academic Publishers, 2001. Vol. 1: *Jewish Messianism in the Early Modern World*. ed. Matt Goldish & Richard H. Popkin. Vol. 2: *Catholic Millenarianism: From Savonarola to the Abbé Grégoire*. ed. Karl A. Kottman. Vol. 3: *The Millenarian Turn: Millenarian Contexts of Science, Politics, and Everyday Anglo-American Life in the Seventeenth and Eighteenth Century*. ed. James E. Force & Richard H. Popkin. Vol. 4: *Continental Millenarians: Protestants, Catholics, Heretics*. ed. John Christian Laursen & Richard H. Popkin.

Porete, Marguerite. 1993. *The Mirror of Simple Souls*. Translated by Ellen L. Babinsky. Mahwah, NJ: Paulist Press.

Post, R.R. 1968. *The modern devotion. Confrontation with Reformation and humanism*. New York: Brill.

Poton, Didier. 1985. *Saint-Jean-de-Gardonnenque. Une communauté reformee à la veille de la Révocation (1663-1685)*.

Potter, David, ed. 1998. *The French Wars of Religion: Selected Documents*. Translated by David Potter. New York: St. Martin's Press.

Powell, C.H. 1965. *Paul Through Modern Eyes*. London.

Prestwich, Menna, ed. 1985. *International Calvinism, 1541-1715*. Oxford: Clarendon Press of Oxford University Press.

Prosperi, Adriano. 1992. New Heaven and New Earth: Prophesy and Propaganda at the Time of the Discovery and Conquest of the Americas. In *Prophetic Rome in the High Renaissance Period*, ed. Reeves, 279–303. Oxford: Oxford University Press.

de Quehen, Hugo, ed. 1996. *Lucy Hutchinson's Translation of Lucretius:* ***De rerum natura****. London*. Duckworth/Ann Arbor: University of Michigan Press.

Quéniart, Jean. 1985. *La Révocation de l'Édit de Nantes: protestants et catholiques français en France de 1598 à 1685*. Paris: Desclée de Brouwer.

Racault, Jean-Michel. 1996. La pensée utopique des protestants français à la veille de la Révocation. *Revue canadienne de littérature comparée* 23 (2): 403–412.

Rapley, Elizabeth. 1990. *The Dévotes: women and Church in Seventeenth-Century France*. Toronto: McGill-Queen's University Press (Studies in the History of Religion.

Raymond, Joad. Tongues of Angels: Mysticism and Theological Politics, 1640–1660. *Conversations with Angels*, 9-10 September, 2005, interdisciplinary conference at CRASSH, Cambridge. http://www.crassh.cam.ac.uk/events/2004-5/angels.html.

Redekop, Benjamin W., and Calvin W. Redekop. 2001. *Power, Authority, and the Anabaptist Tradition*. Baltimore, MD: Johns Hopkins University Press.

Redekop, Calvin. 1989. *Mennonite Society*. Baltimore: Johns Hopkins University Press.

Reeves, Marjorie, ed. 1992. *Prophetic Rome in the High Renaissance Period*. Oxford: Oxford University Press.

Reid, David. 1982. *The Party-Colored Mind: Selected Prose relating to the Conflict between Church and State in 17th-Century Scotland*. Edinburgh: Scottish Academic Press.

Reitzenstein, Richard. 2018. *Hellenistic Mystery-Religions: Their Basic Ideas and Significance*. Translated by John E. Steely. Waco, TX: Baylor University Press.

Richard, Michel-Edmond. 1994. *La vie des protestants français de l'Édit de Nantes à la Révolution, 1598-1789*. Paris: Éditions de Paris.

Riesner, Rainer. 1998. *Paul's Early Period: Chronology, Mission Strategy*. Eerdmans: Theology, Grand Rapids, MI.

Ritschl, Albrecht. 1966. *Geschichte des Pietismus*. Vol. 3. Bonn: Marcus, 1880-1886, repr. Berlin.

Robinson, Marilynne. 2019. Which Way to the City on a Hill. *New York Review of Books* 66 (12): 43–45. (Colonial and state constitutions, 1611-1651).

Roquebert, Michel. 1999. *Histoire des Cathares: Hérésie, Croisade, Inquisition, du XIe au XIVe siècle*. Paris: Libraire Académique Perrin.
Round, Phillip H. 1999. *By Nature and by Custom Cursed: Transatlantic Civil Discourse and New England Cultural Production, 1620-1660*. Hanover, NH: University Press of New England.
Rowland, Ingrid. The Ecstatic Journey of Athanasius Kircher, 1656. *Conversations with Angels*, 9-10 September, 2005, interdisciplinary conference at CRASSH, Cambridge, http://www.crassh.cam.ac.uk/events/2004-5/angels.html.
Rowlands, Alison. 2008. 'Superstition', Magic, and Clerical Polemic in Seventeenth-Century Germany. *The Religion of Fools? Superstition Past and Present; Past & Present* 199 (Supplement 3): 157–177. http://past.oxfordjournals.org/content/vol199/suppl_3/index.dtl?etoc.
Rummel, Erika. 2000. *The Confessionalization of Humanism in Reformation Germany*, Oxford Studies in Historical Theology. New York: Oxford University Press. (a source of anti-intellectualism).
Russell, Jeffrey Burton. 1987. *The Devil (1977); Satan (1977); Lucifer (1984); Mephistopheles*. Ithaca, NY: Cornell University Press.
Russell, Paul A. 1986. *Lay Theology in the Reformation: Popular Pamphleteers in Southwest Germany, 1521-1525*. Cambridge: Cambridge University Press.
Rutman, Darrett B. 1965. *Winthrop's Boston*. Chapel Hill: University of North Carolina Press.
Rymatzki, Christoph. 2004. *Hallische Pietismus und Judenmission*. Tübingen.
Sachse, Julius F. 1895. *The German Pietists of Provincial Pennsylvania, 1694-1708*. Philadelphia.
Savonarola, Girolamo. 1955. In *Prediche sopra l'Esodo*, ed. Giorgio Ricci, vol. 2. Rome, 1956.
———. 1846. *Sermone e prediche di fra Girolamo Savonarola*. Florence.
———. 1962. In *Prediche sopra Ruth e Michea*, ed. V. Romano. Rome.
Schering, Ernst. 1982. Pietismus und die Renaissance der Mystik. Pierre Poiret als Interpret und Wegbereiter der romantischen Mystik in Deutschland. In *Pietismus-Herrentum-Erweckungs-bewegung*, ed. Dietrich Meter. Cologne.
Schilling, Heinz. 1987. Calvinismus und Freiheitsrechte. *Bijdragen en Medelingen betreffende de Geschiedenis der Niederlanden* 102: p404–p434.
Schmidt, Martin. 2008. *Pietismus. (1983)*. 3rd ed. Kohlhammer Verlag.
———. 1975. In *Der Pietismus in Gestalten und Wirkungen. Martin Schmidt zum 65. Geburtstag*, ed. Heinrich Bornkamm, F. Heyer, and A. Schindler. Bielefeld.
Schwartz, Sally. 1987. *"A Mixed Multitude": The Struggle for Toleration in Colonial Pennsylvania*. New York: New York University Press.
Schweitzer, Albert. 1998a. *The Mysticism of Paul the Apostle*. (1931) Translated by William Montgomery. Baltimore, MD: Johns Hopkins University Press.
———. 1998b. *The Quest of the Historical Jesus: A Critical Study of Its Progress from Reimarus to Wrede*. Vol. 1906. Baltimore, MD: Johns Hopkins University Press.
Scott, Tom. 1989. *Thomas Müntzer, Theology and Revolution in the German Reformation*. New York: St. Martin's.
Scougal, Henry (1650-1678). 1677. *The Life of God in the Soul of Man*. Grand Rapids, MI: Christian Classics Ethereal Library. Accessed 14 Oct 2003.
Screech, M.A. 1994. *Clément Marot: A Renaissance Poet Discovers the Gospel [Marot évangélique]*. New York: E.J. Brill.
Scribner, Bob, Roy Porter, and Mikulas Teich, eds. 1994. *The Reformation in National Context*. Cambridge: Cambridge University Press.
Selinger, Suzanne. 1984. *Calvin Against Himself: An Inquiry in Intellectual History*. Hamden, CT: Archon.
Sellars, John. 2011. Is God a Mindless Vegetable? Cudworth on Stoic Theology. *Intellectual History Review* 21 (2): 121–134.
Shaw, George Bernard. 1916. *Androcles and the Lion*. Vol. 1911. New York: Brentano's.
Sheehan, Jonathan. 2006a. Introduction: Thinking about Idols in Early Modern Europe. *Journal of the History of Ideas* 67 (4): 561–570.

———. 2006b. The Altars of the Idols: Religion, Sacrifice, and the Early Modern Polity. *Journal of the History of Ideas* 67 (4): 649–674.

Sheils, W.J. 1979. *The Puritans In The Diocese Of Peterborough, 1558-1610*. Northamptonshire Record Society.

Singer, Isaac Bashevis. 1997. Isaac Singer's Promised City. *City Journal*.

Shuffelton, Frank. 1977. *Thomas Hooker, 1586-1647*. Princeton, NJ: Princeton University Press.

Shulman, George M. 1989. *Radicalism and Reverence: The Political Thought of Gerrard Winstanley*. Berkeley, CA: University of California Press.

Sider, R.J. 1974. *Andreas Bodenstein von Karlstadt. The development of his thought, 1517-1525*. New York: Brill.

Silk, Mark. 2004. Numa Pompilius and the Idea of Civil Religion in the West. *Journal of the American Academy of Religion* 72 (4).

Simons, Menno. 1983. *Complete Works Of Menno Simons*. Translated by John Funk (1871), repr. Pathway Pub.

Skinner, Quentin. 1980. The Origins of the Calvinist Theory of Revolution. In *After the Reformation*, ed. Barbara C. Malament, p309–p330. Philadelphia.

Smith, David L. 1992. *Oliver Cromwell: Politics and Religion in the English Revolution, 1640-1658*. Cambridge: Cambridge University Press.

Sole, J. *Le débat entre Protestants et Catholiques Français de 1598 à 1685. 4 tomes*, 1985. Paris: Amateurs des livres.

Sommerville, C. John. 1992. *The Discovery of Childhood in Puritan England*. Athens: University of Georgia Press.

———. 1977. *Popular Religion in Restoration England*. University Press of Florida (University of Florida Monographs, Social Sciences No. 59).

Sorbière, Samuel. 2002. *Discours sceptiques. Édition critique établie et présentée par Sophie Gouverneur*. Vol. 10. Geneva: Slatkine, coll. "Libre pensée et littérature clandestine,".

Spellman, W.M. 1993. *The Latitudinarians and the Church of England, 1660-1700*. Athens: University of Georgia Press.

Spener, Philipp Jakob. 1964, 2002. *Pia Desideria* [*Pious wishes, or Heartfelt Desire / for a God-pleasing Reform / of the true Evangelical Church, / Together with Several Simple Christian Proposals / Looking Toward this End*] (German, 1675, Latin 1678), Translated by Theodore G. Tappert, Eugene, OR: Wipf and Stock.

Sproul, R. C.. 2016. *What is Reformed Theology? Understanding the Basics*. [of Calvinism] Baker Books.

Sprunger, K.L. 1982. *Dutch Puritanism. A history of English and Scottish churches of the Netherlands in the sixteenth and seventeenth centuries*. New York: Brill.

Spurr, John. 1992. *The Restoration Church of England, 1646-1689*. New Haven: Yale University Press.

Stam, F.P. van (Frans Pieter). 1988. *The Controversy over the Theology of Saumur, 1635-1650: Disrupting Debates among the Huguenots in Complicated Circumstances*. Amsterdam: APA-Holland University Press.

Stankiewicz, W.J. 1960. *Politics and Religion in Seventeenth Century France: A Study of Political Ideas from the Monarchomachs to Bayle, as Reflected in the Toleration Controversy*. Berkeley: University of California Press; Greenwood Press, 1977.

Stark, Rodney. 1996. *The Rise of Christianity: A Sociologist Reconsiders History*. Princeton, NJ: Princeton University Press. (40CE to 300CE).

———. 2001. *One True God: Historical Consequences of Monotheism*, 2003. Princeton, NJ: Princeton University Press.

———. 2003. *One True God: Historical Consequences of Monotheism. Princeton. For the Glory of God: How Monotheism Led to Reformations, Science, Witch-Hunts, and the End of Slavery*, 2004. Princeton, NJ: Princeton University Press.

———. 2005. *The Victory of Reason: How Christianity Led to Freedom, Capitalism, and Western Success*. New York: Random House.

———. 2011. *The Triumph of Christianity: How the Jesus Movement Became the World's Largest Religion*. HarperOne.
Starr, G.A. 1971. *Defoe and Spiritual Autobiography. (1965)*. Gordian Pr Inc. reprint.
Stauffer, Richard. 1962. *Moïse Amyraut, un précurseur français de l'œcuménisme*. Paris: Librairie Protestante.
———. 1969. *L'Affaire d'Huisseau, Une controverse protestante au sujet de la réunion des chrétiens*. Paris: Presses universitaires de France.
Stavely, Keith W.F. 1987. *Puritan Legacies: Paradise Lost and the New England Tradition, 1630-1890*. Ithaca, NY: Cornell University Press.
Stayer, James. 1992. *The German Peasants' War and Anabaptist Community of Goods*. Toronto: McGill-Queen's University Press (Studies in the History of Religion).
Stegmann, André, ed. 1979. *Edits des guerres de religion*. (Textes et Documents de La Renaissance). Paris: Vrin.
Steinmetz, David. 1995. *Calvin in Context*. New York: Oxford University Press.
———. 1986. *Luther in Context*. Indiana University Press.
Stocker, Margarita. 1987. *The Apocalyptic Marvell: The Second Coming in Seventeenth-Century Poetry*. Athens: Ohio University Press.
Stoeffler, F. Ernest. 1973. *German Pietism During the Eighteenth Century. v24 of Studies in the History of Religion*. E. J. Brill: Leiden.
———. 2007. *The Rise of Evangelical Pietism. (1965)*. Eugene, OR: Wipf & Stock.
———. 1976. *Continental Pietism and Early American Christianity*. Grand Rapids, MI: Eerdmans.
Stoever, William K.B. 1978. *"A Faire and Easie Way to Heaven": Covenant Theology and Antinomianism in Early Massachusetts*. Middletown, CT: Wesleyan University Press.
Stout, Harry S. 1986. *The New England Soul: Preaching and Religious Culture in Colonial New England*. New York: Oxford University Press.
Stowell, Marion B. 1977. *Early American Almanacs: The Colonial Weekday Bible*. New York.
Stoyanov, Yuri. 2000. *The Other God: Dualist Religions from Antiquity to the Cathar Heresy*. New York: Walker & Co.; New Haven, CT: Yale University Press, pb 2000.
Strayer, Brian E. 2001. *Huguenots and Camisards as Aliens in France, 1589-1789: The Struggle for Religious Toleration*. Vol. 50. Lewiston/New York: E. Mellen, coll. "Studies in Religion and Society,".
Strickland, Lloyd. *Proofs of God in Early Modern Europe: An Anthology*. Waco, TX: Baylor University Press.
Struck, Peter T. 2016. A Cognitive History of Divination in Ancient Greece. *Journal of the History of Ideas* 77 (1): 1–25.
Stuart, Gilbert. 1805. *The History of the Establishment of the Reformation of Religion in Scotland*. (1780) Edinburgh.
Stuurman, Siep. 2000. From Feminism to Biblical Criticism: The Theological Trajectory of François Poulain de la Barre. *Eighteenth-Century Studies* 33 (3): 367–382.
Suso, Henry. (1295-1366).1989. In *Henry Suso: The Exemplar, with Two German Sermons (Classics of Western Spirituality)*, ed. Frank Tobin. Mahwah, NJ: Paulist Press.
Swensson, Eric. Reception of the Doctrine of Justification among German Lutheran Pietists. www.holytrinitynewrochelle.org/yourti89645.html. Accessed 6 Feb 05.
Sykes, Norman. 2008. *Old Priest and New Presbyter*. Cambridge: Cambridge University Press.
Tardieu, Michel. 1984. *Ecrits gnostiques. Le codex de Berlin*. Paris: Le Cerf.
Targoff, Ramie. 2001. *Common Prayer: The Language of Public Devotion in Early Modern England*. Chicago: University of Chicago Press.
Taubes, Jacob. 2003. *The Political Theology of Paul. Translated by Dana Hollander*. Stanford, CA: Stanford University Press (Cultural Memories in the Present).
Tauler, Johannes (c1300-1361). 1985. *Sermons (Classics of Western Spirituality)*. Translated by Maria Shrady. Introduced by Josef Schmidt. Mahwah, NJ: Paulist Press.

Taylor, Larissa J. 1991. *Soldiers of Christ: Preaching in Late Medieval and Reformation France*. New York: Oxford University Press.
Thomas, Keith. 1971. *Religion and the Decline of Magic*. New York: Scribner's.
Thompson, Augustine. 1992. *Revival Preachers and Politics in Thirteenth-Century Italy: The Great Devotion of 1233*. Oxford: Clarendon Press; New York: Oxford University Press.
———. 2006. *Cities of God: The Religion of the Italian Communes, 1125-1325*. University Park, PA: Penn State University Press.
Thornton, John K. 1992. *Africa and the Africans in the Making of the Atlantic World, 1400-1680*. Cambridge: Cambridge University Press.
Todd, Margo. 1987. *Christian Humanism and the Puritan Social Order*. New York: Cambridge University Press.
Tolles, Frederick B. 1960. *Quakers and the Atlantic Culture*. New York: Macmillan.
———. 1963. *Meeting House and Counting House: The Quaker Merchants of Colonial Philadelphia 1682-1763*. New York: W. W. Norton.
Tracy, James D. 2000. *Europe's Reformations, 1450-1650*. Lanham, MD: Rowman & Littlefield.
Trevor-Roper, Hugh. 1988. *Catholics, Anglicans, and Puritans: Seventeenth Century Essays*. Chicago: University of Chicago Press.
Trexler, R.C. 1974. *The spiritual power. Republican Florence under interdict*. New York, Brill.
Tulloch, John. 1872. *Rational Theology: Christian Philosophy in England in the Seventeenth Century*. Vol. 2. Blackwood.
Tyacke, Nicholas. 1987. *Anti-Calvinists: The Rise of English Arminianism, c1590-1640*. Oxford: Oxford University Press.
Urner, Hans. 1952. *Der Pietismus*. Gladbeck: Heilmann.
Underdown, David. 1992. *Fire From Heaven: Dorchester in the Seventeenth Century*. New Haven, CT: Yale University Press.
Underwood, Ted Leroy. 1997. *Primitivism, Radicalism, and the Lamb's War: The Baptist-Quaker Conflict in Seventeenth-Century England*. New York: Oxford University Press.
———. 2000. *The Acts of the Witnesses: The Autobiography of Lodowick Muggleton and Other Early Muggletonian Writings*. New York: Oxford University Press.
Valone, James. 1995. *Huguenot Politics, 1601-1622*. Lewiston, New York: Edwin Mellen Press.
Van Engen, John, ed. 2014. *Sisters and Brothers of the Common Life: The Devotio Moderna and the World of the Later Middle Ages*, The Middle Ages Series. Universityof Pennsylvania Press.
Van Engen, ed. 1988. *Devotio Moderna: Basic Writings* (Classics of Western Spirituality). Mahwah, NJ: Paulist Press. (Sources in English, Middle Dutch and Latin)
Van Ruymbeke, Bertrand. A Dominion of True Believers: French Colonial Religious Policy and the Early Settlement of Colonial Louisiana. *Colonial Louisiana Symposium*, University of Southern Mississippi, 3–6 March, 1999.
Vasoli, Cesare. 1974. Profezie e profeti nella vita religiosa e politica fiorentina. In *Magia, astrologia, e religione nel Rinascimento*, 16–29. Wroclaw.
Verbeke, Werner, et al., eds. 1988. *The Use and Abuse of Eschatology in the Middle Ages*. Leuven.
Verge-Franceschi, Michel. 1992. *Abraham Duquesne: Huguenot et marin du Roi-Soleil*. Paris: France-Empire.
Vickers, B., ed. 1984. *Occult and Scientific Mentalities in the Renaissance*. Cambridge: Cambridge University Press.
Villani, Stefano. 2011. 17th-century Italy and English radical movements. In *Varieties of Seventeenth- and Early Eighteenth-Century English Radicalism in Context*, ed. Hessayon and Finnegan. London: Ashgate.
Vissière, Isabelle, and Jean-Louis Vissière, eds. 2000. *Lettres édifiantes et curieuses des jésuites de l'Inde au dix-huitième siècle*. Saint-Étienne: Publications de l'Université de Saint-Étienne, coll. "Lire le dix-huitième siècle,".
Voeltzel, René. 1955. *Vraie et fausse Eglise selon les théologiens protestants français du XVIIe siècle*. Paris: Presses universitaires de France.

Voth, H.J. 1994. Seasonality of Conceptions as a Source for Historical Time-Budget Analysis: Tracing the Disappearance of Holy Days in Early Modern England. *Historical Methods* 27 (3): 127–132.
Walker, D.P. 1964. *The Decline of Hell: Seventeenth-Century Discussions of Eternal Torment.* Chicago: University of Chicago Press.
———. 1984. Valentine Greatrakes, the Irish Stroker and the Question of Miracles. In *Mélanges sur la littérature de la Renaissance à la mémoire de V.-L. Saulnier*. Geneva.
———. 1983. La cessazione dei miracoli. *Intersezioni* 3: 285–301.
Wallace, Dewey D., Jr. 1982. *Puritans and Predestination: Grace in English Protestant Theology, 1525-1695.* Chapel Hill, NC: University of North Carolina Press.
Walter, John. 2004. 'Abolishing Superstition with Sedition'? The Politics of Popular Iconoclasm in England 1640-1642. *Past & Present* 183 (1): 79–123.
Walvin, James. 1998. *The Quakers: Money and Morals.* North Pomfret, VT: John Murray/ Trafalgar Square.
Walwyn, William. 1988. In *The Writings of William Walwyn*, ed. Jack R. McMichael and Barbara Taft. Athens, GA: University of Georgia Press.
Walzer, Michael. 1982. *Revolution of the Saints: A Study in the Origins of Radical Politics. (1965).* 2nd ed. Cambridge, MA: Harvard University Press.
Ward, William Reginald. 1998. *The Protestant Evangelical Awakening.* Vol. 1991, 1992. Cambridge: Cambridge University Press.
———. 1993a. Mysticism and Revival: The Case of Gerhard Tersteegen. FS John Walsh. *Revival and Religion since 1700.* Jane Garnett and Colin Matthew. London.
———. 1993b. German Pietism, 1670-1750. *Journal of Ecclesiastical History* 44: 479–505. (bibliographical survey).
———. 1999. *Christianity Under the Ancien Régime, 1648-1789.* Cambridge: Cambridge University Press.
———. 2006. *Early Evangelicalism: A Global Intellectual History, 1670-1789.* Cambridge: Cambridge University Press.
Warfield, Benjamin Breckinridge. 1887. (1851-1921) Translation of Augustine. *Anti-Pelagian Writings.* In *Select Library of the Nicene and Post-Nicene Fathers of the Christian Church*, ed. Philip Schaff. New York: The Christian Literature Company.
———. Augustine and the Pelagian Controversy. (Christian Literature Company, 1887), CrossReach Publications. 2018.
Washington, Joseph Reed, Jr. 1988. *Puritan Race Virtue, Vice, and Values 1620-1820.* New York: Peter Lang.
Watt, Tessa. 1991. *Cheap Print and Popular Piety, 1550-1640.* Cambridge: Cambridge University Press.
Watts, Michael R. 1986. *The Dissenters: Volume I: From the Reformation to the French Revolution.* Oxford: Clarendon Press of Oxford University Press.
Weaver, Rebecca Harden. 1996. *Divine Grace and Human Agency: A Study of the Semi-Pelagian Controversy*, 1998. Macon, GA: Mercer University Press.
Weber, Max Die. 2002. *The Protestant Ethic and the Spirit of Capitalism.* (*Die protestantische Ethik und der Geist des Kapitalismus).* (1904-05) Translated by Gordon C. Wells & Peter Baehr. Penguin.
Weeks, Stephen Beauregard. 1892. *The Religious Development in the Province of North Carolina.* Baltimore: Johns Hopkins University Press.
Wegner, Daniel. 2002. *The Illusion of Conscious Will.* Cambridge, MA: MIT Press.
Weigelt, Horst. 1965. *Pietismus Studien.* Stuttgart.
———. 2001. *Geschichte des Pietismus in Bayern.* Vandenhoeck & Ruprecht: Göttingen.
———. 2012. *Spiritualistische Tradition im Protestantismus.* (1973) Reprint. De Gruyter (Arbeiten Zur Kirchengeschichte).
Weinstein, Donald, and Valerie R. Hotchkiss. 1994. *Girolamo Savonarola: Piety, Prophecy and Politics in Renaissance Florence.* Dallas, TX.

Weir, David A. 1990. *The Origins of the Federal Theology in Sixteenth-Century Reformation Thought*. New York: Clarendon Press of Oxford University Press.
Wellhausen, Julius (1844-1918). 2002. *Pharisees and Sadducees*. Translated by Mark E. Biddle, Mercer University Press.
Westerkamp, Marilyn J. 1988. *Triumph of the Laity: Scots-Irish Piety and the Great Awakening, 1625-1760*. New York: Oxford University Press.
———. 1999. *Women and Religion in Early America, 1600-1850: The Puritan and Evangelical Traditions*. London and New York: Routledge (Christianity and Society in the Modern World.
Whelan, Ruth. 1992. From Christian Apologetics to Enlightened Deism: The Case of Abbadie, Jacques (1656-1727). *Modern Language Review (G.B.)* 87: p32.
———. 1999Liberté de culte, liberté de conscience? Les huguenots en Irlande 1662-1702. dans Jens Häseler & Antony McKenna, eds. *la Vie intellectuelle aux Refuges protestants. Actes de la Table ronde de Münster du 25 juillet 1995*. Paris: Champion, coll. "Vie des Huguenots," 5, p. 69-83.
White, P.O.G. 1992. *Predestination, Policy and Polemic: Conflict and Consensus in the English Church from the Reformation to the Civil War*. New York: Cambridge University Press.
Whiting, Robert. 1989. *The Blind Devotion of the People: Popular Religion and the English Reformation*. Cambridge: Cambridge University Press.
Whitley, W.T. 1928. *The Baptists of London, 1612-1928*. London: Kingsgate Press.
Wigglesworth, Michael. 1965. In *The Diary of Michael Wigglesworth, 1653-1657: The Conscience of a Puritan*, ed. S. Edmund. New York: Morgan.
Wiles, Maurice. 2001. *Archetypal Heresy: Arianism through the Centuries*. New York: Oxford University Press.
Wilken, Robert Louis. 2003a. *The Spirit of Early Christian Thought: Seeking the Face of God*. New Haven, CT: Yale University Press.
———. 2003b. *The Christians as the Romans Saw Them (1984)*. 2nd ed. New Haven, CT: Yale University Press.
Williams, George H. 1992. *The Radical Reformation*. Kirksville, MO.
Williams, Roger. 1987. In *The Correspondance of Roger Williams*, ed. Glenn W. LaFantasie. I, 1629-53 & II, 1654-82. Hanover, NH: University Press of New England.
Williams, Selma. 1981. *Divine Rebel: The Life of Anne Marbury Hutchinson*. New York.
Wills, Garry. 2006. *What Paul Meant*. New York: Viking Penguin.
———. 1999. *Saint Augustine*. New York: Viking Penguin/Lipper.
Wilson, John F. 1969. *Pulpit in Parliament: Puritanism during the English Civil Wars, 1640-1648*. Princeton, NJ: Princeton University Press.
Winship, Michael P. 2002. *Making Heretics: Militant Protestantism and Free Grace in Massachusetts, 1636-1641*. Princeton, NJ: Princeton University Press.
Wintermeyer, Rolf. 1994. L'autobiographie piétiste, remède, rite d'initiation ou œuvre littéraire. In *Littérature et civilisation à l'agrégation d'allemand*, 85–121.
Winthrop, John. 1997. *Journal*. Vol. 3. Cambridge, MA: Harvard University Press.
Wolfe, Michael. 1993. *The Conversion of Henri IV: Politics, Power, and Religious Belief in Early Modern France*. Cambridge, MA: Harvard Historical Studies.
Wright, S. *Parish, Church and People: Local Studies in Lay Religion, 1350-1750*. Hutchinson Radius, 1988.
Wrightson, Keith, and David Levine. 1995. *Poverty and Piety in an English Village: Terling, 1525-1700*. New York: Oxford University Press.
Yardeni, Myriam. 2002. *le Refuge huguenot: assimilation et culture*, 22. Geneva: Slatkine, coll. "La vie des huguenots,".
———. 1987. French Calvinist Political Thought, 1534-1715. In *International Calvinism, 1541-1715*, ed. Menna Prestwich, p315–p337. Oxford: Clarendon Press of Oxford University Press.

———. 2000. *Repenser l'histoire: aspects de l'historiographie huguenote des guerres de religion à la Révolution française*, 11. Paris: Champion, coll. "La vie des huguenots,".

Zakai, Avihu. 1992. *Exile and Kingdom: History and Apocalypse in the Puritan Migration to America*. New York: Cambridge University Press.

Zaret, David. 1985. *The Heavenly Contract: Ideology and Organization in Pre-Revolutionary Puritanism*. Chicago: University of Chicago Press.

Zwicker, Steve. 2000. That Most Unlikely of Conversions: Dryden's Catholicism in the Spring of 1687. American Society for Eighteenth-Century Studies, 31st Annual Meeting, University of Pennsylvania.

Chapter 4
The Crucible of the Counter-Enlightenment, II

Abstract Jonathan Edwards, the Atlantic Great Awakening. The Atlantic Enlightenment and Counter-Enlightenment contest and combine. Calvinist Protestantism, and grace.

In the chain of conversion experiences that founded the Protestant Christian evangelical world, Jonathan Edwards's was early. He was 19, not yet ordained, but doing the job as the fill-in minister at a breakaway Presbyterian church near the docks on William Street, in New York City. On the 12th of January, 1722, he confided to the *Diary* he had begun to keep in December, that he had just "solemnly renewed my baptismal covenant."

> I have given every power to him; so that, for the future, I'll challenge no right in myself, in no respect whatever. I have expressly promised him, and I do now promise Almighty God, that by his grace I will not. I have this morning told him that I did take him for my whole portion and felicity, looking on nothing else as any part of my happiness, nor acting as if it were; and his law, for the constant rule of my obedience; and would fight with all my might against the world, the flesh, and the devil, to the end of my life; and that I did believe in Jesus Christ, and did receive him as a Prince and Saviour; and that I would adhere to the faith and obedience of the gospel, however hazardous and difficult the confession and practice of it may be; and that I did receive the blessed Spirit as my Teacher, Sanctifier, and only Comforter, and cherish all his motions to enlighten, purify, confirm, comfort, and assist me.[1]

The eve of a Christian Sabbath, it was a Saturday Edwards never forgot, and it was the experience he remembered in his 1740 *Personal Narrative* as having marked his final conversion. He did remember that there had been a couple of false positives, beginning when he was 9, walking the woods and fields and discerning Wordsworthian intimations of immortality before relapsing into boyish battles of settlers and Indians; but after January, 1722, his repeated struggles with "dulness" seemed over, grace became less uncertain, his own will given up, and he could finally believe he had been predestined to eternal life in heaven and saved from eternal punishment in hell. Edwards remembered the day in spite of changes in the

[1] Jonathan Edwards, *Diary*, Saturday, January 12, 1722 (O.S.) in *Works*, ed., Edward Hickman, 1834, Volume 1, Chapter IV @ http://www.ccel.org/ccel/edwards/works1.i.iv.html.

W. R. Everdell, *The Evangelical Counter-Enlightenment*, Boston Studies in Philosophy, Religion and Public Life 9,
https://doi.org/10.1007/978-3-030-69762-4_4

whole English dating system, with the adoption by the British world of a Catholic invention we call the Gregorian calendar, erasing 11 days in 1752, and moving New Year's Day back from March 25 to January 1, which retroactively changed the year of Edwards's conversion to 1723.

He was in no way the first to encounter the divine in this way. "Awakening," in the mind of the Calvinists of New England, was when you became conscious that you were depraved and began truly fearing damnation. This was "salutary" (the word means productive of salvation) because it would lead to self-examination and changes in behavior, in the course of which your soul would realize (by encountering God as Jesus) that it was among the few who had been predestined to grace and were converted—or among the many who were not. Awakenings had come to Jonathan Edwards more than once, beginning when he was 9, but a subsequent ecstasy, an access of grace, if any, had not lasted. The last and ultimately effective awakening had begun in 1720 when Edwards was 16. A contemporary Sufi Muslim might have linked them together in a *tariqa* or "way" of approaching the divine, but for Edwards, the Calvinist, it could not be his way of approaching God; it had to be God's way of approaching him. As one experimental awakening to his sinful depravity succeeded another, anxiety and inspiration followed by relapse, Edwards felt at last assured of saving grace, that God had "wrought" that work, a "conversion" that he could not possibly deserve or earn, but which he came to affirm when he abandoned his will to God's on January 12, 1723. Nearly continual godly behavior thereafter would provide some fragile evidence of the reality of his ecstatic experience of the divine.

But this crucial turning point for Edwards turned out not to be for Edwards alone. It was to go far beyond the New England frontier and the inward struggles of Edwards's own consciousness. Unlike the conversion experiences of most English Calvinists (Puritans, Congregationals and Presbyterians, later Baptists and other Dissenters), Jonathan Edwards would make his own conversion reverberate around the Western world when he called, a decade later, for similar conversions in his own congregants and in his New England countrymen, and inspired other Christians by his accounts of these calls and responses. Protestants in North America and in England began to convert themselves and others, increasingly during open-air services and ecstatic mass meetings, not yet called "revivals," conducted by traveling preachers in what historians call the Great Awakening in America and the "evangelical" movement among the world's Protestants.[2]

The Moravians were already organized when Edwards received grace in 1723, but they were 4 years away from their first experience of mass conversion, and their first worldwide evangelizing mission. The Wesleys and Whitefield were still in

[2]The newest scholarly account of the "Great Awakening," as a fully Atlantic event, with more attention paid to the Native and African Americans, and the pre-Edwards awakenings among Moravians and in Frelinghuysen's New Jersey, is John Howard Smith, *The First Great Awakening: Redefining Religion in British America, 1725-1775* (Madison, NJ: Fairleigh Dickinson U.P., 2015). The most comprehensive account of the Great Awakening by a modern historian remains *The Great Awakening: The Roots of Evangelical Christianity in Colonial America* (New Haven, CT, Yale University Press, 2007) by Thomas Kidd who combines a doctorate from Catholic Notre Dame with a professorship at southern Baptist Baylor.

school. Moravians and Wesleyans would encounter Edwards's message on both sides of the Atlantic, and George Whitefield would encounter Edwards himself, probably doing more than any other preacher to extend his message; but not until 1740, over a decade later. Late in 1706 refugee Protestant rebels from Catholic-controlled southern France, called the "French Prophets," had landed in London claiming sudden divine inspiration, and organized a millennial, pre-Pentecostal sect. They had made a distinctly bad impression on Enlightenment opinion-makers like Shaftesbury in 1707, but did not constitute a movement.[3] In continental Europe the Augustinian Catholics called Jansenists had already arisen and been crushed in 1709 by the Pope and the King, but the Jansenists had yet to cause schism in the Netherlands or an outbreak of ecstatic prophecy in France. Israel Ben Eliezer would not become the Baal Shem in Miedzyboz, Poland for another 15 years; and Muhammad Ibn Abd al-Wahhab, born in 'Uyaynah, Arabia in 1703 (the same year as Edwards and John Wesley), had yet to make his *hijra* to Mecca. None of the latter four would ever hear of Edwards's message (though leaders of both Jansenists and the French Prophets did meet with Moravians). Nevertheless, their conclusions about access to divine grace and the freedom of the human will would be similar, and their response to those conclusions would produce ecstatics in equal measure—and as many reactionaries as rationalists.

Jonathan Edwards, who got in at the start of so much of this counter-Enlightenment religious activity, remains a giant in the American history of ideas, even for twentieth- and twenty-first-century historians who have not been "saved," and have never wished to be. He was an intellectual of a high order. George W. Marsden, a moderate evangelical, begins his hefty new scholarly biography with this judgment: "By many estimates, he was the most acute early American philosopher and the most brilliant of all American theologians."[4] Philosopher F. J. E. Woodbridge, who had little sympathy for Edwards's idealism, wrote in 1904 that Edwards "was distinctly a great man. He did not merely express the thought of his time, or meet it simply in the spirit of his tradition. He stemmed it and moulded it ... His time does not explain him."[5]

---

[3] NS [Anthony Ashley Cooper, 3rd Earl of Shaftesbury], "A Letter Concerning Enthusiasm to Lord Somers" (September, 1707) *Characteristics of Men, Manners, Opinions, Times* (1708) London: Grant Richards, 1900, v1, Sec. 7, p. 37. The refugee Protestant "French Prophets" reminded the English of the Puritans defeated in England and relegated to North America in the previous century. By 1709, when Richard Kingston, published *Enthusiastik Imposters, No Divinely inspir'd Prophets, the second part* (London, 1709) the Prophets had made some very specific prophecies that were not fulfilled and had passed their moment. Five years after Shaftesbury's "Letter," Joseph Addison's *Spectator* essay called "religious enthusiasm" an error comparable to "superstition," and recommended replacing both with religious "devotion." (*Spectator* #201, Oct 20, 1711).

[4] George W. Marsden, *Jonathan Edwards, A Life* (New Haven, CT: Yale University Press, 2003), Introduction, p. 1. Marsden wrote what is now the definitive biography, but his claim for it was modest: "Presenting Edwards's life in terms that he would recognize and a wide variety of readers can understand may be a sufficient end in itself." (Marsden, *Edwards*, Introduction, Kindle ed. loc. 144).

[5] F. J. E. Woodbridge, "Jonathan Edwards," *The Philosophical Review*, 13(1904), p. 405.

His time, of course, was the Enlightenment, which our own time usually sums up as Newtonian science and Voltairean anticlericalism, and celebrates as the millennial defeat of "superstition" and "fanaticism." And in fact Edwards's great academic champion, Perry Miller,[6] no Puritan, championed Edwards as a philosophical pioneer, a student of the empirical Enlightenment ideas of Locke and Newton who overturned them by resurrecting epistemological Idealism, rejecting both materialist empiricism and pre-Enlightenment substance ontologies for an ontology based on mind—an ontology which is a prerequisite for acknowledging ecstatic experience. The insight appears first in one of his notebooks, written in the summer of 1723, some months after his conversion, in his father's house in East Windsor, Connecticut.

> nothing has any existence anywhere else but in consciousness.[7]

That philosophical premise, the idealist ontology on which Edwards built his theology, was exemplified in his own time only by the philosopher George Berkeley. "Metaphysically," Perry Miller asserted, "this led to the immense conclusion that the entire universe exists in the divine idea,"[8] and he described what he called Edwards's "great discovery . . . that an idea in the mind is not only a form of perception but is also a determination of love and hate."[9]

In the event, though, it was not Edwards's ontology (what is in being, and how) or epistemology (how we know what we know) that put him at the center of change, but his psychology, his insights into how we think and feel.[10] It was his psychology, his religious thinking, his practice, and his preaching, that ended up making history in the eighteenth century and extending his influence for centuries afterward.

That psychology, that thinking, and those practices both influenced and were influenced by the new culture his preaching came from, which was the English frontier whose line then lay just west of the Connecticut River Valley. Edwards never doubted he was English, a member of the state that had been the Protestant champion in centuries of religious wars and the king- and bishop-free Puritan Commonwealth (republic) of two generations before. Born in 1703, to the Reverend Timothy Edwards and the daughter of the Reverend Solomon Stoddard—ministers were the aristocrats of New England—he had spent his infancy and childhood on a

---

[6] Miller's contemporary Alfred Kazin, called Miller "the master of American intellectual history." (in Vicki Luker and Brij Lal, *Telling Pacific lives: prisms of process* (2008) p 14).

[7] in Marsden, *Jonathan Edwards*, Chap 4. Marsden views it as "momentous" and "startling."

[8] Perry Miller, *Jonathan Edwards*, p. 63.

[9] Perry Miller, *Errand into the Wilderness*, p. 179, quoted by Rivka Maizlish, "Perry Miller and the Puritans: An Introduction," S-USIH (http://s-usih.org/2013/05/perry-miller-and-the-puritans-an-introduction.html), 8 May, 2013.

[10] John De Witt wrote in 1912 that "Jonathan Edwards changed what I may call the centre of thought in American theological thinking…More than to any other man, to Edwards is due the importance which, in American Christianity, is attributed to the conscious experience of the penitent sinner, as he passes into the membership of the Invisible Church…" (John De Witt, "Jonathan Edwards: A Study" in *Biblical and Theological Studies by Members of the Faculty of Princeton Theological Seminary*, 1912, pp. 130, 136).

disputed frontier just east of the Catholic French and the pagan Indians. A middle child in a tall family, he had grown to be a six-footer, and he was the only boy among ten sisters in a society too reflexively patriarchal (despite the insistence of their religion on the equality of all believers before God) to allow women in its colleges or pulpits. (Or, for that matter, to prohibit slavery.)

It was, however, a society which educated women in the Bible, and sometimes the classics as well, and the Reverend Timothy sent all but one of the ten Edwards sisters away to "finishing" school in Boston. Education was essential. It was, indeed, a publicly financed public good, because of how unlikely the Puritans thought you were, if male, to enter the leadership class of ministers and public officials without it—or what was very much more important, to find salvation. In the eyes of New England, children were willful—full of will—a will that would not be free until its possessor recognized that it was not free at all, but predestined by God. Until then, the soul was not only undisciplined but also "depraved" by nature, "reprobate," meaning as yet unvisited by God or Christ, unaffected by his grace, and thus unsaved from hell.[11] The English Puritan churches, like the mother congregation founded by Calvin in Geneva, had begun by excluding any persons from full membership who could not prove they had been awakened to the overwhelming question, and then saved by an access of grace that could be demonstrated to the congregation's elders and pastors. This exclusion was still thought to be right in the eighteenth century by many Calvinist ministers, especially in New England.

It's not impossible for a gently raised early twenty-first-century American to see how grace, undeserved and irresistible, and its interlocking web of Augustinian-Calvinist companion doctrines would act in the mind and heart of an eighteenth-century would-be believer, especially one who had been presented since childhood with a vivid picture of redemption as heaven and especially of perdition as Hell, complete with eternal—that is, infinitely long-lasting—punishments of the kind that only the voice of God (and/or the human imagination) can begin to make real. The Muslims had a Hell but seemed to have feared it less, and the Jews' idea of it had always been meager, but for the Edwards sort of Christian, a fearful childhood would be succeeded by an adolescence beset by more than the usual anguish, full of doubt, not only about the truth of the doctrines one ought to believe, but about whether one actually did believe them, or whether, if one didn't, one could hope ever to receive the grace one needed to believe them. No merit could earn that grace—God's intervention—because there was no such thing, in this god's eyes, as human merit. No effort could achieve it, because no human had the capacity,

[11] Philip Greven has written resoundingly and convincingly about the difference in child-raising methods between the Anglican-deist Tidewater elite and the New England Calvinists, the one indulgent and negligent, the other retributive and demanding. Greven, *The Protestant Temperament: Patterns of Child-Rearing, Religious Experience, and the Self in Early America.* (New York: Knopf, 1977).

without God's intervention, to achieve any such goal.[12] And what outward sign, what change of mind, what feelings, if any, could be relied on as evidence of that divine intervention?

Having escaped the terrifying child mortality rates of the era, and arrived at adulthood (or "adolescence," as we now call it) you would either be assured of grace by memorable, often ecstatic, experiences, closely adapted to you, "awakened" to a knowledge of your sin, "convicted" by "legal terrors," as you perceived how the law of God condemned you, "believing" that the sacrifice of the Son of God could and would redeem you, and "converted," "born again" so to speak and thereby insured (and hopefully not hardened) against others' criticism or your own doubt.

Or it could go another way. You might come out of this spiritual-psychological turmoil deprived of assurance and thus bereft of dignity within a community of believers. Some souls, brave or lazy, might seek relief in being an unrepentant reprobate, sometimes leaving the community for good; others might opt for a lifelong and secret hypocrisy; and still others, tiring of the struggle, might settle for indifference, or a deadened faith—bad faith—within an outward conformity. Some might reach for the Arminian solution, if solution it was, where you denied that you were helpless and gave yourself at least some credit for your own striving to live as a Christian and achieve grace.

That grace might be achieved was, of course, heresy to Calvinists; but along the same Arminian lines, some might succeed in convincing themselves that grace had come to them by becoming outwardly strict (and inwardly anxious) observers of the law—the classic stance of the fundamentalist, then called a legalist and in Jesus's time, a Pharisee. Either way what would such adults do about the children, children who were born, not saved but depraved? How would they bring the next generation to salvation, if, as they believed, they had no power to bring themselves to it? No wonder they set such store by education.

[12] I attempt here to answer the question sent me by one of my Saint Ann's students, Ingrid Norton, after she went south to college, "In terms of Calvinism, the sense that our flaws and the world's are inevitable and engrained and that therefore all we can do is seek salvation once we recognize them, rather than change fault and improve our lot and rather we have to pray and try to be purged in terms of perfection of church and Christ—where does that come from?" (Norton to the author, 9Aug06) A shorter answer than mine would be "Augustine," but his book is longer. So was Edwards's. In 1751, not long before his sudden death from disease, Jonathan Edwards completed the manuscript of the large, logical and philosophical treatise against the Arminian belief in free will. It was published posthumously in 1754 as *A Careful and Strict Enquiry into the Modern Prevailing Notions of that Freedom of the Will, Which Is Supposed to be Essential to Moral Agency, Vertue and Vice, Reward and Punishment, Praise and Blame*. Samuel Taylor Coleridge attacked it in his 1825 *Aids to Reflection* to whose first American edition in 1829 the President of the University of Vermont, James Marsh, wrote a preface invoking Coleridge to help him show that Edwards was wrong and that the will was indeed free. American Transcendentalism is often said to have begun with it. (Brad Bannon, "President Edwards and the Sage of Highgate: Determinism, Depravity, and the Supernatural Will," *Journal of the History of Ideas* 77:1(Jan, 2016), pp. 27–48, p. 27–28).

In New England toward the end of the eighteenth century, this web of doctrines around grace came to be called "Old Calvinism."[13] At least that's what its friends called it. Old Calvinism is a very rare bird now; but in the 16th, 17th and early eighteenth centuries it was an engine of change as powerful as emerging commercial capitalism. Indeed, as American social scientists still remind us, Max Weber, the early twentieth-century pioneer of sociology, thought Calvinism was a major cause of the rise of capitalism, and even an English socialist, R. H. Tawney, agreed.[14] Calvinism was also, more than any other version of Protestantism, a principal cause of the century-long European civil wars of religion. Having brought us religious war, it also harassed kings and occasionally brought back an ancient form of government with no kings at all—the Commonwealth, or republic. (The tombstones of some of those regicidal Puritan revolutionaries stand today on New Haven green in Connecticut, and the state of Massachusetts is still styled "The Commonwealth.")[15]

The Old Calvinist teachings about grace can be shown to have underlain almost all of those changes. Some of Calvinism's dynamism was due to the assurance of the first generations of Calvinists; but much was clearly also the result of a new, less parochial, less ostentatious, more effective, more polyarchic, and more egalitarian form of church organization, patterned on that of Calvin's republican city of Geneva. Presbyterian church government, and Congregational, were not merely republican but decentralized, confederated, self-governing, organized by Calvin to propagate themselves, first to France, then to Holland, Zeeland, Prussia, England, Scotland, Connecticut and Massachusetts, among others, often enduring, and usually surviving, violent opposition by the state, not to mention other enemies, including several denominations of Christianity.

The North American Calvinists, the Pilgrims and Puritans, would eventually include their direct descendants the Independents or Congregationals (nowadays brought together as the United Church of Christ), the Presbyterians (Scots and English mostly), the Dutch, German and French "Reformed" churches (French Calvinists like Paul Revere's father had got the name "Huguenots"), and the Baptists, organized in Rhode Island by Roger Williams, and now the largest religious

---

[13] New England Protestants argued fiercely about the purity of Calvinism and the Particular Baptist branch of the new Baptists came up with the following "Five-Point" **TULIP** formula:

Five-Point CalvinismTotal Depravity (also known as *Total Inability and Original Sin*)

***U**nconditional Election*
***L**imited Atonement* (also known as *Particular Atonement*)
***I**rresistible Grace*
***P**erseverance of the Saints* (also known as *Once Saved Always Saved*)

[14] Max Weber, *The Protestant Ethic and the Spirit of Capitalism* (1904–05); R. H. Tawney, *Religion and the Rise of Capitalism* (1926).

[15] This republican, anti-monarchical aspect of Puritanism is the theme of several indispensable histories by the great English historian Christopher Hill (a socialist), especially perhaps his *Society and Puritanism in Pre-Revolutionary England* (New York: Schocken Books, 1964). It took an American, Ralph Barton Perry, to make the most complete case so far that Puritanism was not only republican but also democratic, especially in America. (*Puritanism and Democracy*. New York: Vanguard Press, 1944; pb New York: Harper Torchbooks, 1964).

denomination in the United States. In ever-multicultural New York, for example, the first Calvinist denomination in colonial Manhattan and Albany was Dutch Reformed, in New Rochelle it was Huguenot (*Église Réformée*) and on eastern Long Island, Congregational. In New England, Harvard was founded to train Calvinists for the Puritan ministry in Massachusetts, and when Harvard's standards began to seem too lax, Yale was founded in New Haven to do the same for Connecticut and points west, and the College of New Jersey in Princeton to train Presbyterians for points south and west, where the Scots-Irish were settling. (Edwards himself took his degrees at Yale, challenged Harvard at its commencement, and ended his career as the President of Princeton.) Rhode Island and Providence Plantations, founded by the highly educated Roger Williams, had no college until 1764, partly because the Baptist branch of Calvinism that emerged with him there argued (sometimes by educational experiments) that for those with too much book learning, grace was actually harder to come by, and that an unprofessional—but converted—clergy was more likely to save souls than one that was trained, paid and established.

After the awakenings began, Calvinism, especially the Baptist denomination, spread to the American South, converting the unwashed in colonies where the propertied elites tended to Deism and their colleges remained Anglican, and then on to the Appalachian and trans-Appalachian West where there were as yet no establishments and no colleges to speak of. American Calvinists would also come to include, as we shall see, the great evangelical denominations, like the Methodists and later Pentecostals as they became dependent on a view of grace that, because it derived from Calvin, became more and more constrained by Calvinism's excluded middle. Either you were saved or damned, and your hope was to find out you were saved before you died.

The prerequisites for this eruption of ecstatic religious awakenings, commitments and conversions were thus in place in New England in the first decades of the eighteenth century, as Edwards grew up on the rapidly settling Connecticut River frontier. Well downriver from his father's East Windsor church just south of Hartford was the Collegiate School, the Puritan seminary-college newly moved to the port of New Haven and renamed for its benefactor Elihu Yale, where Edwards spoke as Latin valedictorian of his baccalaureate class in 1720. After sailing back from his preacher's stint and final conversion in New York City in 1723, he received his MA from Yale and orated his thesis (on divine grace versus human helplessness) at Commencement in September, joining the Yale faculty forthwith as a tutor/teacher. Called to his first ordained ministry at the undistinguished congregation of Bolton, just east of Hartford, in 1723, Edwards did his duty for a few months until May, 1724, when Yale called him back to tutor again. In 1727, he married the daughter of one of the ministers who had founded Yale, not long after the suitable pulpit had finally turned up for him in Northampton, also on the Connecticut River but well north of Hartford in the colony of Massachusetts Bay. Edwards's maternal grandfather, Solomon Stoddard, a man whom his fellow anti-Catholics ironically called the "Pope" of the New England frontier, had appointed him assistant minister.

It was at Northampton that the Reverend Edwards came into his own as a minister, and where he would begin to preach awakening, but not right away. He would

Fig. 4.1 Jonathan Edwards in Congregational "Geneva" gown and preaching tabs/bands. Public Domain, https://commons.wikimedia.org/w/index.php?curid=68036

have to hold his tongue until his grandfather died, because he did not agree with him about how to deal with those in a congregation who could not give evidence that they had received grace. Solomon Stoddard, born in Boston soon after its founding and celebrated by the Massachusetts establishment, did not believe in separating the saved from the not-yet-saved at the communion service. He thought that sharing the bread and wine that commemorated the body and blood of the crucified and risen Christ would help raise the consciousness of the reprobate and bring her or him closer to an awakening of the need for grace. This view, part of what is sometimes called the Half-Way Covenant, had helped newer generations of New England Puritans to cope with having their children face exclusion from the communion table of their parents' churches. The view had not prevented Stoddard from leading successful awakenings; he had in fact preached five of them, most recently in 1712 and 1718, but Jonathan Edwards, like his father the Reverend Timothy, who had also preached an awakening in East Windsor in 1712, thought Stoddard was wrong. For the kind of awakenings he wanted to preach, Jonathan Edwards wanted to begin with a repudiation of the reprobates.

Stoddard did die, in February, 1729–1730, and Edwards took over. He seems to have thought it was impolitic to begin by excluding the old man's loyal parishioners; but he preached reform of manners to the young and may well have preached on "legal terrors." Five years later, with almost no warning—and no repudiations—the ecstatic "awakening" happened, and Edwards was thrilled. It seemed to him not just one of Northampton's periodic revivals but one of a constellation of simultaneous outpourings of grace everywhere in the world of reformed (Calvinist) Christianity. He wrote an account that began as a letter and became a book that was read all over the western world and put America at the center of a Protestant Christian global movement. The book is still the foundational text of evangelical revivalism.

A Faithful Narrative of the Surprizing Work of God in the Conversion of Many Hundred Souls in Northampton, and in the Neighboring Towns and Villages of New [sic] *Hampshire in New England* began in 1735 as a letter from a young minister in Hampshire County, Massachusetts Bay Colony—Jonathan Edwards—to an open-minded Puritan minister in Boston, where, since Cotton Mather had died, such *surprising works of God* were less often discerned. The minister forwarded the letter to the Reverend Dr. Guyse, a well-connected Congregational minister in London, it produced a request for publication, seconded by the famous Nonconformist (non-Church of England) hymn-writer, Isaac Watts. Revised and expanded by Edwards and prefaced by Watts and Guyse, it was published in London in 1737. By 1738 it had reached its first German, first Scottish, and third American editions, just as John Wesley hit upon the 1737 London edition and began making notes for what eventually became a training manual for Methodist revival preachers. It would continue to be read all over the western world, putting an event involving a few hundred citizens of a handful of small towns in provincial America at the focus of what was new and hopeful in all of Protestant Christianity. The book that coined the term "Great Awakening" was in the libraries of Protestant missionaries all over the world for two centuries, and it remains the foundational text of what is today called "evangelical revivalism."

A Faithful Narrative is Edwards's close study of the events in his own congregation with reports by his ministerial colleagues of similar events. The latter reads rather like a newspaper report of unusual weather; but Edwards's account of his own congregation and its members has a concern for fact, numbers and social situation that foreshadows the work of the pioneers of anthropology. The whole elegantly meshes the Enlightenment with what would become the Counter-Enlightenment. It showed a scientifically minded wariness of the emotional excess and associated self-delusion that the Enlightenment, following Shaftesbury, Swift and Hume, would continue to stigmatize as "enthusiasm"[16] Edwards wrote:

[16] Shaftesbury, "Letter concerning Enthusiasm," 1708 (datelined September, 1707). According to a manual that takes a less Enlightened view of passion and religion, published by one John Dennis in 1704, the "Enthusiastick Passions" consisted of "Admiration, Terror, Horror, Sadness, Joy, and Desire" The "two chief" ones, Admiration and Terror "make the principal Greatness of Poetry," and "are to bear proportion with the Ideas from which they are deriv'd, and that consequently the greatest must flow from religious Ideas." (John Dennis, *The Grounds of Criticism in Poetry*, London: Geo. Strahan and Bernard Lintott, 1704; cited by David Radcliffe, C18-L, 1Dec98).

> I am very sensible, how apt many would be, if they should see the account I have here given, presently to think with themselves that I am very fond of making a great many converts, and of magnifying the matter; and to think that for want of judgment, I take every religious pang, and enthusiastic conceit, for saving conversion.[17]

At the same time the account has surprising psychological depth, and unabashed appreciation for what the Enlightenment would condemn as "fanaticism" and "superstition"—religious experience. And the evidence for that religious experience Edwards unhesitatingly found in piety—the heart's affections and loving behavior of the convert.[18]

> Many have spoken much of their hearts being drawn out in love to God and Christ; and of their minds being wrapt up in delightful contemplation of the glory and wonderful grace of God, the excellency and dying love of Jesus Christ; and of their souls going forth in longing desires after God and Christ. Several of our young children have expressed much of this; and have manifested a willingness to leave father and mother and all things in the world, to go and be with Christ; some persons having had such longing desires after Christ, or which have risen to such degree, as to take away their natural strength. Some have been so overcome with a sense of the dying love of Christ to such poor, wretched, and unworthy creatures, as to weaken the body. Several persons have had so great a sense of the glory of God, and excellency of Christ, that nature and life seemed almost to sink under it; and in all probability, if God had showed them a little more of Himself, it would have dissolved their frame. [...] Their sense of their exceeding littleness and vileness, and their disposition to abase themselves before God, has appeared to be great in proportion to their light and joy.
>
> Such persons amongst us as have been thus distinguished with the most extraordinary discoveries, [...] are eminent for a spirit of meekness, modesty, self-diffidence, and a low opinion of themselves. ...[19]

There are six individual stories in *A Faithful Narrative*, which we might call conversion case studies, the longest of which, and to us, perhaps, the most curious, is the story of little Phebe Bartlet, which Edwards collected from her mother. Phebe was only four when she was first "awakened" to her sinfulness in talks with her 11-year old brother. God only knows what sins a 4-year-old, or even an 11-year-old,

---

[17] Jonathan Edwards, *A Faithful Narrative of the Surprizing Work of God in the Conversion of Many Hundred Souls in Northampton, and the Neighboring Towns and Villages of the County of Hampshire, in the Province of Massachusetts-Bay in New England*, ed., Benjamin Colman, London: John Oswald, 1737, in *Works*, v4, *The Great Awakening*, ed., C. C. Goen, New Haven: Yale U. Press, 1972, p. 159–160. Edwards's wariness of "enthusiasm" also appears on page?: "I have seen some [converts], and conversed with them in such frames, who have certainly been perfectly sober, and very remote from any thing like **enthusiastic** wildness." "[They] have commonly nowise appeared with the assuming, self-conceited, and self-sufficient airs of **enthusiasts**, but exceedingly the contrary." John Wesley reprinted *A Faithful Narrative* in his *Christan Library*.

[18] For an up-to-date review of all that's been written academically about the psychological originality of Edwards's thought, see Ray S. Yeo, *Renewing Spiritual Perception with Jonathan Edwards: Contemporary Philosophy and the Theological Psychology*, "2. Spiritual Perception and the theological psychology of converting grace," NY: Routledge, 2016, pp. 13ff. The consensus remains that Edwards was fairly early but hardly original in abandoning the older "faculty psychology," nor was his reworking of what is being called "theological psychology," through a renewal of parts of the older biblical diction to describe actual reported experience much of an advance on what European Pietists and Jansenists had done in the seventeenth century. In the English American context, however, it was a giant step.

[19] Edwards, *A Faithful Narrative* (1737), in *Works*, v4, ed., C. C. Goen, Yale U. Press, 1972, p. 181–182.

should feel guilty of[20]; but once she was awakened, Phebe, whose family home seems to have had a private room or "closet" for such things, went off by herself at regular intervals to pray in it—sometimes "five or six times a day." As Edwards reports:

> Her parents did not know of it at that time, and were not wont, in the counsels they gave to their children, particularly to direct themselves to her, being so young, and, as they supposed, not capable of understanding. But after her brother had talked to her, they observed her very earnestly listen to the advice they gave to the other children; and she was observed very constantly to retire, several times in a day, as was concluded, for secret prayer. She grew more and more engaged in religion, and was more frequent in her closet; till at last she was wont to visit it five or six times a day: and was so engaged in it, that nothing would at any time divert her from her stated closet exercises. Her mother often observed and watched her, when such things occurred as she thought most likely to divert her, either by putting it out of her thoughts, or otherwise engaging her inclinations; but never could observe her to fail.[21]

To her mother, whose tactful indulgence might seem un-Puritan to us, Phebe described this as her search for God. It did not go well for a while. She said anxiously, she "could not find God." One day, her mother told Edwards, she heard Phebe praying aloud:

> which was unusual, and never had been observed before. And her voice seemed to be as of one exceedingly importunate and engaged; but her mother could distinctly hear only these words, spoken in a childish manner, but with extraordinary earnestness, and out of distress of soul, *pray, blessed Lord, give me salvation! I pray, beg, pardon all my sins!*

When she came out she was "writhing" in "anguish."

> When the child had done prayer, she came out of the closet, sat down by her mother, and cried out aloud. Her mother very earnestly asked her several times what the matter was, before she would make any answer; but she continued crying, and writhing her body to and fro, like one in anguish of spirit. Her mother then asked her, *whether she was afraid that God would not give her salvation.* She then answered, *Yes, I am afraid I shall go to hell!* Her mother then endeavored to quiet her, and told her *she would not have her cry, she must be a good girl, and pray every day, and she hoped God would give her salvation.* But this did not quiet her at all; she continued thus earnestly crying, and taking on for some time, till at length she suddenly ceased crying, and began to smile, and presently said with a smiling countenance, *Mother, the kingdom of heaven is come to me!* Her mother was surprised at the sudden alteration, and at the speech; and knew not what to make of it; but at first said nothing to her.
>
> The child presently spake again, and said, *There is another come to me, and there is another, there is three*; and being asked what she meant, she answered, *One is, Thy will be done, and there is another, Enjoy Him for ever*; by which it seems, that when the child said, There is three come to me; she meant three passages of her catechism that came to her mind.
>
> After the child had said this, she retired again into her closet, and her mother went over to her brother's, who was next neighbor; and when she came back, the child, being come out of the closet, meets her mother with this cheerful speech; *I can find God now!*

[20] We may never be able to know this now that the Western understanding of children has changed so utterly. How New England brought "legal terrors" to the raising of children (while Tidewater didn't) is deeply documented in Philip Greven's *The Protestant Temperament: Patterns of Child-Rearing, Religious Experience, and the Self in Early America.* (NY: Knopf, 1977).

[21] Phebe's story begins at Edwards, *A Faithful Narrative* (1737), in *Works*, v4, ed., C. C. Goen, Yale University Press, 1972, p. 199.

This, Edwards reasoned, was not her imagination, but a genuine encounter with the divine. It was a conversion. Four years after her birth, little Phebe had been born again.[22]

> Then her elder sister, referring to her saying she could find God now, asked her, *where she could find God.* She answered, *In heaven. Why*, said she, *have you been in heaven? No*, said the child. By this it seems not to have been any imagination of any thing seen with bodily eyes, that she called God, when she said, *I can find God now.*[23]

She had suddenly lost entirely that fear of hell that had awakened her in the first place.

> Her mother asked her, whether she was afraid of going to hell, and if that had made her cry? She answered, *Yes, I was; but now I shan't.* Her mother asked her, whether she thought that God had given her salvation: she answered, *Yes*. Her mother asked her. *When?* She answered, *Today.*

And before the day was out she had begun her own course of evangelism to try to get others saved, starting with three of her older sisters, Nabby, Eunice and Amy.

> The same day the elder children, when they came home from school, seemed much affected with the extraordinary change that seemed to be made in Phebe. And her sister Abigail standing by, her mother took occasion to counsel her, now to improve her time, to prepare for another world. On which Phebe burst out in tears, and cried out, *Poor Nabby!* Her mother told her, she would not have to cry; she hoped that God would give Nabby salvation; but that did not quiet her, she continued earnestly crying for some time. When she had in a measure ceased, her sister Eunice being by her, she burst out again, and cried, *Poor Eunice!* and cried exceedingly; and when she had almost done, she went into another room, and there looked upon her sister Naomi: and burst out again, crying, *Poor Amy!* Her mother was greatly affected at such a behavior in a child, and knew not what to say to her. One of the neighbors coming in a little after, asked her what she had cried for. She seemed at first backward to tell the reason: her mother told her she might tell that person, for he had given her an apple: upon which she said, *she cried because she was afraid they would go to hell.*

Phebe's conversion was a lasting one (unlike what Edwards had experienced at age 9) with only a few later moments of doubt. In 1736:

> She still continues very constant in secret prayer, so far as can be observed, for she seems to have no desire that others should observe her when she retires, being a child of a reserved temper. [...] She sometimes appears to be in doubt about the condition of her soul; and when asked, whether she thinks that she is prepared for death, speaks something doubtfully about it. At other times she seems to have no doubt, but when asked, replies, *Yes*, without hesitation.[24]

And a note added to a later edition of *A Faithful Narrative* describes Phebe as remaining a "true convert" in 1789, 65 years later.

Edwards felt that the awakening of Northampton had begun in December, 1734, with the unexpected confession by the town's most incorrigible "company-keeper" (what the next century would call a "loose woman") that she had experienced

---

[22] Doubtless this is the worst place to quote the anti-evangelical Tee-shirt slogan: "It is easier to be born again than to grow up." (North Star catalogue, May, 1999).

[23] Susannah Kühnel had reported the same experiences in Herrenhut in 1727, but she was 11.

[24] Phebe's story ends at Edwards, *A Faithful Narrative* (1737) in *Works*, v4, ed., C. C. Goen, Yale U. Press, 1972, p. 205.

conversion. At ecstasy's peak in March and April of 1734–1735, Edwards wrote of seeing the conversion in Northampton "at least of four persons in a day; or near thirty in a week, take one with another, for five or six weeks together," for a total of 150–170, with 80 appearing at a single communion service. 32 children between age 9 and 14, one between ages 4 and 9 (Phebe Bartlet), 50 over 40, including two over 70, as many men as women, and "Negroes," too, were "born again." Edwards reckoned that about 300 were converted in this extraordinary half-year, until he could count 620 saved communicants in his 200-family congregation, "almost all our adult persons." Striving mightily to exhibit the humility that he was sure had been the precondition of his receiving grace and the putatively irresistible consequence of his having received it. Edwards did his best to assign responsibility for what happened in his Northampton parish in 1734 and 1735 to God rather than to his own ministry. His pre-awakening efforts to turn the town's young people away from "frolics" and "company-keeping" on Sunday nights are cast in the passive voice: "a sermon was now preached on the sabbath before the lecture, to show the evil tendency of the practice, and to persuade them to reform it." Also in passive voice is his uncompromising stand against Arminian breaches of the bottom-line Protestant doctrine "There were some things said publicly on that occasion, concerning *justification by faith alone*."

Edwards's attempts to suppress his pastoral ego was recommended by the ethics of both Christianity, which exalts humility, and science, which demands the routine admission of error. The newly Enlightened eighteenth-century Western intellectual world required the firsthand testimony of a trained and skeptical observer, and Edwards was the only one in Northampton who could provide that. As a reader of Locke and a would-be contributor to the *Philosophical Transactions* of the Royal Society in London, Edwards tried and often succeeded in making his account conform to the models provided by contemporary scientific literature. He did his best to provide evidence of what he thought God was wreaking in his parishioners' souls. He tried not to exaggerate what he nevertheless considered, as a lifelong student of the biblical book of *Apocalypse* or *Revelation*, to be a crucial event in the history of the world, a foretaste of the Second Coming and the Last Judgment.

Somewhat less scientifically, Edwards conflated into a single movement all the towns whose ministers had preached awakening to their congregations in 1734 and were reporting more than the usual number of conversions. From Preston, in the east of the small colony of Connecticut, to Woodbury in the west, and from Enfield and Northfield in the far north of Massachusetts Bay to Stratford, New Haven and Guilford along the south coast of Connecticut, there were only about two dozen of them, all about three generations old and rather small, even by the standards of eighteenth-century civilization. It was long before any post-industrial population explosion would lead to the coming of "the masses," and only two towns had more than 4000 inhabitants and three of them had fewer than 1000. When some two hundred or more residents of such a town claimed suddenly to have had that long-contemplated ecstatic conversion experience, it could easily look like a miraculous act of God to all the residents, including to the ones who were still unsaved, and certainly to the minister who had preached awakening. If, in addition, a careful examination of each convert's "soul" (the ancient Greek word had been *psyche*) revealed thoughts, feelings, and even visions that were overwhelming, or as we say today, "life-changing," and repeated the steps in the process that past ministers had identified, the conclusion would be almost unavoidable.

To Edwards it seemed that the curtain fell on the great awakening in Northampton with two suicide attempts in May. One attempt, by Town Clerk Joseph Hawley, II, husband of Edwards's aunt, was successful. Edwards's awakener rhetoric may have paled after that.[25] He did stop preaching for a while after the suicides when he took a trip south "for my health" in the summer of 1735 and met his fellow Awakeners, the Tennents.

The awakening was clearly not for everybody.[26] While the Connecticut Valley was undergoing conversion, New York City newsman John Peter Zenger was getting indicted for seditious libel against Governor William (Bill?) Cosby. It makes for an arresting contrast between front-page news in New England and the Middle Colonies: political faction and high-minded constitutional law in the city (where Edwards had been living when he privately recorded his conversion), but salvation and church government in New England. Nevertheless, in Raritan, New Jersey, across the bay from New York, a Dutch Reformed minister from the Netherlands, Theodorus Frelinghuysen (c1691–c1747), had been preaching awakening, conviction and conversion for a dozen years before the movement had hit Northampton. Frelinghuysen, who had been raised, like Zinzendorf, in the "heart religion" of German Pietism, had arrived in January, 1719–1720, 3 years before Edwards was approaching his encounter with the divine in New York. Jonathan Edwards, a strict Congregational, didn't hear of the man he referred to as "Freelinghousa" until his trip south in 1735; but in *A Faithful Narrative*, he annexed Frelinghuysen's work to his own, attributing both to God, without ever meeting Frelinghuysen or learning how to spell his name.

On the same trip, Edwards also met and made alliance with William Tennent and his son Gilbert. In western New Jersey and Pennsylvania, Scots-Irish immigrants who were Calvinist and Presbyterian, had already found their awakeners in the

---

[25] Edwards's account of Hawley, added to *A Faithful Narrative*, reads: "he grew much discouraged, and melancholy grew again upon him, till he was wholly overpowered by it, and was in a great measure past a capacity of receiving advice, or being reasoned with to any purpose. The devil took the advantage, and drove him into despairing thoughts. He was kept awake at nights, meditating terror, so that he had scarce any sleep at all for a long time together; and it was observed at last, that he was scarcely well capable of managing his ordinary business, and was judged delirious by the coroner's inquest". Edwards, *A Faithful Narrative* (1737), in *Works*, v4, ed., C. C. Goen, Yale U. Press, 1972, p. 206. Robert Lowell put this directly into verse of ironic Yankee sobriety in his poem "After the Surprising Conversions":

> In the latter part of May
> He cut his throat. And though the coroner
> Judged him delirious, soon a noisome stir
> Palsied our village. At Jehovah's nod
> Satan seemed more let loose amongst us: God
> Abandoned us to Satan, and he pressed
> Us hard, until we thought we could not rest
> Till we had done with life....
> (Robert Lowell, *Lord Weary's Castle*, 1944, 1946)

[26] The estimate that "about one-third" of Connecticut's churches and "one-fifth of those in Massachusetts" were "eventually" awakened in total is in Marsden, *Edwards*, Kindle ed., loc. 3894.

Tennent family. William Tennent, born in Scotland in 1673, and originally a priest in the Anglican Church of Ireland, had gone over to the Presbyterians and emigrated to Philadelphia in 1718 together with his four sons, all eventually ministers. William, the family patriarch, took up a pastorate in Warminster, Bucks County, Pennsylvania, in 1726. A year later, William Tennent set up the famous Log College there, where he educated his sons and others in Calvinist theology, Presbyterian church government and how to minister to a congregation. By 1734, he and all four of his sons, Gilbert, Charles, John and William Junior (the last three had graduated from the Log College), had been preaching awakening, conviction and conversion for the better part of a decade. Together, they covered the Middle Colonies' east side, from Charles's parish in Delaware to William senior's in southeastern Pennsylvania, north to the Jerseys to the "Old Scots" church of John and his successor William junior in Freehold, to Gilbert's presbytery in New Brunswick.

Before his conversion, William junior had become so "convicted" of sin that he lost his health, starving himself into a 3-day coma from which he recovered only just in time to prevent his own funeral from taking place. Amnesia followed and his convalescence was long, but he did feel assured of the conversion that resulted and he preached awakening, conviction and conversion for the rest of his life.

Gilbert, the oldest brother, became the family's itinerant. He traveled to many other congregations from his own in New Brunswick giving sermons and "lectures" on the question of grace. In 1741–1742, he was preaching awakening with George Whitefield well east of the Jerseys at the mouth of the Connecticut River in Lyme.[27] The year before he had preached and published a sermon, "The Dangers of an Unconverted Ministry," that tore into unsaved preachers as "Pharisee-shepherds" and "Pharisee-teachers," graceless hypocrites who would put their congregants in danger of eternal damnation by failing to preach awakening or to understand one when it happened.[28] Gilbert's travels from congregation to congregation, preaching awakening to sin and condemnation of unconverted ministers provoked the governing council of his church, the Presbytery of Philadelphia, to prohibit any preacher from preaching in another's parish without an invitation, and caused a Presbyterian schism that lasted 17 years and extended to an even longer-lasting division between "Old Light" and "New Light" Presbyterians about the very value of awakening and "enthusiasm."

By attaching the Tennents and Frelinghuysen to the last draft of his *Faithful Narrative* in 1736, Edwards tried to make all their awakenings part of a single major event in the salvation history of the world. The success of *A Faithful Narrative* made

[27] Gilbert Tennent and George Whitefield both preached at Lyme, Connecticut, in 1741–1742, resulting in a reported 150 conversions. Their preaching in nearby New London provoked a reported 80 conversions. (In 1731, the Rev. Jonathan Parsons' congregation in Lyme, catching its new minister by surprise, had plunged into an awakening; but Jonathan Edwards left Lyme out of his 1736 letter, *A Faithful Narrative*. He also left out New London, but New London, it appears, was yet to be awakened in 1735.)

[28] It was Benjamin Franklin, unsaved but always alert for bestsellers, who published it. Gilbert Tennent, A.M., *The Danger of an Unconverted Ministry, Considered in a SERMON on Mark VI. 34. Preached at Nottingham, in Pennsylvania, March 8. Anno 1739*, Philadelphia: Benjamin Franklin, 1740 (Rare Book and Special Collections Division, Library of Congress (73)).

that happen in the minds of so many mid-eighteenth-century Christians that historians ever since have treated all the post-Northampton awakenings as a single event—the Great Awakening—whether or not they assigned the responsibility for it to God.[29] Edwards carefully noted that awakenings, with "saving conversions," "outpourings of grace," and "ingathering of souls," had happened before, and that they had only been locally known, like the five ingatherings that Edwards counted in his grandfather Stoddard's congregation (now his own), and the "four or five" in his father Timothy's. In 1734–1735, by contrast, news went from town to town in "a swift and extraordinary propagation," so that "continual news kept alive the talk of religion, and did greatly quicken and rejoice the hearts of God's people, and much awakened those who looked on themselves as still left behind."[30]

Whether it is word of mouth, improved social integration of New England, the new emotional packaging of Calvinist grace, or even the Holy Spirit, I think we must agree that something was moving faster than the mails in 1734–1735. Adding to Edwards's two dozen Connecticut Valley towns that year was at least one awakening that Edwards failed to report, overseen by the Reverend Jonathan Parsons, one of the Yale undergraduates whom Edwards had tutored, at Lyme. And we might add that the first conversion experience among the later founders of Methodism, George Whitefield's, occurred in Whitefield's Oxford room that spring; or that even a Church of England minister, the Reverend Daniel Rowland, and his layman friend Howell Harris, had conversion experiences and began outdoor itinerant preaching before Whitefield or Wesley did in 1735.[31]

John Wesley read *A Faithful Narrative* in October, 1738, 6 months after his own conversion experience at the Moravian chapel in London's Aldersgate Street in May. The awakening-conviction-conversion sequence was new to him, but America was not. He had returned from his first mission trip to America in February, 1738. In fact he had begun that trip by landing in Georgia with his brother Charles and with David Nitschmann's Moravians in February, 1736, when Edwards was writing and editing the various versions of *A Faithful Narrative*. Whitefield, for his part, arrived in America for the first time in May, beginning a career of itinerant outdoor field-preaching that provided the model for what would come to be called "revival." With the beginning of Whitefield's American missions, there came a wave of

---

[29] The "Great Awakening" is a nineteenth-century coinage, and it remains an outsize target for historiographical revisionism. Jonathan Butler argued that although it existed, it was neither national nor big but rather "a short-lived Calvinist revival in New England in the 1740s" which removes New England Calvinism from center stage where Edwards had put it (Butler, "Enthusiasm Described and Decried: The Great Awakening as Interpretive Fiction." in *Journal of American History*, 69(1982), 305–25; and *Awash in a Sea of Faith*). (Cambridge: Harvard University Press, 1992). Frank Lambert's *Inventing the "Great Awakening"* (Princeton, NJ: Princeton University Press, 1999) argued that the Awakening was an idea "constructed" by "colonial revivalists themselves ... —not the term, but the idea of a coherent, intercolonial revival." (Lambert, p. 6). That is, it was an interpretive link, constructed by preachers who knew more of each other than their parishioners did. Historians may warily recognize that constructing this sort of link is a tool habitually deployed by historians.

[30] Edwards, *A Faithful Narrative*, in *Works*, v4, ed., C. C. Goen, Yale U. Press, 1972, p. 153–154.

[31] Isabel Rivers, "Review Essay: Writing the History of Early Evangelicalism," *History of European Ideas* 35:1(March, 2009), p. 105–111, p. 106.

conversions in Protestant congregations in British America, followed by the Methodist outbreak at home in England and Scotland, and so much awakening that opposition began to organize.

Edwards had helped inspire that opposition before the Northampton awakening. Two years after succeeding Solomon Stoddard, in 1731, he had preached at the annual assembly of Congregational ministers in Boston that was held around the Harvard College commencement. The sermon, "God Glorified in Man's Dependence," was a sustained attack on the Arminian view that human beings might have some effect of their own on God's sovereign power to give or to withhold grace. In this, the first work of his to be published, Edwards said that even the redeemed, (the saved or converted) were helpless. Expounding on a verse from Saint Paul's first Epistle to the Corinthians, he began by pointing to the irony that Corinth had been one of the home cities of ancient Greek philosophy, but that even ancient Greek wisdom was limited and human.

Ten years later, with Whitefield on the march and awakeners inspiring ecstasies all over New England, Edwards, fresh from his over-the-top awakening sermon at Enfield, "Sinners in the Hands of an Angry God," gave the Commencement sermon at his alma mater Yale. His text was the warning from the Gospel of John: "Beloved, believe not every spirit, but try the spirits whether they are of God; because many false prophets are gone out into the world." Both the text and his title, "The Distinguishing Marks of a Work of the Spirit of God," created an expectation that he would offer his hearers ways of weeding out the devilish counterfeits from the true and godly awakening and conversion experiences.

Among the "Distinguishing Marks," however, were almost all the behaviors that Yale's governing Old Lights were questioning as counterfeits. Even as Edwards granted (against the rebellious New Lights) that not all the affections, or passions, were religious, he argued that revivals and their itinerant preachers were good things. Edwards objected that you could not say it was the Devil's work simply because it was "carried on in a way very unusual and extraordinary" or because of "any Effects on the bodies of Men; such as Tears, Trembling, Groans, loud Outcries, Agonies of Body, or the Failing of bodily Strength" or because the people affected were affected with "great Imprudences and Irregularities in their Conduct" like, for example, Saint Paul's highly irregular Corinthians, or because the work of God had some of the Devil's work mixed in, or because some with extraordinary gifts of God "fall away into gross Errors or scandalous Practices." Most importantly:

> It is no Argument that a Work is not from the Spirit of GOD, *That is it promoted by Ministers inſiſting very much on the Terrors of God's holy Law, and that with a great deal of* Pathos *and Earneſtneſs.* If there be really a Hell of dreadful and never-ending Torments, which Multitu[d]es are in great Danger of, and which the bigger Part of Men in Christian Countries do actually from Generation to Generation fall into, for Want of a Senſe of the Terribleneſs of it, and their Danger, and ſo for Want of taking due Care to avoid it; then why is it not proper for thoſe that have the Care of Souls to take great Pains to make Men ſenſible of it? why ſhould not they be told as much of the Truth as can be?[32]

[32] John Wesley, *The Distinguishing Marks of a Work of the Spirit of God. Extracted from Mr. Edwards. Minister of Northampton, in New-England* [edited] *By John Wesley*. (1742) 2nd ed. London: Henry Cock, 1755, p. 18.

Edwards's sermon was published in Boston almost immediately and in Philadelphia, London, Edinburgh and Glasgow by the end of 1742. John Wesley would publish his own editions of it in 1742.[33] But in the same month in 1741, when Edwards spoke at Yale, Charles Chauncy gave the commencement sermon at Harvard. "Enthusiasm Described and Cautioned Against," also on a text from *Corinthians*, was an indictment of "enthusiasm," familiar since the early Enlightenment of Shaftesbury and Swift, and directed at the new indulgence of extreme "religious affections," attitudes and behaviors. Though he mentioned no particular details, it was clear that Chauncy's target was Jonathan Edwards and his ilk, and with them the whole Awakening.[34]

> I. I am in the first place, to give you some account of **Enthusias**m.... The word, from it's Etymology, carries in it a good meaning, as signifying inspiration from GOD: in which sense, the prophets under the old testament, and the apostles under the new, might properly be called **Enthusias**ts. [...]
>
> But the word is more commonly used in a bad sense, as intending an imaginary, not a real inspiration: according to which sense, the **Enthusias**t is one, who has a conceit of himself as a person favoured with the extraordinary presence of the Deity. He mistakes the workings of his own passions for divine communications, and fancies himself immediately inspired by the SPIRIT of GOD, when all the while, he is under no other influence than that of an over-heated imagination.
>
> The cause of this **enthusias**m is a bad temperament of the blood and spirits; 'tis properly a disease, a sort of madness.... And various are the ways in which their **enthusias**m discovers itself.
>
> [...]
>
> They are likewise positive and dogmatical, vainly fond of their own imaginations, and invincibly set upon propagating them: And in the doing of this,...they sometimes exert themselves with a sort of extatic violence: And 'tis this that gives them the advantage, among the less knowing and judicious, of those who are modest, suspicious of themselves, and not too assuming in matters of conscience and salvation. The extraordinary fervour of their mind, accompanied with uncommon bodily motions, and an excessive confidence and assurance, gains them great reputation among the populace; who speak of them as men of GOD in distinction from all others, and too commonly hearken to, and revere their dictates as tho' they really were, as they pretend, immediately communicated to them from the DIVINE SPIRIT.
>
> This is the nature of *Enthusiasm*, and this is operation, in a less or greater degree, in all who are under the influence of it. 'Tis a kind of religious Phrenzy, and evidently discovers it self to be so, whenever it rises to any great height....[35]

---

[33] Wesley, *The Distinguishing Marks of a Work of the Spirit of God. Extracted from Mr. Edwards. Minister of Northampton, in New-England* [edited] *By John Wesley*, London: S. Mason, 1742; Glasgow: R. Smith, 1742.

[34] Ned C. Landsman, "Edwards versus Chauncy: The Great Debate," in *From Colonials to Provincials: American Thought and Culture, 1680-1760*. (Ithaca, NY: Cornell University Press, 1997), pp. 105ff.

[35] "Enthusiasm Described and Caution'd Against, by Charles Chauncy," from *Puritan Rhetoric: The Issue of Emotion in Religion*, p. 103 ff, posted 6 September, 2011 @ The Sound of Shaking Paper (blog), http://papershake.blogspot.com/2011/09/enthusiasm-described-and-cautiond.html.

Edwards replied in 1742 with *Some Thoughts Concerning the Present Revival of Religion in New-England*, in which he tried to show that not only was reason not enough to make a believer, it was not fit to bridle the affections, as conventional wisdom taught, because the affections were the soul's true means of belief. He attacked what he called "pious zealots" for trying to suppress a work of God that they could not understand. The legislatures of Massachusetts Bay and Connecticut chimed in in May, 1742, by banning uninvited itinerants, and Chauncy came back in September, 1743 with a pamphlet *The Late Religious Commotions in New-England considered. An Answer To the Reverend Mr. Jonathan Edwards' Sermon*, and the encyclopedic *Seasonable Thoughts on the State of Religion in New England*. When Edwards began his great text on the psychology of conversion, *A Treatise Concerning Religious Affections*, with a series of sermons in 1743, it was an answer to the critique of enthusiasm, inspiration and vision made by the Enlightenment champion, Chauncy.[36]

All this came long before the invention of college sports but at this point it may not be totally incongruous to invoke the Yale-Harvard Game. The paper war between Harvard's Chauncy and his Old Lights and Yale's Edwards and his New Lights began with those two commencement sermons and lasted for years. The struggle over which feelings were God-inspired and which were delusions, or which behaviors were godly and which devilish, resulted in the secession and splitting of congregations, the founding of new denominations, and ecstasies of every kind. Laymen answered the call to preach. So did children—and laywomen! Congregants screamed, twirled, barked, fell into fits, and fainted dead away. In his zeal to awaken New England to sin, Congregational minister James Davenport, first in his class at Yale back in 1732, who left his church in 1741 to become an itinerant like Whitefield, was found by the Connecticut legislature in 1742 to be "under the influences of enthusiastical impressions and impulses, and thereby disturb'd in the rational faculties of his mind, and therefore to be pittied and compassionated, and not to be treated as otherwise he might be."[37] In 1743, Davenport tried to stage a bonfire of the vanities *à la* Savonarola in New London, Connecticut, but was persuaded at the last minute that the sacrifice of books and fancy clothing was not necessary for salvation. Leaving the pyre unlighted, he retrieved both the books and his own overfancy

[36] Edwards, *Some Thoughts Concerning the Present Revival of Religion in New-England*, Boston: Kneeland and Green, 1742 (republished in Edinburgh in 1743. This is an early use of the word "revival" to describe an awakening.) Charles Chauncy, *The Late Religious Commotions in New-England considered. An Answer To the Reverend Mr. Jonathan Edwards' Sermon, Entitled The Distinguishing Marks of a Work of the Spirit of God, applied to that uncommon Operation that has appeared in the Minds of many of the People of the Lord*, Boston, 1743, and Chauncy, *Seasonable Thoughts on the State of Religion in New England*, Boston, 1743.

[37] in Richard L. Bushman, ed., *The Great Awakening: Documents on the Revival of Religion, 1740-1745* (1970), (Chapel Hill, NC: U. of North Carolina Press, 1989), p. 46.

pants.[38] A year later he published a formal apology for his extremism in the pursuit of salvation, and blamed his behavior on possession by "demonic spirits," but that was after Edwards had led a delegation of New Light ministers to New London to counsel him.[39] Today, we might be reminded of the "Burning Man" festival.

Pastors resigned, were dismissed, imprisoned, or exiled from their colonies, others became itinerants, and still others were appointed and reassigned. James Davenport himself was banished from Connecticut to Southhold, Long Island, in 1742,[40] and Edwards himself was dismissed by his own congregation in 1750. Edwards, like Whitefield, Gilbert Tennent, and the other leading preachers of awakening, stuck to his convictions, and never became what we will call a fundamentalist, always holding the conversion of the heart above the letter of the law, even in the 1742–1743 moral code he made his congregants agree to, known as the Northampton Covenant.[41] The spirit of the law was especially at the forefront in Edwards's 1742–1743 sermon series that later became *A Treatise Concerning the Religious Affections*. In that classic book, his only concession to outward conformity was to argue that one of the signs of having true religious affections would be the tendency to live a Christian life of love, joy, and hope.[42]

---

[38] A thoroughly unawakened traveler, Maryland lawyer, Dr. Alexander Hamilton, wrote later about hearing the story, which must have been pretty well embellished by then: "Deacon Green's son came to see me. He entertained me with the history of the behaviour of one Davenport, a fanatick preacher there who told his flock in one of his enthusiastic rhapsodies that in order to be saved they ought to burn all their idols. They began this conflagration with a pile of books in the public street, among which were [Church of England Archbishop] Tillotson's *Sermons*, [CofE Bishop] Beveridge's *Thoughts*, Drillincourt [Charles Drelincourt] on Death, [Thomas] Sherlock [who had tried to historicize the Resurrection] and many other excellent authors, and sung psalms and hymns over the pile while it was a burning. They did not stop here, but the women made up a lofty pile of hoop petticoats, silk gown, short cloaks, cambrick caps, red heeld shoes, fans, necklaces, gloves and other such apparrell, and what was merry enough, Davenport's own idol with which he topped the pile, was a pair of old, wore out, plush breaches. But this bone fire was happily prevented by one more moderate than the rest, who found means to perswade them that making such a sacrifice was not necessary for their salvation, and so everyone carried of[f] their idols, again, which was lucky for Davenport who, had fire been put to the pile, would have been obliged to strutt about barearsed, for the devil another pair of breeches had he but these same old plush ones which were going to be offered up as an expiatory sacrifise". (Dr. A. Hamilton, "Journal," Gentleman's Progress, (n.p., n.d.), 161–163, in Page Smith, ed., *Religious Origins of the American Revolution*, Missoula, Montana, Scholars Press for American Academy of Religion, 1976, p. 136).

[39] James Davenport, *Confession and Retractations*, 1744. See Thomas S. Kidd, *The Great Awakening: A Brief History with Documents* (New York: Bedford/St. Martin's, 2008).

[40] According to a letter to a Boston newspaper from an observer in Hartford, the Connecticut legislature concluded "that the said Davenport is under the influences of enthusiastical impressions and impulses, and thereby disturb'd in the rational faculties of his mind, and therefore to be pittied and compassionated, and not to be treated as otherwise he might be." ("Anti-Enthusiasticus" letter from Hartford, Connecticut, in *Boston Weekly Newsletter*, 1 July, 1742, in Bushman, ed. *The Great Awakening: Documents*, p. 46).

[41] Edwards, "The Northampton Covenant," March 16, 1742–43, in Bushman, ed. *The Great Awakening: Documents*. #39.

[42] Edwards, *A Treatise Concerning the Religious Affections* (1746) Online Edition by: International Outreach, Inc. PO Box 1286, Ames, Iowa 50014 @ http://www.jonathan-edwards.org/ReligiousAffections.pdf.

Older, but perhaps not wiser, Edwards in 1744 bravely disciplined and tried to awaken a new generation of young men of Northampton. They had begun reading *Aristotle's Master Piece, Or, The Secrets of Nature Displayed*, the most available English sex manual of the eighteenth century, and they were teasing (harassing?) the young women with it. Unfortunately for Edwards this generation of young people seemed not to have come to Awakening the way their counterparts had in 1734–1735, and their elders began criticizing Edwards for indiscretion and intolerance, opening the way for them to form a determined opposition in 1748 when he reversed his grandfather's Halfway Covenant policy and tried to exclude from communion the unsaved who could make no "profession of the things wherein godliness consists."[43] With the concurrence of a council of ministers, the Northampton congregation dismissed Edwards in June, 1750, and he went off to Stockbridge in the fall to minister to the Christian Housatonic Indians, learning how the Moravians had done it.

Edwards, as he aged, was tempted by the letter but stayed with the spirit and piety. The rest of the Congregational and Presbyterian clergy of New England and the Jerseys, however, split down the middle and the letter of the law triumphed with many, as it has since. For many, both awakeners and awakened, it could be hard to maintain assurance of grace. As for Charles Chauncy, he ended by going wholly over to the Enlightenment, eventually giving up the Calvinist doctrine of election entirely and all that went with it, concluding, at first secretly, that everyone was saved. After thus becoming the first American Universalist, Chauncy, still the pastor of Boston's foundational First Church, emerged in the 1780s as one of the founders of the Unitarian denomination, a deistical Christianity without a divine Christ that traced its origins to Poland but would later be defined (possibly by Edgar Allan Poe of Baltimore and New York) as "The Fatherhood of God, the Brotherhood of Man, and the Neighborhood of Boston." The stage had been set in 1735–1741 for a permanent conflict as important as the Awakening itself, a long argument about whether and how humans could experience the divine.

The argument ran parallel with the earlier philosophical debate between the Ancients and Moderns, and the aesthetic one that followed between the Classic (Enlightenment) and Romantic (Counter-Enlightenment) ideals of art. Was religion rational or emotional? Was it natural or unnatural? Unchanging or progressive? Delusional or demonstrable? Was it neither, or could it be both? What Jonathan Edwards did for the argument was to give it a religious form with the potential to last three centuries.

---

[43] Edwards, "Farewell Sermon," July, 1, 1750, preached in Northampton, MA, after his dismissal in June by a council of ministers from 9 churches. It would be published in 1751. (@ https://chapellibrary.org:8443/pdf/books/fsoj.pdf). In the previous year, Edwards had published *An Account of the Life of the Reverend Mr. David Brainerd, with Reflections and Observations thereon* (Boston, 1749) in which he had renewed his faith in his own saving conversion by recounting the life of a younger convert, whose journals of self-examination he had read after Brainerd died of tuberculosis in the Edwards home.

Bibliography

Backus, Isaac. 1979. In *The Diary of Isaac Backus*, ed. William G. McLoughlin. Providence.

Baker, Frank. January 1965. Early American Methodism; A Key Document. *Methodist History* 3: 3–15.

———. October 1970. Whitefield's Break with the Wesleys. *Church Quarterly Review* 3: 103–13.

———, ed. 1976. *From Wesley to Asbury: Studies in Early American Methodism*. Durham, NC: Duke University Press.

———. January 1984. The Origins, Character, and Influence of John Wesley's Thoughts Upon Slavery. *Methodist History* 22 (2): 75–86.

Bannon, Brad. January 2016. President Edwards and the Sage of Highgate: Determinism, Depravity, and the Supernatural Will. *Journal of the History of Ideas* 77 (1): 27–48.

Benedict, Philip. 2002. *Christ's Churches Purely Reformed: A Social History of Calvinism*. New Haven, CT: Yale University Press.

Benes, Peter, and Philip D. Zimmerman. 1979. *New England Meeting House and Church: 1630-1850*. Boston.

Bergamasco, Lucia. May 12–13, 2000. Cotton Mather and English Protestant Hagiography: A Reading of *Magnalia Christi Americana*. Conference paper, *Colonial Saints: Hagiography in the Americas, 1500-1800*. University of Toronto.

Berk, Stephen E. 1974. *Calvinism versus Democracy: Timothy Dwight and the Origins of American Evangelical Orthodoxy*. Hamden, CT: Archon Books.

Bilhartz, Terry D. 1986. *Urban Religion and the Second Great Awakening: Church and Society in Early National Baltimore*. Rutherford, NJ: Fairleigh Dickinson University Press; Toronto: Associated University Presses.

Blaikie, Alexander. 1881. *A History of Presbyterianism in New England*. Boston.

Boles, John B. 1972. *The Great Revival, 1787-1805: The Origins of the Southern Evangelical Mind*. Lexington, KY: University Press of Kentucky; pb. 1996. *The Great Revival: Beginnings of the Bible Belt*. Lexington, KY: University Press of Kentucky.

———. 1983. *Black Southerners, 1619-1869*. Lexington, KY: University Press of Kentucky.

———., ed. 1988. *Master and Slaves in the House of the Lord: Race and Religion in the American South, 1740-1870*. Lexington, KY: University Press of Kentucky.

———. 1995. *Religion in Antebellum Kentucky*. Lexington, KY: University Press of Kentucky.

Bolton, S. Charles. 1982. *Southern Anglicanism: The Church of England in Colonial South Carolina*. Westport, CT: Greenwood Press.

Bonomi, Patricia U. 1986. *Under the Cope of Heaven: Religion, Society, and Politics in Colonial America*. New York: Oxford University Press.

———. 1991. 'A Just Opposition': The Great Awakening as a Radical Model. In *The Origins of Anglo-American Radicalism*, ed. Margaret C. Jacob and James R. Jacob, vol. 1984, 226–239. Atlantic Highlands, NJ: Humanities Press.

———. 1996. 'Hippocrates' Twins': Religion and Politics in the American Revolution. *History Teacher* 29: 137–144.

Boyd, William K., ed. 1927. *Some Eighteenth Century Tracts concerning North Carolina*. Raleigh, NC.

Bozeman, Theodore Dwight. 1977. *Protestants in an Age of Science: The Baconian Ideal and Ante-bellum American Religious Thought*. Chapel Hill, NC: University of North Carolina Press, ("beatification of Bacon" in Second Great Awakening).

Brantley, Richard E. 1984. *Locke, Wesley and the Method of English Romanticism*. Gainesville, FL: University Press of Florida.

———. 1990. The Common Ground of Wesley and Edwards. *Harvard Theological Review* 83: 271–303.

Bratt, James D. Spring 2004. Religious Anti-Revivalism in Antebellum America. *Journal of the Early Republic* 24 (1): 65–106.

———., ed. 2006. *Antirevivalism in Antebellum America: A Collection of Religious Voices*. New Brunswick, NJ: Rutgers University Press.

Breidenthal, Rev. Thomas. March 21, 2007. Princeton's Revivalist Roots: Religion on the campus from the Great Awakening to the 'interfaith awakening'. *Princeton Alumni Weekly* 24–27.

Bressler, Anne Lee. 2001. *The Universalist Movement in America, 1770-1880*. New York: Oxford University Press.

Bridenbaugh, Carl. 1962. *Mitre and Sceptre: Transatlantic Faiths, Ideas, Personalities, and Politics*, 1689-1775. New York: .

———. 1981. 'The Famous Infamous Vagrant' Tom Bell. In *Early Americans*. New York.

Brown, Robert E. 2002. *Jonathan Edwards and the Bible*. Bloomington: Indiana University Press.

Brown-Lawson, Albert. 1994. *John Wesley and the Anglican Evangelicals of the Eighteenth Century: A Study in Cooperation and Separation with Special Reference to the Calvinistic Controversies*. Edinburgh: Pentland.

Buchanan, Richard W., Jr. 1977. The Justice of America's Cause: Revolutionary Rhetoric in the Sermons of Samuel Cooper. *New England Quarterly* 50: 101–124.

Bucke, Emory, ed. 1964. *The History of American Methodism. 3v*. New York/Nashville: Abingdon.

Bumstead, J.M. 1967. Revivalism and Separatism in New England: The First Society of Norwich, Connecticut, as a Case Study. *William and Mary Quarterly* 24: 600ff.

Bumstead, J.M., and John E. Van de Wetering. 1976. *What Must I Do To Be Saved? The Great Awakening in Colonial America*. Hinsdale, IL: Dryden Press.

Bushman, Richard L. 1967. *From Puritan to Yankee: Character and the Social Order in Connecticut, 1690-1763*. Cambridge, MA: Harvard University Press; New York: Norton pb, 1970.

———. 1970. *From Puritan to Yankee: Character. ed. The Great Awakening: Documents on the Revival of Religion, 1740-1745*. New York: Atheneum; Chapel Hill: University of North Carolina Press, 1989.

Bushman, Richard L[yman]. 1988. *Joseph Smith and the Beginnings of Mormonism*. Urbana-Champaign: University of Illinois Press.

Bushman, Richard L. 2007. *Joseph Smith: Rough Stone Rolling*. New York: Vintage.

Butler, Jon[athan]. 1982. Enthusiasm Described and Decried: The Great Awakening as Interpretive Fiction. *Journal of American History* 69: 305–325. ("a short-lived Calvinist revival in New England in the 1740s").

———. 1990. *Awash in a Sea of Faith: Christianizing the American People*. Cambridge, MA: Harvard University Press.

———. *The 'New Evangelical Thesis' in American Historiography: A Description and Critique*, AHA 12/30/92. Washington, DC.

Cady, Edwin H. 1966. *John Woolman The Mind of the Quaker Saint*. New York: Washington Square Press.

Caldwell, Patricia. 1983. *The Puritan Conversion Narrative: The Beginnings of American Expression*. New York.

Calhoon, Robert M. 1988. *Evangelicals and Conservatives in the Early South, 1740-1861*. Columbia: University of South Carolina Press. Rvw by Matthews, Donald G. August 1990. *Journal of Southern History* 56 (3): 515–516.

Capp, Kristin, Sieglinde Geisel, and Rod Slemmons. 1998. *Hutterite: A World of Grace*. Edition Stemmle.

Caricchio, Mario. 2011. News from the New Jerusalem: Giles Calvert and the Radical Experience. In *Varieties of Seventeenth- and Early Eighteenth-Century English Radicalism in Context*, ed. A. Hessayon and D. Finnegan. New York: Ashgate.

Carroll, Peter, ed. 1970. *Religion and the Coming of the American Revolution*. Waltham, MA.

Carroll, Bret E., ed. 2001. *The Routledge Historical Atlas of American Religion*. New York: Routledge.

Carwardine, Richard J. 1978. *Transatlantic Revivalism: Popular Evangelicalism in Britain and America, 1790-1865*. Westport, CT: Greenwood Press.

———. 1993. *Evangelicals and Politics in Antebellum America*. New Haven, CT: Yale University Press.
Caudle, James Joseph. 1996. *Measures of Allegiance: Sermon Culture & the Creation of a Public Discourse of Obedience & Resistance in Georgian Britain, 1714-1760*. diss't. Yale University.
Chai, Leon. 1989. *The Romantic Foundations of the American Renaissance*. Ithaca, NY: Cornell University Press.
———. 1998. *Jonathan Edwards and the Limits of Enlightenment Philosophy*. New York: Oxford University Press.
Chauncy, Charles. 1743a. *The Late Religious Commotions in New-England considered. An Answer To the Reverend Mr. Jonathan Edwards' Sermon, Entitled The Distinguishing Marks of a Work of the Spirit of God, applied to that uncommon Operation that has appeared in the Minds of many of the People of the Lord*. Boston.
———. 1743b. *Seasonable Thoughts on the State of Religion in New England*. Boston.
———. 1972. Enthusiasm Described and Caution'd Against, by Charles Chauncy. In *Puritan Rhetoric: The Issue of Emotion in Religion*, ed. Eugene E. White. Carbondale, IL: Southern Illinois University Press, pb 2009, p. 103–118 @ http://papershake.blogspot.com/2011/09/enthusiasm-described-and-cautiond.html.
Cherry, Conrad, ed. 1971. *God's New Israel: Religious Interpretations of American Destiny*. Englewood Cliffs, NJ: Prentice-Hall. (millennialists).
———. 1990. *The Theology of Jonathan Edwards: A Reappraisal*. Bloomington: Indiana University Press.
Chute, Anthony L. 2005. *A Piety above the Common Standard: Jesse Mercer and Evangelistic Calvinism*. Macon, GA: Mercer University Press.
Clapper, Gregory S. Fall 1984. "True Religion" and the Affections: A Study of John Wesley's Abridgement of Jonathan Edward's Treatises on Religious Affections. *Wesleyan Theological Journal* 19 (2): 77–89.
Clark, J.C.D. 1993. *The Language of Liberty, 1660-1832: Political Discourse and Social Dynamics in the Anglo-American World*. Cambridge: Cambridge University Press.
———. 1994. *English Society 1688-1832: Ideology, Social Structure and Political Practice During the Ancien Régime*, 235–247. Cambridge: Cambridge University Press. (the "confessional state").
———. 2000. *English Society, 1660-1832: Religion, Ideology, and Politics During the Ancien Regime*. Cambridge: Cambridge University Press. Reviewed for H-Albion <H-Albion@h-net.msu.edu> (December, 2000) by Marilyn Morris.
Clarke, Erskine. 1996. *Our Southern Zion: A History of Calvinism in the South Carolina Low Country, 1690-1990*. Tuscaloosa, AL: University of Alabama Press.
Cleveland, Catharine C. 1916. *The Great Revival In The West, 1797-1805*. diss't, University of Chicago Libraries; Chicago: University of Chicago Press.
Clifford, Alan C. 26 April 1990. *Atonement and Justification: English Evangelical Theology 1640-1790: An Evaluation*. New York: Oxford University Press.
Coalter, Milton J., Jr. 1986. *Gilbert Tennent, Son of Thunder: A Case Study of Continental Pietism's Impact on the First Great Awakening in the Middle Colonies*. New York: Greenwood Press.
Cogliano, Francis. 1996. *No King, No Popery: Anti-Catholicism in Revolutionary New England*. New York: Praeger.
Cohen, Daniel. 1975. *The Spirit of the Lord: Revivalism in America*. New York: Four Winds Press.
Cohen, Charles Lloyd. 1986. *God's Caress: The Psychology of Puritan Religious Experience*. New York: Oxford University Press.
Cohen, I. Bernard, et al., eds. 1990. *Puritanism and the Rise of Modern Science: The Merton Thesis*. New Brunswick: Rutgers University Press.
Cole, Charles C., Jr. 1994. *Lion of the Forest: James B. Finley, Frontier Reformer*. Lexington: University Press of Kentucky.

Coleridge, Samuel Taylor. n.d. *Aids to Reflection* [London, 1825]: *With a Preliminary Essay* [by James Marsh]. (1st American ed. Burlington: Chauncy Goodrich, 1829). Fourth edition, 1839. Loschberg: Jazzybee Verlag, Printed North Charleston, SC: CreateSpace.

Conforti, Joseph A. 1995. *Jonathan Edwards, Religious Tradition, and American Culture*. Chapel Hill: University of North Carolina Press. (the Awakening was not big or national but "**a reification** that served the cultural and polemical needs of the leaders of the *Second* Great Awakening," i.e. 1830s revivalists).

———. 2008. *Samuel Hopkins and the New Divinity Movement: Calvinism and Reform in New England Between the Great Awakenings*. Repr. Eugene, OR: Wipf & Stock (Jonathan Edwards Classic Studies).

Conkin, Paul K. 1989. *Cane Ridge: America's Pentecost, (Curti Lectures)*, 1990. Madison: University of Wisconsin Press.

———. 1995. *The Uneasy Center: Reformed Christianity in Antebellum America*. Chapel Hill: University of North Carolina Press.

Cooke, Edward M., Jr. 1976. *The Fathers of the Towns: Leadership and Community Structure in Eighteenth-Century New England*. Baltimore.

Cooper, Frederick. October 1996. "Race, Ideology, and the Perils of Comparative History" review of Frederickson, *Black Liberation*, and Campbell, *Songs of Zion*, 1995. *American Historical Review* 101 (4): 1122–1138.

Cooper, James F., Jr. 1999. *Tenacious of Their Liberties: The Congregationalists in Colonial Massachusetts*. New York: Oxford University Press.

Corrigan, John. 1987. *The Hidden Balance: Religion and the Social Theories of Charles Chauncy and Jonathan Mayhew*. New York: Cambridge University Press.

Cott, Nancy F. 1977. *The Bonds of Womanhood: "Woman's Sphere" in New England, 1780-1835*. New Haven, CT: Yale University Press.

Crawford, Michael J. 1991. *Seasons of Grace: Colonial New England's Revival Tradition in Its British Context*. New York: Oxford University Press.

Creel, Margaret Washington. 1988. *"A Peculiar People": Slave Religion and Community-Culture among the Gullahs*. New York: New York University Press.

Cross, Arthur Lyon. 1964. *The Anglican Episcopate and the American Colonies (1902)*. Hamden, CT: Archon.

Curry, Thomas J. 1986. *The First Freedom: Church and State in America to the Passage of the First Amendment*. New York: Oxford University Press.

Daniel, Stephen H. 1994. *The Philosophy of Jonathan Edwards: A Study in Divine Semiotics*. Bloomington: Indiana University Press.

Davenport, James. (1716–1757). *The Reverend Mr. James Davenport's confession & retractations*. Boston: Printed and sold by S. Kneeland and T. Green, in Queenstreet, 1744; Text Creation Partnership @ http://name.umdl.umich.edu/n04347.0001.001.

Davidson, James West. 1977. *The Logic of Millennial Thought: Eighteenth-Century New England*. New Haven, CT: Yale University Press.

Davis, Richard Beale, ed. 1967. *The Colonial Virginia Satirist: Mid-Eighteenth-Century Commentaries on Politics, Religion, and Society*. Philadelphia.

De Benneville, K. Ludwig. 1902. Memorabilia of the Tennents. *Journal of Presbyterian History* 1: 344–354.

De Prospo, R.C. c1985. *Theism in the Discourse of Jonathan Edwards*. Newark, DE: University of Delaware Press; London/Cranbury, NJ: Associated University Presses.

De Witt, John. 1912. Jonathan Edwards: A Study. In *Biblical and Theological Studies by Members of the Faculty of Princeton Theological Seminary*, 130–136.

Deconinck-Brossard, Françoise. 2002. "Sermons protestants dans l'Europe des Lumières", *le Spectateur européen. The European Spectator* 4: 13–24.

Delbanco, Andrew. 1989. *The Puritan Ordeal*. Cambridge, MA: Harvard University Press.

———. 1995. *The Death of Satan: How Americans Have Lost the Sense of Evil*. New York: Farrar Straus & Giroux.

———, ed. 2001. *Writing New England: An Anthology from the Puritans to the Present.* Cambridge, MA: Harvard University Press.

Demos, John. 1970. *A Little Commonwealth: Family Life in the Plymouth Colony*. New York.

———, ed. n.d. *Remarkable Providences.*

Dennis, John. 1704. *The Grounds of Criticism in Poetry*. London: Geo. Strahan and Bernard Lintott.

Dorgan, Howard. 1988. *Giving Glory to God in Appalachia: Worship Practices of Six Baptist Subdenominations*. Knoxville: University of Tennessee Press.

Dow, Lorenzo. 1860. *History of the Cosmopolite; or, The Writings of Rev. Lorenzo Dow, containing His Experiences and Travels, in Europe and America, up to near His Fiftieth Year*. (Revised ed. Cincinnati).

Downey, James. 1969. *The Eighteenth Century Pulpit: a study of the sermons of Butler, Berkeley, Secker, Sterne, Whitefield and Wesley*. Oxford: Clarendon Press.

Dreyer, Frederick. Fall 1983. Faith and Experience in the Thought of John Wesley. *The American Historical Review* 88: 12–30.

———. 1987. Evangelical Thought: John Wesley and Jonathan Edwards. *Albion* 19: 177–192.

Edmunds, R. David. 1983. *The Shawnee Prophet*. Lincoln, NE: University of Nebraska Press.

Edmunds, Julie. May 1987. *Apocalyptic Thinking in Eighteenth-Century America*. Thesis, Yale University History Dept.

Edwards, Jonathan. 1742. *The Great Awakening*. v4 of *The Works of Jonathan Edwards*, ed. C.C. Goen. New Haven. *Some Thoughts Concerning the Present Revival of Religion in New-England*. Boston: Kneeland and Green (republished, Edinburgh, 1743). @ http://revival-library.org/index.php/catalogues-menu/1725/some-thoughts-concerning-the-present-revival-of-religion-in-new-england.

———. 1750. "Farewell Sermon," July, 1, 1750, @ https://chapellibrary.org:8443/pdf/books/fsoj.pdf.

———. 1834. *The Great Awakening*. v4 of *The Works of Jonathan Edwards*, ed. C.C. Goen. New Haven. *Works*. ed. Edward Hickman. 1834 @ http://www.ccel.org/ccel/edwards/works.

———. 1972aff. *The Works of Jonathan Edwards*, ed. C.C. Goen. 21v. New Haven, CT: Yale University Press.

———. 1972b. *The Great Awakening*. v4 of *The Works of Jonathan Edwards*, ed. C.C. Goen. New Haven, CT: Yale University Press.

———. 1972c. *The Great Awakening*. v4 of *The Works of Jonathan Edwards*, ed. C.C. Goen. New Haven. *A Faithful Narrative of the Surprizing Work of God in the Conversion of Many Hundred Souls in Northampton, and the Neighboring Towns and Villages of the County of Hampshire, in the Province of Massachusetts-Bay in New England*, ed. Benjamin Colman, London: John Oswald, 1737, in *Works*. v4, *The Great Awakening*, ed. C.C. Goen, New Haven: Yale University Press.

———. 1977. *Apocalyptic Writings: "Notes on the Apocalypse" and "An Humble Attempt,"* ed. Stephen J. Stein. New Haven, CT: Yale University Press.

———. 1984a. *The Great Awakening*. v4 of *The Works of Jonathan Edwards*, ed. C.C. Goen. New Haven. *An Account of the Life of the Reverend Mr. David Brainerd, with Reflections and Observations thereon* (Boston, 1749) v7 of *The Works of Jonathan Edwards*. New Haven, CT: Yale University Press.

———. 1984b. *An Account of the Life of the Reverend Mr. David Brainerd, with Reflections and Observations thereon* (Boston, 1749) *The Works of Jonathan Edwards*. v7.

———. 1995, 1998. *The Sermons of Jonathan Edwards: A Reader*, ed. Wilson H. Kimnach. *A Jonathan Edwards Reader*, ed. John E. Smith, Harry S. Stout and Kenneth P. Minkema. New Haven, CT: Yale University Press.

———. 1999. In *The Sermons of Jonathan Edwards: A Reader*, ed. Wilson H. Kimnach, Kenneth P. Minkema, and Douglas A. Sweeney. New Haven, CT: Yale University Press.

———. 2003. *The Great Awakening*. v4 of *The Works of Jonathan Edwards*, ed. C.C. Goen. New Haven. *Sermons and Discourses, 1739-1742*. v22 of *The Works of Jonathan Edwards*, ed. Nathan O. Hatch. New Haven, CT: Yale University Press.

———. 2009a. *Religious Affections*. ed. John E. Smith. v2 of *The Works of Jonathan Edwards*. New Haven, CT: Yale University Press.

———. 2009b. *An Account of the Life of the Reverend Mr. David Brainerd. A Careful and Strict Enquiry into the Modern Prevailing Notions of that Freedom of the Will, Which Is Supposed to be Essential to Moral Agency, Vertue and Vice, Reward and Punishment, Praise and Blame*. (1754) in *Freedom of the Will*, ed. Paul Ramsey. v1 of *The Works of Jonathan Edwards*. New Haven, CT: Yale University Press.

———. n.d. *Religious Affections*, ed. John E. Smith. v2 of *The Works of Jonathan Edwards*. New Haven. *A Treatise Concerning the Religious Affections*. Online Edition by: International Outreach, Inc. PO Box 1286, Ames, Iowa 50014 @ http://www.jonathan-edwards.org/ReligiousAffections.pdf.

Eisenstadt, Peter R. 1982. Church Adherence in the Eighteenth-Century British American Colonies. *William and Mary Quarterly* 3rd ser. 39: 245–246.

Elder, Robert. May 2016. *The Sacred Mirror: Evangelicalism, Honor, and Identity in the Deep South, 1790-1860*. Chapel Hill: University of North Carolina Press.

Elliot, Nathan, ed. 1808. *The Columbian Preacher: or, a Collection of Original Sermons from Preachers of Eminence in the United States, Embracing the Distinguishing Doctrines of Grace*. Catskill, NY: Nathan Elliot.

Elwell, Walter A., ed. 1984. *Evangelical Dictionary of Theology*. Grand Rapids, MI: Baker Book House.

———., ed. 1993. *Handbook of Evangelical Theologians*. Grand Rapids, MI: Baker.

Emerson, Michael O., and Christian Smith. 2000. *Divided by Faith: Evangelical Religion and the Problem of Race in America*. New York: Oxford University Press, pb, 2001.

(Ephrata). 1976. *Chronicon Ephratense: A History of the Community of the Seventh-Day Baptists at Ephrata*. Trans. J. Max Hark. New York: Burt Franklin.

Eslinger, Ellen. c1999. *Citizens of Zion: the Social Origins of Camp Meeting Revivalism*. Knoxville: University of Tennessee Press.

Essig, James David. 1982. *The Bonds of Wickedness: American Evangelicals Against Slavery, 1770-1808*. Philadelphia, PA: Temple University Press.

Estep, William R. 1990. *Revolution Within the Revolution: The First Amendment in Historical Context, 1612-1789*. Grand Rapids, MI: Eerdman's.

Fabend, Firth Haring. 2000. *Zion on the Hudson: Dutch New York and New Jersey in the Age of Revivals*. New Brunswick, NJ: Rutgers University Press.

Fiering, Norman. October 1972. Will and Intellect in the New England Mind. *William and Mary Quarterly* XXIX: 515–558. Referred to neo-Arminian American "Calvinists" as partisans of "intellectualism." (Greven noticed and copied.).

———. 1976. The Transatlantic Republic of Letters. *William and Mary Quarterly* 3rd ser. 33: 642–660.

Finke, Roger. 1989. How the Upstart Sects Won America: 1776-1850. *Journal for the Scientific Study of Religion* 28: 27–44.

Finke, Roger, and Rodney Stark. 1993. *The Churching of America, 1776-1990: Winners and Losers in Our Religious Economy*. New Brunswick, NJ: Rutgers University Press.

Fischer, David Hackett. 1989. *Albion's Seed: Four British Folkways in America. (Volume 1 of America: a cultural history.)*. New York: Oxford University Press. (East Anglia to Massachusetts, South of England to Virginia, North Midlands to the Delaware Valley, Borderlands to the Backcountry).

Fisher, Miles Mark. 1963. *Negro Slave Songs in the United States*. Ithaca, NY: Cornell University Press.

Fisher, Elizabeth W. 1985. 'Prophecies and Revelations': German Cabalists in Early Pennsylvania. *Pennsylvania Magazine of History and Biography* 109: 299–333.

Fishwick, Marshall. 1992. *Great Awakenings*. Hayworth.

Fitzgerald, Allan D. O.S.A. ed. 1999. *Augustine Through the Ages: An Encyclopedia*. Grand Rapids, MI: Eerdmans.

Flaherty, David H. 1972. *Privacy in Colonial New England*. Charlottesville, VA: University Press of Virginia.

Fliegelman, Jay. 1982. *Prodigals and Pilgrims: The American Revolution against Patriarchal Authority, 1750-1800*. Cambridge: Cambridge University Press.

Fogel, Robert William. 2000. *The Fourth Great Awakening & the Future of Egalitarianism*. Chicago: University of Chicago Press.

Fogleman, Aaron Spencer. August 2015. *Two Troubled Souls: An Eighteenth-Century Couple's Spiritual Journey in the Atlantic World*. Chapel Hill: University of North Carolina Press.

Forbes, Bruce David, and Jeffrey H. Mahan, eds. 2000–2005. *Religion and Popular Culture in America*. Berkeley: University of California Press.

Foster, Walter R. 1958. *Bishop and Presbytery: The Church of Scotland, 1661-1688*. London.

Foster, Charles I. 1958–1960. *An Errand of Mercy: The Evangelical United Front, 1790-1837*. Chapel Hill, NC: University of North Carolina Press.

Foster, Stephen. 1991. *The Long Argument: English Puritanism and the Shaping of New England Culture, 1570-1700*. Chapel Hill: University of North Carolina Press.

Foster, F.H. 2015. *A Genetic History of the New England Theology, (1907)*. New York: Routledge.

Frantz, John B. April 1976. The Awakening of Religion among the German Settlers in the Middle Colonies. *William and Mary Quarterly* 3rd ser. 33 (2): 266–288.

Frelinghuysen, Theodorus Jacobus. 2000. In *Forerunner of the Great Awakening: Sermons by Theodorus Jacobus Frelinghuysen (1691-1747)*, ed. Joel R. Beeke. Grand Rapids, MI: Eerdmans.

Frey, Sylvia R., and Betty Wood. 1998. *Come Shouting to Zion: African American Protestantism in the American South and British Caribbean to 1830*. Chapel Hill: University of North Carolina Press.

Fulop, Timothy E., and Albert J. Raboteau. 1997. *African-American Religion: Interpretive Essays in History and Culture*. New York: Routledge.

Gallay, Alan. August 1987. The Origins of Slaveholders' Paternalism: George Whitefield, the Bryan Family, and the Great Awakening in the South. *Journal of Southern History* 53: 369–394.

Gardner, Robert G. 1989. The Statistics of Early American Baptists: A Second Look. *Baptist History and Heritage* 24 (4): 29–44.

Gaustad, Edwin S. 1957. *Great Awakening in New England*. New York.

———. 1987. *Faith of the Founders: Religion and the New Nation, 1776-1826*. New York: Harper & Row. Foreword by Randall Balmer. Waco, TX: Baylor University Press, September 2011.

———. 1991. *Liberty of Conscience: Roger Williams in America*. Grand Rapids, MI: Eerdmans.

———. 2001. *New Historical Atlas of Religion in America*. 3rd ed. New York: Oxford University Press.

Gaustad, Edwin Scott, and Philip L. Barlow, eds. 2001. *New Historical Atlas of Religion in America*. New York: Oxford University Press.

Gaustad, Edwin S., and Leigh E. Schmidt. 2015. *The Religious History of America: The Heart of the American Story from Colonial Times to Today*. (Revised ed.). HarperOne.

Genovese, Eugene D. 1974. *Roll, Jordan, Roll: The World the Slaves Made*. New York.

———. 1980. *From Rebellion to Revolution: Afro-American Slave Revolts in the Making of the Modern World*. Baton Rouge, LA: Louisiana State University Press.

German, J.D. December 1995. The social utility of wicked self-love: Calvinism, capitalism, and public policy in revolutionary New England. *Journal of American History* 82 (3): 965–998.

Gewehr, Wesley M. 1930. *The Great Awakening in Virginia, 1740-1790*. Durham, NC: Duke University Press; reprint, LLC, June, 2011.

Ghosh, P. 2003. Max Weber's idea of 'Puritanism': a case study in the empirical construction of the Protestant ethic. *History of European Ideas* 29 (2): 183–222.

Gibbs, F.W. 1967. *Joseph Priestley: Revolutions of the Eighteenth Century*. New York: Doubleday.

Gildrie, Richard P. 1975. *Salem, Massachusetts, 1626-1682: A Covenant Community*. Charlottesville: University of Virgina Press.

Gillies, Rev. John, ed. 1845. *Historical Collections Relating to Remarkable Periods of the Success of the Gospel*. (2v, Glasgow, 1754; Appendix, 1761, Supplement in 1786) Edinburgh & London (@ https://archive.org/details/historicalcollec00gill).

Girardeau, John L. 1998. *Calvinism and Evangelical Arminianism (1890)*. Hess Publications.

Godbeer, Richard. 1992. *The Devil's Dominion: Magic and Religion in Early New England*. New York: Cambridge University Press.

———. 2002. *Sexual Revolution in Early America*. Baltimore, MD: Johns Hopkins University Press.

Goen, C.C. 1962. *Revivalism and Separatism in New England, 1740-1800: Strict Congregationalists and Separate Baptists in the Great Awakening*. New Haven, CT: Yale University Press; Waco, TX: Baylor University Press, August 2012.

———. 1985. *Broken Churches, Broken Nation: Denominational Schisms and the Coming of the Civil War*. Macon, GA: Mercer University Press.

Goren, C.C., ed. 1972. *The Great Awakening*. New Haven, CT: Yale University Press.

Gould, Philip. 1996. *Covenant and Republic: Historical Romance and the Politics of Puritanism*. (Cambridge Studies in American Literature and Culture #103), Cambridge: Cambridge University Press.

Grant, Charles S. 1972. *Democracy in the Connecticut Frontier Town of Kent (1961)*. New York: Norton.

Grasso, Christopher. 1999. *A Speaking Aristocracy: Transforming Public Discourse in 18th-Century Connecticut*. Chapel Hill: University of North Carolina Press.

———. Autumn, 2002. Skepticism and American Faith: Infidels, Converts, and Religious Doubt in the Early Nineteenth Century. *Journal of the Early Republic* 22 (3): 465–508.

Greene, Lorenzo J. 1942. *The Negro in Colonial New England, 1620-1776*. New York.

Greven, Philip. 1977. *The Protestant Temperament: Patterns of Child-Rearing, Religious Experience and the Self in Early America*. Chicago: University of Chicago Press.

Guelzo, Allen C. 1989. *Edwards on the Will: A Century of American Theological Debate*. Middletown, CT: Wesleyan University Press.

———. July 1995. From Calvinist Metaphysics to Republican Theory: Jonathan Edwards and James Dana on the Freedom of the Will. *Journal of the History of Ideas* 56 (3): 399–418.

Hackett, David G. 1991. *The Rude Hand of Innovation: Religion and Social Order in Albany, New York, 1625–1836*. New York: Oxford University Press.

———., ed. 1995. *Religion and American Culture: A Reader*. London and New York: Routledge.

Hale, Christopher G. February 17, 2001. *The Rhetoric of Jonathan Edwards: Inventing the Revolution*. DeBartolo Conference.

Hall, David D. 1972. *The Faithful Shepherd: A History of the New England Ministry in the Seventeenth Century*. Chapel Hill: University of North Carolina Press, Omohundro Institute.

Hall, Timothy D. 1994. *Contested Boundaries: Itineracy and the Reshaping of the Colonial American Religious World*. Durham, NC: Duke University Press.

Hall, Mark David. 2013. The Religious Beliefs of America's Founders: Reason, Revelation, and Revolution. *Journal of American History* 99: 1226–1227.

Hambrick-Stowe, Charles E. 1982. *The Practice of Piety: Puritan Devotional Disciplines in Seventeenth-Century New England*. Chapel Hill: University of North Carolina Press.

Hamilton, Alexander. 1976. Dr. A. Hamilton, "Journal," *Gentleman's Progress*. (n.p., n.d.), 161–163. In *Religious Origins of the American Revolution*, Page Smith, ed. Missoula, Montana: Scholars Press for American Academy of Religion, p. 136.

Hancock, Ralph C. 1989. *Calvin and the Foundations of Modern Politics*. Ithaca, NY: Cornell University Press.

Hanson, Charles P. 1998. *Necessary Virtue: The Pragmatic Origins of Religious Liberty in New England*. Charlottesville/London: University Press of Virginia.

Haroutunian, Joseph. 1932. *Piety versus Moralism: The Passing of the New England Theology*. New York: Henry Holt.

Harris, Marc L. July 1993. Revelation and the American Republic: Timothy Dwight's Civic Participation. *Journal of the History of Ideas* 54 (3).
Hatch, Nathan O. 1977. *The Sacred Cause of Liberty: Republican Thought and the Millennium in Revolutionary New England*. New Haven, CT: Yale University Press.
———. 1984. Evangelicalism as a Democratic Movement. In *Evangelicalism and Modern America*, ed. Marsden, 71–82. Grand Rapids, MI: Eerdmans.
———. 1989. *The Democratization of American Christianity*. New Haven, CT: Yale University Press, pb 1991.
———. 1994. *The Democratization of American Christianity*. New Haven. "The Puzzle of American Methodism". *Church History* 63: 175–189.
Hatch, Nathan O., and Harry S. Stout, eds. 1988. *Jonathan Edwards and the American Experience*. New York: Oxford University Press.
Hatch, Nathan O., and John Wigger, eds. 2001. *Methodism and the Shaping of American Culture*. Nashville, TN: Kingswood Books.
Heideking, J. Fall–Winter 1994. The Federal Processions of 1788 and the Origins of American Civil Religion. *Soundings* 77 (3–4): 367–388.
Heimert, Alan. 1966. *Religion and the American Mind from the Great Awakening to the Revolution*. Cambridge, MA: Harvard University Press.
Heimert, Alan, and Andrew Delbanco, eds. 1985. *The Puritans in America: A Narrative Anthology*. Cambridge, MA: Harvard University Press.
Heimert, Alan, and Perry Miller, eds. 1967. *The Great Awakening*. Indianapolis, IN: Bobbs-Merrill.
Heitzenrater, Richard P. January 1990. The Second Rise of Methodism: Georgia [J Wesley's journals]. *Methodist History* 28 (2): 117–132.
Helm, Paul. 2004. *John Calvin's Ideas. [6: Free Will, 12: Equity, Natural Law, and Common Grace]*. New York: Oxford University Press.
Herbert, T. Walter. c1977. *Moby-Dick and Calvinism: A World Dismantled*. New Brunswick, NJ: Rutgers University Press.
Hill, Christopher. 1964. *Society and Puritanism in Pre-Revolutionary England*. New York: Schocken Books.
———. 1965. *Intellectual Origins of the English Revolution. (Ford Lectures, 1962)*. New York: Oxford University Press, pb 1980.
———. 1997. *Intellectual Origins of the English Revolution, Revisited*. New York: Oxford University Press.
Hindmarsh, D. Bruce. 2008. *The Evangelical Conversion Narrative: Spiritual Autobiography in Early Modern England*. New York: Oxford University Press.
———. 2018. *The Spirit of Early Evangelicalism: True Religion in a Modern World*. New York: Oxford University Press.
Hirrel, Leo P. 1998. *Children of Wrath: New School Calvinism and Antebellum Reform*. Lexington: University Press of Kentucky.
Holmes, Oliver Wendell. 1890. "The Pulpit and the Pew" (on Jonathan Edwards) in *Pages from an Old Volume of Life: A Collection of Essays, 1857-1881*. New York: Houghton, Mifflin. 1890 @ https://www.gutenberg.org/files/2699/2699-0.txt.
Hooker, Richard J. 1953. In *The Carolina Backcountry on the Eve of the Revolution: The Journal and Other Writings of Charles Woodmason, Anglican Itinerant*, ed. Charles Woodmason. Chapel Hill: University of North Carolina Press.
Horowitz, Helen Lefkowitz. 2006. *Attitudes toward Sex in Antebellum America: A Brief History with Documents*. New York: Palgrave Macmillan.
Horton, James P. 1839. *A Narrative of the Early Life, Remarkable Conversion, and Spiritual Labors of James P. Horton, Who Has Been a Member of the Methodist Episcopal Church upward of Forty Years*. n.p.
Howe, Daniel Walker. 1989. Religion and Politics in the Antebellum North. In *Religion and American Politics*, ed. Noll, 124.

———. 1997. *Making the American Self: Jonathan Edwards to Abraham Lincoln*. Cambridge, MA: Harvard University Press, Studies in Cultural History.

Irons, Charles F. 2008. *The Origins of Proslavery Christianity: White and Black Evangelicals in Colonial and Antebellum Virginia*. Chapel Hill, NC: University of North Carolina Press.

Isaac, Rhys. July 1974. Evangelical Revolt: The Nature of the Baptists' Challenge to the Traditional Order in Virginia, 1765-1775. *William and Mary Quarterly* 3rd ser. 31: 345–368.

———. 1982. *The Transformation of Virginia, 1740-1790*. Chapel Hill: University of North Carolina Press.

Jacobsen, Douglas G. 1991. *An Unprov'd Experiment: Religious Pluralism in Colonial New Jersey*. Chicago: University of Chicago Press.

Jarratt, Devereux. 1806. *The Life of the Reverend Devereux Jarratt, Rector of Bath Parish, Dinwiddie County, Virginia, Written by Himself.* Baltimore.

Jedrey, Christopher M. 1979. *The World of John Cleaveland: Family and Community in Eighteenth-Century New England*. New York.

Jenson, Robert W. 1987. *America's Theologian: A Recommendation of Jonathan Edwards*. New York: Oxford University Press.

Jernegan, Marcus W. 1916. Slavery and Conversion in the American Colonies. *American Historical Review* 21: 504–527.

Johnson, Harvey. (1842–1923). 1885. *History of Baptist Churches in Maryland, 1742–1885*. Baltimore: J.F. Weishampel Jr.

Johnson, Richard O. January 1981. The Development of the Love Feast in Early American Methodism. *Methodist History* 19 (2): 67–83.

Johnson, Curtis D. 1989. *Islands of Holiness: Rural Religion in Upstate New York, 1790-1860*. New York: Fall Creek Books.

Johnson, Charles A. 1995. *The Frontier Camp Meeting: Religion's Harvest Time*. Dallas, TX: Southern Methodist University Press.

Jones, Douglas. 1981. *Village and Seaport: Migration and Society in Eighteenth-Century Massachusetts*. Hanover, NH: University Press of New England.

Juster, Susan. 1994. *Disorderly Women: Sexual Politics and Evangelicalism in Revolutionary New England*. Ithaca, NY: Cornell University Press.

———. 2003. *Doomsayers: Anglo-American Prophecy in the Age of Revolution*. Philadelphia: University of Pennsylvania Press.

Juster, Susan, and Lisa MacFarlane, eds. 1996. *A Mighty Baptism: Race, Gender, and the Creation of American Protestantism*. Ithaca, NY: Cornell University Press.

Kamensky, Jane. 1998. *Governing the Tongue: The Politics of Speech in Early New England*. New York: Oxford University Press.

Kamil, Neil. 2013. The Science of the Soul in Colonial New England. *Journal of American History* 99: 1216–1217.

Keller, Charles Roy. 1942. *The Second Great Awakening in Connecticut*. New Haven, CT: Yale University Press.

Kidd, Thomas S. June 2003. 'Let Hell and Rome Do Their Worst': World News, Anti-Catholicism, and International Protestantism in Early-Eighteenth-Century Boston. *The New England Quarterly* 76 (2): 265–290.

———. 2007. *The Great Awakening: The Roots of Evangelical Christianity in Colonial America*. New Haven, CT: Yale University Press.

———. 2008. *The Great Awakening: A Brief History with Documents*. New York: Bedford/St. Martin's.

Kidd, Thomas S., and Barry G. Hankins. 2015. *Baptists in America: A History*. New York: Oxford University Press, pb, 2018.

Kingston, Richard. 1709. *Enthusiastik Imposters, No Divinely inspir'd Prophets, the second part*. London.

Kitson, Peter, ed. 1999. *Slavery, Abolition and Emancipation*. London: Pickering & Chatto. (v2 (of 8): includes Ramsay, Clarkson, Newton, Wilberforce, Beckford, Harris).

Kitson, Peter, and Debbie Lee, eds. 1999. *Slavery, Abolition and Emancipation*. London: Pickering & Chatto. (v1 (of 8) includes Sancho, Equiano, Cugoano, Prince, Seacole, Wedderburn, Gronniosaw).
Kling, David W. 1993. *A Field of Divine Wonders: The New Divinity and Village Revivals in Northwestern Connecticut, 1792-1822*. University Park, PA: Pennsylvania State University Press.
Knight, Janice. 1995. *Orthodoxies in Massachusetts: Rereading American Puritanism*. Cambridge: Harvard University Press.
Knott, John R., Jr. 1980. *The Sword of the Spirit: Puritan Responses to the Bible*. Chicago: University of Chicago Press.
Koch, G. Adolf. 1933. *Religion of the American Enlightenment*. New York: Thomas Y. Crowell, Apollo pb, 1968, repr. of *Republican Religion: The American Revolution and the Cult of Reason*. New York.
Koefoed, Jonathan. August 2017. Transcendental Trinitarian: James Marsh, the Free Will Problem, and the American Intellectual Context of Coleridge's *Aids to Reflection*. Religions 8 (9): 172 (MDPI) @ https://www.mdpi.com/2077-1444/8/9/172.
Kramnick, Isaac, and R. Lawrence Moore. 1996. *The Godless Constitution: The Case Against Religious Correctness*. New York: Norton.
Kraybill, Donald B. 1989. *The Riddle of Amish Culture*. Baltimore: Johns Hopkins University Press; rev, ed. Baltimore, MD: Johns Hopkins University Press, 2001.
———. 1993a. *Old Order Amish: Their Enduring Way of Life. photographs by Lucian Niemeyer*. Baltimore: Johns Hopkins University Press.
———., ed. 1993b. *The Amish and the State*. Baltimore: Johns Hopkins University Press.
Kraybill, Donald B., and F. Carl. 2001. *Bowman. On the Backroad to Heaven: Old Order Hutterites, Mennonites, Amish, and Brethren*. Baltimore, MD: Johns Hopkins University Press.
Kuklick, Bruce. 1985. *Churchmen and Philosophers: From Jonathan Edwards to John Dewey*. New Haven, CT: Yale University Press.
Lambert, Frank. 1993a. *"Pedlar in Divinity" George Whitefield and the Transatlantic Revivals, 1737-1770*, c1994. Princeton, NJ: Princeton University Press. Whitefield made full use of 18thC state-of-the-art commercial merchandising and publicity.
———. July 1993b. Subscribing for Profits and Piety: The Friendship of Benjamin Franklin and George Whitefield. *William and Mary Quarterly* 50 (3): 529–554.
———. 1999. *Inventing the "Great Awakening"*. Princeton, NJ: Princeton University Press.
———. Winter 2002. 'I Saw the Book Talk': Slave Readings of the First Great Awakening. *The Journal of African American History, The Past before Us* 87: 12–25.
Landsman, Ned C. 1982. Revivalism and Nativism in the Middle Colonies: The Great Awakening and the Scots Community in East New Jersey. *American Quarterly* 34: p149–p164.
———. 1985. *Scotland and Its First American Colony, 1683-1765*. Princeton, NJ: Princeton University Press.
———. 1997. Edwards versus Chauncy: The Great Debate. In *From Colonials to Provincials: American Thought and Culture, 1680-1760*, 105ff. Ithaca, NY: Cornell University Press.
Larson, Rebecca. 1999. *Daughters of Light: Quaker Women Preaching and Prophesying in the Colonies and Abroad, 1700-1775*. New York: Knopf; Chapel Hill: University of North Carolina Press, pb 2000.
Le Beau, B.F. 2006. *Jonathan Dickinson and the Formative Years of American Presbyterianism*. University Press of Kentucky.
Le Jau, Francis. 1956. In *The Carolina Chronicle of Dr. Francis Le Jau, 1706-1717*, ed. Frank J. Klingberg. Berkeley: University of California Press.
Lebsock, Suzanne D. 1984. *The Free Women of Petersburg: Status and Culture in a Southern Town, 1784-1860*. New York: W. W. Norton.
Lee, Jesse. 1810. *A Short History of the Methodists, in the United States of America; beginning in 1766, and Continued till 1809*. Baltimore, MD: Magill & Clime; facsimile, Miami, FL: Hard Press, 2017.

Lemons, J. Stanley. 2019. *Retracing Baptists in Rhode Island: Identity, Formation, and History*. Waco, TX: Baylor University Press.
Lepore, Jill. 1998. *The Name of War: King Philip's War and the Origins of American Identity*. New York: Knopf.
Lesser, M. X. November 1994. *Jonathan Edwards: An Annotated Bibliography, 1979-1993*. Westport, CT: Greenwood Press.
Levin, David, ed. 1963. *The Puritan in the Enlightenment: Franklin and Edwards*. Chicago: Rand McNally (Berkeley Series in American History).
———, ed. 1969. *Jonathan Edwards: A Profile*. New York: Hill & Wang.
Levy, Leonard W. 1986. *The Establishment Clause: Religion and the First Amendment*. New York.
Lewis, Donald, ed. 1995. *A Dictionary of Evangelical Biography*. Cambridge, MA: Blackwell.
Lincoln, C. Eric, and Lawrence H. Mamiya. 1990. *The Black Church in the African American Experience*. Durham, NC: Duke University Press.
Lippy, Charles H., and Peter W. Williams, eds. 1988. *Encyclopedia of the American Religious Experience: Studies of Traditions and Movements*. New York: Scribner's.
Lipson, Dorothy Ann. 1977. *Freemasonry in Federalist Connecticut, 1789-1835*. Princeton, NJ: Princeton University Press.
Little, Thomas J. 2015. *The Origins of Southern Evangelicalism: Religious Revivalism in the South Carolina Lowcountry, 1670–1760*. University of South Carolina Press.
Lockridge, Kenneth Ross. 1985. *A New England Town, The First Hundred Years: Dedham, Massachusetts, 1636-1736*. (Expanded ed.). New York.
Longenecker, Stephen L. 2002. *Shenandoah Religion: Outsiders and the Mainstream, 1716-1865*. Waco, TX: Baylor University Press.
Louis, Jeanne Henriette. 1998. "La sainte expérience de la Pennsylvanie (1682-1756) gage de la royauté spirituelle et de la France-Amérique" dans Frank Lestringant (édit.), *la France-Amérique (XVIe-XVIIIe siècle). Actes du XXXVe colloque intenational d'études humanistes*. Paris: Honoré Champion, coll. "Travaux du Centre d'études supérieures de la Renaissance de Tours. Le savoir de Mantice," 5: 541–551.
Love, William D. 1895. *The Fast and Thanksgiving Days of New England*. Boston.
Lovejoy, David S. 1969. *Religious Enthusiasm and the Great Awakening*. Englewood Cliffs, NJ: Prentice-Hall.
———. 1985. *Religious Enthusiasm in the New World: Heresy to Revolution*. Cambridge, MA: Harvard University Press.
———. 1991. 'Desperate Enthusiasm': Early Signs of American Radicalism. In *The Origins of Anglo-American Radicalism (1984)*, ed. Margaret C. Jacob and James R. Jacob, 214–225. Atlantic Highlands, NJ: Humanities Press.
Loveland, Anne C. 1980. *Southern Evangelicals and the Social Order, 1800-1860*. Baton Rouge, LA: Louisiana State University Press.
Lowell, Robert. 1946. *Lord Weary's Castle*. New York: Harcourt, Brace.
Lucas, Paul R. 1976. *Valley of Discord: Church and Society along the Connecticut River, 1636-1725*. Hanover, NH: University Press of New England.
Luchetti, Cathy. 1989. *Under God's Spell: Frontier Evangelists, 1722-1915*. New York: Harcourt Brace Jovanovich.
Luker, Vicki, and Brij V. Lal. 2010. *Telling Pacific Lives: Prisms of Process*. ANU E Press.
Lumpkin, William L. 1959. *Baptist Confessions of Faith*. Valley Forge, PA: Judson Press.
Lyttle, David. c1983. *Studies in religion in early American literature: Edwards, Poe, Channing, Emerson, some minor transcendentalists, Hawthorne, and Thoreau*. Lanham, MD: University Press of America.
MacMaster, Richard K. 1973. Thomas Rankin and the American Colonists. *Proceedings of the Wesley Historical Association (G.B.)* 39 (2): 25–33.
Magnuson, Norris A., and William G. Travis. 1990a. *American Evangelicalism: An Annotated Bibliography*. West Cornwall, CT: Locust Hill Press.

———. 1990b. *American Evangelicalism II: First Bibliographical Supplement, 1990-1996*. West Cornwall, CT: Locust Hill Press.
Maizlish, Rivka. 2013. Perry Miller and the Puritans: An Introduction. S-USIH @ http://s-usih.org/2013/05/perry-miller-and-the-puritans-an-introduction.html. Accessed 8 May 2013.
Makemie, Francis. (1658–1708). 1999. *The Life and Writings of Francis Makemie*, ed. Boyd S. Schlenther (Philadelphia, 1971). Lewiston, NY: Edwin Mellen Press.
Mapp, Alf, Jr. 2003. *The Faiths of Our Fathers: What the Founders Really Believed*. Lanham, MD: Rowman & Littlefield.
Marietta, Jack D. 1984. *The Reformation of American Quakerism, 1748-1783*. Philadelphia.
Maring, Norman H. 1964. *Baptists in New Jersey: A Study in Transition*. Valley Forge, PA: Judson Press.
Maring, Norman H., and Winthrop S. Hudson. 1965, 1981. *A Short Baptist Manual of Polity and Practice*. (Revised ed.). Valley Forge, PA: Judson Press.
Marini, Stephen A. 1982. *Radical Sects of Revolutionary New England*. Cambridge, MA.
———. June 2002. Hymnody as History: Early Evangelical Hymns and the Recovery of American Popular Religion. *Church History* 71 (2): 273–306.
Marsden, George M. June 1977. Fundamentalism as an American Phenomenon: A Comparison with British Evangelicalism. *Church History* 46.
———. 2001. *Religion and American Culture*. 2nd ed. San Diego: Harcourt College Publishers.
———. 2003. *Jonathan Edwards: A Life*. New Haven, CT: Yale University Press.
Marsh, James. n.d. "Preliminary Essay" to Coleridge, *Aids to Reflection*. Burlington: Chauncy Goodrich, 1829. Fourth edition, 1839. Loschberg: Jazzybee Verlag, Printed North Charleston, SC: CreateSpace.
Marty, Martin E. 1970. *Righteous Empire: The Protestant Experience in America*. New York: Dial.
———. 1984. *Pilgrims in Their Own Land: 500 Years of Religion in America*. New York/London: Penguin Books.
Marty, Martin, and R. Scott Appleby, eds. 1991. *Fundamentalisms Observed. The Fundamentalism Project*. Vol. 1. Chicago: University of Chicago Press.
———, eds. 1995. *Fundamentalisms Comprehended. The Fundamentalism Project*. Vol. 5. Chicago: University of Chicago Press, pb, 2004.
Mathews, Donald G. 1965. *Slavery and Methodism: A Chapter in American Morality, 1780-1845*. Princeton, NJ: Princeton University Press.
———. 1969. The Second Great Awakening as an Organizing Process, 1780-1830: An Hypothesis. *American Quarterly* 21: 23–43.
———. 1977. *Religion in the Old South*. Chicago: University of Chicago Press.
———. 1980. Religion and Slavery: The Case of the American South. In *Anti-Slavery, Religion and Reform*, ed. Bolt and Drescher, 207–232. London: Wm Dawson/Hamden, CT: Archon Books.
Mathisen, Robert R., ed. c2001. *Critical Issues in American Religious History: A Reader*. Waco, TX: Baylor University Press. Incl. Martha T. Blauvelt & Rosemary Skinner Keller, "Women and Revivalism: The Puritan and Wesleyan Traditions".
Matossian, Mary Kilbourne. 1989. Great Awakening or Great Sickening. In *Poisons of the Past: Molds, Epidemics and History*. New Haven, CT: Yale University Press.
Maxson, C[harles] H[artshorn]. 2019. *The Great Awakening in the Middle Colonies (1920)*. Kindle Edition.
May, Henry F. 1976. *The Enlightenment in America*. New York: Oxford University Press.
———. 1991. *The Divided Heart: Essays on Protestantism and the Enlightenment in America*. New York: Oxford.
Mayhew, Jonathan. 1995. *Sermons*. North Stratford, NH: Ayer.
McBeth, H. Leon, ed. 2004. *A Sourcebook for Baptist Heritage*. Nashville, TN: Broadman Press.
McCauley, Deborah Vansau. 1995. *Appalachian Mountain Religion: A History*. Urbana: University of Illinois Press.
McFerrin, John B. 1888. *History of Methodism in Tennessee*. Vol. 1. Publishing House of the M. E. Church.

McGarvie, Mark. 2013. The Religious Roots of the First Amendment: Dissenting Protestants and the Separation of Church and State. *Journal of American History* 99: 1221.
McKibbens, Thomas R., ed. 2017. *Baptists in Early North America—First Baptist Church.* Vol. IV. Boston, MA: Mercer University Press.
McKim, Donald K, ed. 1992. *Encyclopedia of the Reformed Faith.* Louisville, KY: Westminster/ John Knox Press; Edinburgh: Saint Andrew Press.
McLoughlin, William G. 1961. Pietism and the American Character. *American Quarterly* 13.
———. 1967–1970. *Isaac Backus and the American Pietist Tradition.* Boston: Little, Brown.
———. 1971. *New England Dissent, 1630-1833: The Baptists and the Separation of Church and State.* 2 vols. Cambridge, MA: Harvard University Press.
———. 1974. Revivalism. In *The Rise of Adventism*, ed. Gaustad, 119–153. New York: Harper.
———., ed. 1976. *The American Evangelicals, 1800–1900: An Anthology.*
———. 1978–1980. *Revivals, Awakenings, and Reform: An Essay on Religion and Social Change in America, 1607-1977.* Chicago: University of Chicago Press (Chicago History of American Religion).
———. 1984. *Cherokees and Missionaries, 1789-1839.* New Haven, CT: Yale University Press.
———. 1991. *Soul Liberty: The Baptists' Struggle in New England, 1630-1833.* Hanover, NH: University Press of New England (Brown).
Melton, J. Gordon. 1983. *Biographical Dictionary of American Cult and Sect Leaders.* New York: Garland.
———. 1983–1992. *Encyclopedic Handbook of Cults in America.* New York: Garland.
———. 1998. *The Encyclopedia of American Religions.* MI: Gale Research.
Mickeljohn, George. 1927. "On the Important Duty of Subjection to the Civil Powers," New Bern, NC, 1768, sermon in Boyd. In *Some Eighteenth Century Tracts concerning North Carolina*, ed. K. William. Raleigh, NC.
Middlekauff, Robert. 1999. *The Mathers: Three Generations of Puritan Intellectuals, 1696-1728. pb.* Berkeley: University of California Press.
Miller, Perry. 1939. *The New England Mind: The Seventeenth Century.* New York: Harcourt.
———. 1948. "Jonathan Edwards' Sociology of the Great Awakening". *New England Quarterly* 21.
———. 1953. *The New England Mind: From Colony to Province.* Cambridge, MA: Harvard University Press.
———. 1956a. *The New England Mind: From Colony to Province.* Cambridge. *The New England Mind: From Colony to Province.* Cambridge. *Errand Into the Wilderness.* New York: Harper Torchbooks; Cambridge, MA: Harvard University Press.
———. 1956b. *The American Puritans; Their Prose and Poetry.* Garden City, New York: Doubleday Anchor Books.
———. 1961. From the Covenant to the Revival. In *The Shaping of American Religion*,, ed. James Ward Smith and A. Leland Jamison. Volume I: *Religion in American Life.* Princeton, NJ: Princeton University Press, pp. 322–368.
Minkema, Kenneth P. 1997. Jonathan Edwards on Slavery and the Slave Trade. *William and Mary Quarterly, 3d ser.* 54: 823–834.
Minutes and Letters of the Coetus of the German Reformed Congregations in Pennsylvania, 1747-1792, Philadelphia, 1903.
Moore, Frank, ed. 1862. *The Patriot Preachers of the American Revolution.* New York.
Moran, Gerald F. 1973. *The Puritan Saint: Religious Experience, Church Membership, and Piety in Connecticut, 1636-1776.* PhD diss't, Rutgers University.
———. 2013. Godly Republicanism: Puritans, Pilgrims, and a City on a Hill. *Journal of American History* 99: 1215–1216.
Morgan, Edmund S. 1958. *Visible Saints: The History of a Puritan Idea. Ithaca. Visible Saints: The History of a Puritan Idea. Ithaca. The Puritan Dilemma: The Story of John Winthrop (1958).* Boston: Little, Brown, pb.
———. 1963. *Visible Saints: The History of a Puritan Idea.* Ithaca, NY: Cornell University Press.

———. 1966. *Visible Saints: The History of a Puritan Idea. Ithaca. Visible Saints: The History of a Puritan Idea. Ithaca. The Puritan Family: Religion and Domestic Relations in Seventeenth-Century New England (1944).* New York: Harpoer Torchbooks.
———. 1975. *American Slavery, American Freedom: The Ordeal of Colonial Virginia.* New York.
Morris, William Sparkes. 1991. *The Young Jonathan Edwards: A Reconstruction.* Chicago: University of Chicago Press.
Muller, Richard A. 1999. *The Unaccommodated Calvin: Studies in the Foundation of a Theological Tradition.* New York: Oxford University Press.
Murdock, Kenneth Ballard. 1963. *Literature & theology in colonial New England (1949).* New York: Harper.
Murphy, Larry G. J. Gordon Melton & Gary L. Ward. eds. 1999. Encyclopedia of African-American Religions. Hamden, CT: Garland.
Murray, Iain H. 1971. *The Puritan Hope: Revival and the Interpretation of Prophecy.* Edinburgh: Banner of Truth.
———. 1988. *Jonathan Edwards: A New Biography.*
———. 1994. *Revival and Revivalism: The Making and Marring of American Evangelicalism 1750–1858.* Edinburgh: Banner of Truth.
Neele, Adriaan C. 2019. *Before Jonathan Edwards: Sources of New England Theology.* New York: Oxford University Press.
Niebuhr, H. Richard. 1929. *The Social Sources of Denominationalism.* New York: Henry Holt; Cleveland, OH: World/Meridian pb, 1957.
Nissenbaum, Stephen. 1996a. *The Battle for Christmas.* New York: Knopf.
———. April 1996b. Christmas in early New Engand, 1620-1820: Puritanism, popular culture, and the printed word. *Proceedings of the American Antiquarian Society* 106 (1): 79–164.
Noll, Mark A[llan]. 1977. *Christians in the American Revolution.* Washington, DC/Grand Rapids, MI: Christian University Press.
———. 1989. *Princeton and the Republic, 1768-1822: The Search for a Christian Enlightenment in the Era of Samuel Stanhope Smith.* Princeton, NJ: Princeton University Press.
———. 1991. Evaluating North Atlantic Religious History, 1640-1859: A Review Article. *Comparative Studies in Society and History* 33: 415–425.
———. 1992a. Contexts: Comparative Evangelical History. *Evangelical Studies Bulletin* 9: 5–9.
———. 1992b. *A History of Christianity in the United States and Canada.* Grand Rapids, MI: Eerdmans.
———. Winter 1993. The American Revolution and Protestant Evangelicalism. *Journal of Interdisciplinary History* 23 (3): 615–638. (Cambridge, MA: MIT Press).
———. 2002. *America's God: From Jonathan Edwards to Abraham Lincoln.* New York: Oxford University Press.
———. 2003. *The Rise of Evangelicalism: The Age of Edwards, Whitefield and the Wesleys (A History of Evangelicalism: People, Movements and Ideas in the English-Speaking World, Book 1).* Downers Grove, IL: InterVarsity Press.
———. 2007. Rvw of Paul Harvey. Freedom's Coming: Religious Culture and the Shaping of the South from the Civil War through the Civil Rights Era. *Journal of the American Academy of Religion* 75: 473–477.
Noll, Mark A., David W. Bebbington, and George A. Rawlyk, eds. 1994. *Evangelicalism: Comparative Studies of Popular Protestantism in North America, the British Isles, and Beyond, 1700-1990.* New York: Oxford University Press. Rvw by Martin Marty. May 1995. *Journal of Southern History* 61 (2): 363–365.
Noll, Mark A., Nathan O. Hatch, George M. Marsden, David F. Wells, and John D. Woodbridge, eds. 1983. *Eerdman's Handbook to Christianity in America.* Grand Rapids, MI: Eerdmans'.
Noonan, John T., Jr. 1998. *The Lustre of Our Country: The American Experience of Religious Freedom.* Berkeley: University of California Press, pb, 2000.
———. 1995. Development in Moral Doctrine. In *Theological Studies 54 (Dec 1993) and as a chapter in The Context of Casuistry.* Georgetown.

Norwood, Frederick A. 1974. *The Story of American Methodism*. Nashville, TN: Abingdon Press.

O'Brien, Susan. 1986. A Transatlantic Community of Saints: The Great Awakening and the First Evangelical Network. *American Historical Review* 91: 811–832.

Oak Bluffs Historical Society, with Chris Stoddard. 2000. *A Centennial History of Cottage City*. Oak Bluffs, MA: Oak Bluffs Historical Commission.

Oberg, Barbara B., and Harry S. Stout, eds. 1993. *Benjamin Franklin, Jonathan Edwards and the Representation of American Culture*. New York: Oxford University Press.

Perry, Ralph Barton. 1944. *Puritanism and Democracy*. New York: Vanguard Press; pb New York: Harper Torchbooks, 1964.

Pilcher, George W. 1971. *Samuel Davies: Apostle of Dissent in Colonial Virginia*. Knoxville.

Pilmore, Joseph. 1969. In *The Journal of Joseph Pilmore, Methodist Itinerant for the Years August 1, 1769 to January 2, 1774*, ed. Frederick E. Maser and Howard T. Maag. Philadelphia.

Pitts, Walter F. 1993. *Old Ship of Zion: The Afro-Baptist Ritual in the African Diaspora*. New York: Oxford University Press.

Pointer, Richard W. 1988. *Protestant Pluralism and the New York Experience: A Study of Eighteenth-Century Religious Diversity*. Bloomington, IN: Indiana University Press.

Pope, Robert G. 1969. *The Half-Way Covenant: Church Membership in Puritan New England*. Princeton, NJ: Princeton University Press.

———. 1969–1970. New England versus the New England Mind: The Myth of Declension. *Journal of Social History* 3: 95–108.

Potash, P. Jeffey. 1991. *Vermont's Burned-Over District: Patterns of Community Development and Religious Activity, 1761-1850*. Chicago: University of Chicago Press.

Powell, Sumner Chilton. 1963. *Puritan Village: The Formation of a New England Town*. Middletown, CT: Wesleyan University Press.

(Presbyterian Church). 1904. *Records of the Presbyterian Church in the United States of America [...] 1706-1788*. Philadelphia.

Prestwich, Menna, ed. 1986. *International Calvinism, 1541-1715*, esp. pp. 315–337.

Prince, Rev. Thomas, Jr., publisher; Thomas Prince Jr. ed. 1744. *The Christian History, Containing Accounts of the **Revival** and Propagation of Religion in Great-Britain & America for the Year 1743* I:1(March, 1743), Boston: Kneeland & Green. Hard Press, Kindle Edition, 2018.

———., publisher; Thomas Prince Jr. ed. 1745. *The Christian History Containing Accounts of the Revival and Propagation of Religion in Great-Britain and America for the Year 1744*, 5. Boston.

Prothero, Stephen. 2003. *American Jesus: How the Son of God Became a National Icon*. New York: Farrar, Straus and Giroux.

Queen, E.L., Stephen R. Prothero, and Gardiner H. Shattuck, Jr. 1996. *The Encyclopedia of American Religious History*. 2v.

Raboteau, Albert J. 1978–1980. *Slave Religion: The 'Invisible Institution' in the Antebellum South*. New York: Oxford University Press.

———. 1995. *A Fire in the Bones: Reflections on African-American Religious History*. Boston: Beacon Press.

Rawlyk, George A. 1984. *Ravished by the Spirit: Religious Revival, Baptists, and Henry Alline*. Kingston, ON.

———. 1994. *The Canada Fire: Radical Evangelicalism in British North America, 1775-1812*. Montreal: McGill-Queen's University Press.

Rawlyk, George A., and Mark A. Noll, eds. c1993. *Amazing Grace: Evangelicalism in Australia, Britain, Canada, and the United States*. Grand Rapids, MI: Baker Books; Toronto: McGill-Queen's University Press (Studies in the History of Religion), 1994.

Reid-Maroney, Nina. 2001. *Philadelphia's Enightenment, 1740-1800: Kingdom of Christ, Empire of Reason*. Westport, CT: Greenwood Press.

Robbins, Keith, ed. 1990. *Protestant Evangelicalism: England, Ireland, Germany and America, c. 1750-c. 1950, Essays in Honor of W.R. Ward*. Cambridge, MA: Blackwell.

Roeber, A.G. 1993. *Palatines, Liberty, and Property: German Lutherans in Colonial British America, Baltimore and London*. Baltimore: Johns Hopkins University Press.

Rogers, Charles. Allen. Winter 1966. John Wesley and Jonathan Edwards. *Duke Divinity School Bulletin* 31: 20–38.
Rohrer, James R. 1995. *Keepers of the Covenant: Frontier Missions and the Decline of Congregationalism, 1774-1818*. New York: Oxford University Press.
Rothermund, Dietmar. 1961. *The Layman's Progress: Religious and Political Experience in Colonial Pennsylvania, 1740-1770*. Philadelphia.
Rubin, Julius H. 1994. *Religious Melancholy and Protestant Experience in America*. New York: Oxford University Press.
Ruffin, J., and A. Rixey. 2008. *Paradise of Reason: William Bentley and Enlightenment Christianity in the Early Republic*. New York: Oxford University Press. ("Christian naturalism". Summer 2011. Rvw by Jonathan M. Yeager in *Eighteenth-Century Studies* 44 (4): 547–548).
Rutman, Darret B. 1963. *Winthrop's Boston: Portrait of a Puritan Town*. Chapel Hill: University of North Carolina Press.
———. 1977. *American Puritanism: Faith and Practice. Philadelphia, 1970; pb.* New York: W. W. Norton.
Sachse, Julius F. 1895. *The German Pietists of Provincial Pennsylvania, 1694-1708*. Philadelphia; Reprint, Metalmark, 2015.
Scarberry, Mark S. John Leland and James Madison: Religious Influence on the Ratification of the Constitution and on the Proposal of the Bill of Rights. *Penn State Law Review* 113 (3): 733–800.
Schelbert, Leo. 1980. From Reformed Preacher in the Palatinate to Pietist Monk in Pennsylvania: The Spiritual Path of Johann Peter Muller, 1709-1796. In *Germany and America: Essays on Problems of International Relations and Immigration*, ed. Hans Trefousse. New York.
Schmidt, Leigh Eric. 1986. 'A Second and Glorious Reformation': The New Light Extremism of Andrew Croswell. *William and Mary Quarterly* 3rd ser. 43: 222.
———. 1989. *Holy Fairs: Scottish Communions and American Revivals in the Early Modern Period*. 2nd ed. Princeton, NJ: Princeton University Press. pb. Grand Rapids, MI: Eerdmans, 2001.
———. 2000. *Hearing Things: Religion, Illusion, and the American Enlightenment*. Cambridge, MA: Harvard University Press, pb, 2002.
———. 2016. *Village Atheists: How American Unbelievers Made Their Way in a Godly Nation*. Princeton, NJ: Princeton University Press.
Schwartz, Sally. 1987. *"A Mixed Multitude": The Struggle for Toleration in Colonial Pennsylvania*. New York: NYU Press.
Scott, Donald M. 1978. *From Office to Profession: The New England Ministry, 1750-1850*. Philadelphia, PA: University of Pennsylvania Press.
Seeman, Erik R. Summer 1995. The Spiritual Labour of John Barnard: An 18th-Century Artisan Constructs His Piety. *Religion and American Culture* 5 (2): 181–216.
———. 1999. *Pious Persuasions: Laity and Clergy in Eighteenth-Century New England*. Baltimore, MD: Johns Hopkins University Press.
Selement, George. 1984. *Keepers of the Vineyard: The Puritan Ministry and Collective Culture in Colonial New England*. Lanham, MD: University Press of America.
Semple, Robert A. 1810. *History of the Rise and Progress of Baptists in Virginia*. Richmond, VA: John O'Lynch. (revised, ed. Rev. Beale, Richmond: Pitt and Dickinson, 1894).
Sernett, Milton C., ed. 1999. *African-American Religious History: A Documentary Witness*. Durham, NC: Duke University Press.
Shaftesbury (Anthony Ashley Cooper, 3rd Earl of Shaftesbury). 1900. *A Letter Concerning Enthusiasm to Lord Somers (September, 1707) Characteristics of Men, Manners, Opinions, Times. (1708)*. London: Grant Richards.
Shain, Barry Alan. 1994. *The Myth of American Individualism: The Protestant Origins of American Political Thought*. Princeton, NJ: Princeton University Press.
Sidbury, James. 1997. *Ploughshares into Swords: Race, Rebellion, and Identity in Gabriel's Virginia, 1730-1810*. New York: Cambridge University Press.
Simpson, Alan. 1955. *Puritanism in Old and New England*. Chicago: University of Chicago Press.

Simpson, George Eaton. 1978. *Black Religion in the New World*. New York: Columbia University Press.

Skinner, Quentin. 1980. The Origins of the Calvinist Theory of Revolution. In *After the Reformation*, ed. Barbara C. Malament, 309–330. Philadelphia.

Smith, Henry. 1848. In *Recollections and Reflections of an Old Itinerant: A series of letters originally published in the Christian Advocate and Journal and the Western Christian Advocate*, ed. George Peck. New York: Lane & Tippett, for the M. E. Church.

Smith, Timothy L. 1957. *Revivalism and Social Reform: American Protestantism on the Eve of the Civil War*. Nashville: Abingdon Press; pb. New York: Harper Torchbooks, 1965; Baltimore, MD: Johns Hopkins University Press, 1980.

———. 1974. The Holiness Crusade. In *History of American Methodism*, ed. Emory S. Bucke. Nashville, TN: Abingdon Press.

Smith, Page, ed. 1976. *Religious Origins of the American Revolution*. Missoula, Montana: Scholars Press for American Academy of Religion.

Smith, Robert D. 1990. John Wesley and Jonathan Edwards on Religious Experience: A Comparative Analysis. *Wesleyan Theological Journal* 25 (1): 130–146.

Smith, John E. 1993. *Jonathan Edwards: Puritan, Preacher, Philosopher*. Notre Dame, IN: University of Notre Dame Press.

Smith, John Howard. 2015. *The First Great Awakening: Redefining Religion in British America, 1725-1775*. Madison, NJ: Fairleigh Dickinson U.P.

Smith, James Ward, and A. Leland Jamison, eds. 1961. *The Shaping of American Religion. Volume 1: Religion in American Life*. Princeton, NJ: Princeton University Press.

Smylie, J.H. Autumn 1995. Madison and Witherspoon: Theological Roots of American Political Thought. *American Presbyterians* 73 (3): 155–164.

Sobel, Mechal. 1979a. *Trabelin' On: The Slave Journey to an Afro-Baptist Faith*. Westport, CT: Greenwood Press.

———. 1979b. 'They Can Never Prosper Together': Black and White Baptists in Nashville, Tennessee. *Tennessee Historical Quarterly* 38: p296–p307.

———. 1987. *The World They Made Together: Black and White Values in Eighteenth-Century Virginia*. Princeton, NJ: Princeton University Press.

Soderlund, Jean R. 1985. *Quakers and Slavery: A Divided Spirit*. Princeton, NJ: Princeton University Press.

———. 2013. John Woolman's Path to the Peaceable Kingdom: A Quaker in the British Empire. *Journal of American History* 99: 1217–1218.

Stauffer, Vernon. 1918. *New England and the Bavarian Illuminati*. New York: Columbia University Press.

Stavely, Keith W.F. 1987. *Puritan Legacies: Paradise Lost and the New England Tradition, 1630-1890*. Ithaca, NY: Cornell University Press.

Steele, Richard B. 1994. *Gracious Affection & True Virtue According to Jonathan Edwards & John Wesley*. Metuchen, NJ: Scarecrow.

———. Spring 1995. John Wesley's Synthesis of the Revival Practices of Jonathan Edwards, George Whitefield, Nicholas von Zinzendorf. *Wesleyan Theological Journal* 30 (1): 154–172.

Stein, Stephen J. 1975. An Apocalyptic Rationale for the American Revolution. *Early American Literature* 9: 211–225.

———. 1984. Transatlantic Extensions: Apocalyptic in Early New England. In *Apocalypse in English Renaissance Thought and Literature: Patterns, Antecedents, and Repercussions*, ed. Patrides and Wittreich. Manchester, UK: Manchester University Press.

———. 1992. *The Shaker Experience in America: A History of the United Society of Believers*, 1993. New Haven, CT: Yale University Press.

———., ed. 1996. *Jonathan Edwards's Writings; Text, Context, Interpretation*. Bloomington: Indiana University Press. Rvw by Amy Plantinga Pauw. Summer, 1998. *Journal of the History of the Behavioral Sciences* 34 (3): 338.

Stiles, Ezra. 1910. In *The Literary Diary of Ezra Stiles*, ed. Franklin B. Dexter. New York.

———. 1916. In *Extracts from the Itineraries and Other Miscellanies of Ezra Stiles*, ed. Franklin B. Dexter. New Haven, CT: Yale University Press.
Stoeffler, F. Ernest, ed. 1976. *Continental Pietism and Early American Christianity*. Eerdmans: Grand Rapids, MI.
Stoever, William K.B. 1978. *"A Faire and Easie Way to Heaven": Covenant Theology and Antinomianism in Early Massachusetts*. Middletown, CT: Wesleyan University Press.
Stone, Robert. March 26, 1998. "American Apostle," review of Kazin, *God and the American Writer*. *New York Review of Books* 45 (5): 25–28.
Stout, Harry S. 1975. Ethnicity: The Vital Center of Religion in America. *Ethnicity* 2: 2.
———. October 1977. "Religion, Communication, and the Ideological Origins of the American Revolution," *William and Mary Quarterly* 3rd ser. 34: 519–541.
———. 1986. *The New England Soul: Preaching and Religious Culture in Colonial New England*. New York: Oxford University Press.
———. 1991. *The Divine Dramatist: George Whitefield and the Rise of Modern Evangelism*. Library of Religious Biography. Grand Rapids, MI: William B. Eerdmans.
Stout, Harry S., and D.G. Hart, eds. 1997. *New Directions in American Religious History*, 1999. New York: Oxford University Press.
Stout, Harry S., and Peter Onuf. 1983–1984. James Davenport and the Great Awakening in New London. *Journal of American History* 70: 556–578.
Sutton, William R. Winter 1992. Benevolent Calvinism and the Moral Government of God: The Influence of Nathaniel W. Taylor on Revivalism in the Second Great Awakening. *Religion and American Culture: A Journal of Interpretation* 2: 24?.
———. 1998. *Journeymen for Jesus: Evangelical Artisans Confront Capitalism in Jacksonian Baltimore*. University Park: Pennsylvania State University Press.
Sweet, William Warren, ed. 1935. *Men of Zeal: The romance of American Methodist Beginnings*. Abingdon Press.
———, ed. 1952a. *Religion in the Development of American Culture, 1765-1840*. New York: Charles Scribner's Sons.
———, ed. 1952b. *Religion of the American Frontier. Vol. 2, The Presbyterians, 1783-1840: A Collection of Source Materials. ed. Religion of the American Frontier. Vol. 2, The Presbyterians, 1783-1840: A Collection of Source Materials. Religion in the Development of American Culture, 1765-1840*. New York: Charles Scribner's Sons; Reprint, Literary Licensing, LLC, 2012.
———, ed. 1961. *Methodism in American History (1933)*. Abingdon Press (1953 ed. revised).
———, ed. 1964a. *Religion of the American Frontier, 1783-1840. vol. 4, The Methodists, a Collection of Source Materials. (1946)*. New York: Cooper Square.
———, ed. 1964b. *Religion on the American Frontier: The Baptists, 1783-1830. (1931)*. New York: Cooper Square Publishers.
———, ed. 1964c. *Religion of the American Frontier*. Vol. 2, *The Presbyterians, 1783-1840: A Collection of Source Materials (1936)*.
———, ed. 1965. *Religion of the American Frontier*. Vol. 2, *The Presbyterians, 1783-1840: A Collection of Source Materials*. ed. *Religion of the American Frontier*. Vol. 2, *The Presbyterians, 1783-1840: A Collection of Source Materials. Revivalism in America: Its Origin, Growth and Decline (1944)*. Peter Smith.
———, ed. 2015. *Religion of the American Frontier*. Vol. 2, *The Presbyterians, 1783-1840: A Collection of Source Materials*. ed. *Religion of the American Frontier*. Vol. 2, *The Presbyterians, 1783-1840: A Collection of Source Materials. Religion in Colonial America (1942)*. Andesite Press.
———, ed. 2018. *Religion of the American Frontier*. Vol. 2, *The Presbyterians, 1783-1840: A Collection of Source Materials*. ed. *Religion of the American Frontier*. Vol. 2, *The Presbyterians, 1783-1840: A Collection of Source Materials*. ed. *Religion on the American Frontier, 1783-1850*. Vol. 3, *The Congregationalists: A Collection of Source Materials (1939)*. Classic Reprint.

Sweet, William Warren, and Erie Prior. 1955. *Virginia Methodism: A History*. Whittet & Shepperson.

Tanis, James. 1968. *Dutch Calvinistic Pietism in the Middle Colonies: A Study of the Life of Theodorus Jacobus Frelinghuysen*. The Hague.

Taves, Ann, ed. 1989. *Religion and Domestic Violence in Early New England: The Memoirs of Abigail Abbot Bailey*. Bloomington: Indiana University Press.

———, ed. 1999. *Fits, Trances, & Visions: Experiencing Religion and Explaining Experience from Wesley to James*. Princeton, NJ: Princeton University Press.

Tawney, R.H. 2015. *Religion and the Rise of Capitalism. [1926]*. New York: Verso.

Tennent, William. [Sr. 1673–1746]. *Sermons* MSS, 1706–1740, *William Tennent Papers* at the Presbyterian Historical Society, 425 Lombard Street, Philadelphia, Pennsylvania.

Tennent, Gilbert A.M. 1740. *The Danger of an Unconverted Ministry, Considered in a SERMON on Mark VI. 34. Preached at Nottingham, in Pennsylvania, March 8. Anno 1739*. Philadelphia: Benjamin Franklin.

Tennent, William. 1940. William Tennent's Sacramental Sermon. *Journal of Presbyterian History* 19: 149n.

Tennent, William, Jr. 1810. *Memoirs of the Life of William Tennent [...] An Account of His Being Three Days in a Trance and Apparently Living*. Trenton, NJ.

The Querists; or, An Extract of Sundry Passages Taken Out of Mr. Whitefield's Printed Sermons, Journals and Letters. 1740. Philadelphia.

The Querists. Part III. 1741. Philadelphia.

Thuesen, Peter. 2009. *Predestination: The American Career of a Contentious Doctrine*. New York: Oxford University Press.

Tigert, John James. 1898. *The making of Methodism: studies in the genesis of institutions*. Nashville, TN: Pub. House of the Methodist Episcopal Church, South.

Tipton, Baird. 1975. How can the religious experience of the past be recovered? The examples of Puritanism and Pietism. *Journal of the American Academy of Religion* 43 (4): 695–707.

Tolles, Frederick B. 1960. Quietism Versus Enthusiasm: The Philadelphia Quakers and the Great Awakening. In *Pennsylvania Magazine of History 69(1945), p26–49; and as Ch6 in Quakers and the Atlantic Culture*. New York: Macmillan.

Torbet, Robert G. 1963. *History of the Baptists* (Revised ed.). Valley Forge, PA: Judson Press.

Toulouse, Teresa. 1987. *The Art of Prophesying: New England Sermons and the Shaping of Belief. Athens*. University of Georgia Press.

Townsend, Leah. 2007. *South Carolina Baptists, 1670-1805 (1935)*. Clearfield.

Tracy, Patricia J. 1980. *Jonathan Edwards, Pastor: Religion and Society in Eighteenth-Century Northampton*. New York.

Tracy, Joseph. 2019 *The Great Awakening: A History of the Revival of Religion in the Time of Edwards and Whitefield.* (Boston, 1841) Banner of Truth, 2019; Kindle Edition.

Trinterud, Leonard J. 1949. *The Forming of an American Tradition: A Reexamination of Colonial Presbyterianism*. Philadelphia.

Truth, Sojourner. 1991. *Narrative of Sojourner Truth, A Bondswoman of Olden Time, with a History of Her Labors and Correspondance Drawn from Her "Book of Life" (1850)*. New York: Oxford University Press.

Tull, James C. 1973. *Shapers of Baptist Thought*. Valley Forge, PA: Judson Press.

Tuveson, Ernest Lee. 1968. *Redeemer Nation*. Chicago: University of Chicago Press.

Tweed, Thomas A. ed. 1997. *Retelling U.S. Religious History*. Berkeley: University of California Press, pb.

Valeri, Mark. 1994. *Law and Providence in Joseph Bellamy's New England: The Origins of the New Divinity in Revolutionary America*. New York: Oxford University Press. (vs Haroutunian).

VanAnglin, R.P. 1993. *The New England Milton: Literary Reception and Cultural Authority in the Early Republic*. Pennsylvania State University Press.

Vann, Richard T. 1969. *The Social Development of English Quakerism, 1655-1755*. Cambridge, MA.

Vaughan, Alden T., ed. 1997. *The Puritan Tradition in America, 1620-1730*. University Press of New England.

Wainwright, William J. 1995. *Reason and the Heart: A prolegomenon to a critique of passional reason*. Ithaca, NY: Cornell University Press. (Edwards).

Waldrep, Christopher. June 1994. The Making of a Border State Society: James McGready, the Great Revival, and the Prosecution of Profanity in Kentucky. *American Historical Review* 99 (3).

Wallace, Dewey D., Jr. 1982. *Puritans and Predestination: Grace in English Protestant Theology, 1525-1695*. Chapel Hill, NC: University of North Carolina Press.

Walvin, James. 1998. *The Quakers: Money and Morals*. North Pomfret, VT: John Murray/ Trafalgar Square.

Ward, W[illiam] R[eginald]. 1991-1992. *The Protestant Evangelical Awakening*. Cambridge: Cambridge University Press.

———. 2006. *Early Evangelicalism: A Global Intellectual History, 1670-1789*. Cambridge: Cambridge University Press.

Warfield, Benjamin B. Edwards and the New England Theology. In *The Works of Benjamin B. Warfield*. Vol. IX: *Studies in Theology*.

Warner, Michael, ed. 1999. *American Sermons: The Pilgrims to Martin Luther King, Jr*. New York: Library of America.

Washington, Joseph Reed, Jr. 1988. *Puritan Race Virtue, Vice, and Values 1620-1820*. New York: Peter Lang.

Weber, Donald. 1988. *Rhetoric and History in Revolutionary New England*. New York: Oxford University Press.

Weber, Max. 2002. *The Protestant Ethic and the Spirit of Capitalism [1904–05]: and Other Writings*. Penguin.

Webster, Richard. 2004. *A History of the Presbyterian Church in America: From Its Origin Until the Year 1760, with Biographical Sketches of Its Early Ministers*. (1857) repr. Tentmaker Publications.

Weir, David A. 1990. *The Origins of the Federal Theology in Sixteenth-Century Reformation Thought*. New York: Clarendon Press of Oxford University Press.

Wells, Colin. April 2002. *The Devil and Doctor Dwight: Satire and Theology in the Early American Republic*. Chapel Hill: University of North Carolina Press.

Werner, Julia Stewart. 1984. *The Primitive Methodist Connexion: Its Background and Early History*. Madison: University of Wisconsin Press.

Wesley, John. 1755. *The Distinguishing Marks of a Work of the Spirit of God. Extracted from Mr. Edwards. Minister of Northampton, in New-England [edited] By John Wesley. London: S. Mason, 1742; Glasgow: R. Smith, 1742; London: William Strahan, 1744; 2nd ed.* London: Henry Cock.

Westerkamp, Marilyn J. 1988. *Triumph of the Laity: Scots-Irish Piety and the Great Awakening, 1625-1760*. New York: Oxford University Press.

———. 1999. *Women and Religion in Early America, 1600-1850: The Puritan and Evangelical Traditions. Christianity and Society in the Modern World*. London and New York: Routledge.

White, Eugene E. 1972. *Puritan Rhetoric: The Issue of Emotion in Religion*. Carbondale, IL: Southern Illinois University Press, pb 2009.

White, Henry Alexander. 2000. *Southern Presbyterian Leaders: 1683-1911*. Edinburgh: Banner of Truth Trust.

Wigger, John H. 1997–1998. *Taking Heaven by Storm: Methodism and the Rise of Popular Christianity in America. Religion in America Series*. New York/Oxford: Oxford University Press.

Williams, William H. 1984. *The Garden of American Methodism: The Delmarva Peninsula, 1769-1820*. Wilmington, DE.

Williams, Peter W. 1989. *Popular Religion in America: Symbolic Change and the Modernization Process in Historical Perspective*. Champaign, IL: University of Illinois Press.

———. 2001. *America's Religions: From Their Origins to the Twenty-First Century*. Urbana/ Chicago: University of Illinois Press.

Williams, Peter W., and Charles H. Lippy, eds. *Encyclopedia of the American Religious Experience*.

Wilson, John F. 1986. *Church and State in America: A Bibliographical Guide. Vol. 1: The Colonial and Early National Periods*. Westport, CT: Greenwood Press.

———. 1989. Religion, Government, and Power in the New American Nation. In *Religion and American Politics: From the Colonial Period to the 1980s*, ed. Noll, 77–91. New York: Oxford University Press.

Wind, James P., and James W. Lewis, eds. 1995. *American Congregations. 2v*. Chicago: University of Chicago Press.

Winiarski, Douglas L. March 2017, February 2019. *Darkness Falls on the Land of Light: Experiencing Religious Awakenings in Eighteenth-Century New England*. Chapel Hill: Omohundro Institute of Early American History and Culture/University of North Carolina Press.

Winthrop, John. 1997. *Journal. 3v*. Cambridge, MA: Harvard University Press.

Woodbridge, F.J.E. 1904. Jonathan Edwards. *The Philosophical Review* 13: 405.

Woodmason, Charles. 1953. In *The Carolina Backcountry on the Eve of the Revolution: The Journal and Other Writings of Charles Woodmason, Anglican Itinerant*, ed. Richard J. Hooker. Chapel Hill, NC: University of North Carolina Press.

Woolverton, John F. 1984. *Colonial Anglicanism in North America*. Detroit: Wayne State University Press.

Wright, Charles Conrad. 1976. *The Beginnings of Unitarianism in America (1955)*. Archon Books.

Yarborough, Stephen R., and John C. Adams. 1993. *Delightful Conviction: Jonathan Edwards and the Rhetoric of Conversion*. Westport, CT: Greenwood Press.

Yeo, Ray S. 2016. 2. Spiritual Perception and the theological psychology of converting grace. In *Renewing Spiritual Perception with Jonathan Edwards: Contemporary Philosophy and the Theological Psychology*, 13ff. New York: Routledge.

Youngs, J., and T. William. 1976. *God's Messengers: Religious Leadership in Colonial New England, 1700-1750*. Baltimore.

Zakai, Avihu. 1992. *Exile and Kingdom: History and Apocalypse in the Puritan Migration to America*. New York: Cambridge University Press.

Zaret, David. 1985. *The Heavenly Contract: Ideology and Organization in Pre-Revolutionary Puritanism*. Chicago: University of Chicago Press.

Ziff, Larzer. 1973. *Puritanism in America: New Culture in a New World*. New York: Viking Press; pb 1974.

Zuckerman, Michael. 1978. *Peacable Kingdoms: New England Towns in the Eighteenth Century (1970)*. New York: W. W. Norton pb.

Zwelling, Shomer S. Fall 1986. Robert Carter's Journey: From Colonial Patriarch to New Nation Mystic. *American Quarterly* 38: 613–636.

Chapter 5
The Crucible of the Counter-Enlightenment, III

Abstract John Wesley, George Whitefield, Methodism, and the Transatlantic Awakening. Augustinians and Arminians.

The largest single evangelical-ecstatic movement in the English-speaking world was led and organized by John Wesley (1704–1791). That could not have been predicted. He had been ordained priest by ancient ritual in a government-established church that banned itinerant preaching out of doors or inside of churches, and had become suspicious of "enthusiasm" in the Enlightened eighteenth century. The Anglican Bishop of London wrote warily, in the year of Wesley's conversion, that Enthusiasm was "A strong persuasion on the mind of persons that they are guided, in an extraordinary manner, by immediate impressions and impulses of the Spirit of God. And this is owing chiefly to the want of distinguishing aright between the ordinary and extraordinary operations of the Holy Spirit."[1] Wesley admitted that others preached grace and inspired ecstasy better than he did. Besides, it was his singular and edifying fate to experience his "conversion" not before but *after* he went out to convert others. When he first went soul-saving in 1735 at the edge of European empire in America, Jonathan Edwards was preaching awakening in New England, but Wesley had yet to be infused with enthusiasm, and had yet to receive the "grace" so longed for by Protestant Christians in the two centuries since Luther.

Wesley's trip to James Oglethorpe's evangelical colony of Georgia from 1735 to 1737 had been something of a surprise to his father, the parish priest of Epworth, Lincolnshire, who had groomed him from his youth to secure a high post in the Church of England, the officially established church which had been Protestant since Henry VIII but was governed by royal appointees. The Reverend Samuel Wesley's 15th child, had been a fellow and lecturer at the bastion of Anglican conservatism where C of E priests were trained—Oxford University. He had been ordained in 1728, serving 2 years as his father's assistant minister for Epworth, and

[1] Edmund Gibson, Bishop of London, "Lukewarmness and Enthusiasm," pastoral letter published 1739, (in James Paterson Gledstone, *The Life and Travels of George Whitefield, M.A.* London: Longmans, Green, 1871, p. 162, quoted in Knox, *Enthusiasm.* from the 1900 edition of Gledstone).

W. R. Everdell, *The Evangelical Counter-Enlightenment*, Boston Studies in Philosophy, Religion and Public Life 9,
https://doi.org/10.1007/978-3-030-69762-4_5

he had just preached a prize sermon series at Oxford.[2] Late in 1734, at the age of 31, he was offered a good "living" as his father's successor at Epworth, where he had been born, to boost him on a comfortable and eventually prestigious clerical career; but he turned it down, writing to his father a letter in which the 16th of 26 numbered paragraphs reads:

> If you say, "The love of the people of Epworth" to me "may balance these advantages," I ask, How long will it last? Only till I come to tell them plainly that their deeds are evil, and particularly to apply that general sentence, to say to each, Thou art the man![3]

John Wesley not only took his duties seriously, and had enough fair-mindedness to apply to himself the categories of evildoing he would find in others, he also took seriously the doctrines of Protestant Christianity: God had given to sinful man in his son Jesus, not only a model of sinlessness, but also a means of avoiding eternal punishment, and to some the grace to believe it. Indeed, John Wesley took everything seriously, and seems to have done so until the end of his life. Gravity came naturally to him even in youth, familiarity only when he had grown old, and though he was capable of wit, he was very chary of indulging in it. Like his antireligious contemporary Thomas Jefferson, he had a solemnity quite immune to the delights of paradox and seems never to have been heard to laugh at himself. In this leader of thousands of ecstatics, decorum would chronically trump ecstasy.

Returning to Oxford to take up his fellowship, John Wesley found that his brother Charles had founded a small society of young Oxfordians who were trying to take Christianity seriously in an Enlightenment college town. The Godly Club met from 6 a.m. to 9, prayed on the hour, fasted 3 days a week, took Communion every Sunday, distributed part of their allowances as alms, and visited people who were sick and in prison. John Wesley unhesitatingly joined and inevitably came to lead the group. Devout and practicing young male Christians without titles at establishment Oxford in the eighteenth-century were automatically suspected of ill breeding, and possibly even Dissent. (Dissenters were members of the Puritan Protestant Christian denominations, Presbyterian and Congregational, and their offshoots like Baptist and Quaker, which flourished in Scotland and North America, but were disenfranchised in England because they had spearheaded the rebellion that beheaded King Charles I in the seventeenth century.) Indeed, Oxford wits had a lot of fun with Wesley's "little society" mockingly calling it "The Holy Club," the "Sacramentarians," "The Enthusiasts or The Reforming Club" or "Methodist and Supererogation Men, and so on."[4] Their behavior was socially beneath them. If the

---

[2] John Wesley, "The Circumcision of the Heart," on Romans 2:29, the third of these university sermons, was preached on January 1, 1733, at St. Mary's, Oxford (#17 in John Wesley, *Works*. v1, ed.. Outler, 1984.

[3] John Wesley to the Rev. Samuel Wesley, Sr., in John Wesley, *Works*. 1984, v19, p. 39–45, p. 43. Original publication: John Wesley, *An Extract of the Rev'd Mr John Wesley's Journal from August 12, 1738, To Nov. 1, 1739*. Bristol: Felix Farley, 1742. See also: *The Works of John Wesley*. v25, *Letters I*. (1721–1739), ed. Frank Baker. Nashville, TN: Abingdon Press, 1984, p. 397–409.

[4] John Wesley to Richard Morgan, 18 Oct, 1732, addition of 1 Dec, 1732, in Wesley, "The Letters of John Wesley". The Wesley Center Online. Accessed 30 July, 2014.

term had existed, the Oxford establishment would certainly have been pleased to call "The Holy Club" "counter-enlightened." Not that the members were mystics or visionaries; they reported no ecstasy, no encounter with the divine beyond prayer, and very little disappointment about that lack. Wesley, even more than his fellow Holy Clubmen, also took theological doctrines seriously. One doctrine in particular bothered Wesley to near obsession, and that was the doctrine of grace, with its long and tortuous history since Paul and Augustine. How could a sinner be saved from Hell if he or she continued to offend God by sinning? Could you really be saved by God by simply believing that you were saved (as Luther had deduced from *Romans*)? And—perhaps the hardest question—how could you tell?

They were also ambitious. Around 1735, they began to conclude that "doing good" and loving one's neighbor (and possibly even the pursuit of grace) must require not only the reformation of one's own life and those of a few friends, but reforming the whole Christian establishment, and bringing the promise of salvation to as many people as possible who were without it. Whether you were saved yourself, whether your doing of good was or was not evidence of grace, could remain a private matter. Hence Wesley's decision to preach to the natives and the settlers in the newly founded North American English colony of Georgia.

Aboard ship in October, 1735, heading for Georgia with his recently ordained brother Charles, who was secretary to Georgia's founder Oglethorpe, John Wesley had encountered Zinzendorf's Herrnhuter Moravians for the first time. Led by the Moravian stalwart, David Nitschmann, they were on a mission to the same colony—Savannah was not to be settled without them. Learning German to speak with them, Wesley was impressed by their piety, and even more impressed by their conviction. Among Nitschmann's Moravians there seemed to be no doubters; this was a "society" of people who knew they were saved.

> At seven I went to the Germans. I had long before observed the great seriousness of their behavior. Of their humility they had given a continual proof, by performing those servile offices for the other passengers which none of the English would undertake [...] saying "it was good for their proud hearts," and "their loving Savior had done more for them." [...] no complaint was found in their mouth. [...] In the midst of the psalm wherewith their service began, wherein we were mentioning the power of God, the sea broke over, split the mainsail in pieces, covered the ship, and poured in between the decks, as if the great deep had already swallowed us up. A terrible screaming began among the English. The Germans looked up, and without intermission calmly sang on. I asked one of them afterwards, "Was you not afraid?" He answered, "I thank God, no." I asked, "But were not your women and children afraid?" He replied mildly, "No, our women and children are not afraid to die."[5]

Once in Georgia, Wesley took over the "cure" of new Church of England parishes in Savannah and Frederica and promptly separated out from them the "little societies," conventicles of the most earnest salvation seekers that he had learned to join and found at Oxford and whose informal developing liturgy reflected Moravian and

[5] John Wesley, *Journal* (25 January, 1736), v1, p. 142ff, in G. W. Forell, tr. & ed. *Zinzendorf: Nine Public Lectures on Important Subjects in Religion Preached in Fetter Lane Chapel in London in the Year 1746* (Iowa City: University of Iowa Press, 1973; Eugene, OR: Wipf and Stock, 1998), p. x.

earlier Pietist practices. His contact with the Moravians continued and so did his envious admiration of them, especially after he met their American bishop, August Spangenberg, whom Zinzendorf had sent to oversee the new Moravian community at Savannah. Georgia did not yet permit slavery by law, so Wesley made a mission trip to South Carolina, where he converted slaveowners and—with their permission—their slaves, whose ignorance of Christian redemption distressed him somewhat more than their enslavement did.

His mission still looked fairly conventional to contemporaries. Wesley's small meetings of the converted outside of churches—conventicles—were not permitted by the established Church of England, but they had been well known and sometimes tolerated from Puritan and Pietist times.[6] Outdoor mass confession and communion services, however, were not so old. They had been pioneered by the Presbyterian Church of Scotland a hundred years before.[7] In the Connecticut Valley in New England, centering on Jonathan Edwards's Northampton, there had already been news of outbreaks of loud public enthusiasm and fervor among young Congregationals[8] in December, 1734, which later historians would call the "Little Awakening." In England, a Church of England minister named Daniel Rowland and one of his parishioners, Howell Harris, had had simultaneous conversion experiences and begun outdoor itinerant preaching in 1735.[9] Outdoor mass conversions (later called "revivals" when they had ceased being novel), however, were too new and unorthodox for John Wesley to try them in Georgia in 1735. Among the

[6] In May–June, 1736, John Wesley gathered "serious" parishioners in Frederica, Georgia, as he had in Savannah, into a "sort of little society" meeting once or twice a week. It is now called the second American Methodist society, and was held by Wesley later to be one of the three "beginnings of Methodism." It was largely borrowed from Moravian practice. (in Sylvia R. Frey & Betty Wood, *Come Shouting to Zion: African American Protestantism in the American South and British Caribbean to 1830* (Chapel Hill: U. of North Carolina Press, 1998), p. 88).

[7] The best work on this important Scottish contribution to the rise of Christian evangelicalism is Leigh Eric Schmidt, *Holy Fairs: Scottish Communions and American Revivals in the Early Modern Period* (Princeton, 1989) 2nd ed., pb, Grand Rapids, MI: Eerdmans, 2001. Revival in Scotland had started long before George Whitefield preached in Scotland in 1741. Scholars have added information about much earlier outdoor confession and communion services among the Scots-Irish in northern Ireland in the 1620s. After one in 1625, a minister wrote: "I have seen them myself stricken, and swoon with the Word—yes. A dozen in one day carried out of doors as dead, so marvelous was the power of God smiting their hearts for sin, condemning and killing; and some of these were none of the weaker sex or sprit, but indeed some of the boldest spirits." (quoted in Marilyn J. Westerkamp, "Enthusiastic Piety—From Scots-Irish Revivals to the Great Awakening," 70, in: Philip R. Vandermcer, and Robert P. Swierenga (Eds.) *Belief and Behavior: Essays in the New Religious History* (New Brunswick: Rutgers University Press, [c.1991], in William L. De Arteaga (an "Anglican Pentecostal"), "The Lord's Supper and Revival: The Scottish example," 15 November, 2013. http://anglicalpentecostal.blogspot.com/2013/11/the-lords-supper-and-revival-scottish.html.

[8] "Congregational" was the Dissenter established (state) church of Massachusetts and Connecticut, named for its decentralized form of church government.

[9] Isabel Rivers, "Review Essay: Writing the History of Early Evangelicalism," *History of European Ideas* 35:1(March, 2009), p. 106.

unconverted of another continent, Wesley was still preaching, as it were, indoors and to the choir.

Wesley's reasonableness, reminiscent of the English Enlightenment moralist Shaftesbury, leaps from the journals he obsessively kept and often published.[10] So does his social life, with its many relationships, seldom heated. The three thwarted courtships of the founder of Methodism provided Ronald Knox's anti-Methodist masterpiece, *Enthusiasm* with more than enough material to make a fool of him. Wesley's first love, Sophia Hopkey, was 18, and he was 23, when he met her in 1735 on the ship coming over to America. He taught her French and read to her—from books of theology and church history. He never did get around to telling her that he loved her because one of the Moravian ministers for whom young Wesley had so much respect staged what we would now call an intervention and convinced Wesley that it was "not God's will for him."[11] Sophia responded by breaking up with him and declaring that she would never marry. Sensibly, she got engaged within the year, to which Wesley reacted by sending her a solemn letter "taxing her with inconsistency," and banning her from Communion in his parish. Sophia and her new husband replied with a lawsuit; a mistrial resulted; and at about this time Wesley felt God's call to return to England.

In December, 1737, knowing his mission was nearly over, he wrote to a younger and more enthusiastic minister he knew back in England, George Whitefield (1714–1770), a member of the Oxford "Holy Club," suggesting that he might be the one to come overseas and take on the task of saving American souls (and implying he might do a better job than Wesley had). "What if thou art the man, Mr. Whitefield?" he ended the letter. Whitefield had just graduated from Oxford as a lowly "servitor" and dated his access of grace (conversion) to a prayer (Jesus's "I thirst!") answered in his rooms on campus during a long fast in 1735.[12] He had graduated from Oxford

---

[10] Cf. [Anthony Ashley Cooper, 3rd Earl of Shaftesbury], *Characteristicks of Men, Manners, Opinions, Times*, 1711, 1713, 1732, 1737. Shaftesbury's *A Letter concerning Enthusiasm to Lord Somers*, datelined September, 1707, was published anonymously in 1708, and again in *Characteristicks*, 1711, 1713, 1732 and 1737. A classic of the English Enlightenment, it had pointed out the dangers of "enthusiasm" by arguing that "Inspiration is a real feeling of the Divine Presence, and Enthusiasm a false one," and that nevertheless there were such things as "*Enthusiastical atheists*." Very lukewarm, if not cool. Indeed this and other works of Shaftesbury have a faint echo in the way international English has preserved and used the American jazz term, "cool."

[11] Ronald A. Knox, *Enthusiasm: A Chapter in the History of Religion, With Special Reference to the seventeenth and eighteenth centuries* (1949), NY: Oxford U.P. Galaxy pb, 1961, p. 445.

[12] "One Day, perceiving an uncommon Drought and a disagreeable Clamminess in my Mouth, and using Things to allay my Thirst, but in vain, it was suggested to me, that when Jesus Christ cried out, "I thirst," his Sufferings were near at an End. Upon which, I cast myself down on the Bed, crying out, I thirst! I thirst!—Soon after this, I found and felt in myself that I was delivered from the Burden that had so heavily oppressed me! The Spirit of Mourning was taken from me, and I knew what it was truly to rejoice in God my Saviour, and, for some Time, could not avoid singing Psalms wherever I was" (Whitefield, *Journals* first edition v2.qxp: *Complete Journals* 14 04 2009 Quinta Press pdf. This is the 1740 version. 1756 is quite different, omitting the thirsting). Whitefield never forgot the event. "I know the place.... Whenever I go to Oxford, I cannot help running to the spot where Jesus Christ first revealed himself to me and gave me the new birth. (in "George Whitefield," *Christian Classics Ethereal Library*. http://www.ccel.org/ccel/whitefield, 5 Aug 14).

and given his first sermon in Gloucester in June, 1736,[13] only a year before Wesley's invitation; but his response to Wesley was immediate: "My heart leaped within me, and, as it were, echoed to the call."[14] In fact Whitefield's ship set sail for America from the English port of Deal on 31 January, 1737–38, just half a day before Wesley's homebound ship dropped anchor in the same harbor on the first day of February. As it turned out, Whitefield's mission to America, unlike Wesley's was to be epically successful, and Wesley's in England, thanks to Whitefield's example, would be no less so.

By the time he had returned to England in 1737–1738, John Wesley was convinced that although saving souls might well be his vocation, he was still not saved himself. The grace-contented Moravians kept turning up. Zinzendorf himself was preaching in Berlin in early 1738, but he had been in London in 1737 discussing relations with the Church of England, and Zinzendorf's appointee, Bishop Peter Böhler, a converted Moravian destined for America, was still at Oxford. When John Wesley paid a visit to his brother Charles who was recovering from a lung infection, he encountered Böhler at Charles's bedside, and proceeded to solicit his instruction.

> I found my brother at Oxford recovering from his pleurisy, and with him Peter Böhler, by whom (in the hand of the great God) I was, on Sunday the 5th, clearly convinced of unbelief, of the want of faith whereby alone we are saved. Immediately it struck into my mind, "Leave off preaching. How can you preach to others, who have no faith yourself?" I asked Böhler whether he thought I should leave it off or not. He answered, "By no means." I asked, "But what can I preach?" He said, "Preach faith till you have it; and then, because you have it, you will preach faith."[15]

By his own account he was feeling particularly sinful and unregenerate in the months after his first mission and those encounters with so many saved Moravians. On May 24, 1738 he went to a meeting of one of his "little societies" of salvation-seeking English in a Moravian conventicle in London:

> In the evening, I went very unwilling to a society in Aldersgate Street where one was reading Luther's "Preface" to the *Epistle to the Romans*. About a quarter before nine, while he was describing the change which God works in the heart through faith in Christ, I felt my heart strangely warmed. I felt that I did trust in Christ, Christ alone for salvation, and an assurance was given me, that he had taken away my sins, even mine, and saved me from the law of sin and death.[16]

By now we should know why the reading had to be from Martin Luther, and that the piece being read had to be Luther's reaction to Paul's letter to the Romans, where

---

[13] Whitefield remembered his maiden sermon as a success: "Some few mocked; but most for the present seemed struck: and I have since heard, that a complaint had been made to the Bishop, that I drove fifteen mad." —Whitefield, *George Whitefield's Journal*, in Jerome Dean Mahaffey, *The Accidental Revolutionary: George Whitefield and the Creation of America* (Waco, TX: Baylor University Press, 2011), p. 15.

[14] The exchange is quoted in Frey & Wood, *Come Shouting to Zion* (Chapel Hill: U. of North Carolina Press, 1998), p. 91.

[15] John Wesley, *Journal*, v1, p. 442, in Forell, ed., p. xi.

[16] John Wesley, *Journal*, 24 May, 1738.

that hitherto unforgivable sixteenth-century monk had made his first discovery of the Protestant core concept of unearned and undeserved grace–"justification by faith." Compared to Luther's or the BESHT's, conversion, however, Wesley's produced no fireworks. It "warmed," in his words, but it did not burn. It was not really a vision, and it did not qualify as a mystic encounter with the divine; but neither, it seems clear, was it imposture. And if it was self-delusion, it was certainly comprehensive. Wesley himself never doubted it. In October he began taking notes on Edwards's *A Faithful Narrative*, with its case studies of saving grace; and at 3:00 in the morning on the first of January, 1738–1739, he did, at last, have an ecstatic experience with a small group of fellow worshipers at a Moravian "love-feast," in Fetter Lane, one which he would later speak of as an indication that he was not only saved but on the road to "perfection."[17] It all provided the conviction necessary for the pioneer of English evangelical Christianity to undertake what eventually amounted to the largest "conversion" effort in the history of the English-speaking world—an effort that never flagged until Wesley's death in 1791 at the age of 87.

Indeed, it may well be that what makes sense of John Wesley's extraordinary success, more conversions of others and a larger organization of followers than any other single evangelical of his time, is his immunity from ecstasy. At the ecstatic Fetter Lane conventicle on January 1, 1738–1739, Wesley reported that "many cried out [...] and many fell to the ground," but these "many"s do not include Wesley. Indefatigable commitment, he had, even doggedness, but it was his congregants, not he, who displayed what the Enlightenment stigmatized as "enthusiasm" in England or "fanatisme" in France[18] Wesley became both the preacher and the organizer of the spreading of ecstasy and "new birth" in the English-speaking world; but so far from being the sectarian "enthusiast" he was accused of being by everyone from the Oxford wits to the Bishop of London, the founder of Methodism was as deliberate, reasonable and empirical as his Enlightenment contemporaries, David Hume, Adam Smith, Ben Franklin and Voltaire. Sentimental but unmystical, he often seems Victorian before Victoria.[19] "Methodist" is the putdown he early accepted as the

[17] On January 1, 1739, John Wesley wrote that he, "Mr. Hall, Kinchin, Ingham, Whitefield, Hutchins, and my brother Charles, were present at our love-feast in Fetter Lane, with about 60 of our brethren. About three in the morning, as we were continuing instant in prayer, the power of God came mightily upon us, inasmuch that many cried out for exceeding joy, and many fell to the ground. As soon as we recovered a little from that awe and amazement at the presence of His Majesty, we broke out with one voice, "We praise thee, O God; we acknowledge thee to be the Lord." (John Wesley, *Journal*, in *Works*, ed., Outler, v1, p. 170).

[18] [Anthony Ashley Cooper, 3rd Earl of Shaftesbury], *A Letter concerning Enthusiasm to Lord Somers*, London, 1708, and in *Characteristicks*, 1711, 1713, 1732 and 1737.

[19] Wesley seemed less of an enthusiast than his increasingly large band of followers, but it is notable that what Anglican Bishop Gibson of London wrote in 1738 about "Enthusiasm" arising from "extraordinary operations of the Holy Spirit" was more characteristic of 18th-century Methodism than later expressions. That was especially true in America, where one estimate finds that about "one-third" of the first generation of Mormon converts (that would include Brigham Young and Joseph Smith himself), had become "enthusiastic" Methodists not long before accepting the supernaturalistic Mormon revelation of the Golden Plates. (Christopher Jones, "'It's Like Methodism, Only More': Mormon Conversion and Narratives of the Great Apostasy," *Patheos*, February 4, 2013.https://www.patheos.com/blogs/peculiarpeople/2013/02/its-like-methodism-only-more-mormon-conversion-and-narratives-of-the-great-apostasy/).

Fig. 5.1 George Whitefield in "Geneva" gown and preaching bands/tabs. His crossed eye is deemphasized. Portrait by John Russell, 1745–1806, https://commons.wikimedia.org/w/index.php?curid=5977749

name of his movement, and "methodical" seems an almost ideal word for the man who became the peerless indefatigable administrator of an ever-growing organization of societies, official and unofficial, which were preached to indoors and out by an ever-increasing cadre of itinerant circuit-riding ministers in every part of Britain and North America.

But this is to reckon without Whitefield. George Whitefield proved to be a natural, the member of the Holy Club who could reach the most people at one time. That reach was estimated by his friend, Benjamin Franklin, at over 20,000 people, for a sermon Whitefield preached outdoors in Philadelphia, probably on 28 November, 1739, from the center of a circle whose radius was 1/10 of a mile.[20] Of course, Franklin was also Whitefield's publisher, and might have exaggerated; but Whitefield, a small man with permanently crossed eyes, was a phenomenon who punched far above his weight. Short and odd-looking he might be, but his voice and dramatic range were inimitable, and by most accounts he was the most sensational preacher of his generation, or even the century.[21] He did not invent extemporaneous open-air preaching (Saint Francis of Assisi had done a lot of it back in the thirteenth century and the more radical Protestants had followed suit) but he made himself an expert at it at a time when Wesley, the leader of the Holy Club, was still in Georgia, preaching to small groups under solid roofs (like most other Protestant ministers) and tutoring Sophia Hopkey.

Returned from his first trip to America in early 1739, Whitefield set out for Bristol and immediately held a crowd of 4000 for a sermon preached in the fields. What he preached was the necessity of enthusiasm, a sign of grace.[22] Wesley went

[20] Franklin, in his very Enlightened fashion, measured it, famously reporting in his *Autobiography*, that when Whitefield "preach'd one Evening from the Top of the Court House Steps, which are in the middle of Market Street, and on the West Side of Second Street which crosses it at right angles. Both Streets were fill'd with his Hearers to a considerable Distance. Being among the hindmost in Market Street, I had the Curiosity to learn how far he could be heard, by retiring backwards down the Street towards the River; and I found his Voice distinct till I came near Front Street, when some Noise in that Street, obscur'd it. Imagining then a Semicircle, of which my Distance should be the Radius, and that it were fill'd with Auditors, to each of whom I allow'd two square feet, I computed that he might well be heard by more than Thirty Thousand. This reconcil'd me to the Newspaper Accounts of his having preach'd to 25,000 People in the Fields, and to the ancient Histories of Generals haranguing whole Armies, of which I had sometimes doubted." (Franklin, *Autobiography* in *Writings*, Library of America, 1987. p. 1408–1409).

[21] Franklin published several of Whitefield's sermons, adjusting their titles to American thinking, and even had his account of his voyage ready soon after Whitefield arrived in 1739: Whitefield, *A Journal of a Voyage from Gibraltar to Georgia*, Philadelphia: Franklin, 1739. Whitefield's sermon "On Regeneration" (originally "The Nature and Necessity of Our New Birth in Christ Jesus," 1737), appeared in *Sermons on Various Subjects*, v1, Philadelphia: Franklin, 1740. Frank Lambert's fine study of George Whitefield (*"Pedlar in Divinity" George Whitefield and the Transatlantic Revivals, 1737–1770*. Princeton, NJ: Princeton University Press, 1993) centers on the printing and sale of sermons and tracts in partnership with Franklin. That rather secular business was very successful, but does not, even for Lambert, qualify as Whitefield's main motive for preaching salvation across British America.

[22] On 24 June, 1739, Whitefield preached a sermon published as "An Exhortation to the People of God not to be discouraged in their Way, by the Scoffs and Contempt of wicked Men." It is an uncompromising argument for ecstatic religious experience, as this passage makes clear: "The letter-learned Scribes and Pharisees of this day, look on us as madmen and enthusiasts; but though they make so much noise about the world enthusiast, it means no more than this, one in God; and what Christian can say, he is not in God, and God in him? And if this is to be an enthusiast, God grant I may be more and more so; if we being in Christ, and Christ in us, makes us enthusiasts. I would to God we were all more and more enthusiasts." (Whitefield, "Sermon 56" in *The Works of the Reverend George Whitefield* [microform]. Published by E. and C. Dilly, 1771–1772, London.)

out to Bath and Bristol, where he observed Whitefield preaching to the Kingswood miners on April 1. Surprised, impressed (and possibly envious), he fell back on the prejudice of a Church-of-England curate.

> I could scarce reconcile myself at first to this strange way of preaching in the fields, of which he set an example on Sunday, having been all my life (till very lately) so tenacious of every point relating to decency and order that I should have thought the saving of souls almost a sin if it had not been done in a church.[23]

Whitefield invited Wesley to replace him as the revival preacher after he should go back to America again, but Wesley demurred. "The idea was repugnant to the correct and proper presbyter of the Church of England."[24] But the very next day, despite his misgivings, Wesley tried open-air preaching for himself, to what he estimated were over 2000 hearers. This Bristol sermon became the first of what were to be some 50,000 such appearances, and Wesley never looked back. Though he was not Whitefield, and for a long time Whitefield's crowds remained larger,[25] Wesley was immediately successful, writing in his published journal and to friends in April that he had had audiences of 2000, 2500 and eventually 6–7000. "Many," he reported were "convinced." On April 17, he preached indoors, but there were so many in the audience that the floor collapsed. In May he was causing hearers to fall

[23] John Wesley, *Journal*, in *Works*, 1984, v19, p. 46.

[24] He continued with the same phrases: "The idea was repugnant to the correct and proper presbyter of the Church of England, who declared that he had not been so tenacious of every point relating to decency and order, that I should have thought the saving of souls almost a sin if it had not been done in a church." (John Wesley, *Journal*, March 31, 1739, in *Works*, v2, *Sermons II–IV* ed. Outler, 1984, p. 167).

[25] Wesley wrote from Bristol on 2 April, 1739, to his Moravian fellow-worshiper, James Hutton, who was also Whitefield's pubisher: "At eight our dear brother, Whitefield expounded in Weavers' Hall to about a thousand souls; on Sunday morning to six or seven thousand at the Bowling Green; at noon to much the same number at Hanham Mount; and at five to, I believe, thirty thousand from a little mount on Rose Green. At one to-day he left Bristol. I am straitened for time. Pray ye, my dear brethren, that some portion of his spirit may be given to

"Your poor, weak brother.

"Dear Jemmy, none of my things are come. I want my gown and cassock every day. Oh how is God manifested in our brother Whitefield! I have seen none like him—no, not in Herrnhut!" (http://wesley.nnu.edu/john-wesley/the-letters-of-john-wesley/wesleys-letters-1739/) A new and helpful book compares the two preachers' sermon structures, delivery styles and doctrines: Ian J. Maddock, *Men of One Book: A Comparison of Two Methodist Preachers, John Wesley and George Whitefield* (Cambridge, UK: Lutterworth Press, 2011).

"thunder-struck" and receive the assurance of grace.[26] By May he was able to hold such large, attentive crowds spellbound, even in the rain.[27]

In August, he lost heart a bit, and in a letter to James Hutton, the English convert to Moravianism who was Whitefield's publisher, Wesley discreetly and unfavorably compared himself to Whitefield, who seemed to be having a much easier time convicting sinners.[28] In the same month he wrote to his fellow Holy Clubber James Hervey to enlist him in the new work; but Hervey turned him down flatly, echoing his initial suspicion of social and liturgical unorthodoxy. "I a thundering Boanerges! I a speaking-trumpet from heaven! [...] Besides, I freely own I cannot approve of itinerant-preaching. I think it is repugnant to the Apostolical as well as to the English Constitution."[29] Wesley, however, had gotten over his first worries that it was tantamount to sin to preach outside of a church, and committed, despite his training, to

---

[26] As John Wesley reported to his brother Samuel in May, "While we were praying at a Society here, on Tuesday the 1st instant, the power of God (so I call it) came so mightily among us that one, and another, and another fell down as thunder-struck. In that hour many that were in deep anguish of spirit were all filled with peace and joy. Ten persons, till then in sin, doubt, and fear, found such a change that sin had no more dominion over them; and, instead of the spirit of fear, they are now filled with that of love and joy and a sound mind. A Quaker who stood by was very angry at them, and was biting his lips and knitting his brows, when the Spirit of God came upon him also, so that he fell down as one dead. We prayed over him, and he soon lifted up his head with joy and joined with us in thanksgiving.

"A bystander, one John Haydon, was quite enraged at this, and, being unable to deny something supernatural in it, labored beyond measure to convince all his acquaintance that it was a delusion of the devil. I was met in the street the next day by one who informed me that John Haydon was fallen raving mad. It seems he had sat down to dinner, but wanted first to make an end of a sermon he was reading. At the last page he suddenly changed color, fell off his chair, and began screaming terribly and beating himself against the ground. I found him on the floor, the room being full of people, whom his wife would have kept away; but he cried out, 'No; let them all come; let all the world see the just judgment of God.'" (John Wesley to Samuel Wesley, Bristol, 10 May, 1739. http://wesley.nnu.edu/john-wesley/the-letters-of-john-wesley/wesleys-letters-1739/).

[27] "Twelve or fifteen hundred stayed" in the rain to hear Wesley on 16 May (John Wesley to James Hutton, Bristol, 28 May, 1739. http://wesley.nnu.edu/john-wesley/the-letters-of-john-wesley/wesleys-letters-1739/). On 15 April, the rain had held off while he preached to (he estimated) 5000. (John Wesley to James Hutton, Bristol, 16 April, 1739 in *The Letters of John Wesley* ed. Telford, 1931. http://wesley.nnu.edu/john-wesley/the-letters-of-john-wesley/wesleys-letters-1739/).

[28] According to Wesley, he and Whitefield met in Bristol, where Whitefield said he "had been told these things [conversions] were owing to my encouraging them, and that if they were not encouraged no such thing would ever be. But the next day, no sooner had he himself begun to call all sinners to be in Christ, than four were seized before him in a moment. One of them dropped down and lay without motion; a second trembled exceeding; the third was in strong convulsions, but made no noise unless by groans; the fourth, equally convulsed, called upon God with strong cries and tears also." (John Wesley to James Hutton, 3 Aug, 1739 in *The Letters of John Wesley* ed. Telford, 1931. http://wesley.nnu.edu/john-wesley/the-letters-of-john-wesley/wesleys-letters-1739/).

[29] James Hervey to John Wesley, 21 Aug 1739 in *The Letters of John Wesley* ed. Telford, 1931. http://wesley.nnu.edu/john-wesley/the-letters-of-john-wesley/wesleys-letters-1739/).

Fig. 5.2 John Wesley in "Geneva" gown and tabs, preaching in the open outside a church. Wikimedia Commons https://commons.wikimedia.org (from https://wellcomeimages.org/indexplus/obf_images/32/1b/2cc571d981947dadf12de2ffd11

the new enthusiastic, dramatic way of doing it.[30] On 16 September, he reported preaching the same sermon twice, out of doors, both times, with 10,000 in the first audience and over 20,000 in the second—but the sermon was not on the usual sin, death, grace and salvation, but an explanation and defense of Methodism, its doctrines and demands.[31]

[30] John Wesley to James Hutton, Bristol, 16 April, 1739 in *The Letters of John Wesley* ed. Telford, 1931. http://wesley.nnu.edu/john-wesley/the-letters-of-john-wesley/wesleys-letters-1739/).

[31] "Sunday, the 16th, I preached at Moorfields to about 10,000, and at Kennington Common to between twenty and thirty thousand, on those words, 'We desire to hear of thee what thou thinkest: for as concerning this sect, we know it is everywhere spoken against.' At both places I described in very plain terms the difference between true old Christianity, commonly called by the new name of Methodism, and the Christianity now generally taught." (JWesley to CWesley, Islington, 21 Sep 1739 in *The Letters of John Wesley* ed. Telford, 1931. http://wesley.nnu.edu/john-wesley/the-letters-of-john-wesley/wesleys-letters-1739/).

Indeed Wesley did what he first said plainly he would not do, and took over Whitefield's task and his English turf (notably the Bowling Green at Bristol) when Whitefield returned to America in the fall of 1739. As Whitefield, the pioneer, worked harder and harder, Wesley got better and better at his new vocation, holding enormous religious services outside of the Church of England and its church buildings, and holding audiences for his message of damnation and grace that made them feel both deeply guilty and eager for ecstatic experience.

Whitefield, of course, was just getting started. Back in the colonies from November, 1739, to January, 1741, Whitefield preached, according to one count based on his regularly published journals, memoirs and letters, 350 times to audiences that numbered from 100 to 20,000, traveling 2000 miles on horseback and 3000 by boat to over 75 cities and towns from Savannah, Georgia, north to Boston, Massachusetts, and connecting with a remarkable range of Americans, from Benjamin Franklin (his grace-deprived publisher and friend), Peter Böhler (John Wesley's Moravian confessor then working in America), William and Gilbert Tennent (Presbyterian father and son who founded their own Log College to train awakened ministers), and Congregational Jonathan Edwards, whose Connecticut Valley revivals, beginning in 1734 and exploding after March, 1739, had been the first in what American historians would eventually call The Great Awakening. From 1741 to 1744, Whitefield field-preached to huge effect all over England, Scotland, and Ireland, founding an organization in Wales to organize itinerant preachers. Surviving criticism, raillery, riots—even an assassination attempt by a noble rake with a sword in the summer of 1744—not to mention bans on itinerant preaching by bishops, synods and the states of Massachusetts and Connecticut, Whitefield returned to British North America in the fall of 1744 for a third tour that would reach thousands more and last until 1748.

On his second trip in 1740, Whitefield preached near Harvard College, where Dissenting ministers had been trained for a century to staff the colonial established churches. Harvard, Whitefield observed disapprovingly in his *Journals* published in 1741, included a goodly share of young men who were merely frivolous, but it also had more than its share of Arminians (who thought people could achieve grace by effort), as well as undercover Unitarians (believing God has one, not three, persons), Universalists (heaven is for everybody) and Deists (God exists, but reveals himself in natural law alone, obeys the rule of law, and takes no part in people's lives).[32] In reply to Whitefield's criticism, both explicit and implicit, Arminians, "Old Side"

[32] "The chief college for training the sons of the prophets in New England [...] Discipline is at a low ebb. Bad books are become fashionable among the tutors and students. Tillotson and Clark are read, instead of Shepard, Stoddard, and such-like evangelical writers; and, therefore, I chose to preach from these words—'We are not as many, who corrupt the Word of God.'" (Whitefield, *Journals*, London, 1741, in Richard L. Bushman, ed. *The Great Awakening: Documents on the Revival of Religion, 1740–1745*. (1970) Chapel Hill: University of North Carolina Press, 1989, p. 30).

Presbyterians, disdainful Anglicans of the English establishment and Congregationals of the New England establishment invoked law, custom, *hauteur* and good manners, and published replies, but Whitefield's influence only grew greater. Beset Baptists (dissenters from Dissent) split the Boston First Baptist congregation for and against the Awakening, and escalated their argument for separation of church and state. Some graduated from the pursuit of ecstasy to real ritual excess, like Congregational minister James Davenport who went from top of his class at Yale in 1732 to the small-time itinerant who would throw his plush pants on a bonfire of the vanities in 1743. He was, declared the Connecticut legislature, "under the influences of *enthusiastical* impressions and impulses, and thereby disturb'd in the rational faculties of his mind..."[33]

In every case of deviation or opposition Whitefield invoked the English tradition of toleration, the American custom of interchurch cooperation, and his own transparent unselfishness, candor and honesty, to rise above it. Even a Deist like Franklin found that although his friend Whitefield repeatedly failed to convince him to fall into enthusiastic terror and decide for Christ, the great preacher could easily persuade him to empty his pockets into a collection box for his Savannah orphans' home. As for the Reverend Charles Chauncy of Boston, leader of the Congregational establishment, who was no longer entirely sure that God had more than one Person, and had even begun to stray from Calvin's reprobate many and chosen few to the possibility that God might offer salvation free of charge to everybody,[34] confined himself to insulting Whitefield's unbridled enthusiasm and unconcern for church law and decorum to a friendly audience at the Harvard Commencement, months after Whitefield had left Boston for Savannah.[35] At still-Calvinist Yale, the commencement sermon was preached by Jonathan Edwards, who thought what Whitefield was doing was a work of God. Indeed, the 1741 commencement sermons of Chauncy at Harvard and Edwards at Yale resulted in a scorching pamphlet war on the subject of revivals and enthusiasm under the emerging party names "Old Side" or "Old Lights" and "New Side (Lights)" who accepted at least some enthusiasm in the hope of holding on to Calvin's irresistible grace and the chosen few who could receive it. The Harvard-Yale rivalry is a lot older than football, and in the eighteenth century it touched both enthusiasm and eternity. As for Princeton, it was founded in

[33] Connecticut's report is in Thomas S. Kidd, *The Great Awakening: A Brief History with Documents* (New York: Bedford/St. Martin's, 2008) and Bushman, ed. *The Great Awakening: Documents*, p. 46. Italics mine.

[34] Charles Chauncy, *The New Creature Describ'd and Consider'd*, Boston, 1741. Chauncy professed here not to know whether all might be saved or not: children might be saved in childhood. Chauncy would eventually out himself as a Universalist (or universal-salvationist) in 1784. On that account John Calvin would have probably called for his execution.

[35] Charles Chauncy, *Enthusiasm Described and Cautioned Against*, Boston, 1742, the Harvard Commencement sermon of September, 1741, published early in 1742. Chauncy said: "the enthusiast [...] when all the while, he is under no other influence than that of an overheated imagination [...] enthusiasm [is] bad temperament of the blood and spirits; 'tis properly a disease, a sort of madness [...] God [...] cannot be suppos'd to be the author of any private revelations." Chauncy, "Enthusiasm ...," Boston, 1742, p. 3 (in Wright, *Beginnings of Unitarianism*, p. 53).

the years after the pamphlet war as the College of New Jersey for the training of "New Side" Presbyterian ministers. It chose Edwards as its third president, and Whitefield raised some of its founding funds, putting it at the forefront of the American Great Awakening. Princeton is hardly sleeping now, but the issues that brought about its awakening are.

As for bemused American Deists, undercover Unitarians and Universalists, and wary Quakers, they kept their heads down and found Whitefield deserving of tolerance, more sincere and effectual for good morals than mistaken or dangerous to them.[36] They opposed even his ever-proliferating, ever more enthusiastic disciples, including ever more numerous approved but unordained lay preachers, with circumspection. Meanwhile in Britain, Whitefield was tolerated more by opponents of enthusiasm, or of Calvinism, or even by the opponents of religion, than by the established church of which he continued to be a loyal though critical member. Lord Chesterfield, well-known for his gentlemanly irreligion, heard a sermon or two by Whitefield courtesy of the preacher's aristocratic patron, Selina, Countess of Huntingdon. And the publicly Deist and privately atheist David Hume, who wrote disparagingly "Of Superstition and Enthusiasm" in 1741, attended part of a Whitefield sermon in his native Edinburgh and concluded that Whitefield was worth traveling 20 miles to hear.[37] Whitefield, by contrast, could accuse an Archbishop of

[36] James Logan, a well-known Philadelphia Quaker, wrote: "None can be long a stranger to George Whitefield. All I have to say of him is, that be good language, a better utterance, an engaging manner, and a powerful voice, he gained much at first on most sorts of people… It must be confessed his preaching has a good effect in reclaiming many dissolute people, but from his countenancing of so very much the most hot-headed predestinarians, and those of them, principally, who had been accounted by the more sober as little better than madmen, he and they have actually driven divers[e] into despair, and some into perfect madness. In short, it is apprehended by the more judicious that the whole will end in confusion, to the great prejudice of the cause of virtue and solid religion; his doctrine turning on the danger of good works without such a degree of sanctifying faith as comes up to his gauge. (quoted from E. R. Beadle, *The Old and the New, 1743–1876*, Philadelphia, 1876, p. 18, by Frederick B. Tolles, *Quakers and the Atlantic Culture*. New York: Macmillan, 1960, p. 100).

[37] An intimate friend of the infidel Hume, asked him what he thought of Whitefield's preaching; for he had listened to the latter part of one of his sermons at Edinburg. "He is, sir," said Mr. Hume, "the most ingenious preacher I ever heard. It is worthwhile to go 20 miles to hear him." He then repeated the following passage which he heard towards the close of that discourse: "After a solemn pause, Mr. Whitefield thus addressed his numerous audience;—'The attendant angel is just about to leave the threshold, and ascend to heaven. And shall he ascend and not bear with him the news of one sinner, among all this multitude, reclaimed from the error of his ways?' To give greater effect to this exclamation, he stamped with his foot, lifted up his hands and eyes to heaven, and with gushing tears, cried aloud, '*Stop, Gabriel*! *Stop, Gabriel*! Stop, ere you enter the sacred portals, and yet carry with you the news of one sinner converted to God! He then, in the most simple, but energetic language, described a Savior's dying love to sinful man; so that almost the whole assembly melted into tears. This address was accompanied with such animated, yet natural action, that it surpassed anything I ever saw or heard in any other preacher." (first pub. in few words in a footnote in Gillies, *Memoirs of George Whitefield*, 1772, p175nU; first pub. in full by Impartialitas, "George Whitefield, and *The Minor*," in *The Monthly Mirror*, (May, 1808), p. 384; in full in footnote to Gillies, *Memoirs of George Whitefield*, 1853, pp. 197–198; *Wellman's Miscellany*, 1871, p. 13; A. Belden, *George Whitefield, the Awakener*, p. 170, in Knox, p. 491).

Canterbury of not being saved.[38] A Church of England bishop in 1755 tried to officially prohibit Whitefield from preaching at Long Acre chapel, the tabernacle his supporters had built for him in London. Then, when he couldn't close down the services, the bishop seems to have arranged a campaign of harassment:

> A number of soldiers, drummers, and many other malicious persons were employed to make a noise in an adjoining house, or yard [...]: these raised a dreadful uproar, and that as often as Mr. Whitefield preached. They were hired by subscription, and supplied with drums, bells &c., thus keeping up a continual din, from the beginning to the end of the sermon. Thus mobs were excited to riot at the doors of the chapel, insulting and abusing both preacher and hearers, as soon as the service was over. They repeatedly broke the windows with large stones, by which several of the congregation were severely wounded.[39]

Whitefield replied by writing to the bishop, politely but not obsequiously, and threatening, like St. Paul, to appeal "unto Caesar" for redress. John Wesley also faced establishment opposition, but he was no help to Whitefield. When Wesley met with the Bishop of Bristol, Joseph Butler, in 1739, and Butler said, "Sir, the pretending to extraordinary revelations and gifts of the Holy Ghost is a horrid thing, a very horrid thing," Wesley replied, "My lord, for what Mr. Whitefield says, Mr. Whitefield and not I is accountable. I pretend to no extraordinary revelations or gifts of the Holy Ghost."[40]

Official censorship and prosecution worked better in France, where, as we shall see, the leading atheists of the French Enlightenment, like Diderot and the Baron d'Holbach, faced the same official repression from church and state as the Jansenist convulsionaries and the other enthusiasts and purveyors of enthusiasm whom they snorted at. Nevertheless, although you could snub dissenters in Britain, or insult them, or disenfranchise them by excluding them from colleges and government office, or even jail them for lawbreaking, you couldn't hang them or burn them or confiscate their property, or censor them except in the theater. The lessened fear of draconian punishment in this world may or may not, by comparison, have decreased the fear of eternal punishment in the next, but it seems to have had no effect on their zeal, nor did it mute their enthusiasm.

Whitefield did, however, come to a disagreement with Wesley himself, one as important for theology in general as for their emerging Methodist movement, a

---

[38] Whitefield accused the late Archbishop of Canterbury, Primate of England John Tillotson, of never having experienced New Birth, and of knowing less of **grace** than "Mohamet." (Harry S. Stout. *The Divine Dramatist: George Whitefield and the Rise of Modern Evangelism.* Grand Rapids, MI: William B. Eerdmans, 1991, pp. 100–101).

[39] John Gillies, *Memoirs of the Life of the Reverend George Whitefield, M.A...* London: Dilly, 1772, p. 215–216. The passage continues: "In consequence of these unwarrantable proceedings, Whitefield wrote several spirited letters to the bishop of B_______; in one of them he thanks his lordship for his candor, favorable opinion, and good wishes, the bishop having answered his first letter; but yet, in a manly style, and with a just sense of British liberty, defended his own conduct, and powerfully remonstrated against the riotous proceedings of his enemies [...] 'If no more noise is made on their part, I assure your lordship, , no further resentment shall be made on mine. But, if they persist, I have the authority of the apostle, on a like occasion, to appeal unto Caesar; and thanks be to God, we have a Caesar to appeal to [...]'" (Gillies, 1772, p. 216).

[40] John Wesley, *Journal* 29 April, 1739, in *Works*, 1984, v19, p. 471; *Works*, v9, p47, says it was July.

disagreement over which point of view, Arminian or Calvinist, was the right way to understand the crucial question of access to grace, to belief and to salvation. In the first flush of his success at field-preaching, on April 29, 1739, Wesley had preached a sermon in Bristol called "Free Grace," attacking predestination.[41] He had come to believe that once you had credible evidence of an access of grace, you were capable of "perfection," which Wesley defined as the assurance that you could work your way free of sin.[42] Whitefield tried to prevent Wesley from publishing it. He saw "perfection" as Arminian, meaning it made it possible for people to work their way into heaven, or worse, to feel smugly that access was guaranteed whether you worked at goodness or not. Such a view would make mincemeat of Calvin's classic doctrine of election—that your salvation, or the lack of it, had been determined in advance by God alone. Whitefield wrote to Wesley that publication "shocks me to think of it," and when Wesley went forward anyway Whitefield wrote that the heart

[41] "I declared the free grace of God to about four thousand people [...] From Clifton we went to Rose Green, where were (by computation) near seven thousand, and thence to Gloucester Lane Society. After which was our first love-feast in Baldwin Street. O how God has renewed my strength!" (John Wesley, *Journal*, in *Works*, 1984, v19, p. 52) Wesley's letter to James Hutton on 30 April, 1739, says the sermon was directed by the Moravian "lot," and that it "declared openly for the first hour against 'the horrible decree'" of predestination.

[42] Wesley's published "Free Grace" sermon was on Paul's classic text, *Romans* 8:32. It took on predestination in paragraph 9 and summed up the "perfectionist" alternative in paragraphs 15 and 16. "9. Call it therefore by whatever name you please, election, preterition, predestination, or reprobation, it comes in the end to the same thing. The sense of all is plainly this,—by virtue of an eternal, unchangeable, irresistible decree of God, one part of mankind are infallibly saved, and the rest infallibly damned; it being impossible that any of the former should be damned. or that any of the latter should be saved. [...] I appeal to any of you who hold this doctrine, to say, between God and your own hearts, whether you have not often a return of doubts and fears concerning your election or perseverance! If you ask, "Who has not" I answer, Very few of those that hold this doctrine; but many, very many, of those that hold it not, in all parts of the earth;—many of these have enjoyed the uninterrupted witness of his Spirit, the continual light of his countenance, from the moment wherein they first believed, for many months or years, to this day. [...] 16. That assurance of faith which these enjoy excludes all doubt and fear, It excludes all kinds of doubt and fear concerning their future perseverance; though it is not properly, as was said before, an assurance of what is future, but only of what now is. And this needs not for its support a speculative belief, that whoever is once ordained to life must live; for it is wrought from hour to hour, by the mighty power of God, "by the Holy Ghost which is given unto them." And therefore that doctrine [reprobation or predestination] is not of God, because it tends to obstruct, if not destroy, this great work of the Holy Ghost, whence flows the chief comfort of religion, the happiness of Christianity." (John Wesley, "Free Grace," (Bristol, 29 April, 1739), London, (August) 1739 (Sermon #110 in *Works*, v1, *Sermons* I, 1–33 [*Sermons on Several Occasions*, 1746], ed., Outler, 1984, and can be found at http://wesley.nnu.edu/john-wesley/the-sermons-of-john-wesley-1872-edition/sermon-128-free-grace/). The 1739 printed version, a 24-page pamphlet, has "annexed to it a hymn by Charles Wesley on *Universal Redemption*." (Iain Murray on Whitefield and Wesley in the 1960 edition of *Whitefield's Journals*, The Banner of Truth Trust, 1960. http://www.spurgeon.org/~phil/wesley/murray.htm).

inside his body felt "like melted wax."[43] In the event, Wesley waited until Whitefield had taken ship for America in August, 1739, and then immediately published the sermon. Whitefield had little vindictiveness in his character, but he understood the role that the fear of eternal damnation played in his calls for conviction and "conversion." The two parted ways theologically, and although the disagreement did not end their friendship or their commonality of enthusiasm, it ended their close collaboration for good.

Less than a year later Wesley, who had made the trip to Herrnhut, Saxony back in 1738 to meet Zinzendorf himself, also broke with the Moravians. The point of theology was the same, the "doctrine of reprobation" (all are justly condemned to damnation, with grace given only to an otherwise undeserving elect) but this time it was Zinzendorf who was cast as the Arminian rather than Wesley, and Wesley who did the casting.[44] The move had the effect of interrupting the Moravian-led ecumenical movement for the cooperation and eventual union of the awakened of all denominations.[45] In June, 1740, Wesley read a lecture to the combined Moravian/Methodist conventicle of Fetter Lane, where he himself had been first overcome by enthusiasm a year and a half before, and explicitly upheld reprobation against Moravian (and Arminian) free grace. This broke the Fetter Lane Society in two, and Wesley took the members who agreed with his stricter view of grace away to join his new

[43] Whitefield wrote to Wesley on June 25, 1739: "I hear, honoured sir, you are about to print a sermon on predestination. It shocks me to think of it; what will be the consequences but controversy? If people ask me my opinion, what shall I do? I have a critical part to act, God enable me to behave aright! Silence on both sides will be best. It is noised abroad already, that there is a division between you and me. Oh, my heart within me is grieved I …" On July 2, Whitefield followed up with: "Dear, honoured sir, if you have any regard for the peace of the church, keep in your sermon on predestination. But you have cast a lot. Oh! my heart, in the midst of my body, is like melted wax. The Lord direct us all! …" (in Iain Murray on Whitefield and Wesley in the 1960 edition of Whitefield's *Journals*, The Banner of Truth Trust, 1960).

[44] Hutton's view of the dispute is found in his *Memoirs*: "Wesley desired to give a prominent place in his system of the Christian religion to the doctrine of *an active love*, proceeding from the new birth and faith; and manifesting itself in *striving* after *holiness* and *christian perfection*, and to the doctrine of the furtherance of this *active* love by the *means of gracel in the church*. Zinzendorf on the other hand allowed of none other than a *grateful love*, proceeding from the experience of the heart of a *pardoned* sinner; he condemmed [sic] all self-made holiness, and every merely legal duty, and act of self-denial. He had even publicly, as bishop and guardian of the Church of the Brethren, called the two Wesleys 'false teachers and deceivers of souls, on account of their doctrine of *christian perfection*.'" (Daniel Benham, *Memoirs of James Hutton*, London: Hamilton, Adams, 1856, p. 112, in John R. Weinlick, *Count Zinzendorf: The Story of His Life and Leadership in the Renewed Moravian Church*, Abingdon Press, 1956; Bethlehem, PA: Moravian Church in America, pb, 1989, p. 181).

[45] The evangelicals' ecumenical movement reached a somewhat quixotic peak when Scotch Presbyterian John Erskine published a *Memorial* calling for an international, transatlantic day of common prayer, Moravians agreed, Whitefield's deputy in Wales, Howel Harris, began organizing it, and Jonathan Edwards in New England published *A Humble Attempt to Promote Explicit Agreement and Visible Union of God's People in Extraordinary Prayer for the Revival of Religion and the Advancement of Christ's Kingdom on earth, pursuant to Scripture Promises and Prophecies concerning the Last Time* in 1747.

Foundry Society, the first "Methodist" Society. James Hutton, a Moravian of Fetter Lane (and Whitefield's publisher), conveyed his anger with Wesley in an account that was published later:

> John Wesley, displeased at not being thought so much of as formerly, and offended, as he said, with the easy way of salvation as taught by the Brethren, publicly spoke against our doctrine in his sermons, and his friends did the same. [...] We asked his forgiveness [but] he became our declared opponent, and the two societies of the Brethren and the Methodists thenceforward were separated and became independent upon each other.[46]

Three years later, Hutton reports, Zinzendorf rounded on Whitefield for his insistence on predestination, which he called an "*abominable doctrine*, so contrary to sound reason." "You must, said Zinzendorf to Whitefield, "first formally recant, and preach openly *free grace* in the blood of the Lamb, and an *election of grace* as taught in the Scriptures, which is quite different from the doctrine of predestination which you teach; and if not, our church must necessarily be opposed to you."[47] (In later years Wesley would soften, titling the official Methodist journal he founded in 1778 *The Arminian Magazine*.)

If we were talking about Freudians or Marxists, we would suspect that this was a struggle for leadership dignified by arguments from principle, and it may be that the difference between science and religion (not to mention politics and the rest of the "social sciences") is that bids for scientific leadership cannot involve differences over principle. In any case Zinzendorf's Brethren went into the background, and Whitefield, despite his enormous charisma, did the same. Zinzendorf's movement was the most international, stretching from Baltic Livonia to Germany, and Greenland to the East and West Indies, but his many organizational "conferences"

---

[46] "John Wesley, displeased at not being thought so much of as formerly, and offended, as he said, with the easy way of salvation as taught by the Brethren, publicly spoke against our doctrine in his sermons, and his friends did the same. In June, 1740, he formed his 'Foundry Society,' in opposition to the one which met at Fetter Lane, and which had become a Moravian Society. Many of our usual hearers left us, especially the females. We asked his forgiveness if in anything we had aggrieved him, but he continued full of wrath, accusing the Brethren, that in following Luther without discrimination, they, by dwelling exclusively on the doctrine of faith, neglected the law and zeal for sanctification. In short, he became our declared opponent, and the two societies of the Brethren and the Methodists thenceforward were separated and became independent upon each other." (Benham, *Memoirs of James Hutton*, London, 1856, p. 54, in Forell, ed., Zinzendorf, *Nine Lectures*, p. xv). Hutton's account seems more retrospective than it was because of its much later publication, but Wesley's account of the quarrel in his *Journals* for November, 1739 was not published until 1744. John Wesley, *Journal*, part 4, London, 1744, in *The Works of John Wesley*, v19, *Journals and Diaries II (1738–1743)*. (Nashville, TN: Abingdon Press, 1990).

[47] Hutton's account of Zinzendorf's meeting with Whitefield is found in his *Memoirs*: "Not less severe was his declaration against Whitefield, with whom he had a friendly conversation in London, and whom he had heard preach on the subject of *reprobation*. He renounced all connexion with him, on account of this '*abominable doctrine*, so contrary to sound reason.' 'You must first formally recant, and preach openly *free grace* in the blood of the Lamb, and an *election of grace* as taught in the Scriptures, which is quite different from the doctrine of predestination which you teach ; and if not, our church must necessarily be opposed to you.'" (Benham, *Memoirs of James Hutton*, 1856, p. 112, in Weinlick, *Count Zinzendorf*, pb, 1989, p. 181).

concentrated power in him and his appointees, often family members. Conferences were not revival meetings. The Moravians busied themselves founding utopian religious communities, and did not do outdoor revival preaching, which meant their organization did not grow nearly as fast.[48] Although Whitefield convened the pro-predestination Methodists in what should be called the first Methodist organizational conference, the Joint Association of English and Welsh Calvinistic Methodism, at Watford in Whitefield-evangelized Wales in January, 1743, Whitefield was away in America in the fall of 1744, when the Association needed him, and this hiatus would be repeated. Indeed, Whitefield was in America when he died in 1770, on his seventh tour. Wesley, on the other hand, having founded the first Methodist Society at the Foundry in London in June, 1740, when Whitefield was away in America, went on to convene what he called, and history still calls, the "first Methodist Conference" in the Foundry on 25 June, 1744, when Whitefield was again overseas. The Conference's agenda began with doctrine (faith, justification, assurance of salvation, and sanctification) and ended with organization, unlike Whitefield's Association which had led with organization.

In this muffled competition, the annual successors of the Methodist Conference, chaired by Wesley, outlasted the annual conferences of Whitefield's Joint Association, such that it was under Wesley's leadership that the Methodist movement moved into its period of institutionalization and eventual separation from the Church of England as an independent Protestant denomination, evangelical to the core.[49]

America got a local Methodist Conference of its own for the first time in 1774, only after its national preacher, Whitefield, had died. The United States of America did not get a national Methodist Conference until 1783, and at the second Conference, meeting in Baltimore on Christmas Eve, 1784, Francis Asbury, one of America's leading preachers (and Wesley's personal appointee), moved and carried a resolution ending Methodism's republican church government, naming Wesley as American Methodism's chief executive, and solemnly agreeing: "During the life of the Rev. Mr. Wesley we acknowledge ourselves his sons in the gospel, ready in matters of church government to obey his commands."[50] This was the first step in making Wesley the head of a new church, but also in making a new church able to head itself when he died. At the Conference in America in 1787, Asbury would be titled "Bishop" and the Methodists would become Episcopalian, a system which outlasted Wesley's control, and Wesley himself. A Methodist Conference 4 years after Wesley died agreed to the "Plan of Pacification" which completed the separation by giving

---

[48] "Traditional freedom of speech and assembly had prepared the people of the British Isles for mass revival techniques. The Methodists were ready to capitalize on it. The Moravians were not. Revivalism of that kind did not come to Germany until the rise of free churches in the mid-nineteenth century. [...] Zinzendorf actually called the Methodist revival meetings 'mobs'." (Weinlick, *Count Zinzendorf*, pb, 1989, p. 217).

[49] Rack, Henry D. *Reasonable Enthusiast; John Wesley and the Rise of Methodism*. London: Epworth, 1989.

[50] In Ferguson, *Organizing to Beat the Devil*, 1971, p. 42.

the Methodist Conferences discretion to approve and ordain its ministers and bishops and power to the ministers to administer the sacraments.

Whatever the organization, Methodism did the job of summoning grace, circuit preaching in unlicensed churches and out under the blue sky inspired thousands to repent and "catch the spirit," beginning with impromptu prayer and then moving to screaming, singing, cheering, and sometimes jerking, falling as if dead, and foaming at the mouth. It inspired hundreds, both lay and ordained, to go out and try to evoke the same response. Wales or Georgia, Scotland or Tennessee, even in Puritan Boston, Quaker Philadelphia, urbane Edinburgh, boisterous multicultural New York and Enlightened London, the Methodists drew their crowds and made their converts, usually among those whom later centuries would call "the masses." They were democratic before political democracy, classless for their times, and disrespectful of all hierarchies, not excluding their own church leadership.[51] Even slave and free got grace together in South Carolina (as they had in the Virgin Islands with Zinzendorf), and Wesley (though not Whitefield, who bought a slave plantation in South Carolina in 1744) finally came out against slavery itself in the 1770s, branding it a threat to the salvation of both slave and owner.

Other denominations either rallied to Methodist methods or came over to the new denomination, and Virginia's unchurched backwoods became a new mission country. Samuel Davies (1723–1761), converted at 15 and becoming a New Side Presbyterian, got the first license to preach ever awarded a Dissenter in Anglican Virginia which he used to itinerate from vacant parish to vacant parish, raising the roof and bringing in the sheep. He founded the first southern Presbyterian synod and ended his preaching career as President of New Side Princeton in succession to Jonathan Edwards. His assistant, John Todd, founded Providence Church for the saved and would-be saved living near Payne's Mill in Louisa County. In Brunswick County, the Reverend Devereaux Jarratt of the Church of England cooperated wholeheartedly with the Methodist Societies in his parish, and described the ecstatic results he got in 1775: "cries and tears" "panting and groaning" and then sanctification "instantaneously, and by simple faith."[52] In 1790 the Baptist itinerant John Leland (1754–1841), born Congregational in Massachusetts, wary of false enthusi-

---

[51] Élie Halévy, the French liberal historian, became fascinated by Methodism's democratic aspects and tendencies, and suggested in his histories of early nineteenth century England that if it had not been for the success of Methodism cathecting popular grievance, England would have had a Revolution much like the French. Cf Halévy, "The Birth of Methodism in England," (in *La Revue de Paris*, 1906), tr. Bernard Semmel, Chicago: U. of Chicago Press, 1971) and the considerable scholarly discussions of the "Halévy Thesis" that have followed. Nathan O. Hatch may be said to have brought a Halévy Thesis to American historiography with his groundbreaking *The Democratization of American Christianity*. (New Haven, CT: Yale University Press, 1989).

[52] "Many were 'panting and groaning for pardon' while others were 'entreating God with strong cries and tears to save them from the remains of inbred sin, to sanctify them throughout…' Numbers of them testified to having been sanctified 'instantaneously, and by simple faith.'" (Vinson Synan. *The Holiness-Pentecostal Movement in the United States*. 1971, p. 9, quoting Devereaux Jarratt, *A Brief Narrative of the Revival of Religion in Virginia, in a Letter to a Friend…*, 4th ed., London: R. Hawes, 1779, pp. 7–12).

asm, and a fierce opponent of government-sponsored religion, described services of the new evangelical southern New Light "Separate" Baptists he had seen 2 or 3 years before while itinerating in Virginia. Whereas the Regular Baptists:

> were orthodox Calvanists [sic], and the work under them was solemn and rational; but the Separates were the most zealous, and the work among them was very noisy. The people would cry out, "fall down," and, for a time, lose the use of their limbs; which exercise made the bystanders marvel; some thought they were deceitful, others, that they were bewitched, and many being convinced of all, would report that God was with them of a truth.[53]

And some in them were trying to repeat the ecstatic experience of receiving grace:

> This exercise is not confined to the newly convicted, and newly converted, but persons who have been professors a number of years, at such lively meetings, not only jump up, strike their hands together, and shout aloud, but will embrace one another, and fall to the floor.[54]

Dissenting, non-established churches took up the cause of enthusiasm and the system of unlicensed outdoor preaching. In 1754, Shubal Stearns, converted from a Connecticut Congregational to a Separate Baptist, met Daniel Marshall in rural Berkeley County, Virginia, from whence they traveled further south, building a meeting house in Sandy Creek, in backwoods Guilford County, North Carolina, where they began ministering enthusiastically to 16 even more enthusiastic communicants. Stearns and Marshall founded the so-called "Primitive" Baptists, preaching free grace rather than reprobation, welcoming to the mostly unchurched slaves and the poor, unlanded whites who were often their overseers, and substituting the ecstatic experience of conversion and behavior like trances and visions, for dogma and catechism. Blacks (who often outnumbered whites at revival tents) found trance and Spirit possession familiar to them but fainting, groaning, and barking seemingly unfamiliar and white. Whites saw blacks' energy of possession and "shout" as unfamiliar, but together they found common ground in ecstatic ritual.[55] The gigantic

---

[53] John Leland, *The Writings of the Late Elder John Leland Including Some Events in His Life*, ed., L. F. Greene, NY: G. W. Wood, 1845, p. 14, (Frey & Wood, p100, mistakenly locate this observation on page 105).

[54] Leland, "The Virginia Chronicle" (1790) in *The Writings of the Late Elder John Leland*, ed., Greene, 1845, p. 114–115, Taves quotes it in Taves, p. 86n49). Leland was aware that this sort of behavior was suspected by the respectable of encouraging sexual misadventure, so he continued his account: ". I have never known the rules of decency broken so far as for persons of different sexes, thus to embrace and fall at meetings."

[55] Walter F. Pitts, *Old Ship of Zion: The Afro-Baptist Ritual in the African Diaspora*, NY: Oxford U.P., 1993, p. 43. These services, it bears repeating, included blacks and whites together. For a cautiously approving eyewitness account of how blacks differed from whites at early American evangelical worship there is Leland: "When they attempt to preach, they seldom fail of being very zealous; their language is broken, but they understand each other, and the whites may gain their ideas. A few of them have undertaken to administer baptism, but it generally ends in confusion. They commonly are more noisy, in time of preaching, than the whites, and are more subject to bodily exercise, and if they meet with any encouragement in these things, they often grow extravagant." (*The Writings of the Late Elder John Leland*, ed., Greene, 1845, p. 98).

1800 revival at Cane Ridge, Tennessee, can be traced to the little Sandy Creek ministry of Stearns and Marshall.[56]

Perhaps the most striking story of Methodist-inspired evangelicalism in Virginia centers not on a democrat but on an aristocrat, Robert Carter III, one of Virginia's largest slaveowners, grandson and heir of Robert "King" Carter of Nomony Hall and plantations in the Northern Neck of Virginia. On the 12th of June, 1777, Robert III, recovering from smallpox and meditating on (what else?) the words of an epistle of Saint Paul, had "a most gracious Illumination,"[57] a mystical experience of grace that led him to leave the Church of England, his "deistical Opinion,"[58] his place on the Governor's Council of Virginia, and eventually his residence in Virginia and the bulk of his inheritance. He spent the next 15 months, with the Revolutionary War raging around him, fervidly exploring all religious traditions, and keeping the results in religious daybooks. He decided to commit himself to the Revolution, and on 6 September, 1778, Robert Carter was rebaptized a Baptist by Rev. Lewis Lunsford in Totuskey Creek before 400 rejoicing witnesses. He signed his name on the rolls of the saved as #61, below the names of slaves, in the register of one of the tiny new unlicensed churches, the Morattico Baptist Church, built on his land partly with his funds. When Morattico restricted its members' voting rights to free males, Carter wrote a charter for a new more egalitarian and democratic Yeocomico Baptist Church and joined this one, too, signing below the slaves. Then, beginning in 1791, he applied all his legal expertise to apply the new Virginia Manumission Act of 1782, and contrive a court-approved Deed of Gift that would free all 452 of his slaves within his own lifetime. He succeeded—a unique distinction in British America—despite the opposition of his dispossessed family and his suspicious slaveowning neighbors. Carter ended his life in Baltimore, a member of the new American Swedenborgian church, founded in Philadelphia in 1784.

Having begun in the 1730s with misgivings about the exclusion of slaves from churches, and then persuading two South Carolina slaveowners to allow him to preach to their slaves, Wesley moved (as Whitefield did not) to opposition to the slave trade and to slavery itself as unchristian and unscriptural, as well as inhuman. Finally in 1774, 2 years after the Somerset case made slavery illegal in England, and after meeting with the slave ship captain turned priest, John Newton, who would write "Amazing Grace" about his own conversion, Wesley published *Thoughts*

[56] Paul Harvey, *Redeeming the South: Religious Cultures and Racial Identities among Southern Baptists, 1865–1925*, Chapel Hill: U. of North Carolina Press, 1997, p. 99. Sylvia R. Frey & Betty Wood, *Come Shouting to Zion: African American Protestantism in the American South and British Caribbean to 1830*, Chapel Hill: U. of North Carolina Press, 1998, p. 102.

[57] Carter described it as: "'a most gracious Illumination [in which he felt] the truth contained in the followi[n]g scripture, where Paul declares—"That he, Paul, was alive without the Law once: but when the Comandment came, sin revived, and he died." (Andrew Levy, *The First Emancipator: Slavery, Religion, and the Quiet Revolution of Robert Carter* (2005), NY: Random House pb 2007, p. 80).

[58] Levy, *The First Emancipator*, p. 90.

Upon Slavery, a summary history of slavery and its multitude of evils, which ended with a thoroughly evangelical imputation of guilt and a call to repentance.

> **V-3.** May I speak plainly to you? I must. Love constrains me; love to you, as well as to those you are concerned with. Is there a God? You know there is. Is he a just God? Then there must be a state of retribution; a state wherein the just God will reward every man according to his works. Then what reward will he render to you? O think betimes! before you drop into eternity! Think now, "He shall have judgment without mercy that showed no mercy."[59]

A year later, in 1775, Wesley came out against the American Revolution, in large part because, as the dean of English Enlightenment writers, Samuel Johnson, had already charged, the demand of the American revolutionaries for freedom was a demand that came from slaveowners.[60] One of Wesley's last sermons was the one he preached against slavery in 1788, the only one that seems to have inspired what we might call counter-conversions. He preached it in Bristol, where he and Whitefield had begun their successful careers as open-air itinerant evangelists—invokers of grace—but Bristol, like Liverpool, was one of Britain's leading slave-trading ports, and in the middle of the sermon the crowd quite suddenly lost its attentiveness. A clearly unsanctified panic "shot like lightening through the whole congregation" with "inexpressible … terror and confusion," and violence broke out that might have killed him.[61] Wesley was unharmed, but when he died 3 years later, in 1791, the

---

[59] John Wesley. "Thoughts upon Slavery," (London: 1774); repr. Philadelphia: Joseph Crukshank, 1774, p. 52. https://docsouth.unc.edu/church/wesley/wesley.html.

[60] "The writer [of the pamphlet Wesley is attacking] asserts twenty times, 'He that is taxd without his own consent, that is, without being represented, is a slave.' I answer, No; I have no representative in Parliament; but I am taxd; yet I am no slave. Yea, nine in ten throughout England have no representative, no vote; yet they are no slaves; they enjoy both civil and religious liberty to the utmost extent. He replies, 'But they may have votes if they will; they may purchase freeholds.' What! Can every man in England purchase a freehold? No, not one in an hundred. But, be that as it may, they have no vote now; yet they are no slaves, they are the freest men in the whole world. 'Who then is a slave?' Look into America, and you may easily see. See that Negro, fainting under the load, bleeding under the lash! He is a slave. And is there 'no difference' between him and his master? Yes; the one is screaming, "Murder! Slavery!" the other silently bleeds and dies!" —John Wesley, "A Calm Address to Our American Colonies," 1775, in *The Works of John Wesley*, Volume 11: *The Appeals to Men of Reason and Religion and Certain Related Open Letters*, ed. Gerald R. Cragg. (Nashville, TN: Abingdon Press, 1975, 1987). Wesley withdrew his Methodist missionaries from America after the Declaration of Independence, but he diplomatically accepted the Revolution once it was over.

[61] "About the middle of the discourse, while there was on every side attention still as night, a vehement noise arose, none could tell why, and shot like lightening through the whole congregation. The terror and confusion were inexpressible. You might have imagined it was a city taken by storm. The people rushed upon each other with the utmost violence; the benches were broke in pieces, and nine-tenths of the congregation appeared to be struck with the same panic." (John Wesley, *Jnl*, 1788).

last of his many letters was to William Wilberforce, the evangelical who had become the Parliamentary leader of the movement to abolish the slave trade.[62]

The American Methodist Annual Conference of 1784 formally agreed to expel any slaveowner who did not emancipate all his slaves in the ensuing 2-year interval, but that seems to have been a bridge too far. Even free black and white Methodists perceived differences greater than grace could bridge. By 1800, the Methodist "connection" in North America included two black congregations preparing their own independent inter-congregational associations: the African Methodist Episcopal Church spreading from Philadelphia and the African Methodist Episcopal Zion Church which began in New York. By 1816 they and other congregations had constituted themselves the first General Conference of the African Methodist Episcopal Church, no longer a part of white Methodism. White Methodists in the slaveholding states of North America found themselves unable to accept Wesley's uncompromising view of slavery, and in 1844 the Methodist Church, South seceded from the Methodist Episcopal Church in the United States, renaming itself the Methodist Church of the Confederate States of America from 1861 to 1865. Southern Baptists followed suit in 1845. Reconciliation has been slow, and it was only in 2012 that the Southern Baptist convention elected its first black president; but one reading of the history suggests that what Wesley derived from his limited experience of the ecstatic reception of grace has continued not only to move others to such experiences, but also to move the evangelicals of the Anglophone world in the great political conflicts with hierarchy and slavery, toward democracy and liberty.

British Enlightenment writers like Smollett and Fielding made fun of it, and Hume tried to ignore it, but it goes without saying that Methodism endures and Methodist enthusiasm is regularly revived. Counter-Enlightenment thinking in England betrays a reluctant admiration and sympathy, not to mention philosophical attunement. The Romantic and erstwhile radical Robert Southey wrote its history, and his friend Samuel Taylor Coleridge, not yet the Christian conservative who translated (and plagiarized) German Counter-Enlightenment philosophers, wrote a note in the margins of his copy of Southey:

> How many and many an hour of self-oblivion do I owe to this Life of Wesley; and how often have I argued with it […] then again listened, and cried Right! Excellent!—and in yet heavier hours intreated it, as it were, to continue talking to me—for that I heard and listened, and was soothed, though I could make no reply. […][63].

[62] Wesley famously wrote: "O be not weary of well-doing! Go on, in the name of GOD and in the power of his might, till even American slavery (the vilest that ever saw the sun) shall vanish away before it." http://place.asburyseminary.edu/cgi/viewcontent.cgi?article=1009&context=engaginggovernmentpapers. The Act of Parliament against the slave trade did pass, but not until 1807. Brycchan Carey's neat summary of Wesley's slavery views, "John Wesley (1703–1791)" 2002, can be found at http://www.brycchancarey.com/abolition/wesley.htm. Carey's summary follows from his major work, *British Abolitionism and the Rhetoric of Sensibility: Writing, Sentiment, and Slavery, 1760–1807* (Basingstoke: Palgrave Macmillan, 2005).

[63] Coleridge, marginal note, printed in the 3rd ed. of Robert Southey, *Life of Wesley and Rise and Progress of Methodism*. (1820) London: Longmans, 1846, v1, p. xv. https://archive.org/details/lifewesleyandri01soutgoog).

Bibliography

(The) Querists; or, An Extract of Sundry Passages Taken Out of Mr. Whitefield's Printed Sermons, Journals and Letters, Philadelphia: Benjamin Franklin, 1740.

———. Part III, Philadelphia: Benjamin Franklin, 1741.

Abbott, Benjamin. 1832. In *The Experience and Gospel Labours of the Rev. Benjamin Abbott*, ed. John Firth (1805 1807), 239. Butler, NY.

Abelove, Henry. 1992. *The Evangelist of Desire: John Wesley and the Methodists*. Stanford, CA: Stanford University Press.

Acornley, John H. 1909. *A History of the Primitive Methodist Church in the United States of America*. Fall River, MA: N.W. Matthews.

Airhart, Phyllis D. 1992. *Serving the Present Age: Revivalism, Progressivism, and the Methodist Tradition in Canada*. Toronto: McGill-Queen's University Press (Studies in the History of Religion). isbn:0-7735-0882-1.

Anderson, Misty. 2000. (University Tennessee), Getting into the habit: Methodistical sisters in mid-century England. In *ASECS 31st Annual Meeting*, University of Pennsylvania.

Andrews, Doris E. 1986. *Popular Religion and the Revolution in the Middle Atlantic Ports: The Rise of the Methodists, 1770–1800*. PhD dissertation, University of Pennsylvania.

Andrews, Dee E. 2000. *The Methodists and Revolutionary America, 1760–1800: The Shaping of an Evangelical Culture*. Princeton: Princeton University Press.

Armstrong, Anthony. 1973. *The Church of England, the Methodists and Society, 1700–1850*. London: University of London Press.

Baker, Frank. 1957. *Methodism and the Love Feast*. London, England: Epworth.

———. 1962. Wesley's Puritan ancestry. *London Quarterly & Holborn Review* 187: 180–186.

———. 1963. Aldersgate 1738–1963; The challenge of Aldersgate [Address]. *Duke Divinity School Bulletin* 28: 67–80.

———. 1965. Early American methodism; A key document. *Methodist History* 3: 3–15.

———. 1966a. *A Union Catalogue of the Publications of John and Charles Wesley*. Stone Mountain, GA: George Zimmerman, 1991.

———. 1966b. Aldersgate and Wesley's editors. *London Quarterly & Holborn Review* 191: 310–319.

———. 1966c. John Wesley's first marriage. *Duke Divinity School Bulletin* 31: 175–188.

———. 1970a. *John Wesley and the Church of England*. Nashville, TN: Abingdon.

———. 1970b. Whitefield's break with the Wesleys. *Church Quarterly Review* 3: 103–113.

———. 1975. Shaping of John Wesley's "Calm Address" [1775]. *Methodist History* 14: 3–12.

———, ed. 1976. *From Wesley to Asbury: Studies in Early American Methodism*. Durham, NC: Duke University Press.

———. 1984. The origins, character, and influence of John Wesley's thoughts upon slavery. *Methodist History* 22 (2): 75–86.

———. 1988. *Charles Wesley's verse: An introduction*. 2nd ed. London: Epworth Press.

———. 1990. Eye-witnesses to early methodism [representative extracts from John Wesley, 1725–1785]. *Methodist History* 28 (2): 92–103.

Bamford, Samuel. 1788–1872. *Early Days*. (1848). https://minorvictorianwriters.org.uk/bamford/c_radical_(1).htm.

———. 1984. *Passages in the Life of a Radical* (1843). Oxford: Oxford University Press. https://archive.org/details/passagesinlifeof0000bamf/page/n1/mode/1up.

Barry, Jonathan and Kenneth Morgan. 1994. *Reformation and Revival in Eighteenth-Century Bristol*. Stroud, Gloucestershire: Printed for the Bristol Record Society.

Bassett, Paul M. 1973. Conservative Wesleyan theology and the challenge of secular humanism. *Wesleyan Theological Journal* 8: 73–82.

———. 1983. The holiness movement and the protestant principle. *Wesleyan Theological Journal* 18 (1): 7–29.

———. ed. 1989. [John Wesley's Aldersgate experience]. *Wesleyan Theological Journal* 24: 7–73.

Beadle, Elias R. 1876. *The Old and the New, 1743–1876*. Philadelphia, (Philadelphia local history).

Bebbington, David W. 1989. *Evangelicalism in Modern Britain: A History from the 1730s to the 1980s*. NY/London: Unwin Hyman.

———. 1991. Evangelical christianity and the enlightenment, In Eden & Wells.

Belden, Albert D. 1940. *George Whitefield, the Awakener*. Sampson Low: Marston & Co.

Benham, Daniel. 1856. *Memoirs of James Hutton; Comprising the Annals of his Life, and Connection with the United Brethren*. London: Hamilton, Adams. Reprint, Miami, FL: Hard Press, 2017.

Bennett, G.V. 1957. *White Kennett, 1660–1728*. London: Bishop of Peterborough.

———. 1975. *White Kennett. The Tory Crisis in Church and State, 1688–1730: The Career of Francis Atterbury, Bishop of Rochester*. Oxford: Oxford University Press.

Bennett G. V. and J. D Walsh, eds. 1966. *Essays in Modern English Church History*. London.

Bertrand, Claude Jean. 1971. *Le méthodisme*. Paris: Colin.

Blackwell History of Music in Britain. 1990. In *The, v4: The Eighteenth Century*, ed. H. Diack Johnstone and Roger Fiske. Oxford: Basil Blackwell.

Blanning, T. C. W. and Peter Wende. 1999. *Reform in Great Britain and Germany, 1750–1850*. British Academy.

Bogue, David and J. Bennett. 1809. *History of Dissenters: From the Revolution in 1688 to the Year* 1808. (4v), vol. 2, London. https://books.googleusercontent.com/books/content?req=AKW5QafVjgvhb3zNu_Zu5yp_sWsdXoKfyGTDkeXf9LxRJ0DQJ-Jq3w7AwYkyiIilHd21EGqFsu54mmg9yJAsRujQ3n2mAoUiBIsw_yp4m5ABTbEKu-WmewP2Zqn5AgaDzDubgndgS3wFiYNkq1yyoEjCR14F7_t0x8JHAEYkdreo8Y-DiVbEy43Iev9L0jNXreQVMHN9UuuKFPERObvOgSoeNjkG4HfXmMVSwseAC9L-HKGCGsprIWxvjc5PkrS3KNJG8rKZkztJRq2inpxY8t4JSK390B0GE5V1RXQFi64WcEuPi-dPkw-rzQ.

Bolam, C. G. et al. 1968. *English Presbyterians from Elizabethan Puritanism to Modern Unitarianism*. London.

Bourignon, Antoinette. 1717. *Les oeuvres de Mlle. Antoinette Bourignon, contenues en dix-neuf volumes*. ed. Pierre Poiret Naudé, Volumes I-XIX. Amsterdam: Pieter Arentsz & Jan Rieuwerts, 1676–1684. (Repr. Amsterdam: John Wetstein, 1679–1686 & Amsterdam: Wetstein).

———. 1825. *Treatise of Solid Virtue*. (Letters 1–25, 1699) ed. & abbr. John Wesley, in *A Christian Library: Extracts from and Abridgments of the Choicest Pieces of Practical Divinity Which Have Been Published in the English Tongue* #36 (1750) Vol. 21, London: J. Kershaw. https://ht.whdl.org/sites/default/files/publications/A%20Christian%20Library%20vol%2021.pdf.

Bowmer, John C. 1961. *The Lord's Supper in Methodism, 1791–1960*. London: Epworth Press.

Bradley, James E. 1990. *Religions, Revolution, and English Radicalism: Non-conformity in Eighteenth-Century Politics and Society*. Cambridge: Cambridge University Press.

Brantley, Richard E. 1975. *Wordsworth's "Natural Methodism"*. New Haven, CT: Yale University Press.

———. 1976–1977. Johnson's Wesleyan connection. *Eighteenth-Century Studies* 10 (2): 143–168.

———. 1984. *Locke, Wesley and the Method of English Romanticism*. Gainesville, FL: University Press of Florida.

———. 1987. Charles Wesley's experimental art. *Eighteenth Century Life* 11: 1–11.

———. 1990. The common ground of Wesley and Edwards. *Harvard Theological Review* 83: 271–303.

Bray, Thomas, D.D. 1701. *A Memorial, Representing the Present State of Religion, on the Continent of North-America*. London: Printed by John Brudenell, for the Author. http://anglicanhistory.org/england/tbray/memorial1701.html.

Bridwell Library. 2003. *Wesley in America: An exhibition celebrating the 300th Anniversary of the birth of John Wesley*, curated by Richard P. Heitzenrater and Peter S. Forsasith, Exhibit Catalogue, Dallas, TX: Bridwell Library, Southern Methodist Unuversity. isbn:941881-30-X. Includes Whitefield's original folding pulpit, owned by the American Tract Society, Garland, Texas.

Brown, Earl Kent. 1985. Feminist theology and the women of Mr. Wesley's methodism. In *Wesleyan Theology Today*, ed. Theodore H. Runyon, 143–150. Nashville, TN: Kingswood.

Brown, Dale W. 1989. The Wesleyan revival from a pietist perspective. *Wesleyan Theological Journal* 24: 7–17.
Brown, Dave, *Whitefield and Wesley on Grace and Predestination.*
Brown, Ford K. Fathers of the Victorians: The Age of Wilberforce. 1961. Cambridge: Cambridge University Press. Chapters on: George Eliot, Francis Newman, T.D. Weld, Sarah Grimké/E.C. Stanton/Frances Willard, Van Gogh, Edmund Gosse, James Baldwin. Mentions of: Ruskin, Samuel, son of CWesley, Moses Harmon, Samuel Porter Putnam, Alfred C. Kinsey, Herbert Asbury, Lucy Stone, children of Clapham Sectarians, "'[...] Macaulay and De Quincy, the sons of Babington and Gisborne and Stephen, the four sons of Wilberforce, the three daughters of Patrick Brontë Marian Evans [...] John Henry Newman, the son or sons of Charles Grant, Lord Teignmouth, Buxton, Lady Emily Pusey, Benjamin Harrison, Sir James Graham, John Gladstone, Sir Robert Peel and William Manning.
Brown-Lawson, Albert. 1994. *John Wesley and the Anglican Evangelicals of the Eighteenth Century: A Study in Cooperation and Separation with Special Reference to the Calvinistic Controversies*. Edinburgh: Pentland.
Bryne, Brendan. 1986. Ignatius Loyola and John Wesley: Experience and strategies of conversion. *Colloquium: The Australian and New Zealand Theological Review* 19 (1): 54–66.
Bucke, Emory, ed. 1964. *The History of American Methodism*. Vol. 3v. Nashville, TN: Abingdon.
Burtt, Shelley. 1992. *Virtue Transformed: Political Argument in England, 1688–1740*. Cambridge: Cambridge University Press.
Bushaway, Bob. 1982. *By Rite: Custom, Ceremony, and Community in England, 1700–1880*. London: Junction & Atlantic Highlands, NJ: Humanities Press.
Campbell, James T. 1995. *Songs of Zion: The African Methodist Episcopal Church in the United States and South Africa*. New York: Oxford University Press.
Cannon, William R. 1974. Methodism in a philosophy of history. *Methodist History* 12 (4): 27–43.
Carey, Brycchan. 2002. John Wesley (1703–1791). http://www.brycchancarey.com/abolition/wesley.htm.
———. 2003. William Wilberforce's sentimental rhetoric: Parliamentary reportage and the abolition speech of 1789. In *The Age of Johnson: A Scholarly Annual*, ed. Paul J. Korshin and Jack Lynch, vol. 14, 281–305. New York: AMS Press.
———. 2005. *British Abolitionism and the Rhetoric of Sensibility: Writing, Sentiment, and Slavery, 1760–1807*. Basingstoke: Palgrave Macmillan.
Carwardine, Richard J. 1978. *Transatlantic Revivalism: Popular Evangelicalism in Britain and America, 1790–1865*. Westport, CT: Greenwood Press.
Caudle, James J. 1996. *Measures of Allegiance: Sermon Culture & the Creation of a Public Discourse of Obedience & Resistance in Georgian Britain, 1714–1760*. Dissertation, Yale University.
Cell, George C. 1935. *The Rediscovery of John Wesley*. New York: H. Holt and Company.
Chamberlain, Jeffrey S. 1993. Moralism, justification and the controversy over methodism. *Journal of Ecclesiastical History* 44 (4): 652–678.
Champion, J.A.I. 1992. *The Pillars of Priestcraft Shaken: The Church of England and its Enemies, 1660–1730*. Cambridge: Cambridge University Press.
Chauncy, Charles. 1741. *The New Creature Describ'd and Consider'd*. Boston.
———. 1742. *Enthusiasm Described and Cautioned Against*, Boston.
Chilcote, Paul W. 1991. *John Wesley and the Women Preachers of Early Methodism*. Metuchen, NJ: Scarecrow.
———. 1993. *She Offered Them Christ: The Legacy of Women Preachers in Early Methodism*. Nashville, TN: Abingdon Press.
Clapper, Gregory S. 1984. "True religion" and the affections: A study of John Wesley's abridgement of Jonathan Edward's treatises on religious affections. *Wesleyan Theological Journal* 19 (2): 77–89.
———. 1989. *John Wesley on Religious Affections: His Views on Experience and Emotion and their Role in the Christian Life and Theology*. Metuchen, NJ: Scarecrow Press.

———. 1990. Orthokardia: The practical theology of John Wesley's heart religion. *Quarterly Review* 10: 49–66.

Clark, J.C.D. 1993. *The Language of Liberty, 1660–1832: Political Discourse and Social Dynamics in the Anglo-American World*. Cambridge: Cambridge University Press.

———. 1994. *English Society 1688–1832: Ideology, Social Structure and Political Practice During the Ancien Régime*, 235–247. Cambridge: Cambridge University Press. (a controversial politico-theologico-historical account oriented towards the "confessional state").

Clark, J. C. D 2000. *English Society, 1660–1832: Religion, Ideology, and Politics During the Ancient Regime*. Cambridge: Cambridge University Press, 2000. Reviewed for H-Albion <H-Albion@h-net.msu.edu> (December, 2000) by Marilyn Morris.

Clarke, Adam. 1923. *Memoirs of the Wesley Family: Collected Principally from Original Documents*. London: Printed by J & T Clark and sold by J. Kershaw.

Clarke, W. K. Lowther. 1944. *Eighteenth-Century Piety*. London.

———. 1959. *A History of the S. P. C. K.* [Society for the Promotion of Christian Knowledge]. London.

Clarke, Basil F. W. 1963. *The Building of the Eighteenth-Century Church*. London.

Clarkson, G.E. 1973. John Wesley and William Law's Mysticism. *Religion in Life* 42: 537–544.

Clifford, Alan C. 1990. *Atonement and Justification. English Evangelical Theology, 1640–1790: An Evaluation*. Oxford: Clarendon Press.

Collins, Kenneth J. 1988. The Continuing Significance of Aldersgate [response to "John Wesley against Aldersgate" by T W Jennings, 8:3–22 1988; rejoinder, 100–105]. *Quarterly Review* 8: 90–99.

———. 1989. The Continuing Significance of Aldersgate [response to "John Wesley against Aldersgate" by T W Jennings]. "Twentieth-century Interpretations of John Wesley's Aldersgate Experience: Coherence and Confusion?". *Wesleyan Theological Journal* 24: 18–31.

———. 1990. The Continuing Significance of Aldersgate [response to "John Wesley against Aldersgate" by T W Jennings]. "The Influence of Early German Pietism on John Wesley [Arndt and Francke]". *The Covenant Quarterly* 48: 23–42.

———. 1991. The Continuing Significance of Aldersgate [response to "John Wesley against Aldersgate" by T W Jennings]. "Other Thoughts on Aldersgate: Has the Conversionist Paradigm Collapsed?". *Methodist History* 30 (1): 10–25.

———. 1992. The Continuing Significance of Aldersgate [response to "John Wesley against Aldersgate" by T W Jennings]. "John Wesley's Critical Appropriation of Early German Pietism". *Wesleyan Theological Journal* 27 (1 and 2): 57–92.

———. 1993. The Continuing Significance of Aldersgate [response to "John Wesley against Aldersgate" by T W Jennings]. "John Wesley's Assessment of Christian Mysticism". *Lexington Theological Quarterly* 28 (4): 299–318.

———. 2003. *John Wesley: A Theological Journey*. Nashville, TN: Abingdon Press.

———. 2020. *A Wesley Bibliography*. 9th ed. Wilmore: First Fruits Press. https://issuu.com/asburytheologicalseminary/docs/wesley_bib_nw.

Colón-Emeric, Edgardo A. 2018. *Wesley, Aquinas, and Christian Perfection: An Ecumenical Dialogue*. Waco, TX: Baylor University Press.

Cooke, John. 1783. *The Preacher's Assistant: (after the manner of Mr. Letsome) containing a series of the texts of sermons and discourses published either singly, or in volumes, by divines of the Church of England, and by the dissenting clergy, since the Restoration to the present time*. Oxford: printed for the editor, at the Clarendon-Press—and sold by Mess. Fletcher, D. Prince and J. Cooke, R. Bliss, and S. Arnold, Oxford—Mess. Merrill—and Deighton, Cambridge. (2 volumes 8vo. arranged by book of the bible, and (separately) by special occasion eg Jan 31st. breaks out authors, places of publication, sermon subjects, etc. In libraries called *Pulpit Publications 1660–1782*.

Cosmos, Georgia. 2005. *Huguenot Prophecy and Clandestine Worship in the Eighteenth Century: 'The Sacred Theatre of the Cévennes'*. Aldershot and Burlington, VT: Ashgate.

Coupland, Sir Reginald. 1923. *Wilberforce: A Narrative*. London: Oxford University Press.

Cowley, T. 1969. Les Débuts du Méthodisme et les Courants Évangéliques dans la Société Britannique. *Istina* 14: 387–412.

Cox, Leo George. 1964. *John Wesley's Concept of Perfection*. Kansas City, MO: Beacon Hill Press.

Cunliffe, C., ed. 1992. *Joseph Butler's Moral and Religious Thought: Tercentenary Essays*. Oxford: Clarendon Press.

Cushman, Robert Earl. 1947. Salvation for all: John Wesley and calvinism. In *Methodism*, ed. W.K. Anderson, 103–115. New York, NY: Methodist Publishing House.

Dallimore, Arnold A. 1970. *George Whitefield: The Life and Times of the Great Evangelist of the Eighteenth-Century Revival*. Vol. 2v, 1979. Westchester, IL: The Banner of Truth Trust.

Danker, Ryan N. 2016. *Wesley and the Anglicans: Political Division in Early Evangelicalism*. Westmont: InterVarsity Press.

Davenport, James. 1716–1757. *The Reverend Mr. James Davenport's Confession & Retractations*. Boston: Printed and sold by S. Kneeland and T. Green, in Queenstreet, 1744; Text Creation Partnership. http://name.umdl.umich.edu/n04347.0001.001.

Davie, Donald. 1978. *A Gathered Church: The Literature of the English Dissenting Interest, 1700–1930*. Oxford: Oxford University Press.

———. 1982. *Dissentient Voice: Enlightenment and Christian Dissent: The Ward-Phillips Lectures for 1980 with some Related Pieces*. Notre Dame, IN: University of Notre Dame Press.

———. 1993. *The 18th-Century Hymn in England*. Cambridge: Cambridge University Press.

Davies, Horton. 1961. *Worship and theology in England*, From Watts and Wesley to Maurice, 1690–1850. Vol. III. Princeton, NJ: Princeton University Press.

———. 1975. *Worship and Theology in England, Vol. II, From Andrews to Baxter and Fox, 1603–1690*. Princeton, NJ: Princeton University Press.

Davies, Rupert E. 1981. Justification, sanctification, and the liberation of the person. In *Sanctification and Liberation*, ed. Theodore H. Runyon, 64–82. Nashville, TN: Abingdon.

———. 1985. *Methodism*. London: Epworth.

Davies, Horton. 1992. Charles Wesley and the calvinist tradition. In *Charles Wesley: Poet and Theologian*, ed. S.T. Kimbrough Jr., 186–203. Nashville, TN: Kingwood Books.

Davies, Rupert E., A. Raymond George and E. Gordon Rupp, eds. 1989. *History of the Methodist Church in Great Britain*. Volume 4: Part One *Documents and Source Material*, Part Two *Bibliography*. London.

———, eds. 2017. *A History of the Methodist Church in Great Britain*. Volume One (1965) and Volume Two (1978) pb reprint. Eugene, OR: Wipf and Stock.

Dayfoot, Arthur C. 2000. *The Shaping of the West Indian Church, 1492–1962*. Gainesville: University of Florida Press.

De Arteaga, William L. 2013. The Lord's supper and revival: The Scottish example. http://anglical-pentecostal.blogspot.com/2013/11/the-lords-supper-and-revival-scottish.html.

de la Mothe Guyon, Mme J. B.. 1767–1768. *Lettres Chrétiennes et spirituelles*, 5v, London. (Ward, *Early Evan.* Ch3).

———.. 1775. *The Exemplary Life of the pious Lady Guion translated from ... the original French ...* Dublin. (Ward, *Early Evan.* Ch3).

———.. 1801. *Poems Translated from the French of Mme de la Mothe Guyon by the late William Cowper Esq.* Newport: Pagnell. (Ward, *Early Evan.* Ch3).

Deconinck-Brossard, Françoise. 2002. "Sermons protestants dans l'Europe des Lumières", *le Spectateur européen. The European Spectator* 4: 13–24.

Dedieu, J. 1920. *Le rôle politique des Protestants français de 1685 à 1715*. Paris: Bloud & Gay.

Dimond, Sydney G. 1926. *The Psychology of the Methodist Revival*. London: Humphrey Milford.

———. 1932. *The Psychology of Methodism*. London: Epworth Press.

Donaldson, Gordon. 1985. *Scottish Church History*. Edinburgh: Scottish Academic Press.

Dorr, Donal J. 1964. Total corruption and the Wesleyan tradition. *Irish Theological Quarterly* 31: 303–321.

———. 1965. Wesley's teaching on the nature of holiness. *London Quarterly & Holborn Review* 190: p234–p239.

Doughty, W.L. 1955. *John Wesley, Preacher*. London: Epworth.

Downey, James. 1969a. *The Eighteenth Century Pulpit: A Study of the Sermons of Butler, Berkeley, Secker, Sterne, Whitefield and Wesley*. Oxford: Clarendon Press.

———. 1969b. John Wesley. In *The Eighteenth Century Pulpit*, 189–225. Oxford: Clarendon.

Drescher, Seymour. 1980. Two variants of anti-slavery: Religious organization and social mobilization in Britain and France, 1780–1870. In *Anti-Slavery, Religion and Reform*, ed. Bolt and Drescher, 43–63. London: Wm Dawson/Hamden, CT: Archon Books.

Dreyer, Frederick. 1983. Faith and experience in the thought of John Wesley. *The American Historical Review* 88: 12–30.

———. 1987. Evangelical thought: John Wesley and Jonathan Edwards. *Albion* 19: 177–192.

Driver, Cecil. 1946. *Tory Radical: The Life of Richard Oastler*. Oxford: Oxford University Press. Oastler (1789–1861) was educated in England by Moravians 1798–1806, he was against Catholic Emancipation and parliamentary Reform, but also, though called the "Factory King," he was against slavery, against the New Poor Law, and proponent of the Ten-Hour Factory Act, which limited child labor.

Duffy, Eamon. 1977. Primitive christianity revived: Religious renewal in Augustan England. In *Renaissance and Renewal in Christian History*, ed. D. Baker. Oxford: Blackwell.

Dunn, Samuel. 1996. Wesleyan Christianity: A Religion for the Third Millennium. online.

Edwards, Jonathan. 1747. *A Humble Attempt to Promote Explicit Agreement and Visible Union of God's People in Extraordinary Prayer for the Revival of Religion and the Advancement of Christ's Kingdom on earth, pursuant to Scripture Promises and Prophecies concerning the Last Time*. Boston.

Edwards, Maldwyn L. 1933. *John Wesley and the Eighteenth Century: A Study of His Social and Political Influence*. New York: Abingdon Press.

Eli, R. George. 1993. *Social Holiness: John Wesley's Thinking on Christian Community and its Relationship to the Social Order*. New York: P Lang Pubs.

Ellenzweig, Sarah. 2008. *The Fringes of Belief: English Literature, Ancient Heresy, and the Politics of Freethinking, 1660–1760*. Stanford, CA: Stanford University Press. (Rochester, Blount, Behn, Fontenelle, Swift, Pope).

English, John C. 1989. John Wesley and the english enlightenment: An 'appeal to men of reason and religion'. *Studies on Voltaire and the Eighteenth Century* 263: 400–403.

Ethridge, Willie S. 1971. *Strange Fires: The True Story of John Wesley's Love Affair in Georgia*. Birmingham, AL: Vanguard.

Fairchild, Hoxie N. 1939. *Religious Trends in English Poetry, v1, 1700–1740, Protestantism and the Cult of Sentiment*. New York: Columbia University Press.

Faulkner, John Alfred. 1909. The socialism of John Welsey. In *Social Ideals*, 103–124. London: Robert Culley.

Feilla, Cecilia. 2002. Performing virtue: *Pamela* on the French revolutionary stage, 1793. *Eighteenth Century: Theory and Interpretation* 43 (3): 286–305.

Ferrars, E. X. 2003. *Wesley and the Wesleyans: Religion in Eighteenth-Century Britain*. http://www.amazon.com/exec/obidos/ASIN/0521455324/enlightenmentweb.

Ferrel, Lowell O. 1988. John Wesley and the Enthusiasts [roots of Holiness-Pentecostal tensions]. *Wesleyan Theological Journal* 23 (1–2): 180–187.

Ferrell, Lori A. & Claydon, eds. 1999. *The English Sermon Revised*, Manchester—Robert Ingram, C18-L.

Field, Clive D. 1977. Bibliography of methodist historical literature, 1974, 1975. *Proceedings of the Wesley Historical Society (G.B.)* 1976.

Fitzgerald, Allan D. O. S. A, ed. 1999. *Augustine Through the Ages: An Encyclopedia*. Grand Rapids, MI: Eerdmans.

Flew, R. Newton. 1934. *The Idea of Perfection in Christian Theology*. London: Oxford University Press.

Follett, Richard R. 2002. *Evangelicalism, Penal Theory and the Politics of Criminal Law Reform in England, 1808–1830*.

Forbes, A.M. 1995. Ultimate reality and ethical meaning: Theological utilitarianism in 18th-century England. *Ultimate Reality and Meaning* 18 (2): 119–138.
Franklin, Benjamin. 1987. *Autobiography in Writings*, 1306–1469. New York: Library of America.
Frey, Sylvia R., and Betty Wood. 1998. *Come Shouting to Zion: African American Protestantism in the American South and British Caribbean to 1830*. Chapel Hill: U. of North Carolina Press.
Furneaux, Robin. 1974. *William Wilberforce*. London: Hamish Hamilton.
Garrettson, Freeborn. 1984. In *American Methodist Pioneer: The Life and Journals of the Rev. Freeborn Garrettson, 1752–1827*, ed. D. Robert. Rutland, VT: Simpson.
Gibson, Edmund. Bishop of London, "Lukewarmness and Enthusiasm," pastoral letter (1739). In *The Life and Travels of George Whitefield, M.A*, ed. James Paterson Gledstone, 1871. London: Longmans, Green.
Gilbert, Alan D. 1976. *Religion and Society in Industrial England: Church, Chapel and Social Change*, 1740–1914.
Gill, Frederick C. 1954. *The Romantic Movement and Methodism: A Study of English Romanticism and the Evangelical Revival (1937)*. London: Epworth Press (E. C. Barton).
Gill, Stephen. 1989. *William Wordsworth: A Life*. Oxford: Clarendon Press/Oxford University Press.
Gillies, John. 1712–1796. *Memoirs of the Life and Character of the Late Reverend George Whitefield: of Pembroke College, Oxford, and chaplain to the Right Hon. the Countess of Huntingdon. Faithfully selected from his original papers, journals, and letters, illustrated by a variety of anecdotes, from the best authorities/Originally compiled by the late Rev. John Gillies*. London: Dilly, 1772; 4th ed, ed. Aaron C. Seymour, Philadelphia: Simon Probasco, 1820.
Gledstone, James P. 1871. *The Life and Travels of George Whitefield, M.A.* London: Longmans, Green.
Gravely, Will B. 1985. African methodisms and the rise of black nationalism. In *Rethinking Methodist History: A Bicentennial Historical Consultation*, ed. Russell E. Richey and Kenneth E. Rowe. Nashville: Kingswood Books.
Graves, Richard. 1715–1804. *The Spiritual Quixote, or the Summer's Ramble of Mr. Geoffry Wildgoose, a Comic Romance* (anon.), 1772, 1773, 1774 (two later editions, 1783 and 1808). Satire on John Wesley, George Whitefield, and Methodism in general, which Graves saw as a threat to his Anglican congregation.
Green, J. Brazier. 1945. *John Wesley and William Law*. London: Epworth Press.
Green, V.H.H. 1961. *The Young Mr. Wesley: A Study of John Wesley and Oxford*. New York: St. Martin's Press.
———. 1987. *John Wesley*. Lanham, MD: University Press of America. Reprint of 1964 edition.
Greene, Donald. 1990. How 'degraded' was eighteenth-century anglicanism?". *ECS* 24:1.
Greig, Martin. 1993. The reasonableness of christianity: Gilbert Burnet and the trinitarian controversy of the 1690s. *Journal of Ecclesiastical History* 44 (4): 631–651.
Gunter, W. Stephen. 1989. *The Limits of "Love Divine": John Wesley's Response to Antinomianism and Enthusiasm*. Nashville, TN: Kingswood Books.
Gurses, Derya. 2003. The Hutchinsonian defence of an old testament Trinitarian Christianity: the controversy over Elahim, 1735–1773. *History of European Ideas* 29: 393–409.
Gwynn, Robin D. 1985. *Huguenot Heritage: The History and Contribution of the Huguenots in Britain*. New York: Routledge.
———. 1998. *The Huguenots of London*. Brighton: Alpha. 67 pp. isbn:1-898595-24-0 (paper) [and see brief untitled review by Adrian Tahourdin, TLS, 5000 (January 29, 1999): 36].
Haas, John W., Jr. 1994a. Eighteenth century evangelical responses to science: John Wesley's enduring legacy. *Science and Christian Belief* 6: 83–100.
———. 1994b. John Wesley's views on science and christianity: An examination of the charge of anti-science. *Church History* 63: 378–392.
Halévy, Elie. 1961. *History of the English People in the Nineteenth Century*, Vol. 1, *England in 1815* (1912). Translated by E. I. Watkin & D. A. Barker (1949). New York: Barnes & Noble.
———. 1971. [The Birth of Methodism in England] (article in La Revue de Paris. 1906) tr. & ed. Bernard Semmel. Chicago: University of Chicago Press.

Hampson, John. 2013. *Memoirs of the Late Rev. John Wesley, A.M.: With a Review of his Life and Writings, and a History of Methodism, from its Commencement in 1729, to the Present Time*. Cambridge: Cambridge University Press.
Hampton, Stephen. 2008. *Anti-Arminians: The Anglican Reformed Tradition from Charles II to George I*. (Oxford Theology and Religion Monographs). New York: Oxford University Press.
Harrison, G.E. 1937a. *Haworth Parsonage: Study of Wesley & the Brontes*. Folcroft, PA: Folcroft Press.
Harrison, G. Elsie. 1937b. *Son to Susanna: The Private Life of John Wesley*. R West: Baton Rouge, LA.
Harvey, Paul. 1997. *Redeeming the South: Religious Cultures and Racial Identities among Southern Baptists, 1865–1925*. Chapel Hill: U. of North Carolina Press.
Hatch, Nathan O. 1989. *The Democratization of American Christianity*. New Haven, CT: Yale University Press.
———. 1994. The puzzle of American methodism. *Church History* 63: 175–189.
Hatch, Nathan O., and John Wigger, eds. 2001. *Methodism and the Shaping of American Culture*. Nashville, TN: Kingswood Books.
Hauerwas, Stanley. 1976. Christianizing perfection: Second thoughts on character and sanctification. In *Wesleyan Theology Today*, ed. Theodore C. Runyon, 251–263. New York: AMS Press; repr. Nashville, TN: Kingswood, 1985.
Haverly, Thomas P. 1989. Conversion narratives: Wesley's Aldersgate narrative and the portrait of Peter in the Gospel of Mark. *Wesleyan Theological Journal* 24: 54–73.
Haydon, C. 1993. In *The Church of England c. 1689-c. 1833*, ed. J. Walsh and S. Taylor. Cambridge: Cambridge University Press.
Haykin, M.A.G., and K.J. Stewart, eds. 2008. *Bebbington's Evangelicalism in Modern Britain: The Emergence of Evangelicalism: Exploring Historical Continuities*. Nottingham.
Heitzenrater, Richard P. 1974. Oxford diaries and the first rise of methodism. *Methodist History* 12: 110–135.
———. 1984. *The Elusive Mr. Wesley*. Vol. 2. Nashville, TN: Abingdon Press.
———. 1988. Wesley and his diary. In *John Wesley: Contemporary Perspectives*, ed. John Stacey, 11–22. London: Epworth.
———. 1989a. At full liberty: Doctrinal standards in early American methodism. In *Mirror and Memory: Reflections on Early Methodism*, ed. Richard P. Heitzenrater, 189–204. Nashville, TN: Kingswood Books.
———., ed. 1989b. *Mirror and Memory: Reflections on Early Methodism*. Nashville, TN: Kingswood Books.
———. 1990. The Second Rise of Methodism: Georgia [J Wesley's journals]. *Methodist History* 28 (2): 117–132.
———. 1995. *Wesley and the People Called Methodists*, 2013. Nashville, TN: Abingdon Press.
———. The *Imitatio Christi* and the Great Commandment: Virtue and obligation in Wesley's Ministry with the poor. In *The Portion of the Poor*, ed. M. Douglas, 1994. Nashville, TN: Kingswood.
Hempton, David N. 1984. *Methodism and Politics in British Society, 1750–1850*. Stanford, CA: Stanford University Press.
———. 1993. John Wesley and England's 'Ancien Regime'. In *Modern Religious Beliefs*, ed. Stuart Mews, 36–55. London: Epworth.
———. 1996a. *Religion and Political Culture in Britain and Ireland: From the Glorious Revolution to the Decline of Empire*. New York: Cambridge University Press.
———. 1996b. *The Religion of the People: Methodism and Popular Religion, c. 1750–1900*. New York: Routledge.
———. 2005. *The Religion of the People: Methodism. The Religion of the People: Methodism. Methodism: Empire of the Spirit*. New Haven, CT: Yale University Press. (international-Rivers).
———. 2008. *The Religion of the People: Methodism. The Religion of the People: Methodism. Methodism: Empire of the Spirit*. New Haven. *The Religion of the People: Methodism. Methodism: Empire of the Spirit*. New Haven. *Evangelical Disenchantment: 9 Portraits of Faith and Doubt*. New Haven, CT: Yale University Press (important from Toby).

Henry, Stuart C. 1957. *George Whitefield: Wayfaring Witness*. Nashville, Abingdon Press.
Heyrman, Christine L. *Southern Cross: The Beginnings of the Bible Belt*. New York: Knopf, 1997; Chapel Hill, NC: UNC Press, pb, 1998. Rvws by Ruth Alden Doan in *Journal of the Early Republic* 18:4(1998), p735–737; by R. Stephen Warner in *Social Forces* 78:4: 1587–1588.
Hildebrandt, Franz. 1951. *From Luther to Wesley*. London: Lutterworth.
———. 1956. *Christianity According to the Wesleys*. London: Epworth.
Hilton, Boyd. 1988. *The Age of Atonement: The Influence of Evangelicalism on Social and Economic Thought, 1785–1865*. Oxford: Clarendon Press/NY: Oxford University Press.
Hindley, J.C. 1957. A study in the origins of 'experimental theology'. *London Quarterly & Holborn Review* 182: 99–109. and (July 1957): 199–210.
Hindmarsh, D. Bruce. 1994. 'I am a sort of middle-man': The politically correct evangelicalism of John Newton, in George Rawlyk & Mark A. Noll, eds. *Amazing Grace: Evangelicalism in Australia, Britain, Canada, and the United States*. Grand Rapids, MI: Baker Books, c1993; Toronto: McGill-Queen's University Press (Studies in the History of Religion), 29.
———. 1997. 'My chains fell off, my heart was free': Early Methodist Conversion Narrative, c.1735–1745. London Modern Religious History Seminar.
———. 2001. *John Newton and the English Evangelical Tradition: Between the Conversions of Wesley and Wilberforce*. New York: Oxford University Press, 1996; Grand Rapids, MI: Eerdman's.
———. 2005. *The Evangelical Conversion Narrative: Spiritual Autobiography in Early Modern England*. New York: Oxford University Press. (See rvw by Noll).
———. 2018. *The Spirit of Early Evangelicalism: True Religion in a Modern World*. New York: Oxford University Press.
Hobhouse, Stephen. 1936. '*Fides et ratio*', the book [by Poiret] which introduced Jacob Boehme to William Law. *The Journal of Theological Studies* 37: 350–368.
Hobsbawm, E. J. 1964. Methodism and the threat of revolution in Britain. (History Today, Feb, 1957) in Hobsbawm, *Labouring Men, Studies in the History of Labour*. New York: Basic Books.
Hobsbawm, E.J. 1965. *Primitive Rebels*. Vol. 1959. New York: Norton.
Hochschild, Adam. 2004. *Bury the Chains: Prophets, Slaves, and Rebels in the First Human Rights Crusade*. Boston: Houghton Mifflin.
Hole, Robert. 1989. *Pulpits, Politics and Public Order in England, 1760–1832*. New York: Cambridge University Press.
Holland, Bernard G. 1971. The conversions of John and Charles Wesley and their place in methodist tradition. *The Proceedings of the Wesley Historical Society* 38: 45–53. 65–71.
———. 1973. 'A Species of Madness': The Effect of John Wesley's Early Preaching. *Proceedings of the Wesley Historical Society* 39: 77–85.
Holmes, Geoffrey. 1973. *The Trial of Dr Sacheverell*. London: Eyre Methuen.
Hopkins, James K. 1982. *A Woman to Serve Her People: Joanna Southcott and English Millenarianism in an Era of Revolution*. Austin, TX: University of Texas Press.
Horton, James P. 1839. *A Narrative of the Early Life, Remarkable Conversion, and Spiritual Labors of James P. Horton, Who Has Been a Member of the Methodist Episcopal Church upward of Forty Years*, n.p.
Houston, Joel. 2019. *Wesley, Whitefield and the 'Free Grace' Controversy: The Crucible of Methodism*. (Routledge Methodist Studies Series) Routledge.
Howard, Harry L. 1992. John Wesley: Tory or democrat? *Methodist History* 31 (1): 38–46.
Hoyles, John. "Nature and Enthusiasm," The Edges of Augustanism. Springer International Archives of the History of Ideas Archives internationales d'Histoire des Idees (ARCH, vol. 53), 123–132.
Hughes, Robert D. 1975. Wesley roots of Christian socialism. *The Ecumenist* 13: 49–53.
Hulley, Leonard D. 1987. *Wesley: A Plain Man for Plain People*. Westville, South Africa: Methodist Church of South Africa.
———. 1988. *To Be and To Do: Exploring Wesley's Thought on Ethical Behavior*. Pretoria: University of South Africa.
Hutin, Serge. 1960. *Les Disciples anglais de Jacob Boehme au 17e et 18e siècles*. Paris: Denoël.

Hutton, James (1715–1795). *Memoirs of James Hutton: Comprising the Annals of His Life and Connection with the United Brethren*. (1856), ed. Daniel Benham, 112. Nabu Press, 2011.
Hynson, Leon O. 1979. John Wesley and the "Unitas Fratrum": A theological analysis. *Methodist History* 18: 26–60.
———. 1984. *To Reform the Nation: Theological Foundations of Wesley's Ethics*. Grand Rapids, MI: Zondervan.
———.. Whitefield and Wesley Perfectionism—A Response to [Timothy] Smith.
Impartialitas. 1808. George Whitefield, and *The Minor*, in *The Monthly Mirror*, 384.
Irlam, Shaun. 1999. *Elations: The Poetics of Enthusiasm in Eighteenth-Century Britain*. Stanford, CA: Stanford University Press.
Isaac, Robert. 1840. In *The Correspondence of William Wilberforce*, ed. Samuel Wilberforce, vol. 2v. London: John Murray.
Isaac, Robert, and Samuel Wilberforce. 1838. *The Life of William Wilberforce*. Vol. 5v. London: John Murray.
Itzkin, Elissa S. 1975. The Halévy thesis—A working hypothesis? English revivalism: Antidote for revolution and radicalism 1789–1815. *Church History* 44 (1): 47–56.
Jarratt, Devereaux. 1779. *A Brief Narrative of the Revival of Religion in Virginia, in a Letter to a Friend....* 4th ed. London: R. Hawes.
Jennings, Theodore W., Jr. 1988. John Wesley against Aldersgate. *Quarterly Review* 8: 3–22.
———. 1991. John Wesley on the origin of methodism. *Methodist History* 29 (2): 76–86.
Johnson, Richard O. 1981. The development of the love feast in early American methodism. *Methodist History* 19 (2): 67–83.
Johnson, W. Stanley. 1988. John Wesley's concept of enthusiasm. *Kardia* 3: 27–38.
Jones, B.E. 1964. Reason and religion joined; The place of reason in Wesley's thought. *London Quarterly & Holborn Review* 189: 110–113.
Jones, D. C. 2004. *"A Glorious Work in the World": Welsh Methodism and the International Evangelical Revival, 1735–1750*, Cardiff.
Jones, Christopher. 2013. 'It's like methodism, only more': Mormon conversion and narratives of the great apostasy. *Patheos*. https://www.patheos.com/blogs/peculiarpeople/2013/02/its-like-methodism-only-more-mormon-conversion-and-narratives-of-the-great-apostasy/.
Jordan, W.K. 1965. *The Development of Religious Toleration in England*. Vol. 3v. New York: Peter Smith repr.
Kassler, Michael, and Philip Olleson. 2005. *Samuel Wesley (1766–1837): A Source Book*. Burlington, VT: Ashgate.
Katz, David S. 1986. John Wesley and English Arminianism. *Evangelical Journal* 4 (1): 15–28.
———. 1987. Characteristics of Wesley's Arminianism. *Wesleyan Theological Journal* 22 (1): 88–100.
———. 1988. (Tel Aviv University), *Sabbath and Sectarianism in Seventeenth-Century England*. New York: E.J. Brill.
———.. 1990. Characteristics of Wesley's Arminianism. *Wesleyan Theological Journal* 22. "John Wesley, The Methodists, and Social Reform in England." *Wesleyan Theological Journal* 25(1): 7–20.
———. 1994. *The Jews in the History of England, 1485–1850*. Oxford: Clartendon Press.
———.. 2000. Aestheticizing Scripture; Anaesthetizing Revolution: The Damping Down of Millenarianism in Eighteenth-Century England. *Cambridge History of Medicine Seminar*, 5:00 p.m. in Seminar Room 1, Department of History and Philosophy of Science, Free School Lane, Cambridge CB2 3RH.
Keefer, Luke L. 1984. John Wesley: Disciple of early Christianity [reply, H A Snyder, C. L. Bence]. *Wesleyan Theological Journal* 19 (1): 23–32.
Kendall, H.B. 1906. *History of the Primitive Methodist Church*. Vol. 2v. London.
Kent, John H.S. 1974. Methodism and revolution. *Methodist History* 12 (4): 136–144. (Halévy thesis).
Kent, John. 2002. *Wesley and the Wesleyans: Religion in Eighteenth-Century Britain*. New York: Cambridge University Press.

Keymer, Tom. 2004. *Richardson's 'Clarissa' and the Eighteenth-Century Reader*. New York: Cambridge University Press.
Kidd, Colin. 1997. The Kirk, the French Revolution and the Burden of Scottish Whiggery. dans Nigel Aston (édit.), *Religious Change in Europe 1650–1914: Essays for John McManners*. Oxford.
Kinkel, Gary Steven. 1990. The big chill: The theological disagreement which separated John Wesley and Count Zinzendorf. *Unitas fratrum* 27–28: 89–112.
Kirkham, Donald H. 1975. John Wesley's "Calm Address": The response of the critics. *Methodist History* 14: 13–23.
Kitson, Peter. eds. 1999. *Slavery, Abolition and Emancipation*. London: Pickering & Chatto; v2 (of 8): includes Ramsay, Clarkson, Newton, Wilberforce, Beckford, Harris, etc.
Kitson, Peter & Debbie Lee, eds. 1999. *Slavery, Abolition and Emancipation*. London: Pickering & Chatto; v1 (of 8): includes Sancho, Equiano, Cugoano, Prince, Seacole, Wedderburn, Gronniosaw, etc.
Klein, Milton M. 2004. *Amazing Grace: John Thornton & the Clapham Sect*, 160 pp.
Knight, Henry H. 1992. *The Presence of God in the Christian Life: John Wesley and the Means of Grace*. Metuchen, NJ: Scarecrow Press.
Knox, Ronald A. 1961. *Enthusiasm: A Chapter in the History of Religion, with Special Reference to the Seventeenth and Eighteenth Centuries (1950)*. New York: Oxford University Press Galaxy.
Knox-Shaw, Peter. 2004. *Jane Austen and the Enlightenment*. New York: Cambridge University Press.
Koch, Mark. 2013. 'A spectacle pleasing to god and man': Sympathy and the show of charity in the restoration spittle [St. Mary's Hospital] sermons. *Eighteenth-Century Studies* 46 (4): 479–497.
Koerber, Carolo. 1967. *The Theology of Conversion According to John Wesley*. Rome: Neo-Eboraci.
Koretsky, Deanna P. 2013. Sarah Wesley, British methodism, and the Feminist question, again. *Eighteenth-Century Studies* 46 (2): 223–238. (Charles Wesley's daughter as a forgotten early and counter-enlightenment feminist).
Krutch, Joseph Wood. 1949. *Comedy and Conscience after the Restoration*. New York: Columbia University Press.
Laborie, Lionel. 2015. *Enlightening Enthusiasm: Prophecy and Religious Experience in Early Eighteenth-Century England*. Manchester, UK: Manchester University Press.
Lambert, Frank. 1990. 'Pedlar in divinity': George Whitefield and the great awakening, 1737–1745. *The Journal of American History* 77 (3): 812–837.
———. 1993a. *"Pedlar in Divinity" George Whitefield and the Transatlantic Revivals, 1737–1770*, c1994. Princeton, NJ: Princeton University Press.
———. 1993b. Subscribing for profits and piety: The friendship of Benjamin Franklin and George Whitefield. *William and Mary Quarterly* 50 (3): 529–554.
Lavington, George. 1754. *Enthusiasm of methodists and papists compared*, 3pts in 2v. London: J. & P. Knapton.
Lawson, John. 1988. The conversion of the Wesleys: 1738 reconsidered. *The Asbury Theological Journal* 43 (2): 7–44.
Lean, Garth. 1979. *Strangely Warmed*. Wheaton, IL: Tyndale.
Lee, Umphrey. 1931. *Historical Backgrounds of Early Methodist Enthusiasm*. New York, NY: AMS Press.
Legg, J. Wickham. 1914. *English Church Life from the Restoration to the Tractarian Movement*. London.
Leland, John. 1845. *The Writings of the Late Elder John Leland Including Some Events in His Life*, ed., L. F. Greene, New York: G. W. Wood.
Leland, Scott. 1974. The Message of Early American Methodism. *In History of American Methodism*, ed. Emory S. Bucke, vol. 1, 291–359. Nashville, TN: Abingdon Press.
Lessenich, Rolf P. 1972. *Elements of pulpit oratory in eighteenth-century England (1660–1800)*. Bohlau, 1.
Levy, Andrew. *The First Emancipator: Slavery, Religion, and the Quiet Revolution of Robert Carter* (2005), New York: Random House 2007.

Lewis, Donald, ed. 1995. *A Dictionary of Evangelical Biography*. Cambridge, MA: Blackwell.
Lincoln, Anthony. 1938. *Some Political and Social Ideas of English Dissent*. Cambridge: Cambridge University Press.
Lindstrom, Harald. 1946. *Wesley and Sanctification: A Study in the Doctrine of Salvation*, 1982. Grand Rapids, MI: Francis Asbury Press of Zondervan Publishing House. Reprint of 1950 edition.
Luker, David. 1986. Revivalism in theory and practice: The case of Cornish methodism [1791–1871]. *The Journal of Ecclesiastical History* 37 (4): 603–619.
Lyerly, Cynthia Lynn. 1998. *Methodism and the Southern Mind, 1770–1810*. New York: Oxford University Press.
Lyles, Albert M. 2015. *Methodism Mocked: The Satiric Reaction to Methodism in the Eighteenth Century*. Eugene, OR: Wipf & Stock.
Maas, Robin. 1989. *Crucified Love: The Practice of Christian Perfection*. Nashville, TN: Abingdon Press.
MacMaster, Richard K. 1973. Thomas Rankin and the American colonists. *Proceedings of the Wesley Historical Association (G.B.)* 39 (2): 25–33.
Maddock, Ian J. 2011. *Men of One Book: A Comparison of Two Methodist Preachers, John Wesley and George Whitefield*. Cambridge, UK: Lutterworth Press.
Maddox, Randy L., ed. 1990. *Aldersgate Reconsidered*. Nashville, TN: Kingswood Books.
Maddox, Randy L., and Jason E. Vickers. 2009. *The Cambridge Companion to John Wesley*. Cambridge: Cambridge University Press.
Mahaffey, Jerome D. 2007. *Preaching Politics: The Religious Rhetoric of George Whitefield and the Founding of a New Nation*. Waco, TX: Baylor University Press.
———. 2011. *The Accidental Revolutionary: George Whitefield and the Creation of America*. Waco, TX: Baylor University Press.
Marshall, I.H. 1962. Sanctification in the teaching of John Wesley and John Calvin. *The Evangelical Quarterly* 34: 75–82.
Mastromarino, Mark A. 1996. *Taking Heaven by Storm: Methodism and the Popularization of American Christianity 1770–1820*. New York: Oxford University Press, forthcoming.
Mathews, Donald G. 1965. *Slavery and Methodism: A Chapter in American Morality, 1780–1845*. Princeton, NJ: Princeton University Press.
———. 1969. The second great awakening as an organizing process, 1780–1830: An hypothesis. *American Quarterly* 21: 23–43.
———. 1980. Religion and slavery: The case of the American south. In *Anti-Slavery, Religion and Reform*, ed. Bolt and Drescher, p207–p232. London: Wm Dawson/Hamden, CT: Archon Books.
May, Cedrick. 2004. John Marrant and the narrative construction of an early black methodist evangelical. *African American Review* 38 (4): 553–570.
McBride, I.R. 1999. *Scripture politics: Ulster presbyterians and Irish radicalism in the late eighteenth century*. New York: Oxford University Press.
McCarthy, William, and Elizabeth Kraft, eds. 1994. *The Poems of Anna Letitia Barbauld*. Athens: University of Georgia Press. children's education.
McCullough, Peter & Lori Anne Ferrell, eds. 2000. *The English Sermon Revised: Religion, Literature and History 1600–1750*. (Politics, Culture and Society in Early Modern Britain, 9). Manchester and New York: Manchester University Press.
McFerrin, John B. 1888. *History of Methodism in Tennessee*, v1. Publishing House of the M. E. Church.
McGever, Sean. 2020. *Born Again: The Evangelical Theology of Conversion in John Wesley and George Whitefield* (Studies in Historical and Systematic Theology) pb.
McGinty, J. Walter. 2003. *Robert Burns and Religion*. Burlington, VT: Ashgate.
McGonigle, Herbert B. 1988. *The Arminianism of John Wesley*. Derbys, England: Moorley's Bookshop.
———.. 2001. *Sufficient Saving Grace: John Wesley's Evangelical Arminianism*. (Studies in Evangelical History and Thought), Paternoster.

McIlvanney, L. 1995. Robert Burns and the Calvinist Radical Tradition. *History Workshop Journal* 40: 133–150.
McKenzie, Alan T. 1990. *Certain, Lively Episodes: The Articulation of Passion in Eighteenth-Century Prose*. Athens: University of Georgia Press.
McLeister, Ira F. 1976. *Conscience and Commitment: The History of the Wesleyan Methodist Church of America*. Wesleyan History Series, Vol. 1. 4th revised ed. Marion, IN: Wesley Press.
Michalson, Carl. 1982. The hermeneutics of holiness in Wesley. In *God's Word for Today*, ed. Wayne McCown and James E. Massey, 31–52. Anderson, IN: Warner.
Miguez Bonino, J. 1981. Wesley's doctrine of sanctification from a liberationist perspective. In *Sanctification and Liberation*, ed. Theodore H. Runyon, 49–63. Nashville, TN: Abingdon.
Miller, John. 1986. *Religion in the Popular Prints*. Cambridge: Chadwyck-Healey. includes "The Scheming Triumvirate," a 1760 print (BMC 3730) satirizing George Whitefield, Laurence Sterne, and Samuel Foote, Plate 71, p 202–03.
Monk, Robert C. 1966. *John Wesley: His Puritan Heritage*. Nashville, TN: Abingdon Press.
Moore, D. Marselle. 1985. Development in Wesley's thought on sanctification and perfection. *Wesleyan Theological Journal* 20 (2): 29–53.
Mounsey, Chris. 2001. *Christopher smart: Clown of God*. Bucknell University Press. (Bucknell Studies in Eighteenth-Century Literature and Culture).
Nagler, A. W. 1918. *Pietism and Methodism: OR The Significance of German Pietism in the Origin and Early Development of Methodism*. Nashville, TN: Publishing House, Methodist Church South. https://archive.org/stream/pietismmethodism00nagl/pietismmethodism00nagl_djvu.txt.
Nelson, James D. 1988. The strangeness of Wesley's warming. *Journal of Theology* (United Theological Seminary) 92: 12–24.
Nettles, Thomas J. 1995. John Welsey's contention with calvinism: Interactions then and now. In *The Grace of God, the bondage of the will*, ed. T.R. Schreiner and B.A. Ware, vol. 2, 297–332. Grand Rapids, MI: Baker.
Newman, Richard S. *Freedom's Prophet: Bishop Richard Allen, the AME Church, and the Black Founding Fathers*. New York: New York University Press, 359 pp. $34.95.
Newton, John A. 1964. *Methodism and the puritans*. London: Dr. William's Library Trust.
Nicholson, Roy S. 1952. John Wesley's personal experience of Christian perfection. *The Asbury Seminarian* 6 (1): 65–89.
Nockles, Peter B. 1996. *The Oxford Movement in Context: Anglican High Churchmanship, 1760–1857*, 1994. New York: Cambridge University Press.
Noll, Mark A[llan]. 1974. Romanticism and the Hymns of Charles Wesley. *The Evangelical Quarterly* 46: 195–223.
———. 1975. John Wesley and the doctrine of assurance. *Bibliotheca Sacra* 132: 161–177.
———. 2003. *The Rise of Evangelicalism: The Age of Edwards, Whitefield and the Wesleys* (*A History of Evangelicalism: People, Movements and Ideas in the English-Speaking World*, Book 1). Downers Grove, IL: InterVarsity Press.
———. 2007. Rvw of D. Bruce Hindmarsh, The evangelical conversion narrative: Spiritual autobiography in early modern England. *Journal of the American Academy of Religion* 75: 470–473.
Noll, Mark A., David W. Bebbington, and George A. Rawlyk, eds. 1994. *Evangelicalism: Comparative Studies of Popular Protestantism in North America, the British Isles, and Beyond, 1700–1990*. New York: Oxford University Press. Rvw by Martin Marty, *Journal of Southern History* 61:2(May, 1995), p363–365.
Norwood, Frederick A. 1974. *The Story of American Methodism*. Nashville, TN: Abingdon Press. No Arminianism.
Nott, George F. 1803. *Religious Enthusiasm Considered; in Eight Sermons, preached before the University of Oxford, in the year MDCCCII. at the lecture founded by John Bampton, A.M. Canon of Salisbury*. Oxford: The University Press for the author; sold by W. Hanwell and J. Parker.
Nuttall, F. 1981. Methodism and the older dissent: Some perspectives. *Journal of the United Reformed Church History Society* 2: 259–274.

Nuttall, Geoffrey F., et al, eds. 1964. *The Beginnings of Nonconformity*. London.
O'Brien, Susan. 1986. A transatlantic community of saints: The great awakening and the first evangelical network. *American Historical Review* 91: 811–832.
O'Malley, J. Steven. 1986. Recovering the vision of holiness: Wesley's epistemic basis. *The Asbury Theological Journal* 41 (1): 3–17.
———. 1994. Pietist influences in the eschatological thought of John Wesley and Jurgen Moltmann. *Wesleyan Theological Journal* 29 (1): 127–139.
Oglethorpe, James E. 1990. *Some Account of the Design of the Trustees for establishing Colonys in America. (1733)*. Athens: University of Georgia Press.
Ong, Walter J. 1953. Peter Ramus and the naming of methodism. *Journal of the History of Ideas* 14: 235–248.
Orcibal, Jean. 1965. The theological originality of John Wesley and continental spirituality. In *A History of the Methodist Church in Great Britain*, ed. R.E. Davies and E.G. Rupp, vol. I, 83–111. London: Epworth.
Orentas, Rimas J. 1995. *George Whitefield—Lightning Rod of the Great Awakening*.
Outler, Albert C., ed. 1964. *John Wesley*. New York: Oxford University Press.
———. 1971. *Evangelism in the Wesleyan Spirit*. Nashville, TN: Tidings. See especially Chapter 3, "A Third Great Awakening?".
———. 1975. *Theology in the Wesleyan Spirit*. Nashville, TN: Discipleship Resources.
———. 1989. Pietism and enlightenment: Alternatives to tradition. In *Christian Spirituality III*, ed. Louis Dupre and Don Saliers, 240–256. New York: Crossroad.
———. 1991. *The Wesleyan Theological Heritage: Essays of Albert C. Outler*. Grand Rapids, MI: Zondervan.
Paley, William. 1998. *The Works of William Paley; with Additional Sermons and a Corrected Account of the Life and Writings of the Author* (1830), intr. Victor Nuovo, 6v. Bristol, UK: Thoemmes Press.
Pelton, Samuel. 1822. *The absurdities of Methodism* (debate w/minister Lawrence Kean, 1821). New York: Bliss & White.
Peters, John L. 1985. *Christian Perfection and American Methodism*. Grand Rapids, MI: Francis Asbury Press of Zondervan Publishing House. Reprint of the 1956 edition with a new foreword by Albert C. Outler.
Pilmore, Joseph. 1969. In *The Journal of Joseph Pilmore, Methodist Itinerant for the Years August 1, 1769 to January 2, 1774, ed*, ed. Frederick E. Maser and T. Howard. Philadelphia: Maag.
Pitts, Walter F. 1993. *Old Ship of Zion: The Afro-Baptist Ritual in the African Diaspora*. New York: Oxford University Press.
Podmore, Colin. 1998. *The Moravian Church in England, 1728–1760*. New York: Oxford University Press.
Pollock, John Charles. 1972. *George Whitefield and the Great Awakening*. Garden City. New York: Doubleday; London: Hodder & Staughton, 1973.
Portius, G. V. 1912. *Caritas Anglicana, or, an Historical Inquiry into Those Religious and Philanthropical Societies That Flourished in England Between the Years 1678 and 1740*.
Priestley, Joseph. 2002. In *Memoirs and Correspondence of Joseph Priestley*, ed. J.T. Rutt. Bristol, UK: Thoemmes. Priestley's unfinished autobiography and correspondence with Theophilus Lindsey and Thomas Belsham among others. www.thoemmes.com/theology/priestley_life.htm.
Prince, Michael. 1996. *Philosophical Dialogue in the British Enlightenment: Theology, Aesthetics and the Novel*. Cambridge: Cambridge University Press.
Prince, Thomas Jr., publisher; Thomas Prince Jr. 1745. *The Christian History Containing Accounts of the Revival and Propagation of Religion in Great-Britain and America for the Year 1744*, 5, Boston.
———., publisher; Thomas Prince Jr., ed. 2018. *The Christian History, Containing Accounts of the Revival and Propagation of Religion in Great-Britain & America for the Year 1743* I:1(March, 1743), Boston: Kneeland & Green, 1744. Reprint, Hard Press, Kindle Edition.
Pucelik, Thomas M. 1963. *Christian Perfection According to John Wesley*. Rome: Officium Libri Catholici.

Rack, Henry Derman. 1987. Religious societies and the origin of methodism [Societies for the reformation of manners]. *The Journal of Ecclesiastical History* 38: 582–595.
———. 1993. *Reasonable Enthusiast: John Wesley and the Rise of Methodism*. London: Epworth Press, 1989; Nashville, TN: Abingdon Press.
Rattenbury, J. Ernest. 1928. *Wesley's Legacy to the World: Six Studies in the Permanent Values of the Evangelical Revival*. London: Epworth Press (J. A. Sharp.
———. 1938. *The Conversion of the Wesleys: A Critical Study*.
———. 1941. *The Evangelical Doctrines of Charles Wesley's Hymns*.
Rawlyk, George A. and Mark A. Noll, eds. 1994. *Amazing Grace: Evangelicalism in Australia, Britain, Canada, and the United States*. Grand Rapids, MI: Baker Books, c1993; Toronto: McGill-Queen's University Press (Studies in the History of Religion).
Reisinger, Ernest. *Whitefield, Calvinism and Evangelism*.
Reist, I.W. 1975. John Wesley and George Whitefield: A study in the integrity of two theologies of grace. *The Evangelical Quarterly* 47: 26–40.
Richetti, John, ed. 2005. *The Cambridge History of English Literature, 1660–1780*, 2012. New York: Cambridge University Press.
Richey, Russell E. 1991. *Early American Methodism*. Bloomington: Indiana University Press.
Richey, Russell E., and Kenneth E. Rowe, eds. 1985. *Rethinking Methodist History: A Bicentennial Historical Consultation*. Nashville, TN: Kingswood Books.
Richey, Russell E., Kenneth E. Rowe, and Jean Miller Schmidt. 1993. *Perspectives on American Methodism: Interpretive Essays*. Nashville, TN: Kingswood Books.
Rivers, Isabel. 1982. Dissenting and methodist books of practical divinity. In *Books and Their Readers in Eighteenth Century England*, ed. Isabel Rivers, 127–164. New York: St. Martins.
———. 1991. *Reason, Grace, and Sentiment: A Study of the Language of Religion and Ethics in England, 1660–1780*, vol I, *Whichcote to Wesley*. Cambridge: Cambridge University Press (Cambridge Studies in Eighteenth-Century English Literature and Thought #8).
———. 2000. *Reason, Grace and Sentiment: A Study of the Language of Religion and Ethics in England, 1660–1780*, vol V, *Shaftesbury to Hume*. Cambridge: Cambridge University Press (Cambridge Studies in Eighteenth-Century English Literature and Thought #37).
———. 2005. Religion and literature. In *The Cambridge History of English Literature, 1660–1780*, ed. Richetti, 467. New York: Cambridge University Press.
———. 2009. Review essay: Writing the history of early evangelicalism. *History of European Ideas* 35 (1): 105–111.
———. 2018. *Vanity Fair and the Celestial City: Dissenting, Methodist, and Evangelical Literary Culture in England 1720–1800*. Oxford: Oxford University Press.
Rix, Robert. William Blake and the Radical Swedenborgians. http://esoteric.msu.edu/VolumeV/Blake.htm.
Robbins, Keith, ed. 1990. *Protestant Evangelicalism: England, Ireland, Germany and America, c. 1750-c. 1950, Essays in Honor of W.R. Ward*. Cambridge, MA: Blackwell.
Rogal, Samuel J. 1983. *John and Charles Wesley*. New York, NY: Macmillan.
———. 1988a. *John Wesley's London: A Guidebook*. Lewiston, NY: E Mellen.
———. 1988b. *John Wesley's Mission to Scotland*. Lewiston, NY: E Mellen.
———. 1989. Electricity: John Wesley's curious and important subject. *Eighteenth Century Life* 13: 79–90.
———. 1991. *A bibliographical dictionary of 18th-century Methodism*, v1 (A-D), v2 (E-H), Lewiston. New York: Mellen Press.
———. 1993a. *A bibliographical dictionary of 18th-century methodism. John Wesley in Ireland, 1747–1789*. Vol. 2 pts. Lewiston, NY: E Mellen.
———. 1993b. *A bibliographical dictionary of 18th-century Methodism. John Wesley in Wales, 1739–1790: Lions & Lambs*. Lewiston, NY: E Mellen.
———. 1994. A bibliographical dictionary of 18th-century methodism. Ladies Huntingdon, Glenorchy, and Maxwell: Militant methodist women. *Methodist History* 32: 126–132.
———. 2000. For the love of Bach: The Charles Burney—Samuel Wesley correspondence," *BACH*, 23(1): 31–37. "Wesley deified Bach, and named his oldest illegitimate son Samuel Sebastian." —Laura Kennelly, C18-L, 6Dec00.

Rogers, Charles Allen. 1966. John Wesley and Jonathan Edwards. *Duke Divinity School Bulletin* 31: 20–38.
Rosman, Doreen. 2004. *The Evolution of the English Churches 1500–2000.*
Ross, Valentine Simon. 1998. Significant inroads into 'Satan's Seat'—early methodism in Bradford, 1740–1760. *Proceedings of the Wesley Historical Society* 51 (5): 141–154. ("love feasts" and collapsing floors).
Rott, Ludwig. 1968. *Die englischen Beziehungen der Erweckungsbewegung und die Anfänge des Wesleyanischen Methodismus in Deutschland.* Frankfurt a/Main: Studiengemeinschaft für Geschichte des Methodismus; Stuttgart: Auslieferung durch das Christliche Verlagshaus.
Rowe, Kenneth E, ed. 1980. *The Place of Wesley in the Christian Tradition.* (1976) Revised ed. with updated bibliography. Metuchen, NJ: Scarecrow Press.
———. 1976. The search for the historical Wesley. In *The Place of Wesley in the Christian Tradition*, ed. Kenneth E. Rowe, 11–38. Metuchen, NJ: Scarecrow.
Roxburgh, Kenneth B.E. 1994. The Scottish evangelical awakening of 1742 and the religious societies. *Journal of the United Reformed Church History Society* 5: 260–273.
Rudolph, L. C. 1966. *Francis Asbury.* Nashville, TN.
Runyon, Theodore H. 1981a. Wesley and the theologies of liberation. In *Sanctification and Liberation: Liberation in the Light of the Wesleyan Tradition*, ed. Theodore H. Runyon, 9–48. Nashville, TN: Abington.
———. 1981b. *Sanctification and Liberation: A Reexamination in the Light of the Wesleyan Tradition (1977).* Nashville, TN: Abingdon Press.
Rupp, E. Gordon. 1965. Methodists, Anglicans, and Orthodox. In *We Belong to One Another: Methodist, Anglican and Orthodox*, ed. A.M. Allchin, 13–29. London: Epworth.
———. 1971. Paul and Wesley. In *De Dertende Apostel en het Elfde Gebod*, ed. G.C. Berkouwer and H.A. Oberman, 102–110. Kampen: K.H. Kok.
———. 1987. *Religion in England, 1688–1791* (Oxford History of the Christian Church), 1st ed. Oxford: Clarendon Press.
Ryan, Robert M. 1997. *The Romantic Reformation: Religious Politics in English Literature, 1789–1824*, 2000. New York: Cambridge University Press.
Ryder, Mary R. 1985. Avoiding the "many-headed Monster": Wesley and Johnson on enthusiasm. *Methodist History* 23 (4): 214–222.
Ryle, J. C. 1816–1900. George Whitefield and his Ministry. Ch1 of *Christian Leaders of the 18th Century.* London: T. Nelson, 1878. https://banneroftruth.org/us/store/history-biography/christian-leaders-of-the-18th-century/.
Sambrook, James. 1993. *The Eighteenth Century: The Intellectual and Cultural Context of English Literature, 1700–1789*, 2nd ed. Middleton.
Sangster, William E. 1984. *The Path to Perfection: An Examination and Restatement of John Wesley's Doctrine of Christian Perfection.* (1943) Repr. London: Epworth Press.
Sasson, Diane. 1983. *The Shaker Spiritual Narrative.* Knoxville: University of Tennessee Press.
Schmidt, Martin. 1958. *The Young Wesley: Missionary and Theologian of Missions.* London: Epworth.
———. 1962–1973. *John Wesley: A Theological Biography.* Vol. 2. Nashville, TN: Abingdon Press.
Schmidt, Leigh Eric. 2001. *Holy Fairs: Scottish Communions and American Revivals in the Early Modern Period (Princeton, 1989)*, 2nd ed. Grand Rapids, MI: Eerdmans.
Schneider, A. Gregory. 1993. *The Way of the Cross Leads Home: The Domestication of American Methodism*, Bloomington: Indiana University Press, "family religion".
Schofield, Robert E. 1953. John Wesley and science in 18th century England. *Isis* 44: 331–340.
Schwartz, Hillel. 1978. *Knaves, Fools, Madmen, and that Subtile Effluvium: A Study of the Opposition to the French Prophets in England, 1706–1710.* Gainsville, FL: University Presses of Florida.
———. 1980. *The French Prophets: The History of a Millenarian Group in Eighteenth-Century England.* Berkeley: University of California Press.
Scotland, Nigel Adrian D. 1997a. Methodism and the English labour movement, 1800–1906. *Anvil* 14: 36–48. (Halévy Thesis).

———. 1997b. The role of Methodism in the Chartist movement. *Wesley Historical Society Bristol Branch Bulletin* 77: 1–14. (Halévy Thesis).

Scouloudi, Irene, ed. 1987. *Huguenots in Britain and Their French Background, 1550–1800*.

Sell, Alan P.F., ed. 2004a. *Protestant Nonconformist Texts, v2, The Eighteenth Century*. Burlington, VT: Ashgate.

———., ed. 2004b. *Testimony and Tradition: Studies in Reformed and Dissenting Thought*. Burlington, VT: Ashgate.

Semmel, Bernard. 1971a. The Halévy Thesis. *Encounter* 37 (1): 44–56.

———. ed. & tr. Élie Halévy. *The Birth of Methodism in England*. Chicago: University of Chicago Press, 1971b.

———. 1972. *The Methodist Revolution*. New York: Basic Books. (London: Heinemann, 1974).

Semple, Neil. 1996. *The Lord's Dominion: The History of Canadian Methodism*. Toronto: McGill-Queen's University Press (Studies in the History of Religion). isbn:0-7735-1400-7; Cloth isbn:0-7735-1367-1.

Shaftesbury [Anthony Ashley Cooper, 3rd Earl of Shaftesbury], *Characteristics of Men, Manners, Opinions, Times*, 1711, 1713, 1732, 1737. Shaftesbury's *A Letter concerning Enthusiasm to Lord Somers*, 1707, published anonymously in 1708, appeared in all editions.

Shepherd, Thomas B. 1940. *Methodism and the Literature of the Eighteenth Century*. London: Epworth Press (Edgar C. Barton).

———. 1969. *Methodism & the Literature of the 18th Century. (1940)*. Brooklyn, NY: M S G Haskell House.

Simon, J. W. 1921. *John Wesley and the Religious Societies*.

Slaatte, Howard. 1983. *Fire in the Brand: An Introduction to the Creative Work and Theology of John Wesley*. Lanham, MD: University Press of America.

Smith, Timothy L. 1974. The holiness crusade. In *History of American Methodism*, ed. Emory S. Bucke, vol. 2, 608–627. Nashville, TN: Abingdon Press.

Smith, Warren Thomas. 1979. The Wesleys in Georgia: An evaluation. *The Journal of the Interdenominational Theological Center* 6: 157–167.

———. 1981. Sketches of early black methodists. *The Journal of the Interdenominational Theological Center* 9: 1–18.

Smith, Timothy L. 1984. George Whitefield and Wesleyan Perfectionism [reply to L. O. Hynson]. *Wesleyan Theological Journal* 19 (1): 63–85.

———., ed. 1986a. *Whitefield and Wesley on the New Birth*. Grand Rapids, MI: Zondervan.

Smith, Warren Thomas. 1986b. *John Wesley and Slavery*. Nashville, TN: Abingdon.

———. 1986c. Eighteenth century encounters: Methodist-Moravian. *Methodist History* 24 (3): 141–156.

Smith, Robert D. 1990. John Wesley and Jonathan Edwards on religious experience: A comparative analysis. *Wesleyan Theological Journal* 25 (1): 130–146.

Snape, Michael Francis. 1998. Anti-methodism in 18th-century England: The Pendle forest riots of 1748. *Journal of Ecclesiastical History* 49 (2): 257–281.

Snyder, Howard A. 1987. *The Radical Wesley: Pattern for Church Renewal (1980)*. Grand Rapids, MI: Zondervan.

Soupel, Serge. 1993. Richardson as a source for Baculard d'Arnaud's Novelle. *R.L.C.* 67: 207–217.

———. 1998. "Les romans du XVIIIe siècle: rencontres franco-britanniques; rencontrer, assimiler, copier," dans Max Véga-Ritter (édit.), *l'Un(e) miroir de l'autre*, Clermont-Ferrand: Université Blaise-Pascal, Centre de recherches sur les littératures modernes et contemporaines, coll. "Cahiers de recherches du CRLMC": 123–133.

Southey, Robert. 1846. *Life of Wesley and the Rise of Methodism*. (2v. 1820). London: Longman, Brown, Green, and Longmans. https://archive.org/details/lifewesleyandri01soutgoog.

Spellman, W.M. 1993. *The Latitudinarians and the Church of England, 1660–1700*. Athens: University of Georgia Press.

Spring, David. 1961. The Clapham sect: Some social and political aspects. *Victorian Studies* 5 (1): 35–48.

Starkie, Andrew. 2007. *The Church of England and the Bangorian Controversy, 1716–1721*. Boydell Press pdf, (Cambridge Univ PhD.26293).
Stechner, Henry F. 1973. *Elizabeth Singer Rowe, the Poetess of Frome: A Study of 18th Century Pietism*. Bern: Peter Lang.
Steele, Richard B. 1994. *Gracious Affection & True Virtue According to Jonathan Edwards & John Wesley*. Metuchen, NJ: Scarecrow.
———. 1995. John Wesley's synthesis of the revival practices of Jonathan Edwards, George Whitefield, Nicholas von Zinzendorf. *Wesleyan Theological Journal* 30 (1): 154–172.
Stephen, Leslie. 1962. *History of English Thought in the Eighteenth Century* (1876, 3rd ed. 1902), 2v. New York: Harcourt, Brace & World/Harbinger.
Stephens, W.P. 1988. Wesley and the Moravians. In *John Wesley: Contemporary Perspectives*, ed. John Stacey, 23–36. London: Epworth.
Stigant, P. 1971. Wesleyan Methodism and Working-Class Radicalism in the North, 1792–1821. In *Northern History*, v6.
Stoeffler, F. Ernest. 1976a. Tradition and renewal in the ecclesiology of John Wesley. In *Traditio—Krisis—Renovatio aus theologischer Sicht*, ed. B. Jaspert and R. Mohr, 298–316. Elwert: Marburg.
———. 1976b. Pietism, the Wesleys and methodist beginnings in America. In *Continental Pietism and Early American Christianity*, ed. F. Ernest Stoeffler, 184–221. Grand Rapids, MI: Wm. B. Eerdmans.
———, ed. 1976c. *Continental Pietism and Early American Christianity*. Grand Rapids, MI: Eerdmans.
———. 1986. Religious roots of the early Moravian and methodist movements. *Methodist History* 24 (3): 132–140.
Stout, Harry S. 1991. *The Divine Dramatist: George Whitefield and the Rise of Modern Evangelism*, Library of Religious Biography. Grand Rapids, MI: William B. Eerdmans.
Stromberg, Roland N. 1954. *Religious Liberalism in Eighteenth-Century England*, xi + 192. London: Oxford University Press. quotes Clarendon.
Sullivan, Robert E. 1982. *John Toland and the Deist Controversy: A Study in Adaptations*. Cambridge, MA.
Sweet, William Warren, ed. 1935a. *Men of Zeal: The Romance of American Methodist Beginnings*. Nashville, TN: Abingdon Press.
———, ed. 1935b. *Men of Zeal: The Romance of American Methodist Beginnings*. Nashville, TN: Abingdon Press.
———. 1961. *Methodism in American history*. (1933) Nashville, TN: Abingdon Press (1953 ed. revised).
———, ed. 1964a. *Religion of the American Frontier, 1783–1840*, vol. 4, *The Methodists, a Collection of Source Materials*. (1946) New York: Cooper Square.
———. ed. 1964b. *Religion on the American Frontier: The Baptists, 1783–1830*. (1931) New York: Cooper Square Publishers.
———. ed. 1964c. *Religion on the American Frontier (Vol. 2) the Presbyterians 1783–1840 a Collection of Source Materials*. (1936).
———. 1965a. *Revivalism in America: Its Origin, Growth and Decline* (1944), Peter Smith.
———. 1965b. *Men of Zeal: The Romance of American Methodist Beginnings*. Nashville.
———, ed. 1986. *Whitefield and Wesley on the New Birth*. Grand Rapids, MI: Francis Asbury Press of Zondervan Publishing House.
———. 2015. *Religion in Colonial America*. (1942) Andesite Press.
———. ed. 2018. *Religion on the American Frontier, 1783–1850, Vol. 3: The Congregationalists; A Collection of Source Materials*. (1939) Classic Reprint.
Sweet, William Warren, and Erie Prior. 1955. *Virginia Methodism: A History*. Richmond: Whittet & Shepperson.
Sykes, Norman. 2018. *Church & State in England in the XVIIIth Century*. (1934) reprint, Forgotten Books.

Synan, Vinson. 1971. *The Holiness-Pentecostal Movement in the United States*. Grand Rapids, MI: Eerdmans.

Tamez, Elsa. 1985. Wesley as read by the poor. In *The Future of the Methodist Theological Traditions*, ed. M. Douglas Meeks, 67–84. Nashville, TN: Abingdon.

Taro, K.M. 1996. Denominated 'Savage': Methodism, writing, and identity in the works of William Apess, a Pequot. *American Quarterly* 48 (4): 653–679.

Taylor, John Tinnon. 2014. *Early Opposition to the English Novel: The Popular Reaction from 1760 to 1830* (1943), ed. Aleks Matza, Kindle ed.

Telford, John. 1898. *The Life of John Wesley*. New York: Eaton & Mains; Cincinnati: Jennings and Pye.

Thomas, Roger, The breakup of nonconformity," in Nuttall et al, eds. *The Beginnings of Nonconformity*, London, 1964.

Thompson, H. P. 1951. *Thomas Bray. Into All Lands: A History of the Society for the Propagation of the Gospel in Foreign Parts, 1701–1950*. London.

———. 1954. *Thomas Bray*, London.

Thompson, E. P. 1966. *The Making of the English Working Class* (1963). New York: Vintage.

———.. 1993. *Witness against the Beast: William Blake and the Moral Law*, Foreword by Christopher Hill. New York: Cambridge University Press.

Thorsen, Donald A. *The Wesleyan Quadrilateral: Scripture, Tradition, Reason & Experience as a Model of Evangelical Theology*. Grand Rapids, MI: Francis Asbury.

Thun, Nils. 1948. *The Behmenists and the Philadelphians: A Contribution to the Study of English Mysticism in the 17th and 18th Centuries*. Uppsala.

Tigert, John James. 1898. *The Making of Methodism: Studies in the Genesis of Institutions*. Nashville, TN: House of the Methodist Episcopal Church, South.

Timpe, Randie L. 1985. John Wesley and B. F. Skinner: Casuality, freedom, and responsibility [bibliog]. *Journal of Psychology and Christianity* 4 (3): 28–34.

Tolles, Frederick B. 1945. Quietism versus enthusiasm: The Philadelphia quakers and the great awakening. In *Pennsylvania Magazine of History* 69, 26–49; and as Ch6 in *Quakers and the Atlantic Culture*. New York: Macmillan, 1960.

———. 1960. *Quakers and the Atlantic Culture*. New York: Macmillan.

Tomkins, Stephen. 2007. *William Wilberforce: A Biography*. Wm. B. Eerdmans Publishing.

———. 2010. *The Clapham Sect: How Wilberforce's Circle Changed Britain*. Oxford: Lion Hudson.

Towlson, Clifford W. 1957. *Moravian and Methodist: Relationships and Influences in the Eighteenth Century*. London: Epworth Press.

Townsend, W. J., H. B. Workman and George Eayrs. 2009. A New History of Methodism. (2v. 1909). BiblioBazaar.

Tracy, Joseph. 2019. *The Great Awakening: A History of the Revival of Religion in the Time of Edwards and Whitefield*. (Boston, 1841) Banner of Truth, 2019; Kindle Edition, 2019 (Perhaps the coiner of the term "Great Awakening").

Tucker, Karen B. Westfield. 2001. *American Methodist Worship*. New York: Oxford University Press.

Tull, James C. 1973. *Shapers of Baptist Thought*. Valley Forge, PA: Judson Press.

Tumbleson, Raymond D. 1996. 'Reason and Religion': The Science of Anglicanism. *Journal of the History of Ideas* 57 (1): 131. (1685–89).

———. 1998. *Catholicism in the English Protestant Imagination: Nationalism, Religion, and Literature, 1600–1745*. Cambridge: Cambridge University Press.

Turley, David. 1992. *The Culture of English Antislavery, 1780–1860*. New York: Routledge.

Tuttle, Robert G., Jr. 1989. *Mysticism in the Wesleyan Tradition*. Grand Rapids, MI: Francis Asbury Press of Zondervan Publishing House.

Tyacke, Nicholas. 1987. *Anti-Calvinists: The Rise of English Arminianism, c1590–1640*. Oxford: Oxford University Press.

Tyerman, Luke. 1871–1876. *The Life and Times of the Rev. John Wesley, Founder of the Methodists*, 3v, London: Hodder and Stoughton.

———. 1873. *The Oxford Methodists: Memoirs of the Rev. Messrs. Clayton, Ingham, Gambold, Hervey and Broughton, with Biographical Notices of Others*. London: Hodder and Stoughton.
———. 2014. *The Life and Times of the Rev. Samuel Wesley, M.A., Rector of Epworth, and Father of the Revs. John and Charles Wesley, the Founders of The Methodists*. (1866) HardPress Publishing (Kindle ed.).
Tyson, John R. 1982. John Wesley and William law: A reappraisal [Appendices]. *Wesleyan Theological Journal* 17 (2): 58–78.
———. 1986. *Charles Wesley on Sanctification: A Biographical and Theological Study*. Grand Rapids, MI: Francis Asbury Press of Zondervan Publishing House.
———., ed. 1989. *Charles Wesley: A Reader*. New York: Oxford University Press.
Underwood, Alfred C. 1947. *A History of the English Baptists*, London.
van den Berg, Johannes. 1971. John Wesley's contacten met Nederland. *Leyden*: 36–96.
Vandermcer, Philip R. & Robert P. Swierenga, eds. *Belief and Behavior: Essays in the New Religious History*. New Brunswick: Rutgers University Press, [c.1991].
Vann, Richard T. 1969. *The Social Development of English Quakerism, 1655–1755*. Cambridge, MA.
Vickers, John Ashley. 1996. *Methodism and the Wesleys: A Reader's Guide*. 4th ed. Emsworth: WMHS Publications.
———. 1997. Recent American methodist scholarship: A review article. *Epworth Review* 245 (3): 118–123.
Vickers, Jason E. 2013. *The Cambridge Companion to American Methodism* (Cambridge Companions to Religion).
Viswanathan, Gauri. 1998. *Outside the Fold: Conversion, Modernity, and Belief*. Princeton, NJ: Princeton University Press. (conversions in Britain and British India).
Wainwright, Geoffrey. 1987. *Geoffrey Wainwright on Wesley and Calvin: Sources for Theology, Liturgy and Spirituality*. Melbourne: Uniting Church Press.
Wakefield, Gordon. 1966. *Methodist Devotions: The Spiritual Life in the Methodist Tradition, 1791–1945*. London: Epworth Press.
———, ed. 1976. *The Fire of Love: The Spirituality of John Wesley*. London: Darton, Longman and Todd.
Wakeley, J[oseph] B[eaumont]. 1871. *The Prince of Pulpit Orators: A Portraiture of Rev. George Whitefield, M. A*. 2nd ed. New York: Carlton & Lanahan; San Francisco: E. Thomas.
Walker, G. Clinton. 1993. *John Wesley's Doctrine of Justification in Relation to Two Classical Anglican Theologians: Richard Hooker and Lancelot Andrewes*. Ph.D. Dissertation, Baylor University.
Walls, Jerry L. 1981. John Wesley's critique of Martin Luther. *Methodist History* 20 (1): 29–41.
———. 1984. The free will defense, calvinism, Wesley, and the goodness of God. *Christian Scholar's Review* 13 (1): 19–33.
Walsh, John D. 1966. Origins of the evangelical revival. In G. V. Bennett & J. D Walsh, eds. *Essays in Modern English Church History*. London. —Ian Welch, Ianwelch@coombs.anu.edu.au, H-AMREL, 30Apr02.
———. 1975. Elie Halévy and the birth of methodism. *Transactions of the Royal Historical Society (G.B.)* 25: 1–20.
———. 1986. Religious societies: Methodist and evangelical, 1738–1800. In Sheils & Wood, 1986, pp 279ff. —Ian Welch, Ianwelch@coombs.anu.edu.au, H-AMREL, 30Apr02.
Walsh, FS John. 1993. Revival and Religion since 1700, ed. Jane Garnett and Colin Matthew. London. (Ward, *Early Evan.* Ch3).
Walsh, John D. *Methodism and the Mob*.
Walsh, John, Stephen Taylor, et al., eds. 1993. *The Church of England, c. 1689-c. 1833: From Toleration to Tractarianism*. Cambridge: Cambridge University Press.
Ward, W[illiam] R[eginald]. 1976. *Early Victorian Methodism*.
———. 1992. *The Protestant Evangelical Awakening*. Cambridge: Cambridge University Press, 1991.

———. 2006. *Early Evangelicalism: A Global Intellectual History, 1670–1789*. Cambridge: Cambridge University Press.

Warner, Wellman Joel. 1967. *The Wesleyan Movement in the Industrial Revolution*. New York/Berkeley, CA: Russell & Russell.

Watson, David L. 1985. *The Early Methodist Class Meeting: Its Origins and Significance*. Nashville, TN: Discipleship Resources.

Watson, Philip S. 1990. *Anatomy of a Conversion*. Grand Rapids, MI: Zondervan.

Watts, Michael R. 1986. *The Dissenters*, From the Reformation to the French Revolution. Vol. I. Oxford: Clarendon Press of Oxford University Press.

Wearmouth, Robert Featherstone. 1937. *Methodism and the Working Class Movements of England, 1800–1850*. London.

———. 1945. *Methodism and the Common People of the Eighteenth Century*. London.

Weinlick, John R. 1989. *Count Zinzendorf: The Story of His Life and Leadership in the Renewed Moravian Church*, Abingdon Press, 1956; Bethlehem, PA: Moravian Church in America.

Welch, Barbara Ann. 1971. *Charles Wesley and the Celebration of the Evangelical Experience*. Ph.D. Dissertation, University of Michagan.

Werner, Julia Stewart. 1984. *The Primitive Methodist Connexion: Its Background and Early History*. Madison: University of Wisconsin Press.

Wesley, John. 1774. *The Political Writings of John Wesley*. "Thoughts upon Slavery," London; repr. Philadelphia: Joseph Crukshank. https://docsouth.unc.edu/church/wesley/wesley.html.

———. 1776. *An Extract of the Life of Madam Guion*. London.

———, ed. 1819–1827. *A Christian Library: consisting of Extracts from and Abridgements of the Choices Pieces of Practical Divinity which have been Publish'd in the English Tongue*, 50 vols. Bristol: printed by E. Farley, 1754; *A Christian Library, Consisting of Extracts from and Abridgements of the Choicest Pieces of Practical Divinity which have been published in the English Tongue*, 30v. London: T. Blanshard, 1819–1827.

———. 1909–1916. *The Works of John Wesley. The Journal of Rev. John Wesley*, ed. Nehemiah Curnock, 8v. London: Epworth Press.

———. 1931a. *The Letters of John Wesley*. Edited by John Telford. London: Epworth Press. The Wesley Center Online. http://wesley.nnu.edu/john-wesley/the-letters-of-john-wesley/.

———. 1931b. *The Letters of the Rev. John Wesley*, ed. John Telford, 8v. London: Epworth Press.

———. 1975. *A Plain Account of Christian Perfection*. London: Epworth Press. *Explanatory Notes upon the Old Testament*, 3v, Bristol: William Pine, 1765. Facsimile reprint, Salem, OH: Schmul Publishers.

———. 1977. *Devotions and Prayers of John Wesley*. Grand Rapids, MI: Baker Book House.

———. 1978. *The Works of John Wesley. The Works of Rev. John Wesley*, ed. Thomas Jackson, 14v. London: Wesleyan Methodist Book Room, 1829–1831. Reprinted Grand Rapids, MI: Baker Book House.

———. 1980. *The Works of John Wesley, . The Journals of Rev. Charles Wesley*, ed. Thomas Jackson, 2v. London: John Mason, 1949. Reprinted Grand Rapids, MI: Baker Book House.

———. 1984a. *The Works of John Wesley*, Bicentennial ed. v1, *Sermons I, 1–33* [*Sermons on Several Occasions*, 1746], ed. Albert C. Outler. Nashville, TN: Abingdon Press.

———. 1984b. *The Works of John Wesley. The Works of John Wesley*, Bicentennial ed. v9, *The Methodist Societies: History, Nature and Design*, ed. Rupert E. Davies. Nashville, TN: Abingdon Press, 1989.

———. 1984c. *The Works of John Wesley. The Works of John Wesley*, Bicentennial ed. v25: *Letters I*. (1721–1739), ed. Frank Baker. Nashville, TN: Abingdon Press, 1980.

———. 1984d. *The Works of John Wesley*, Bicentennial ed. v32: *Oxford Diaries*, ed. Richard P. Heitzenrater. Nashville, TN: Abingdon Press.

———. 1984e. *An Extract of the Life of Madam Guion*. "The Circumcision of the Heart," on *Romans* 2:29, preached on January 1, 1733, at St. Mary's, Oxford. #17 in *The Works of John Wesley*. v1, ed. Outler.

———. 1984–1987. *The Works of John Wesley*, Bicentennial ed. v2–4, *Sermons II -IV* ed. Albert C. Outler. Nashville, TN: Abingdon Press.

———. 1987a. *The Works of John Wesley. The Works of John Wesley*, Bicentennial ed. v11: *The Appeals to Men of Reason and Religion and Certain Related Open Letters*, ed. Gerald R. Cragg. Nashville, TN: Abingdon Press, 1975.
———. 1987b. *The Journal of John Wesley: A Selection*. Ed. Elizabeth Jay. New York: Oxford University Press.
———. 1987c. *A Plain Account of Christian Perfection*. London: Epworth Press. *Explanatory Notes upon the New Testament*. London: William Bowyer, 1755. Most recent reprint. Grand Rapids, MI: Baker Book House.
———. 1988. *The Works of John Wesley. The Works of John Wesley*, Bicentennial ed. v18: *Journals and Diaries I* (1735–1738), ed. W. Reginald Ward, & Richard P. Heitzenrater. Nashville, TN: Abingdon Press.
Wesley, Charles. 1989a. In *Charles Wesley: A Reader*, ed. John R. Tyson. New York: Oxford.
Wesley, John. 1989b. *The Works of John Wesley*, Bicentennial ed. v7: *A Collection of Hymns for the Use of the People Called Methodists*, ed. Franz Hildebrandt & Oliver Beckerlegge. Nashville, TN: Abingdon Press, 1983.
———. 1990a. *The Works of John Wesley. The Works of John Wesley*, Bicentennial ed. v19, *Journals and Diaries II* (1738–1743). ed. W. Reginald Ward & Richard P. Heizenrater. ed. Frank Baker et al. Nashville, TN: Abingdon Press, 1984.
———. 1990b. *A Plain Account of Christian Perfection*. London: Epworth Press; Philadelphia: Trinity Press International.
———. 1991. *The Works of John Wesley. The Works of John Wesley*, Bicentennial ed. v20: *Journals and Diaries III* (1743–1754). ed. W. Reginald Ward, & Richard P. Heitzenrater. Nashville, TN: Abingdon Press.
———. 1992a. *The Works of John Wesley. The Works of John Wesley*, Bicentennial ed. v21: *Journals and Diaries IV* (1733–1765), ed. W. Reginald Ward & Richard P. Heizenrater. Nashville, TN: Abingdon Press.
———. 1992b. *Wesley's Forms of Prayers*, Library of Methodist Classics. Nashville, TN: United Methodist Publishing House.
———. 1993. *The Works of John Wesley. The Works of John Wesley*, Bicentennial ed. v22: *Journals and Diaries V* (1765–1775) ed. W. Reginald Ward, & Richard P. Heitzenrater. Nashville, TN: Abingdon Press.
———. 1995. *The Works of John Wesley. The Works of John Wesley*, Bicentennial ed. v23: *Journals and Diaries VI (1776–1786), ed. W. Reginald Ward & Richard P. Heizenrater*. Nashville, TN: Abingdon Press.
———. 1998. In *The Political Writings of John Wesley*, ed. Graham Maddox. Herndon, VA: Thoemmes Press.
———. 2003a. *The Works of John Wesley. The Works of John Wesley* v24: *Journals and Diaries VII* (1787–1791), ed. W. Reginald Ward & Richard P. Heizenrater, 2003.
———. 2003b. *The Works of John Wesley. The Works of John Wesley*, v26: *Letters II* (1740–1755), ed. W. Reginald Ward & Richard P. Heizenrater. Nashville, TN: Abingdon Press.
———. 2011. *The Works of John Wesley*, v10, *The Methodist Societies; The Minutes of Conference*, ed. Henry Rack. Nashville, TN: Abingdon Press.
———. 2013. *The Works of John Wesley* v13: *Doctrinal and Controversial Treatises II* ed. Paul Wesley Chelcotte & Kenneth J. Collins, Nashville, TN: Abingdon Press.
———. 2015. *The Works of John Wesley. The Works of John Wesley*. v27, *Letters III* (1756–1765) ed. W. Reginald Ward, & Richard P. Heitzenrater. Nashville, TN: Abingdon Press.
———. 2020. *The Works of John Wesley*, v17: *Oxford Diaries*, ed. Richard P. Heitzenrater. Nashville, TN: Abingdon Press.
Wesley Historical Society, *Proceedings*.
Westerkamp, Marilyn J. 1991. Enthusiastic Piety—From Scots-Irish revivals to the great awakening, 70. In Vandermcer, and Robert P. Swierenga (Eds.) *Belief and Behavior: Essays in the New Religious History*. New Brunswick: Rutgers University Press.
Whitefield, George. 1739. *A Journal of a Voyage from Gibraltar to Georgia*. Philadelphia: Franklin.
———. 1740a. *A Short Account of God's Dealings with the Reverend Mr. George Whitefield*. London.

———. 1740b. *A Journal of a Voyage from Gibraltar to Georgia*. "On Regeneration" ("The Nature and Necessity of Our New Birth in Christ Jesus," 1737). In *Sermons on Various Subjects*, v1. Philadelphia: Franklin.
———. 1771–1772. *The Works of the Reverend George Whitefield*. London: E. and C. Dilly [microform].
———. 1771–1772. *A Journal of a Voyage from Gibraltar to Georgia*. "Sermon 56". In *The Works of the Reverend George Whitefield*. London: E. and C. Dilly [microform].
———. 1858. *"Rev. George Whitefield's Conviction and Conversion,"* in Weishampel, J. F. Sr. *The Testimony of a Hundred Witnesses: Or, The Instrumentalities by Which Sinners Are Brought To Embrace the Religion of Jesus Christ. From Christians of Different Denominations. Compiled by Elder J. F. Weishampel, Sen*. Baltimore: J. F. Weishampel Jr.
———. 1960. In *George Whitefield's Journals*, ed. Iain Murray. London: The Banner of Truth Trust.
———. 2009. *Complete Journals*. Quinta Press. https://quintapress.webmate.me/PDF_Books/Whitefield/Complete_Journals_WIP.pdf.
———. n.d. In *Whitefield's Journals. To Which Is Prefixed His "Short Account" and "Further Accounts"*, ed. William Wale. London: Henry J. Drane.
Whitely, J. H. 1938. *Wesley's England: A Survey of Eighteenth-Century Social and Cultural Conditions*. London.
Wigger, John H. 1998. *Taking Heaven by Storm: Methodism and the Rise of Popular Christianity in America*, Religion in America Series. NY/Oxford: Oxford University Press, 1997.
Williams, William H. 1984. *The Garden of American Methodism: The Delmarva Peninsula, 1769–1820*. Wilmington, DE.
Williams, George H. 2004. The Bible Reading of Samuel Bradburn, Itinerant Methodist Minister, ASECS, Boston.
Wilson, W. 1808–1814. *The History and Antiquities of Dissenting Churches and Meeting Houses in London*. v1. London: for the author.
Wilson, David D. 1968. *The Influence of Mysticism on John Wesley*. Ph.D. Dissertation, Leeds University.
———. 1969. *Many Waters Cannot Quench: A Study of the Sufferings of Eighteenth-century Methodism and their Significance for John Wesley and the First Methodists*. London: Epworth.
Wilson, Douglas. 1991. Wrestling with Wesley. *Antithesis*.
Winckles, Andrew O. 2013. 'Excuse what deficiencies you will find': Methodist Women and Public Space in John Wesley's *Arminian Magazine*. *Eighteenth-Century Studies* 46 (3): 415–430.
Wood, A. Skevington. 1978. *The Burning Heart: John Wesley, Evangelist*. Minneapolis, MN: Bethany House.
———. 1981. The eighteenth century methodist revival reconsidered. *The Evangelical Quarterly* 53: 130–148.
———. 1986. *Love Excluding Sin: Wesley's Doctrine of Sanctification*. Derbys, England: Moorley's Bookshop.
———. 1992. *Revelation and Reason: Wesleyan Responses to Eighteenth-Century Rationalism*. Bulkington: The Wesley Fellowship.
Worden, Barbara S. 1983. The emotional Evangelical: Blake and Wesley. *Wesleyan Theological Journal* 18 (2): 67–79.
Wright, Charles Conrad. 1976. *The Beginnings of Unitarianism in America*. (1955) Archon Books.
Wykes, David. 1994. Friends, parliament, and the toleration act. *Journal of Ecclesiastical History* 45: 42–63.
Yates, A. S. 2015. *The Doctrine of Assurance With Special Reference to John Wesley*. (1952) Wipf & Stock reprint.
Young, Frances. 1988. The significance of John Wesley's conversion experience. In *John Wesley: Contemporary Perspectives*, ed. John Stacy, 37–46. London: Epworth.
Zehrer, Karl. 1979. The relationship between Pietism in Halle and early methodism; trans. by James A Dwyer. *Methodist History* 17: 211–224.
Zinzendorf, Nikolaus Ludwig Graf von. 1998. *Nine Public Lectures on Important Subjects in Religion Preached in Fetter Lane Chapel in London in the Year 1746*. Translated and edited by G. W. Forell. University of Iowa Press, 1973; Eugene, OR: Wipf and Stock.

Chapter 6
The Crucible of the Counter-Enlightenment, IV

Abstract The Jansenist Convulsionaries. A Catholic Counter-Enlightenment? Augustinian and Jansenist Catholics, Zinzendorf again and Jean-Jacques Rousseau, Charismatic and Sentimental Catholics (Lamourette).

The first convulsion to be reported came late in July, 1731. A certain abbé Bescherand, a canon of the diocese of Montpellier who had been born a cripple with one leg useless and shorter than the other, visited the tomb of a recently deceased church deacon named Pâris in the parish of Saint Médard in the city of Paris, where miraculous cures had begun to be reported almost as soon as Pâris had been interred in it in 1728. Bescherand was not the first to experience convulsion in addition to (or instead of) a cure; but he seems to have been the first one to make the papers, and raise the great questions of what convulsions might mean and whether or not they were authentic. As the industrious and skeptical contemporary diarist, Barbier, reported:

> From time to time convulsions seized him, convulsions so dreadful that his pulse stopped; he became pale, he foamed at the mouth and with effort raised himself a foot above the tomb, in spite of those who held him [...] It is said that he had not been able to walk, and that he walked [...] and that he limped much less; others say he limped the same; that his convulsions came from forcing himself, in his hope for a cure, to extend and straighten the leg, and that the pains that this caused him made him elevate himself thus; others say that in all of tradition one had never seen the miracles of God and his apostles [...] take so long to be effected or to be accompanied by convulsions; others in the end believed that this was all sorcery by the Jansenists. One may say that the truth of a religion is not much at ease when between two parties that are trying to destroy each other.[1]

[1] Barbier, *Chronique de la régence et du règne de Louis XV (1718–1763), ou Journal de Barbier*, 1ère éd., Paris: Charpentier, 1857–1866, v2, p199, September, 1731. Edmond Jean François Barbier, a lawyer-diarist who was not a sympathetic observer, seems to have been the first to write the word "convulsion," until then a medical term, to describe the phenomena to be observed at the tomb of Deacon Pâris; or so writes Catherine-Laurence Maire, who reprints this Barbier passage in her *Les convulsionnaires de Saint-Médard: Miracles, convulsions et prophéties à Paris au XVIIIe siècle* (Paris: Gallimard/Julliard Archives 1985), pp15, 107. This outstanding documents

W. R. Everdell, *The Evangelical Counter-Enlightenment*, Boston Studies in Philosophy, Religion and Public Life 9,
https://doi.org/10.1007/978-3-030-69762-4_6

Indeed, Abbé Bescherand belonged to a party in the national Catholic Church of France called "Jansenists." Bescherand's bishop, Charles-Joachim Colbert de Croissy of Montpellier, was a "Jansenist Appelant," the signer of a recent appeal over the head of the Pope in behalf of this party. And Deacon Pâris himself, a very minor clergyman, had been a Jansenist until he died at 37, largely because of his extraordinary regimen of ascetic penances. Deacon Pâris's bishop had been Cardinal Louis-Antoine de Noailles (1651–1729), Archbishop of Paris, and he too had been known as a jansenist sympathizer. The jansenist view that emerged in 1728 was that these miracles and convulsions were God's way of endorsing the doctrinal interpretations of the Jansenists. Noailles, however, had died not long after Pâris, and the new bishop of the capital city, Vintimille, in whose diocese the convulsions had begun, was not only not a Jansenist, but when it came to Jansenism-proving miracles, he quickly concluded that there was no way that God could be their author, and became more and more determined to prove that they were false (Fig. 6.1).

The Jansenist convulsionaries of the 1730s made it clear that Catholics, too, might find grace and ecstasy, and not just Jews, Sufi Muslims, and evangelical Protestants. In November, 1719, three years before the first refugee Moravians arrived at his Saxon manor, and began to experience their contact with the divine, the 19-year old Zinzendorf had visited France, there to be introduced by an Oratorian Order priest to a 68-year-old pillar of the French Catholic establishment, none other than Cardinal Archbishop de Noailles.[2] On the simplest level this was a young eighteenth-century aristocrat meeting a fellow noble on his postgraduate Grand Tour; but it was quite odd for a German Lutheran to meet with a French Catholic archbishop, and especially one who was at odds with his king and his Pope. Noailles had gone on record three years in a row, with an official appeal against a papal bull titled *Unigenitus* that he saw as anti-Augustinian and anti-Jansenist. What did they talk about in their long and earnest conversation? What did the two of them share? We have no transcript, but Zinzendorf's first biographer reports the Count's own

book brings together a large and diverse selection the source material for eighteenth-century Jansenism with a sophisticated linking narrative.

[2] The source of all sources for Zinzendorf is Bishop August Spangenberg, whose *Leben des Herrn Nicolaus Ludwig, Grafen und Herrn von Zinzendorf und Pottendorf, beschrieben von August Gottlieb Spangenberg*: in 8 Theilen, 1772–1775, exists in a modern edition (8 Bände in 4 Bänden, NY: Olms, 1971) and in an abridged English translation as *The Life of N. L. Count Zinzendorf, Translated* [and Abridged] *from the German, by S. Jackson* (London: Holdsworth, 1838), pp20–22. This is where the story of Zinzendorf's encounter with the jansenist and jansenist-leaning clergy enters historiography. It is Spangenberg who mentions a meeting with "Cardinal Bussy," repeated by all subsequent biographers, but unless he meant "Bissy," Henri-Pons de Thiard de Bissy (1657–1737), the anti-jansenist Cardinal Bishop of Meaux, there was no such Cardinal in 1719–1720. A short biography in English, John R. Weinlick, *Count Zinzendorf: The Story of His Life and Leadership in the Renewed Moravian Church* (Abingdon Press, 1956; Bethlehem, PA: Moravian Church in America, pb, 1989), has the encounter without enough background (p45); F. Ernest Stoeffler, *The Rise of Evangelical Pietism*, 1965; 2nd ed., 1971, puts the Noailles meeting in 1720. A more recent popular biography by Erika Geiger, *Nikolaus Ludwig Graf von Zinzendorf: Seine Lebensgeschichte* (Hänssler Verlag, 1999), does not mention any other French clergy except for the Oratorian Father LaTour, who arranged the meeting with Noailles.

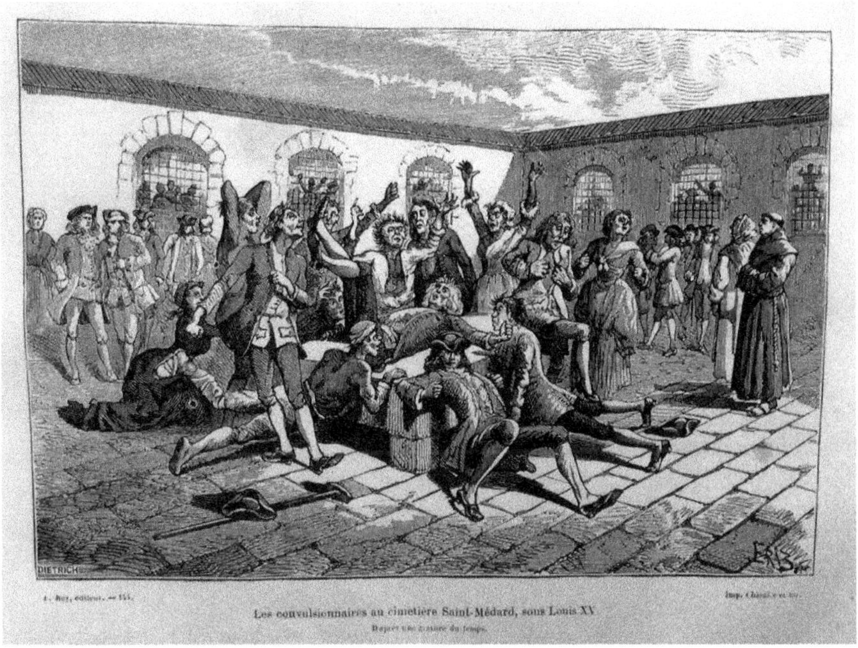

Fig. 6.1 *Convulsionnaires* at the tomb of Deacon Pâris at the Cemetery of Saint Médard. (Contemporary engraving @ https://oliviermarchal.blogspot.com/2015/09/convulsions-au-cimetiere-saint-medard-1.html)

reminiscences and implies that the main subjects of this meeting between the aged Cardinal Archbishop of Paris and the teenage future founder of the earliest evangelical Protestant sect were Catholic-Protestant cooperation in the saving of souls, and the means of that salvation, which they agreed was grace (Fig. 6.2).

Grace is the action of the Abrahamic God to make the impossible possible by electing and enabling sinners to encounter the divine, repent and be saved. The two men may have reached some agreement about the availability of grace, but neither party emerged a convert—or in any sense an ecstatic enthusiast—nor did Catholic and Protestant reconcile. Zinzendorf remained a Lutheran and a Pietist, strictly augustinian on the subject of the irresistibility of grace. But Noailles would remain Zinzendorf's correspondent, would join Zinzendorf's secret Order of the Grain of Mustard Seed, and eventually become godfather to his son, the unfortunate Christian Renatus. What brought them together, besides their common membership in the European nobility, was their agreement that the grace of God was not given to everyone, that humans were helpless without it, and that they could neither command it nor resist it.

Nearly all Protestants at the time had this augustinian view on grace, but Noailles was far from being the only contemporary Catholic Augustinian. Notable in the previous century (the seventeenth) had been the Dutchman Cornelis Jansen, author of the theological treatise *Augustinus* (1640), Jansen's friend Jean Duvergier de

Fig. 6.2 Nikolaus Ludwig, Graf von Zinzendorf und Pottendorf (1700–1760) in a scholar's coif. (Engraving by an unknown author—from the book *Zweihundert deutsche Männer in Bildnissen und Lebensbeschreibungen* (Two hundred German men in portraits and biographies), Leipzig 1854, Public Domain)

Hauranne, the abbé of St. Cyran, confessor of the Port-Royal convent outside of Paris, St. Cyran's friend Pierre de Bérulle and the Oratorian order of teaching friars that Bérulle had founded, the Arnauld family of lawyers and academics one of whom was Abbess of Port-Royal, Jean Racine, the classic tragic playwright who had been schooled at Port-Royal, and the great mathematician Blaise Pascal, whose sister was a nun there, and who had had his own ecstatic encounter with God. More recently there had been Pasquier Quesnel, author of a book favoring Jansen that had been condemned by a bull from the Pope titled *Unigenitus Dei Filius* in 1713.

All that makes the timing of the Zinzendorf-Noailles meeting doubly interesting. Zinzendorf also met with two Oratorian priests, two other preeminent French bishops, and separately with another French Cardinal, Bishop de Bissy. Bissy was defending orthodoxy against Noailles, but the two other Bishops, Langlet and Colbert,[3] like the Oratorians, were on Noailles's side. Like Noailles they were dissidents, leaders of the widespread doctrinal dissent in Catholic Christianity, which the French had long been calling *jansénisme* after Cornelis Jansen; and in 1719 Jansenism's pot was beginning to boil once again.[4] It was six years after the classic second crisis of the Jansenism movement in 1713, the order by King Louis XIV imposing the bull of Pope Clement XI, *Unigenitus Dei Filius* on the Church of France, and *Unigenitus*, also promulgated in 1713, was precisely designed to extirpate that jansenist view of grace. Cardinal de Noailles had been the first of a dozen prominent clergymen to appeal from the royal order in 1717, when four bishops, including Langlet and Colbert, had put their names to jointly published diocesan letters appealing to the Pope against the bull.[5] Noailles repeated his appeal in 1718, and in January of the year he met Count Zinzendorf, in 1719, Noailles had published a pastoral letter denying the authority of both the Pope and the bull;[6] but in 1720, less than a year after the Zinzendorf meeting, Noailles would acquiesce and endorse the *Unigenitus* bull, deeply disappointing the Count.[7]

Unigenitus, like several of its predecessor ant-Jansenist decrees, was an attempt to brand as heresy the full augustinian view—that God asked fallen humans for more than they could deliver and did not provide all of them with the irresistible grace that they needed to deliver it. It condemned 101 propositions which it identified in the newest (1695) edition of a devotional book for laypeople first published

[3] Pierre Langlet, Bishop of Boulogne and Charles-Joachim Colbert de Croissy, Bishop of Montpellier.

[4] Spangenberg writes in Zinzendorf's biography that the Count "himself" said at the time, "'I was not altogether safe in Paris, in consequence of the affair of the Constitution, which was at that time much agitated; and hence my governor was extremely anxious respecting me.' It seems that he narrowly escaped being poisoned by a person, who could not bear his zeal for the appealing bishops; for immediately afterwards he felt its effects, fell dangerously ill, and retained the marks of it in his face until his end." (Spangenberg, *The Life of N. L. Count Zinzendorf*, 1838, p22).

[5] *Mandement de Messeigneurs les évêques de Mirepoix, de Senez, de Montpellier, et de Boulogne*, Amsterdam: Jean Potgieter, 1719. The four Jansenist bishops were Langlet, Soanen, Colbert de Croissy and La Broue. The subtitle of the printed appeal translates as "For the publication of the act by which they [these bishops] lodge an appeal to a General Council through letters from Our Holy Father, Pope Clement XI, addressed to all the faithful, published at Rome on 8 September, 1718; & renew the appeal already lodged on the bull *Unigenitus*."

[6] Cardinal de Bissy, by contrast, was emphatically not a party to the appeal of the Bull. He had written a two-volume comprehensive treatise defending *Unigenitus*, called *Traité Théologique sur la constitution Unigenitus*, Spangenberg does not say what his meeting with Zinzendorf was like.

[7] On leaving Paris in 1720, Zinzendorf wrote to Noailles, "I hereby bid you adieu forever" (Spangenberg (1838), p21; Weinlick, p46–47). The Count was made uneasy by the great muted struggle over the *Unigenitus* bull, called the "Constitution": "I was not altogether safe in Paris, in consequence of the affair of the Constitution, which was in that time much agitated; and hence my governor was extremely anxious respecting me." He seems to have been right about this, surviving an attempt by (he believed) an anti-jansenist to poison him. (Spangenberg, *The Life of N. L. Count Zinzendorf*, 1838, p22n).

in 1668 (and endorsed later by Noailles), whose innocent title translates as *The New Testament In French With Moral Reflections On Each Verse Intended To Make Reading And Meditation Easier*, by Pasquier Quesnel.[8] Quesnel (1643–1719), a French priest of the Oratorian order who had died in exile in Amsterdam the year before Zinzendorf's meeting with the jansenist bishops, had been branded a Jansenist and expelled from his order over thirty years before. What his publications had done to attract the Pope's condemnation was to revive—for ordinary Catholics—the arguments of the earliest jansenist text, the 80-year-old *Augustinus* by Jansen himself, whose name had become shorthand for the movement. Quesnel's and Jansen's views of human helplessness and divine grace had become heretical in 1713, by papal bull and in France by royal decree. Clergy who were inclined to the doctrine now needed all their ingenuity to avoid being identified as heretics, especially when the Jesuit order, with its distinctive "Molinist," concept of grace, "casuist" or situational approach to morals, and its considerable intellectual muscle, was collaborating with the French absolute monarchy against them.[9]

Indeed it seems to have been Jesuits who pushed Pope Clement XI to issue *Unigenitus* in the first place, and that puts Jesuits to the frontlines of the crisis. Historians like Ulrich Lehner by and large agree that amid the fierce anticlericalism of the continental *philosophes* there was a Catholic Enlightenment going on. If so, it was spearheaded by Jesuit intellectuals who did not disown the *Lumières*. That, in turn, suggests that if we are to discern a Catholic Counter-Enlightenment (retronymically), we must look for its leaders among the Jansenists, who were the Jesuits' declared enemies.[10]

The Jansenists' first gambit in this new crisis had been Archbishop Noailles' attempt to steer the General Assembly of the Clergy of France to head off the bull, *Unigenitus*, or to impose conditions on it. Back in 1653, a different papal bull (*Cum occasione*) had located five propositions in Jansen's 1640 book, *Augustinus* and found them to be heretical; but forty years before *Unigenitus* one could argue that,

[8] Pasquier Quesnel (1643–1719), *Le Nouveau Testament en Français, avec des Réflexions morales sur chaque verset, pour en rendre la lecture plus utile et la méditation plus aisée*, 4v, 1693, revised, 1695, usually referred to as *Réflexions morales* (Moral Reflections), was the edition cited by critics. The first edition of this key jansenist text had appeared without much notice in 1668. Quesnel's principal works also include *La Tradition de l'Église Romaine sur la prédestination des Saints et sur la grâce efficace*. (Cologne, 1687–1690), a three-volume theological treatise of augustinian grace and predestination.

[9] Molinism is named for a sixteenth-century Jesuit theologian named Luis de Molina who thought that God intended humans to have free will, and that since they were thus not irredeemably helpless, they could have some agency in obtaining grace, a position which led Jansenists to think of him as a sort of Catholic Arminius, or as Augustine's contemporaries might have said, a Pelagius.

[10] Ulrich Lehner. *The Catholic Enlightenment: The Forgotten History of a Global Movement*. (Oxford: Oxford University Press, 2016). Pascal's satire, *Provincial Letters* (*Provinciales*, 1656–1657) is still the basic text for the Jesuit attack on augustinian grace. John Ralston Saul reminds us, in the course of casting the Jesuits as the forerunners of Enlightenment bureaucratic dispassion, that one of the Jesuits' founding documents, Loyola's instructions to the Society, contains a prohibition against calling a "heretic" an "evangelical." Cf. Saul, *Voltaire's Bastards: The Dictatorship of Reason in the West* (New York: Vintage, 1992), p46.

even if those five propositions were heretical, only one of them could be found verbatim in the actual texts of Jansen. As the seventeenth-century Jansenist lay leader Antoine Arnauld had annoyingly pointed out at the time (seconded by the Jansenist satirist, mystic and mathematical genius Pascal), even if one could not dissent from the Pope on heresy, one could certainly dissent from a Pope who asserted, no matter how solemnly, that something was there when it wasn't. Unfortunately for the Jansenists of 1713 the 101 propositions deemed heretical by *Unigenitus* were indeed there, though not in Jansen. The bull had quoted all 101 verbatim from Quesnel's *Moral Reflections*.

Thus Noailles could not make Arnauld's ingenious point, and he had been forced to reverse field, arguing instead that only some of the propositions were heretical, but not all; and he could not get the Assembly of the Clergy of France either to quibble or to delay. Noailles could only send a pastoral letter to the clergy of his own diocese which disapproved of the Assembly's decision. Affronted by the letter, Pope Clement, had thereupon prepared two ultimatums, one harsher and one milder, demanding the bishop to conform or risk derogation (being fired), and sent them to King Louis XIV. The King, careful to preserve the independence of the clergy of the Church of France (not to mention his power to appoint them), had served neither of the ultimata before he died in 1715. Supported by Jansenists, the Regent for Louis XIV's great-grandson and successor, 5-year-old Louis XV, had waffled on the matter. A large and ingenious opposition to *Unigenitus* arose, firmly based on sentiments that were not only augustinian but hospitable to mystic experience. They were also clearly patriotic and anti-papal, as well as somewhat anticlerical and anti-monarchic.

Dissent had mounted pretty quickly. The French universities, headed by Paris, moved to repeal their own "registrations," or acceptances, of *Unigenitus*. Then the French royal courts—the *parlements* which Louis XIV had persuaded to enter the papal bull on their official registers of French law in 1714, began to resist it. Jansenist lawyers and judges in the *parlements* began to argue that the Pope's writ could not constrain the Church of France because a papal bull, especially one whose registration by the *parlements* was in dispute, could not be a French law. Finally, in 1717, the upper clergy had chimed in with that highly visible "appel" or formal appeal. This was not an appeal to the King to de-register the bull; but something far more consequential, an appeal from the Pope to his theoretical superior, a General Council of the Church, the international Catholic congress, which had not met for 154 years.

Popes had long tried to prevent or quash Councils, and they had usually succeeded. In the eyes of popes they were dangerous; a Council's claim to be superior to popes had more than once threatened to make the Catholic Church a republic instead of a monarchy. Though the last such council, the Council of Trent in the mid-1500s, had organized the Church against Protestantism, the council before Trent, the Council of Basel, had attempted to pass laws that would bind the Church without the Pope's approval; and the Council before Basel, the Council of Constance had threatened the Catholic Church with a thoroughgoing republican revolution in 1415. This Council, more famous for burning Jan Hus, had deposed three popes, elected a fourth, and declared itself permanent. That history was well known to the four French bishops, Langlet, Colbert, La Broue and Soanen, who founded the *appellant* party by publishing their appeal in print. The four bishops knew, too, that they had the sympathies of the Archbishop of Paris, Cardinal Louis-Antoine de Noailles. The lawyers in the French national courts (*parlements*) also knew the history, which tended toward freeing France from the Popes' control, liked the idea of appealing from the Pope to a Council. Not to be undone, the Pope issued a bull, *Pastoralis officii*, excommunicating everyone who had called for an appeal to a General Council of the Church.

The bull backfired. The Appelants proceeded to appeal *Pastoralis officii* itself to a General Council of the Church, and in addition to the original Four, eighteen bishops and three thousand lower clergy supported the appeal. Unfortunately for Jansenism this was only about 10% of the Church of France, the vast majority of whose clergy at all levels became *acceptants* and stuck by the Pope. In 1727 Appelant Bishop Soanen was hauled before an *ad hoc* church council at Embrun and exiled from his bishopric; and in 1728 Noailles recanted his appeal of *Unigenitus*, dying a year later to be replaced by an Acceptant. The bull was not appealed; no Council ever met; and the jansenist opposition, deprived of its most important clerical leadership and united only by a clandestine newsletter, simmered on for decades in covert, principled civil disobedience that prepared the lower clergy to support rebellion right up to the beginning of the French Revolution in 1789.

Such was Catholic Church politics at the end of the West's Early Modern Period. The ecstatic Catholic mystics of the Middle Ages (Hildegarde of Bingen, Mechthild of Magdeburg, Julian of Norwich), and the mystics of the Counter-Reformation (Bérulle, Teresa of Ávila, John of the Cross) had come and gone. The Catholic Church itself remained a monarchy served by a centralized bureaucracy, quite unlike an eighteenth-century Protestant congregation, governed by a presbytery of its own elected elders or by a federal council (synod) of delegates of congregations. Religious experience, and sometimes even religious doctrine, can get lost in such an organization, especially when it's that of a minority, and when the doctrinal side is resurrected as the focus, it obscures the experiential side of the story for twenty-first-century historians. In March, 1730, it looked like the political narrative would end when a grown up Louis XV issued a royal decree making opposition to the Pope's anti-Jansenist bull, *Unigenitus*, contrary to the law of France, and derogating out of their posts and properties all clergy who had not signed the anti-Jansenist *formulaire*. To get the parlements to register the decree, Louis held a medieval "bed of justice" (*lit de justice*), reclining in person at the highest court. Appeals to the courts "on abuse" (*appels comme d'abus*) against the Bull were forbidden. The Acceptant party began to purge the Jansenists, and 300 Appellant priests were interdicted. Their parlements silenced, only a few of the lawyers continued the fight for the Appellant priests.[11] Every avenue seemed at last to be shut to jansenist Augustinianism in the French Catholic Church.

[11] Jeffrey Merrick, "'Disputes Over Words' and Constitutional Conflict in France, 1730–1732" in *French Historical Studies* XIV:4(1986), p. 505, 519.

Then came a surprise. In the same year as the King's *lit de justice*, Jansenism began to burst forth among the ordinary people of France, in a form that had almost nothing to do with doctrine and everything to do with experience. Policymakers in both the French government and the French Catholic upper clergy, already charmed by the Enlightenment critique of enthusiasm, were caught flat-footed by a popular outbreak of miraculous cures, disordered physical performances and visionary experiences—a democratic Counter-Enlightenment which none of them knew how to counter.

The miracles came first. They began in 1727 at the tombs of priests who in life had been Jansenist Appellants, one near Reims and two in Paris. Curates, Canons and Deacons were the lowest rank of ordained secular clergy; but the moral power of Appellants had ways to outflank the political power of the hierarchy. To the tomb in the parish of Avenay of the recently deceased and well-beloved Jansenist Canon, Gerard Rousse, Anne Augier, a peasant woman long afflicted with paralysis, was put in a basket by volunteers from her parish at Mareüil, carried to Rousse's tomb and laid there on July 8, 1727. After a short time, she got up, prayed thanksgiving and walked home restored to full movement, and reminding the whole diocese of Reims that the Church hierarchy had denied the sacraments to Rousse because he had been a Jansenist Appelant.

The most widely reported miracles occurred in the fenced-in graveyard of the parish of Saint Médard, in a Paris left-bank neighborhood in 1728, where the newly entombed deacon was François de Pâris (1690–1727), a law student turned priest whose name was the same as his city's. Pâris was a known Jansenist Appellant, so appreciated by his parishioners that some of them were convinced he had died a saint. He had died young, in part because of his effortful self-denial, starving himself to meet the conditions for a full conviction of sin and an access of grace.[12] The miracles began in Saint Médard the year Pâris was buried, when Marie-Jeanne Orget was laid on his tomb for "about an hour" on the 28th of June, 1728, and cured of what a church investigation called an "erysipelas" but seems to have been paralysis.[13] Miracles attributed to Appelant "saints" began to multiply. Two years later, in 1730, the decree and *lit de justice* of the new king Louis XV turned the *Unigenitus* bull into French law, but the miracles continued to lend moral authority to the bull's longtime opponents. There were 70 reported in 1731, when a story printed in city broadsides claimed that a woman named Anne Le Franc had been miraculously cured the year before by praying at Pâris's tomb, and Bishop Vintimille, successor to the just deceased Noailles, published a pastoral *Mandement* denying Le Franc's cure. Vintimille's letter could not prevent her miracle from becoming a celebrated story, the story that became the first to reach the new clandestine jansenist newspaper; and reopened in public the old debate on grace. A second royal *lit de justice* of

---

[12] Pâris's father Nicolas Pâris had been a member of the Paris Parlement when its long campaign to protect Jansenism from papal decrees had begun.

[13] The report, which was eventually submitted to none other than Cardinal de Noailles, is printed in Catherine-Laurence Maire, *Les convulsionnaires de Saint-Médard: Miracles, convulsions et prophéties à Paris au XVIIIe siècle* (Paris: Gallimard/Julliard Archives 1985), pp82–83.

1732 banning court appeals against *Unigenitus*, and the royal order of the same year that closed the Saint-Médard cemetery to visitors, would stop neither the controversy nor the jansenist miracles.[14]

A year after Anne Le Franc's cure, that first "convulsion" accompanying a cure—abbé Bescherand's—was reported. It was hard to miss. Convulsionaries like Bescherand would contort themselves into postures normally seen only in carnival shows, gesticulate, scream, occasionally disrobe, and go on later to turn prayers into clandestine preaching and prophecy. Students of the Atlantic Great Awakening will recognize these first convulsions immediately as ecstasies and visions, and many observers, both sympathetic and unsympathetic, referred to accesses of grace. It was not the grace to repent that Jonathan Edwards described to the English-speaking world four years later in 1736, but it was associated with that grace's most spectacular effect. Convulsionaries began to be attended by believers (one being Voltaire's anti-Enlightenment brother[15]) intent on recording their prophecies, and occasional non-believers, including the police, intent on demonstrating fraud. Before the police closed it in the name of public order, Saint Médard had become clogged not only with miracle-seekers but also with *assistants*, as the French call spectators. The emerging eighteenth-century skeptics like Barbier dismissed convulsions as they had dismissed most or all of the miracle cures, as dubious spectacles, or as manifestations of a malady so far lacking a natural explanation. Fully "enlightened" commentators alternated between accusations of fraud or delusion and attempts at medical diagnosis. Mainstream Catholic commentators followed accusations of fraud and delusion with attempts to defend against heresy and schism. The Jansenist leaders hailed the events as messages from God, but even the jansenist leadership eventually turned slowly away from the convulsionaries as their numbers began to diminish in later decades, and their physical and oratorical expressions became more outrageous.

As the movement went on, convulsionaries increased their courting of pain, seeking to authenticate their experience of grace by mortifying their bodies, often with the help of others, in spectacular ways. The ways included beating and cutting, a violation of law for which 80 were arrested in 1736. Still later they tried crucifixion with nails, a reminder of Jesus and Saint Peter, and perhaps of Anne Augier, a paralytic cured by an early Pâris miracle in the 1720s after neighbors had proved her insensibility with needles and nails. The convulsionaries and their *assistants* met in secret to see and hear what the ecstatics had to impart and the enthusiasts to perform (thrashing "about on the floor in a state of frenzy, screaming, roaring, trembling and twitching"), treated each other as equals in a hierarchical society, adopted

[14] The diarist Barbier reported the closure quoting the famous anonymously posted distich: De par le roi, defense à Dieu/De faire miracle en ce lieu (By royal order, God's forbidden/From doing miracles herein.).

[15] The brother, Armand Arouet, was a fervent Jansenist and supporter of the convulsionaries. Auguste Gazier, "Le frère de Voltaire", *Revue des Deux Mondes,* vol.32 (1906) 615-https://fr.wikisource.org/wiki/Le_Fr%C3%A8re_de_Voltaire_1685-1745).

pseudonyms to celebrate their special revelations and to avoid the police.[16] Late in the 1730s, Jansenist convulsionaries turned millenarian and apocalyptic, preaching and prophesying the end of the monarchy, the end of the papacy, even the end of the world, a world which had failed to understand those acts of God which had distinguished what they thought of as their own central role in humanity's redemption.[17]

The final triumph of the anti-Augustinians, the King, the Pope, the Jesuits and the now orthodox hierarchy, came after a Paris lawyer, Louis-Basile Carré de Montgéron, converted from deism to Jansenism during a visit to the tomb of Deacon Pâris in September, 1731. He then put together on his own a thorough and quite lawyerly investigation of as many of the miracles as he could find, and many of the early convulsions. He had it printed in 1737 in two volumes, in the Netherlands to avoid French censorship, and went directly to Versailles on July 29 with a presentation copy of volume one, offering it on his knees to King Louis XV himself. That same night Carré de Montgéron was arrested by royal *lettre de cachet*, taken to the Bastille, and imprisoned for the rest of his life.

Nevertheless, in this last of its repeated resurgences, Jansenism became one of the unacknowledged keys to the course of the French Revolution.[18] Jansenist

[16] Brian E. Strayer (*Suffering Saints: Jansenists and Convulsionnaires in France, 1640–1799* (Brighton, UK: Sussex Academic Press, 2008), the newest narrative account of the whole history of Jansenism, fully informed on church-state politics, with the convulsionary part backed up by the *convulsionaire* archives in the Arsénal Library in Paris. The quotation is from the older, but no less well-informed B. Robert Kreiser, *Miracles, convulsions, and ecclesiastical politics in early eighteenth-century Paris*, Princeton, NJ: Princeton U. Press, 1978, p257, bringing together materials in the Arsénal Library like the *Testimony of Denise Regnier*, AN, X-ib 9690.

[17] Kreiser, *Miracles, convulsions, and ecclesiastical politics*, pp265, 268–273. His translation of the ecstatic speech of Soeur La Croix on the eschatologically sacred character of the *parlementaire* opposition is on p. 302.

[18] This complicated but fascinating topic of the relation of Early Modern religion to the Enlightenment and the rise of political republicanism and liberalism was once referred to Préclin (Edmond Préclin, *Les Jansénistes du XVIIIe siècle et la Constitution civile du Clergé: le développement du Richérisme*, Paris, 1929) and Gazier (Augustin Gazier, *Histoire du mouvement janséniste depuis ses origines jusqu'à nos jours*, 2v, Paris: Honoré Champion, 1924); but there is now a great deal of much newer work with a more sympathetic understanding by Catherine-Laurence Maire (*De la cause de Dieu à la cause de la Nation; Le jansénisme au XVIIIe siècle*. Paris: Gallimard, 1998) and the Cottrets: Bernard Cottret, *Le Christ des lumières*. (Paris: Le Cerf, 1990); Monique Cottret, *Jansénismes et Lumières: Pour un autre XVIIIe siècle*. (Paris: Albin Michel, 1998); Monique Cottret, "Aux origines du républicanisme janséniste: Le mythe de l'Église primitive et le primitivisme des lumières," *Revue d'histoire moderne et contemporaine* 31(1984), p99–115; and Bernard Cottret, Monique Cottret & Marie-José Michel (éd.), *Jansénisme et puritanisme, actes du colloque du 15 septembre 2001, tenu au Musée national des Granges de Port-Royal-des-Champs*. préface de Jean Delumeau. (Paris: Nolin 2002). An American, B. Robert Kreiser, ventured into that thicket before the Cottrets and returned with new, transatlantic perspectives (Kreiser, "Religious Enthusiasm in Early Eighteenth-Century Paris: The Convulsionaries of Saint-Médard" in *The Catholic Historical Review* 61:3(1975), p353–385; and *Miracles, convulsions, and ecclesiastical politics* (1978). Three other Americans, Dale van Kley (*The Religious Origins of the French Revolution: From Calvin to the Civil Constitution of the Clergy, 1560–1791*. (New Haven: Yale University Press, 1997), and "The Jansenist constitutional legacy in the French prerevolution," in Keith Michael Baker, ed., *The Political Culture of the Old Regime* (Oxford:

veterans of the convulsionary episode and the church's augustinian opposition party became proponents (sometimes called Richerists after the pre-jansenist cleric and reform writer Edmond Richer) of the presbyterianizing (or republicanization) of the Catholic Church and the election of the Catholic clergy by their parishioners. Ecstatics they were no longer, and indeed they largely abandoned the ever less numerous secretly practicing ecstatics who remained; but once the Revolution began they became the leaders of the new French national church and its constitutional clergy. One of them, a provincial priest named Henri Grégoire (1750–1831), was elected a member of the clerical Estate in the National Assembly in 1789, and then elected Bishop of Blois under the Assembly's new Civil Constitution of the Church. In the National Assembly in 1791, he championed the successful bill that emancipated France's Jews from legal discrimination, and made the motion to allow Haitian black property-owners to vote. Elected to the democratic French National Convention in 1792, he voted to abolish the monarchy and in 1794 became one of the sponsors of the new Republic's decree abolishing slavery. He survived both the dechristianization program of the Terror in 1793, the Restoration of the monarchy in 1815, Napoleon's Concordat with the Pope in 1801 and his proclamation of the Empire in 1804 (both of which he opposed) as a member of the lower houses of four successive national legislatures; and when he died he contrived to receive last rites from a jansenist priest despite a ban by the local bishop.[19]

***

As an intellectual influence on the French Revolution, Jansenism is a bit roundabout, but it is clear that a quite direct influence on the Revolution's second, democratic phase, called The Terror by conservatives, was the influence of Jean-Jacques Rousseau, who became, in the course of a long three-part struggle to come to terms with his religious inheritance, the first Counter-Enlightenment philosopher, and something like an evangelical movement of his own.[20]

Pergamon Press, 1987, pp169–201), Brian E. Strayer (*Suffering Saints,* 2008), and Jan Goldstein ("Enthusiasm or Imagination? Eighteenth-Century Smear Words in Comparative National Context." *Huntington Library Quarterly* 60(1998), pp29–49); and in addition the British historian, William Doyle (*Jansenism: Catholic Resistance to Authority from the Reformation to the French Revolution*, Palgrave Macmillan, 2000) have since contributed a good deal to this once all-French story, the long debate on the historical evaluation of international Jansenism. Kreiser's *Miracles, convulsions, and ecclesiastical politics* is exceptionally thorough, all but definitive in its account of the multiple effects of the dauntingly complicated politics of church and state in eighteenth-century France. Strayer's *Suffering Saints* is the most thoroughly researched and most plausible account of the convulsionaries available in any language.

[19] The remarkable Grégoire had long had only one biographer in English, a good one: Ruth Necheles, *The Abbé Grégoire: 1787–1831: the odyssey of an egalitarian.* (Westport, CT: Greenwood, 1987). Alyssa Goldstein Sepinwall's *Abbé Grégoire and the French Revolution: The making of modern universalism*, incorporated new research and was published by the University of California Press in 2005. There is a helpful collection of evaluations by Jeremy D. and Richard H. Popkin: *The Abbé Grégoire and His World* (Dordrecht: Springer Netherlands, 2015).

[20] Rousseau, of course, has never stopped confounding his readers. Zeev Sternhell thought he was a fundamentally Enlightenment figure, and Kwame Anthony Appiah, reviewing Justin Smith, doubted a year ago if the "Counter-Enlightenment schema" can fit anyone, let alone Rousseau (Appiah, "Dialectics of Enlightenment," Review of Justin Smith, *Irrationality*, in *New York Review*

Surprisingly, Rousseau's odyssey began with an encounter with Augustinianism. Born a Protestant in Calvin's own Geneva two centuries after Calvin's death, he had set off toward Catholic France as a motherless teenager after missing the city's curfew in 1728. Afoot, alone, fifteen years old, and penniless like a midcentury American hipster, he was taken up by a childless older woman, Mme. Louise-Elénore de Warens, a Catholic convert whose marriage had been annulled; and as Rousseau became part of her household, she became his tutor in life and love. Local priests, Mme. de Warens herself, and de Warens's concierge doctor J.-B. Salomon, were to direct the adolescent Rousseau as the future genius began his secondary education. Louise-Elénore (Rousseau came to call her "Maman" at about the same time he became her lover) was herself from a Protestant family in Calvin's Geneva, but she had converted to Catholicism partly to get an annulment and a pension, which suggests a reason why her religious views tended to the Oratory and Port-Royal, the leading augustinian-jansenist, "calvinizing," educators in Catholicism. Rousseau was attracted, ready to learn just about anything (Fig. 6.3).[21]

---

of Books, 9 May, 2019). A recent encounter involved the pre-eminent intellectual historian of the Enlightenment, Jonathan Israel, who uses the term "Counter-Enlightenment" for at least one side of Rousseau, writing that "he always simultaneously exhibited disparate radical, moderate, and Counter-Enlightenment tendencies but mixed in shifting proportions at different times." (Jonathan Israel, "Rousseau, Diderot, and the 'Radical Enlightenment': A Reply to Helena Rosenblatt and Joanna Stalnaker," *Journal of the History of Ideas* 77:4(Oct, 2016), p649–677, p656. (The rest of the symposium includes Rosenblatt, "Rousseau, the 'Traditionalist'," and Stalnaker, "Jonathan Israel in Dialogue.") Earlier, historians Darrin McMahon (*Enemies of the Enlightenment: The French Counter-Enlightenment and the Making of Modernity*, NY: Oxford U.P., 2001), Rob Zaretsky (*Frail Happiness: An Essay on Rousseau*, Penn State U.P., 2001), and Graeme Garrard (*Rousseau's Counter-Enlightenment: A Republican Critique of the Philosophes*, Albany, NY: State U. of New York Press, 2003), have given Rousseau some relatively recent credit for his momentous recasting of religion. Jonathan Israel seems ready to call that recasting a "moderate" move, which makes it more interesting that, despite the immense erudition of Israel's work, he makes so small a place in it for Jansenism (*Radical Enlightenment*, 2001, p19), presenting it entirely in the context of the philosophical struggle between Cartesian and Aristotelian philosophy, and has no place in it at all for Augustinianism or ecstasy, despite the political radicalism they were often associated with.

[21] "I even began to look after books which might better enable me to understand [Salomon's] discourses. Those mingling devotion with science were the most agreeable to me, particularly those emanating from the Oratory and from Port Royal, and I began to read, or rather to devour them. [...]" *The Confessions of Jean-Jacques Rousseau, newly translated into English* (1st ed., Stott, 1891) London: Gibbings, 1907, p241. The original is Rousseau, *Confessions* (MS, 1772), *Œuvres complètes*, v1, p232. It is significant that Rousseau gave his autobiography the same title, *Confessions*, as Augustine had given his, for quite similar reasons. Rousseau did his best to tell the truth, often spectacularly against self-interest, and after repeated scholarly examination, the posthumously published *Confessions* (1778) has been found to be more trustworthy on the facts than might be expected of a polemical self-justification. Monique Cottret brought out the significance of Rousseau's jansenist temptation in chapter 3 of her *Jansénismes et Lumières*, 1998, p89. Patrick Riley, who traced Rousseau's General Will to Jansenist and other dissident religious sources (*The General Will Before Rousseau: The Transformation of the Divine into the Civic*, Princeton, NJ: Princeton U.P., 1986, 1988) is the only commentator I have found who has drawn a bead in English on the contrary effect of Augustine and Augustinianism on Rousseau ("The Inversion of Conversion: Rousseau's Rewriting of Augustinian Autobiography," *Studies in Eighteenth-Century Culture*, 28(1999), p. 229–255). Rousseau expressed suspicion of jansenist insincerity through a

Fig. 6.3 Jean-Jacques Rousseau and Madame de Warens in 1732 after an engraving by Maurice Leloir at http://athena.unige.ch/athena/rousseau/confessions/cn02_044_entrevue_de_jjr_et_mme_de_warens.jpg

So he converted to Mama's convert Catholicism, an augustinian Catholicism which encouraged the reading of jansenist texts, and between 1736 and 1740, before he had reconverted to become a Protestant again, even had a moment of temptation to awakening, conviction and grace.

> The writings of Port-Royal and the Oratory that I read most frequently were making me half-Jansenist and despite all my confidence their hard theology sometimes frightened me. The terror of Hell, which until then I had little feared was troubling my security. [...] I asked myself what state is my soul in? If I were to die this instant, would I be damned? According to my Jansenists the thing was indubitable; but according to my own conscience it seemed that it was not. [...] I told myself I will go throw a stone against that tree I see

character in *La Nouvelle Héloise* (1762), "Quand je vois les mêmes hommes changer les maximes selon les Coteries, molinistes dans l'une, jansénistes dans l'autre ..." (Rousseau, *Julie*, 2e Partie, "Lettre XVI à Julie," *OC*, t2, p241) as noted by Pierre Chaunu, Madeleine Foisil & Françoise de Noirfontaine, *Le Basculement religieux de Paris au XVIIIe siècle* (Paris: Fayard, 1998, p316) and by Strayer in *Suffering Saints* (p229).

> across from me. If I hit it, sign of salvation; if I miss, sign of damnation. Speaking thus I threw the stone with a trembling hand and with a horribly beating heart, but so happily that it hit the very center of the tree, a feat that in truth was not difficult because I had taken care to choose one that was very big and very close. Since then I have had no doubt of my salvation.[22]

This experiment amounts to a parody of the Calvinist understanding of grace (though perhaps not of the Sufist); and except for the trembling hands, there is nothing very ecstatic about it. Expecting to encounter the divine in an external material coincidence rather than in a mystical experience within makes Rousseau sound more Pelagian than Augustinian, at least as he looks back on the event from 30 years on. This however was just the first of three turning points in Rousseau's religious odyssey. Leaving Mama, Rousseau renounced his conversion, and found a living in Paris as a "Grub Street" writer and music copyist, making acquaintances among the Deist and atheist philosophers, or *philosophes*, of the French Enlightenment, and contributing articles on music to the radical *Encyclopédie* whose editor was his friend Denis Diderot.

When Diderot was imprisoned in 1749 for writing an unsigned pamphlet endorsing materialism, Rousseau took a now-famous walk from Paris to the Vincennes prison chateau to visit him, carrying the latest issue of the *Mercure de France*, and on the way, he had his second and personally most momentous of his quasi-ecstatic experiences. Stopping by the road to rest and read the *Mercure*, he discovered an essay contest with a prize sponsored by the Dijon Academy for an answer to the question, "Has progress in the Sciences and the Arts contributed to the corruption or to the improvement of morals?" "Within an instant of reading this," he wrote nearly thirty years later in his autobiography, "I saw another universe and became another man."[23] Tears filled his eyes as he realized that he did not believe progress in the arts and sciences had improved morals at all. No, he thought, morals were worse; and it was "Progress" in science and art that had made them worse. This sudden overarching insight can be thought of as a counter-Augustinian conversion experience. When Rousseau arrived at the prison, Diderot noticed his "nearly delirious" excitement and advised him to enter the Dijon contest. Rousseau did so, and won the prize and lasting fame, not to mention the fundamental theme for all his subsequent writing.

[22] Rousseau, *Confessions* (1778) in *Œuvres completes*. Paris: Gallimard/Pléiade, v1, 1959, pp. 242–243. My translation. (The 1891 English translation of *Confessions* left all that out.) Cf. Cottret, *Jansénismes et Lumières*. 1998, p89.

[23] Rousseau, *Confessions* (1778), in *Œuvres complètes*, Paris: Gallimard/Pléiade, v1, 1959, p. 351. We can recognize "another universe" as an echo of Paul's rapture in *II Corinthians*; and "another man" as a more distant echo of Jesus's "born again." Rousseau would have known those stories, but he was hardly more than a deist at the time of this "conversion." Rousseau's first account of his "vision" in the second of his 1762 letters to Malesherbes, did not use the trope of becoming "another man," but as Rousseau remarks in *Confessions*, he usually forgot things after he had written them down. ("Lettres à Malesherbes" (1762) in *Œuvres completes*. Paris: Gallimard/Pléiade, v1, 1959, pp. 1130–1147).

In fact, he later concluded, "The whole rest of my life and my troubles was the inevitable effect of that instant of straying [*égarement*]."[24]

Strayed he had. This latter revelation of Rousseau's was a Pelagian, Arminian, and most un-Augustinian one, a conversion from pessimism about human nature to optimism, instead of the other way around. In Rousseau's mind, it was not God who dominated man, but society, rewarding egotism over solidarity and cynicism over moral effort, increasing inequality, and evoking, encouraging and indulging the most frivolous of human wants until they became enslaving needs. That first prize essay, *Discourse on the Arts and Sciences*, published in 1750, not only made Rousseau's reputation, it also set the stage for all of his entire groundbreaking literary work, including the essays *On the Origin of Inequality* (1755), on theatrical performances in Geneva (*Lettre à d'Alembert sur les spectacles*, 1758), *On the Social Contract* (1762), the novels *Julie, Or the New Heloïse* (1761), *Émile, Or Education* (1762), the posthumously published memoirs *Rousseau Judge of Jean-Jacques*, *Reveries of a Solitary Walker*, and the *Confessions* themselves, because, as Rousseau himself asserted, all of them were approaches to a solution of the problem he had discovered on the road to Vincennes. Rousseau had come in a sudden rush to believe that human nature was not intrinsically bad, as Pelagius had claimed so long ago to Augustine (and Arminius to the Dutch Calvinists), but that developed human societies were intrinsically malevolent: that humans did not need to be saved from themselves so much as to be saved from being corrupted by the society of other humans.[25]

The Catholic Church saw this immediately and Christophe de Beaumont, the Archbishop of Paris who had finally reversed the Jansenist policies of his predecessor Noailles, officially condemned Rousseau's *Essay on the Origin of Inequality* as "Pelagian" on its publication in 1755, which was probably not the reason why Rousseau reconverted to Protestantism that October and was restored to citizenship in his home town of Geneva. Nevertheless, seven years later in 1762 when the newly published *Émile* was criminally condemned by the Paris Parlement ("impious and detestable principles"), by the Sorbonne Faculty of Theology ("contrary to faith and morals"), by Archbishop de Beaumont in an official *Mandement* ("insinuates the poison of sensuality while pretending to proscribe it"), and by the city council of Geneva, which burned Rousseau's *Social Contract* on the same pyre ("reckless, scandalous, impious and tending to destroy Christianity and governments"), Rousseau centered his public and polemical reply to the Archbishop's *Mandement*, his *Lettre à Christophe de Beaumont* (1763), on a Pelagian denial of the ancient

[24] Rousseau, *Confessions* (1778), in *Œuvres complètes*, Paris: Gallimard/Pléiade, v1, 1959, p. 351. "Strayed" (*égaré*) is a word for what sinners have done, particularly Protestant sinners, appearing in the General Confession in English Prayer Books, but the verb *égarer*, with its involuntary echo, does not seem to appear in confessions used by the Calvinist Church of Geneva. (Jean-René Moret, "Les réformateurs face à la confession," *La Revue réformée* 63:261(January, 2012) @ http://larevuereformee.net/articlerr/n261/les-reformateurs-face-a-la-confession).

[25] It is worth noting that *Moral Man and Immoral Society* (1932), the talismanic treatise by the American Lutheran social democrat, Reinhold Niebuhr, put a rather similar thesis in his title.

doctrine of original sin.[26] It then became clear that Rousseau was neither an Augustinian nor a Jansenist, and that it was as much the Pelagianism of his religious view as it was the anti-absolutist politics he had derived from it, that would make him an outlaw and an exile, unwelcome among French-speaking Catholics and Protestants alike.

The overturning of traditional Christian grace did not make Rousseau a visionary, or a mystic with personal contact with the divine. The nearest of his works to a vision might be the authoritarian democratic republic of *On the Social Contract*, his "good society," which produces citizens of irreproachable virtue and unbending interpersonal loyalty by imposing an equal Spartan austerity on every last one of them. Rousseau scholars have, often grudgingly, come to agree with J. L. Talmon that the democratic republic Rousseau imagined in *The Social Contract* was an anticipation of the Terror and of all the subsequent totalitarianisms which have democratically allowed the "general will" to subordinate—or trump—debate, compromise and the rule of law.[27]

We can not even think of Rousseau as a nature mystic—a pre-Romantic believer that personal contact with the divine is mediated by natural beauty. In 1762, the same year as *The Social Contract* was published, Rousseau published *Émile, or On Education*, which contained, in volume 4, the "Profession of Faith of a Savoyard Vicar" made to the young protagonist Émile. This Savoy Confession (to echo an old Protestant term) amounts to Rousseau's third and last word on the matters of salvation and religious conversion. It was Rousseau's "good religion," adapted to his long-term project of getting his "natural" man—good by nature—into a corrupting society without giving up too much of his natural goodness. The project doesn't sound very challenging today, but it was so Pelagian and so anti-dogmatic that it got the whole novel (like the previous *Essay on Inequality*) banned by the pro-Jansenist Parlement of Catholic Paris and burnt by order of his own Protestant city of Geneva, sending Rousseau into exile for more than five years.

---

[26] The argument for *Emile* in Rousseau's *Letter to Christophe de Beaumont begins* several pages in: "The fundamental principle of all morals, on which I have reasoned in all my writings, and which I have developed in this last one with all the clarity of which I am capable, is that man is a being who is naturally good, loving justice and order; that there is no original perversity in the human heart, and that the first promptings of nature are always right." A bit later, it continues, "First, it is necessary, in my view, that this doctrine of original sin, subject to such terrible difficulties, not be found either as clearly or as harshly in Scripture as it has pleased the Latin Rhetor Augustine, and our theologians to construct it." Rousseau, *Lettre à Christophe de Beaumont, Archévêque de Paris* (1763) *Œuvres complètes*, v4, p. 935–36, 937–38, my translation.

[27] J[acob] L[eib] Talmon, *The Origins of Totalitarian Democracy* (London: Secker & Warburg, 1952). Rousseau's first written account of his 1749 "vision," in the second of his 1762 letters to Malesherbes, described a "giddiness (*étourdissement*) resembling drunkenness" as ideas like the goodness of humankind crowded his mind while he lay weeping under a tree (https://fr.m.wikisource.org/wiki/Lettres_%C3%A0_Malesherbes). Isaiah Berlin cited this 1762 account to open his case in the same year as Talmon, 1952, for the totalitarian "lunacy" of Rousseau's *Social Contract*. (Berlin, "Rousseau" in *Freedom and Its Betrayal*, 2nd ed. Princeton, NJ: Princeton University Press, 2014, p. 38–39.)

The Savoyard Vicar is a Catholic priest, a vicar, or paid deputy, whom the late adolescent Émile is sent to find in a parish between Switzerland and Italy in the mountains of Savoy. The unnamed[28] Vicar has come to his unorthodox religion not by sudden ecstatic conversion, or revelation, but through a long and logical meditation on his reason and his feelings (*sentiments*). This he relates to Émile at exemplary length, opening with the standard eighteenth-century philosophical wisdom (empiricism) that the observation of external nature by the senses gives rise to all internal sensation, as well as to the ideas preserved by memory and compared by judgment using reason, which is innate. The Vicar then reasons his way to the conclusion that the truth of revealed religions, including his own, cannot be grasped by "my bewildered understanding convinced of its own weakness," but that the truth of natural religion (as both the apologists and the *philosophes* had agreed in calling it) can. He finds this reasoned proof of natural religion in the observing of order in the universe, but much more in the innate and indubitably human ability to compare people's actions based on moral sentiment, which implies, since it so regularly conflicts with self-interest, that a moral conscience ("the voice of the soul") must exist in every human.[29] That thoroughly Pelagian premise leads him not to postulate the existence of a god by reason, but to "feel" that there is one God, the author of his conscience, on whom his existence therefore depends, and to respond with grateful, worshipful sentiment and an effort to follow his conscience with his independent free will.[30]

---

[28] The editors of the *Œuvres complètes* collect the evidence for Rousseau's conflation of two different actual Catholic vicars he had known in the character of the Savoyard: one he had met in Turin, Jean-Claude Gaime (1692–1761), and another named Gâtier. (Rousseau, *Confessions*, *OC*, v1, pp. 91, 119). Gaime is known to have had jansenist leanings.

[29] "Conscience is the voice of the soul,—the passions are the voice of the body. Is it surprising that these two voices should sometimes contradict each other, or can it be doubted, when they do, which ought to be obeyed? Reason deceives us but too often, and has given us a right to distrust her conclusions; but conscience never deceives us. She is to the soul what instinct is to the body,—she is man's truest and safest guide." Rousseau, *Émile*, Book 4, in *Œuvres complètes*, v4, p. 594; Harvard Classics ¶91 (Rousseau generalized "human" with the word "man" throughout his work, but unlike most of his contemporaries who did the same, he was charged with sexism long before he died, with the principal evidence being *Émile,* and its sequel, *Émile et Sophie*.)

[30] Rousseau continued to read jansenist writings (Strayer, *Suffering Saints*, p229), though he found the convulsionaries deplorable; but he seems not to have read English Protestants, whether Calvinist or Universalist. What would the Protestant evangelical leaders, Zinzendorf, Edwards, Whitefield and Wesley have thought of *Émile*, a novel in French by a self-described Protestant, condemned as heterodox by the Churches of France and Geneva? Zinzendorf had died in 1760, but Jonathan Edwards seems not to have noticed the book, and George Whitefield (d.1770) for all his travel and international connections, never mentioned it. John Wesley did get around to reading it in 1770, and found, despite his Arminian view of divine grace and human goodness, that the "celebrated book" was "whimsical to the last degree, grounded neither upon reason nor experience," and its author to be a "cynic," a "misanthrope" and a "consummate coxcomb." (Wesley, *Journals*, 3Feb, 1770 @ https://www.ccel.org/ccel/wesley/journal.vi.xv.vi.html) Attacks on Rousseau by English-speaking Protestant intellectuals could be harsh but most came from after the French Revolution. Rousseau was attacked by the Jansenist weekly *Nouvelles Ecclésiastiques* as another "*prétendu philosophe*," but not for his theology, or for his austerity.

The Vicar's religion thus turns out to assert no knowledge at all of the supernatural or the divine, and even less about the revelations, rituals and doctrines of religions, or even the consensus (*sensus communis*) of humankind. He reduces all that to what he considers reasonable and provable (and Deist) assertions that the order of the universe implies an orderer, that humans have free will and conscience, and that Jesus Christ is such a model for good conscience that his life and death are those of a God, which sentiment (or is it a judgment?) provoked believers as much as it did Deists.[31]

Beyond that, the Vicar has no doctrines to press on Émile, much less any liturgy or ritual, but only feelings to evoke. The infinite in magnitude he finds no less beyond reason than Pascal had in the previous century. With no assurance about anything beyond experience, reason and sentiment, and seeing self-imposed limits to at least the first two, he has no way of being anything but tolerant of the resulting diversity of opinion and behavior. He remains a member of a "revealed" faith, he considers uniformity of belief desirable but not attainable; and he would like to believe that God is one; but he can find no assurance that the Catholic Christian revelation, or any other revelation, is true.

The model for an apologia or defense of Catholic Christianity had been standardized a century before *Émile*, starting with "natural religion," followed by "revelation," its "prophecies" confirmed by "miracles" which are "witnessed" by trustable believers, who confirm doctrine and morals. (A standard apologia usually filled three volumes.[32]) Halfway through his "Profession," the Vicar summarily reduces the standard apologia to a dismissive interpolated dialogue between *Inspiré* (Inspired) and *Raisonneur* (Reasoner) to whom grace, says *Inspiré*, "does not speak," and who dismantles the apologetic structure piece by piece in three pages.[33] Not even salvation and damnation, or "future rewards and punishments" as Enlightened Deists and other natural religionists had taken to calling them, survive this critique, and revealed religion does no better, which means that grace, or intervention of the divine, with ecstasy or without, is not only impossible but useless. No wonder the book was burned by both Catholics and Protestants. As for Jews and Muslims (Rousseau mentioned both), they would not have liked it any better had they known about it at the time.

Rousseau and his Vicar put forward once again the Augustinian principle that since humans have free will, all evil must come from human action, but also the Pelagian principle that humans are quite capable of good action without divine intervention—grace. They essentially propose that only feeling can be trusted to affirm a religious belief or behavior. Rousseau's gambit was (somewhat like Unitarian Universalism) a way around the Enlightenment's loss of faith in the old

[31] "if the life and death of Socrates are those of a sage, the life and death of Jesus are those of a God." Rousseau, *Émile*, Book 4, in *Œuvres complètes*, v4, p626; tr. Harvard Classics ¶223.

[32] W. R. Everdell, *Christian Apologetics in France, 1750–1801* (diss't 1971, Lewiston, NY: Edwin Mellen Press, 1987).

[33] Rousseau, *Émile*, Book 4, in *OC*, v4, pp. 614–617, tr. Harvard Classics ¶127–131, 135–144, 160–186.

epistemology of religious experience. At the height of the subsequent Revolution, the Catholic abbé Lamourette who coined "Christian democracy" would try to pull the clerical and anticlerical French together on that basis.[34] Indeed, it was the Counter-Enlightenment highway by which the Romantic generations of the early nineteenth century succeeded in giving Christianity, and indeed all religion in the West, a new lease on life. Feeling made its debut as a proof of faith, and the way was paved for feeling to become the justification of religious experience all by itself. When he based religion on feeling Rousseau looked back to Saint Paul's Corinthians and Zinzendorf's Moravians and forward to the hippies, providing a new range of possibilities for ecstasy in the West.

Bibliography

Abercrombie, Nigel. 1936. *Origins of Jansenism*. Oxford: Clarendon Press.

———. 1938. *Saint Augustine and French Classical Thought*. New York: Russell and Russell, 1972.

Adam, Antoine. 1968. *Du mysticisme à la révolte: Les jansénistes du XVIIe siècle*. Paris: Fayard.

Albertan-Coppola, Sylviane. 2010. *L'abbé Nicolas-Sylvestre Bergier, 1718–1790 - des Monts-Jura à Versailles, le parcours d'un apologiste du XVIIIe*. Paris: Honoré Champion.

Anderson, Allan. 2001. *African Reformation: African Initiated Christianity in the Twentieth Century*. Trenton, NJ: Africa World Press.

Armogathe, Jean-Robert. 1971. A propos des miracles de Saint Médard: les preuves de Carré de Montgeron et le positivisme des Lumières. *Revue de l'Histoire des Religions* 180 (2): 135–160.

———. 1985. *Croire en liberté: Eglise catholique et la révocation de l'Edit de Nantes*. Paris: O.E.I.L.

———. 1999. À propos de Nicolas Sylvestre Bergier. In *Etre matérialiste à l'Âge des Lumières. Mélanges offerts à Roland Desné*, ed. Beatrice Fink and Gerhardt Stenger. Paris: Presses Universitaires de France.

Aston, Nigel, ed. 1997. *Religious Change in Europe, 1650–1914: Essays for John McManners*. Cambridge: Cambridge University Press.

———. 1998. Religion in Eighteenth-Century France. *European History Quarterly* 28 (4): 515–526. [Review essay].

Atkinson, Geoffroy. 1970. *The Sentimental Revolution: French Writers of 1690–1740*. Seattle, WA: University of Washington Press.

Attali, Jacques. 2000. *Blaise Pascal: Le Génie Français*. Paris: Fayard.

Baker, Keith Michael, ed. 1987. *The Political Culture of the Old Regime*. Oxford: Pergamon Press.

Barbier, Edmond Jean François. 1857–1866. *Chronique de la régence et du règne de Louis XV (1718–1763), ou Journal de Barbier*. 1st ed. Paris: Charpentier.

Barker, John. 1976. *Strange Contrarieties. Pascal in England During the Age of Reason*. Montreal: McGill-Queens University Press.

[34] Everdell, "Revealed Religion is Natural Too, Lamourette" Chapter 10 of *Christian Apologetics in France*. pp. 213–224. Lamourette was a great admirer of Rousseau. Chapter 6 of David Sorkin's *The Religious Enlightenment: Protestants, Jews, and Catholics from London to Vienna*. (Princeton, NJ: Princeton University Press, 2008), pp. 263–309, gives a newer and better account of Lamourette, but Sorkin groups him with Moses Mendelssohn in the "religious Enlightenment" rather than in a Counter-Enlightenment conceived as Isaiah Berlin (and I) did that would separate him from Mendelssohn. Both categories are abstract enough to provoke arguments both long and somewhat metaphysical.

Barnett, S.J. 2003. France: The Revolt of Democratic Christianity and the Rise of Public Opinion, Chapter 4. In *The Enlightenment and Religion: The Myths of Modernity*, 130–167. Manchester, UK/New York: Manchester University Press. New York: Oxford University Press, 2013

Barny, Roger. 1985. *Prélude idéologique à la Révolution Française: Le Rousseauisme avant 1789*. Paris: Belles Lettres.

Bartha, Paul, and Lawrence Pasternack. 2018. *Pascal's Wager*. Cambridge: Cambridge University Press.

Batllori, Miguel. 1966. *La cultura hispano-italiana de los jesuitas expulsos: espanoles, hispano-americanos, filipinos*. Madrid: Gredos.

Bayley, Peter. 1980. *French Pulpit Oratory, 1598–1650: A Study of Themes and Styles, with a Descriptive Catalogue of Printed Texts*. Cambridge: Cambridge University Press.

Beckwith, Francis J. 2019. *Never Doubt Thomas: The Catholic Aquinas as Evangelical and Protestant*. Waco, TX: Baylor University Press.

Benedict, P. 1991. *The Huguenot Population of France, 1600–1685: The Demographic Fate and Customs of a Religious Minority*, Transactions of the American Philosophical Society. Vol. 81, pt 5. Philadelphia: American Philosophical Society.

Bergier, N.-S. 1765. *Le déisme réfuté par lui-même: ou Examen, en forme de Lettres, des Principes d'incrédulité répandus dans les divers Ouvrages de M. Rousseau*. Paris: Vrin, 1999.

Berkvens-Stevelinck, Christiane. 1999. De La Haye à Berlin en passant par Londres. In *La Vie intellectuelle aux Refuges protestants. Actes de la Table ronde de Münster du 25 juillet 1995*, Vie des Huguenots, ed. Jens Häseler and Antony McKenna, vol. 5, 85–98. Paris: Honoré Champion Éditeur.

Berlin, Isaiah. 1952. Rousseau. In *Freedom and Its Betrayal*. 2nd ed., 28–52. Princeton, NJ: Princeton University Press, 2014.

Besse, Guy. 1996. Une lettre du chanoine Bergier (1774). *Dix-Huitième Siècle* 28: 259–266.

Birn, Raymond. 2001. *Forging Rousseau*, Studies on Voltaire and the Eighteenth Century. Vol. 8. Oxford: Voltaire Foundation.

Birnstiel, Eckart, and avec la collaboration de Chrystel Bernat ed. 2001. *La Diaspora des huguenots. Les réfugiés protestants de France et leur dispersion dans le monde (XVIe–XVIIIe siècles)*, La vie des huguenots. Vol. 17. Paris: Honoré Champion.

Bishops Langlet, Soanen, Colbert de Croissy, and La Broue. 1719. *Mandement de Messeigneurs les évêques de Mirepoix, de Senez, de Montpellier, et de Boulogne*. Amsterdam: Jean Potgieter.

Bissy, Cardinal Henri-Pons de Thiard de. 1722. *Traité Théologique adressé au clergé du diocèse de Meaux [sur la constitution Unigenitus]*, 1722. Paris: Mazières.

Blanc, Hippolyte. 1865. *Le merveilleux dans le Jansénisme, le magnétisme, le Méthodisme et le Baptisme américains, l'épidémie de Morzine, le spiritisme; recherches nouvelles par Hippolyte Blanc*. Paris: Plon.

Bokobza Kahan, Michèle. 2000. *Libertinage et folie dans le roman du 18e siècle*. Louvain: Peeters.

Bosc, Henri. 1985–1993. *La Guerre des Cévennes 1702–1710*. 6 vols. Montpellier: Presses de Languedoc.

Bost, Hubert. 1999. L'histoire des églises réformées de France dans le *Dictionnaire* de Bayle. In *La Vie intellectuelle aux Refuges protestants. Actes de la Table ronde de Münster du 25 juillet 1995*, Vie des Huguenots, ed. Jens Häseler and Antony McKenna, vol. 5, 227–252. Paris: Honoré Champion Éditeur.

———. 2001. *Ces messieurs de la R.P.R. Histoires et écritures des huguenots, XVIIe–XVIIIe siècles*, La vie des huguenots. Vol. 18. Paris: Honoré Champion.

———. 2002. La superstition pire que l'athéisme ? Quelques réactions aux paradoxes de Bayle dans l'Europe protestante au XVIIIe siècle. *The European Spectator* 3: 17–45.

Bost, Hubert, and Claude Lauriol, eds. 1998. *Entre désert et Europe. Le pasteur Antoine Court (1695–1760). Actes du colloque de Nîmes, 3–4 novembre 1995*, La vie des Huguenots. Vol. 3. Paris: Éditions Honoré Champion.

Bots, J.A. Hans. 1999. Les pasteurs français au Refuge des Provinces-Unies: un groupe socio-professionnel tout particulier, 1680–1710. In *La Vie intellectuelle aux Refuges protestants.*

Actes de la Table ronde de Münster du 25 juillet 1995, Vie des Huguenots, ed. Jens Häseler and Antony McKenna, vol. 5, 9–68. Paris: Honoré Champion.

Boulard, F., and G. Cholvy, eds. 1992. *Matériaux pour l'histoire religieuse du peuple français, 19e-20e siècles*. 3 vols. Paris: Editions de l'Ecole des Hautes Etudes en Sciences Sociales.

Boutin, Pierre. 1998. La philosophie naturelle comme enjeu institutionnel: l'opposition de l'Église catholique à la franc-maçonnerie. *Dix-Huitième Siècle* 30: 397–411.

Burson, Jeffrey D. 2010. *The Rise and Fall of Theological Enlightenment, Jean-Martin de Prades and Religious Polarization in Eighteenth-Century France*. Notre Dame, IN: University of Notre Dame Press.

———. 2008. Towards a New Comparative History of European Enlightenments: The Problem of Enlightenment Theology in France and the Study of Eighteenth-Century Europe. *Intellectual History Review* 18 (2): 173–187.

Carey, Patrick W. 1982. *An Immigrant Bishop: John England's Adaptation of Irish Catholicism to American Republicanism*. Yonkers, NY: U.S. Catholic Historical Society.

———. 1983. Republicanism in American Catholicism, 1785–1860. *Journal of the Early Republic* 3: 413–437.

———. 1987. *People, Priests, and Prelates: Ecclesiastical Democracy and the Tensions of Trusteeism*. Notre Dame, IN: University of Notre Dame Press.

Carré de Montgéron, Louis-Basile. 1737. *La Vérité des Miracles Operés à l'intercession de M. de Pâris & autres Appelans Démontrée contre M. l'Archevêque de Sens. Dédié au Roi. Et présenté à Sa Majeste' le 29. Juillet 1737*. Par M. Carre' de Montgeron, Conseiller au Parlement. Tome Premier, s.l. sans éd.

———. 1741. *Continuation des Démonstrations des miracles Opérés à l'intercession de M. de Paris & autres Appelans. Observations sur l'Oeuvre des Convulsions et sur l'état des Convulsionnaires*. Tome Second, s.l. sans éd.

Chantin, Jean-Pierre. 1996. *Le jansénisme*. Paris: CERF.

Chaunu, Pierre, Madeleine Foisil, and Françoise de Noirfontaine. 1998. *Le Basculement religieux de Paris au XVIIIe siècle*. Paris: Fayard.

Chevallier, Pierre. 1974. *Histoire de la franc-maçonnerie française. La maçonnerie, école de l'égalité, 1725–1799*. Paris: Fayard.

———. 1994. *Les Ducs sous l'Acacia*. 2e ed. Repr. Geneva: Slatkine. (Postface: dialogues between Ramsay and M. de Geusau on Freemasonry).

Cognet, Louis. 1967. *Le jansénisme*, Que sais-je? Paris: PUF.

Colloque de Paris. 1985. *La Révocation de l'Edit de Nantes et le protestantisme français en 1685: actes du colloque de Paris (15–19 octobre 1985)*. réunis par Roger Zuber et Laurent Theis. Paris: au siège de la Société, 1986.

Colonia, Dominique de S.J. 1722. *Bibliothèque janséniste ou catalogue alphabétique des principaux livres jansénistes ou suspects de jansénisme, qui ont paru depuis la naissance de cette hérésie*. 2nd ed. Bruxelles: S. T'Sertetevens, 1739.

———. 1752. *Dictionnaire des livres jansénistes, ou qui favorisent le jansénisme*. 4 vols. Anvers: J.-B. Verdussen. Charleston: Nabu Press, 2012.

Cook, Alexandra. 1997. Rousseau's *Spectacle de la Nature* as Counterpoint to the *Théâtre du Monde*: An Analysis of the *Lettre à d'Alembert* from the Standpoint of Natural History. *Pensée libre* 6: 23–32.

Coppola, Silviane. 1981. *Recherches sur la littérature apologétique catholique en France de 1730 à 1770*. Thèse de doctorat, 3ème cycle, Paris-Sorbonne IV.

Corrigan, John. 1991. *The Prism of Piety: Catholick Congregational Clergy at the Beginning of the Enlightenment*. New York: Oxford University Press.

Cosmos, Georgia. 2005. *Huguenot Prophecy and Clandestine Worship in the Eighteenth Century: 'The Sacred Theatre of the Cévennes'*. Aldershot and Burlington, VT: Ashgate.

Cossy, Valérie, and Deidre Dawson, eds. 2001. *Progrès et violence au XVIIIe siècle*, Études internationales sur le dix-huitième siècle. Vol. 3. Paris: Honoré Champion.

Costelloe, Timothy M. 2003. The Theater of Morals: Culture and Community in Rousseau's *Lettre à M. d'Alembert*. *Eighteenth-Century Life* 27 (1): 52–71.

Cottret, Monique. 1979. Piété populaire et clandestinité: le cas des convulsionnaires parisiens au XVIIIe siècle. *Histoire et clandestinité Albi*: 169–173.

———. 1984. Aux origines du républicanisme janséniste: Le mythe de l'Église primitive et le primitivisme des lumières. *Revue d'histoire moderne et contemporaine* 31: 99–115.

Cottret, Bernard. 1990. *Le Christ des lumières*. Paris: Le Cerf.

Cottret, B.J. 1992a. *The Huguenots in England: Immigration and Settlement, 1640–1700*. New York: Cambridge University Press.

Cottret, Bernard. 1992b. *Cromwell*. Paris: Fayard.

———. 1995. *Calvin*, Lattès; (German) 1998. Paris: Payot, 1999.

Cottret, B.J. 1996. Les pères et la religion du Père: les oeuvres d'un mémorialiste protestante, Jacques Fontaine (1658–1728). *Études théologiques et religieuses* 71 (4): 511–522.

Cottret, Monique. 1998. *Jansénismes et Lumières. Pour un autre XVIIIe siècle*, Bibliothèque histoire. Paris: Albin Michel.

———. 2002. *Culture et politique dans la France des lumières (1715–1792)*. Paris: Armand Colin.

———. 2006. Voltaire au risque du jansénisme: *le Siècle de Louis XIV* à l'épreuve du jansénisme. *SVEC* 10: 387–397.

Cottret, Bernard, Monique Cottret, and Marie-José Michel, eds. 2002. *Jansénisme et puritanisme, actes du colloque du 15 septembre 2001, tenu au Musée national des Granges de Port-Royal-des-Champs*, préface de Jean Delumeau. Paris: Nolin. (Including articles by: Hubert Bost, Audrey Chazalviel, Bernard Cottret, Monique Cottret, Liliane Crété, Tony Gheeraert, Jacques Gres-Gayer, Christopher Haigh, Marie-Jose Michel, Jean-Louis Quantin, Christophe Tournu et Frédérick Vanhoorne).

Coudreuse, Anne, ed. 2001. *le Refus du pathos au XVIIIe siècle*, Babeliana. Vol. 3. Paris: Éditions Honoré Champion.

Court, Antoine. 2002. *Histoire des troubles des Cévennes*. Montpellier: Presses du Languedoc. Présentation par Otto Selles. "Antoine Court, pasteur et historien: l'histoire des camisards et la lutte pour la liberté religieuse," 13–32.

Cragg, Gerald R. 1960. *Penguin History of the Church*. Vol. 4 of The Church and the Age of Reason, 1648–1789. New York: Penguin, 1990.

Crogiez, Michèle. 1997. *Rousseau et la paradoxe*. Paris: Éditions Honoré Champion.

Dancourt. 1996. *la Fête de village ou les Bourgeoises de qualité*. Édition et présentation de Judith et Ross Curtis, Espace Théâtre. Vol. 34. Montpellier: Éditions Espaces.

Darnton, Robert. 1968 *Mesmerism and the End of the Enlightenment in France*. Cambridge, MA. New York: Schocken, 1970. (Convulsionaries, 36, 42; jansenists, 36, 61).

David, Zdeněk V. 2014. The Views of Hus and Utraquism in the Bohemian Catholic Enlightenment. *XIth Symposium on the Bohemian Reformation and Religious Practice* Under the Auspices of the Collegium Europaeum of the Faculty of Arts of the Charles University and the Institute of Philosophy of the Academy of Sciences of the Czech Republic Academic Conference Centre Jilská 1/Husova 4 a Praha 1, June 18–20.

Davidson, Hugh M., and Pierre H. Dube. 1975. *A Concordance to Pascal's Pensées*. Ithaca, NY: Cornell University Press.

de Boer, Wietse. 2001. *The Conquest of the Soul: Confession, Discipline, and Public Order in Counter-Reformation Milan*. Boston: Brill.

de Dainville-Barbiche, S. 1992. *Le Clergé paroissal de Paris de 1789 à janvier 1791: Répertoire biographique*. Paris: Klincksieck.

De McKenna, A. 1990. *Pascal à Voltaire: le rôle des 'Pensées' de Pascal dans l'histoire des idées entre 1670 et 1734*, Studies on Voltaire and the Eighteenth Century. Vol. 276, 277. Oxford: Voltaire Foundation.

Deconinck-Brossard, Françoise. 2002. Sermons protestants dans l'Europe des Lumières. *The European Spectator* 4: 13–24.

Dedieu, J. 1920. *Le rôle politique des Protestants français de 1685 à 1715*. Paris: Bloud & Gay.
Deguise, Pierre. 1966. *Benjamin Constant méconnu: le livre "De la Religion"*. Geneva: Droz.
Deimling, Katherine. 2000. *Teaching Vice: Mentors and Students in the Eighteenth-Century French Novel*. Thèse de doctorat, New York, Columbia University, Dir.: Gita May.
Deism, French, article électronique. 1996. *The Internet Encyclopedia of Philosophy*. Localisation: http://www.utm.edu/research/iep/d/deismfre.htm.
Delumeau, Jean. 1975. Au sujet de la déchristianisation. *Revue d'Histoire Moderne et Contemporaine* 22: 52–60.
———. 1977. *Catholicism Between Luther and Voltaire: A New View of the Eighteenth Century*. Trans. J. Moiser. London: Burns & Oates.
———. 1995. *Jurieu*. Paris: Imprimerie Nationale/Acteurs de l'Histoire.
———. 1997. *Des religions et des hommes*. Paris: Desclée de Brouwer.
———. 2000. *Que reste-t-il du paradis?* Paris: Fayard.
Dent, N.J.H. 1992. *A Rousseau Dictionary*. Oxford: Blackwell.
Desan, Suzanne. 1991. *Reclaiming the Sacred: Lay Religion and Popular Politics in Revolutionary France*. Ithaca, NY: Cornell University Press.
———. 2000. What's after Political Culture? Recent French Revolutionary Historiography. *French Historical Studies* 23 (1): 163–196.
Dinet, Dominique. 1993. La ferveur religieuse dans la France du XVIIIe siècle. *Revue d'Histoire de l'Église de France* 79 (203): 275–299.
Dodge, Guy Howard. 1947. *The Political Theory of the Huguenots of the Dispersion, with special reference to the thought and influence of Pierre Jurieu*. New York: Columbia University Press.
Dodge, Guy. 1980. *Benjamin Constant's Philosophy of Liberalism: A Study in Politics and Religion*. Chapel Hill, NC: University of North Carolina Press.
Does, Marthe van der. 1974. *Antoinette Bourignon 1616–1680: La vie et l'oeuvre d'une Mystique chrétienne*. Amsterdam: Holland University Press.
Doyle, William. 1994. *Jansenism, Catholic Resistance to Authority from the Reformation to the French Revolution, A Global-Historical Interpretation*. Cambridge: Cambridge University Press. Repr., London & New York: Palgrave Macmillan, 2000; New York: St. Martin's, 2001.
Drescher, Seymour. 1980. Two Variants of Anti-Slavery: Religious Organization and Social Mobilization in Britain and France, 1780–1870. In *Anti-Slavery, Religion and Reform*, ed. C. Bolt and S. Drescher, 43–63. London: Wm Dawson. Hamden, CT: Archon Books.
Ducasse, André. 1962. *La guerre des Camisards: La résistance huguenote sous Louis XIV*. Limbourg, Belgium: Marabout, 1978.
Dumas, Robert. 2005. L'abbé Grégoire, révolutionnaire parce que prêtre. *Médium* 4: 122–135.
Edwards, Tom T. 1960. *Jansenism in Church and State*. PhD Dissertation, Harvard University.
Egret, Jean. 1977. *The French Prerevolution, 1787–1788*. Chicago: University of Chicago Press.
Engels, J.I. 1996. Une grammaire de vérité: les miracles jansénistes en Provence au XVIIIe siècle selon les *Nouvelles ecclésiastiques*, 1728–1750. *Revue d'histoire ecclésiastique* 91 (2): 436–464.
Everdell, William R. 1971. *Christian Apologetics in France, 1730–1790* [1750–1801]*: The Roots of Romantic Religion*. Diss't, New York University. Lewiston, NY: Edwin Mellen Press, 1987.
———. 1975. The *Rosières* Movement and the French Revolutionary Cults. *French Historical Studies* 9 (1): 23–36.
———. Revealed Religion is Natural Too, Lamourette, Chapter 10. In *Christian Apologetics in France*, 213–224. New York: Mellen Press.
Fabre-Koechlin, Madeleine. 1999. Le père Pierre-François Le Courayer dans son refuge anglais: un parcours insolite de l'abbaye de Sainte-Geneviève à celle de Westminster: 1728–1776. In *la Vie intellectuelle aux Refuges protestants. Actes de la Table ronde de Münster du 25 juillet 1995*, Vie des Huguenots, ed. Jens Häseler and Antony McKenna, vol. 5, 289–304. Paris: Honoré Champion.
Feilla, Cecilia. 2002. Performing Virtue: *Pamela* on the French Revolutionary Stage, 1793. *Eighteenth Century: Theory and Interpretation* 43 (3): 286–305.

Gardiner, Anne Barbeau. 1999. Catholic Authors and Liberty of Conscience: 1649–1771. *Catholic Dossier* 5 (4): 17–22.
Garrard, Graeme. 2003. *Rousseau's Counter-Enlightenment: A Republican Critique of the Philosophes*. Albany, NY: State University of New York Press.
Garrioch, David. 1996. *The Formation of the Parisian Bourgeoisie, 1690–1830. Part One: The Jansenist Years*. Cambridge, MA: Harvard University Press.
Gazier, Auguste. 1906. Le frère de Voltaire. *Revue des Deux Mondes* 32: 615. https://fr.wikisource.org/wiki/Le_Fr%C3%A8re_de_Voltaire_1685-1745.
Gazier, Augustin. 1924. *Histoire du mouvement janséniste depuis ses origines jusqu'à nos jours*. 2 vols. Paris: Honoré Champion.
Geiger, Erika. 1999. *Nikolaus Ludwig Graf von Zinzendorf: Seine Lebensgeschichte*. Holzgerlingen: Hänssler Verlag.
Gérard, Alain. 2000. *"Par principe d'humanité": la Terreur et la Vendée*. Paris: Fayard.
Gérard, Nauroy, Pierre Halen, and Anne Spica, eds. 2003. *le Désert, un espace paradoxal. Actes du colloque de l'Université de Metz (13–15 septembre 2001)*, Recherches en littérature et spiritualité. Vol. 2. Berne, Berlin, Bruxelles, Francfort, New York, Oxford et Vienne: Peter Lang.
Gerhards, Agnès. 1998. *Dictionnaire historique des ordres religieux*. Paris: Fayard.
Goddard, Jean-Christophe. 2003. Le Dieu de Fichte et le Dieu de Rousseau. *Fichte und die Aufklärung/Fichte e l'illuminismo*. Conference, Bologna, 11 April.
Goldmann, Lucien. 1959. *Le Dieu caché. Etude sur la vision tragique dans les Pensées de Pascal et dans le théatre de Racine*. Paris: Gallimard.
Goldstein, Jan. 1998. Enthusiasm or Imagination? Eighteenth-Century Smear Words in Comparative National Context. *Huntington Library Quarterly* 60: 29–49.
Gondal, Marie-Louise. 1989. *Madame Guyon (1648–1717): Un nouveau visage*. Paris: Beauchesne.
Gouzi, Christine. 2007. *L'art et le jansénisme au XVIIIe siècle*. Paris: Nolin.
Grégoire, abbé Henri. 1810. *Histoire des sectes religieuses [...] depuis le commencement du siècle jusqu'à l'époque actuelle*. Paris: Potey.
———. 1988. *Essai sur la régénération des Juifs*. Paris: Stock.
Grieder, Josephine. 1975. *Translations of French Sentimental Prose Fiction in Late 18th Century England: The History of a Literary Vogue*. Durham, NC: Duke University Press.
Guyon, Mme J. B. de la Mothe. 1767–1768. *Lettres Chrétiennes et spirituelles*. 5 vols. London, n.p.
Haag, Eugene. 1846–1859. *La France protestante*. 10 vols. Paris/Genève: J. Cherbuliez.
———. 1861–1869. *La France protestante*. 10 vols. Paris: Sandoz et Fischbacker.
Hastings, Derek. 2010. *Catholicism & the Roots of Nazism: Religious Identity & National Socialism*. New York: Oxford University Press.
Havinga, Jan. 1925. *Les «Nouvelles ecclésiastiques» dans leur lutte contre l'esprit philosophique*. Amersfoort: S. W. Melchior.
Heppe, H.L.J. 1875. *Geschichte der quietistischen Mystik der katholischen Kirche*. Berlin: Wilhelm Hertz. Repr., New York: Hildesheim, 1978.
———. 1879. *Geschichte des Pietismus und der Mystik in der Reformirten Kirche, namentlich der Niederlande*. Inktank Publishing, 2019.
Hermon-Belot, Rita. 2000. *L'abbé Grégoire: La politique et la vérité*. Paris: Seuil UH.
Hildesheimer, Françoise. 1992. *Le Jansénisme en France aux XVIIe et XVIIIe siècles*. Paris/Marseilles: Publisud.
Hillenaar, Henk. 1978. L'Augustinisme de Fénelon face à l'Augustinisme des jansénistes. In *Jansenismus, Quitismus, Pietismus*, ed. Helmut Lehmann, Heinz Schilling, and H.-J. Schrader. Göttingen: Vandenhoeck & Ruprecht, 2002.
Hobson, Marian, J.T.A. Leigh, Robert Wokler, and R.A. Leigh, eds. 1992. *Rousseau and the Eighteenth Century. Essays in Memory of R. A. Leigh*. Oxford: Voltaire Foundation.
Hoffman, Philip T. 1984. *Church and Community in the Diocese of Lyon, 1500–1789*. New Haven, CT: Yale University Press.
Howells, Robin. 1995. Rousseau and Voltaire: A Literary Comparison of Two *Professions de foi. French Studies* 49 (4): 397–409.

Hulliung, Mark. 1994. *The Autocritique of Enlightenment: Rousseau and the Philosophes*. Cambridge: Harvard University Press.

Ida, Hisashi. 2001. *Genèse d'une morale matérialiste: les passions et le contrôle de soi chez Diderot*, Les dix-huitièmes siècles. Vol. 53. Paris: Honoré Champion.

Inguenaud, Marie-Thérèse. 1998. La famille de Nicolas-Antoine Boullanger et les milieux jansénistes. *Dix-huitième siècle* 30: 361–372.

Israel, Jonathan. 2001. *Radical Enlightenment: Philosophy and the Making of Modernity, 1650–1750*. New York: Oxford University Press.

———. 2016. Rousseau, Diderot, and the 'Radical Enlightenment': A Reply to Helena Rosenblatt and Joanna Stalnaker. *Journal of the History of Ideas* 77 (4): 649–677.

Jalliet, Aline. 1994. Loaisel de Tréogate, romancier féministe? *Dix-huitième siècle* 26: 475–485.

Jenkins, Philip. 2002. *The Next Christendom: The Coming of Global Christianity*. Oxford: Oxford University Press.

Jennings, Lawrence C. 2000. *French Anti-Slavery: The Movement for the Abolition of Slavery in France, 1802–1848*. New York: Cambridge University Press.

Joblin, Alain. 1999. La religion populaire et la Révolution française dans le Nord-Ouest de la France (1789–1799). *Annales historiques de la Révolution française* 316: 271–300.

Jonas, Raymond. 1998. Sacred Mysteries and Holy Memories: Counter-Revolutionary France and the Sacré-Coeur. In *Symbols, Myths & Images of the French Revolution*, ed. Ian Germani and Robin Swales. Regina: The Canadian Plains Research Center, University of Regina.

———. 2000. *France and the Cult of the Sacred Heart: An Epic Tale for Modern Times*, Studies on the History of Society & Culture. Vol. 39. Berkeley: University of California Press.

Joutard, Philippe. 1965. *Journaux camisards 1700–1715*. Paris: Union générale d'éditions.

———. 1977a. Les déserts 1685–1800. In *Histoire des Protestants de France*. Toulouse: Privat.

———. 1977b. *La Légende des Camisards: une sensibilité au passé*. Paris: Gallimard.

Kahan, Michèle Bokobza. 2007. Les Lumières au service des miracles. *Dix-Huitième Siècle* 39: 175–188.

———. 2010. Ethos in Testimony: The Case of Carré de Montgeron, a Jansenist and a Convulsionary in the Century of Enlightenment. *Eighteenth-Century Studies* 43 (4): 419–433.

Kamuf, Peggy. 1995. The Rhetoric of Ruin: L'Abbé Grégoire and La Harpe. *Western Society for Eighteenth-Century Studies*.

Kiernan, V. 1952. Evangelicalism and the French Revolution. *Past and Present* 1: 44–56.

Kley, Dale K. van. 1975. *The Jansenists and the Expulsion of the Jesuits from France, 1757–1765*. New Haven, CT: Yale University Press.

———. 1987a. The Jansenist Constitutional Legacy in the French Prerevolution. In *The Political Culture of the Old Regime*, ed. Keith Michael Baker, 169–201. Oxford: Pergamon Press.

———. 1987b. Pierre Nicole, Jansenism, and the Morality of Enlightened Self-Interest. In *Anticipations of Enlightenment in England, France, and Germany*, ed. Alan Charles Kors and Paul J. Korshin. Philadelphia: University of Pennsylvania Press.

———. 1991. *From Calvin to Quesnel: Religion, Politics, and Some Long-Term Origins of the French Revolution*. Vancouver: Society for French Historical Studies.

———. 1997. From Calvin to Quesnel: Religion. In *The Religious Origins of the French Revolution: From Calvin to the Civil Constitution of the Clergy, 1560–1791*. New Haven, CT: Yale University Press.

Knee, Philippe. 2001. Images de Jean-Jacques Rousseau: duplicité et liberté. *Lumen* XX: 137–146.

Kneubühler, Michel. ed. De la tolérance aux droits de l'homme—Écrits sur la liberté de conscience, des guerres de religion à la Révolution française, suivis de La laïcité entre la tolérance et la liberté de Jean Baubérot. Grigny: Éditions Paroles d'aube, coll. "Inventaires," 1998.

Kolakowski, Leszek. 1995. *God Owes Us Nothing: A Brief Remark on Pascal's Writing and the Spirit of Jansenism*. Chicago: University of Chicago Press. Rev. Bruno Neveu. 1996. Grace before deserts. *TLS* 4843: 29.

Kors, Alan C., and Paul Korshin, eds. 1987. *Anticipations of Enlightenment in England, France, and Germany*. Philadelphia: University of Pennsylvania Press.

Kreiser, B. Robert. 1975. Religious Enthusiasm in Early Eighteenth-Century Paris: The Convulsionaries of Saint-Médard. *The Catholic Historical Review* 61 (3): 353–385.

———. 1978. *Miracles, Convulsions, and Ecclesiastical Politics in Early Eighteenth-Century Paris*. Princeton, NJ: Princeton University Press.

Krumenacker, Yves. 1997. *les Protestants du Poitou au XVIIIe siècle (1681–1789)*, La vie des Huguenots. Vol. 1. Paris: Éditions Honoré Champion.

———. 2002. *Des protestants au Siècle des lumières. Le modèle lyonnais*, La vie des huguenots. Vol. 21. Paris: Honoré Champion.

Kruse, Elaine. *The Mother Will Reign: Religious Enthusiasm and the Politics of the Terror*. Washington, DC: American Historical Association.

L'Aminot, Tanguy. 1997. Quelques réflexions sur l'enfance dans les *Rêveries*. *Op. cit.—Revue de littératures française et comparée* 9.

Labrosse, Claude. 2000. La religion dans les *Mémoires de Trévoux*: essai d'utilisation d'une base de données. In *Journalisme et religion (1685–1785)*, Eighteenth-Century French Intellectual History, ed. Jacques Wagner, vol. 6. New York, Berne, Berlin, Bruxelles, Francfort, Oxford & Vienne: Peter Lang.

———. 2001. Nouveauté de *la Nouvelle Héloïse*. *Eighteenth-Century Fiction* 13 (2–3): 235–246.

Lahouati, Gérard. 1997. Le nombre et l'harmonie. *Les Rêveries du promeneur solitaire*: des consolations des misères de ma vie au matérialisme du sage. *Op. cit.—Revue de littératures française et comparée* 9.

Lambrechts, Mathijs, and L. Kennis, eds. 1994. *L'Augustinisme à l'ancienne Faculté de Théologie de Louvain*. Centre pour l'Étude du Jansénisme de la Katholieke Universiteit Leuven, Conference celebrating the 350th anniversary of *Augustinus*, 7–9 November 1990. Leuven: Leuven University Press & Uitgeverij Peeters.

Lavillat, Bernard. 1977. *l'Enseignement à Besançon au XVIIIe siècle*, Cahier d'études comtoises, 23. Annales littéraires de l'Université de Besançon, 184. Paris: Belles Lettres.

Lecercle, Jean-Louis. 1999. Le matérialisme du sage selon Rousseau. In *Etre matérialiste à l'Âge des Lumières. Mélanges offerts à Roland Desné*, ed. Beatrice Fink and Gerhardt Stenger. Paris: Presses universitaires de France.

Leduc-Fayette, Denise, ed. 1996. *Fénelon. Philosophie et spiritualité. Actes du colloque de la Sorbonne de mai 1994*, Histoire des idées et critique littéraire. Vol. 353. Geneva: Droz.

Lefebvre, Philippe. 1992. *Les Pouvoirs de la Parole: L'Eglise et Rousseau, 1762–1848*. Paris: Cerf.

Lehmann, Hartmut, Heinz Schilling, and H.-J. Schrader, eds. 1977. *Jansenismus, Quietismus, Pietismus*. Göttingen: Vandenhoeck & Ruprecht, 2002.

Lehner, Ulrich L. 2016. *The Catholic Enlightenment: The Forgotten History of a Global Movement*. Oxford: Oxford University Press.

Lesaulnier, Jean. 1996. Les manuscrits port-royalistes et jansénistes. *XVIIe siècle* 48 (3): 461–476.

Lichtheim, George. 1966. Rousseau and De Maistre. *New Statesman*: 398–399.

Ligou, Daniel. 1968. *Le Protestantisme en France de 1598 à 1715*. Paris: Société d'édition d'enseignement supérieure.

———. 1991. Le chevalier Ramsay précurseur de *l'Encyclopédie* ou aventurier religieux? In *L'encyclopédisme, actes du colloque de Caen, 12–16 janvier 1987*, ed. Annie Becq, 169–182. Paris: Aux amateurs de livres.

Louis, Jeanne Henriette. 1998. La sainte expérience de la Pennsylvanie (1682–1756) gage de la royauté spirituelle et de la France-Amérique. In *la France-Amérique (XVIe–XVIIIe siècle). Actes du XXXVe colloque intenational d'études humanistes*, Travaux du Centre d'études supérieures de la Renaissance de Tours. Le savoir de Mantice, ed. Frank Lestringant, vol. 5, 541–551. Paris: Honoré Champion.

MacKenna, Antony. 1990. *De Pascal à Voltaire: Le rôle des Pensées dans l'histoire des idées entre 1670 et 1734*, Studies on Voltaire and the Eighteenth Century. Vol. 2. Oxford: Voltaire Foundation.

Maire, Catherine-Laurence. 1981. *Les Possédées de Morzine (1857–1873)*. Lyon: Presses Universitaires de Lyon.

———, ed. 1985. *Les convulsionnaires de Saint-Médard: miracles, convulsions et prophéties à Paris au XVIIIe siècle*. Paris: Gallimard/Julliard Archives.

———. 1998. *De la cause de Dieu à la cause de la nation. Le jansénisme au XVIIIe siècle*. Paris: Gallimard.

———. 2002. Les jansénistes face aux convulsionnaires (1732–1747). In *Foi, croyances, superstitions dans l'Europe des Lumières*, le Spectateur européen. The European Spectator, ed. Clotilde Prunier, vol. 4, 131–144. Montpellier: Presses Universitaires de la Méditerranée.

Mall, Laurence. 2000. Des monstres et d'un prodige: les commencements de l'*Émile*. *Revue de métaphysique et de morale* 3: 363–380.

Mander, J. 1999. Julie or the New Heloise: Letters of Two Lovers who Live in a Small Town at the Foot of the Alps. *History Workshop* 48: 258–264.

Mandrou, Robert, et al. 1977. *Histoire des protestants en France*. Toulouse: Privat.

Marso, L.J. 1998. The Stories of Citizens: Rousseau, Montesquieu, and de Staël Challenge Enlightenment Reason. *Polity* 30 (3): 435s.

Martin, David. 1993. *Tongues of Fire: The Explosion of Protestantism in Latin America*. Oxford, UK & Cambridge, MA: Blackwell.

Masseau, Didier. 1994. *L'Invention de l'intellectuel dans l'Europe du XVIIIe siècle*. Paris: PUF.

———. 2000. *Les Ennemis des philosophes. L'antiphilosophie au temps des Lumières*. Paris: Albin Michel. Paris: Honoré Champion, 2001.

Masson, Pierre-Maurice. 1916 Rousseau et la restauration religieuse. In *La Religion de Jean-Jacques Rousseau*. 3 vols. Paris: Hachette. Repr., Geneva: Slatkine, 1970.

Mathiez, Albert. 1904. *Les Origines des cultes révolutionnaires (1789-1792)*. Paris: Société nouvelle de librairie et d'édition.

Maza, Sarah. 1995. *Private Lives and Public Affairs: The Causes Célèbres of Prerevolutionary France*, Studies on the History of Society and Culture. Vol. 18. Berkeley: University of California Press.

McEachern, (Rousseau) Jo-Ann E, ed. 1989–1993. *Bibliography of the writings of Jean Jacques Rousseau to 1800*. vols. 1–2, (of 8 vol projected). Oxford: Voltaire Foundation.

McMahon, Darrin. 2001. *Enemies of the Enlightenment: The French Counter-Enlightenment and the Making of Modernity*. New York: Oxford University Press.

McManners, John. 1998a. *Church and Society in Eighteenth-Century France*, The Clerical Establishment and its Social Ramifications. Vol. 1. New York: Oxford University Press. http://www.amazon.com/exec/obidos/ASIN/0198270038/enlightenmentnet/.

———. 1998b. *Church and Society in Eighteenth-Century France*, The Religion of the People and the Politics of Religion. Vol. 2. New York: Oxford University Press. http://www.amazon.com/exec/obidos/ASIN/0198270046/enlightenmentnet.

Mentzer, Raymond A., Jr. 2000. Morals and Moral Regulation in Protestant France. *Journal of Interdisciplinary History* 31 (1): 1.

Mercier-Faivre, Anne-Marie. 1995. Les protestants français du XVIIIe siècle à la recherche d'une identité. In *Le roi, le protestant et la république*, 35–47. France: Éditions Cêtre.

———. 1997. Les traités sur la tolérance: Voltaire et les protestants français, une confrontation. *Studies on Voltaire and the Eighteenth Century*: 613–630.

———. 1998. Le rêve des origines: du protestantisme à la franc-maçonnerie. In *Franc-maçonnerie et religion dans l'Europe des Lumières*, 57–76. Paris: Champion.

Merrick, Jeffrey W. 1986. 'Disputes Over Words' and Constitutional Conflict in France, 1730–1732. *French Historical Studies* XIV (4): 497–520.

———. 1990. *The Desacralization of the French Monarchy in the Eighteenth Century*. Baton Rouge: LSU Press. (Jansenism as republican).

Michel, Marie-José. 2000. *Jansénisme et*. Paris: Klincksieck.

Michelet, Jules. 1853. *Histoire de la Révolution française, bk3, ch11–12*. Paris: Chamerot. (l'Être Suprème).

Michon, Hélène. 2006. Voltaire, lecteur de Pascal ou la question du langage équivoque. *SVEC* 10: 349–359.

Migne, Jacques-Paul, ed. 1847. *Dictionnaire des Hérésies, des Schismes, des Auteurs et des Livres Jansénistes, des Ouvrages Mis à l'Index, des Propositions Condamnées par l'Église, et des Ouvrages Condamnés par les Tribunaux Français*. tome 2, vol. 12 of *Encyclopédie théologique, ou Série de dictionnaires sur toutes les parties de la science religieuse*. 50 vols. Paris: Ateliers Catholiques Migne.

Mobarek, Yasmina. 1998. La vérité et ses mises en scène dans la 'Profession de foi du vicaire savoyard'. In *Religion and French Literature*, French Literature Series, vol. 25. The Netherlands: Brill. (Rousseau).

Montesquieu. 1944. *Un carnet inédit. le Spicilège*. Paris: Flammarion. (Jansenist *convulsionnaires*).

Moret, Jean-René. 2012. Les réformateurs face à la confession. *La Revue réformée* 63: 261. http://larevuereformee.net/articlerr/n261/les-reformateurs-face-a-la-confession.

Mornet, Daniel. 1907. *le Sentiment de la nature en France, de J.-J. Rousseau à Bernardin de Saint-Pierre.* Essai sur les rapports de la littérature et des moeurs, 586. Paris: Réimpression de l'édition de. Repr., Genève: Slatkine Reprints, 2000.

———. 1912. *le Romantisme en France au XVIIIe siècle*, vol. 298. Paris: Réimpression de l'édition de. Repr., Genève: Slatkine Reprints, 2000.

———. 1933. *Les Origines intellectuelles de la Révolution Française, 1715–1787*. 6th ed. Paris: Armand Colin, 1967.

Mortier, Roland. Prélude à la fête révolutionnaire: la "fête bocagère" dans la poésie descriptive de la fin du XVIIIe siècle. In *Le Coeur et la Raison*. Oxford: Voltaire Foundation.

Mothu, Alain. 1997. Un curé "janséniste" lecteur et auteur de manuscrits clandestins: Guillaume Maleville. *la Lettre clandestine* 6.

Necheles, Ruth. 1987. *The Abbé Grégoire: 1787–1831: The Odyssey of an Egalitarian*. Westport, CT: Greenwood.

Nowak, Kurt. 1993. *Der umstrittene Burger von Genf: Zur Wirkungsgeschichte Rousseaus im deutschen Protestantismus des 18. Jahrhunderts*. Berlin: Akademie Verlag.

O'Brien, Charles H. 1985. The Jansenist Campaign for Toleration of Protestants in Late Eighteenth-Century France: Sacred or Secular? *Journal of the History of Ideas* 46 (4): 523–538.

O'Connell, Marvin R. 1997. *Blaise Pascal: Reasons of the Heart*. Grand Rapids, MI: Eerdmans.

O'Keefe, Cyril B. 1974. Contemporary Reactions to the Enlightenment (1728–1762): A Study of Three Critical Journals, the Jesuit *Journal de Trévoux*, the Jansenist *Nouvelles Ecclésiastiques*, and the Secular *Journal Des Savants*. Thesis, University of Toronto.

Oakley, Francis. 1982–1989. "Conciliar Theory" and "Councils, Western (1311–1449)". Articles in *The Dictionary of the Middle Ages*, vol 3, 510–523, 642–656. 13 vols. New York: Charles Scribner's Sons.

———. 1984. *Natural Law, Conciliarism, and Consent in the Late Middle Ages: Studies in Ecclesiastical and Intellectual History*. London: Variorum Reprints.

———. 1997. Locke, Natural Law and God—Again. *History of Political Thought* 18 (4): 624–651.

———. 1998a. The Absolute and Ordained Power of God in Sixteenth- and Seventeenth-Century Theology. *Journal of the History of Ideas* 59 (3): 437–462.

———. 1998b. The Absolute and Ordained Power of God and King in the Sixteenth and Seventeenth Centuries: Philosophy, Science, Politics, and Law. *Journal of the History of Ideas* 59 (4): 669–690.

———. 1999. Bronze-Age Conciliarism: Edmond Richer's Encounters with Cajetan and Bellarmine. *History of Political Thought* 20 (1): 65–86.

Orcibal, Jean. 1947. *Les Origines du jansénisme*, vols II & III, Jean Duvergier de Hauranne abbé de Saint-Cyran et son temps: 1531–1638. 3 vols. Louvain: Bureaux de la Revue.

———. 1948a. *Les origines du jansénisme*. Vol. 5 vols. Paris: Vrin.

———. 1948b. *État present des recherches sur la repartition géographique des Nouveaux Catholiques à la fin du XVIIe siècle*. Paris: J. Vrin.

———. 1951. The Theological Originality of John Wesley. "Les spirituals français et espagnols chez John Wesley et ses contemporains". *Revue d'histoire des religions* 139: 50–109.

———. 1965. The Theological Originality of John Wesley and Continental Spirituality. Trans. R.J.A. Sharp in *A History of the Methodist Church in Great Britain*, ed. Davies & Rupp, 83–111.
Ozouf, Mona. 1988. *Festivals and the French Revolution*. Trans. A. Sheridan. Cambridge, MA: Harvard University Press.
Palissot de Montenoy, Charles. 1730–1814. *Les Philosophes*. Comedy in 3 acts and in verse Comédie Française, 2 May 1760.
Pallavidini, R. 1997. The Structures of Social Subjectivity in Rousseau, the "Aesthetics" of Shaftesbury, and the British Culture of "Sentimentality". *Filosofia* 48 (3): 427–464. (In Italian).
Palmer, Robert R. 1966. *Catholics and Unbelievers in Eighteenth-Century France*. Princeton, NJ: Princeton University Press.
Pappas, John. 1999. Buffon matérialiste? Les critiques de Berthier, Feller, et les *Nouvelles ecclésiastiques*. In *Etre matérialiste à l'Âge des Lumières. Mélanges offerts à Roland Desné*, ed. Beatrice Fink and Gerhardt Stenger. Paris: Presses universitaires de France.
Parny, Évariste de. 2002. *la Guerre des dieux*. Édition critique par Jacques-Charles Lemaire. *L'âge des Lumières*. Paris: Honoré Champion.
Pascal, Blaise. 1963. Lettres Provinciales. (1656–57). In *Œuvres completes*, 371–469. Paris: Seuil.
Pintard, René. 1943. *Le Libertinage érudit dans la première moitié du XVIIe siècle*. Paris: Boivin. Repr., Genève/Paris: Slatkine, 1983.
Pister, Danielle, ed. 2001. *l'Image du prêtre dans la littérature classique (XVIIe–XVIIIe siècles). Actes du colloque organisé par le Centre Michel Baude - Littérature et spiritualité de l'Université de Metz, 20–21 novembre 1998*, Recherches en littérature et spiritualité. Vol. 1. Berne, Berlin, Bruxelles, Francfort, New York, Oxford et Vienne: Peter Lang.
Pitassi, Maria Christina. 1992. *De l'Orthodoxie aux Lumières: Genève 1670–1737*. Geneva: Labor et Fidès.
Pitassi, Maria-Cristina, and Laurence Bergon. 1999. Jean-Alphonse Turrettini, correspondant de l'Europe savante et ecclésiastique au début des Lumières. In *la Vie intellectuelle aux Refuges protestants. Actes de la Table ronde de Münster du 25 juillet 1995*, Vie des Huguenots, ed. Jens Häseler and Antony McKenna, vol. 5, 157–171. Paris: Honoré Champion éditeur.
Pitt, Alan. 2000. The Religion of the Moderns: Freedom and Authenticity in Constant's *De la Religion. History of Political Thought* 21 (1): 67–87.
Plongeron, Bernard. 1969. *Conscience religieuse en Révolution: Regards sur l'historiographie de la Revolution francaise*. Paris: Editions A. & J. Picard.
———. 1973. *Théologie et politique au Siècle des Lumières (1770–1820)*, Travaux d'histoire éthico-politiques. Vol. 25. Geneva: Droz.
———. 1977. La Vie quotidienne du clergé français au xviiie siècle, 1974. *Annales historiques de la Révolution française* 227: 119–124.
———. 1989. *L'abbé Grégoire (1750–1831) ou l'Arche de la fraternité*. Paris: Letouzey et Ané.
———. 1996. Sur Grégoire régicide d'après les documents pris pour sources. *Annales historiques de la Révolution française* 305: 535–536.
———. 2001. *L'abbé Grégoire et la République des savants*. Paris: Editions du CTHS.
Poewe, Karla, ed. 1994. *Charismatic Christianity as a Global Culture*. Columbia, SC: University of South Carolina Press.
Porterfield, Amanda, and Rev. George M. Marsden. 1991. Understanding Fundamentalism and Evangelicalism, in Sociological Analysis. *Religious Movements and Social Movements* 52 (4): 419–420.
Post, Steef. 1993. De bekering van Bernard Nieuwentijt. *De Achttiende Eeuw* 25 (2): 211–214. [Re: N's 1715 conversion].
Pouzet, Régine, ed. 2001. *Chronique des Pascal. "Les affaires du monde" d'Étienne Pascal à Marguerite Périer (1588–1733)*. Préface de Jean Mesnard. Vol. 30 of Lumières classiques. Paris: Éditions Honoré Champion.
Préclin, Edmond. 1929. *Les Jansénistes du XVIIIe siècle et la Constitution civile du Clergé: le développement du Richérisme*. Paris: Éditeur inconnu.

———. 1930. Edmond Richer (1559–1631): Sa vie, Son oeuvre et le Richérisme. *Revue d'histoire moderne* 5: 241–269, 321–336.
Préclin, Edmond, and Eugène Jarry. 1955. *Les luttes politiques et doctrinales aux XVIIe et XVIIIe siècles*. Paris: Bloud & Gay.
Pressly, William L. 1999. *The French Revolution and Blasphemy: Johann Zoffany's Paintings of the Massacre at Paris August 10, 1792*. Berkeley: University of California Press.
Prothero, Stephen. 2008. *Religious Literacy: What Every American Needs to Know—and Doesn't*. New York: HarperCollins.
Quesnel, Pasquier. 1668. *Le Nouveau Testament en Français, avec des Réflexions morales sur chaque verset, pour en rendre la lecture plus utile et la méditation plus aisée*. (*Réflexions morales*, 1st ed.), 4 vols, 1693, revised, 1695. A Paris: chez André Pralard.
———. 1687–1690. *La Tradition de l'Église Romaine sur la prédestination des Saints et sur la grâce efficace*. Cologne: Chez Nicolas Schouten.
Ramsay, chevalier Andrew Michael. 1737. *Discours prononcé à la réception des francs-maçons par le chevalier André-Michael de Ramsay*. Édition de Georges Lamoine. Toulouse: Éditions SNES, 1999.
———. 2002a. *les Principes philosophiques de la religion naturelle et révélée dévoilés selon le mode géométrique*. (1748–1749) Traduction, introduction, notes et index par Georges Lamoine. Vol. 18 of L'âge des lumières. Geneva: Slatkine.
———. 2002b. *les Voyages de Cyrus. Avec un discours sur la mythologie*. (1727) Édition critique établie par Georges Lamoine. Vol. 17 of L'âge des lumières. Geneva: Slatkine.
Randall, C. 1997. The "Protestant's Progress": Reading Reformed Travel Literature in Early Modern France. *Religion & Literature* 29 (3): 21–42.
Renwick, John, Lucette Pérol, and with Jean Ehrard. 1999. *Deux bibliothèques oratoriennes à la fin du XVIIIe siècle: Riom et Effiat*. Saint-Étienne: Publications de l'Université de Saint-Étienne.
Riley, Patrick. 1986. *The General Will Before Rousseau: The Transformation of the Divine into the Civic*. Princeton, NJ: Princeton University Press, 1988.
———. 1999. The Inversion of Conversion: Rousseau's Rewriting of Augustinian Autobiography. *Studies in Eighteenth-Century Culture* 28: 229–255.
Rogers, Ben, and Bernard Rogers. 1999. *Pascal: The Great Philosophers*. New York: Routledge.
Rosenblatt, Helena. 1998. The Language of Genevan Calvinism in the Eighteenth Century. In *Reconceptualizing Nature, Science, and Aesthetics: Contribution à une nouvelle approche des Lumières helvétiques*, Travaux sur la Suisse des Lumières, vol. 1. Geneva: Éditions Slatkine.
———. 2004a. Re-Evaluating Benjamin Constant's Liberalism: Industrialism, Saint-Simonianism and the Restoration Years. *History of European Ideas* 30 (1): 23–37.
———. 2004b. Why Constant? A Critical Overview of the Constant Revival. *Modern Intellectual History* I (3): 359–385.
———. 2016. Rousseau, the 'Traditionalist'. *Journal of the History of Ideas* 77 (4): 627–635.
Rousseau, Jean-Jacques. 1761a. *The Confessions of Jean-Jacques Rousseau. Emile*. http://www.ilt.columbia.edu/Projects/emile/emile.html.
———. 1761b. *The Confessions of Jean-Jacques Rousseau. Émile*, Book 4 in *Œuvres completes*, vol 4. Paris: Gallimard Pléiade, 1969.
———. 1762. The Confessions of Jean-Jacques Rousseau. "Lettres à Malesherbes". In *Œuvres complètes*, vol. 1, 1130–1147. Paris, Gallimard/Pléiade, 1959. https://fr.m.wikisource.org/wiki/Lettres_%C3%A0_Malesherbes.
———. 1763. Lettre à Christophe de Beaumont, Archévêque de Paris. *Œuvres complètes* 4: 935–938.
———. 1778. Confessions. In *Œuvres complètes*, vol. 1. Paris: Gallimard/Pléiade, 1959.
———. 1907. *The Confessions of Jean-Jacques Rousseau, newly translated into English*. London: Gibbings. 1st ed. 1891 by Stott.
———. 1909–1914. *The Confessions of Jean-Jacques Rousseau. Profession of Faith of a Savoyard Vicar*. Vol. XXXIV, Part 4 of The Harvard Classics. New York: P.F. Collier & Son.

———. 1959–1995. *Œuvres completes*. Ed. Bernard Gagnebin, Marcel Raymond et al. 5 vols. Paris: Gallimard Pléiade.
———. 1965–1995. *Correspondance complète de Jean Jacques Rousseau*. vols. 1–51 (of 52 expected). Geneva: Institut et Musée Voltaire. Oxford: Voltaire Foundation.
———. 1978. *Profession de foi du vicaire savoyard*. "Vicaire 76", ed. A. Robinet, Tableaux, Concordances. Paris: Vrin.
———. 2002. *De la Suisse suivi du Journal (septembre 1764) de J. C. von Zinzendorf.* Édition critique par Frédéric S. Eigeldinger. Vol. 20 of L'âge des Lumières. Paris: Honoré Champion.
Roussin, Philippe, ed. 1998. *Critique et affaires de blasphème à l'époque des Lumières*. Paris: Honoré Champion.
Saul, John Ralston. 1992. *Voltaire's Bastards: The Dictatorship of Reason in the West*. New York: Vintage.
Schmaltz, Tad M. 1999. What Has Cartesianism To Do with Jansenism? *Journal of the History of Ideas* 60 (1): 37–56. (Arnauld; Desgabets; Noël; Mesland; Petau; Bayle; Rohault; Le Bossu; de Cordemoy; Fromentier; Maignan; Fabri; Du Vaucel; Ferrier; Le Moine, &c.).
Schwartz, Joel. 1984. *The Sexual Politics of Jean-Jacques Rousseau*. Chicago: University of Chicago Press.
Sedgwick, Alexander. 1977. *Jansenism in Seventeenth Century France*. Charlottesville, VA: University Press of Virginia.
Seillière, Ernest. 1920. Joseph de Maistre et Rousseau. *Comptes rendues des séances de l'Academie des Sciences Morales et Politiques* 194: 321–363.
Séité, Yannick. 2002. *Du livre au lire: la Nouvelle Héloïse, roman des Lumières*, Les dix-huitièmes siècles. Vol. 67. Paris: Honoré Champion.
Selles, Otto H. 1998. Des convulsions à Paris et dans les Cévennes: le jansénisme convulsionnaire et le protestantisme prophétique selon Louis-Basile Carré de Montgeron et Maximilien Misson. *Chroniques de Port Royal* 47: 405–428.
Sgard, Jean. 1998. Diderot vu par les Nouvelles ecclésiastiques. *Recherches sur Diderot et sur l'Encyclopédie* 25: 9–19.
Shelford, Aril G. 2002. Thinking Geometrically in Pierre-Daniel Huet's *Demonstratio evangelica* (1679). *Journal of the History of Ideas* 63 (4): 599–618.
Shennan, J. 1998. *The Parlement of Paris*. Stroud: Sutton Press.
Silvestrini, Gabriella. 2009. Religion naturelle, droit naturel et tolérance dans la 'Profession de foi du Vicaire Savoyard'. *Archives de Philosophie* LXXII (1): 31–54.
Soboul, Albert. 1956. Sentiment religieux et cultes populaires pendant la Révolution. *Archives de Sociologie des Religions* 2.
———. 1957. Religious Sentiments and Popular Cults: Patriot Saints and Martyrs of Liberty. *Annales Historiques de la Révolution Française* 3: 193–213. Transl. A.A. Knutson in Soboul, *Understanding the French Revolution*, New York: International Publishers, 1988.
———. 1982. Sur les « curés rouges » dans la Révolution Française. *Annales historiques de la Révolution française* 249: 349–363. https://doi.org/10.3406/ahrf.1982.3847. www.persee.fr/doc/ahrf_0003-4436_1982_num_249_1_3847. ["On the 'Red Priests' in the French Revolution" Trans. A.A. Knutson in Soboul, *Understanding the French Revolution*. New York: International Publishers, 1988].
Soëtard, M. 1997. La révolution épistémologique de l'*Émile*. *Études Jean-Jacques Rousseau* 9.
Sosso, P. 1992. Rousseau Caught Between St. Paul and So-Called Natural Religion [in Italian]. *Studi Francesi* 36 (3): 525–530.
Soupel, Serge. 1993. Richardson as a Source for Baculard d'Arnaud's Novelle. *R.L.C.* 67: 207–217.
———. 1998. Les romans du XVIIIe siècle: rencontres franco-britanniques; rencontrer, assimiler, copier. In *l'Un(e) miroir de l'autre*, Cahiers de recherches du CRLMC, ed. Max Véga-Ritter, 123–133. Clermont-Ferrand: Université Blaise-Pascal, Centre de recherches sur les littératures modernes et contemporaines.
Spangenberg, August. 1971. *Leben des Herrn Nicolaus Ludwig, Grafen und Herrn von Zinzendorf und Pottendorf, beschrieben von August Gottlieb Spangenberg*. (1772–1775) 8 Volumes in 4.

New York: Olms. Abridged English translation: *The Life of N. L. Count Zinzendorf*, Translated from the German, by S. Jackson, London: Holdsworth, 1838.
Steinberger, Deborah. 1999. A New Look at the *comédie larmoyante*. *l'Esprit créateur* 39 (3): 64–75.
Stewart, H.F. 2012. *The Holiness of Pascal*. Cambridge: Cambridge University Press.
Stoeffler, F. Ernest. 1965. *The Rise of Evangelical Pietism*. 2nd ed., 1971. Brill: Netherlands
Strayer, Brian E. 2001. *Huguenots and Camisards as Aliens in France, 1589–1789: The Struggle for Religious Toleration*, Studies in Religion and Society. Vol. 50. Lewiston, NY: E. Mellen.
———. 2008. *Suffering Saints: Jansenism and Convulsionaires in France, 1640–1799*. Brighton, UK: Sussex Academic Press.
Swenson, James. 2000. *On Jean-Jacques Rousseau Considered as One of the First Authors of the Revolution*, Atopia. Stanford, CA: Stanford University Press.
Switzer, R., ed. 1970. *Chateaubriand: Actes du Congrés de Wisconsin (1968)*. Geneva: Droz.
Tackett, Timothy. 1977. *Priest and Parish in 18th Century France: A Social and Political Study of the Curés in a Diocese of Dauphiné*. Princeton, NJ: Princeton University Press.
———. 1986. *Religion, Revolution, and Regional Culture in 18th Century France: The Ecclesiastical Oath of 1791*. Princeton, NJ: Princeton University Press.
Talmon, J[acob] L[eib]. 1952. *The Rise of Totalitarian Democracy*. Boston: Beacon Press. (*The Origins of Totalitarian Democracy*, London: Secker & Warburg, 1960).
Tans, J.A.G. 1956. Les idées politiques des jansénistes. *Neophilologus* XC: 1–18.
Taveneaux, R. 1960. *Le Jansénisme en Lorraine (1640–1789)*. Paris: Vrin.
———. 1965. *Jansénisme et politique*. Paris: A. Colin.
———. 1977. *Jansénisme et prêt à intérêt*. Paris: Vrin.
———. 1985. *La Vie quotidienne des jansénistes aux xviie et xviiie siècles*. Paris: Hachette.
Thiery, Robert. 1992. *l'Emile et la Révolution*. Paris: Universitas.
———. 1995. In *Jean-Jacques, politique et nation. Actes du IIe Colloque international de Montmorency*, ed. le Musée Jean-Jacques Rousseau. Paris: Éditions Honoré Champion, 2001.
Todorov, Tzevtan. 2001. *Frail Happiness: An Essay on Rousseau*. Trans. J.T. Scott and R.T. Zaretsky. University Park, PA: Penn State University Press.
Touitou, Béatrice. 1997. *Baculard d'Arnaud*, Bibliographica. Bibliographie des écrivains français. Vol. 9. Paris/Rome: Memini.
Trouille, Mary. 1997. *Sexual Politics in the Enlightenment: Women Writers Read Rousseau*. Albany: State University of New York Press.
Trousson, Raymond. 1967. *Socrate devant Voltaire, Diderot et Rousseau*. Paris: Minard, "Thèmes et mythes".
———. 1970. Jean-Jacques Rousseau traducteur de Tacite. *Studi Francesi* 16: 231–242.
———. 1990. Rousseau traducteur de Sénèque. *Travaux de Littérature* 3: 139–151.
———. 1992. Quinze années d'études rousseauistes (II). *Dix-huitième siècle* 24: 421–489.
———. 1995. *Défenseurs et adversaires de J.-J. Rousseau. D'Isabelle de Charrière à Charles Maurras*. Paris: Champion.
———. 1997. *Images de Diderot en France*. Paris: Champion.
———. 2001a. Le *Dolbreuse* de Loaisel de Tréogate: du roman libertin au 'roman utile'. *Eighteenth-Century Fiction* 13 (2–3): 301–313.
———. 2001b. *Visages de Voltaire (XVIIIe–XIXe siècles)*, Les dix-huitièmes siècles. Vol. 63. Paris: Honoré Champion.
Trousson, Raymond, and Frédéric Eigeldinger. 1998. *Jean-Jacques Rousseau au jour de jour. Chronologie*. Paris: Éditions Honoré Champion.
Truchet, J. 1974. Deux imitations des *Femmes savantes* au Siècle des Lumières, ou Molière anti-philosophe et contre-révolutionnaire. In *Approches des Lumières, Mélanges offerts à Jean Fabre*. Paris: Klincksieck.
Van Crugten-André, Valérie. 1997. *Le Roman du libertinage 1782–1815: redécouverte et réhabilitation*. Paris: Honoré Champion.

Venard, Marc. 1979. Popular Religion in the Eighteenth Century. In *Church and Society in Catholic Europe of the Eighteenth Century*, ed. W.J. Callahan and D. Higgs. Cambridge: Cambridge University Press.

Vidal, Daniel. 1977. *L'ablatif absolu: théorie du prophétisme: le discours camisard en Europe (1706–1713)*. Paris: Anthropos.

———. 1983. *Le Malheur et son prophète: inspirés et sectaires en Languedoc calviniste 1685–1725*. Paris: Payot.

———. 1986. *Miracles et convulsions jansénistes au XVIIIe siècle, Le mal et sa connaissance.* Paris: PUF, 1987.

Wagner, Jacques, ed. 2000. *Journalisme et religion: 1685–1785*, Eighteenth-Century French Intellectural History. Vol. 6. New York: Peter Lang.

———, ed. 2002. *Roman et religion en France (1713–1866)*, Colloques sur le 18e. Paris: Honoré Champion.

Weil, Françoise. 1997. *Les livres persécutés en France de 1720 à 1770*, la Lettre clandestine. Vol. 6. Paris: Publication des Presses de l'Université de Paris-Sorbonne.

———. 1999. L'état civil des protestants en 1778. In *Gazettes et information politique sous l'Ancien Régime*, Lire le dix-huitième siècle, ed. Henri Duranton and Pierre Rétat. Saint-Étienne: Publications de l'Université de Saint-Étienne.

Weinlick, John R. 1956. *Count Zinzendorf: The Story of His Life and Leadership in the Renewed Moravian Church.* Nashville, TN: Abingdon Press. Repr., Bethlehem, PA: Moravian Church in America, 1989.

Whatmore, Richard. 2006. Rousseau and the *Représentants*: The Politics of the *Lettres écrites de la montagne. Modern Intellectual History* 3 (3): 385–413.

Whelan, Ruth. 1992. From Christian Apologetics to Enlightened Deism: The Case of Abbadie, Jacques (1656–1727). *Modern Language Review* 87: 32ff.

Willaert, Léopold. 1948. *Les origines du Jansénisme dans les Pays-Bas catholiques.* Bruxelles: Palais des Académies.

Williams, Huntington. 1983. *Rousseau and Romantic Autobiography.* Oxford University Press: New York.

Wright, Johnson Kent, Helen Rosenblatt, Christopher Kelly, Robert Wokler, and James Miller. 2006. Forum: Reading Rousseau, The *Second Discourse. Modern Intellectual History* 3 (1): 65–109.

Yardeni, Myriam. 1987. French Calvinist Political Thought, 1534–1715. In *International Calvinism, 1541–1715*, ed. Menna Prestwich, 315–337. Oxford: Oxford University Press.

———. 2000. *Repenser l'histoire: aspects de l'historiographie huguenote des guerres de religion à la Révolution française*, La vie des huguenots. Vol. 11. Paris: Honoré Champion.

Zaretsky, Rob. 2001. *Frail Happiness: An Essay on Rousseau.* Philadelphia: Penn State U.P.

Zatorska Iza. 2001. *Réflexions de T****** sur les égarements de sa jeunesse.* Édition établie et présentée par Jean Sgard. Texte de 1729. *XVIIIe siècle.* Paris: Desjonquères.

Zoberman, Pierre. 1999. *les Cérémonies de la parole. L'éloquence d'apparat en France dans le dernier quart du XVIIe siècle.* Paris: Honoré Champion.

Chapter 7
The Crucible of the Counter-Enlightenment V

Abstract Israel Ba'al Shem Tov, Hasidism and the Judaic Counter-Enlightenment. Jewish Antecedents: Sabbatian Judaism. The Medieval Torah: Paquda and piety, Maimonides's Enlightenment, De Leon's *Zohar* and Kabbalism. Hasidim between Mithnagdim and Maskilim.

In 1740, the American Awakening was about to become Great, and George Whitefield had begun his third and most sensational mission to British America where he would finally meet Jonathan Edwards in fully awakened Northampton. Zinzendorf's Moravian mission to Georgia was giving up and moving on to Pennsylvania, and one of his missionaries in New York converted his first Mahican native. The Count himself, just back from the West Indies, was in Marienborn, Germany, about to found the Order of the Little Fools. At the same time, several hundred miles east of Marienborn, in the fortified trading town of Międzybóż, in what was then the Podolia province in the east of the vast Kingdom of Lithuania-Poland,[1] a remarkable religious ecstatic named Israel Ben Eliezer (1698–1760) took up residence. Israel, a widowed forty-year-old innkeeper turned itinerant teacher, had come from Tłuste (Tovste), west of Międzybóż in the Carpathian Mountain province of Galicia—farm country—where he had been working for the last ten

[1] Międzybóż is the Polish name of an old town not far from the modern city of Khmelnitsky, is now (2009) in the Khmelnytskyi province in the west of the newly independent and currently embattled Republic of Ukraine. Because this was the town name that was preferred by the Polish-Lithuanian elite who used the Latin alphabet and ruled Międzybóż in the mid-eighteenth century, I use it here, and with accents attached. The Yiddish name, מעזשביזש is transliterated into the Latin alphabet as Mezhbizh. Międzybóż, now officially transliterated (from the Ukrainian) as Medzhybizh, comes from "mezhbuzhye" which we are told means "between the Buzhenka River (and the Bug River)," between the two rivers rather like "Mesopotamia." Orthography remains challenging in eastern Europe and transliteration more so. Alternate spellings include those of all of Międzybóż's various ruling states: Russian: Меджибож, transliterated into English as Medzhibozh; Polish: Międzybóż or Międzybórz; German: Medschybisch; and most recently Ukrainian: Меджибіж, transliterated into English as Medzhybizh (which is the one used by Google Maps). Never consistently spelled—other English transliterations include Medzibezh, Mezhybozhe, Mezshbozsh and Miedjyborz—Międzybóż is easier to pin down on a map than it is on Google, and it can still be found at 49°27′N, 27°25′E. The latest census reports a population of 4614.

W. R. Everdell, *The Evangelical Counter-Enlightenment*, Boston Studies in Philosophy, Religion and Public Life 9,
https://doi.org/10.1007/978-3-030-69762-4_7

years or so as a scripture teacher.[2] Tłuste was a very small town. Międzybóż was larger, and it was growing. The gentile population had increased by 44% since 1722, and the Jewish community, the *kahal*, had grown by 67%, all despite the fact that the town they called Mezhbizh was, like most of eastern Europe before the nineteenth century, still in feudal tenure, the property of the Polish noble family of Czartoryski, who had acquired it from the Sieniawski, and who conducted the census that carefully distinguished Jew from Gentile. Here, the new arrival Israel Ben Eliezer was put up in the house belonging to Międzybóż's flourishing Yiddish-speaking Jewish *kahal*, which called their home town Mezhbizh. He appeared in Polish records of the Czartoryski overlords as "*kantorski wnim kabalista*" (cantor and Kabbalist), and in 1742 as "Balsem."[3] It was in fact, in Międzybóż/Mezhbizh that Israel the son of Eliezer would become the Ba'al Shem Tov or "Master of the Good Name," the founder of Hasidic Judaism.

Ḥasid, (חסיד), sometimes transliterated Chassid, means "pious one" in Hebrew, and as we shall see, Hasidism for Jews arose out of a renewal of mysticism in much the same way as did Pietism for Protestants, Sufism for Muslims and Jansenism for Catholics.[4] The twentieth-century Reform Jew Martin Buber, awed by early Hasidism's mystic transcendence, did not see the parallels when he wrote, "The Hasidic movement, which came to life somewhat suddenly in Eastern European Jewry in the middle of the eighteenth century, must be seen as the last intensive effort in modern history to rejuvenate a religion."[5] The similarities are still easy to overlook in the twenty-first century in the United States and the rest of the industrialized world, where the Ḥasidim (חסידים) have become part of the fascination of

---

[2] Tłuste, now usually called Tovtse, was in Habsburg Galicia and called Tłuste after 1548 by administrators from Poland-Lithuania. It is now (2014) in Ukraine, west of Międzybóż. It's still small and no census I can find reports its population, but its synagogue has been gone since World War 2. (Another small town named Tłuste is in central Poland.)

[3] Moshe Rosman, in Gershon D. Hundert, ed., *Essential Papers on Hasidism: Origins to Present.* NY: New York U.P., c1991, p217. Moshe Rosman, *Founder of Hasidism: A Quest for the Historical Ba'al Shem Tov*, Berkeley: U. of California Press, 1996, Chapter 10, pp 159–170.

[4] Introducing the first comprehensive history of Hasidism in English, David Biale and his team of seven authors clear the historiography by asserting a premise not too different from that of this book: "We are accustomed to think of the Enlightenment and its critique of religion as representing modernity, while seeing movements of religious revival as reactionary, throwbacks to an earlier age.

"Yet the story of modernity is more complex. As we now know, the trajectory of history did not lead in a straight line from religion to secularism, 'darkness' to 'light': religion is as much a part of the modern world as it was of the medieval. As much as religion typically claims to stand for tradition, even the most seemingly 'orthodox' or 'fundamentalist' forms of religion in the modern world are themselves products of their age. Just as secularism was incubated in the womb of religion, so religion since the eighteenth century is a product of its interaction with secularism." (David Biale, David Assaf, Benjamin Brown, Uriel Gellman, Samuel Heilman, Moshe Rosman, Gadi Sagiv, Marcin Wodziński, and Arthur Green, *Hasidism: A New History*, Princeton, NJ: Princeton University Press. 2017, Kindle Edition, p1).

[5] Martin Buber, "Rabbi Nachman's Journey to Palestine," in Buber, *The Tales of Rabbi Nachman* (1906), tr. Maurice Friedman (1956), NY: Avon Discus ed., 1970, p180.

living in a polyglot, multicultural, modern city, and where, even in that setting, they can seem like dwellers in an alternate universe. Dressed in the height of a vanished fashion, the men in long, frock coats cut in the European style of the 1790s, with prayer shawls peeping from the tails, broad-brimmed black fur hats, hiding the *kippes* (skullcaps) underneath, and revealing long *pais*, or earlocks, the women in long-sleeved dresses and wigs, both sexes flaunting fur trim even in summer's heat, they faithfully carry out each and every *mitzvah* or injunction from the Torah (Law) as they find them interpreted by the rest of the (Hebrew) Bible, the Talmud, and their particular Hasidic community's *rebbe* (rabbi, teacher, mayor, community head). This last source of authority is one that distinguishes the Ḥasidim from what have been called the Orthodox and even the "Ultra-Orthodox" among Jews, even more than their men's fashions, designed by former rebbes to pin Hasidism to eighteenth-century Poland, and thereby attach eternal significance to the time and place of their founders.

The Ḥasidim have been known to irritate non-Ḥasidim, both Jewish and Gentile non-Ḥasidim, and this is not only because of their oddness, their visibility, or their seeming rejection of modernity. Some of Hasidism's most stubbornly held beliefs, doctrines, and liturgies can seem wrong to Jews as much as to non-Jews. Ḥasidim believe that liturgy is malleable, that prayer may not be scheduled, that salvation is attainable through actions that transcend the learning of Torah, that the coming of the Messiah—Moshiach—and the world's renewal are to be expected at world's end; that direct revelation has persisted into the latter days, and most importantly that immediate grace (*ḥesed*) in the form of *devekut*—ecstasy, rapture and vision, is also expectable, even in the midst of life, such that it can bring any believer into immediacy with God.[6] From this comes the most obvious outward sign of grace for the Ḥasidim. It is the custom of dancing rapturously before the Lord of Hosts on special occasions, as the Bible says King David danced when the Ark of the Covenant was brought into Jerusalem.[7] Inspired dance is the clearest remaining mark of what the Ba'al Shem Tov brought to Międzybóż/Mezhbizh in the 1740s, which was nothing less than religious ecstasy.

The Ḥasidim see their history the way the Sufis see their *tariq*, as a set of dynasties of rebbes, each rebbe a *ẓaddiḳ* or *tsadik*, a "just one" or "friend of God" in close communication with the divine, each succeeding his predecessor as leader of the congregation, in a line descending from teacher to student or from father to son—or

[6] The key terms for Hasidic mysticism are, in Hebrew, *devekut* ("ecstatic union"), *ha'alat nitzotzot* ("raising of sparks"), *avodah be-gashmiyut* ("worship through the material") and, of course, Hasid ("pious one") so that Hasidism, simply means the practice of "piety". Gershom Scholem added another earlier Kabbalistic notion, *bittul ha-yesh* ("annihilation of reality"). (Biale, et al., *Hasidism: A New History*, PUP Kindle Edition, p. 1, 5). "For some Hasidic teachers, *devekut* meant the union of the worshipper with God, while for others, it meant less self-effacing communion." Biale, et al., *Hasidism*, p. 6.

[7] 2 Samuel 6:14–16

both—(only once among women have the Ḥasidim found inspiration);[8] with each and every Hasidic dynasty ultimately tracing itself back to that odd new teacher of Międzybóż/Mezhbizh in the 1740s, Israel Ben Eliezer, the Ba'al Shem Tov, who made no dynasty.

The Ḥasidim from their beginnings have also followed a custom prohibited by seventeenth-century authorities to both Jews and Christians, the practice of holding some religious services privately, in houses or otherwise removed from officially recognized places of worship. In 1741, a year after the Ba'al Shem arrived in Międzybóż/Mezhbizh, the records tell us that one Asher ben Moshe, a resident, faced resistance from the *kahal* for assembling a *minyan*, the biblical quorum for prayer, in his own home. This was, in fact, a conventicle (to use the English word), of the sort prohibited by church and state alike to Baptists in England, and Pietists in Germany.[9] Was the intent to provide a pulpit for the newly arrived "cantor and Kabbalist," Israel Ben Eliezer? The records do not say, and the Ba'al Shem's legend has been so regularly revised that his history is at best distorted and at worst, beyond hope of reconstruction. Religious commitment has a way of turning reliance on oral tradition and any other kind of evidence into an act of faith; making the historian all the more grateful for the note in the Czartoryski records for 1742 referring to the recent immigrant Israel Ben Eliezer as "Balsem." After all, "Balsem" is not a bad approximation, for a Polish tax accountant, to the Hebrew for "Master of the Holy Name."[10]

Israel Ben Eliezer had not become the Ba'al Shem Tov overnight. He had been a peasant, a transient healer, a synagogue sexton, a teacher of Jewish children. Some

---

[8] Gershom Scholem, a man who knew the documents better than any before, or perhaps since, devoted three paragraphs of his large assessment, *Major Trends in Jewish Mysticism* (1938, NY: Schocken Books, 1995), to the Ḥasidim's overwhelming masculinity, (NY, 1995, pp. 37–38), with a single footnote (#38, page 355) mentioning the only known female *ẓaddiḳ*, Hannah Rachel, the nineteenth-century "Maid of Ludomir." A rather recent book by Ada Rapoport-Albert, *Women and the Messianic Heresy of Sabbatai Zevi, 1666–1816* (tr. Deborah Greniman, Oxford/Portland, OR: Littman Library of Jewish Civilization, 2011) reminds us that the Sabbatian movement was less excluding of women than its Hasidic successor, something Gershom Scholem missed in his other masterpiece, *Sabbatai Sevi: The Mystical Messiah* (Princeton, NJ: Princeton U.P., 1973). Muslim Sufism has many more female adepts, but over many more centuries. For visionary women, Christianity would seem to have the best record of opportunity among the Abrahamics (but all three Abrahamics fall short of several other religions on this score).

[9] Rosman, *Op. cit.*, in Hundert, ed., *Essential Papers*, p215–216.

[10] On the difficulties presented by Hasidic historiography in general, one starts with Gershom Scholem, *Major Trends in Jewish Mysticism*; but at present the most judicious work in English on the founding Ḥasid is Moshe Rosman's *Founder of Hasidism* (Berkeley: U. of California Press, 1996). Other English accounts are Immanuel Etkes, *The Besht: Magician, Mystic, and Leader* (tr. Saadya Sternberg, Waltham, Mass., and Hanover, N.H., 2005), and Moshe Idel, *Hasidism: Between Ecstasy and Magic* (Albany, N.Y.: SUNY Press? 1995). The first comprehensive history of Hasidism in English—the third in any language since Shmuel Abba Horodezky's in 1922 and Simon Dubnow's 90-year old classic in Hebrew, (*Toldot ha-ḥasidut*, 3v, Tel Aviv, 1930–1932, also published in German), is *Hasidism: A New History* (Princeton, NJ: Princeton University Press. 2017) by the team of David Biale, David Assaf, Benjamin Brown, Uriel Gellman, Samuel Heilman, Moshe Rosman, Gadi Sagiv, Marcin Wodziński, and Arthur Green.

six years before he appeared in the Międzybóż census, he did indeed have a conversion experience. That seems to have taken place in 1734, while Israel Ben Eliezer was still teaching in Tłuste and no longer living with his wife. It was a conversion by special revelation. According to the story, he had been receiving instruction from a contemporary of King David (that would make the instructor some 26 centuries years older than the student), and then, after ten years of this Davidic instruction, on his 36th birthday (the rabbinical date was the 18th of Elul, 5494) there had been:

> revealed to the Ba'al Shem Tov from on High that he had a unique mission in this existence … to bring a new light and instill a new spirit in our people through a somewhat different approach to our faith … a way of life which we now call Chasidus.[11]

We are told that God's revelation of a prophetic vocation had not been altogether welcome to the future Ba'al Shem:

> He was most reluctant to undertake this mission. The simple, sublime life he led in the Carpathian Mountains, far from the teeming cities … the indescribable bliss of learning Torah from a true Prophet of G_d … made life a veritable Gan Eden for him.[12]

Of course such reluctance in the one called was well known to guarantee that the call was authentic, like those of Moses, Amos and Isaiah in the Bible. In any case, a year or so later, the legend has Israel Ben Eliezer of Tłuste, not yet housed by the Jewish *kahal* of Międzybóż/Mezhbizh, revealing himself in public as *ba'al shem* or Master of the Name, a man able to work "wonders" (miracles) by the use of an art since called "practical Kabbala."

Israel was not the only *ba'al shem* in his eighteenth-century village world. In the previous century Rabbi Eliyahu, the Ba'al Shem of Khelem (Chełm, now in Poland) had been reputed to have defeated 100,000 witches in order to rescue an infant stolen by Lilith.[13] Eliyahu's student, a Rabbi Yoel had been reputed a *ba'al shem*, working wonders, commanding demons and charming amulets in a town called Zamość, in southern Poland.[14] In the past two decades Hebrew language books had been published in Europe, containing what has been called practical Kabbala for *ba'alei shem*, known as "wonder-workers" to make finds, cures or miracles.[15]

[11] Zalman Aryeh Hilsenrad (compiled and translated), *The Baal Shem Tov: A Brief Biography of Rabbi Israel Baal Shem Tov The Founder of Chasidus* (Brooklyn, Kehot Publication Society, 5759/1999), p.43. "revealed … from on High" are, of course, the words of Hilsenrad, a Hasidic writer.

[12] Hilsenrad, *The Baal Shem Tov*, p43.

[13] *Yivo Encyclopedia of Jews in Eastern Europe*, Article "Magic," @ http://www.yivoencyclopedia.org/article.aspx/Magic (Accessed 9 August, 2014).

[14] "Yoel Ba'al Shem I," *Wikipedia*, 10 Aug 14. *Wikipedia* lists its source as the memoir of Rabbi Yosef Yitzchak Schneerson (1880–1950) @ http://www.hebrewbooks.org/pagefeed/hebrewbooks_org_15614_96.pdf, but the name Schneerson suggests a Lubavitcher point of view.

[15] Simon Dubnow, *Die Weltgeschichte des juedischen Volkes*, [*World History of the Jewish People*] (10v, Germany, 1925–29; tr., Moshe Spiegel as *History of the Jews*, 5 vols., South Brunswick, N.J., 1967–1973), in Hundert, ed., *Essential Papers*, p31. Among the books are *Amtaḥat Binyamin* (1716), *Toldot adam* (1720), *Mif'alot Elohim* [Works of God] (1725); cf., *Yivo Encyclopedia of Jews in Eastern Europe*, Article "Magic," @ http://www.yivoencyclopedia.org/article.aspx/Magic (Accessed 9 August, 2012).

Among Israel Ben Eliezer's accomplishments in Tłuste had been common medical remedies, like bleeding with leech and lancet, folk religious staples, like driving out demons with prayers or oaths, and selling homemade amulets with the names of angels written on parchment to put in a tin box on a neck chain. Occasionally he had traveled from Tłuste to minister to people in towns like Horodenka, Kutów and others in Podolia and Galicia, Zaslaw, and others in Volhynia, or Sluck in Lithuania. He had become known, we are told, for praying with such animation and joy that barrels danced, and for making prophecies using the fundamental text of Jewish *Kabbala*, the *Zohar*.[16] Stories of his special understanding of the divine had already begun to spread, possibly including this curious gloss on Creation, preserved in a source long postdating the 1740s:

> The light God created in the first six days was sufficient (according to the legend in the Talmud) to enable one to see from one end of the universe to the other. When God saw that the earth was too puny to require so much light, He tucked some of it away for the righteous to use in times to come. And where did he hide it? In the Torah, and that is why when I open the book of the *Zohar* I can see anywhere in the world.[17]

Pausing here to run the clock backward, we see a pattern in Judaism, like the one in Christianity, that runs much deeper than the eighteenth-century Enlightenment. The word "zohar," Hebrew for "shining" or "splendor" of light, as in the first fiat of Genesis, "Let there be light," makes Ben Eliezer's account instantly recognizable as Kabbalistic. There was a book called Zohar, *Sefer Ha-Zohar*, or *Book of Splendor*, a series of commentaries on the Torah, written partly in the Aramaic language of second-century Judea. It was reputed to be a highly respectable fifteen hundred years old in the Ba'al Shem's time, but it wasn't. No one seems to have suspected that it was only a third that old, compiled and most likely composed in Muslim-governed Andalusia (Spain) late in the thirteenth century.[18] Kabbala was a lot more than folk magic, even in the mid-eighteenth century. It was the name of the heterodox biblical interpretation found throughout the *Zohar*, which had become a general term for Jewish scriptural interpretation that was esoteric, or hidden, leading to a mystical knowledge, learned almost entirely in states of ecstasy, of things which, like the nature of God, were unknowable to believers in principle (as Sufis would understand.)

Kabbala also became associated with some of its methods, adumbrated by earlier jewish mystics and specified in the writings of the extravagant thirteenth-century Kabbalist rabbi, Abraham Abulafia, of decoding the meanings of scripture, often using numerations and rearrangements of letters. But that was method. The object of the method, as the *Zohar* used it, was mysticism, immediate and ecstatic

---

[16] Dubnow, *World History of the Jewish People,* in Hundert, ed., *Essential Papers*, pp. 32–33. The source published closest to the birth of Hasidism is *Shivhei ha-BESHT* [*Shivchei Habesht*, or *Praise of the Ba'al Shem Tov*], Kapust (Lithuania)/Berdyczew (Ukraine), 1815.

[17] *Shivei ha-BESHT* [Stories of the Ba'al Shem], p6b, in Dubnow, in Hundert, ed., *Essential Papers*, p33n.19.

[18] Joseph Jacobs & Isaac Broydé. "Zohar". *Jewish Encyclopedia.* Funk & Wagnalls Company. http://www.jewishencyclopedia.com/view.jsp?artid=142&letter=Z#406.

knowledge of God, and whether the writing in the *Sefer Ha-Zohar* was fifteen centuries old, or four (or both), in the Ba'al Shem's eighteenth century it was reputed to have distilled more than a thousand years of the Jewish mystical tradition. The book had also had several remarkable episodes of efflorescence since its publication, with both direct and indirect effects on the diaspora community of Old World Jewry that were enormous. The *Zohar* and its Kabbala went very deep; and everything we are told of the Ba'al Shem Tov makes it clear that what he had found in the tradition was not remedies and nostrums, but how to encounter the Most High. *Zohar* was unquestionably intoxicating. It should not surprise any reader, including Jewish readers, that the human appetite for myth and personification may trump the First Commandment even among the people to whom the Commandments were originally addressed. The *Zohar* replied discouragingly[19] to would-be guardians of the Commandments like Moses Maimonides (Mosheh ben Maimon ca. 1135–1204). Maimonides and other rationalist Jews had struggled against the book without success soon after its appearance in the thirteenth century, much as Sephardic rabbis would struggle against the Kabbalistic mystics of Safed in the sixteenth century and the rabbis called *Mithnagdim* together with the new enlightenment *Maskilim*, would struggle again against the Hasidic mystics in the eighteenth.

Judaism, the original Abrahamic religion, had come long before Christianity and Islam, and had long lived within them without an Empire Christendom or Caliphate of its own. Its ancient scripture provided no less than Abraham himself and the Torah-giver Moses as examples of ecstatic experience leading to moral reformation—and a body of law handed down directly from the one God. Antinomianism (or we might say, anti-legalism) is very far from the mainstream of a religion like Judaism, which claims, after all, that Law (*Torah*) is precisely the form in which God is revealed to humans. The Law, enlarged by Talmudic scholarship, became utterly central to Judaism. Even so, it did not prevent Jewish thinkers in later eras from taking antinomian stances, distinguishing piety from legalism, reintroducing mysticism, and arguing that there was more to Judaism than obedience to the commandments. A Jewish antinomianism did show itself in the Middle Ages, sometimes in overt collaboration with Islam, or even with Christianity, and it did lead to mysticism.

An early example had been Bahya ben Joseph ibn Paquda, who had lived in the late eleventh century in Muslim-governed Andalusia, the medieval Spanish state where all three Abrahamic religions were allowed to flourish. Ibn Paquda's manuscript was called *Al Hidayah ila Faraid al-Qulub* (*The Book of Direction to the Duties of the Heart*). Addressed to his fellow Jews about 1180, it had nonetheless been written in Arabic and framed as a dialogue (*midrash* is the Hebrew word)

[19] "Woe unto those who see in the Law nothing but simple narratives and ordinary words .... Every word of the Law contains an elevated sense and a sublime mystery .... The narratives of the Law are but the raiment in which the (higher) Law is clothed. Woe unto him who mistakes the garment for the Law itself. It was to avert such a calamity that David prayed, 'Open my eyes that I might behold wonderous things out of Thy Law'" (*Zohar*, Introduction, ed. & tr., Simon, Sperling, Levertoff, Soncino Press, v1, p?).

between a Jew and a Ṣufi Muslim.[20] It had raised simple piety (*hasidut*, in the Hebrew translation) over the following of law, or even the pursuit of justice (*zaddik*). Its antinomianism had been clear; in its introduction, according to Gershom Scholem "Bahya says … that he wished to fill a great need in Jewish literature; he felt that neither the rabbis of the Talmud nor subsequent rabbis adequately brought all the ethical teachings of Judaism into a coherent system."[21] Bahya felt that many Jews paid attention only to the outward observance of Jewish law, "the duties to be performed by the parts of the body" ('*Hovot ha-evarim*'), without regard to the inner ideas and sentiments that should be embodied in this way of life, "the duties of the heart ('*Hovot ha-lev*')."[22] When it had been translated into Hebrew more than a century later, the translator had been a rabbi, Judah ben Joseph ibn Tibbon (1120–c1190). And Rabbi Judah ben Joseph was a Kabbalist who acted "on the initiative" of the contemporary Kabbalists of Lunel and their leader.[23]

This was the strongest link between the antinomian and the mystical. A century after Paquda's ethical tract, rabbis had begun a renaissance of sorts, resurrecting what they thought were rabbinical commentaries of the first century—Kabbala, or "what has been received." Among the earliest were *Sefer Raza Rabba* ("The Book of the Great Secret") a manuscript midrash or dialogue possibly going back to the ninth century, of which only fragments survive, and another manuscript midrash called *Sefer Ha-Bahir* (The Book of the Brightness), probably largely written in the twelfth century CE but assumed at that time to be from the first century and thus 1200 years old.[24] Both of these works move into the realm here called "ecstasy," reinterpreting a very old religious tradition to prescribe, justify and make room for

---

[20] Ibn Paquda's book may derive in part from earlier Ṣufi Muslim manuals, also in Arabic, one by Abū Talib al-Makki (d. 996), *Qut al-qulub* (*Food of Hearts*) and another, the more esoteric *'Ilm al-qulub* (*Knowledge of the Hearts*, as suggested by John Baldock in *The Essence of Sufism*, Arcturus, 2004 Kindle ed. p56). Indeed, *Duties of the Heart* has just received a major treatment in English in Diana Lobel's *A Sufi-Jewish Dialogue: Philosophy and Mysticism in Bahya ibn Paquda's* ***Duties of the Heart***, Philadelphia: University of Pennsylvania Press, 2020); and Lobel could rely on what is still the only English translation from the eleventh-century Arabic: Bahya Ben Joseph Ibn Pakuda, *The Book of Direction to the Duties of the Heart* (*al-hidâya ilâ farâ'id al-qulûb*, ca. 1080) introduction, translation and notes by Menahem Mansoor with Sara Arenson and Shoshanna Dannhauser. (London: Routledge & Kegan Paul, Littmann Library of Jewish Civilization, 1973).

[21] Gershom Scholem, *Kabbalah*, p36. The transliterated Hebrew is *Chovot ha-Levavot*, and the author's name may also be transliterated as Pakuda or Pachuda.

[22] *Ibid.*

[23] Judah ben Joseph ibn Tibbon's Hebrew translation of Paquda's *Ḥovot ha-levavot*, (MS 1161) is translated into English as: Bachya Ben Joseph Ibn Pakuda. *Duties of the Heart*. Translated by Yaakov Feldman (Northvale, NJ: Jason Aronson, 1996).

[24] *Encyclopedia Judaica*, article, "Bahir," Keter Publishing. Up to date on the bibliographic issues is AICE's Jewish Virtual Library @ https://www.jewishvirtuallibrary.org/sefer-ha-bahir & https://www.jewishvirtuallibrary.org/sefer-raza-rabba. It is notable that the "Hermetic" books acquired the same sort of uncritical veneration by being mistakenly attributed to pre-Mosaic Egyptians by Renaissance Christians.

a mystical approach to God. Out of materials like these, classic Hebrew Kabbalism was taking shape.

Rabbi Yitzhak Saggi Nehor or Isaac the Blind of Provence, had taken up the standard, as had his student Azriel ben Menahem of Gerona[25] and the twelfth-century authors of the pseudepigraphical *Book of Brightness*. They had slowly built among them an ever more elaborate theology, beginning with a non-canonical name for God, transliterated as *Ayn* or *Ein Sof* and meaning "the endless," with a number, eventually ten, of *sefirot* ("emanations" as they called them to avoid any implication of polytheism) emanating from Ein Sof. Knowing the sefirot, a believer might ascend through them mystically—and Platonically—to union with the divine.

Late in the twelfth century there had arisen a fundamentalizing reaction against the trend represented by these early Kabbalists and ibn Tibbon's translation of Pequda's Arabic ethics. Its most prominent member had been Maimonides. In his time he had been the leading rabbi of the Jews of Egypt, a subject of the Abbasid Caliph, but he would eventually become (for us) the iconic Jewish thinker of the Middle Ages and an intellectual mentor of the eighteenth-century Jewish Enlightenment. Maimonides's *Guide for the Perplexed*, another Jewish classic, had been very different from Kabbala.[26] Gershom Scholem called the *Guide* "in almost every respect the antithesis" of Kabbalism's central text.[27] And unlike Paquda's *The Book of Direction to the Duties of the Heart*, Maimonides's *Guide* was to the duties of the intellect, rationalizing ethics and putting mysticism of any kind under the most severe suspicion and the burden of proof. Having lived as a rabbi under Muslim rule in Spain, Morocco, Palestine and finally Egypt, Maimonides had said little or nothing definitive about God, perhaps preferring (like many believers in all religions today) to be as silent as Wittgenstein on what he could not speak about. His book had indeed made some room for special revelation in Judaism's past prophets and given some elaborate esoteric interpretations of biblical details, like the chariot of Ezekiel; but Maimonides's purpose had evolved as he wrote.

> in the Book of Harmony [...] we intended to examine all the passages in the Midrash which, if taken literally, appear to be inconsistent with truth and common sense, and must therefore be taken figuratively. [...] I had proceeded but a short way when 1 became dissatisfied with my original plan. For I observed that by expounding these passages by means of allegorical

---

[25] Girona was a town north of Barcelona where it seems that a preponderance of Jews were involved in mystical Kabbala in the twelfth century.

[26] Mosheh ben Maimon (Maimonides), *Dalālat al-ḥā'irīn*, known in English as *The Guide for the Perplexed*. translated from Arabic by M. Friedlander, 2nd ed. revised, 1904 (http://teachittome.com/seforim2/seforim/the_guide_for_the_perplexed.pdf). It was written originally in Arabic, like Paquda's *Duties of the Heart*, and later translated into Hebrew as *More nevukhim*. Interestingly, its Hebrew translator was Samuel ben Judah ibn Tibbon, the son of Paquda's translator, Judah ben Saul ibn Tibbon. Mosheh ben Maimon (ca. 1135–1204), an exemplary product of the polyreligious world of the medieval Mediterranean, was known as Mūsā ibn Maymūn ibn Abdallah al-Kurtubi al-Israili in Arabic, and Moses Maimonides in Greek and Latin. The Hebrew spelling of ben Maimon's name is רבי משה בן מיימון, and his full Arabic name is spelled موسى بن ميمون بن عبد الله القرطبي الإسرائيلي.

[27] Gershom Scholem, ed., *Zohar, The Book of Splendor: Basic Readings from the Kabbalah*, NY: Schocken Books, 1963, p7.

> and mystical terms, we do not explain anything, but merely substitute one thing for another of the same nature, [...] a person who is both religious and well educated [...] cannot escape the following dilemma: either he takes [the passages] literally, and questions the abilities of the author and the soundness of his mind-doing thereby nothing which is opposed to the principles of our faith,—or he will acquiesce in assuming that the passages in question have some secret meaning, and he will continue to hold the author in high estimation whether he understood the allegory or not.[28]

In all his many books and especially in the *Guide*, Maimonides had stood "for an austerely intellectual doctrinal Judaism, the castigation of all forms of idolatry and the combining of Jewish learning with secular science and philosophy (in his [Maimonides's] own times, this meant the Classics, and especially Aristotle)."[29] As Maimonides himself had put it, "He [...] who begins with Metaphysics, will not only become confused in matters of religion, but will fall into complete infidelity."[30] Like Thomas Aquinas, the medieval Christian he most resembles (and indeed most influenced), Maimonides warns in his book against esoteric learning and refers to ecstatic meditation in a way that makes it clear that he had had no personal experience of it to speak of.

Late in the thirteenth century, however, a hundred years after Maimonides's *Guide* and ibn Tibbon's Hebrew *Duties of the Heart*, two Jewish thinkers, Abraham Abulafia and Moses de León, had moved the Kabbala's game of codes definitively into the realm of ecstasy. Abulafia, born in Muslim Spain, had lived in Italy, Greece and Ottoman Palestine (now Israel), wandered all around the Mediterranean meditating on the letters of the Torah. In 1280 Abulafia had tried to lobby the papacy and been jailed by Pope Nicholas III. He had escaped being burned at the stake only because the Pope had died before he could order his execution. After his release Abulafia had continued his ecstatic Kabbalist mission, focusing on the letters of Scripture and free-associating with them so as to move by meditation beyond abstract truths to the music of pure thought. Exiled for a presumption to prophesy, and, more dangerously, to identify himself as a messiah, he had ended up on a tiny island in the Mediterranean. Diaspora rabbis who had heard of him were divided; Solomon Adret in Barcelona had condemned him as a charlatan. In Ottoman Palestine his ideas would come to be combined with the mystical *tariqat* (*turuq*), or Ways, of Ṣufi Islam. It may be argued that Abulafia's dedication to the cause and his apostolic travels were partly responsible for preventing Maimonides's view from prevailing.

---

[28] Maimonides, *Guide for the Perplexed*, tr. M. Friedlander, 1904, http://teachittome.com/seforim2/seforim/the_guide_for_the_perplexed.pdf, Introduction, p75.

[29] Karen Armstrong, *The Case for God* (NY: Knopf, 2009), p138. For Maimonides's theology of what-God-is-not, or God-circumspection, Armstrong uses the helpful term "apophatic."

[30] "He [...] who begins with Metaphysics, will not only become confused in matters of religion, but will fall into complete infidelity. I compare such a person to an infant fed with wheaten bread, meat and wine; it will undoubtedly die, not because such food is naturally unfit for the human body, but because of the weakness of the child, who is unable to digest the food, and cannot derive benefit from it." Maimonides, *Guide for the Perplexed*, http://teachittome.com/seforim2/seforim/the_guide_for_the_perplexed.pdf, Chapter 33, p123.

In any case, at this time the *Zohar* was prevailing over Maimonides. *Zohar*, Kabbala's key text, had appeared only a few years after Abulafia's exile. In 1286, a manuscript had begun to circulate among interested rabbis in Muslim Spain, a manuscript they had referred to as *Sefer ha-Zohar*—the Book of Illumination, or Splendor (not to say enlightenment). Its form was a midrashic conversation in a combination of Hebrew and first-century Aramaic summarizing *Kabbalah*, the lore of the Jewish diaspora. They had supposed it to be a copy of an original from the circle of a rabbi who was known to have sat at the feet of the famous first-century rabbi Akiva.[31] One of those Spanish rabbis, Moses de León,[32] had acknowledged having made the copy, but since Gershom Scholem's work[33] the conclusion has become inescapable that de León copied very little of it, and instead wrote almost all of it himself, making it a pseudepigraphon—a writing with a faked origin.

De León's pseudepigraphical composition of *Sefer ha-Zohar* had soon revealed itself to be a major literary achievement. The book struck reader after reader as a theological revelation of the highest order and came to be called *Ha-Zohar ha-Qadosh* [The Holy Zohar]. It remains the *locus classicus* of all the terms that make Kabbalist mysticism so seductively complicated. A quick summary of De León's dizzyingly complex construction illustrates how mysticism typically lends itself to catalogs. The de Léon *Zohar* fully identifies the names and functions of the ten *sefirot* emanating from *Ein Sof* [endless]: *Ayin* [nothingness], *Keter* [crown] (of Adam Qadmon), *Hokhmah* [wisdom], *Binah* [understanding] (also called *Teshuvah* [return] which gives birth to *Hesed* [love] and *Gevurah* [power] also known as *Din* [judgment]. If *Din* is not softened by *Hesed* then the 4th *sefirah*, *Sitra Ahra* [the other side], or evil, can threaten life. The 5th *sefirah* is *Tif'eret* [beauty] or *Rahamim* (compassion), and is called "Heaven," "Sun," "King" or "Holy One, blessed be He, son of *Hokhmah* and *Binah*." The 7th and 8th Sefirot are *Netsah* [eternity], and *Hod* [splendor], symbolized by two legs of the mystical body. The 9th is *Yesod* [foundation] also called *Tsaddiq* [righteous one], which is the phallus (because God is male?) of the mystical body and the pivot of the cosmos (*axis mundi*). The 10th and last of the Sefirot is *Malkhut* [kingdom] also called *Shekhinah* [presence] representative of the immanence of God in the material world as daughter of Binah and bride of Tif'eret.[34]

In short, De León's Zohar had used, and introduced into Kabbala ("what is received") terms not in the Torah or the Talmud, like *Ein Sof*, for the infinite,

[31] The disciple's name was given as Rabbi Shim'on bar Yohai. The original source for nearly every trustworthy fact about Kabbala's origins is, of course, Gershom Scholem.

[32] His full name in transliterated Hebrew was Moshe ben Shem Tov de León. Joseph Jacobs & Isaac Broydé. "Zohar". *Jewish Encyclopedia*. Funk & Wagnalls Company. http://www.jewishencyclopedia.com/view.jsp?artid=142&letter=Z#406.

[33] Gershom Scholem (1897–1982), *Origins of the Kabbalah*, tr., Arkush, ed., Werblowsky, Princeton, NJ: Princeton U.P., 1987.

[34] *Zohar*, ed. & tr., Simon, Sperling & Levertoff, 5v, Soncino Press, 1996, v.?, II 42b. Just a little of this can be found in Gershom Scholem's English reader's abridgement, *Zohar, The Book of Splendor* (NY: Schocken Books, 1963), pp77–81. (There will *not* be a quiz.)

unknowable essence of Nothing—or God before Creation—and *Sefiroth* for the "emanations" of the Creator, ending in *Shekinah* for God realized in Creation. Evil in the world was what interfered with this cosmic moral structure. Messiah's advent and Jewish obedience would bring the *Tikkun*, or redemption, of the universe.

Moreover, in *Zohar*'s extravagant metaphysical articulation of the cosmos, materials abound for moving outside the self and into the "oceanic feeling" of cosmic dependence, as a Jewish atheist once called it. (That would be Freud, of course, though Freud would surely have snorted at the sefirotic details.) Kabbala study had provided Hebrew terms for the goals of mysticism, *bittul* or *bitul ha-yesh* (annihilation of the self or being), *hafikhat ha-ani le-ayin* (making the ego into nothing) and total absorption in God (*hitkal'lut*), terms and ideas that the Ḥasidim would seize upon in the eighteenth century. When the Spanish Kabbalist Joseph Taitsatak had settled in Salonika, in Ottoman Greece, around the time that Spain expelled its Jews in 1492, the future of Kabbalistic mysticism within a Judaism under stress had been assured. It had spread like wildfire among a people newly subject to successive exiles and the disabilities imposed by the rising modern anti-Muslim monarchies north of the Mediterranean. Attempts like that of Maimonides to return to a non-ecstatic "rational" and "rabbinic" Judaism had continued, but without an organized institution able to set standards, the result could only be dissidence and debate. Thus had the stage been set for extraordinary outbreaks of antinomian ecstasy, with a false Messiah in the seventeenth century and the Ḥasidim in the eighteenth.

Sefer Ha-Zohar and its teachings had brought the entire Judaic universe to a millennial crisis in the seventeenth century. In early 1665 an ecstatic Jewish Kabbalist had proclaimed another ecstatic Jew to be the Messiah. The designee had accepted his messiahship in spring, welcomed the homage of most of the diaspora of Jewish communities during the summer and the following year, and then, in September, 1666, had suddenly, publicly, accepted Islam and ceased to be a Jew.

This was Sabbatai Zevi.[35] A rabbi and a wanderer among the cities of the polyreligious Empire of the Ottoman Turks, he had been born in 1626 in the Greek-speaking city of Smyrna (Izmir), on the coast of Turkey. Expelled as a heretic by Smyrna's Jewish community around 1650, he had spent the next 15 years going around the Ottoman Empire. Salonika, a town on the Greek coast with a Jewish majority, had welcomed him at first, then got suspicious in 1657, when he changed the liturgy to "uplift the Shekhinah," probably by abolishing the Service of Rachel, a nighttime service of mourning for the Shekhinah, started by the sixteenth-century Kabbalists (Cordovero and Luria) of Safed in Galilee.[36] The last straw for the rabbis of Salonika, had come when Zevi invited them to a banquet at which he brought out

[35] Or "Sevi," as Gershom Scholem transliterated it in his *Sabbatai Sevi: The Mystical Messiah*. Other spellings and transliterations include, but may not be limited to: Shabtai, Shabbetai, Shabbatai, Sabatai, Sabethai, Sabetha, Sabbathai Sabatei; Sebi, Sevi, Tzvi, Tzevi, Zwi, and Zvi. (A Googler may have to try them all.) Sabbatai was the second son of Mordecai Zevi, a merchant from Smyrna (now Izmir in Turkey), whose name suggests descent from the Ashkenazim, the Jews of central and eastern Europe.

[36] Scholem, *Sabbatai Sevi*, p. 158–166.

a Torah, took it under a wedding canopy and married it. This did not, on reflection, strike the rabbis as the sort of thing a Messiah would do, or even a Torah-observant Jew, and they expelled him from the city.

In 1658, after showing up in Athens and possibly also Larissa and Thebes. Zevi is known to have made his first appearance in Constantinople, the Ottoman capital on the Bosporus, where Jews had lived even before it was called Byzantium.[37] There Sabbatai Zevi had put a fish in a cradle to symbolize (it was said) the birth of Messiah under the constellation of Pisces. He had invited rabbis to see it, and the rabbinic court had reacted by sentencing him to forty lashes. This chastisement, however, had not discouraged some leading Constantinople Jews from befriending Zevi and undertaking to teach him Lurianic Kabbala. One of these, David Ḥabillo, had even followed along with Zevi when he left Constantinople after a year and returned to his home town of Smyrna/Izmir.[38] Each of Zevi's odd acts, however frowned on by the rabbinic establishment, had only added to his charisma with lay and less established Jews; and this would go on, willy-nilly, throughout his life.

Again on the move in the spring of 1662, Rabbi Sabbatai Zevi had gone to Cairo, the Muslim capital of Egypt, via Rhodes and probably Alexandria. In the summer, he had left Cairo for Jerusalem.[39] He was on the point of returning to Cairo in the fall of 1663 to question his Egyptian taxes, when he met the man who changed his destiny. Passing through Gaza on a short pilgrimage to the Cave of the Patriarchs in Hebron where the grave of Abraham is still visited, he met a young Kabbala student named Abraham Nathan Ashkenazi, soon to become known as Nathan of Gaza.[40] Nathan had already convinced himself that Zevi was the man that he had known was coming. He bound himself without hesitation to Zevi and began to talk of him as the long-expected Anointed One—the Messiah. Unsurprisingly, the putative Messiah's prophet was even more a Kabbalist mystic than the Messiah himself. He had had a conversion experience that had extinguished his material senses for an entire day, and given him a mystical vision of the *merkabah* of the *sefiroth* (the palace of God and of God's ten aspects). This experience and others, which had come to him as a teenager, had confirmed him in his reading and study of the new sixteenth-century Kabbalist interpretations by Moses Cordovero, Cordovero's followers Taitsatak and Eliezer, and most importantly of Isaac Luria and his disciples—the Lurianic Kabbala—with its paradoxical hope that Messiah's imminent arrival would uplift the Shekinah and in effect reconstruct the universe.[41]

Around his meeting of Zevi, this ecstatic young rabbi in training began to have further visions. There had been a mystical vision of Zevi as the promised Savior (Moshiach or Messiah?) during the eve of Purim (the Esther festival), and more

---

[37] Scholem, *Sabbatai Sevi*, p160. In Zevi's time these Jews were mostly Karaite and Romaniote, but there were new Sephardic and Italian immigrants. Scholem's account of Sabbatai Sevi's last visit to Constantinople in 1665, and his triumph and imprisonment there, is in *Sabbatai Sevi*, pp433–460.

[38] Scholem, *Sabbatai Sevi*, p174; Freely, p36.

[39] Scholem, *Sabbatai Sevi*, p. 197–199; Freely, p40–43.

[40] He was seen there by a reliable witness, Abraham Cuenque. Scholem, *Sabbatai Sevi*, p. 191.

[41] Freely, p45–47; Scholem, *Sabbatai Sevi*, p. 202–207.

recently another vision of Zevi in the *merkabah* among the *sefiroth*. Somewhat less visionary, Rabbi Sabbatai Zevi himself went on to Cairo, where he married a woman named Sarah on the 31st of March, 1664 (5 Nisan, 5424). Jews had always expected the Messiah of the Jews to be a man, but (as Christians are often surprised to learn) the Messiah was not expected by God's people to be unmarried. As for Sarah, she was an orphan of the 1648 massacres of the Jews in Chmielnicki, Poland, and she had always said she was destined to be married to Messiah.[42]

Meanwhile, Nathan's ecstatic visions from the eve of Purim and of Zevi and the *sefiroth* convinced him to go public. He had identified Zevi as the Messiah while Zevi was still in Cairo; and on May 28, 1665, after the newlyweds had returned from Cairo to Palestine, Nathan of Gaza, who was staying with them, had convinced Zevi to proclaim his messiahship himself. May 28 was the eve of the Shavuot holy days, but Sabbatai Zevi had refused to say the liturgy and had retired for the night, leaving Nathan of Gaza at the service, where he had had yet another of his ecstatic visions.[43] He had torn off his clothes, collapsed on the floor, and spoken as if in a trance.[44] After he recovered he had written to his rabbinic correspondents in Egypt, Aleppo and Smyrna that Zevi was the real thing and would proceed not only to lead a war of independence against the Ottoman Sultan, but also a migration (*aliyah* or ascent) to the Holy Land in Palestine.

Nathan had dedicated himself to prophesying and preaching the messiahship of Sabbatai Zevi. Zevi had let him do it, but asked of those who might subscribe to his mission that they observe the rites of Lurianic Kabbalism as proclaimed by the school of Safed. In most other cases Zevi had proved himself to be antinomian by calling for non-observance—and even specific counter-observances—of Jewish law (Torah) or complete transcendance of it (like Jesus as St. Paul had rendered him, or James Davenport, the minister who would one day burn the vanities in New London, Connecticut). Many diaspora Jews had greeted the news with celebration and eschatological preparations. Some had sold their homes and possessions, rolled in nettles, feasted on fast days, immersed themselves in icy water and given away much or all of what they had in extraordinary alms. "It was," writes religious historian Barbara Armstrong, "one of the first of many Great Awakenings of early modernity, when people instinctively sensed the coming of major change."[45]

The dénouement had come quickly and was not pleasant. In February, 1666, the newly self-proclaimed Messiah had set out to confront the Ottoman Sultan; but in the end it would be the Sultan's Privy Council that confronted the Messiah. Sultan Mehmet IV had had Zevi arrested near Gallipoli, brought east to his new capital city of Edirne, and interrogated by his Council as the Sultan himself watched from behind a screen. Zevi was offered the choice of being executed or being converted

[42] Freely, p47; Scholem, *Sabbatai Sevi*, p. 191–198.

[43] Nathan, *Book of Creation*, Barbara Armstrong. *The Battle for God*. (New York: Alfred Knopf, 2000), p27, Scholem, *Sabbatai Sevi*, p. 217–219.

[44] Freely, p55; Scholem, *Sabbatai Sevi*, p. 217–219.

[45] Armstrong. *Battle for God*. p27.

to Islam. With unbecoming haste he had chosen conversion. Taking the name of Aziz Mehmet Efendi, he had accepted appointment as head palace gatekeeper (*kapicibashi*) to the Sultan, from which post he began to study the Muslim *shari'ah* in an effort to put Islam, Judaism and Christianity together—surely the most ambitious religious syncretism (a more popular term is mashup) before the twentieth century.[46]

Gershom Scholem, the intellectual historian who singlehandedly restored Sabbatai Zevi from mythography to history, has made it possible to explain to modern atheists, anticlericals and non-observant Jews why there is, even now, nothing funny about the episode. Having reconstructed the long history of Jewish mysticism and defined Kabbalism, Scholem removed any doubt that Zevi was a Lurianic Kabbalist, as was Nathan of Gaza, the prophet of his advent. Scholem also came to the conclusion that Zevi was a bipolar personality, subject, by his own account, to regular bouts of mania and depression. The combination of mania with Kabbalistic millennialism was explosive. Isaac Luria's reading of the *Zohar* around 1300 had not only made Messiah's coming imminent, it had justified the paradoxical Kabbalistic view that the salvation of Jewry and the redemption of the world could be brought about by destined individuals transgressing the Torah and breaking the moral law—an antinomian revolution.

Sabbatai Zevi had altered several Jewish liturgies and prayers during his brief advent, and he had cavalierly advocated doctrines that were heterodox, not to say heretical; but his supreme act of antinomian transgression had been to abjure Judaism altogether. Jews across Europe and the Middle East, many of whom had given up their homes and lives to share in the millennium, were faced with a daunting choice: either Zevi was a fraud and they his dupes, and the redemption of Jewry would never come, or Zevi was, somehow, even after his apostasy, the real thing. After all, could there be any better example of the Kabbalistic idea of redemptive sin than the renunciation of Judaism by the Jewish Messiah? Indeed, for many Jews the apostate *had to be* the Messiah, because he would not otherwise have apostasized.

Following 1666, the Kabbalist movement in Judaism, indeed most of Judaism itself, had split into several streams. One had repudiated Zevi and maintained Kabbala, purging it of its apocalyptic messianism. Another had held on to Zevi's messiahship, either hoping for Zevi to return from his "going under," or following his lead into antinomianism (law-repudiation) and various kinds of apostasy. One group, followers of Rabbi Jacob Frank, called Frankists, who had neighbors among the Jews of southern Poland, took holy sinning so far that they all converted to Catholicism in 1759.

Gershom Scholem was never dismissive of visionaries and ecstatics, but in his view the route to Frankism, via the false Messiah and the long linked chain of apostasies, had been an unmitigated disaster for his faith. The *Jewish Encyclopedia* of Scholem's time summed up the story as follows:

[46]Armstrong, p28–29, Freely, chapter 13; Scholem weighs the evidence for all the possible scenarios in *Sabbatai Sevi*, Chapter 6.

> The disastrous effects of the Shabbethai Ẓebi movement, which was greatly fostered by the obnoxious influences of the *Zohar*, damped the enthusiasm that had been felt for the book, and the representatives of Talmudic Judaism began to look upon it with suspicion. Especially was this the case when the Shabbethaian movement had degenerated into religious mysticism and had produced the anti-Talmudic sectaries who styled themselves "Zoharites," and who, under the leadership of Jacob Frank, finished by embracing Christianity.[47]

The minority of Jewish thinkers who rejected Kabbalism struggled to discredit the movement Zevi had inspired (now called Sabbatian), forcing it underground together with antinomianism, pantheism, polytheism and other previously known heretic tendencies of Judaism, including even prophetic inspiration and ecstasy. Some Yemenite Jews and most of the Sephardic Jews in exile from what had become Christian Spain usually followed the great Maimonides in rejecting Kabbala, although of course the compiler and probable author of the *Zohar*, Moses De León, had been, like Maimonides, a thirteenth-century Spanish Jew.[48] One anti-Kabbalist, post-Sabbatian, proto-*maskil* rabbi, Jacob Emden, wrote a book, *Miṭpaḥat Sefarim*, targeting the *Zohar* itself as a forgery; and Emden did not scruple to deploy textual criticisms first set out only three years after Sabbatai Zevi's apostasy by a French Catholic cleric.[49] Nor should we overlook Sabbatai Zevi's great contemporary, fellow-Jew and fellow excommunicate, Baruch Spinoza, who was expelled from his Amsterdam synagogue in 1656 for the opposite of mysticism, the launching of wholesale historical criticism, not of the *Zohar*, but of the Torah itself, and for conceiving of God as nothing more personal than Nature itself, the law-abiding universe.[50]

---

[47] Joseph Jacobs & Isaac Broydé, "Zohar". *Jewish Encyclopedia*. Funk & Wagnalls Company. http://www.jewishencyclopedia.com/view.jsp?artid=142&letter=Z#406.

[48] "There is a small group among the Orthodox who refuse to accept the *Zohar*, known as Dor Daim (דרדעים). They are mainly from the Jewish community in Yemen, and claim that the *Zohar* cannot be true because its ideas clash with the ideas of the Rambam (Maimonides), the great medieval rabbi and rationalist, Rabbi Saadiah Gaon, and other early representatives of the Jewish faith. The *Zohar* is rejected by almost all Spanish and Portuguese Jews. Some among them believe the *Zohar* is collection of ideas based on Midrasim and misinterpretation of midrashic concepts." (Joseph Jacobs & Isaac Broydé. "Zohar," *Jewish Encyclopedia*. Funk & Wagnalls Company. http://www.jewishencyclopedia.com/view.jsp?artid=142&letter=Z#406.)

[49] The cleric, Jean Morin, had noticed, for example, a suspect reference in the *Zohar* to the crusades against the Muslims, suspect because neither crusades nor Muslims existed in the second century when the *Zohar*'s purported author was supposed to have lived. Cf., Jean Morin, *Exercitationes Biblicæ*, Paris, 1669, pp. 359 et seq. "These and other objections of Emden's, which were largely borrowed from […] Morin […] were refuted by Moses ben Menahem Kunitz, who, in a work entitled "Ben Yoḥai" (Budapest, 1815).

[50] Descartes's contemporary Baruch Spinoza (1632–1677), unlike Sabbatai Zevi (1626–1676), has lately returned to prominence in the canon of Western philosophers, thanks in part to Yirmiyahu Yovel's two volumes, *Spinoza and Other Heretics*, Volume 1: *The Marrano of Reason*, and Volume 2: *The Adventures of Immanence* (Princeton: Princeton University Press; Reprint edition, 1992), together with Jonathan Israel's two larger volumes which lay the Enlightenment's entire left wing on Spinoza's doorstep: *Radical Enlightenment: Philosophy and the Making of Modernity 1650–1750* (NY: Oxford University Press pb, 2002) and *Enlightenment Contested: Philosophy, Modernity, and the Emancipation of Man 1670–1752* (NY: Oxford U.P., 2009). The best popular books about Spinoza are by Matthew Stewart, *The Courtier and the Heretic: Leibniz, Spinoza, and*

But despite the disgrace and the attacks, Kabbalism had survived. Indeed, by 1700 it had begun to flourish, notably on the fringes of the Ottoman Empire and beyond in what we now call Eastern Europe. It flourished especially where it was able to dissociate itself entirely from Sabbatai Zevi and the messianic movement he had inspired, maintaining its respect for the traditional Scripture and ritual, as the Sufis had, while preaching and practicing rapture.

It was, in essence, non-Sabbatian Kabbalist mysticism, a religion of ecstasy, grace and the heart, which reached Mezhbizh in 1740 with Israel Ben Eliezer, the Ba'al Shem Tov, who gave new *devekut* to the Jews and made the barrels dance in Międzybóż.[51]

Międzybóż and its province of Podolia had actually been part of the Muslim Ottoman Empire in one decade of the previous century (1672–1682), but that was a mere episode, like the Cossack (Khazakh) pogroms in 1648–1664. It had been subject for longer periods in the sixteenth and seventeenth centuries to Lithuania-Poland and the feudal tenure of the Sieniawski and Czartoryski families.[52] After Hasidism rose the Russians would take the region over in the Second Partition of Poland in 1792, and, thereafter Podolia would be repeatedly shuffled among Russia, Poland, Moldova, Romania, the Soviet Union and Ukraine. Understandably, local and religious loyalties there came to trump national and even regional ones in a region that historian Timothy Snyder has recently titled the Bloodlands.[53] The new movement which began on such a small scale in Międzybóż/Mezhbizh would soon be able to focus the loyalty and devotion of many communities of Jews nearly everywhere in the Bloodlands, producing Hasidic *rebbe*s with their "courts" and "dynasties" in towns from Bessarabia and Hungary in the south to Lithuania in the north, centering in what is now Ukraine, Poland and Belarus—half the Jews in eastern Europe, according to one historian. Having, in these times, no state to enforce orthodoxy, Judaism would continue its millennial debate over the proper

the Fate of God in the Modern World (NY: Norton, 2006) and Rebecca Goldstein, *Betraying Spinoza: The Renegade Jew Who Gave Us Modernity* (Jewish Encounters, Schocken pb, 2009). Spinoza's part in the German Counter-Enlightenment is fundamental, beginning with a famous debate on his religious position that began in 1785 among Moses Mendelssohn (1729–1786), Friedrich Heinrich Jacobi (1743–1819), and Johann Gottfried von Herder (1744–1803).

[51] As Jacobs and Broydé continue their *Jewish Encyclopedia* article: "However, the *Zohar* is still held in great reverence by many Orthodox Jews, especially the Ḥasidim, who, under its influence, assign the first place in religion not to dogma and ritual, but to the sentiment and the emotion of faith." Joseph Jacobs & Isaac Broydé, "Zohar" http://www.jewishencyclopedia.com/view.jsp?artid=142&letter=Z#406.

[52] In the even more distant past the region had been subject to the famously Jewish, Turkic-speaking, Khazar Khans from the seventh to the tenth centuries, to pagan Pechenegs, Alans and Orthodox Christian Kievan Rus' in the tenth to the twelfth centuries, and to Mongol Khans and Galician princes in the thirteenth and fourteenth centuries. The city of Odessa, on the Black Sea coast, was its window on Constantinople, Christian until 1453, and the Muslim empires to the south.

[53] Timothy Snyder, *Bloodlands: Europe Between Hitler and Stalin*, NY: Basic Books, 2010. Indeed, very little national loyalty of any kind has been able to survive in this area through the twentieth century. Ukraine, the state that was born in 1917 and now contains the birthplace of Hasidism, faced dismemberment by pro-Russian rebels immediately on its proclamation, and again almost exactly a century later, in 2014.

relationship of Jews with God and how best to foster it. The debate not only eventually separated Orthodoxy from Haskalah and the Enlightenment, it also separated Hasidic communities that welcomed antinomian enthusiasm, and those that wanted it damped down. It also politically atomized the Ḥasidim of eastern Europe, and divided them further into Zionist and anti-Zionist. It continues to this day, having survived the formation of a "Jewish state," and helps account for the remarkable variety of Jews in the twenty-first-century world.

In Międzybóż/Mezhbizh, in the middle of the "enlightened" eighteenth century, however, these stories had yet to unfold. On September 15, 1746, Rosh Hashanah, the first day of the new Jewish year of 5507, the Ba'al Shem Tov (the BESHT, for short), locally venerated since 1733 for dreaming dreams, seeing visions, praying joyful non-canonical prayers at all hours and occasionally performing what local Jews called miracles, had a vision in Mezhbizh of the Messiah himself. According to a letter to his brother-in-law published thirty-five years after the event by one of his disciples, Ben Eliezer met and conversed with Messiah and asked when he would finally come, receiving the reply, "When your sources spread out beyond."[54] It was a clear invitation to the BESHT to spread the word—evangelize.

He did so, much like his contemporary, the Moravian leader Zinzendorf, acquiring disciples and encouraging them to go forth and lead new Hasidic communities.[55] The most influential of these disciples was Rabbi Dov Ber (1704/1710?–1772), called the Maggid (itinerant parable-preacher) of Mezeritch. This is the Dov Ber whose collected sermons, posthumously published, make up the Hasidic classic, *Magid devarav le-Ya'akov* (1781).[56] He was the nearest thing to a successor of the BESHT, whom he probably met in 1752, and not only in the rebbe-ship of Mezhbizh. By founding a group he called Chevra Kaddisha, the Holy Society, to bring rabbis committed to the new joyful ecstasy, *ḥasidus*, together in the common evangelizing enterprise, Dov Ber became, for a while, the John Wesley of Hasidic Judaism, rebbe of most of the many towns all over eastern Europe to which Hasidism had begun to spread. Dov Ber's disciples, in turn, had their visions, danced their prayers, preached evangelically and became rebbes in their turn. The three most famous of those early

---

[54] בסופו אגרת הבעש"ט לגיסו ה"ר גרשון קיטוווער אודות עלית הנשמה שלו Israel Ben Eliezer to Rabbi Gershon Kitover, in Rabbi Jacob Joseph (Hacohen), *Ben Porath Yosseph* (*Ben Poras Yosef*), Koretz, Ukraine, 1781, p207–08 @ http://hebrewbooks.org/pdfpager.aspx?req=24560&st=&pgnum=207

As translated into English by a Ḥasid: "On Rosh Hashanah of the year 5507 I made an 'ascent of soul'... I ascended level after level until I reached the chamber of the Moshiach... And I asked Moshiach: "When will the Master come?" And the Moshiach replied: "When your teachings will be disseminated and revealed in the world, and your wellsprings will spread outside..." (in Jacob Joseph, *Ben Poras Yosef*), Koretz, 1781, trans. @ http://www.chabad.org/kabbalah/article_cdo/aid/380401/jewish/The-Chamber-of-Mashiach.htm).

Another translation: "When will the Master come down to earth to redeem us?"

"When your fountains will spread to the outside." (in Hilsenrad, p45).

And in French: "lorsque tes sources se répandront à l'extérieur'." (*Lexique du hassidisme* @ www.modia.org/lexhassid/lexhassid.html).

[55] The Moravian headquarters of Herrnhut was about 1000 kilometers west of Międzybóż, just over the current Polish border with Germany.

[56] Published posthumously in Korets, Ukraine, in 1781.

disciples were probably Ya'akov Yosef of Polnoye (1710–1784), Menachem Mendel of Vitebsk (1730–1788), and Shneur (or Schneur) Zalman of Liadi (1745–1812) who, though he rose to leadership of the Hasidic movement after the death of Dov Ber, had thought of Menachem Mendel as his rebbe.

Ya'akov Yosef of Polnoye died some 20 years after the Ba'al Shem Tov in 1784. He began as an ascetic whose fasts, self-seclusions and legalist stringencies were extreme enough to get him expelled from his community. He fetched up in the nearby town of Międzybóż/Mezhbizh and there met the Ba'al Shem Tov, whose example convinced him to leave his astringencies at the gate and dance instead. The BESHT also seems to have convinced Ya'akov Yosef not to emigrate to Palestine and to become the Rabbi of another community in Podolia instead, which he did. Ya'akov Yosef also wrote the first Hasidic book to be printed, *Toldot Ya'akov Yosef* (1780), sermons with a supplement called, "Words I Heard from My Master." Published in Ya'akov Yosef's lifetime, it is the closest a historian can come, at this writing, to what all those disciples must have found in the Ba'al Shem Tov.[57]

As for Menachem Mendel, he held forth at Minsk, now the capital of Belarus, and later at Vitebsk, inspiring many in the region to Hasidism's Kabbala-based mysticism. In the winter of 1772 he and Shneur Zalman mounted a joint effort to visit and make a friend of a very distinguished, very learned rabbi in Vilna, also named Zalman, Eliyahu ben Shelomoh Zalman (1720–1797), called the Gaon (genius) of Vilna. The Gaon, too, was titled the pious one (Ḥasid). His learning included Kabbala,[58] and he had described personal mystical experiences, encompassing migrations of the soul and revelations of *magidim* (angelic teachers). Nevertheless, what he had heard about the Ḥasidim did not suggest either study of Torah or contemplation of mysteries. These Ḥasidim had, for example, made what the Gaon judged a heretical new misinterpretation the *Zohar* itself. They were, he judged, neglecting, even discouraging, mandatory study of the Torah, disparaging scholars (a sin in the Talmud) and establishing conventicles, new prayer groups disassociated from existing *minyanim* and synagogues from which they recruited new Ḥasidim. And they were dancing and somersaulting during prayer, ecstatic exercises which the Ḥasidim, like the Sufis, prized as acts of humility, but which the Gaon considered a spectacle that was idolatrous as well as unedifying (Figs. 7.1 and 7.2).[59]

He was not alone. A movement against Hasidism was already springing up among many established rabbis of eastern Europe a group that would soon be called the "opponents," or, in Hebrew, *mithnagdim.* They certainly did not condemn *ḥasidus* (exceptional piety); no more did they condemn Kabbala or Kabbalistic

[57] On the difficulties presented by Hasidic historiography in general, one starts with Scholem, but for the Baal Shem himself one starts with Moshe Rosman's *Founder of Hasidism.* (Berkeley: U. of California Press, 1996).

[58] His Kabbalistic texts, posthumously published, include *Tikune Zohar, Sefer yetsirah,* and *Sifra' di-tseni'uta.* (Immanuel Etkes, "Eliyahu ben Shelomoh Zalman," trans., David Strauss, *YIVO Encyclopedia of the Jews in Eastern Europe*, online @ http://www.yivoencyclopedia.org/article.aspx/Eliyahu_ben_Shelomoh_Zalman, accessed 14 Aug 12).

[59] Etkes, "Eliyahu ben Shelomoh Zalman," *YIVO Encyclopedia of the Jews in Eastern Europe*, online @ http://www.yivoencyclopedia.org/article.aspx/Eliyahu_ben_Shelomoh_Zalman, accessed 14 Aug 12).

Fig. 7.1 Lubavitcher Rebbe Shneur Zalman of Liadi (1745–1812), painted by Boris Schatz in 1878 (no contemporary pictures of Hasidic founders is known to exist). (http://en.wikipedia.org/wiki/Image:Schneur_Zalman_of_Liadi.jpg, Public Domain, https://commons.wikimedia.org/w/index.php?curid=3404264)

Fig. 7.2 Exterior of the Baal Shem Tov's synagogue (shul) in Medzhybizh, circa 1915. This building was destroyed by the Nazis, but an exact replica has been erected on its original site as a museum. (Photo: Wikipedia Commons @ https://en.wikipedia.org/wiki/Baal_Shem_Tov#/media/File:Besht_Shul1_Medzhibozh.jpg)

learning. What bothered them was the insistence of the new Ḥasidim and their rabbis that any Jew, at any level of Torah scholarship, could manage the practice of Kabbalistic worship and pursue its mystical goals, whether or not he—invariably "he"—understood the Lurianic terminology. It was the vulgarization of Kabbala, undignified, democratic, and wildly optimistic about human capacities, that they rejected, together with the shade of Sabbatai Zevi. According to one of them, Phinehas ben Judah of Polotsk, the new Ḥasidim were acting out or exaggerating a consciousness they could not understand, and might not even be experiencing. In Rabbi Phinehas's view they were:

> tainted sectarians who act out publicly even with regard to the most private of religious duties and who try to demonstrate to all the purity of their heart and inner intentions: and they reveal very strange gesticulations and loud moans in their prayers, and they gesture with their hands and with their fingers so that all will know of the purity of their hearts. Behold that theirs is a false deception. So, escape from their path, and understand from this that all of their worship is insincere and idolatrous.[60]

Rabbi Avigdor of Pinsk compared the ways the Ḥasidim prayed to the way a presumptuous peasant might address a noble as an equal—in a letter to no less a noble than the Czar of Russia:

> As for their claim that during prayer the divine and the human become completely intermingled, this is a false delusion .... The very opposite is true, as we find in the case of Moses, who said: "I then appealed to God"; and God answered him: "Enough! Do not continue to speak to me of this matter." It is clear from this that they did not become one with God in their prayers. Prayer is similar to the case of a very simple man who speaks to an honored nobleman; can he really imagine that he becomes completely united with him?[61]

The Gaon's vast learning was mostly traditional, his piety ascetic, and he was deeply suspicious of enthusiasm—at least of anyone else's enthusiasm. He refused to meet with Shneur Zalman and Mendel, and instead issued a decree proclaiming that the Ḥasidim were heretics. This was a call on the secular authorities, as well as the Jewish orthodox community, and they set upon the Ḥasidim in Vilna during the Passover holy days. Thus was the Gaon installed as leader of the Jewish anti-Hasidic movement, the *mithnagdim*, dedicated to establishing ritual and doctrine over ecstasy, unless the Ḥasidim did it themselves.

Menachem Mendel of Vitebsk emigrated not long after, in 1777, to his Holy Land with 300 followers, settling in the old Galilean town of Safed where first Rabbi Moses ben Jacob Cordovero (1522–1570) and then Isaac Luria had founded their contrary schools of Kabbala study two centuries before. (It was also one of the places where Kabbalist Nathan of Gaza had saluted Sabbatai Zevi as Messiah.) These were not the first, and far from the last Ḥasidim to move to the Ottoman provinces we now call Israel and Palestine, but Mendel's emigration left the Ḥasidim of

---

[60] Phinehas ben Judah of Polotsk, *Rosh Ha-Giveah* [ethical will], Vilna, 1820, p2b, in Allan Nadler, *The Faith of the Mithnagdim: Rabbinic Responses to Hasidic Rapture*, Baltimore, MD: Johns Hopkins U.P., 1997, p71.

[61] In M. Wilensky, *Ḥasidim u-Mithnagdim: le-Toledoth ha-Pulmus Beynehem*, (Jerusalem: Mossad Bialik, 1970), vol. 1, p248, quoted in Nadler, *The Faith of the Mithnagdim*, p77.

eastern Europe to membership in multiplying communities, and Shneur Zalman's special claim to the legacy of the BESHT left them with a less assured leadership.

The Gaon died twenty-five years later, in 1797, and although he had made disciples, they had neither the numbers nor the energy needed to carry the battle with the Ḥasidim on to victory.[62] The most prominent of the Gaon's disciples, in fact, Ḥayim of Volozhin, publicly retracted the charge of heresy against the Ḥasidim, at a time when Hasidism itself was beginning a long journey back to orthodoxy.

Shneur Zalman was if anything a more enthusiastic visionary than the BESHT. He was only 19 in 1764 when he became a disciple of Rabbi Dov Ber, and he was appointed maggid of the Jews of Liozna at 22; but already in his teens he had become a respected student of Lurianic Kabbala; and in time his book meshing Torah with Kabbala, *Likute amarim* (*Compilation of Teachings*, 1797), and familiarly called the *Tanya*, would be the canonical text of the Chabad (Ḥabad) Ḥasidim read by every branch of the Hasidic movement.[63] He was also well-known for his enthusiasm in prayer, hitting "his fist so hard on the wall while praying that he sometimes literally bled from his hand," and for dancing and singing, sometimes music of his own composition.[64]

Although Shneur Zalman thought of himself as a religiously gifted *ẓaddiḳ* (just man) it seems that he did not believe, as many of his followers did, that he had supernatural powers. Unlike many of the emerging rebbes, he did not expect to be a living mediator between his Ḥasidim and God, or even that he should assume the fundamentally political role of providing for his community's material needs. Few of the thousands of Ḥasidim and would-be Ḥasidim he attracted to his "court," however, saw it that way, and he compromised by setting himself up with an elaborate annual schedule as personal adviser and confessor to every Ḥasid who requested it.

Like his predecessor, Rebbe Shneur Zalman was not a son and heir when he founded the Chabad movement in the small town of Liozna, then moved it to the equally small town of Liadi. He was the youngest disciple of the disciple of the founder of Hasidism, the Baal Shem Tov. He had, however, no fear of changing the inheritance. A devout student of the Law and its commentary, the Talmud, Shneur Zalman tried to find rational premises supporting Kabbala and Hasidism. His idea, set forth in the Chabad's canonical text, the *Likute amarim* or *Tanya*, ("Tanya," the

[62] "The death of the preachers Yisra'el Leibel of Slutsk (ca. 1800) and David of Makeve (Maków; d. 1814), who had considered themselves to be the Gaon's personal emissaries in their vigorous anti-Hasidic activities, also added to the decline of the campaign." (David Assaf, "Hasidism: Historical Overview," *YIVO Encyclopedia of the Jews in Eastern Europe*, online @ http://www.yivoencyclopedia.org/article.aspx/Hasidism/Historical_Overview, accessed 11–13 Aug 12).

[63] *Likute amarim* (*Compilation of Teachings*, 1797) has been called *Sefer Shel Beinonim* (Book of the Average or Intermediate Man), after the title of chapter 12, and the title of one of the 5 parts that *Tanya* was divided into in the 1814 edition.

[64] "Strashelye (Hasidic dynasty)," *Wikipedia*, accessed 13 Aug 12.

first word in the book, means "We have learned") was to create what Chabad now calls Jewish "rational-mysticism".[65]

According to Shneur Zalman's *Tanya*, the intellect consists of [*c*]*hokhmah, binah,* and *da'at* (reductively: intellect or wisdom, contemplation or understanding, and revealed knowledge) yielding a Hebrew acronym that transliterates as CHaBaD. The *Tanya* holds that the three are equal and that together they are as important to a Jew's relationship to God as is the "heart." Indeed, the CHaBaD of intellect must lead the heart. The *Tanya* argues that "understanding [Binah] is the mother of fear and love for God."[66] God, says *Tanya*, "desires the heart," but God also desires the mind, and the mind is the "gateway" to the heart. In *Tanya* Shneur Zalman called for *moach shalit al halev*, "ruling the brain with the heart," but slowly reversing that order.[67]

Thus it was Shneur Zalman, the Alter (Old) Rebbe as Chabad calls him today, who took the first step toward the rationalization, or re-rationalization, of emotional ecstasy in Hasidic Judaism. He began a transition that has not ended, from piety to moralism/legalism. Ḥasidim still pray with enthusiasm, dance before the Lord, and expect miracles; but their antinomian openness is mostly gone and the distance between one dynasty of rebbes and another threatens to become unbridgeable.

Worse, by the time of the Alter Rebbe, the Ḥasidim were being challenged by a new force in their ancient religion, not the Mithnagdim of orthodoxy but the "maskilim" of "Ḥaskalah," the "Jewish Enlightenment." The words "maskilim" and "maskil" meaning Jewish partisan(s) of Enlightenment, had appeared before 1780 to refer to the those who would try to approach God's revelation, the Law, with rational methods that welcomed moral universalism, and to do it using a modern Hebrew that was derived from the Bible instead of from the debate of medieval rabbis. There had been maskilim since Moses Mendelssohn of the German Enlightenment in the 1750s, and the term first appeared in print in a Jewish journal in 1783.[68] The maskilim take on piety and mysticism was disdainful, and even contemptuous, much like Spinoza's attitude which had fueled the original Western Enlightenment back in the seventeenth century. Maskil ridicule of the Ḥasidim would begin with satires by maskillim Joseph Perl in 1819 and Isaac Baer

[65] Nissan Mindel, *The Philosophy of Chabad*, 2. Introduction, Brooklyn: Kehot Publication Society, 1985.

[66] Shneur Zalman of Liadi, *Tanya* (*Likute amarim* or *Compilation of Teachings*), Chapter 13, in "Chabad," *Wikipedia*, 14 Aug 17.

[67] Shneur Zalman, *Tanya*, Chabad English translation Chapter 12 (*Sefer Shel Beinonim*) @ http://www.chabad.org/library/tanya/tanya_cdo/aid/1028911/jewish/Chapter-12.htm.

[68] Isaac Euchel, ed., Ha-Meassef, vol 1, No. 1 (1 October, 1783). The historic conflict between Ḥaskalah (השכלה, wisdom, erudition) and Ḥasidut (חסידות, piety) in eighteenth and nineteenth-century Judaism is covered in detail in Raphael Mahler, *Hasidism and the Jewish Enlightenment* [Ḥaskalah]*: Their Confrontation in Galicia and Poland in the First Half of the Nineteenth Century*, Chapel Hill: U. of North Carolina Press, 1984. (Originally published in part in Yiddish, NY: YIVO, 1942; and in Hebrew as *Sifriyat Po'alim*, 1961).

Levinsohn.[69] Ḥaskalah did not receive its name until a century after Mendelssohn when the term "Ḥaskalah," meaning "wisdom," was used in 1860 by a friendly journal that was written in a modern reestablished biblical Hebrew. By then a term for a Jewish Enlightenment had become necessary because so many Enlightenment intellectuals, some of them Jewish, had proved so stubbornly dismissive of all "revealed" religions, including Judaism and even the liberal Reform Judaism that emerged among the maskilim after 1800.

Thus did the Counter-Enlightenment character of Hasidic Judaism, established in the teeth of Jewish orthodoxy just as the larger Western Enlightenment became dominant, but before the initiation of the Jewish Enlightenment, begin its retreat from mystic ecstasies, unritualized spontaneous liturgy and antinomian interpretation of God's Law. A renewal of mysticism by Rebbe Naḥman of Bratslav (1772–1810), the Ba'al Shem's great-grandson, did not prevail, and over the next two centuries the rule of the Hasidic heart over the brain would be slowly but substantially reversed.

Bibliography

(Maimonides) Jacob Goldenthal (1815–1868). 1845. Ed. Kalonymus. *Mesharet Mosheh.* Commentary on Maimonides' system of Divine Providence, with his explanation of Ps. xix. and xxxvii.

Alfasi, Yitshak. 758 [1997]. *ha-Yahid be-dorot: Maran Rabenu Rabi Yisrael Baal Shem Tov: toldatav, torato, tseetsaav, talmidav vena-baim be-mehitsato.* Tel Aviv: Mekhon Telipot.

Altmann, Alexander. 1973. *Moses Mendelssohn: A Biographical Study.* Philadelphia: The Jewish Publication Society.

———. 1981a. M. Mendelssohn on Miracles. In *Essays in Jewish Intellectual History*, ed. Alexander Altmann, 142–153. Hanover/London: Brandeis University Press.

———. 1981b. *Essays in Jewish Intellectual History.* Hanover/London: Brandeis University Press.

Armstrong, Barbara. 2000. *The Battle for God.* New York: Alfred Knopf.

Assaf, David. 2002. *The Regal Way: The Life and Times of Rabbi Israel of Ruzhin.* Stanford, CA: Stanford University Press.

———. 2012. Hasidism: Historical Overview. In *YIVO Encyclopedia of the Jews in Eastern Europe.* http://www.yivoencyclopedia.org/article.aspx/Hasidism/Historical_Overview.

Assaf, David, and Ada Rapoport-Albert, eds. 2009. *Let the Old Make Way for the New: Studies in the Social and Cultural History of Eastern European Jewry.* Vol. 2. Jerusalem: The Zalman Shazar Center for Jewish History.

Bartal, Israel, Rachel Elior, and Chone Shmeruk, eds. 1994. *Tsadikim ve-anshe ma'aseh: Meḥkarim be-ḥasidut Polin.* Jerusalem.

Baskin, Judith R., and Kenneth Seeskin. 2010. *The Cambridge Guide to Jewish History, Religion, and Culture.* Cambridge: Cambridge University Press.

Belcove-Shalin, Janet, ed. 1995. *New World Hasidim: Ethnographic Studies of Hasidic Jews in America.* New York: State University of New York Press.

[69] Perl, *Megaleh Tmirin* (Revealer of Secrets), 1819, Levinsohn, *Divre tsadikim* (or *Dibre Ẓaddiḳim*, Words of the Righteous), 1830, and Levinsohn *'Emek refa'im* (Valley of the Ghosts), published posthumously in 1867. Levinsohn wrote from his birthplace of Kremnetz, Ukraine, the same province as the Międzybóż/Mezhbizh of the Ba'al Shem Tov and Shneur Zalman.

Ber (Baer), Dov (Maggid of Mezritsch). 1967. In *Levi Yitshaq of Berditchev*, ed. Or ha-Emet. Bnei Brak: Yahadut.
Bernstein, Alan E. 2017. *Hell and Its Rivals: Death and Retribution Among Christians, Jews, and Muslims in the Early Middle Ages*. Ithaca, NY: Cornell University Press.
Biale, David, David Assaf, Benjamin Brown, Uriel Gellman, Samuel Heilman, Moshe Rosman, Gadi Sagiv, Marcin Wodziński, and Arthur Green. 2017. *Hasidism: A New History*. Princeton, NJ: Princeton University Press.
Blau, Joseph Leon. 1944. *The Christian Interpretation of the Cabala in the Renaissance*. New York: Columbia University Press.
Borden, Morton. 2011. *Jews, Turks, and Infidels*. Chapel Hill: University of North Carolina Press.
Bourel, Dominique. 2006. Y a-t-il des Lumières juives ou qu'est-ce que la *Haskalah*? *SVEC* 12: 113–123.
Breuer, Mordechai, and Michael Graetz. 1996. Tradition and Enlightenment 1600–1780. In *German-Jewish History in Modern Times*, vol. 1, ed. Michael Meyer and Michael Brenner. Study of the Leo Baeck Institute. Trans. William Templer. New York: Columbia University Press.
Buber, Martin. 1904. *An der Geschichte* (.... On the History of the Problem of Individuation: Nicholas of Cusa and Jakob Böhme). Diss't, University of Vienna.
———. 1906. *Tales of Rabbi Nachman* [*Die Geschichten des Rabbi Nachman*]. Trans. Maurice Friedman. New York: Horizon Press, 1956. New York: Avon Discus, 1970.
———. 1908. *The Legend of the Baal-Shem-Tov* [*Die Legende des Baalschem*]. New York: Harper, 1955.
———. 1909. *Ecstatic Confessions* [*Ekstatische Konfessionen*. Jena: Eugen Diederichs]. Trans. Esther Cameron and ed. Paul Mendes-Flohr. Syracuse, NY: Syracuse University Press, 1996.
———. 1910. *The Sayings and Parables of Chuang-tzu* [*Reden und Gleichnisse des Tschuang-Tse*]. Leipzig: Insel.
———. 1911a. *Chinese Ghost and Love Stories* [*Chinesische Geister—und Liebesgeschichten*]. Frankfurt: Rütten & Loening
———. 1911b. *Three Addresses on Judaism.*
———. 1914a. *Kalewala: Das Nationalepos der Finnen*. München: G. Müller.
———. 1914b. *Die vier Zweige des Mabinogi: Ein keltische Sagenbuch*. Leipzig: Insel.
———. 1914c. *Mit ein Monist* [With a Monist].
———. 1923. *Ich und Du* [I and Thou]. Leipzig: Insel
———. 1958. *Hasidism and Modern Man*. Vol. 1 of *Hasidism and the Way of Man*. Ed. and trans. Maurice Friedman. New York: Horizon. Collects 30 years of his essays.
———. 1960. *The Origin and Meaning of Hasidism*. Vol. 2 of *Hasidism and the Way of Man*. Ed. and trans. Maurice Friedman. New York: Horizon. Collects 30 years of his essays.
———. 1961. *Tales of the Hasidim*. 2 vols. Vol. 1 of The Early Masters. Vol. 2 of The Later Masters. New York: Schocken.
———. 2002. *The Martin Buber Reader: Essential Writings*. Ed. Asher D. Biemann. New York: Palgrave.
Buber, Martin, and Maurice Friedman. 1995. *The Legend of the Baal Shem*. Book 131 of 5: Mythos: The Princeton/Bollingen Series in World Mythology. Princeton, NJ: Princeton University Press.
Burnett, Stephen. 1996. *From Christian Hebraism to Jewish Studies: Johannes Buxtorf (1564–1629) and Hebrew Learning in the Seventeenth Century*. Leiden/New York: Brill.
Buxbaum, Yitzhak. 2006. *The Light and Fire of the Baal Shem Tov*. New York: Continuum.
Carlebach, Elisheva. 1990. *Pursuit of Heresy: Rabbi Moses Hagiz and the Sabbatian Controversy*. New York: Columbia University Press.
Carmilly-Weinberger, Moshe. 1977. *Censorship and Freedom of Expression in Jewish History*. New York: Sepher-Hermon Press with Yeshiva University Press.
Chazan, Robert. 2017. *From Anti-Judaism to Anti-Semitism: Ancient and Medieval Christian Constructions of Jewish History*. Cambridge: Cambridge University Press.
———. 2018. *The Cambridge History of Judaism*. Vol. 6 of The Middle Ages: The Christian World. Cambridge: Cambridge University Press.

Cohen, Shaye D. 2001. *The Beginnings of Jewishness: Boundaries, Varieties, Uncertainties*. Berkeley, CA: University of California Press.
Cohen, Steven M., and Arnold M. Eisen. 2000. *The Jew Within: Self, Family, and Community in America*. Bloomington: Indiana University Press.
Cohn-Sherbok, Dan. 2006a. *The Politics of Apocalypse: The History and Influence of Christian Zionism*. Oxford, UK: Oneworld.
———, ed. 2006b. *Kabbalah & Jewish Mysticism: An Anthology*. Oxford, UK: Oneworld.
Dan, Joseph, ed. 1997. *The Christian Kabbalah*. Cambridge, MA: Harvard College Library.
Dauber, Jeremy Asher. 2004. *Antonio's Devils: Writers of the Jewish Enlightenment and the Birth of Modern Hebrew and Yiddish Literature*. Stanford, CA: Stanford University Press.
Davies, W.D., and Louis Finkelstein. 1990. *The Cambridge History of Judaism*. Vol. 2 of The Hellenistic Age. Cambridge: Cambridge University Press.
Davis, Robert C., and Benjamin David, eds. 2001. *The Jews of Early Modern Venice*. Baltimore, MD: Johns Hopkins University Press.
Dubnow, Simon. 1916–1920. *History of the Jews in Russia and Poland: From the Earliest Times to the Present Day*. Trans. Israel Friedlaender. 3 vols. Philadelphia: Jewish Publication Society.
———. 1925–1929. *Die Weltgeschichte des juedischen Volkes* [World History of the Jewish People]. 10 vols, Germany, 1925–1929 (Hebrew, 1923–1938; Yiddish, 1948–1958; version in the Russian original, 1934, 1938). Vol. 11 in Hebrew, 1940, updating the work to World War II.
———. 1930–1932. *Die Weltgeschichte des juedischen Volkes* [World History of the Jewish People]. 10 vols. *Toldot ha-ḥasidut* [History of Hasidism in the Period of its Rise and Growth]. 3 vols. Tel Aviv: Dvir.
———. 1958. *Nationalism and History: Essays on Old and New Judaism*. Ed. S. Koppel. Philadelphia: Pinson.
———. 1967–1973. *Die Weltgeschichte des juedischen Volkes* [World History of the Jewish People]. 10 vols. *History of the Jews*. Trans. Moshe Spiegel. 5 vols. South Brunswick, NJ: Yoseloff.
Dynner, Glenn. 2006. *Men of Silk: The Hasidic Conquest of Polish Jewish Society*. Oxford: Oxford University Press.
Etkes, Immanuel. 1988. Hasidism as a Movement—The First Stage. In *Hasidism: Continuity or Innovation*, ed. Bezalel Safran. London. Cambridge, MA: Harvard University Press: Harvard University Center for Jewish Studies.
———. 2002. *The Gaon of Vilna: The Man and His Image*. Berkeley: University of California Press.
———. 2005. *The Besht: Magician, Mystic, and Leader*. Trans. Saadya Sternberg. Waltham, MA: Brandeis University Press. Hanover, NH: University Press of New England
Feiner, Shmuel. 2002. *Haskalah and History: The Emergence of a Modern Jewish Historical Consciousness*. Trans. Chaya Naor and Sondra Silverston. Oxford/Portland, OR: Littman Library of Jewish Civilization, (*maskilim* vs *hasidim*, *Heilsgeschichte*, Zionist nationalism).
———. 2004. *The Jewish Enlightenment*. Trans. Chaya Naor. Philadelphia: University of Pennsylvania Press.
———. 2005. *Moses Mendelssohn: Sage of Modernity*. Trans. Anthony Berris. New Haven, CT: Yale University Press, 2010.
Frank, Daniel H., and Oliver Leaman. 2003. *The Cambridge Companion to Medieval Jewish Philosophy*. Cambridge: Cambridge University Press.
Freely, John. 2001. *The Lost Messiah: In Search of Sabbatai Sevi*. New York: Penguin/Viking.
Garb, Jonathan. 2011. The Circle of Moshe Hayyim Luzzatto in Its Eighteenth-Century Context. *Eighteenth-Century Studies* 44 (2): 189–202.
Gitelman, Zvi. 2012. *Jewish Identities in Postcommunist Russia and Ukraine: An Uncertain Ethnicity*. Cambridge: Cambridge University Press.
Goldenthal, Jacob (1815–1868). 1838. Ed. Al-Ghazali. *Mozene Ẓedeḳ*. MS treatise on philosophical ethics, Hebrew translation by Abraham ibn Ḥasdai, with an introduction on the lives and works of Al-Ghazali and Ibn Ḥasdai. By a Principal of a Jewish school in Bessarabia after 1843, and professor of Rabbinica and Oriental languages at the University of Vienna from

Sept. 1849 until his death in 1868. Upon the nomination of Hammer-Purgstall he was elected corresponding member of the Vienna Academy of Sciences.

———. 1842. Ed. Averroës. *Bi'ur ibn Roshd.* Averroes' commentary on Aristotle's "Rhetorica," Hebrew translation by Todrosi with a historical and philosophical introduction. By Principal of Jewish school in Bessarabia after 1843, and professor of Rabbinica and Oriental languages at the University of Vienna from Sept. 1849 until his death in 1868. Upon the nomination of Hammer-Purgstall he was elected corresponding member of the Vienna Academy of Sciences.

———. 1845. Ed. Kalonymus. *Mesharet Mosheh.* Commentary on Maimonides' system of Divine Providence, with his explanation of Ps. xix. and xxxvii.

Goldstein, Rebecca. 2009. *Betraying Spinoza: The Renegade Jew Who Gave Us Modernity*, Jewish Encounters. New York: Schocken Publishing.

Green, Arthur. 2004. *A Guide to the Zohar*. Stanford, CA: Stanford University Press.

Hasdai, Yaacov. 1982. … *Tzaddikim* and *Hasidim'*…. *Zion* XLVII: 253–292.

———. 1988. The Origin of the Conflict Between Hasidim and Mitnagdim. In *Hasidism: Continuity or Innovation*, ed. Bezalel Safran. London. Cambridge, MA: Harvard University Press: Harvard University Center for Jewish Studies.

Heschel, Abraham Joshua. 1984. *The Circle of the Baal Shem Tov: Studies in Hasidism*. Chicago: University of Chicago Press.

Heschel, Susannah. 1998. *Abraham Geiger and the Jewish Jesus*. Chicago: University of Chicago Press.

Hilsenrad, Zalman Aryeh (compiled and translated). 1999. *The Baal Shem Tov: A Brief Biography of Rabbi Israel Baal Shem Tov The Founder of Chasidus*. Brooklyn: Kehot Publication Society, 5759.

Horbury, William, W.D. Davies, and John Sturdy. 1999. *The Cambridge History of Judaism*. Vol. 3 of The Early Roman Period. Cambridge: Cambridge University Press.

Hundert, Gershon D., ed. 1991. *Essential Papers on Hasidism: Origins to Present*. New York: New York University Press.

Huss, B. 1998. *Sefer ha-Zohar* as a Canonical, Sacred and Holy Text: Changing Perspectives of the *Book of Splendor* Between the Thirteenth-Century and Eighteenth-Century. *Journal of Jewish Thought and Philosophy* 7 (2): 257–307.

Ibn Pakuda (Paquda, Pachuda), and Bahya Ben Joseph. 1945. *Duties of the Heart*. Trans. Moses Hyamson from Judah ben Saul ibn Tibbon's Hebrew translation, *Ḥovot ha-levavot* (MS, 1161–1180). New York: Bloch Publishing.

———. 1973. *The Book of Direction to the Duties of the Heart* (*al-hidâya ilâ farâ'id al-qulûb*. MS, ca. 1080). Introduction, trans. and notes Menahem Mansoor with Sara Arenson and Shoshanna Dannhauser. London: Routledge & Kegan Paul (Littmann Library of Jewish Civilization). (The only English translation from the original Arabic).

———. 1996. *Duties of the Heart*. Trans. Yaakov Feldman from Judah ben Saul ibn Tibbon's Hebrew translation, *Ḥovot ha-levavot* (MS, 1161–1180). Northvale, NJ: Jason Aronson.

Idel, Moshe. 1987. *The Mystical Experience in Abraham Abulafia*. Albany, NY: SUNY Press.

———. 1988. *Kabbalah: New Perspectives*. New Haven, CT: Yale University Press.

———. 1995. *Hasidism: Between Ecstasy and Magic*. Albany, NY: SUNY Press.

———. 1999. *Messianic Mystics*. New Haven, CT: Yale University Press.

———. 2011. *Kabbalah in Italy, 1280–1510: A Survey*. New Haven, CT: Yale University Press.

Israel, Jonathan. 2002. *Radical Enlightenment: Philosophy and the Making of Modernity 1650–1750*. New York: Oxford University Press.

———. 2009. *Enlightenment Contested: Philosophy, Modernity, and the Emancipation of Man 1670–1752*. New York: Oxford University Press.

Jacobs, Joseph, and Isaac Broydé. Zohar. In *Jewish Encyclopedia*. http://www.jewishencyclopedia.com/view.jsp?artid=142&letter=Z#406.

Joseph, Rabbi Jacob (Hacohen). 1781. *Ben Porath Yosseph* (*Ben Poras Yosef*), 207–208. Koretz, Ukraine. http://hebrewbooks.org/pdfpager.aspx?req=24560&st=&pgnum=207.

Kaplan, Aryeh. 1981. *The Light Beyond: Adventures in Hassidic Thought*, Collection of Chassidic Sayings. New York: Moznaim.

———. 1984. *Chassidic Masters*. New York: Moznaim. (Short biographies and excerpts from works of leading Chassidic rebbes of the 1st and 2nd generation).

Karp, Jonathan, and Adam Sutcliffe. 2018. *The Cambridge History of Judaism*. Vol. 7 of The Early Modern World, 1500–1815. Cambridge: Cambridge University Press, .

Katchen, Aaron. 1985. *Christian Hebraists and Dutch Rabbis: Seventeenth Century Apologetics and the Study of Maimonides' "Mishnah Torah"*. London. Cambridge, MA: Harvard University Press: Harvard University Center for Jewish Studies.

Katz, Steven T. 2006. *The Cambridge History of Judaism*. Vol. 4 of The Late Roman-Rabbinic Period. Cambridge: Cambridge University Press.

Kaufman, Debra Renée. 1991. *Rachel's Daughters: Newly Orthodox Jewish Women*. New Brunswick, NJ: Rutgers University Press.

Kavka, Martin, Zachary Braiterman, and David Novak. 2012. *The Cambridge History of Jewish Philosophy*. Vol. 2 of *The Modern Era*. Cambridge: Cambridge University Press.

Kellner, Menachem. 2011. *Maimonides' Confrontation with Mysticism*. Portland, OR: Littman Library of Jewish Civilization. ("Kabbalistic counter-reformation" provoked.).

León, Moses de. 1988. *Sefer ha-Rimmon* [The Book of the Pomegranate]. Ed. Elliot R. Wolfson. Atlanta, GA: Scholars' Press.

Lerner, Ralph. 2000. *Maimonides' Empire of Light: Popular Enlightenment in an Age of Belief*. Chicago: University of Chicago Press.

Levinsohn, Isaac Baer. 1830. *Divre tsadikim (or Dibre Ẓaddiḳim, Words of the Righteous)*. Vienna: A. Schmid.

———. 1838. *Bet Yehudah* (MS, 1829).

———. 1867. *Divre tsadikim* [and] *'Emek refa'im* [Valley of the Ghosts]. Odessa: Bi-defus L. Niṭshe eṭ A. Tsederboim.

Lexique du hassidisme. www.modia.org/lexhassid/lexhassid.html.

Litvak, Olga. 2012. *Haskalah: The Romantic Movement in Judaism*. New Brunswick, NJ: Rutgers University Press.

Lobel, Diana. 2020. *A Sufi-Jewish Dialogue: Philosophy and Mysticism in Bahya ibn Paquda's Duties of the Heart*. Philadelphia: University of Pennsylvania Press.

Loewenthal, Naftali. 1990. *Communicating the Infinite: The Emergence of the Habad School*. Chicago: University of Chicago Press.

Lotterie, Florence, and Darrin M. McMahon, eds. 2001/2002. *Les lumières européennes dans leur relation avec les autres grandes cultures et religions du XVIIIe siècle*, Études internationales sur le dix-huitième siècle. Vol. 5. Paris: Honoré Champion.

Lustick, Ian S. 1988. *For Land and the Lord: Jewish Fundamentalism in Israel*. New York: Council on Foreign Relations.

Luzzatto, Moshe Chaim (1707–1746). 1740a. *Mesillat Yesharim* or *Mesillas Yeshorim*. (מסילת ישרים lit. "Path of the Upright"). Amsterdam. Trans. Mordecai Kaplan. Philadelphia: Jewish Publication Society. (1738 MS is a dialogue between a *hakham* (wise man) and a *hasid* (pious man) on ethics: Purity (*tahara*) to Piety (*hasidut*) to Holiness (*kedusha*). Changed to a monologue for publication.).

———. 1740b. *Da'at Tevunot*. MS, Amsterdam. (1st ed. Warsaw: Samuel Luria, 1889). Trans. Rabbi Shraga Silverstein. *The Knowing Heart*. Bilingual edition, Feldheim Pub, 2003. (A dialogue between Reason and the Soul on Maimonides's 13 Principles of Faith).

———. 1981. *Derech haShem: The Way of God/Ma'amar halkkarim: An Essay on Fundamentals*. Trans. Aryeh Kaplan. 3rd Corrected ed. Jerusalem: Feldheim.

Luzzatto, S. 1997. Il bacio di Grégoire. La "rigenerazione" degli ebrei nella Francia del 1789. *Studi Settecenteschi* 17: 265–286.

Maciejko, Pawel. 2011. *The Mixed Multitude: Jacob Frank and the Frankist Movement, 1755–1816*. Rev. Sutcliffe. New York, Philadelphia: University of Pennsylvania Press.

MacIntosh, Terence. 2015. Pietists, Jurists, and the Early Enlightenment Critique of Private Confession in Lutheran Germany. *Modern Intellectual History* 12 (3): 627–656.
Magid, Shaul. 2004. *Hasidism on the Margin*. Madison: University of Wisconsin Press.
———. 2014. *Hasidism Incarnate: Hasidism, Christianity, and the Construction of Modern Judaism*. Stanford, CA: Stanford University Press.
Mahler, Raphael. 1984. *Hasidism and the Jewish Enlightenment [Haskalah]: Their Confrontation in Galicia and Poland in the First Half of the Nineteenth Century*. Chapel Hill: University of North Carolina Press. (Published in part in Yiddish. New York: YIVO, 1942; and in Hebrew as *Sifriyat Po'alim*, 1961).
Maimonides (Mosheh ben Maimon). 1904. *The Guide for the Perplexed*. Trans. M. Friedlander from Arabic *Dalālat al-ḥā'irīn*. 2nd ed. revised. http://teachittome.com/seforim2/seforim/the_guide_for_the_perplexed.pdf.
Manuel, Frank E. 1992. *The Broken Staff: Judaism Through Christian Eyes*. Cambridge, MA: Harvard University Press.
Matt, Daniel C. 1996. *The Essential Kabbalah: The Heart of Jewish Mysticism*. San Francisco: Harper San Francisco.
———., trans. 2003. *The Zohar: Pritzker Edition*. 2 vols. Stanford, CA: Stanford University Press, 2004.
Mendelssohn, Moses. 1997. *Philosophical Writings*. Ed. Daniel O. Dahlstrom, Texts in the History of Philosophy. Cambridge: Cambridge University Press.
Mendes-Flohr, Paul. 2019. *Martin Buber: A Life of Faith and Dissent*. New Haven, CT: Yale University Press. Rev. Adam Kirsch, Divine Guidance in *The New Yorker*, May 6, 2019.
Menocal, María Rosa. 2001. *The Ornament of the World: How Muslims, Jews, and Christians Created a Culture of Tolerance in Medieval Spain*. New York: Little, Brown.
Meyer, Michael A., and Michael Brenner, eds. 1996 *German-Jewish History in Modern Times*. Vol. 1 of Tradition and Enlightenment 1600–1780, Mordechai Breuer and Michael Graetz. Trans. William Templer. Study of the Leo Baeck Institute. New York: Columbia University Press.
Mindel, Nissan. 1969. *Rabbi Schneur Zalman of Liadi*. Brooklyn, NY: Kehot Publication Society.
Mintz, Jerome R., and Dan Ben Amos. 1970. *In Praise of the Baal Shem Tov (Shivhei ha-Besht): The Earliest Collections of Legends about the Founder of Hasidism*. Bloomington, IN: Indiana University Press.
Mithridates, Flavius [Samuel ben Nissim Bulfarag]. 1481. *Sermo de Passione Domini*. Studies in the Humanities. English and Latin ed. Ed. Chaim Wirszubski. Jerusalem: The Israel Academy of Sciences and Humanities, 1963. A convert to Christianity, he interprets the Old Testament using Jewish texts.
Morgan, Michael L., and Peter Eli Gordon. 2007. *The Cambridge Companion to Modern Jewish Philosophy*. Cambridge: Cambridge University Press.
Morin, Jean. 1669. *Exercitationes Biblicæ*. Paris.
Nadler, Allan. 1997. *The Faith of the Mithnagdim: The Rabbinic Responses to Hasidic Rapture*. Baltimore, MD: Johns Hopkins University Press, 1999.
Neusner, Jacob. 1999. *The Theology of the Oral Torah: Revealing the Justice of God*, Studies in the History of Religion. Toronto: McGill-Queen's University Press.
Newman, Louis I., ed. 1934. *The Hasidic Anthology*. New York: Schocken Books, 1963.
Newman, A. 1993. The Death of Judaism in German Protestant Thought from Luther to Hegel. *Journal of the American Academy of Religion* 61 (3): 485–504.
Pasternak, Velvel (1933–2019). 1968. *Songs of the Chassidim*. New York: Bloch Publishing? Tara Publications?.
———. 1968–1971. *Songs of the Chassidim II*. New York: Tara Publications.
———. 2017. *Behind the Music: Stories, Anecdotes, Articles and Reflections*. New York: Tara Publications.
Perl, Joseph. 1819. *Megaleh Tmirin*. (Vienna: A Straus). Trans. Dov Taylor and ed. David Assaf, *Joseph Perl's "Revealer of Secrets": The First Hebrew Novel*. Boulder, CO: Westview, 1997.

Petrovsky-Shtern, Yahanan. 2004. The Master of an Evil Name: Hillel Ba'al Shem and his *Sefer Ha-Heshek*. *AJS Review* 28 (2): 217–248.

Pick, Bernhard. 1913. *The Cabala*. Chicago: Open Court Press.

Rapoport-Albert, Ada. 2011. *Women and the Messianic Heresy of Sabbatai Zevi, 1666–1816*. Trans. Deborah Greniman and rev. Sutcliffe. Oxford/Portland, OR: Littman Library of Jewish Civilization, 2015.

Ravitzky, Aviezer, ed. 2008a. *Maimonides: Conservatism, Originality, Revolution*. Vol. 2. Jerusalem: The Zalman Shazar Center for Jewish History.

———, ed. 2008b. *Maimonides: Conservatism, Originality, Revolution*. Vol. 1 of History and Halakha. Jerusalem: The Zalman Shazar Center for Jewish History. (Including: Daniel J. Lasker: "Tradition and Innovation in Maimonides' Attitude towards Other Religions"; Gideon Libson: "Maimonides' Halakhic Writing against the Background of Muslim Law and Jurisprudence of the Period").

———, ed. 2008c. *Maimonides: Conservatism, Originality, Revolution*. Vol. 2 of Thought and Innovation. Jerusalem: The Zalman Shazar Center for Jewish History. (Including: Charles H. Manekin: "The Limitations of Human Knowledge according to Maimonides: Earlier vs. Later Writings"; Lawrence Kaplan: "Monotonically Decreasing Esoterism and the Purpose of the *Guide of the Perplexed*"; Josef Stern: "The Enigma of the *Guide of the Perplexed* I, 68;" Sarah Stroumsa: "Maimonides: A 'Fundamentalist' Thinker?"; Amira Eran: "The Influence of Avicenna and Ghazali on Maimonides' Notion of Intellectual Passion"; Carlos Fraenkel: "From Maimonides to Samuel Ibn Tibbon: Interpreting Judaism as A Philosophical Religion"; James T. Robinson: "Maimonides, Samuel Ibn Tibbon, and the Construction of a Jewish Tradition of Philosophy").

Rengstorf, Karl H. 1994. Die deutschen Pietisten und ihr Bild des Judentums. In *Begegnung von Deutschen und Juden*, ed. J. Katz and K.H. Rengstorf. Niemeyer: Tübingen.

Robberechts, É. 2000. *Les Hassidim*. Paris: Brepols.

Roseman, Murray Jay (Moshe Rosman). 1996. *Founder of Hasidism: A Quest for the Historical Baal Shem Tov*. Berkeley, CA: University of California Press, .

Rubin, Eli. n.d. Immanent Transcendence: Chassidim, mitnagdim, and the debate about *tzimtzum*. http://www.chabad.org/library/article_cdo/aid/2306809/jewish/Immanent-Transcendence.htm#footnote27a2306809.

Ruderman, David B. 2000. *Jewish Enlightenment in an English Key: Anglo-Jewry's Construction of Modern Jewish Thought*. Princeton, NJ: Princeton University Press.

Rymatzki, Christoph. 2004. *Hallische Pietismus und Judenmission*. Tübingen: Verlag der Franckeschen Stiftungen Halle im Max Niemeyer.

Safran, Bezalel. 1988. Maharal and Early Hasidism. In *Hasidism: Continuity or Innovation*, ed. Bezalel Safran. London. Cambridge, MA: Harvard University Press: Harvard University Center for Jewish Studies.

Samuels, M. 2002. *Moses Mendelssohn: The First English Biography and Translations*. New Introd. James Schmidt. Bristol, UK: Thoemmes.

Schama, Simon. 2017. *The Story of the Jews*. Vol. 2 of Belonging: 1492–1900. New York: Ecco.

Schochet, Jacob Immanuel. 1974. *The Great Maggid: The Life and Teachings of the Rabbi Dovber of Mezhirech*. Brooklyn, NY: Kehot Publication Society. 3rd ed., 1990.

Scholem, Gershom (1897–1982). 1941. *Major Trends in Jewish Mysticism*. Rev. ed. New York: Schocken, 1995.

———. 1957. *Origins of the Kabbalah*. Trans. Arkush and ed. Werblowsky. Princeton. *Sabbatai Sevi, the Mystical Messiah, 1626–1676*. Trans. R.J. Zwi Werblowsky. Princeton, NJ: Princeton University Press, 1975, new ed. 2016.

———. 1974. *Origins of the Kabbalah*. Trans. Arkush and ed. Werblowsky. Princeton. *Kabbalah*. Jerusalem: Keter Publishing House; New York: Meridian Plume, 1978.

———. 1987. *Origins of the Kabbalah*. Trans. Arkush and ed. Werblowsky. Princeton, NJ: Princeton University Press.

Schwarzbach, Bertram Eugene. 1997. Remarques sur la date, la bibliographie et la réception des *Opinions des anciens sur les Juifs. la Lettre clandestine* 6: 51–63. Publication des Presses de l'Université de Paris-Sorbonne.
Shneur Zalman. 1797. *Tanya* (*Likute amarim*, or *Compilation of Teachings*). Chabad English translation. https://www.chabad.org/library/tanya/tanya_cdo/aid/1028862/jewish/Tanya.htm.
Socher, Abraham P. 2006. *The Radical Enlightenment of Solomon Maimon: Judaism, Heresy, and Philosophy*. Stanford, CA: Stanford University Press.
Stern, Eliyahu. 2013. *The Genius: Eliyahu of Vilna and the Making of Modern Judaism*. New Haven, CT: Yale University Press.
Stewart, Matthew. 2006. *The Courtier and the Heretic: Leibniz, Spinoza, and the Fate of God in the Modern World*. New York: Norton.
Sutcliffe, Adam. 2004. *Judaism and Enlightenment*. New York: Cambridge University Press, 2005.
———. 2013. Messianism and Modernity: Jacob Frank and the Sexual Politics of Transgression in Jewish Eastern Europe, Review Article on Pawel Maciejko. *The Mixed Multitude: Jacob Frank and the Frankist Movement, 1735–1816* and Ada Rapoport-Albert. Women and the Messianic Heresy of Sabbatai Zevi, 1666–1816. *Eighteenth-Century Studies* 46 (2): 299–302.
The Zohar: Pritzker Edition. 2003. Trans. Matt. 2 vols. Stanford, CA: Stanford University Press, 2004.
Twersky, Isadore, and Bernard Septimus, eds. 1987. *Jewish Thought in the Seventeenth Century*. London.: Cambridge, MA: Harvard University Press: Harvard University Center for Jewish Studies.
Unger, Menasheh. 1963. *R. Yisra'el Ba'al-Shem-Tov*. New York: Harides.
Walzer, Michael. 2012. *In God's Shadow: Politics in the Hebrew Bible*. New Haven: Yale University Press.
Walzer, Michael, Menachem Lorberbaum, Noam J. Zohar, and Ari Ackerman. 2003a. *The Jewish Political Tradition*. Vol. I of Authority. New Haven: Yale University Press.
———. 2003b. *The Jewish Political Tradition*. Vol. II of Membership. New Haven: Yale University Press.
———. *The Jewish Political Tradition*. Vol. III of Community. New Haven: Yale University Press, 2018.
Yivo Encyclopedia of Jews in Eastern Europe. http://www.yivoencyclopedia.org.
Yovel, Yirmiyahu. 1992. *Spinoza and Other Heretics*. Vol. 1 of The Marrano of Reason. Vol. 2 of The Adventures of Immanence. Princeton, NJ: Princeton University Press. Repr. edition.
Zohar. 1996. Ed. and trans. Simon, Sperling and Levertoff. 5 vols. Soncino Press.
Zohar, The Book of Splendor. 1963. Ed. and abridged Gershom Scholem. New York: Schocken Books.

Chapter 8
Muslim Antecedents: Enlightenment and Counter-Enlightenment Before the Eighteenth Century

Abstract From the First Century AH to the seventh: Muhammad and the Companions. Jurists and Theologians. *Fiqh* versus *Falasifa*. Al-Qushayri, Al-Hallaj and Ṣufi mystic sages to al-Ghazali versus Averroës. Ibn 'Arabi and Ibn Taymiyyah.

If the Christian experience of prevenient grace and enthusiastic conversion, Protestant Pietism, Augustinian Catholic mysticism, Jewish Kabbalism, Hasidic special revelation, and philosophical anti-rationalism can be associated with a Counter-Enlightenment, what would count as a Counter-Enlightenment in Islam? Any answer to that must begin with Sufism. The mystics, Christian and Jewish, and other harbingers of the eighteenth-century Counter-Enlightenment in the West are very much outnumbered by the Islamic mystics, the Sufi Muslims of the vast House of Islam.

The word "Ṣufi" seems to have come from "suf" the coarse wool of the clothing worn by a penitent or a voluntary pauper, but the fundamental Ṣufi experience was not asceticism (the Greek *askese*); it was ecstasy—ecstatic unmediated union with Allah, God. With a claim to have begun in the very first Muslim century (the 600s CE), Sufism spread like a flood in Dar al-Islam from the tenth Christian century onwards, and came close to becoming the mainstream of medieval Islam, shaping its relations with all other religions. It exchanged ideas and inspiration with Christians and Jews on its borderlands, from Andalusia in the west to the Ottoman Empire in the east. It claimed (posthumously) only one caliph as a member, Ali; but its adherents included the founders of all four Islamic schools of law (*madhab*).

Sufism, however, posed an implicit antinomian threat to the centrality and prestige of Islamic law (shariʿah), much as Hasidism did to the Torah of Israel. In time Sufism would shape its own opposition, from al-Ghazali in the eleventh century CE to Ibn Taymiyyah in the thirteenth, and produce in the eighteenth century CE what is presented in the next chapter, an anti-Sufi strain of Islam that also opposed "enlightened" reforms in the study and application of Islamic law. This strain was represented by Shah Waliullah and Muhammad ibn ʿAbd al-Waḥhab, and their many successors, including most of today's Muslim terrorists (Fig. 8.1).

W. R. Everdell, *The Evangelical Counter-Enlightenment*, Boston Studies in Philosophy, Religion and Public Life 9,
https://doi.org/10.1007/978-3-030-69762-4_8

Fig. 8.1 Rābiʿa al-ʿAdawiyya (c710–801 CE) an early Sufi woman, grinding wheat. (By Unknown author—http://www.mythinglinks.org/NearEast~3monotheisms~Islam~Rabia.html, Public Domain, https://commons.wikimedia.org/w/index.php?curid=4131728)

An Islamic Enlightenment?

To identify Sufism as the main Islamic form of a Counter-Enlightenment begs an even bigger question: What can the Islamic Enlightenment be? Is there such a thing, and has there ever been one? That is a question which historians of Islam and historians of Western Christianity have hardly approached, even in recent times as global history has begun to displace the histories of single cultures and nations. Some very interesting efforts have been made recently to connect the Euro-American Enlightenment to putative enlightenments in other cultures. These include a highly detailed scholarly (and entertaining) book in which Christopher de Bellaigue enlists biography and narrative to show how the Euro-American or Atlantic Enlightenment can be shown to have changed the intellectual life of the many Muslim nations on the shores of the southern and eastern Mediterranean in the nineteenth (Christian) century.[1]

It is misleading, however, to point to the late nineteenth-century Muslim "jadidist" movement (partisans of the new),[2] or to date, as Christopher de Bellaigue does, the "modernization" of the Islamic world from Napoleon's invasion of Egypt

[1] Christopher de Bellaigue. *The Islamic Enlightenment: The Struggle Between Faith and Reason, 1798 to Modern Times*. (Liveright Kindle Edition, 2017).

[2] Ingeborg Baldauf. "Jadidism in Central Asia within Reformism and Modernism in the Muslim World," *Die Welt des Islams*, New Series, Vol. 41, Issue 1 (Mar. 2001), pp. 72–88.

in 1798 at the very end of the eighteenth Western century,[3] because it identifies modernization—and Enlightenment—too readily with "Westernization," and has the unhistorical effect of branding the twelfth Muslim century as intellectually static or backward.[4] It also distracts the historians' attention from what looks very much like a zenith of intellectual achievement (most of it not implied by religious belief) that Dar al-Islam reached before the epistemological retreat of Muḥammad al-Ghazâlî, the era in the third through the fifth Muslim centuries (the ninth through the eleventh Christian centuries) during which, as the West must still acknowledge, the West was Medieval, if not positively Dark.

We must therefore take account of the fact that long before the West's Enlightenment, the Muslim world had an Enlightenment that did not use that name, however much it may deserve it. The ecumene of Dar al-Islam saw a movement of ideas that sums up as a nominalist, empirical, a posteriori, critical, miracle-free, and anti-mystical approach to nature, one that we may call (though this word did not appear in Europe until about 1580 CE) "scientific." It fits the "common denominator" of what is now confidently called a "family" of European Enlightenments: "the ideal of conceptual clarity paired with critical judgment," with the addition of hostility to "dogmatism, prejudice, superstition, and enthusiasm."[5] It also fits Immanuel Kant's famous definition as "man's emergence from his self-imposed immaturity (*selbstverschuldeten Unmundigkeit*) ... the inability to use one's understanding without ... the resolve and courage to use it without direction from another. Sapere Aude!" (Dare to know!)[6]

It was an enlightenment of this kind that was promoted by the imperial Abbasid caliphs, two of whom, al-Rashid and al-Ma'mun, gathered its teams of translators and scholars by establishing a vast library and graduate university called the House of Wisdom in the new Abbasid capital of Baghdad. Funded by al-Ma'mun to do what at least one historian has called "big science," the scholars came from all over

[3] Ahmed S. Dallal in *Islam without Europe* (University of North Carolina Press. Kindle Edition, 2018) makes this point that although a less prescriptive way of evaluating the Sunnah may begin to qualify as "Enlightenment," it remains misleading to date the intellectual modernization of the Islamic world from Napoleon's invasion of Egypt.

[4] De Bellaigue's concept of "Enlightenment" also ran into this challenge from senior scholar Malise Ruthven (Ruthven, "The Islamic Road to the Modern World (Islam & The Enlightenment)," *New York Review of Books* 44:11(June 22, 2017), pp22–25).

[5] This useful and inclusive current definition is found in Ulrich Lehner's comprehensive article, "Catholic Theology and the Enlightenment (1670–1815)" in *The Oxford Handbook of Catholic Theology*. Eds. Lewis Ayres & Medi-Ann Volpe. (Oxford: Oxford University Press, 2015) paraphrased from David Sorkin's *The Religious Enlightenment: Protestants, Jews, and Catholics from London to Vienna.* (Jews, Christians, and Muslims from the Ancient to the Modern World #42, Princeton, NJ: Princeton University Press, 2008). One might add two challenging exceptions to that definition of "Enlightenment": the prejudice that there is no non-scientific truth and the dogma that when two truths contradict each other, one of them is not a truth.

[6] This translation of Kant's *Beantwortung der Frage: Was ist Aufklarung?* (Answer to the Question; What is Enlightenment? 1784) is by Daniel Fidel Ferrer on the Internet Archive, 2013, @ https://archive.org/stream/AnswerTheQuestionWhatIsEnlightenment/KantEnlightmentDanielFidelFerrer2013_djvu.txt

Dar al-Islam, including Baghdad's Iraqi hinterland, home of the chief translator, Hunayn ibn Ishaq, the reviver of Aristotle, al-Kindi, and al-Haytham, called Alhazen in Europe, who refounded optics and physics.[7] Many, if not most, came from Central Asia, a richly civilized region, still misestimated and ill-understood by westerners, including Al-Biruni, the mathematical geographer and anthropological historian, Avicenna (Ibn Sina) the master of medicine and physiology, and al-Khwarizmi who invented "algebra" and gave it its name.[8] In Islam's far west, Andalusia (now Spain), this Muslim enlightenment reached a peak in the twelfth century CE with Averroës (Ibn Rushd) whose commentaries on Aristotle and the pagan scholarship of Classical Greece, translated into Latin in Muslim-ruled Spain, reached the new European universities and helped unleash a European "Renaissance of the Twelfth Century" in medieval Paris where Aristotle began to be titled The Philosopher. Many of these thinkers contributed to Islamic theology, law and ethics, but they stayed clear of doctrinal orthodoxies. The trend in Muslim scholarship until the thirteenth century CE has long been judged by modern standards as this-worldly and scientific. It continued even after the Mongols destroyed the House of Wisdom in 1258 CE and burnt its books (Figs. 8.2 and 8.3).

The next year, 1259, in fact, Muslim scientists began to build an observatory in Maragha in north Persia at the orders of the conqueror of Baghdad himself, the Mongol Hulagu. Its chief astronomer, the Persian Muslim Nasir al-Din al-Tusi, saw no particular implication for his astronomy in either Hulagu's Buddhism or his own minority faith, Twelver Shi'ah Islam. At Maragha he would revise Ptolemy's Greek astronomical model, using his new trigonometry to eliminate the messy "equants" in the planetary orbits, a key advance that Copernicus would use to reach his own great discovery—published centuries later—that the planets orbited the sun rather than the earth. Maragha was abandoned in the early 1300s when it lost its political patronage but cutting-edge astronomy and several other sciences continued in Islam until the sixteenth-century European Renaissance surpassed it.[9] Like the

---

[7] The story of the House of Wisdom, like many in this impossibly brief section on the Islamic Enlightenment is told at length with verve in English in a popular book by a practicing scientist named Jim al-Khalili, who grew up in Iraq, teaches in England, and trained himself as a historian of science: *Pathfinders*, later published as *The House of Wisdom: How Arabic Science Saved Ancient Knowledge and Gave Us the Renaissance* (New York: Penguin, 2011). Khalili argues that it is not an Islamic Enlightenment, or even an Enlightenment, but simply "Arabic science," because all "science" is the same, and only the language it is written in changes. It's certainly true that "Jewish science" and "Christian science" (or, for that matter, "Christian Science") have deeply misleading and historically prejudicial connotations. And one might say the same about "Christian" and indeed "Islamic" "Enlightenment." But sciences are always to an extent derived from cultures, and in our increasingly ecumenical global history, one automatically identifies cultures reductively if one identifies them with either a religion or a language.

[8] An unprecedented, thorough study in English of the Islamic Enlightenment in Central Asia has the added advantage of using the term in its title: S. Frederick Starr. *Lost Enlightenment: Central Asia's Golden Age from the Arab Conquest to Tamerlane*. (Princeton, NJ: Princeton University Press, 2013, Kindle ed.) For the Islamic Enlightenment in the West, one can begin with the best-seller: María Rosa Menocal. *The Ornament of the World: How Muslims, Jews, and Christians Created a Culture of Tolerance in Medieval Spain*. (New York: Little, Brown, 2001).

[9] Al-Tusi's story is one of those told at length by Jim al-Khalili in *The House of Wisdom* (New York: Penguin, 2011). The astronomer, it should be noted, came from al-Ghazali's home district of Tus in northern Iran.

Enlightenment of the seventeenth and eighteenth-centuries in the West this Muslim enlightenment avoided any appeal to the irrational, to infinites, miracles, or divine revelation.[10] Both Islam and the West have come to call it the Golden Age.

An Islamic Counter-Enlightenment?

What happened to the Golden Age, I think, was the growth of a conflict between a rising Ṣufi antinomian mysticism and an increasingly legalistic Islam that led to a discrediting of the natural sciences, a reduced confidence in the experimental, empirical, critical approach to the world of experience—the intellectual stance that the modern world has learned to call the "scientific attitude." Instead of a model for the many other traditionally legitimate ways of acquiring knowledge, the natural sciences came to be seen as a perversion of them that would inevitably lead to unbelief. Something closely resembling the later European Counter-Enlightenment set in, initially favoring Sufism over science but thereafter reinvigorating Islamic orthodoxy in theology (*kalam*) and jurisprudence (*fiqh*) to the detriment of both Sufism and science.[11]

---

[10] The Greek scientific and philosophical heritage in the intellectual world of ninth–eleventh-century Islam (*falasifah* was the Arabic neologism) even produced a few *philosophe*-like anticlericals, skeptics and *zindiq*s (heretics) in spite of the death penalty regularly demanded for religious apostasy. Among them were one of *falasifah*'s founders, Al-Kindi (Abu Yusuf Ya'qub ibn Ishaq al-Kindi, d. c870), and the great medical man Rhazes (Abūbakr Muḥammad ibn Zakaria ar-Rāzī, d. 925 CE). According to Ibn Warraq (*Leaving Islam: Apostates Speak Out*. New York: Prometheus Books, 2003) and Sarah Stroumsa (*Freethinkers of Medieval Islam: Ibn Al-Rawandi, Abu Bakr Al-Razi and Their Impact on Islamic Thought*. Brill, 1999) there were other heretics, including Ibn al-Muqaffa' (executed 760), Bashshar Ibn Burd (executed 783), Ahmad Ibn al-Tayyib all-Sarakhsi, (executed 899), Abū ʿĪsā Muḥammad ibn Hārūn al-Warrāq (d. 862?), Ibn al-Rawandi (Abu al-Hasan Ahmad ibn Yahya ibn Ishaq al-Rawandi, 827–911), and Al-Marri (Abū l-ʿAlāʾ al-Maʿarri, 973–1057 CE).

[11] A review by Lahouari Addi of Ali Humayun Akhtar's *Philosophers, Sufis, and Caliphs* offers a brief but helpful reading of this metaphysical maelstrom:

"To better understand the evolution of Muslim thought, one must recall what is at stake in these debates between the 9th and 12th centuries and identify the three groups of protagonists. There were the orthodox theologians, called *moutakalimoune*, who specialized in the Word (*Kalam*) of God, among them Ibn Hanbal, al Ash'ari, and al-Ghazali. The second protagonists were the philosophers, whose initiative started with al-Kindi and al Farabi, who resorted to Greek philosophy to vindicate the veracity and rationality of the quranic message. The third protagonists are the Sufis. Steeped in platonic metaphysics, to the point of caricature or even alienation, they managed to propagate their spiritual sensibility among the mass of believers. Sufism flourished after the 12th century, giving rise to strong and popular grassroots brotherhoods.

These three currents—Kalam, philosophy, and Sufism—share the same metaphysical source: platonic dualism, or what Akhtar calls the "Graeco-Arab philosophy." The moutakalimoune are Platonists who are unaware of it; the philosophers are Platonists who claim to be so; and finally, the Sufis pushed Platonism to the state of alienation. Philosophy was defeated and implicitly integrated into the Kalam. Since then, Muslim culture has been trapped in the confrontation between moutakalimounes and Sufis, both platonic metaphysicians." (Lahouari Addi, Review of Ali Humayun Akhtar. *Philosophers, Sufis, and Caliphs: Politics and Authority from Cordoba to Cairo and Baghdad*. Cambridge: Cambridge University Press, 2017, in *Reading Religion*, 18 July, 2018 @ https://readingreligion.org/books/philosophers-sufis-and-caliphs.

In the eleventh century CE, as what historians call the High Middle Ages were beginning in Europe, and the Golden Age of Arabic science reached an apogee, Sufism also reached its height of acceptance in Dar al-Islam. This was when Sufism produced its classic summaries and manuals for the apprentice ecstatic and the student of religion. The one most often invoked is the *Treatise* or *Epistle on Sufism* (*Al-Risala al-qushayriyya fi 'ilm al-taṣawwuf*) by ʿAbd al-Karim ibn Hawazin al-Qushayri, a comprehensive textbook that began circulating in about 1045 C.E., and has shaped the education of Ṣufi adherents for nearly ten centuries.[12]

All the great Ṣufi sages had brought a rich lexicon of Arabic and Persian words to the task of describing an experience which they called indescribable, but strove to interpret as a placeless, timeless, one-becoming union with the *tawhid*—the oneness—of the One God. The experience for them would come during a station (*maqam*) on what they hoped to be a spiritual progress. Twenty-First-century minds anchored in our century's science might bridle at how the experiences were described by those who experienced them, but it would not have been easy in any terminology. Some described it coming in "flashes" (*luma' or lawami'*),[13] and others as in a "moment" (*waqt*), though moments might be or seem eternal. Such flashes were distinguished as: *khatrat* (enlightenment, in the sense of illumination), *sama* (ecstatic hearing), *dhawq* (ecstatic taste), *shirb* (ecstatic drinking), *sukr* (ecstatic intoxication), *jadhbat* (ecstatic attraction), *hal* (ecstatic state or feeling), *ghaybat* (ecstatic absence from self), *wajd* (ecstatic intuition), *ghalaba* (ecstasy itself, or rapture), *ma'rifa* (gnosis), *'irfan* (gnosis), *laisiyah* (state of nonbeing), *fana'* or *fanaa* (transmutation or annihilation of self, passing-away, the ecstasy of nothingness).[14] Muslim theology, uncompromisingly monotheist and deeply suspicious of any claims of "association" with God, required its believers to understand this oneness as a loss or extinction of self, *fana'*; but no one should hesitate to call the defining Ṣufi experience "mystic," a word devised by the Greeks to mean "initiates," those who could see the polytheist Mysteries of Eleusis with their eyes shut.

---

[12]*Al-Risala al-qushayriyya fi 'ilm al-taṣawwuf*, and thereafter called, simply, *Al-Risala*, or *The Treatise*, by the Sufi sage Abd al-Karīm ibn Hūzān Abū al-Qāsim al-Qushayrī al-Naysābūrī and recently translated into English by Alexander Knysh as *Al-Qushayri's Epistle on Sufism* (Garnet Publishing, Great Books of Islamic Civilization, 2007).

[13]An especially formative Ṣufi text, two generations earlier than Al-Qushayri's *Treatise*, is *The Book of Flashes*, by Abu Nasr as-Sarraj (*Kitab al-Luma'*, ca. 980 CE), English translation excerpted in Michael A. Sells, ed. *Early Islamic Mysticism: Ṣufim Qur'an, Mi'raj, Poetic and Theological Writings*, (New York: Paulist Press Classics of Western Spirituality, 1996), p196.

[14]Most of these terms for "words of ecstasy" (*shathiyat*), mystical states (*ahwal*), and spiritual stations (*maqamat*) are discussed in this order in the encyclopedic third chapter of al-Qushayri's *Al-Risala* (*Al-Qushayri's Epistle on Sufism*. Translated by Alexander Knysh, Garnet Publishing, 2007). A more recent, more philosophically modern (and even more extensive) account that is still notably dependent on al-Qushayrī, is by the Nimatullahi Ṣufi, Javad Nurbakhsh (Ğawād Nūrbaḫš), *Ṣufi Symbolism: The Nurbakhsh Encyclopedia of Ṣufi Terminology*, Volumes 8–12, *Spiritual States and Mystical Stations* (Khaniqahi Nimatullahi Publications (KNP), 1994–1997. There is some more in *The Nurbakhsh Encyclopedia*, Volume 2 (1987) and Volume 7 (1993).

Fifteen centuries after the last decline of paganism, ecstasy is still the best word for it.[15]

In addition to these anatomies of ecstasy, canonical compilations of Ṣufi biography (or hagiography) came in the eleventh century from al-Sulami (including a collective biography of eighty-two Ṣufi women) and Abu Nu'aym of Isfahan.[16] A book by ʿAbdullah ʿAnṣārī of Herāt titled *Sad Maydan* [*The Hundred Grounds*] became, in 1057, the first Ṣufi didactic text in Dari-Persian; and the *Kashf al-Mahjûb*, by Hujwiri, which was circulating in the 1070s, was not only a manual like al-Qushayri's, but also listed Ṣufi "ways" (*tariqat*, meaning Ṣufi societies with a common ritual and inherited leadership) including ten which Hujwiri called accepted (*maqbul*) and two which were not (*mardud*), which leaves one to wonder what body might be responsible for "accepting" a Ṣufi denomination or why.[17] In all these books, the deceased Ṣufi sages are collectively called "waliya Allah," 'friends of God' (*awaliya'*) and are sharply distinguished from the rich and politically powerful, no matter how punctilious the elite might be about Islamic practice.[18]

Sufism, however, does not seem to have opposed Golden Age Arabic science, not, at least, until it reached a notable turning point in November, 1095 (the same month, as it happens, that the Christian Pope first preached Crusade), when one of

---

[15] The recasting of Ṣufi texts for English-speaking enthusiasts has gone on for more than a century, with the ultimate source always being al-Qushayri's eleventh-century *Al-Risala*. In 1914 R. A. Nicholson wrote: "Among the metaphorical terms commonly employed by the Ṣufis as, more or less, equivalent to 'ecstasy' are *fan'a* (passing-away), *wajd* (feeling), *sama* (hearing), *dhawq* (taste), *shirb* (drinking), *ghaybat* (absence from self), *jadhbat* (attraction), *sukr* (intoxication) and *hal* (emotion)." (Nicholson, *The Mystics of Islam*, 1914, repr., Arkana Books, 1989; World Wisdom, 2002, p. 43). In 1993 Idries Shah wrote: "True ecstasy is known by the technical term *wajd*, and paves the way to *Khatrat*—illumination. Here the mind and soul are liberated from the body, and knowledge and power take the place of the base thoughts of which the mind has been purified. In the Chisthi Order, music is used to induce the ecstatic state; [...] In the ecstatic state Ṣufis are believed to be able to overcome all barriers of time, space and thought..." (Idries Shah, *Oriental Magic*, Arkana Books, 1993; p. 70) An exceptional digest of many early texts from Ṣufi and non-Ṣufi Islamic mysticism in English is Michael A. Sells's edition, *Early Islamic Mysticism: Ṣufi, Qur'an, Mi'raj, Poetic and Theological Writings* (tr. & ed., Michael A. Sells, NY: Paulist Press, 1996).

[16] Both Abu ʿAbd al-Rahman as-Sulami (or ar-Rahman as-Sulami, 937/942–1021) and Ahmad ibn 'Abdullah ibn Ahmad, *Abu Nu'aym* al-Isfahani, or al-Asbahani (948–1038) flourished at the turn of the first millennium in 1000 C.E. Their books have English translations: as-Sulami, *Early Sufi Women: A bilingual critical edition of as-Sulami's Dhikr an-niswa al-muta 'abbidat as sufiyyat*. (Translated by Rkia Elaroui Cornell. Louisville, KY: Fons Vitae, 2005), and al-Isfahani, *Adornment of the Friends of God* (*Hilayat al-awliya'*. Cairo 1932–1938). There is a brief account of al-Isfahani in the standard survey in English of the rich Sufi tradition: Julian Baldick's *Mystical Islam: An Introduction to Sufism*. (New York: New York University Press, 1989), p57–58.

[17] Abul Hassan Ali Ibn Usman al-Jullabi al-Hajvery al-Ghaznawi is particularly hard for English speakers to research. His dates are 990 to either 1074 or 1077, the differences so far irreconcilable. His name may be given in transliteration as Abul Hassan Ali Hujwiri, (or Hajweri, or Hajveri, or Hajvery), with fellow Persians sometimes referring to him as Daata Ganj Bakhsh (Persian/Punjabi, meaning "the master who bestows treasures") or Daata Sahib (Persian/Urdu for "respected master").

[18] The *Sad Maydan* [*The Hundred Grounds*] by ʿAbdullah 'Ansari of Herat became, in 1057, the first Ṣufi didactic text in Dari-Persian.

the great minds of Islamic history rather suddenly resigned his teaching post, disposed of his property and became a Ṣufi, searching for that union with God, which would allow him at last to be certain of something.

His name was Abu Hamid Muḥammad ibn Muḥammad al Tusi al-Ghazâlî (1058–1111), known familiarly as Al-Ghazali or in medieval Europe as Algazel. Al-Ghazali was the chief professor at the Nizamiyya in Baghdad (the city where Ibn Sina (Avicenna) had set the highest standard for natural science, and where al-Khwarizmi (Algoritmi) had invented *al-jabr*—algebra). Al-Ghazali loved learning, writing in the first chapter of his final encyclopedic summa, *The Revival of the Religious Sciences* (*Iḥyā' 'Ulūm al-Dīn*), the sentence: "Great then is the state of knowledge which ranks next to prophethood and stands over martyrdom."[19] More than four centuries after the revelation to the Prophet, al-Ghazali, an immigrant to the capital from Central Asia, was at the peak of a brilliant academic career in what was then an intellectual center of the world; but he could not stop questioning what he knew and how. His questioning was deep and skeptical closely resembling that of Descartes six centuries later. The intellectual turnaround that resulted from al-Ghazali's quest, however, was exactly the opposite of Descartes'. Becoming the anti-Descartes of Dar al-Islam, al-Ghazali did not fall back on reason; he gave up on it. He also gave in to the irrational, and he seems to have come to that surrender by trying to achieve ecstasy and never fully succeeding.

By 1095, al-Ghazali's ceaseless search for intellectual certainty (*'ilm al-yaqin*) had passed through the study of Kalam—the way of divine-law orthodoxy, *al-Batiniyyah*—the Batinite way of Shiʿi esoterism and the infallibility of the Shiʿi Imam, and Philosophy—which for al-Ghazali was the way of logic and science going back to Aristotle and Pythagoras. He had finally come to investigate a fourth way, the Ṣufi way, which, as he already knew, claimed to reach certainty not just through knowledge but through "activity." Al-Ghazali had begun by reading Ṣufi books, because "theory was easier for me than practice." Only then did it dawn on him, as he wrote in his autobiography late in life, "how great a difference there is between your knowing the definition of drunkenness […] and your actually being drunk!" He wrote, "it became clear to me that [the Sufis'] most distinctive

---

[19] Book I of al-Ghazālī's *The Revival of the Religious Sciences* (***Iḥyā' 'Ulūm al-Dīn***), is titled *The Book of Knowledge* (***Kitab al-'Ilm***), and begins with a collection of all the *aḥadith* and salafi injunctions that al-Ghazali could find and footnote in praise of knowledge and non-mystic learning. The judgment from al-Ghazali himself that I quote in the text is from an early paragraph in Section I in the translation by Nabih Amin Faris:

Concerning the superiority of knowledge to worship and martyrdom, the Prophet said, "The superior rank the learned man holds in relation to the worshipper is like the superior rank I hold in relation to the best of men." See how he placed knowledge on an equal footing with prophethood and belittled the value of practice without knowledge, despite the fact that the worshipper may not be ignorant of the worship which he observes. Moreover, without this knowledge there would have been no worship. The Prophet also said, "The superior rank the learned man holds over the worshipper is similar to the superiority of the moon when it is full over the other stars." And again, "They will, on the day of resurrection, intercede [before Allah]: the prophets, then the learned, then the martyrs." **Great then is the state of knowledge which ranks next to prophethood and stands over martyrdom**, the merits of the latter notwithstanding. … . (*The Book of Knowledge: Being a Translation with notes of Kitab al-'Ilm of Al-Ghazzali's Iḥyā' 'Ulūm al-Dīn*, 2005 online @ https://www.ghazali.org/works/bk1-sec-1.htm).

characteristic is something that can be attained, not by study, but rather by fruitful experience and the state of ecstasy and 'the exchange of qualities'."[20] That month of Rajab, in the Muslim year 488 (July, 1095 CE), "the matter passed from choice to compulsion" because al-Ghazali was struck with hysterical speechlessness. Unable to teach at all, he became convinced, however uncomfortably, that he was being driven to Sufism by God—not to study it, but to live it.[21]

He examined his soul. He loved the teaching and scholarship that he was so good at, but, he wondered … was not his goal in teaching irredeemably selfish—his own fame?[22] He reproached himself for having abandoned theology (*'ilm al-kalam*) for philosophy in a vain search for "certain knowledge" (*'ilm al-yaqin*). He would describe this Dantesque mid-life crisis in his late-life autobiography as like "being on the brink of a crumbling bank and already on the verge of falling into the Fire." He made plans to leave Baghdad and academe, but vacillated. "I would put one foot forward, and the other backward."[23] He knew by now he would never be able to apply the Ṣufi way of attaining certainty without "actually engaging in the way"[24] and becoming a Ṣufi ecstatic. He would have to inhale, as a later age might have put it. At last, in the month of November, al-Ghazali dropped everything, put on the wool of the Ṣufi aspirant and left the great city on the road to Damascus, the same ancient town that Saint Paul had gone to recover from his vision. He stayed in Damascus for two years before moving on to a further eight-year pilgrimage through Jerusalem, Hebron, Mecca and Medina (and possibly even Islam's far west, Morocco), praying in seclusion in places like the Dome of the Rock, and "cleansing my heart for the remembrance of God."[25] We have no evidence that he joined an order, or even that he stayed in any Ṣufi *zaouiya*, but "remembrance of God" (*dhikr*) sums up the Ṣufi Way, and al-Ghazali was determined to follow it.

When he returned ten years later, he had tried but not quite succeeded. He was ever more convinced that the Ṣufi Way was the best approach to the divine, but he had been not been able to arrive at the end of it. He had experienced "revelations and visions" and moments of "utter absorption of the heart in the remembrance of God," but it seems clear from his memoir *Deliverance from Error* that he had never become "completely lost in God." He had settled instead for verifying the truth of Ṣufi vision by closely attending to Sufis themselves and their ecstatic experiences. The world had kept intruding on his solitary quest, reminding al-Ghazali of responsibilities in addition to that of saving his soul. He had left children in Baghdad. "Current events

---

[20] al-Ghazālī's words in Arabic are *al-dhawq* (literally, taste) for "fruitional experience," *al-hāl* (literally, state) for "state of ecstasy," and for "exchange of qualities," *tabaddul al-sifāt* (literally, change, or change of moral qualities). (*Al-Ghazali's Path to Sufism: his Deliverance from Error.* (***Al-Munqidh min al-Dalal***). Translated by R. J. McCarthy, SJ, Introduction by William A. Graham, (Louisville, KY: Fons Vitae, 2006), p103nn162–164). The terms *dhawq* and *hāl* for ecstatic experience had appeared in al-Qushayri's great compendium of fifty years earlier (*Al-Qushayri's Epistle on Sufism*, tr., Knysh, Garnet Publishing, 2007).

[21] al-Ghazālī, *Al-Ghazali's Path to Sufism: his Deliverance from Error.* (***Al-Munqidh min al-Dalal***), pp23, 51–55, 89n44, 104n172.

[22] *Al-Ghazali's … Deliverance from Error*, p53.

[23] *Ibid.*

[24] *Al-Ghazali's … Deliverance from Error*, p52.

[25] *Al-Ghazali's … Deliverance from Error*, p56.

and important family matters and gaining the necessities for daily living," he wrote afterward, "had an effect on the way to realize my desire and troubled the serenity of my solitude, and the pure state of ecstasy occurred only intermittently." He did not turn against the Sufis; rather the contrary. He insisted after his return that he had "not ceased to aspire" to ecstasy. "Obstacles," he wrote, "would keep me away from it, but I would return to it."[26]

Thus did al-Ghazali resume the intellectual life. He had, however, learned two things on his incomplete pilgrimage that changed the direction of his teaching forever. First, al-Ghazali had seen the Ṣufi ecstatics as shariʿah-law-abiding rather than antinomian, and had come to the conclusion that casuist arguments of the sort given by the great Ibn Sina for violating a specific stricture of Islam, like the prohibition of alcohol, were specious, as were all arguments that might substitute reason—any more than ecstasy—for simple faith and exact obedience to the laws of Allah. What al-Ghazali's incomplete conversion left him with was a conviction that although Sufi knowledge was a good thing, it was learning, not inspiration, that gave status in heaven, and that the single most important study for a learned Muslim was *fiqh* (Muslim law and jurisprudence). "The foundations of this religion," he wrote (on his own authority, not the Prophet's), is jurisprudence."

> The Prophet also said, 'Allah was not worshipped with anyone better than the learned in religion. Verily a single jurisprudent is more formidable to Satan than a thousand worshippers.'[23] For everything has [its] foundation, and the foundations of this religion is jurisprudence. And again, 'The best part of your faith is [also] the easiest, and the best form of worship is jurisprudence.'[27]

Al-Ghazali concluded further that God had changed his intentions for him, and had moved the Sultan to order him to go to Nishapur in eastern Persia and return to teaching so as to expose and chastise disobedience and Muslim "weakness of faith." Dreams had confirmed him in the decision to obey the Sultan's decree (confirming an entirely worldly event by what he had himself labeled a low entry-level form of prophecy).[28]

Second, and more critically, al-Ghazali had come to the conclusion that many of the most important sciences—sciences including medicine and astronomy that we descendants of Descartes would call "hard"—consisted of knowledge "which could not conceivably be obtained by the intellect alone." Such science did not come from systematic knowledge of nature observed through the senses, but instead from

---

[26] *Al-Ghazali's … Deliverance from Error*, pp 57, 58, 56. Al-Ghazali directs "whoever is not favored with their company [the company of Ṣufi ecstatics] must learn the certain possibility of such mystical states through the evidence of apodeictic demonstration in the way we have mentioned in 'The Book of the Marvels of the Heart'," which is the chapter on this subject in al-Ghazali's own post-pilgrimage encyclopedia of the Muslim faith, *The Revivification of the Religious Sciences*. Another of al-Ghazali's post-pilgrimage works admits that the Sufi sort of knowledge is definitely not law or theology: a "so-called scholar [who] has not tasted the wine of the Truth and is not cognizant of direct knowledge from God (al-'ilm al-laduni), so how can he accept it?!" ("Introduction" to *Al-Ghazali's Treatise on Direct Knowledge from God* (***al-Risalah al-laduniyah***) pp. 87–88, translation © A. Godlas, 1998, @ www.uga.edu/islam/laduni.html).

[27] Al-Ghazâlî, *The Book of Knowledge.* Translated by Nabih Amin Faris, 2005 online @ https://www.ghazali.org/works/bk1-sec-1.htm.

[28] *Al-Ghazali's … Deliverance from Error*, pp 68–71.

knowledge that could not be apprehended without an additional sense, a sense adumbrated in human dreaming, a sense which perceives what may not (yet) be there, a sense which deserves to be called visionary. "This," wrote the redeemed al-Ghazali, "is what is meant by prophecy," the supernal gift of the Prophet who had founded Islam.[29] With this, Islam's most prominent intellectual announced he had given up on empirical science. He proceeded to write several books about why that was a good thing to do and recommending other Muslims to do the same, including the massive critique of metaphysics and natural philosophy, *The Incoherence of the* [Aristotelian] *Philosophers* (*Tahafut al-Falasifah*) and the encyclopedic *Revival of the Religious Sciences*, Islamic classics ever since.[30] "Reason," as Islamic historian Sari Nusseibeh noticed, can defeat itself:

> After having been sparked and then flourishing, reason may ossify—and even turn against its (unacknowledged) sire. Adherents may come to view it as both self-generating and self-sufficient—indeed, as the antithesis of the imagination. Imagination, however self-consciously expressed, whether in poetry or in new and unconventional ideas, then comes to count as the enemy of the rational establishment and the authoritative system of thought. It comes to represent potential danger and a threat to order and stability.[31]

If the Golden Age of Arabic science qualifies as an Enlightenment, then what al-Ghazali launched here was an Islamic Counter-Enlightenment.

Al-Ghazali's late-life memoir, *al Munqidh min al-Dalal* (*Deliverance from Error*, ca. 1110), describes the same corrosive advance of skepticism as would Descartes's *Discourse on Method* (1637) but instead of turning skepticism on its head, as Descartes would, so that "I doubt" could imply "I am," with pure logic establishing the prior existence of self and mind, and only thereafter the existence of God, al-Ghazali concluded that doubt about both the self and the material universe was insurmountable, and instead made religious experience the only source of intellectual certainty. Al-Ghazali made, I would argue, a Counter-Enlightenment move that matches Descartes's Enlightenment one; and he documented his change of mind with *The Incoherence of the Philosophers*. Unfortunately for Muslim science, the refutation of his book, *The Incoherence of the Incoherence* (ca.1160), by the great Muslim Aristotelian, Averroës, would come too late. The future of the "hard" sciences would thereafter lie with the Christian and Jewish borrowers of Arabic learning instead of its Muslim originators.

The conflict al-Ghazali opened in the twelfth century between science and prophecy, or revelation, in Islam has not entirely ended, even when Muslim physicists win Nobel Prizes. The consequences are still fundamental. It continues to be argued that al-Ghazali's turn toward what he called "faith" and away from empirical science is one of the reasons that a conflicted attitude toward the sciences is found in the

---

[29] *Al-Ghazali's ... Deliverance from Error*, p61.

[30] al-Ghazālī, *The Incoherence of the Philosophers*, A parallel English-Arabic Text, translated, introduced, and annotated by Michael E. Marmura, (Islamic Text Society, Provo, Utah: Brigham Young University Press, 2000), p68. Al-Ghazali was read with great interest before the printing press by both Jewish and Christian intellectuals in medieval Europe, including Maimonides and Thomas Aquinas. Dante placed him in Limbo with the virtuous pagan philosophers.

[31] Sari Nusseibeh. *The Story of Reason in Islam*. (Stanford, CA: Stanford University Press, 2017), p. 7.

jihadist and salafist groups in Islam today. For al-Ghazali it had been a consequence of his incomplete conversion to Sufism; but for those Sufis whose ecstasies were more repeatable and whose devotion was continuous and lifelong, conflict with the sciences does not seem to have been an important issue.

For another great mind, however, it was exceptionally important. ʾAbū l-Walīd Muḥammad bin ʾAḥmad bin Rušd (1126–1198), better known simply as Ibn Rushd, and in awakening medieval Europe as Averroës, was outraged by al-Ghazali's *Incoherence of the Philosophers* and he soon replied with a polemical dialogue mischievously titled *Tahafut al Tahafut—The Incoherence of the Incoherence.*[32] Like his Jewish contemporary Maimonides, Averroës was no mystic. He came from the far west of Dar al-Islam, Andalusia (today's Spain and Portugal) which was ruled, together with today's Morocco, by the Almoravid dynasty and later the Almohad. Both these dynasties had been founded by orthodox salafists through wars of conquest, and Averroës eventually ran into a lot of trouble with his Almohad Sultan, Abu Yusuf Yaqub al-Mansur (Jacob the Victorious); but the cultural tradition

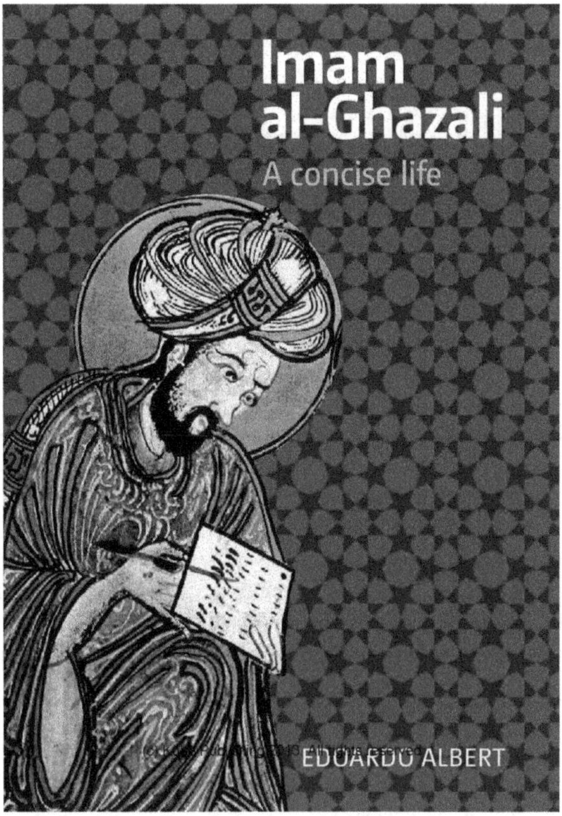

Fig. 8.2 Abū Ḥāmid Muḥammad ibn Muḥammad aṭ-Ṭūsiyy al-Ġazālīy (b. 1056–1059, d. 1111 CE) represented here by a medieval painting of a Muslim scholar. (Image from Kube Publishing)

[32] Averroës (Abū l-Walīd Muḥammad Ibn ʾAḥmad Ibn Rušd). *The Incoherence of the Incoherence* (*Tahafut al Tahafut*, c1180, ed. Maurice Bouyges) tr. Simon van Den Bergh, Gibb Memorial Trust Arabic Studies, 2v, 1954, E-text @ https://antilogicalism.com/wp-content/uploads/2017/07/incoherence.pdf.

Fig. 8.3 Averroës (Abū l-Walīd Muḥammad Ibn ʾAḥmad Ibn Rušd 1126–1198 CE), statue said to be of him in Córdoba, Spain. (Photo by Saleemzohaib, shot personally in Córdoba using my iPhone 5, CC BY 3.0, https://commons.wikimedia.org/w/index.php?curid=39516804)

of Muslim Andalusia was basically multi-ethnic and tolerant, and Averroës was neither a salafist nor a Ṣufi.

Averroës, in fact, was a genuine early scientist, a convinced empiricist and rationalist. Physician to the Almohad Sultan, author of textbooks on medicine, astronomy and three books on physics (kinematics), he had accepted the intellectual legacy of Ibn Sina and made himself Islam's living expert on Aristotle, as well as the Aristotelian heritage of logic and science, which Islam had dubbed "Philosophy"—*Falasifah*.[33] (It was Averroës's commentaries on Aristotle, translated into Latin, that were most responsible for bringing "The Philosopher" back into the Latin West, Greekless for nearly eight centuries.) Averroës's teacher, Ibn Tufail, who had recommended that he write about Aristotle, was a Ṣufi, but Ibn Tufail's most celebrated book is a very unmystical Enlightenment sort of tale in which a marooned infant, with a little help from mute animals, can grow up to understand the material universe (and its divine origin) by reasoning about experience, without the aid of faith

[33] Averroes was also appointed shariah judge (*qadi*) in Seville, and wrote a summary of the Maliki school of jurisprudence, *Bidāyat al-Mujtahid wa Nihāyat al-Muqtaṣid* (بداية المجتهد و نهاية المقتصد, The Distinguished Jurist's Primer).

or prophetic revelation.[34] Ibn Tufail had taken the side of Aristotle and Ibn Sina against al-Ghazali's *Incoherence of the Philosophers* in his own polemic, *Philosophus Autodidactus*, and now Averroës, having written two books on the compatibility of Philosophy with Islam, defended Philosophy against al-Ghazali's misapplied mysticism with *The Incoherence of the Incoherence*.[35]

---

[34] Abu Bakr Muhammad ibn 'Abd al-Malik ibn Muhammad **ibn Tufail** al-Qaisi al-Andalusi, *Hay ibn Yaqsin* (حي بن يقظان *Alive, son of Awake*, 1185) (*Hayy ibn Yaqzan: A Philosophical Tale*, tr., Lenn Evan Goodman, Chicago: U. of Chicago Press, 2009). It has been convincingly shown that this tale, translated into English in 1708, was one of the models for Defoe's *Robinson Crusoe* (1719), as it may have been for Condillac's *Traité des sensations* (1754).

[35] The two books were *Fasl al-Maqal* (The Decisive Treatise) which argued that philosophical investigation was entirely legal under Islamic law, and was indeed prerequisite for study of the Qur'an, and *Kitab al-Kashf* (Book of Unveiling) which argued against the old Ash'arite theology as discredited by Philosophy. For a bit of the flavor of Ghazali's thinking, and Averroës's criticism, I can cite the following from Averroës's *The Incoherence of the Incoherence*.

"The Third Discussion

"Ghazali says, refuting the philosophers:

"'What you affirm are only suppositions and in fact you do nothing but add obscurities to obscurities. If a man were to say that he had seen such things in a dream, it would be a proof of his bad constitution, or if one should advance such arguments in juridical controversies, in which everything under discussion is conjectural, one would say these were stupidities which could not command any assent.'

"I say:

"This is very much the way the ignorant treat the learned and the vulgar the eminent, and in this way, too, the common people behave towards the products of craftsmanship. For, when the artisans show the common people the products of their craftsmanship which possess many qualities from which they draw wonderful actions, the masses scoff at them and regard them as insane, whereas in reality they themselves are insane and ignorant in comparison with the wise. With such utterances as these the learned and the thoughtful need not occupy themselves." (Averroës, *The Incoherence of the Incoherence*, "The Third Discussion," trans. with introduction and notes by Simon van den Bergh (1954), published and distributed by the Trustees of the E. J. W. Gibb Memorial, online @ http://www.muslimphilosophy.com/ir/tt/tt-ch3.htm, 17 July, 2012).

"ABOUT the NATURAL SCIENCES

"The First Discussion

"Ghazali says:

"'According to us the connexion between what is usually believed to be a cause and what is believed to be an effect is not a necessary connexion; each of two things has its own individuality and is not the other, 'and neither the affirmation nor the negation, neither the existence nor the non-existence of the one is implied in the affirmation, negation, existence, and non-existence of the other-e. g. the satisfaction of thirst does not imply drinking, nor satiety eating, nor burning contact with fire, nor light sunrise, nor decapitation death, nor recovery the drinking of medicine, nor evacuation the taking of a purgative, and so on for all the empirical connexions existing in medicine, astronomy, the sciences, and the crafts. For the connexion in these things is based on a prior power of God to create them in a successive order, though not because this connexion is necessary in itself and cannot be disjoined-on the contrary, it is in God's power to create satiety without eating, and death without decapitation, and to let life persist notwithstanding the decapitation, and so on with respect to all connexions. The philosophers, however, deny this possibility and claim that that is impossible. […]'

"I say:

"To deny the existence of efficient causes which are observed in sensible things is sophistry, and he who defends this doctrine either denies with his tongue what is present in his mind or is

It did not carry the day. The dead al-Ghazali had been survived by his ideas, and even the burning of his books by the Almoravid Sultan 'Ali Ibn Yusuf would not stem his influence.[36] Averroës, ever prolific, eloquent and convincing, lost his epic battle with the persistent ghost. Some of Averroës's envious fellow jurists informed on him. Yaqub al-Mansur, his own Almohad Salafist Sultan, got wind of something in Averroës's many writings which struck him as theologically offensive, possibly the phrase, "and it was shown that Venus is one of the gods."[37] He dismissed Averroës as a judge and as his personal physician in 1195 and ordered all his books publicly burned, including 28 works on philosophy, 20 on medicine, 8 on law, 5 on theology, 4 on grammar, the commentary on Plato's *Republic*, and all the commentaries on Aristotle.[38] Only a fraction survived, but every one fell under the suspicion of blasphemy; and Averroës himself, who was officially rehabilitated by his Sultan only a year before his death in 1198, has still not fully recovered his intellectual authority in Islam.

Since post-Crusade Christian intellectuals like Thomas Aquinas could hardly be put off by a philosophy condemned by Islam, Aristotle's logic and science began to flourish in Christendom, making Averroës's Aristotle one of the master keys to the West's recovery of "natural philosophy"—what we eventually came to call "science."[39] Sufism was more threatened by the rational empiricism of Averroës

---

carried away by a sophistical doubt which occurs to him concerning this question. For he who denies this can no longer acknowledge that every act must have an agent. The question whether these causes by themselves are sufficient to perform the acts which proceed from them, or need an external cause for the perfection of their act, whether separate or not, is not self-evident and requires much investigation and research. [...] (Averroës, *The Incoherence of the Incoherence*, "About the Natural Sciences," trans. with introduction and notes by Simon van den Bergh (1954), published and distributed by the Trustees of the E. J. W. Gibb Memorial, online @ http://www.muslimphilosophy.com/ir/tt/tt-ch3.htm, 17 July, 2012).

[36] Janina M. Safran (2014) The politics of book burning in al-Andalus, *Journal of Medieval Iberian Studies*, 6:2, 148–168. She cites Mohammed bin Asaad al-Yafi, *Mir'āt al-jinān wa 'ibrat al-yaqzān fī ma'rifat mā yu'tabar min hawādīth al-zamān*, a book describing events of the year 537 AH (1142 CE), in which 'Ali ibn Yūsuf, the Almoravid ruler, ordered the burning of the book of al-Ghazalī.

[37] This charge is found in 'Abdelwahid al-Marrakushi, *al-Mojib fi Talkhis Akhbar al-Maghrib* [*The Pleasant Book in Summarizing the History of the Maghreb*] (1224), King Saud University, pp.150–151, *quoted in Article "Averroës," Wikipedia, accessed 17 July, 2012.*

[38] The figures are from *the article "Averroës," Wikipedia, accessed 17 July, 2012. That Averroes' works should receive the same punishment as al-Ghazali's has its ironies, but the burnings seem to have had contrary effects.*

[39] Aristotle, in effect, came back to Western Europe on Averroës' passport. The story of his influence illustrates the ultimate unity of the Western religious tradition as well as its scientific one. A Jewish disciple of Maimonides, Jacob Anatoli, translated several of the Aristotelian commentaries of Averroës from Arabic into Hebrew. Many of them were then translated from Hebrew into Latin by two more Jews, Jacob Mantino and Abraham de Balmes, while still others were translated directly from Arabic into Latin by a Christian, Michael Scot, all at the thirteenth-century Neapolitan court of the Frederick II, the Holy Roman Emperor of Christendom famed for his religious heterodoxy. Thomas Aquinas, who called Aristotle "The Philosopher," called Averroës "The Commentator," and Dante placed him with Aristotle and the other virtuous non-Christians in Limbo, the vestibule of *Inferno*. In the Renaissance, Raphael painted him on Plato's side of *The School of Athens*, looking over Pythagoras's shoulder, to the left of Michelangelo as Heraclitus.

than by the friendliness to mysticism of al-Ghazali, but it also survived and flourished. It took time for the path opened to orthodoxy and intolerance by al-Ghazali's intellectual authority became visible to large numbers, and Sufism continued to produce great visionaries who could experience *Hal* without directly threatening either orthodoxy or the sciences. Indeed, it could be said that the "Golden Age" of the Ṣufi Way came in the thirteenth through the sixteenth centuries, C.E.[40] The number of orders proliferated and two Ṣufi sages from opposite ends of Dar al-Islam, Ibn ʿArabī and Rumi, raised for Sufism the most long-lasting of monuments: literature.

Ibn ʿArabī (Abū ʿAbd Allāh Muḥammad ibn ʿAlī ibn Muḥammad ibn ʿArabī, 1165–1240 CE), qualifies as a visionary prodigy as well as one of Islam's great minds.[41] He, too, was born in the Andalusian west of Dar-al-Islam, today's Spain, a subject, like Averroës, of the Almohad Sultan. He was only 16 in 1181 CE when he went into Ṣufiesque seclusion. Around that age Ibn ʿArabī was sent by his father to meet the great Averroës and the boy answered all the Aristotelian philosopher's questions with "Yes" and "No." Said Averroës after the encounter, "I always thought that spiritual knowledge without learning was possible, but I never before met anyone who had experienced it." One of Ibn ʿArabī's formative early visions was of Musa (Moses), Isa (Jesus) and Muḥammad, urging him together to seek God. Ibn ʿArabī himself reported in his book *Rūh al-Quds* that in 1190, as he visited a renowned Ṣufi sage on his deathbed in Córdoba, he saw in a vision all the Prophets from Adam to Muḥammad "in their spiritual reality." One of them, Hūd, named by the *Qur'an* as the first prophet of Arabia, told him that they were all there in order "'to visit [the sage]' "[42] But "according to a tradition passed down by the immediate disciples of Ibn ʿArabī, Hūd explained that the real reason for their gathering was to welcome him (Ibn ʿArabī) as the Seal of Muḥammadan Sainthood (*khatm al-wilāya al-muḥammadiyya*), the supreme heir."[43]

Ibn ʿArabī probably never joined a practicing Ṣufi order, but rather became an unaffiliated adept, for many years a *qalandar* or wandering scholar. Ṣufi disciples came to adopt him, however, and it was Ṣufis who eventually titled him *al-Shaykh al-Akbar*, the Greatest Master. He launched a distinguished and comprehensive writing career in 1194 with *Mashāhid al-Asrār al-Qudusiyya* (Contemplation of the

[40] Article "Ṣufi," *Wikipedia*, accessed 16 June, 2011.

[41] Abū ʿAbdillāh Muḥammad ibn ʿAlī ibn Muḥammad ibn ʿArabī (ʻأبو عبد الله محمد بن علي بن محمد بن عربي) a.k.a. Muhiyuddin Ibn ʿArabi, or Muhyi al-Din ibn al-ʿArabi (1165–1240). The information about him is from "Ibn ʿArabi," *Wikipedia*, accessed 30 January, 2011), some of which is there sourced to two biographies: Stephen Hirtenstein, *The Unlimited Mercifier*, (Anqa Publishing, 1999), and Claude Addas, *Ibn Arabi, ou, La quète du Soufre Rouge* (Paris: Gallimard, n.d.), translated by Peter Kingsley as *Quest for the Red Sulphur: The Life of Ibn Arabi* (Islamic Texts Society, 1993), and *Ibn Arabi et le voyage sans retour* (Paris: Seuil, 1996), translated as *Ibn Arabi: The Voyage of No Return* (Islamic Texts Society, 2000).

[42] Ibn ʿArabi, *Ṣufis of Andalusia: The* **Rūh al-Quds** *and* **al-Durrat al Fakhirah**, tr., Ralph Austin, Roxborough: Beshara Publications, 1971, p116, quoted in Article "Ibn ʿArabī," *Wikipedia*, accessed 30 January, 2011.

[43] Article "ibn ʿArabī," *Wikipedia*, accessed 30 January, 2011, quoting Claude *Addas, Quest for the Red Sulphur: The Life of Ibn Arabi* (Islamic Texts Society, 1993), p76.

Holy Mysteries).[44] His masterpiece, *al-Futûhât al-makkiyya* (*The Meccan Openings* or *Meccan Revelations*), was a Ṣufi *Summa Theologica*, thousands of pages long His philosophical writings made a Ṣufi word out of *wujûd*, an old Arabic epistemological term for perception, by combining simple perceiving with the Ṣufi-derived concept of joy in discovery and the realization—an ecstatic realization—of the presence of the divine in whatever has been discovered to exist, which left him open to the charge of believing that everything all together was God, the heresy of pantheism.[45]

None of Ibn ʿArabī's writings seems to propose, as al-Ghazali had, the dependence of empirical science on supernatural prophecy, despite their author's assumption (an Ash'arite assumption) that all changes in the material world depend on the sustaining will of God. Ibn ʿArabī did not stint on either reasoning or writing, but reason and critical interpretation never seem to have invalidated or interfered with his having visions and appreciating them.[46] In Fez, in 1197 CE, a supernal "light" rendered Ibn ʿArabī totally disoriented as he was leading prayer in the al-Azhar mosque. "'I lost the sense of behind. I no longer had a back or the nape of a neck. While the vision lasted, I had no sense of direction, as if I had been completely spherical (dimensionless).'"[47] In any case, Ibn ʿArabī pursued a busy, intellectual, and quite orthodox life, never anxious that his visions might fail to persist, until he died in Damascus, the city of Paul and al-Ghazali, where he had finally settled in 1240 CE, remaining a model of gentle tolerance for, and openness to, human experience, ecstasy included.[48]

What Ibn ʿArabī was to Sufism in the twelfth (Christian) century Rumi was in the thirteenth. Rumi, too, had visions; indeed, he has been claimed as their founder by the Mawlawiyya or Mevlevi Ṣufi order, the celebrated "whirling dervishes" of Turkey. But the most important thing about Rumi was that he was a consummately gifted poet. At his death in 1273 CE Maulana Jalalu-'d'Din Muḥammad i Rumi (1207–1273) left a classic poem about every aspect of the Ṣufi experience—6 books,

[44] *Tadbīrāt al-Ilāhiyya* (Divine Governance), a text on *fiqh* (law), was another work of the 1190s.

[45] "If on the one hand he speaks of *wujûd* in the standard Avicennan language of necessity and possibility, he simultaneously talks of it—in terms long established by the Ṣufi tradition—as the fullness of divine presence and human consciousness that is achieved in realization." (William Chittick, "Ibn ʿArabi," *Stanford Encyclopedia of Philosophy* online (*August 5, 2008, accessed 15Jul12),* citing R. J. Dobie, "The Phenomenology of *Wujud* in the Thought of Ibn ʿArabi", in A. T. Tymieniecka (ed.), *Timing and Temporality in Islamic Philosophy and Phenomenology of Life* (Dordrecht: Springer, 2007), pp. 313–22.

[46] Chittick's article in the *Stanford Encyclopedia of Philosophy* points out that Ibn ʿArabi never presented himself as a Ṣufi, but judges that he "can be considered the greatest of all Muslim philosophers, provided we understand philosophy in the broad, modern sense and not simply as the discipline of *falsafa*" which is limited in Islamic thought to Classical logic, mathematics and empirical science.

[47] II, 486.

[48] Attacks on Ibn ʿArabi from the doctrinally orthodox continue to this day. Cf., A. A. Tabari, *The Other Side of Sufism* (Revival of Islamic Heritage Society, 1988; posted by Mohammed M. Saleem @ http://www.qss.org/articles/Sufism/toc.html, accessed 5 March, 2012).

25,000 verses and 50,000 lines called the *Mathnawî-yé Ma'nawî*, meaning "Rhyming Couplets (*Mathnawî*) of Deep Spiritual Meaning (*Ma'nawî*)" whose subject, in brief, is humanity, life, love, death, and ecstasy.[49]

> There are thousands of wines
> That can take over our minds
>
> Don't think all ecstasies
> are the same!
>
> Jesus was lost in his love for Allah
> His donkey was drunk with barley.[50]

It had been the work of fifteen years, and it was almost immediately circulating everywhere in the Muslim world, read not only as literature but also as devotional material for practicing Sufis. In India, five centuries after Rumi died, a Ṣufi compendium reports that "a shared recitation of the *Mathnavi* of Rumi" led "one dervish to fall into a state of ecstasy (*hal*)."[51]

Rumi had lived most of his life in the geographical midsection of Islam, the old Byzantine Roman lands we now call Turkey, acquiring his surname which means "Roman"; but Rumi had been born in the east, in Tajikistan, in a family of Hanafi jurists and imams, and he had written in Persian, so his work became a classic for the whole of polyethnic Dar al-Islam, a literary (and religious) achievement that helped many Muslims to get over their midcentury military failures at the hands of the Mongols. He remains today a sort of Persian Shakespeare, a poet both classic *and* popular in his own culture and in a host of foreign and even non-islamic cultures.[52] In 2007, a BBC commentator described Rumi as the "most popular poet in America,"[53] (which may show only that the commentator hadn't been paying attention to the lyrics of U.S. popular music); but among all those, American or not, who appreciate the possibility of what is now called the "spiritual," Rumi has long been Islam's most prominent advocate of piety over moralism/fundamentalism, its most exported reply to rote faith and intolerant salafist orthodoxy (Figs. 8.4, 8.5, 8.6 and 8.7).

---

[49] Maulana Jalalu-'d'Din Muhammad i Rumi (Among variant transliterations are Mevlānā, Mewlānā and Mawlana Jalal ad-din ar-Rumi, Jalal al-Din Muhammad Balkhi al-Rumi.) Among the poem's variants are: *Mesnevi* and *Masnavi i Ma'navi*. www.dar-al-masnavi.org/about_masnavi.html, accessed 2011.

[50] Rumi, "The Many Wines" (from the *Masnavi*) in *The Essential Rumi*, tr. Coleman Barks (1995) with John Moyne, A. J. Arberry & Reynold Nicholson, Edison, NJ: Castle Books, 1997, p6.

[51] Nile Green, *Indian Sufism since he Seventeenth Century*, Kindle ed., loc. 1361, citing Shah Mahmud Awrangabadi, *Malfuzat-e-Naqshabandiyya: Halat-e-Hazrat Baba Shah Musafir Sahib* (Hyderabad: Nizamat-e-'Umur-e-Madhhabi-e-Sarkar-e-ʿAli, 1358/1939–40), p84.

[52] Goethe published a "divan," or cycle of poems of his own in 1819, in imitation of Rumi's fourteenth-century successor, the Persian Ṣufi poet Hafez (Khwāja Shamsu d-Dīn Muhammad Hāfez-e Shīrāzī (1325/1326–1389/1390), under the title *West-östlicher Divan*, or *West-Eastern Cycle*.

[53] Charles Haviland, "The roar of Rumi—800 years on", *BBC News*, 30 Sep, 2007. Quoted in Article "Rumi," *Wikipedia*, accessed 14 July, 2012.

Fig. 8.4 Ibn ʿArabi (1165–1240 CE), al-Shaykh al-Akbar ("the Greatest Master"), with students. Medieval painting. (By Unknown author—http://www.ibnarabisociety.org/articles/treasureofcompassion.html, Public Domain, https://commons.wikimedia.org/w/index.php?curid=4848380)

But at this mid-thirteenth-century moment of triumph, the old suspicion and intolerance of Ṣufi pretensions revived. One cause was the stress that once-triumphant Islam was put under by the invasions of Genghis Khan and his Mongol hordes. In 1258, the Mongols took Baghdad, the capital of the Abbasid caliphs for four centuries, sacked it, razed it, and burnt it to the ground. For good measure, they looted its famous libraries, including the House of Wisdom, putting an end to the Golden Age of Islamic culture, "a psychological blow from which Islam still suffers. Already Islam was turning inward, becoming more suspicious of conflicts between faith and reason and more conservative."[54] (Indeed, Islam's turn inward may be said to have begun a century before with Al-Ghazali.) The Mongols were neither Jewish, nor Christian, nor Muslim nor Buddhist, and although (or maybe because) their descendants would convert to one or another of all these religions, and their dynasts would enlarge the state toleration of religion practiced by the first Muslim caliphs, most Muslims thought of them as an embodiment of evil. Among those was Taqi ad-Din Abul 'Abbās Ahmad ibn ʿAbd al-Halim ibn ʿAbd as-Salam ibn Taymiyya al-Harrānī, (1263–1328), the now notorious Ibn Taymiyyah.[55]

---

[54] Steven Dutch, "The Mongols" @ http://www.uwgb.edu/dutchs/WestTech/xmongol.htm, accessed 11 Jul 2012.

[55] Alternate transliterations include Taymiya, Taymiyya, Taimiya, Teymiyyeh and Taimia. The most extensive secondary sources on Ibn Taymiyyah's ideas in a Western language are Henri Laoust, *Essai sur les doctrines sociales et politiques de Takī-d-Dīn Aḥmad b. Taimīya* (1939), and Laoust, "*La Biographie d'Ibn Taimīya d'après Ibn Kathīr*," in *Bulletin d'Études Orientales,*

Fig. 8.5 The Cairo citadel in front of Muhammad Ali's mosque where Ibn Taymiyyah (1263–1328 CE) was imprisoned in 1306 for writing a book against the Rifāʿiyyah Sufi and the school based on ibn ʿArabī's writing that taught that the Creator and the created become one. (By New York Public Library—Porte de la citadelle et mosquée Mouhammed Aly, No restrictions, https://commons.wikimedia.org/w/index.php?curid=20098811)

Born five years after the destruction of Baghdad, as scion of two generations of Muslim scholars in Rumi's homeland, Turkey, Ibn Taymiyyah was soon on his way to the top of the ranks that had by now become traditional in Dar al-Islam, and he eventually settled in Damascus as a member of its ulema. He was both smart and orthodox, educated in the Sunni way in both theology and law, so well as to be reputed as an international arbiter in this and other ulemas. His legal training was in the older, stricter Hanbali tradition, and he was able to sit as a judge before he was 20 and to teach as a professor of law at 21 (in succession to his father). His *fatwa* decrees were quoted; his judgments were imitated and celebrated; his writings proliferated (166 of them on Muslim law and another 126 on Muslim doctrine). He was intellectually combative enough to be jailed as a heretic by Syria's Egyptian overlords on three separate occasions (during the first two he preached to his fellow-prisoners and during the last he died). A refugee from repeated Mongol attacks, he was physically combative, too, enough to obey his own fatwa against the last Mongol invasion of Syria 1299–1303, by joining the fight himself. He survived and

9(1943), pp115–162. Laoust summarized his broad knowledge of Ibn Taymiyyah in his article on him in the *Encyclopedia Britannica*.

Fig. 8.6 The fort in Damascus where Ibn Taymiyyah (1263–1328) was imprisoned in 1320 for his writing against the ease of divorce, and imprisoned again in 1326 (for writing a book against visiting the tombs of "saints" including the tomb of Muhammad) and where he died in 1328. (By Mewes at German Wikipedia—Transferred from de.wikipedia to Commons, Public Domain, https://commons.wikimedia.org/w/index.php?curid=1825479)

though Taymiyyah's home town in Turkey was destroyed, Damascus was successfully recaptured from the Mongols in time to become his residence.

The invasion inspired Ibn Taymiyyah's most famous argument, that the *ḥadith* of the Prophet (a doubtfully supported hadith) about moving to the greater (*akbar*) jihad from the lesser (*asghar*) jihad after the Battle of Badr in the *Qur'an*, did not mean a shift from physical to moral struggle, as so many others in the twelfth and thirteenth centuries, including the Sufis and his fellow Hanbali jurists, had been saying, but the contrary, a shift from the moral to the physical.[56] And in fact, the most famous of Ibn Taymiyyah's many formal judgments was the "jihad fatwa," issued in 1303 against the Muslims of Mardin who had surrendered to the Mongols in 1260. The fatwa called for holy war against the Ilkhan Mongols of Persia, whose ruler, Ghazan, had recently converted to Islam, but who, instead of imposing shariʿah, had retained his private devotion to Mongol customary law, Mongol shamanism, and state toleration of most of the major religions. When the Ilkhan kingdom enlisted Christian Crusader allies to invade Syria, which was then ruled by the Muslim Mamluks of Egypt, Ibn Taymiyyah's fatwa made armed struggle against this hetero-

[56] The proof texts for the judgment are the similar passages in *Qur'an* 2:193 & 8:38–39.

Fig. 8.7 Maulana Jalalu-'d'Din Muḥammad i Rumi (1207–1273) Sufi master. Statue in Buca, Turkey. (Photographed by Faik Sarıkaya/ wowTURKEY.com—Originally uploaded to www.wowturkey.com. Self-work of a wowturkey user, Attribution, https://commons.wikimedia.org/w/index.php?curid=1799782)

dox combination holy enough not only to be recommended but to be required, the classic full recasting of the obligation of self-defense in law that is much like the recent so-called "stand your ground" obligation now in the law of some U.S. states. Thus the war against the Mongol invasion seems to have been the first Muslim war that a Muslim jurist held it unholy *not* to fight in since the Battle of the Trench in the *Qur'an*.

> Everyone who is with them [the Mongols] in the state over which they rule has to be regarded as belonging to the most evil class of men. He is either an atheist (*zindiq*) and hypocrite who does not believe in the essence of the religion of Islam—this means that he [[only]] outwardly pretends to be a Muslim—or he belongs to that worst class of all people who are the people of [[heretical innovations (*bid'ah*)]] ... They place Muḥammad [[in a position]] equal to [[the position of]] Chinghis-Khan [...][57]

[57] Ibn Taymiyyah, quoted in Richard Bonney, *Jihad: From Quran to Bin Laden* (NY: Palgrave Macmillan, January 9, 2007), p115. Ibn Taymiyyah was author/editor of *Majmu al-Fatawa al-Kubra* (*Majmu'a Fatawa Shaikh ul-Islam Ibn Taymiyya* [Great Compilation of Opinions of Sheikh Ibn Taymiyyah]?) [*A Great Compilation of Fatwa*] (repr. Beirut, 1397/1978, iv, pp331–58), used as recently as 1981 to recommend internal jihad against the Egyptian political class (Rudolf Peters, ed., *Jihad in Classical and Modern Islam*, Princeton, NJ: Markus Wiener, 2nd ed., 2005, p160–161).

And for Ibn Taymiyyah, this is just a particular instance of his general position, derived from the *Qur'an* and selected *aḥadith*, that Muslims are capable of heresy and disobedience to shariʿah and must be fought with violence:

> It has been established on the authority of the Koran, the *Sunna*, and the Consensus of the Community, that those who depart from the law of Islam must be fought, even if they pronounce the two professions of faith. [...] The most serious type of obligatory jihad is the one against the unbelievers and against those who refuse to abide by certain prescriptions of the *Shari'a* ...[58]

In his legal thinking, Taymiyyah claimed to be what's called a *mujtahid* a judge who may rely on *ijtihad*, or individual judgment beyond the precedents. He believed, somewhat paradoxically, that *ijtihad* would return to shariʿah law the flexibility needed to confront an ever increasing number of innovations (*bidat*), including practices like the worship of Ṣufi saints that he saw as polytheistic, heretical, and apostate. He became a Salafist, claiming that the practice of the earliest Muslims (Salafin) might overrule even a ruling by a Companion of Muḥammad, like the decree of Umar, the second caliph, extending toleration to Christians and Jews in the new Muslim empire. He came to accuse even the caliphate of being apostate ever since Ali, because the Muslim community, the *ummah*, must in his judgment be ruled by two and only two at a time: a religious imam and a temporal military emir, and the emir could not launch jihad without the imam's fatwa.[59] He denounced all sorts of heterodoxies as forms of *shirk* or "polytheism," implied or explicit: Mongol converts to Islam, philosophers (*faylasafs*), Shiʿi like the Kasrawan in Lebanon, and Ṣufis, especially Ṣufi visionaries and ecstatics like the Rifa'i (Rifa'iyah), those who prayed to, or through, such ecstatics, and the group or school called *ittihadiyah*, which carried on the teachings of his great predecessor, Ibn ʿArabi, whose views he had clearly studied but which he now joined a growing coalition to attack as heretical.

Ibn Taymiyyah called all Ṣufis *ahl al-bida'* or "innovators"[60] He came to regard "the idea of mystical unity with God and ecstatic aspects of Sufism as explicitly un-Islamic."[61] He publicly rejected the teachings of Ibn ʿArabi, which contained, in his view, a rapturous (or enthusiastic) discussion of the existence of Allah in created

---

See also Ibn Taymiyyah, "*Governance according to God's Law in reforming both the ruler and his flock*" from which a section on *jihad* is quoted in Rudolph Peters, ed., *Jihad: A History in Documents* (1996), Princeton, NJ: Markus Wiener, 2005, pp43–54; and Ibn Taymiyyah, *al-Aqeedah Al-Wasitiyah* [*The Creed to the People of Wasitiyah*] English abridgement @ http://www.scribd.com/doc/7721691/Creed-Sharh-AqeedatIlWasitiyah-Ibn-Taymiyah.

[58] Ibn Taymiyyah, *al-Siyasa al-shar'iyya fi islah al-ra'i wa-al-ra'iyya* [*Governance according to God's Law in reforming both the ruler and his flock*] tr., in Rudolph Peters, ed., *Jihad: A History in Documents* (1996), Princeton, NJ: Princeton U.P., 2005, pp52–53.

[59] "Ibn Taymiyyah," *Wikipedia*, accessed 26 Dec 2007.

[60] Farhad Daftary, (Inst. Ismaili Stu., London), ed., *Mediaeval Isma'ili History and Thought*, Cambridge: Cambridge U.P., pb 2001, p12.

[61] http://muslim-canada.org/wahhabi.htm.

beings and the identification of man with Allah. Pantheistic monism, whereby God is in everything and everything is in God, is an old attempt to square an even older theological circle. Al-Hallaj had been executed for such a claim in 922. Only for mystics can it be reasonable for a transcendent god to be immanent in all created material things—for Allah, that is, to somehow be within his own creation, all of it, or even part of it.[62] To Ibn Taymiyyah such monism seemed not just unreasonable, but flat-out heretical, in the sense of contradicting the oft-asserted singularity, the *tawhid*, of Allah.[63] A "stern critic of antinomian interpretations of Islamic mysticism (Sufism) [who] believed that shariʿah applied to ordinary Muslim and mystic alike," ibn Taymiyyah moved naturally to criticism of the liturgical implications of Sufism, like intercessory prayer, "saint veneration and grave cults."[64]

And yet, stunningly, Ibn Taymiyyah, the paragon of moralism and legalism, was himself a Ṣufi. "I wore the blessed Ṣufi cloak of ʿAbdul Qadir," he was quoted as saying, "there being between him and me two."[65] He was, in fact, a member of the Qadiryah or Qadiri order whose *tariqa* had been founded by sheikh ʿAbd al-Qadir al-Jilani (1077–1166) but whose *silsila* or succession of masters, it was claimed, reached back to Junaid al-Baghdadi, and thence to Ali and finally to Muḥammad himself. Indeed one version took the Qadiryah back to Ali through the first eight of the twelve Shiʿi imams.[66] What then can we make of the fact that not only was Ibn

[62] "Shaykh Ibn Taymiyah (RA)," @ www.central-mosque.com/biographies/taymiyah.htm.

[63] http://muslim-canada.org/wahhabi.htm. Ibn Taymiyyah's book *Risalat al-'ibadaat al-shar'iyya wal-farq baynaha wa bayn al-bid'iyya* [Treatise on?] (in *Majmoo'at al-rasa'il wal- masa'il*, Beirut: Lajnat al-turath al-ʿArabi, 5:83), shows sympathy for Ṣufis but no empathy with *wajd* (ecstasy). ("Ibn Taymiyyah," *Wikipedia*, accessed 26 Dec 2007. That article has been edited since, but the 2007 version could later be found online as "Ibn Taymiyyah," *New World Encyclopedia*, accessed 27 Jul 2012). Ibn Taymiyyah's *Al-Aqeedat-il-Wasitiyah* may be found abridged in English @ http://www.scribd.com/doc/7721691/Creed-Sharh-AqeedatIlWasitiyah-Ibn-Taymiyah. *Enjoining Right and Forbidding Wrong* was to be found @ http://www.java-man.com/pages/books/alhisba.html#INTRODUCTION.

[64] According to the 2007 *Wikipedia* article, "Most scholars (including Salafis) believe that he rejected the creed used by most Ṣufis entirely (the Ash'ari creed). This seems supported by some of his works, especially *al-Aqeedat al-Wasitiyah* wherein he refuted the Asha'ira, the Jahmiyya and the Mu'tazila [theological schools]—the methodology of whom latter day Ṣufi's [sic] have adopted." ("Ibn Taymiyyah," *Wikipedia*, accessed 26 Dec 2007). Ibn Taymiyyah's main work against tombs and tomb veneration is *Risalah Ziyarah Al-Qubur*.

[65] The quotation from Ibn Taymiyyah was recorded in 1772 C.E. in *al-Mas'ala at-Tabriziyya* (MS, Damascus, 1186 H, translated in Hisham Muhammad Kabbani, "Ibn Taymiyya the Ṣufi Shaikh: Answer to Shaikh Adly" (@ http://www.sunniforum.com/forum/showthread.php?6313-Ibn-Taymiyya-the-Ṣufi-!-!). Kabbani is a Lebanese-American Ṣufi Muslim.

[66] Delong-Bas identifies Ibn Taymiyyah as both a Hanbalite and a Ṣufi, as does Christopher Melchert, "The Ḥanābila and the Early Ṣufis," *Arabica* 48:3(2001) and Abdul Hakim I. Al-Matroudi, "The Ḥanbalī school of law and Ibn Taymiyyah: conflict or conciliation," () (Mohammad Sharif Khan, Mohammad Anwar Saleem, *Muslim philosophy and philosophers*, *Aqidah Wasitiyah* vs. Ashariyah; Al-radd ala al-mantiqiyin vs philosophers) Article "Qadiriyya," *Wikipedia*, accessed 14 May, 2006. The Qad**I**riyyah (not to be confused with the Qad**A**rites) believe in the fundamental principles of Islam, especially its rites and shari'a law, but interpreted through mystical experience. The Qadiri order was quite significant. It has become one of the most widespread in Islam, reaching China in 1674, and flourishes today in India, Pakistan, Turkey, the Balkans and East and West

Taymiyyah a Qadiri Ṣufi, but that the Rifa'iyah Ṣufi order which was first among those he specifically condemned was in fact an offshoot of Qadiryah?

Part of the answer may lie in the character of Qadiri, which is one of several *tariqat* that prefer quieter devotion, frown on public displays of enthusiasm, and discourage any antinomian revision or addition to Muslim ritual; but that is not the whole story. Ibn Taymiyyah did not condemn everything Ṣufi, and even wrote defending the Ṣufis for prioritizing love over law and intellect in the approach to Allah:

> As for the Ṣufis, they affirm the love (of Allah), and this is more evident among them than all other issues. The basis of their Way (*tariqa*) is simply will and love. The affirmation of the love of Allah is well-known in the speech of their early and recent masters, just as it is affirmed in the Book and the Sunna and in the agreement of the *salaf*.[67]

The argument here, however, is that Ibn Taymiyyah, like al-Ghazali, never reliably experienced the ecstatic union with Allah that even Qadiri Sufism promised, and that he made a virtue of this necessity. By turning against the Ṣufis, he exonerated himself from failure to achieve their signature aim, and freed himself to be a legalist, a ritualist, in fact a fundamentalist and a heresy hunter. In one of his works, often anthologized, Ibn Taymiyyah goes all the way, raising war in the cause of Islamic orthodoxy to a sixth pillar—a higher duty and a greater religious good than any of the original Five Pillars of Islam (not to mention the Ṣufi ideal of closeness to the Creator, or indeed any general moral duty to show the "compassion" and "mercy"

Africa. The order included Ibn Taymiyyah's "most important student, Ibn al-Qayyim al-Jawziyyah," who went to jail with his teacher and compiled the 350-title bibliography of ibn Taymiyyah's writings; and many of Ibn Taymiyyah's students, though Salafists, were Qadiri Ṣufi and spoke highly of the order's founder al-Jilani. ("Qadiriyya," *Wikipedia*, 14 May 2006).

[67] Ibn Taymiyyah, *Al-ihtijaaj bi al-qadar* (Cairo: al-matba'a al-salafiyya, 1394/1974), p38, in Sh. G. F. Haddad, "Ibn Taymiyya on [al-Jilani/Gilani's] '*Futooh Al-Ghayb*' and Sufism," @ http://www.livingislam.org/n/itaysf_e.html, accessed 20 Mar 1996. Another MS by Ibn Taymiyyah, published in his *Majmu'a Fatawa*, endorses the Ṣufi *fana'* (ego annihilation) as compatible with orthodoxy: "Because that person has vanished in his lover, in *Allah 'azza wa jall*—through the intensity of the love, because He vanished in Allah's love, not his own ego's love. And he will recall Allah, not recalling himself, remember Allah not remembering himself, visualizing Allah [*yastashhid*], not visualizing himself, existing in Allah, not in the existence of himself. When he reaches that stage, he no longer feels his own existence. And that is why he says in this state, "*Ana al-Haqq*" (I am the Truth), or "Subhanee. (Glory to Me!)" [like the martyred al-Hallaj] and he will say "*maa fil jubba ill-Allah*" (there is nothing in this cloak except Allah), because he is drunk in the love of God and this is a pleasure and happiness that he cannot control." (Ibn Taymiyyah, *Majmu'a Fatawa Shaikh ul-Islam Ibn Taymiyya* [Great Compilation of Opinions of Sheikh Ibn Taymiyyah], Book 2, Volume 2, Cairo: Dar ar-Rahmat, 19??, p286, quoted in Kabbani, "Ibn Taymiyya the Ṣufi Shaikh: Answer to Shaikh Adly" @ http://www.sunniforum.com/forum/showthread.php?6313-Ibn-Taymiyya-the-Ṣufi-!-!, Last edited by faqir; 6 May, 2005). Kabbani quotes other works in the same Ibn Taymiyyah collection, *Majmu'a Fatawa*, that endorse some Ṣufi ideas and practices other than pantheism and saint- or tomb-worship: *'Ilm as-Sulook* [The Knowledge of Travelling to Allah] and *At-Tawassuf* [On Tassawuf, Volume 11]. Kabbani also quotes a passage from a different collection, *al-Mukhtasar al-Fatawa al-Masriyya* (al-Madani Publishing House, 1980) which legitimizes "the miracles of saints." (p603).

by which God himself is characterized in the opening of practically every *sura* of the Qur'an).

> Jihad against the disbelievers is the most noble of actions and moreover it is the most important action for the sake of mankind [...]
>
> For whoever has heard the summons of the Messenger of Allah, peace be upon him, and has not responded to it, must be fought.[68]
>
> [...]
>
> [Secondly,] jihad implies all kinds of worship, both in its inner and outer forms. More than any other act it implies love and devotion for Allah, [...] And the individual or community that participates in it, finds itself between two blissful outcomes: either victory and triumph or martyrdom and Paradise.[69]

The scales that had been tipped toward dogmatic faith by al-Ghazali were overturned by Ibn Taymiyyah, whose intellectual descendants have been recognizable in nearly every subsequent era.[70] African Islam recognized Ibn Taymiyyah's influence in the nineteenth century, and his disciples continue to harass heretics in Sudan, northern Nigeria and Chad. In the mid-twentieth century, the Egyptian Salafist and Muslim Brother, Sayyid Qutb, would cite Ibn Taymiyyah against heresy, and Sayyid Qutb's work would become one of the core texts for Ayman al-Zawahiri, Osama bin Laden and the founders of Al Qaeda.[71] In 1981 Muḥammad ʿAbd al-Salam Faraj would use Ibn Taymiyyah's writings to recommend internal jihad against the Egyptian political class. In his new popular English-language history of the development of Muslim law Sadakat Kadri writes that although Ibn Taymiyyah did not quite mean them that way, his famous "*fatwas* against the Mongols [...] are mouthed today to validate murder after murder in Islam's name."[72]

As I wrote this tens of thousands were exiling themselves from the proverbially remote and venerable West African Muslim city of Timbuktu in order to

---

[68] Ibn Taymiyyah, "[The Religious and Moral Doctrine of *Jihad*]," in *al-Siyasa al-shar'iyya fi islah al-Ra'i wa-al-Ra'iyya* [*Governance according to God's Law in reforming both the ruler and his flock*], in Bonney, *Jihad*, p116–117. The same translation, somewhat differently excerpted, is found in Allen, *God's Terrorists*, p46–47.

[69] Ibn Taymiyyah, *Governance according to God's Law* (*al-Siyasa...*) @ http://www.islamist-watch.org/main.html.

[70] The issue remains joined in Islam today, erupting more often than not in an argument between adherents of Ibn Taymiyyah and admirers of Ibn ʿArabi. For a recent attack on Sufism from the Ibn Taymiyyah camp, cf., Br. Yusuf Hijazi, "SUFISM: The Deviated Path," @ http://forums.islamic-awakening.com/f15/Sufism-the-deviated-path-714/ (accessed 24 July, 2012).

[71] Qutb's autobiography-polemic, whose English title is *Milestones*, appeared in 1964. The Taymiyyah-Qutb connection was recognized—and condemned—in a remarkable popular American book, originally titled *The Trouble With Islam: A Muslim's Call for Reform in Her Faith* (NY: St. Martin's, 2004), by the Canadian left-wing gay activist Muslim woman politician and comedian, Irshad Manji. Born in Uganda to an Indian father and an Egyptian mother, graduating high school in the U.S. state of Georgia, Manji, who is neither Wahhabi nor Ṣufi, may represent an alternate future for Islam.

[72] Sadakat Kadri, *Heaven on Earth: A Journey Through Shari'a Law From the Deserts of Ancient Arabia to the Streets of the Modern Muslim World*, NY: Farrar, Straus & Giroux, 2012, in Mohamad Bazzi, "Crime and Punishment," *New York Times Book Review*, 10 Aug 2012.

avoid getting whipped for *bidat*—"innovations," like unaccompanied women walking outside—by a Salafist gang called Ansar Dine, whose first move was to destroy as many as they could find of the tombs of the city's legendary 333 Ṣufi "saints."[73] Ansar Dine had not yet gone on record invoking Ibn Taymiyyah by July, 2012, but observers expected it.[74] Ironically, memorial services of the sort Ibn Taymiyyah condemned for Ṣufi saints, are held for Ibn Taymiyyah even today, and as far away as China.[75] Ibn Taymiyyah may have died in an Egyptian-run prison, as Sayyid Qutb would, but his intellectual legacy, a faith-based assault on faith, a fencing in of extreme religious experience with doctrine and law, lives on in Islam in a strange, backward-looking way that would make everything from a rock concert to the UN Declaration of Human Rights into nothing more than heretical *bidat*.

Ibn Taymiyyah would also be invoked in the eighteenth century, this time by Muslim shari'ah legalists in both west and east. In the east, the widely influential South Asian Muslim cleric Shah Waliullah of Delhi (1703–1762) as he turned from Ṣufi-inspired reconciliation of Islamic sectarianism to Ṣufi heresy-hunting and a jihadist movement in India which would provide energy and justification to a line of Indian *mujahidin* war leaders from Shah Abdul Aziz to Shah Ismail Shaheed. That line has continued straight to the Indian Independence uprising of 1857 and the bombings of Ṣufis by Sunnis in Pakistan in the teens of the twenty-first century.[76]

---

[73] https://goldenagepublication.wordpress.com/2016/09/28/333-saints-of-timbuktu/.

See also, Reuters, "Militants Seek to Destroy Mali Shrines," *New York Times*, 30 June, 2012.

Over the weekend, the Islamists of Ansar Dine—the group that has controlled Timbuktu and much of northern Mali since a coup d'état and a successful revolt against the central authority in March—destroyed at least a half-dozen above-ground mausoleums of religious leaders venerated in Timbuktu as saints. French television stations showed video of men, some armed, resolutely hacking the structures with pickaxes.

[...]

Ansar Dine, which means defenders of the faith, preaches a strict form of Islam that advocates a total ban on alcohol, the flogging of adulterers and the imposition of Shariah, or Islamic law, on a part of Mali that has traditionally practiced religious tolerance. [...]

"It's very simple: It doesn't correspond to the rules of Islam," said a spokesman for Ansar Dine in Timbuktu, Sanda Ould Boumana, explaining the destruction of the monuments. "This is behavior that has nothing to do with Islam."

[74] Irfan Husain, "From here to Timbuktu" *South Asia Citizens Web*, 7 July, 2012 @ http://www.sacw.net/article2722.html, accessed 2 September, 2019. By 2015 some observers had found more evidence: Aly Sergie & Toni Johnson, "Nigeria's Boko Haram and Ansaru"—Council on Foreign Relations http://www.cfr.org/nigeria/boko-haram/p25739 (accessed 2 September, 2019).

[75] www.central-mosque.com/biographies/taymiyah.htm.

[76] Qutb al-Din Ahmad ibn 'Abd al-Rahim Wali Allah al-Dahlawi OR al-Hafidh Imam Hujjatul Allah Shah Ahmad ibn 'Abd ar-Rahim Wali Allah al-Dahlawi (1703–1762). "Shah Waliullah" means "King Friend-of-God." Waliullah's father, Shah 'Abd-ar Rahim, was a Ṣufi, a teacher and school administrator at Madrassa Rahimia, where Waliullah would teach for 12 years, beginning when he was about 17, and which had the goal of reconciling "Muslim philosophers (the Ṣufis and the Mutakallim) and the Muslim jurists (*faqih*)".

And in the west there was al-Waḥhab. As an admirer of Ibn Taymiyyah has written, "almost all historians have recognized his deep impact on the most prominent reformer of the eighteenth century, Sheikh Muḥammad bin ʿAbdul-Waḥhab."[77] Indeed, Ibn ʿAbd al-Waḥhab (1703–1792), the eighteenth-century founder of the official Islam of Saudi Arabia, which its opponents still call "Wahhabism," would invoke Ibn Taymiyyah in arguments for Ṣufi-baiting, heresy-hunting, tomb razing and general Salafi fundamentalism. He and his disciples would also attack an "enlightened" way of interpreting *kalam* that arose in his time in Yemen, next door to Saudi Arabia.[78] And he would further invoke Ibn Taymiyyah in support of a series of wars against fellow-Muslims in the Arabian peninsula, wars which created the Kingdom of Saudi Arabia, razed the Shiʿi tombs in Karbala, Iraq, and after conquering Mecca and Medina in the early 1800s, simply purged them of Sufism and moved from the mandate of religious experience to that of religious law.

Bibliography

'Ansari, 'Abdullah. 1996. *'Abdullah 'Ansari of Herat (1006–1089 C.E.): An Early Sufi Master*. Ed. A.G. Ravan Farhadi. Richmond, UK: Curzon Press.

'Aṭṭar, Farid ud-Din. 1984. *The Conference of the Birds* or *Speech of the Birds*. (Persian منطق الطیر, *Manṭiq-uṭ-Ṭayr*. 1177 CE). Trans. Afkham Darbandi. New York: Penguin Classics.

———. 1990. *Muslim Saints and Mystics: Episodes from the Tadhkirat Al-Auliya'*. Trans. and abridged A.J. Arberry. New York: Penguin Books.

Abdo, Geneive. 2002. *No God But God: Egypt and the Triumph of Islam*. New York: Oxford University Press.

Abu Sway, Mustafa. 1996. *al-Ghazali: A Study in Islamic Epistemology*. Kuala Lumpur: Dewan Bahasa Dan Pustaka.

Abu Sway. 2001. *Muḥammad al-Ghazali*. October. www.cis-ca.org/voices/g/ghaz-mn.htm.

Adamec, Ludwig W. 2005. *Historical Dictionary of Afghan Wars, Revolutions and Insurgencies*. 2nd ed. Lanham, MD: Rowman and Littlefield/Scarecrow Press.

Adamson, Peter. 2015. *Philosophy in the Islamic World: A Very Short Introduction*, Very Short Introductions. New York: Oxford University Press.

Addi, Lahouari, and rvw Ali Humayun Akhtar. 2017. *Philosophers, Sufis, and Caliphs: Politics and Authority from Cordoba to Cairo and Baghdad*. Cambridge: Cambridge University Press. In *Reading Religion*, 2018. https://readingreligion.org/books/philosophers-sufis-and-caliphs.

Afsaruddin, Asma. 2007. *The First Muslims: History and Memory*. Oxford, UK: Oneworld.

---

[77] Jamia Salafia Banaras & Muqtada Hassan Azhari, "Introduction" to ibn Taymiyyah, al-Aqeedat al-Wasitiyah @ http://www.scribd.com/doc/7721691/Creed-Sharh-AqeedatIlWasitiyah-Ibn-Taymiyah (accessed 10 July, 2012).

[78] A leader in this movement for updating Islamic *fiqh*, or jurisprudence, was the Yemeni jurist Al-Shawkani (Muḥammad Ibn Ali ibn Muḥammad ibn Abdullah al-Shawkani, 1759–1839). Cf. Bernard Haykel, *Revival and Reform in Islam: The Legacy of Muḥammad al-Shawkani* (Cambridge Studies in Islamic Civilization. Cambridge: Cambridge University Press, 2003).

Aḥmad, Irfan. 2017. *Religion as Critique: Islamic Critical Thinking from Mecca to the Marketplace*, Islamic Civilization and Muslim Networks Series. Chapel Hill: University of North Carolina Press.

Ajayi, J.F.A., and M. Crowder. 1974. *History of West Africa*, Studies in African History. Vol. 2. New York: Addison-Wesley Longman Ltd.

Akhtar, Ali Humayun. 2017. *Philosophers, Sufis, and Caliphs: Politics and Authority from Cordoba to Cairo and Baghdad.* Cambridge: Cambridge University Press. http://www.cambridge.org/us/academic/subjects/history/middle-east-history/philosophers-sufis-and-caliphs-politics-and-authority-cordoba-cairo-and-baghdad#tlbVKVMUMD5b3j0R.99.

al-Adawiyya, Rabi'a (d. 801), *sayings* in Faridu d-Din 'Attar (d. ca. 1230), ed. 1996. *Memorial of the Friends of God.* (*Tadhikrat al-'Awliya*, in Persian). In *Early Islamic Mysticism*, ed. Michael A. Sells. Classics of Western Spirituality. Mahwah, NJ: Paulist Press.

al-Badawi, Mostafa. 2005. *Sufi Sage of Arabia: Imam Abdallah ibn Alawi al-Haddad*, The Fons Vitae Imam al-Haddad Spiritual Masters series. Louisville, KY: Fons Vitae.

Albertini, Tamara. 2003. The Seductiveness of Certainty: The Destruction of Islam's Intellectual Legacy by the Fundamentalists. *Philosophy East and West* 53 (4): 455–470.

al-Bistami, Abu Yazid (d. 848–849 or 874–875), *shaṭḥyat* (ecstatic sayings), ed. as-Sulami. 1996a. *Tabaqat al-Awliya* [Ranks of the Friends of God]. In *Early Islamic Mysticism*, ed. Michael A. Sells. Mahwah, NJ: Paulist Press (Classics of Western Spirituality).

———, *shaṭḥyat* (ecstatic sayings), ed. as-Sarraj. 1996b. *Kitab al-Luma* [The Book of Flashes]. In *Early Islamic Mysticism*, ed. Michael A. Sells. Classics of Western Spirituality. Mahwah, NJ: Paulist Press.

al-Farabi, Abū Naṣr Muḥammad ibn Muḥammad (Alfarabi). 1998. *On the Perfect State*. Ed. Richard Walzer. Rev. ed. Chicago: Kazi Publications.

———. 2004. *The Political Writings: Selected Aphorisms and Other Texts*. Trans. Charles E. Butterworth. Ithaca, NY: Cornell University Press (Agora Editions).

al-Ghazali, Abu Hamid Muḥammad ibn Muḥammad al Tusi. 1839. *Mozene Ẓedeḳ* [*Mizan al-'Amal*]. Trans. into Hebrew Abraham ibn Ḥasdai. Ed. Jacob Goldenthal. Leipzig. (On philosóphical ethics with Qur'anic references replaced by Biblical, and an introduction on the lives and works of Al-Ghazali and Ibn Ḥasdai, by Goldenthal, professor of rabbinica and Oriental languages at the University of Vienna from Sept. 1849 until his death in 1868.)

———. 1952. *The Logical Part of Al-Ghazali's Maqasid Al-Falasifa, in an Anonymous Hebrew Translation with the Hebrew Commentary of Moses of Narbonne*. Ed. and trans. with Notes and an Introduction and Translated into English by Gershon Baruch Chertoff. Columbia: Columbia University. https://www.ghazali.org/books/chertoff.pdf. (*Maḳaṣid al-Falasifah* or *Aims of the* (Greek) *Philosophers* is al-Ghazali's preliminary treatise to *The Incoherence of the Philosophers* (*Tahâfut al-falâsifa*) dealing with Aristotelian logic, physics, and metaphysics.)

———. 1980. *Al-Ghazali's Path to Sufism: His Deliverance from Error (al-Munqidh min al-Dalal).* Trans. R.J. McCarthy. S.J. Twayne Publishers. Louisville, KY: Fons Vitae, 1999, 2000.

———. 1989. *The Remembrance of Death and the Afterlife* [*Kitab dhikr al-mawt wa-ma ba'dahu*]. Book XL of the *Revival of the Religious Sciences* (Ghazali Series, Bk. 40) [*Iḥyā' 'Ulūm al-Dīn*]. Trans. T.J. Winter. Cambridge: Islamic Texts Society.

———. 1998a. *The Niche of Lights (Mishkat al-Anwar)*, Islamic Translation Series. Trans. David Buchman. Provo, UT: Brigham Young University Press.

———. 1998b. "Introduction" to *Al-Ghazali's Treatise on Direct Knowledge from God* (*al-Risalah al-laduniyah*), 87–88. Trans. A. Godlas. www.uga.edu/islam/laduni.html.

———. 2001. *On Faith in Divine Unity and Trust in Divine Providence: Kitab at-Tawhid wa Tawakul*. Book XXXV of *The Revival of the Religious Sciences* [*Iḥyā' 'Ulūm al-Dīn*]. Trans. David B. Burrell. Louisville, KY: Fons Vitae.

———. 2002. *The Incoherence of the Philosophers (Tahâfut al-falâsifa)*. Rev. ed. Trans. Michael E. Marmura. Islamic Translation Series. Provo, UT: Brigham Young University Press.

———. 2003. *Al-Ghazzali On Enjoining Good and Forbidding Wrong*. ("On Mutual Relations," Part 2, Book XIX of *The Alchemy of Happiness*). Trans. Muḥammad Nur Abdus Salam. Chicago: Kazi Publications.

———. 2005. *The Book of Knowledge: Being a Translation with notes of Kitab al-'Ilm* [Book I] *of Al-Ghazzali's Iḥyā' 'Ulūm al-Dīn* [*The Revival of the Religious Sciences*] *by Nabih Amin Faris*. https://www.ghazali.org/works/bk1-sec-1.htm.

———. 2010. *Al-Ghazali's Kitab Sharh 'Aja'ib al-Qualb: The Marvels of the Heart: Science of the Spirit*. Book XXI of the *Iḥyā' 'Ulūm al-Dīn* [The Revival of the Religious Sciences]. Trans. Walter James Skellie. Louisville, KY: Fons Vitae.

———. 2013. *Al-Ghazzali on Sufism* ("On Meditation," "On Seclusion," and "On Spiritual Poverty" from al-Ghazali, *The Alchemy of Happiness*). Trans. from Persian Muhammad Nur Abdus Salam. Chicago: Kazi Publications.

———. 2014. *Al-Ghazali On The Lawful And The Unlawful*. Book XIV of *The Revival of the Religious Sciences* [*Iḥyā' 'Ulūm al-Dīn*]. Trans. Yusuf Talal Delorenzo. Cambridge: Islamic Texts Society.

———. 2017. *The Alchemy of Happiness [Kimiya-yi Sa'ādat]*. Trans. from Urdu/Persian by Claud Field. Eastford, CT: Martino Fine Books.

al-Ghazzali, Muḥammad. 2001. *The Socio-Political Thought of Shah Wali Allah*. Ed. Abdul Ahad. Islamabad: The International Institute of Islamic Thought. India: Adam Publishers & Distributors, 2008.

al-Ḥallaj, al-Husayn ibn Mansur. 1931. *Le Diwân d'al-Hallaj*. Ed. L. Massignon. *Journal Asiatique* 1–158.

——— (d. 922). 1996a. *Ṭawasin*. In *Early Islamic Mysticism*, ed. Michael A. Sells. Classics of Western Spirituality. Mahwah, NJ: Paulist Press.

———. 1996b. *Akhbar al-Hallaj* [The Sayings of al-Hallaj]. In *Early Islamic Mysticism*, ed. Michael A. Sells. Classics of Western Spirituality. Mahwah, NJ: Paulist Press.

———. 1996c. Diwan. In *Early Islamic Mysticism*, Classics of Western Spirituality, ed. Michael A. Sells. Mahwah, NJ: Paulist Press.

al-Hujwiri, Ali B. 1911. Uthman al-Jullabi. *Kashf Al-Mahjub of Al-Huhwiri: "The Revelation of the Veiled": An Early Persian Treatise on Sufism*. Trans. Reynold Nicholson. Gibb Trust, 2000. Kindle ed.

Ali, Maulana Muhammad. 1941. *A Manual of Hadith*, 2001. Columbus, OH: Ahmadiyya Anjuman Ishaat Islam Lahore.

Ali, Tariq. 2002. *The Clash of Fundamentalisms: Crusades, Jihads and Modernity*. New York: Verso.

Ali, Kecia. 2011. *Imam Shafi'i: Scholar and Saint*, Makers of the Muslim World. Oxford, UK: Oneworld.

al-Iskandari, Shaykh Aḥmad Ibn 'Ata' Allah. 2005a. *The Book of Illumination Including the Sign of Success on the Spiritual Path: Kitab al-Tanwir fi Isqat al-Tadbir*. Louisville, KY: Fons Vitae.

———. 2005b. *The Subtle Blessings in the Saintly Lives of Abul-Abbas al-Mursi: And His Master Abul-Hasan: Kitab Lata'if al-Minan fi manaqib Abul-Abbas al-Mursi wa shaykhihi Abi l-Hasan*. Trans. Nancy Roberts. Louisville, KY: Fons Vitae.

al-Junayd, Abu l-Qasim (d. Baghdad, 910). 1996. Another Point on *Tawḥid*. In *Early Islamic Mysticism*, ed. Michael A. Sells, 1–4. Classics of Western Spirituality. Mahwah, NJ: Paulist Press.

al-Ma'arri, Abū l-'Alā' (973–1057 CE). 2013–2014. *The Epistle of Forgiveness*. Vol. 1 of A Vision of Heaven and Hell Preceded by Ibn al-Qāriḥ's Epistle. Vol. 2 of Hypocrites, Heretics, and Other Sinners. (*Resalat Al-Ghufran*. MS c1033 CE). Ed. and Trans. Geert Jan van Gelder and Gregor Schoeler. New York: New York University Press.
al-Muḥasibi, Abu 'Abd Allah al-Ḥarith ibn Asad (d. Baghdad, 857). 1940. *Kitab al-Ri'aya li Ḥuquq Allah* [The Book on the Observance of the Rights of God]. Ed. Margaret Smith. London: Luzac & Co. E. J. W. Gibb Memorial.
———. 1996. *Kitab ar-ri'aya li ḥuquq Allah* [The Book on the Observance of the Rights of God]. In *Early Islamic Mysticism*, ed. Michael A. Sells. Classics of Western Spirituality. Mahwah, NJ: Paulist Press.
al-Munawi, Muhammad 'Abd al-Ra'uf (1545–1622). 1992. *Les femmes soufies ou la passion de Dieu*. tr. Nelly et Laroussi Amri. éditions Dangles. Excerpts from al-Munawi, *Al-Kawākib ad-durriya fī tarājim as-sāda aṣ-ṣūfiyya* [The resplendent stars or Biographies of the Sufi masters] a.k.a. *Tabaqāt al-Munāwī aṣ-ṣughrā*.
al-Qushayri ('Abd al-Karīm ibn Hūzān Abū al-Qāsim al-Qushayrī al-Naysābūrī, d. 1074). 1996. Treatise. *In Early Islamic Mysticism*, ed. Michael A. Sells. Classics of Western Spirituality. Mahwah, NJ: Paulist Press.
———. 1074). 2007. *Al-Qushayri's Epistle on Sufism* (*Al-Risala al-qushayriyya fi 'ilm al-tasawwuf*, 437 A.H.). Trans. Alexander Knysh. Great Books of Islamic Civilization. Garnet Publishing.
Anjum, Ovamir. 2014. *Politics, Law, and Community in Islamic Thought: The Taymiyyan Moment*, Cambridge Studies in Islamic Civiization. Cambridge: Cambridge University Press.
an-Niffari, Muḥammad ibn 'Abd al-Jabbar ibn al-Hasan (d. 965). 1996. *Kitab al-Mawaqif* [The Book of Standings] #5, 6, 43, 44, 59, 67. In *Early Islamic Mysticism*, ed. Michael A. Sells. Classics of Western Spirituality. Mahwah, NJ: Paulist Press.
Anon. 1967. *Lam' al-Shihab fi sirat Muḥammad Ibn Abd al-Waḥhāb (1817)*. Cairo: Éditions Abu Hakima. (Anonymous and critical).
Aquil, Raziuddin. 2009. *Sufism, Culture, and Politics: Afghans and Islam in Medieval North India*. India: Oxford University Press. Reprint edition, 2012.
———, ed. 2010. *Sufism and Society in Medieval India*, Debates in Indian History and Society. Oxford: Oxford University Press.
———. 2020. *Lovers of God: Sufism and the Politics of Islam in Medieval India*. 1st ed. New York: Routledge.
Aranyosi, Ezgi Ulusoy. 2012. An Enquiry into Sufi Metaphysics. *British Journal for the History of Philosophy* 20 (1): 3–22.
Arberry, A.J. 1950. *Sufism: An Account of the Mystics of Islam*. New York: Dover Publishing, 2002; New Delhi, India: Cosmo Publications, 2004.
———., ed. 1969. *Religion in the Middle East: Three Religions in Concord and Conflict*, Judaism and Christianity. Vol. 1. Cambridge: Cambridge University Press.
Armour, Rollin Sr. 2002. *Islam, Christianity, and the West: A Troubled History*. New York: Orbis Books.
Armstrong, Karen. 1993. *A History of God: The 4,000-Year Quest of Judaism, Christianity and Islam*. New York: Knopf, 1994.
———. 2001. *Islam*. New York: Modern Library Chronicles.
Asani, Ali S. 2004. Ecstasy and Enlightenment: The Ismaili Devotional Literature of South Asia. Rvw Zawahir Moir. *Journal of Islamic Studies* 15 (3): 357–359. http://www3.oup.co.uk/islamj/hdb/Volume_15/Issue_03/eth309.sgm.abs.html.
ash-Shahrastani, Muḥammad ibn 'abd al-Karim (d. 1153). 1996. *Kitab al-Milal wa an-Nihal* [Book of Religious and Philosophical Sects]. In *Early Islamic Mysticism*, ed. Michael A. Sells. Classics of Western Spirituality. Mahwah, NJ: Paulist Press.

Aslan, Reza. 2006. *No God but God: The Origins, Evolution, and Future of Islam*. New York: Random House, 2005.
as-Sadiq, Ja'far. 1996. Sulami Ja'far. In *Early Islamic Mysticism*, Classics of Western Spirituality, ed. Michael A. Sells. Mahwah, NJ: Paulist Press.
as-Sarraj, Abu Nasr of Tus (d. 988). 1996. The Seven Stations (Maqamat) in *Kitab al-Luma* [The Book of Flashes]. In *Early Islamic Mysticism*, ed. Michael A. Sells. Classics of Western Spirituality. Mahwah, NJ: Paulist Press.
as-Sulami, Abu 'Abd ar-Rahman. 1996. *Tabaqat al-Awliya* [Ranks of the Friends of God]. In *Early Islamic Mysticism*, ed. Michael A. Sells. Classics of Western Spirituality. Mahwah, NJ: Paulist Press.
——— (d. 1021). 2005. *Early Sufi Women: A Bilingual Critical Edition of as-Sulami's Dhikr an-niswa al-muta 'abbidat as sufiyyat*. Trans. Rkia Elaroui Cornell. Louisville, KY: Fons Vitae.
Atmaja, Dwi S., Mark Woodward, and Richard C. Martin. 1997. *Defenders of Reason in Islam: Mu'tazililism from Medieval School to Modern Symbol: An Exploration of Fundamentalism in Islam from the Ninth Century to the Present*. London: Oneworld Academic.
at-Tustari, Muḥammad Sahl ibn 'Abdullah (d. Basra, 986). 1996. *Tafsir* (sayings). Ed. Muḥammad ibn Salim (d. 909) in *Early Islamic Mysticism*, ed. Michael A. Sells. Classics of Western Spirituality Mahwah, NJ: Paulist Press.
Averroës (Abū l-Walīd Muḥammad Ibn 'Aḥmad Ibn Rušd). 1842. *On the Harmony of Religions. Averroes on Plato's "Republic"*. Trans. Bi'ur ibn Roshd and ed. Jacob Goldenthal, tr. Todrosi, Leipzig. Averroes' commentary on Aristotle's *Rhetoric*. Hebrew translation with a historical and philosophical introduction by Goldenthal.
———. 1974 *On the Harmony of Religions. Averroes on Plato's "Republic"*. Trans. and ed. Ralph Lerner, Ithaca, NY: Cornell University Press. Agora Editions, 2005.
———. 1978. *The Incoherence of the Incoherence* (*Tahafut al Tahafut*, c1180, ed. Maurice Bouyges). tr. Simon van Den Bergh. Gibb Memorial Trust Arabic Studies, 2 vols, 1954. E-text by Muhammad Hazien. https://antilogicalism.com/wp-content/uploads/2017/07/incoherence.pdf.
———. 2002. *Decisive Treatise and Epistle Dedicatory* [*Kitab fasl al-maqal*, c1190]. Trans. Charles E. Butterworth. Islamic Translation series. Brigham Young University Press.
———. 2019. *On the Harmony of Religions and Philosophy* [*Kitab fasl al-maqal*, c1190]. tr. Independently published.
Axworthy, Michael. 2008. *Empire of the Mind: A History of Iran*. New York: Basic Books.
Aydin, Cemil. 2017. *The Idea of the Muslim World: A Global Intellectual History*. Cambridge, MA: Harvard University Press.
Ayoub, Mahmoud. 2005. *The Crisis of Muslim History: Religion and Politics in Early Islam*. Oxford, UK: Oneworld.
Aziz, Muḥammad Ali. 2011. *Religion and Mysticism in Early Islam: Theology and Sufism in Yemen*, Library of Middle East History. New York: I. B. Tauris.
Baldauf, Ingeborg. 2001. Jadidism in Central Asia within Reformism and Modernism in the Muslim World. *Die Welt des Islams* 41 (1): 72–88. New Series.
Baldick, Julian. 1989. *Mystical Islam: An Introduction to Sufism*. London: I. B. Tauris; New York: New York University Press.
Baldock, John. 2004. *The Essence of Sufism*. Arcturus, Kindle ed.
Ibn Barrajān. 2015. *A Qur'ān Commentary by Ibn Barrajān of Seville (d. 536/1141) Īḍāḥ al-ḥikma bi-aḥkām al-'ibra* [Wisdom Deciphered, the Unseen Discovered]. Ed. and trans. Gerhard Böwering and Yousef Casewit. Texts and Studies on the *Qur'ān* 10. Leiden: Brill.
Bashir, Shahzad. 2003. *Messianic Hope and Mystical Visions: The Nurbakhshiya Between Medieval and Modern Islam*. Columbia: University of South Carolina Press.
———. 2005. *Fazlallah Astarabadi and the Hurufis*, Makers of the Muslim World. Oxford, UK: Oneworld. (Astarabadi and his 14th-century Islamic apocalyptic movement).

———. 2011. *Sufi Bodies: Religion and Society in Medieval Islam*. New York: Columbia University Press. www.ebooks3000.com.

Bearman, P., Th. Bianquis, C.E. Bosworth, E. van Donzel, and W.P. Heinrichs, eds. 2012. *Encyclopaedia of Islam*. 2nd ed. Leiden: Brill, online 2020.

Beckwith, Christopher I. 2009. *Empires of the Silk Road: A History of Central Eurasia from the Bronze Age to the Present*. Princeton, NJ: Princeton University Press.

———. 2012. *Warriors of the Cloisters: The Central Asian Origins of Science in the Medieval World*. Princeton, NJ: Princeton University Press, Kindle ed.

Bellaigue, Christopher de. 2017. *The Islamic Enlightenment: The Struggle Between Faith and Reason, 1798 to Modern Times*. Liveright (Kindle Edition).

Ben Jelloun, Tahar. 2002. *Islam Explained*. New York: New Press.

Benton, William (producer). 1993. *The Glory and the Power: Fundamentalisms Observed*. William Benton Broadcasting Project. (Three part series produced in association with BBC TV and WETA TV for PBS, on the rise and impact of fundamentalisms in Christianity, Judaism, and Islam.)

Berkey, Jonathan P. 2003. *The Formation of Islam, Religion and Society in the Near East, 600–1800*. Cambridge: Cambridge University Press.

Bernstein, Alan E. 2017. *Hell and Its Rivals: Death and Retribution among Christians, Jews, and Muslims in the Early Middle Ages*. Ithaca, NY: Cornell University Press.

Bevilacqua, Alexander. 2018. *The Republic of Arabic Letters: Islam and the European Enlightenment*. Cambridge, MA: Belknap Press of Harvard University Press.

Bonner, Michael. 2006. *Jihad in Islamic History: Doctrines and Practice*. Princeton, NJ: Princeton University Press, Kindle ed.

Bonney, Richard. 2007. *Jihad: From Qu'ran to Bin Laden*. New York: Palgrave Macmillan.

Bowering, Gerhard, ed. 2015. *Islamic Political Thought, An Introduction*. Princeton, NJ: Princeton University Press, Kindle ed.

Bowering, Gerhard, et al., eds. 2012. *The Princeton Encyclopedia of Islamic Political Thought*. Princeton, NJ: Princeton University Press, Kindle ed.

Brenner, Louis. 1987. Muslim Thought in Eighteenth Century West Africa: The Case of Shaykh Uthman b. Fudi [Dan Fodio]. In *Eighteenth-Century Renewal and Reform in Islam*, ed. N. Levtzion and J.O. Voll. Syracuse, NY: Syracuse University Press.

Brown, Peter. 1979. Understanding Islam. *New York Review of Books* 22: 30–33.

Brown, Jonathan A. C. 2010. *Hadith: Oxford Bibliographies Online Research Guide*. (Oxford Bibliographies Online Research Guides)., Kindle ed.

Brown, Jonathan A.C. 2011. *Muḥammad (A Very Short Introduction)*. New York: Oxford University Press, Kindle ed.

———. 2014. *Misquoting Muhammad: The Challenge and Choices of Interpreting the Prophet's Legacy*. Oxford, UK: Oneworld, Kindle ed.

———. 2019. *Slavery & Islam*. Oxford, UK: Oneworld Academic.

Bulliet, Richard. 2004. *The Case for Islamo-Christian Civilization*. Revised ed. New York: Columbia University Press.

Burckhardt, Titus. 1953. *Vom Sufitum—Einführung in die Mystik des Islams*. Munich: Otto Wilhelm Barth-Verlag.

———. 1959. *Introduction to Sufi Doctrine: Commemorative Edition*, Spiritual Classics. Foreword by William C. Chittick. Bloomington, IN: World Wisdom, 2008, Kindle ed.

Callatay, Godefroid de. 2006. *Ikhwan al-Safa': A Brotherhood of Idealists on the Fringe of Orthodox Islam*, 10thC Shi'ah Brethren of Purity. London: Oneworld Academic.

Carey, Brian Todd, and Joshua B. Allfree. 2012. *Road to Manzikert: Byzantine and Islamic Warfare, 527–1071*. Barnsley, UK: Pen and Sword, Kindle ed.

Carré, Olivier, and Paul Dumont, eds. 1985. *Radicalismes islamiques*. 2 vols. Paris: L'Harmattan.

Casale, Giancarlo. 2011. *The Ottoman Age of Exploration*. New York: Oxford University Press, Kindle ed.

Casewit, Yousef. 2017. *The Mystics of al-Andalus: Ibn Barrajān and Islamic Thought in the Twelfth Century*, Cambridge Studies in Islamic Civilization. Cambridge: Cambridge University Press. Adobe eBook Reader. ISBN: 9781316886892. http://www.cambridge.org/us/academic/subjects/history/middle-east-history/mystics-al-andalus-ibn-barrajan-and-islamic-thought-twelfth-century#mxt5kguz1F9qtF8j.99.

Clarke, Peter B. 1982. *West Africa and Islam: A Study of Religious Development from the 8th to the 20th Century*. London: Hodder Arnold.

Coates, Peter. 2002. *Ibn 'Arabi and Modern Thought: The History of Taking Metaphysics Seriously*. Oxford: Anqa Publishing.

Cole, Juan. 2018. *MUHAMMAD: Prophet of Peace Amid the Clash of Empires*. New York: Nation Books.

Cole, Juan R.I., and Nikki R. Keddie, eds. 1986. *Shi'ism and Social Protest*. New Haven, CT: Yale University Press.

Cook, Michael. 2000. *The Koran (A Very Short Introduction)*. New York: Oxford University Press, Kindle ed.

———. 2001. *Commanding Right and Forbidding Wrong in Islamic Thought*. Cambridge: Cambridge University Press, 2003, 2010.

Michael Cook, ed. 2018. *The New Cambridge History of Islam*. 6 vols. Cambridge: Cambridge University Press.

Cook, David. n.d. *Islam and Apocalyptic* (Role of Eschatalogy in Radical Islamic Thought). http://www.mille.org/scholarship/papers/cookabs.html.

Cooperson, Michael (UCLA). 2000. *Classical Arabic Biography: The Heirs of the Prophets*. Cambridge: Cambridge University Press.

Cornell, Vincent J. 1998. *Realm of the Saint: Power and Authority in Moroccan Sufism*. Texas: University of Texas Press.

Cornell, Rkia Elaroui. 2019. *Rabi'a from Narrative to Myth: The Many Faces Of Islam's Most Famous Woman Saint, Rabi'A Al-'Adawiyya*. London: Oneworld Academic.

Crapanzano, Vincent. 1973. *The Hamadsha: A Study in Moroccan Ethnopsychiatry*. Berkeley: University of California Press.

Crone, Patricia. 2004. *Meccan Trade and the Rise of Islam*. Piscataway, NJ: Gorgias Press, Kindle ed.

Daftary, Farhad, ed. 2001. *Medieval Isma'ili History and Thought*. Cambridge: Cambridge University Press.

Dale, Stephen F. 2010. *The Muslim Empire of the Ottomans, Safavids, and Mughals*. Cambridge: Cambridge University Press, Kindle ed.

Doniger, Wendy. 2010. *The Hindus: An Alternative History*. Oxford: Oxford University Press, Kindle ed.

Donner, Fred M. 2010. *Muḥammad and the Believers: At the Origins of Islam*. Cambridge, MA: Belknap Press of Harvard University Press.

Eddin, Sufia M. 2006. *Constructing Bangladesh: Religion, Ethnicity, and Language in an Islamic Nation*, Islamic Civilization and Muslim Networks. Chapel Hill: The University of North Carolina Press.

Edwards, David B. 2002. *Before Taliban: Genealogies of the Afghan Jihad*. Berkeley: University of California Press.

El Fadl, Khaled M. Abou. 2001a. *And God Knows the Soldiers: The Authoritative and Authoritarian in Islamic Discourses*. Lanham, MD: University Press of America.

———. 2001b. *Speaking in God's Name: Islamic Law, Authority, and Women*. Oxford, UK: Oneworld.

El-Hibri, Tayeb. 2018. *Parable and Politics in Early Islamic History: The Rashidun Caliphs*. Columbia: Columbia University Press, Kindle ed.

El-Rouayheb, Khaled. 2015. *Islamic Intellectual History in the Seventeenth Century: Scholarly Currents in the Ottoman Empire and the Maghreb*. Cambridge:

Cambridge University Press. http://www.cambridge.org/us/academic/subjects/history/history-ideas-and-intellectual-history/islamic-intellectual-history-seventeenth-century-scholarly-currents-ottoman-empire-and-maghreb#5wTWwGHOYzfJ1Mz3.99.

Ernst, Carl W. 1985. *Words and Ecstasy in Sufism*. New York: State University of New York Press.

———., ed. and trans. 1999. *Teachings of Sufism*. London: Shambhala.

———. 2011. *Sufism: An Introduction to the Mystical Tradition of Islam*. London: Shambhala.

Ernst, Carl W., and Bruce B. Lawrence. 2002. *Sufi Martyrs of Love: The Chishti Order in South Asia and Beyond*. New York: Palgrave. Rvw Amina M. Steinfels, *Journal of the American Academy of Religion* 2006 74:266–269. http://jaar.oxfordjournals.org/cgi/content/full/74/1/266?etoc.

Fakhry, Majid. 1970. *A History of Islamic Philosophy*, Studies in Asian Culture. Vol. 5. 2nd ed. New York: Columbia University Press, 1983, 2004.

———. 2001. *Averroes: His Life, Works, and Influence*. Oxford, UK: Oneworld.

———. 2002. *Al-Farabi, Founder of Islamic Neoplatonism: His Life, Works, and Influence*, Great Islamic Thinkers. Oxford, UK: Oneworld. Rvw Ayman Shihadeh, *Journal of Islamic Studies* 15:3(September 2004), 347–348 http://www3.oup.co.uk/islamj/hdb/Volume_15/Issue_03/eth304.sgm.abs.html.

Farabi, See al-Farabi.

Farah, Caesar. 2000. *Islam*. 6th ed. New York: Barron's.

Farhadi, A.G. Ravan, ed. 1996. *'Abdullah 'Ansari of Herat (1006–1089 C.E.): An Early Sufi Master*. Richmond, UK: Curzon Press.

Fierro, Maribel. 2010. *The New Cambridge History of Islam*. Vol. 2 of The Western Islamic World, Eleventh to Eighteenth Centuries. Cambridge: Cambridge University Press.

Firestone, Reuven. 1999. *Jihad: The Origin of Holy War in Islam*. New York: Oxford University Press.

Fisher, Humphrey J. 2001. *Slavery in the History of Muslim Black Africa*. London: Hurst.

Flasch, Kurt. 2008. *D'Averroes à Maître Eckhart: Les sources arabes de la mystique allemande*. Conférences Pierre Abelard. Paris: Vrin.

Gairdner, W.H.T. 1980. *Theories, Practices and Training Systems of a Sufi School*. Sufi Research Series. Institute for the Study of Human Knowledge (ISHK) Book Service.

Gall, Le. 2010. Recent Thinking on Sufis and Saints in the Lives of Muslim Societies, Past and Present. *International Journal of Middle East Studies* 42 (4): 673–687.

García-Arenal, Mercedes. 2008. *Aḥmad al-Mansur [r.1578–1603]: The Beginnings of Modern Morocco*, Makers of the Muslim World. Oxford, UK: Oneworld.

Geertz, Clifford. 1971. *Islam Observed: Religious Developments in Morocco and Indonesia (1968)*. Chicago: University of Chicago Press.

———. 2003. Which Way to Mecca? *New York Review of Books* 50 (10): 27–30.

Gellner, Ernest, ed. 1985. *Islamic Dilemmas: Reformers, Nationalists, and Industrialization*. Berlin: Mouton.

Ghod, Saideh. 2004. *Kimia Khatoun*. (Iranian feminist novel of the life of Shams-e Tabrizi, the Sufi mystic who inspired the poetry of Rumi, from the perspective of Tabrizi's discontented wife.)

Glazier, Stephen D., ed. 2001. *Encyclopedia of African and African-American Religions*, Religion and Society Series. Vol. 2. New York: Routedge/Berkshire Publishing Group.

Goldenthal, Jacob (1815–1868), ed. 1845. Kalonymus, *Mesharet Mosheh*. Commentary on Maimonides' system of Divine Providence, with his explanation of Psalms 19 and 37.

Gonzalez Costa, Amina, and Maria Gracia Lopez Anguito. 2010. *Historia del sufismo en al-Andalus: maestros sufíes de al-Andalus y el Magreb*. Córdoba: Almuzara.

Goodman, Lenn E. 2003. *Islamic Humanism*. New York: Oxford University Press. Rvw Oliver Leaman, *Journal of the American Academy of Religion*, 72, 4(December 2004).

Gordon, Stewart. 2007. *When Asia Was the World: Traveling Merchants, Scholars, Warriors, and Monks Who Created the "Riches of the East"*. New York: Da Capo Press, Kindle ed.

Green, Nile. 2006. *Indian Sufism Since the Seventeenth Century: Saints, Books, and Empires in the Muslim Deccan*, Routledge Sufi Series. New York: Routledge, Kindle ed.

———. 2008. Making Sense of Sufism in the Indian Subcontinent. *Religion Compass* 2 (6): 1044–1061.

———. 2012. *Sufism: A Global History*, Blackwell Brief Histories of Religion. Malden, MA: Wiley-Blackwell.

Griffel, Frank. 2009. *Al-Ghazālī's Philosophical Theology*. Oxford: Oxford University Press.

———. 2013. Al-Ghazali. In *The Stanford Encyclopedia of Philosophy*, ed. Edward N. Zalta. Edition online.

Háfiz-i Shírázi, Khwája Shams ud-Dín Muḥammad (d. 1389). 1995. *The Green Sea of Heaven: Fifty Ghazals from the Díwán of Háfiz*. Trans. Elizabeth T. Gray, Jr. Ashland, OR: White Cloud Press.

——— (d. 1389). 2020. *Poems from the Divan of Hafiz*. Trans. Gertrude Lowthian Bell. Kindle ed.

Haider, Najam. 2019. *The Rebel and the Imam in Early Islam: Explorations in Muslim Historiography*. Cambridge: Cambridge University Press.

Haj, Samira. 2008. *Reconfiguring Islamic Tradition: Reform, Rationality, and Modernity*, Cultural Memory in the Present. Stanford, CA: Stanford University Press. (Wahhab and Abduh).

Halevi, Leor. 2004. Wailing for the Dead: The Role of Women in Early Islamic Funerals. *Past & Present* 183 (1): 3–39.

Hassan, Riaz. 2003. *Faithlines: Muslim Conceptions of Islam and Society*. New York: Oxford University Press.

Hatina, Meir. 2015. *Martyrdom in Modern Islam Piety, Power, and Politics*. Cambridge: Cambridge University Press.

Helminski, Camille Adams, ed. 2003. *Women of Sufism, A Hidden Treasure: Writings and Stories of Mystic Poets, Scholars & Saints*. Boston/London: Shambhala.

Hinkel, Leigh G. 2010. *Union with God: Encountering the Beloved: Anthropological Insights: Paul the Apostle, the Spanish Mystics and Sufi Islam*. CreateSpace Independent Publishing Platform.

Hitti, Philip K. 1968. Al-Ghazzali: Greatest Theologian of Islam. In *Makers of Arab History*. New York: Harper Torchbooks, 1971.

Hodgson, Marshall G. S. 1974–1977. *The Venture of Islam: Conscience and History in a World Civilization*. 3 vols. Chicago: University of Chicago Press.

Holland, Tom. 2013. *The Shadow of the Sword: The Birth of Islam and the Rise of the Global Arab Empire*. Kindle ed.

Hoover, Jon S. 2019. *Ibn Taymiyya*. London: Oneworld Academic.

Hourani, Albert H. 1957. The Changing Face of the Fertile Crescent in the XVIIIth Century. *Studia Islamica* 8: 89–122.

Hoyland, Robert G. 2015. *In God's Path: The Arab Conquests and the Creation of an Islamic Empire*. Oxford; New York: Oxford University Press, Kindle ed.

Huda, Qamar-ul. 2003. *Striving for Divine Union: Spiritual Exercises for Suhrawardi Sufis*, Routledge Sufi Series. New York: RoutledgeCurzon. Rvw Arthur F. Buehler, *Journal of Islamic Studies* 15:3(September 2004), 348–350 http://www3.oup.co.uk/islamj/hdb/Volume_15/Issue_03/eth305.sgm.abs.html.

Humayun Akhtar, Ali. 2017. *Philosophers, Sufis, and Caliphs: Politics and Authority from Cordoba to Cairo and Baghdad*. Cambridge, England: Cambridge University Press.

Hunwick, John O., et al. 2008. *The Hidden Treasures of Timbuktu*. New York: Thames & Hudson.

Hurvitz, Nimrod. 2004. The Formation of Hanbalism: Piety into Power. Rvw Wael B. Hallaq. *Journal of Islamic Studies* 15 (3): 345–347. http://www3.oup.co.uk/islamj/hdb/Volume_15/Issue_03/eth303.sgm.abs.html.

Ibn 'Arabi, Mohiudin (Muhiyuddin). 1971. *Sufis of Andalusia*. Trans. R.W.J. Austin, London: Allen & Unwin.

———. 1976. *Treatise on Being* [*Risalat-ul-wujudiyya*]. Trans. T.H. Weir. London: Beshara Pubs.

———. 1977. *"Whoso Knoweth Himself..." from the Treatise on Being: Risale-t-ul-wujudiyyah.* Trans. T.H. Weir BD. Gloucestershire, UK: Beshara Publications.
———. 1980. *The Bezels of Wisdom* [*Fusus al-Hikam*]. Trans. R.W.J. Austin. New York: Paulist Press.
———. 1997. *Les Illuminations de la Mecque: Anthologies présenté par Michel Chodkiewicz,* Spiritualités Vivantes-Poche. Paris: Albin Michel.
———. 2002a. *The Meccan Revelations* [*Kitab Al-Futuhat al-Makkiya*] (Anthology). Ed. Michel Chodkiewicz and Trans. from the Arabic by William C. Chittick, James W. Morris and Denis Gril, Trans. from the French *Les Illuminations de la Mecque* by David Streight, 2 vols. New York: Pir Press.
———. 2002b. *101 Diamonds from the Oral Tradition of the Glorious Messenger Muhammad,* Ibn 'Arabi's hadith anthology. New York: Pir Press.
———. 2003. *Tarjuman al-Ashwaq* [The Interpreter of Desires]. Beirut: Dar Sadir.
———. 2016. *Kernel of the Kernel.* Trans. Ismail Hakki Bursevi and Gloucestershire. England: Beshara Publications.
Ibn 'Arabi, Mohiudin, et al. 1978. *Self-Knowledge; Commentaries on Sufic Songs.* Trans. 'A'isha 'Abd ar-Rahman at-Tarjumana. Diwan Press.
Ibn al-Jawzi, 'Abd al-Raḥmān b. 'Alī b. Muḥammad Abu 'l-Farash. 2016. *Histoires des grands hommes de l'islam. Traduction intégrale de Sifat as safawi.* Trans. Messaoud Boudjenoun. El Bab Éditions.
Ibn al-Rawandi. 1971. *Encyclopaedia of Islam.* Vol. 3, 905. Leiden: Brill. (Abu al-Hasan Ahmad ibn Yahya ibn Ishaq al-Rawandi 827–911 CE, author of *Kitab al-Zumurrud* (*The Book of the Emerald*) questioning miracles and prophecy).
Ibn al-Rawandi (pseudonym). 2000. *Islamic Mysticism: A Secular Perspective.* Prometheus Books, Kindle ed.
Ibn Khallikan. 1843. *Ibn Khallikan's Biographical Dictionary* (*Wafayat al-a'yan*, "Obituaries of Eminent Men"). Trans. Mac Guckin De Slane. 4 vols. Sufi hagiography. Paris: Duprat. London: Allen & Co. https://archive.org/details/WafayatAl-ayantheObituariesOfEminentMenByIbnKhallikan/Vol1Of4WafayatAl-ayantheObituariesOfEminentMenByIbnKhallikan/page/n1/mode/2up.
Ibn Paquda (Pakuda, Pachuda), Bahya ben Joseph. 1945. *Book of Direction to the Duties of the Heart.* Trans. Moses Hyamson from ibn Tibbon's Hebrew *Hovotha-Levavoit* of 1161 to English. New York: Bloch Publishing.
———. 2000. *The Book of Direction to the Duties of the Heart.* (*Al Hidayah ila Faraid al-Qulub*, MS, Arabic, 1040, written in Spain). Trans. Menahem Mansoor. New York: Oxford University Press. (*Al Hidayah* was translated from Arabic to Hebrew by 1161 by Judah ibn Tibbon under the title *Hovotha-Levavoit* or *Chovot ha-Levavot* [Instruction in the Duties of the Heart]).
Ibn Taymiyyah. Taqi ad-Din Abul 'Abbas Aḥmad ibn Abd al-Halim ibn Abd al-Salam al-Numayri al-Ḥarrānī (1263–1328) 1948. *Le Traité de droit public d'Ibn Taimīya* [*Kitāb al-Siyāsah al-sharīyah*]. French trans. Henri Laoust, Beirut: Khayats.
———. 1966. *Ibn Taimiyya on Public and Private Law in Islam, or, Public policy in Islamic jurisprudence.* (*Kitāb al-Siyāsah al-sharīyah*). English trans. Omar A. Farrukh. Beirut: Khayats, 2000.
———. 1996. Governance According to God's Law in Reforming Both the Ruler and His Flock [*al-Siyasa al-shar'iyya fi islah al-ra'i wa-al-ra'iyya*]. In Peters, *Jihad: A History in Documents,* 43–54, ed. Rudolph Peters. Princeton, NJ: Princeton University Press, 2005.
———. 2007. [The Religious and Moral Doctrine of Jihad], in al-Siyasa al-shar'iyya fi islah al-Ra'i wa-al-Ra'iyya [Governance according to God's Law in reforming both the ruler and his flock]. In *Jihad: From Qu'ran to Bin Laden,* 116–117, ed. Richard Bonney. New York: Palgrave Macmillan.

———. 2012a. *The Allies of God and the Allies of the Devil.* Kindle ed.

———. 2012b. *Al-amr bi 'l-ma'ruf wa 'n-nahy 'an al-munkar* [Enjoining Right [al-Ma'ruf] and Forbidding Wrong [al-Munkar]. Trans. Salim Abdallah ibn Morgan in *Fortress of Monotheism.* Kindle ed. https://www.muslim-library.com/english/enjoining-right-amp-forbidding-wrong/ and http://www.java-man.com/pages/books/alhisba.html.

Ibn Warraq (pseudonym) see Warraq.

Insoll, Timothy. 2003. *The Archaeology of Islam in Sub-Saharan Africa.* Cambridge: Cambridge University Press.

Iqbal, Muḥammad. 1920. *The Secrets of the Self.* Trans. Reynold A. Nicholson. Sufism Series. London: Macmillan Publishers, Kindle ed.

Irwin, Robert, ed. 2010. *The New Cambridge History of Islam.* Vol. 4 of Islamic Cultures and Societies to the End of the Eighteenth Century. Cambridge: Cambridge University Press.

Izutsu, Toshihiko. 1980. *God and Man in the Qur'an.* New York: Reprint Books for Libraries.

Jamal, Mahmood, ed. 2010. *Islamic Mystical Poetry: Sufi Verse from the early Mystics to Rumi.* Penguin Classics, Kindle ed.

Jambet, Christian. 2011. *Qu'est-ce que la philosophie islamique?* Paris: Gallimard.

Jami, Nūr ad-Dīn 'Abd ar-Rahmān (1414–1492). 2011. *Fragrant Breezes of Intimate Friendship.* (*Nafahat al-Uns min Hadarat al-Quds* "Breaths of Divine Intimacy from the Presences of Holiness"). Sufi Hagiography. Al Baz Publications.

Kadri, Sadakat. 2012. *Heaven on Earth: A Journey Through Shari'a Law From the Deserts of Ancient Arabia to the Streets of the Modern Muslim World.* New York: Farrar, Straus & Giroux.

Kalin, Ibrahim, ed. 2014. *The Oxford Encyclopedia of Philosophy, Science, and Technology in Islam.* Vol. 1. New York: Oxford University Press.

Karabela, Mehmet. 2014. Ibn al-Rawandi. In *The Oxford Encyclopedia of Philosophy, Science, and Technology in Islam*, ed. Ibrahim Kalin, vol. 1. New York: Oxford University Press.

Karamustafa, Ahmet T. 2006. *God's Unruly Friends: Dervish Groups In The Islamic Middle Period 1200–1550.* London: Oneworld Academic.

———. 2007. *Sufism: The Formative Period.* Berkeley: University of California Press/Edinburgh: Edinburgh University Press.

Kersten, Carool, ed. 2015. *The Caliphate and Islamic Statehood: Formation, Fragmentation and Modern Interpretations.* Critical Surveys in Islamic Studies. Gerlach Press.

———. 2017. *A History of Islam in Indonesia: Unity in Diversity*, New Edinburgh Islamic Surveys. Edinburgh: Edinburgh University Press. New York: Oxford University Press.

Khalidi, Tarif. 2001. *The Muslim Jesus: Sayings and Stories in Islamic Literature.* Cambridge, MA: Harvard University Press.

Knysh, Alexander. 2000. *Islamic Mysticism: A Short History*, Themes in Islamic Studies. Leiden: Brill.

———. 2005. Historiography of Sufi Studies in the West. In *A Companion to the History of the Middle East*, ed. Y.M. Choueiri. Oxford: Wiley-Blackwell.

———. 2016. *Islam in Historical Perspective.* 2nd ed. New York: Routledge.

——— 2017. *Sufism: A New History of Islamic Mysticism.* Repr. Princeton, NJ: Princeton University Press, Kindle ed.

Kohlberg, Etan. 1987. Aspects of Akhbari Thought in the Seventeenth and Eighteenth Centuries. In *Eighteenth-Century Renewal and Reform in Islam*, ed. N. Levtzion and J.O. Voll. Syracuse, NY: Syracuse University Press.

Kokkonen, Taneli. 2014. *Ibn Tufayl: Living the Life of Reason*, Makers of the Muslim World. Oxford, UK: Oneworld.

Krausmüller, Dirk. 2004. Killing at God's Command: Niketas Byzantios' Polemic Against Islam and the Christian Tradition of Divinely Sanctioned Murder. *Al-Masaq: Islam and the Medieval Mediterranean* 16 (1): 163–176.

Krstić, Tijana. 2011. *Contested Conversions to Islam: Narratives of Religious Change in the Early Modern Ottoman Empire.* Stanford, CA: Stanford University Press.

Kugle, Scott. 2007. *Sufis and Saints' Bodies: Mysticism, Corporeality, and Sacred Power in Islam*, Islamic Civilization and Muslim Networks. Chapel Hill: The University of North Carolina Press.

Küng, Hans. 2007. *Islam: Past, Present and Future*. Oxford, UK: Oneworld.

Laoust, Henri. 1939. *Essai sur les doctrines sociales et politiques de Taḳī-d-Dīn Aḥmad b. Taimīya, Canoniste ḥanbalite né à Ḥarrān en 661/1262, mort q Damas en 728/1328*. Cairo: Imprimerie de l'Institut Français d'Archéologie Orientale.

———. 1943. La Biographie d'Ibn Taimīya d'après Ibn Kathīr. *Bulletin d'Études Orientales* 9: 115–162. Complementary notes provided by the historian Ibn Kathīr in the *al-Bidāyah,* on the subject of Ibn Taymīyah's disagreements with his contemporaries.

———. 1965. *Les Schismes dans l'Islam: Introduction à une étude de la religion musulmane*. Paris: Payot, 1977, 1983 (places Ibn Taymīyah in the general development of Islām.)

———. 1971. Ibn Taymiyya, Taḳī al-Dīn Aḥmad. In *Encyclopedia of Islam*, ed. B. Lewis, V.L. Ménage, Ch. Pellat, and J. Schacht, vol. 3, 2nd ed., 951–955. Leiden, The Netherlands: Brill.

Lapidus, Ira M. 1988. *A History of Islamic Societies*. New York: Cambridge University Press. 3rd ed. Cambridge: Cambridge University Press, 2015.

———. 2012. *Islamic Societies to the Nineteenth Century: A Global History*. Cambridge: Cambridge University Press.

Last, Murray. Reform in West Africa: The Jihad Movements of the Nineteenth Century. In *History of West Africa*, Studies in African History, ed. J.F.A. Ajayi and M. Crowder, vol. 2, 1–29. New York: Addison-Wesley Longman Ltd.

Lawrence, Bruce. 1990. *Defenders of God: The Fundamentalist Revolt Against the Modern Age*. University of South Carolina Press, 1995.

———. 2000. *Shattering the Myth: Islam Beyond Violence*. Princeton, NJ: Princeton University Press.

Le Gall, Dina. 2004. *A Culture of Sufism: Naqshbandis in the Ottoman World, 1450–1700*, Suny Series in Medieval Middle East History. New York: State University of New York Press.

Lerner, Ralph, ed. and trans. 2005. *Averroes on Plato's "Republic"*. Ithaca, NY: Cornell University Press (Agora pb).

Lerner, Ralph, and Muhsin Mahdi, eds. 1963. *Medieval Political Philosophy: A Sourcebook*. Rev. ed. Joshua Parens and Joseph C. Macfarland. Ithaca, NY: Cornell University Press, 2011.

Levi, Scott C., and Ron Sela, eds. 2009. *Islamic Central Asia: An Anthology of Historical Sources*. Bloomington: Indiana University Press, Kindle ed. 2012.

Levtzion, Nehemia. 1987. The Eighteenth Century: Background to the Islamic Revolutions in West Africa. In *Eighteenth-Century Renewal and Reform in Islam*, ed. N. Levtzion and J.O. Voll. Syracuse, NY: Syracuse University Press.

Levtzion, Nehemia, and Randall L. Pouwels, eds. 2000. *The History of Islam in Africa*. Athens: Ohio University Press.

Levtzion, Nehemia, and John O. Voll, eds. 1987. *Eighteenth-Century Renewal and Reform in Islam*. Syracuse, NY: Syracuse University Press.

Lewis, Bernard. 1987. *The Jews of Islam*. Kindle ed.

———. 1988. *The Political Language of Islam*. Chicago: University of Chicago Press.

———. 1993. *Islam and the West*. New York: Oxford University Press.

———. 2001. *Cultures in Conflict: Christians, Muslims, and Jews in the Age of Discovery*. New York: Oxford University Press.

Lings, Martin. 1975. *What Is Sufism?* Berkeley: University of California Press, 1977.

Lobel, Diana. 2020. *A Sufi-Jewish Dialogue: Philosophy and Mysticism in Bahya ibn Paquda's Duties of the Heart*. Philadelphia: University of Pennsylvania Press.

Mahdi, Muhsin. 1961. *Alfarabi and the Foundation of Islamic Political Philosophy*. Chicago: University of Chicago Press., 2001.

Makdisi, George. 2005. Ibn Taymīyah. In *Encyclopedia of Religion*, ed. Lindsay Jones, vol. 6, 2nd ed., 4276–4279. Detroit, MI: Macmillan Reference USA.

Margariti, Roxani Eleni. 2007. *Aden and the Indian Ocean Trade: 150 Years in the Life of a Medieval Arabian Arabian Port*, Islamic Civilization and Muslim Networks. Chapel Hill: University of North Carolina Press.

Martin, Richard C. 1997. *Defenders of Reason in Islam: Mu'tazilism and Rational Theology from Medieval School to Modern Symbol*. London: Oneworld, 2016.

Mason, Herbert W. 1995. *Al-Hallaj*. Richmond, Surrey: Curzon Press.

Massignon, Louis. 1975. *La Passion de Husayn ibn Mansûr Hallâj*. Vol. I à IV of Martyr mystique de l'Islam exécuté à bagdad le 26 mars 922. Paris: Gallimard (Tel coffret), 2010.

———. 2019. *The Passion of Al-Hallaj, Mystic and Martyr of Islam*. Trans. Herbert Mason (1972, 1994). Vol. 2 of The Survival of al-Hallaj. Princeton, NJ: Princeton University Press (Princeton Legacy Library pb).

Matar, Nabil. 1998. *Islam in Britain, 1558–1685*. Cambridge: Cambridge University Press.

Matteson, Ingrid. 2013. *The Story of the Qur'an: Its History and Place in Muslim Life*. Kindle ed.

Mbacké, Khadim, Eric Ross, and John O. Hunwick. 2005. *Sufism and Religious Brotherhoods in Senegal*. Princeton, NJ: Markus Wiener.

McAuliffe, Jane Dammen, ed. 2006. *The Cambridge Companion to the Qur'ān*. Cambridge: Cambridge University Press, Kindle ed.

Melchert, Christopher. 2006. *Ahmad Ibn Hanbal*, Makers of the Muslim World. Oxford, UK: Oneworld.

Menchinger, Ethan L. 2016. Free Will, Predestination, and the Fate of the Ottoman Empire. *Journal of the History of Ideas* 77 (3): 445–466. (Lady Mary Wortley Montagu's letter of February, 1718, on hearing that Ottomans were deists.).

Menocal, María Rosa. 2001. *The Ornament of the World: How Muslims, Jews, and Christians Created a Culture of Tolerance in Medieval Spain*. New York: Little, Brown.

Mernissi, Fatema. 1992. *Islam and Democracy: Fear of the Modern World*. Trans. Mary Jo Lakeland. New York: Perseus, 2002. Rvw Toby E. Huff, Rethinking Islam and Fundamentalism, *Sociological Forum* 10 (3) (Sep. 1995), 501–518.

Metcalf, Barbara D., ed. 2009. *Islam in South Asia in Practice*. Princeton, NJ: Princeton University Press, Kindle ed.

Mi'Raj. 1996. Sufi Interpretations of Muhammad's Night Journey. In *Early Islamic Mysticism*, Classics of Western Spirituality, ed. Michael A. Sells. Mahwah, NJ: Paulist Press.

Miles, Jack. 2018. *God in the Qur'an*. New York: Alfred A. Knopf.

Mohammed, Khaleel. 2018. *Islam and Violence*, Cambridge Elements in Religion and Violence. Cambridge: Cambridge University Press.

Moosa, Ebrahim. 2005. *Ghazālī and the Poetics of Imagination*, Islamic Civilization and Muslim Networks. Chapel Hill: The University of North Carolina Press.

Morgan, David O., and Anthony Reid, eds. 2010. *The New Cambridge History of Islam*. Vol. 3 of The Eastern Islamic World, Eleventh to Eighteenth Centuries. Cambridge: Cambridge University Press.

Morris, James W., and rvw Zailan Moris. 2005. Revelation, Intellectual Intuition and Reason in the Philosophy of Mulla Sadra [c1571–1640]: An Analysis of the al-Hikmah al-Arshiyya. (London: RoutledgeCurzon, 2003). *Journal of Islamic Studies* 16: 360–362. http://jis.oxfordjournals.org/cgi/content/full/16/3/360?etoc.

Mortimer, Edward. 1982. *Faith and Power: The Politics of Islam*. New York: Vintage Books.

Nagel, Tilman. 1994. *The History of Islamic Theology: From Muḥammad to the Present*. Munich: C. H. Beck. Trans. Thomas Thornton. Princeton NJ: Markus Wiener, 2000.

Nasr, Sayyed Hossein, ed. 1987. *Islamic Spirituality: Foundations*. New York: Crossroad.

———. 2002. *The Heart of Islam: Enduring Values for Humanity*. San Francisco: HarperSanFrancisco.

Nasr, Seyyed Hossein, Hamid Dabashi, and Seyyed Vali Reza Nasr, eds. 1988a. *Shi'ism: Doctrines, Thought, and Spirituality*. New York: State University of New York Press.

———, eds. 1988b. *Expectation of the Millennium: Shi'ism in History*. New York: State University of New York Press.

Newman, Andrew J. 2006. *Safavid Iran: Portrait of a Persian Empire*. Kindle ed.

Nicholson, R[eynold] A[lleyne]. 1914. *The Mystics of Islam*. World Wisdom, 2003.

Nizami, Khaliq Aḥmad. 1990. The Impact of Ibn Taimiyya on South Asia. *Journal of Islamic Studies* 1 (1): 120–149. https://doi.org/10.1093/jis/1.1.120. http://jis.oxfordjournals.org/cgi/content/citation/1/1/120.

Nurbakhsh, Javad (Ǧawād Nūrbaḫš/Nūrbak̲š, a Nimatullahi Sufi). 1987. *Sufi Symbolism: The Nurbakhsh Encyclopedia of Sufi Terminology*. Vol. II of Love, Lover, Beloved, Allusions and Metaphors. London: Khaniqahi Nimatullahi Publications (KNP).

———. 1988. *Sufi Symbolism: The Nurbakhsh Encyclopedia of Sufi Terminology*. Vol. III of Religious Terminology. London: Khaniqahi Nimatullahi Publications (KNP).

———. 1990. *Sufi Symbolism: The Nurbakhsh Encyclopedia of Sufi Terminology*. Vol. IV of Symbolism of the Natural World. London: Khaniqahi Nimatullahi Publications (KNP).

———. 1991. *Sufi Symbolism: The Nurbakhsh Encyclopedia of Sufi Terminology*. Vol. V of Veils and Clothing, Government, Economics and Commerce, Medicine and Healing. London: Khaniqahi Nimatullahi Publications (KNP).

———. 1992. *Sufi Symbolism: The Nurbakhsh Encyclopedia of Sufi Terminology*. Vol. VI of Titles and Epithets. London: Khaniqahi Nimatullahi Publications (KNP).

———. 1993. *Sufi Symbolism: The Nurbakhsh Encyclopedia of Sufi Terminology*. Vol. VII of Contemplative Disciplines, Visions and Theophanies, Family Relationships, ... Names of Sufi Orders (Farhang-E Nurbakhsh). London: Khaniqahi Nimatullahi Publications (KNP).

———. 1994. *Sufi Symbolism: The Nurbakhsh Encyclopedia of Sufi Terminology*. Vol. VII of Contemplative Disciplines, Sufi Symbolism: The Nurbakhsh Encyclopaedia of Sufi Terminology. Vol. VIII of Spiritual States and Mystical Stations: Inspirations, Revelations, Lights, Charismatic Powers, States and Stations, Praise and Condemnation. London: Khaniqahi Nimatullahi Publications (KNP), 1995.

———. 1995. *Sufi Symbolism: The Nurbakhsh Encyclopedia of Sufi Terminology*. Vol. IX of Spiritual Faculties, Spiritual Organs, Knowledge, Gnosis, Wisdom and Perfection. London: Khaniqahi Nimatullahi Publications (KNP).

———. 1996. *Sufi Symbolism: The Nurbakhsh Encyclopaedia of Sufi Terminology*. Vol. X of Spiritual States and Mystical Stations. London: Khaniqahi Nimatullahi Publications (KNP).

———. 1997a. *Sufi Symbolism: The Nurbakhsh Encyclopaedia of Sufi Terminology*. Vol. XI of Spiritual States and Mystical Stations. London: Khaniqahi Nimatullahi Publications (KNP).

———. 1997b. *Sufi Symbolism: The Nurbakhsh Encyclopaedia of Sufi Terminology*. Vol. XII of Spiritual States and Mystical Stations. London: Khaniqahi Nimatullahi Publications (KNP).

———. 1998. *Sufi Symbolism: The Nurbakhsh Encyclopedia of Sufi Terminology*. Vol. XIII of Scribes, Pens, Tablets, Koranic Letters, Words, Discourse, Speech, Divine Names, Attributes and Essence. London: Khaniqahi Nimatullahi Publications (KNP).

———. 1999. *Sufi Symbolism: The Nurbakhsh Encyclopedia of Sufi Terminology*. Vol. XIV of The Unity of Being. London: Khaniqahi Nimatullahi Publications (KNP).

———. 2000. *Sufi Symbolism: The Nurbakhsh Encyclopedia of Sufi Terminology*. Vol. XV of The Terms Relating to Reality, the Divine Attributes and the Sufi Path. London: Khaniqahi Nimatullahi Publications (KNP).

———. 2003. *Sufi Symbolism: The Nurbakhsh Encyclopedia of Sufi Terminology: General Index*. London: Khaniqahi Nimatullahi Publications (KNP).

Nusseibeh, Sari. 2017. *The Story of Reason in Islam*. Stanford, CA: Stanford University Press.

Ohlander, Erik S. 2008. *Sufism in an Age of Transition: 'umar Al-suhrawardi and the Rise of the Islamic Mystical Brotherhood*, Islamic History and Civilization. Leiden: Brill.

Ormsby, Eric L. 2007. *Ghazali: The Revival of Islam*, Makers of the Muslim World. Oxford, UK: Oneworld.

Otto, Rudolf. 1932. *Mysticism East and West: A Comparative Analysis of the Nature of Mysticism*. Trans. Bertha L. Bracey and Richenda C. Payne. New York: Macmillan.

Patai, Raphael. 1976. *The Arab Mind*. New York: Scribner's, Publishing.

Pemberton, Kelly. 2010. *Women Mystics and Sufi Shrines in India*, Studies in Comparative Religion. Ed. Frederick M. Denny. Columbia: University of South Carolina Press.

Pennel, C.R. Morocco. 2003. *From Empire to Independence*. Oneworld: Oxford, UK.

Peters, F.E. 1994. *The Hajj: The Muslim Pilgrimage to Mecca and the Holy Places*. Princeton, NJ: Princeton University Press, 1995.

Peters, Rudolph, ed. 1996. *Jihad: A History in Documents*. Princeton, NJ: Princeton University Press, 2005.

Peters, F.E. 2003. *The Monotheists: Jews, Christians, and Muslims in Conflict and Competition*. 2 vols. Princeton, NJ: Princeton University Press.

Peters, Rudolph, ed. 2015. *Jihad in Classical and Modern Islam: A Reader*. Princeton, NJ: Markus Wiener.

Pignon, Tatiana. 2018. Averroès et al-Ghazâlî, une controverse entre philosophie et théologie. *Les clés du Moyen-Orient* 22 June 2012. https://www.lesclesdumoyenorient.com/Averroes-et-al-Ghazali-une.html.

Pisani, Emmanuel. 2014. L'approche humaniste d'Abū Ḥamid al-Ghazālī (m. 505/1111). *Studia Islamica* 109 (1): 117–146. https://www.jstor.org/stable/43577559.

Popovic, Alexandre. 1999. *The Revolt of African Slaves in Iraq in the 3rd/9th Century*. Trans. Léon King. Princeton, NJ: Markus Weiner.

Quinn, Charlotte A., and Frederick Quinn. 2003. *Pride, Faith, and Fear: Islam in Sub-Saharan Africa*. New York: Oxford University Press.

Qur'an, Sufi surat. 1996. In *Early Islamic Mysticism*, Classics of Western Spirituality, ed. Michael A. Sells. Mahwah, NJ: Paulist Press.

Quraishi, Asifa. 2008. Taking Shari'a Seriously. Rvw Noah Feldman. In *The Fall and Rise of the Islamic State*. Princeton, NJ: Princeton University Press. In *Constitutional Commentary* 26(2010) University of Minnesota Repository. https://conservancy.umn.edu/bitstream/handle/11299/170642/26_02_BR_Quraishi.pdf;sequence=1.

Rahman, Fazlur. 1999. *Revival and Reform in Islam: A Study of Islamic Fundamentalism*. London: Oneworld Academic.

Rapoport, Yossef, and Shahab Ahmed, eds. 2010. *Ibn Taymiyya and His Times*. Karachi: Oxford University Press.

Reeves, Minou. 2000. *Muhammed in Europe*. Reading, UK: Garnet.

Reid, Megan H. 2017. *Law and Piety in Medieval Islam*, Cambridge Studies in Islamic Civiization. Cambridge: Cambridge University Press.

Renard, John. 2005. *Historical Dictionary of Sufism*, Historical Dictionaries of Religions, Philosophies, and Movements Series. Lanham, MD: Scarecrow Press.

Renard, John, and Ahmet T. Karamustafa, ed. and trans. 2004. *Knowledge of God in Classical Sufism: Foundations of Islamic Mystical Theology*. Classics of Western Spirituality, Vol. 9. Mahwah, NJ: Paulist Press.

Riddell, Peter G. 2017. *Malay Court Religion, Culture and Language. Interpreting the Qurān in 17th Century Aceh*, Texts and Studies on the Qur'ān. Vol. 12. Leiden: Brill.

Ridgeon, Lloyd V.J. 2008. *Sufism: Critical Concepts*, Critical Concepts in Islamic Studies. Vol. 4 vols. New York: Routledge.

———. 2010. *Morals and Mysticism in Persian Sufism: A History of Sufi-Futuwwat in Iran*, Routledge Sufi Series. New York: Routledge.

———. 2015. *The Cambridge Companion to Sufism*. Cambridge: Cambridge University Press.

Rizvi, Sajjad, and Rvw Kiki Kennedy-Day. 2005. *Books of Definition in Islamic Philosophy: The Limit of Words*. (London: RoutledgeCurzon, 2003). *Journal of Islamic Studies* 16: 362–366. http://jis.oxfordjournals.org/cgi/content/full/16/3/362?etoc.

Robinson, Chase F. 2003. *Islamic Historiography*. Cambridge: Cambridge University Press.

———, ed. 2010. *The New Cambridge History of Islam*. Vol. 1 of The Formation of the Islamic World, Sixth to Eleventh Centuries. Cambridge: Cambridge University Press.

Rodinson, Maxime. 2002. *Muhammad*. Trans. Anne Carter. New York: New Press.

Rogerson, Barnaby. 2008. *The Heirs of Muhammad: Islam's First Century and the Origins of the Sunni-Shia Split*. Woodstock: Overlook Press.

Rosen, Lawrence. 2003. *The Culture of Islam: Changing Aspects of Contemporary Muslim Life*. Chicago: University of Chicago Press.

Rousseau, Jean Baptiste Louis Jacques. 1899. *Voyage de Bagdad à Alep*, MS 1808. Ed. Louis Poinssot. Paris: J. André. (Firsthand account of "Wehabis" and "Wehabisme"—Wahhabiya—93–106. https://archive.org/details/voyagedebagdadal00rous/page/114/mode/2up?q=Wehabis).

Roy-Bhattacharya, Joydeep. 2011. *The Storyteller of Marrakesh: A Novel*. New York: Norton, Kindle ed.

Rozehnal, Robert Thomas. 2009. *Islamic Sufism Unbound: Politics and Piety in Twenty-First Century Pakistan*. New York: Palgrave Macmillan.

———. 2019. *Cyber Sufis: Virtual Expressions of the American Muslim Experience*. Oxford, UK: Oneworld.

Rumi, Maulana Jalalu-'d-din Muhammad. 2009. *The Masnavi I Ma'anavi of Rumi, Complete 6 Books*. Ed. E. H. Whinfield. Kindle eBook.

Ruthven, Malise. 1997. *Islam: A Very Short Introduction*. New York: Oxford University Press. Reprint 2000, Kindle ed. 2012.

Sabzvārī, Muḥammad 'Alī. 2007. *Tuhfah-yi 'Abbasi: The Golden Chain of Sufism in Shi'ite Islam*. Trans. Mohammad H. Faghfoory. Lanham, MD: University Press of America.

Sachedina, Abdulaziz. 2000. *The Islamic Roots of Democratic Pluralism*. New York: Oxford University Press.

Safi, Omid. 2006. *The Politics of Knowledge in Premodern Islam: Negotiating Ideology and Religious Inquiry*, Islamic Civilization and Muslim Networks. Chapel Hill: The University of North Carolina Press.

Safran Janina, M. 2014. The Politics of Book Burning in al-Andalus. *Journal of Medieval Iberian Studies* 6 (2): 148–168. https://www.tandfonline.com/doi/abs/10.1080/17546559.2014.925134.

Salaymeh, Lena. 2016. *The Beginnings of Islamic Law: Late Antique Islamicate Legal Traditions*. Cambridge: Cambridge University Press. http://www.cambridge.org/us/academic/subjects/history/middle-east-history/beginnings-islamic-law-late-antique-islamicate-legal-traditions#AJM8o2H8clc6RxLUniversity99.

Schimmel, Annemarie. 1975. *Mystical Dimensions of Islam*. Chapel Hill: University of North Carolina Press. (Sufism).

Segal, Ronald. 2001. *Islam's Black Slaves: The Other Black Diaspora*. New York: Farrar, Straus & Giroux, 2002.

Sells, Michael A., ed. 1996. *Early Islamic Mysticism*, Classics of Western Spirituality. Mahwah, NJ: Paulist Press. (*Qur'an*, *Mi'Raj*, Ja'far as-Sadiq, Sahl at-Tustari, al-Qushayri, Rabi'a, al-Muhasibi, Sarraj, al-Bistami, Junayd, al-Hallaj, Niffari, Shahrastani).

Shah-Kazemi, Reza. 2002. The Notion and Significance of *Ma'rifa* in Sufism. *Journal of Islamic Studies* 13 (2): 155–181.

Shaikh, Sa'diyya. 2012. *Sufi Narratives of Intimacy: Ibn 'Arabī, Gender, and Sexuality*, Islamic Civilization and Muslim Networks. Chapel Hill: The University of North Carolina Press.

Shehadeh, Lamia Rustum. 2003. *The Idea of Women in Fundamentalist Islam*. Gainesville: University Press of Florida.

Shepherd, William H., Jr. 1987. Is There an Islamic Fundamentalism? *Christian Century*: 85. © Christian Century Foundation and used by permission. www.christiancentury.org.

Silvers, Laury. 2010. *A Soaring Minaret: Abu Bakr al-Wasiti [d. 932 CE] and the Rise of Baghdadi Sufism*. New York: State University of New York Press.

Silverstein, Adam J. 2010. *Islamic History (A Very Short Introduction)*. New York: Oxford University Press, Kindle ed.

Sirriyeh, Elizabeth. 2015. *Dreams and Visions in the World of Islam: A History of Muslim Dreaming and Foreknowing*, Library of Modern Religion. London: I. B. Tauris.

Sivan, Emmanuel. 1985. *Radical Islam: Medieval Theory and Modern Politics*. New Haven, CT: Yale University Press.

Smith, Margaret, ed. 1928. *Rabi'a The Mystic and Her Fellow-Saints in Islam*. Cambridge: Cambridge University Press, 2010.

———, ed. 1994. *Readings from the Mystics of Islam*. New York: Pir Press.

———, ed. 2001. *Muslim Women Mystics: The Life and Work of Rabi'a and Other Women Mystics in Islam (1928?)*. Oxford: Oneworld.

———, ed. 2010. *Al-Ghazali the Mystic (1944)*. Delhi: Adam Publishers IND.

———. 2020. Rābiʻa al-ʻAdawiyya al-Qaysiyya. In *Encyclopaedia of Islam*, ed. P. Bearman, Th. Bianquis, C.E. Bosworth, E. van Donzel, and W.P. Heinrichs, vol. 8, 2nd ed. Leiden: Brill. https://referenceworks.brillonline.com/browse/encyclopaedia-of-islam-2/alphaRange/R%20-%20Rg/R.

Starr, S. Frederick. 2013. *Lost Enlightenment: Central Asia's Golden Age from the Arab Conquest to Tamerlane*. Princeton, NJ: Princeton University Press, Kindle ed.

Stroumsa, Sarah. 1999. *Freethinkers of Medieval Islam: Ibn Al-Rawandi, Abu Bakr Al-Razi and Their Impact on Islamic Thought*. Leiden: Brill.

Talbi, Mohamed (b. 1921). 1989. Religious Liberty: A Muslim Perspective. *Liberty and Conscience* I (1): 12–20.

Tamer, George, ed. 2015. *Islam and Rationality: The Impact of al-Ghazali: Papers Collected in his 900th Anniversary*. Vol. 1. Leiden: Brill.

Tetley, G.E. 2014. *The Ghaznavid and Seljuk Turks: Poetry as a Source for Iranian History*, Routledge Studies in the History of Iran and Turkey. New York: Routledge, Kindle ed.

Thornton, John K. 1992. *Africa and the Africans in the Making of the Atlantic World, 1400–1680*. Cambridge: Cambridge University Press.

Trimingham, J. Spencer. 1998. *The Sufi Orders in Islam (1971)*, New foreword by John O. Voll. New York: Oxford University Press, pb.

Trombley, Frank R. 2004. The Arabs in Anatolia and the Islamic Law of War (*fiqh al-jihad*) Seventh-Tenth Centuries. *Al-Masaq: Islam and the Medieval Mediterranean* 16 (1): 147–161.

Wadud, Amina. 1999. *Qur'ān and Woman: Rereading the Sacred Text from a Woman's Perspective*. 2nd ed. New York: Oxford University Press.

Walbridge, John. 2001. *The Wisdom of the Mystic East: Suhrawardi [1154–1191] and Platonic Orientalism*. New York: State University of New York Press. Rvw Mehdi Aminrazavi, *Journal of Islamic Studies* 15:3(September 2004), 350–351. http://www3.oup.co.uk/islamj/hdb/Volume_15/Issue_03/eth306.sgm.abs.html.

Ware, Rudolph T., III. 2014. *The Walking Qur'an: Islamic Education, Embodied Knowledge, and History in West Africa*, Islamic Civilization and Muslim Networks. Chapel Hill: University of North Carolina Press.

Warraq, Ibn. 2001a. *The Quest for the Historical Muhammad*. Trans. Ibn Warraq. New York: Prometheus Books, .

———. 2001b. *What the Koran Really Says: Language, Text, and Commentary*. Trans. Ibn Warraq. New York: Prometheus Books, 2003.
———. 2003. *Leaving Islam: Apostates Speak Out*. New York: Prometheus Books.
———. 2020. *Leaving the Allah Delusion Behind: Atheism and Freethought in Islam*. Berlin: Schiler & Mücke.
Werbner, Pnina. 2002. *Pilgrims of Love: The Anthropology of a Global Sufi Cult*. Bloomington: Indiana University Press.
Wheeler, Brannon. 2006. *Mecca and Eden: Ritual, Relics, and Territory in Islam*. Chicago: University of Chicago Press.
Whitfield, Susan. 2015. *Life Along the Silk Road*. 2nd ed. Berkeley: University of California Press, Kindle ed.
Wills, Garry. 2017. *What the Qur'an Meant: And Why It Matters*. New York: Viking. (Finds the word "Shariah" only once in the Qur'an, meaning, not 'law', but 'path'.).

Chapter 9
The Crucible of the Counter-Enlightenment, VI

Abstract Eighteenth-century reform in Islam, Muhammad Ibn abd al-Wahhab, and Shah Waliullah. Piety to militant moralism. Salafism reborn and its future.

In the 1122nd year of the Hijra of the Prophet Muḥammad, 1744–1745 C.E., as George Whitefield was once again bringing Methodist revivalism to New England and Rousseau was writing music in Paris, a deal was struck in the farming village of al-Dirʿiyah in the arid center of Arabia between two men who shared the Prophet's name, Muḥammad ibn ʿAbd al-Waḥhab (1703–1792), a local Muslim jurist and former Ṣufi, and Muḥammad ibn al-Saʿud (d. 1765), the emir of al-Dirʿiyah. The agreement of the two Muḥammads was to result in the most militantly evangelical movement in Islam since the Almohad conquest of North Africa and Spain in the twelfth century, and to a kingdom, Saudi Arabia, that exists today. With Ibn ʿAbd al-Waḥhab and his descendants as its *imams* (congregation leaders) and al-Saʿud and his heirs as its *emirs* (military and political commanders), it would spread over Arabia, then east to Iraq (and by proxy to Afghanistan and India), meeting its opponents, usually professed fellow Muslims, with fire and sword. The movement would insist on the elimination of all potential diluters of the oneness of Allah, including the Shiʿi Muslims, and perhaps especially, the Ṣufi shaikhs and other marabouts (in arabic, *murabitun*), holy men, their tombs, and the people who revered them. For ibn ʿAbd al-Waḥhab, religious experience had to be subordinated to religious law.

The Waḥhabiya movement followed an older pattern that had begun emerging early in Islam's conflicted political history, in the several forms of Shiʿa, each in expectation of a last imam, and among the Sunni who insisted that all believers must be equal in submission (*islam*) to God so that none could be greater than another, but who nevertheless hoped for a "*mahdi*," a messiah descended from the Prophet of Islam, whose return was to redeem the planet for the true faith. It would produce many more examples, particularly in Africa and the Maghrib, or Islamic West. In fact, Waḥhabism would have a major effect in reestablishing that pattern after the coming of European imperialism.

The paradigmatic story goes something like this: a young man from the provinces who has had a taste of Ṣufi mysticism from a Ṣufi *tariq*, or tradition, studies

W. R. Everdell, *The Evangelical Counter-Enlightenment*, Boston Studies in Philosophy, Religion and Public Life 9,
https://doi.org/10.1007/978-3-030-69762-4_9

God's law (*shariah*) and Muslim jurisprudence (*fiqh*) in one or more of the great university cities of Dar al-Islam. He returns home, dissatisfied with Sufism's ontological uncertainty and unable to make his Ṣufi ecstasies (if any) repeatable, to impose law instead and to bring his neighbors to God's true service. At first he fails and retreats to the less civilized parts of Dar al-Islam, where he is joined by followers, as Muḥammad himself had been joined at Medina. Like first Prophet he returns at the head of an army of his own, or one led by a sympathetic commander (*emir*), to impose the true shariʿah by force both holy and military.[1] Out of the wilderness, filled with the "knowledge of God," these armies of religious certainty had come and worked their will.

The pattern recurs from the far west of Islam in Morocco, Iberia and the Sudan to the far east; from the North African Fatimids of ʿAbdullāh al-Mahdi Billah (909–934) to the Almoravids of Abdullāh ibn Yasin (d. 1059), and the Almohads of Muhammed ibn Tumart (c1080–1130), whose successor burned the books of the great Muslim rationalist, Averroës. Later came the Saadi of Abu Abdallah al-Qaim bi Amrillah (1509–1517), the Fulani of Nasr al-Din (d. 1674), Karamokho Alfa (d. 1751), Usman ibn Fudi or dan Fodio (1754–1817), Seku Amadu (1776–1845), and ʿUmar Tall (c1797–1864). In the 1880s in the eastern Sudan, the self-proclaimed Mahdi, Muḥammad Ahmed (1844–1885), raised a huge army of followers that captured Khartoum with spears and swords, only to be annihilated by an Anglo-Egyptian force armed with rifles and artillery, as holy war against the *kafir* turned into anti-colonial rebellion.[2] Out of south and southeast Asia came jihadists from the India of Shah Waliullah ("King Friend-of-God" 1703–1762), Sayyid Ahmed Barelvi (1786–1831) and Wilayat ʿAlī (1791–1853) to the Sumatra of Tuanku Haji Miskin, whose hijra in 1803 was a haj to Mecca itself, a retreat from which he brought Waḥhabi Islam back to Sumatra, and of Muhamad Saman (or Teungku Chik di Tiro, 1836–1891), who learned to hate colonialism on his own *haj* two generations later.

The stories are rarely put together so that a pattern can emerge, and even when they are, many important commonalities are left out. All those "syeds" or "sayyids" mark the descendants of the sons of Muḥammad's daughter, Fatima, and son-in-law Ali, and those who bear this name and title are therefore in the same family line as the hidden Twelfth Imam of the Twelver Shiʿa, or the Mahdi, the Prophet-descended messiah of Islam. All those self-exiles or withdrawals into the hinterland echo the first *hijra*, the Hegira of the Prophet Muḥammad to Medina in Year One of the Muslim calendar. Moreover, in nearly every case, the founding imam of a new movement will have turned out to be or to have once been a Ṣufi initiate, like al-Ghazali and Ibn Taymiyyah and the Mahdi of Sudan, only to become an exclusivist

---

[1] Nehemia Levtzion, "The Eighteenth Century: Background to the Islamic Revolutions in West Africa," in Levtzion & Voll, eds., *Eighteenth-Century Renewal and Reform in Islam*, Syracuse, NY: Syracuse U.P., 1987.

[2] "Ancient and modern confronted one another." wrote one eyewitness to the Mahdist debacle, a young imperial officer named Winston Churchill, in Chapters 14 and 15 of *A Roving Commission: My Early Life* (New York: Scribner's, 1930).

critic of some of the most central—and ecstatic—of Ṣufi practices. Such was the case of Muḥammad ibn ʿAbd al-Waḥhab of Nejd.

He had been born in 1702 or 1703, in a mid-Arabian town called al-Uyaynah in the arid province of Nejd or Najd, into a family of Muslim jurists, *qadi*s, *muftis* and *ulama* scholars, all of the Hanbali school which puts law above mysticism and speculative theology; and he had set out early to become an expert himself in the wide field of *fiqh*, or Muslim jurisprudence. There is nothing occult or mystical about *fiqh*; it is not knowledge of the divine nature, or experience of it, but knowledge of law and practice, both divinely given as *shari'ah* in the written Recitation (*Qur'an*) of the Word of God and the collected oral "hadiths," the firsthand stories from the lifetime of the Prophet Muḥammad. It had long been axiomatic for Muslims that the *Qur'an* was the supreme authority (as it is still). Muḥammad, who had received it, was the next authority as best it could be known through reports (*aḥadith*) of his acts and sayings. Ibn ʿAbd al-Waḥhab's first teachers had taught him to memorize the Qur'an, which he had done by the age of ten. The next step had been study, which Ibn ʿAbd al-Waḥhab had begun with his father al-Waḥhab, and continued with a hajj pilgrimage to Mecca, followed by a trip to neighboring Medina where the Prophet of Islam, his namesake, had died and been entombed after founding the first *ummah*, or Muslim community more than a thousand years before (Figs. 9.1 and 9.2).

Muḥammad ibn ʿAbd al-Waḥhab had arrived in Mecca at the age of 27, and after performing the rites of the hajj, had gone to Medina, once the Prophet's refuge, now a city of schools and scholars, for two years or more. There he studied the many duties Allah required of a Muslim, and the many ways one might come to know them with certainty. He had had several teachers there, according to the sources, and all of them taught *aḥadith* in the newer way, with more attention to the moral and legal content of the deeds or sayings reported in them than to the authenticity of the report's origins, an attitude which some historians have begun to call an Islamic Enlightenment.[3] One teacher was from al-Waḥhab's own home province of Nejd, Shaikh ʿAbd Allah ibn Ibrahim ibn Sayf.[4] But two others were admirers of that thirteenth-century scholar, Ibn Taymiyyah, who had followed al-Ghazali in denouncing Aristotelian science and who had pronounced the "jihad fatwa" by which no Muslim could remain neutral in a religious war. One of these Taymiyites,[5]

---

[3] For more than one recent scholar of eighteenth-century Islam, this change in ḥadith studies has looked like a sort of Islamic "Enlightenment" (a movement that seems required for the appearance of a Counter-Enlightenment). Among books in English on this are Bernard Haykel's *Revival and Reform in Islam: The Legacy of Muḥammad al-Shawkani* (Cambridge: Cambridge U. P., 2003); and even more recently Ahmed S. Dallal's *Islam without Europe: Traditions of Reform in Eighteenth-Century Islamic Thought* (Islamic Civilization and Muslim Networks) (Chapel Hill: University of North Carolina Press. Kindle Edition, 2018).

[4] Natana J. DeLong-Bas, *Wahhabi Islam: From Revival and Reform to Global Jihad*, (New York: Oxford U.P., 2004), p. 20. A non-western point of view on ʿAbd al-Waḥhab is offered in English by ʿAbd Allah al-Salih ʿUthaymin Darat al-Malik ʿAbd al'Aziz, in *Muḥammad ibn ʿAbd al-Wahhāb: the man and his works*, (London: I.B. Tauris & Co. Ltd, 2009).

[5] I find the coinage "Taymiyite" hard to resist, given the distinctive binary black and white starkness of Ibn Taymiyyah's ethical and intellectual positions, and their tendency to be recalled by

Fig. 9.1 The Tuwaiq Escarpment on the Nejd plateau viewed from the west. The second Saudi capital city, Riyadh, lies just beyond the horizon. (Photo By Baptiste Marcel, Public Domain, https://commons.wikimedia.org/w/index.php?curid=3957052)

Fig. 9.2 al-Uyayna ("the little spring"), birthplace of Muhammad ibn abd al-Wahhab. (no contemporary images of Wahhabi founders is known to exist). (Photo by haitham alfalah—Own work, CC BY 3.0, https://commons.wikimedia.org/w/index.php?curid=22966390)

Muḥammad Ḥayyā al-Sindī, from India, was both a jurist of the Shaf'i school and a Ṣufi of the not-so-ecstatic Naqshabandi *tariqa*, and could have been one of those who exposed ʿAbd al-Waḥhab to Sufism. The other Taymiyite, Ibrahim al-Kurani, was remembered by Shah Waliullah, graduate of a Ṣufi madrassa and Ibn ʿAbd al-Waḥhab's fellow student, as the teacher who introduced him to the ideas of Ibn Taymiyyah in those same years.[6] With teachers like these, Ibn ʿAbd al-Waḥhab spent three or four years in Medina. Then, in 1732, some sources have him drifting off to Iraq, spending the next eight or nine years in al-Majmu'i, a small town near the Shiʿi city of Basra, with a man named Muḥammad, whose ideas are not recorded but who may have been a Ṣufi. From Basra (according to a source more hospitable to legend) Ibn ʿAbd al-Waḥhab is said to have also wandered to Syria, Kurdistan, or as far as the Shiʿi strongholds of Qum and Isfahan in Iran.[7]

---

militants in every century since the fourteenth CE. Of course, any use of the suffixes "-ite" or "-ism" suggests an organized intellectual movement, like the Kharijites who assassinated ʿAli in 661; but it must be stated right here that Taymyites were not organized and that "Taymyism" was neither a sect, nor a school nor a movement, only a recurring and recognizeable referent.

[6] John Voll has provided a carefully articulated roster of 'Abd al-Wahhab's Medinese teachers and fellow-scholars, with their Taymiyite and Naqshabandiya Sufi affiliations, in his article "Muḥammad Ḥayyā al-Sindī and Muḥammad ibn 'Abd al-Waḥhab: An Analysis of an Intellectual Group in Eighteenth-Century Madīna". *Bulletin of the School of Oriental and African Studies, University of London*, (Cambridge University Press) 38:1(1975): 32–39. It follows on Voll's "Linking Groups in the Networks of Eighteenth-Century Revivalist Scholars: The Mizjaji Family in Yemen," in Levtzion & Voll, eds., *Eighteenth-Century Renewal and Reform in Islam*, Syracuse, NY: Syracuse U.P., 1987.

[7] Separating mythography from history is as difficult for al-Waḥhab as it is for the Baal Shem Tov. The preferred, least legendary contemporary source for al-Waḥhab's biography is a superb book by Hammadi Redissi that covers both the founder and his legacy up to the present, *Une histoire du wahhabisme: Comment l'Islam sectaire est devenu l'Islam*, (2007) Paris: Éditions du Seuil (pb Points), 2016. The best contemporary non-Western source for al-Waḥhab's biography is *Unwan al-Majd fi tarikh Najd* (Beirut, 1387 AH (1967–1968)), by contemporary Saudi historian ʿUthman bin ʿAbdullah bin Bishr, which has, unfortunately for me, not been translated into a European language; but ʿAbd Allah al-Salih ʿUthaymin Darat al-Malik ʿAbd al'Aziz makes full use of it in his *Muḥammad ibn 'Abd al-Wahhāb: the man and his works*, (London: I.B. Tauris & Co. Ltd, 2009). The full Saudi point of view presented in English can be found in Jamaal al-Din M. Zarabozo, *The Life, Teachings and Influence of Muḥammad Ibn Abdul-Wahhaab* (Ministry of Islamic Affairs, Endowments, Dawah and Guidance, The Kingdom of Saudi Arabia, 2003) and somewhat less officially in the chapter by ʿAbd Allāh ibn Muḥammad ibn Husayn Abu Dāhish, "The Rise of Muḥammad ibn ʿAbd al-Wahhāb's Da'wa [Mission] in the Southern Arabian Peninsula," Ch. 8 of Fahd al-Semmari, *A History of the Arabian Penisula*, tr., Salma K. Jayyusi (London: I.B. Tauris, in association with the King Abdul Aziz Foundation for Research and Archives, 2010). Hamid Algar, in *Wahhabism: A Critical Essay* (Oneonta, NY: Islamic Publications International, 2002), considers all the travel stories and concludes (based on bin Bishr's account) that ibn ʿAbd al-Wahhab did go to al-Majmu'a (now in Sudan) and Basra (in Shiʿi southern Iraq), but that the 9 years visit to Baghdad is an imitative myth, perpetrated by the anonymous biography of 1817 *Lam' al-Shihab fi sirat Muḥammad Ibn Abd al-Wahhāb* (Cairo: Éditions Abu Hakima, 1967), as are three of the visits to Shiʿa Iran: Kurdistan, Hamadhan and Isfahan. (pp. 12–13). Algar does however think that ibn ʿAbd al-Waḥhab's visit to Qum, which is also a city in Iran, and more Shiʿa than most, was possible. Hammadi Redissi agrees, and adds Basra.

We cannot make much more out of Ibn ʿAbd al-Waḥhab's fragmentary biography. Most contemporary reports of his rise came either from Muslims understandably hostile to his movement, or from non-Muslim Europeans ill-equipped to understand it. No one who saw him, friend or foe, seems to have left any record of what he looked like, and Ibn ʿAbd al-Waḥhab himself might well have thought it idolatrous to wonder. Even today, the official journal of the Waḥhabi ulama of Saudi Arabia follows Hanbali *fiqh* in refusing to print complete pictures of any of Allah's creatures, especially human beings. However, we can safely assume that the reformer had a beard, since one of the injunctions in his legal works forbids cutting one off.

The beard is easy to determine, but we cannot so safely assume the reasons that brought Ibn ʿAbd al-Waḥhab to define so many of his fellow Muslims as *kafir*, non-Muslims, idolaters outside the true faith, on whom a true Muslim like himself had a duty to make war. It seems possible only to guess, according to the precedent pattern, that during his studies with the Naqshabandi Ṣufi scholar Ḥayyā al-Sindī at Medina and the Shiʿi scholars of Qum and Basra, Muḥammad ibn ʿAbd al-Waḥhab had taken a close look at Islam's ecstatic practices and doctrines, possibly even tried them, and emerged disappointed, unsympathetic and ultimately hostile. About the only thing that Sufism might have given him is the courage to trust his own religious experience—or the lack of such experience—in his own way. We know from his later writings that he had decided, contrary to wisdom received in most of Islamic jurisprudence since the tenth century that his own reason and judgment (*ijtihad*) could contradict decisions that the four schools of Islamic *fiqh* might have concluded from the Sunna (tradition). The first and most important of his handful of books, *Kitab al-Tawhid* (Book of the Singleness, Unicity, of God), 66 short chapters of *aḥadith*, compiled without much commentary, is an effort to demonstrate that the idolatry condemned by the Prophet and the *Qur'an* must include time-honored practices like the veneration of tombs, and the "saints" within, whether they be Ṣufi or Salafi.

Neither this *Book of Unicity* nor any other of al-Waḥhab's works can honestly be called extensive.[8] Hamid Algar, a scholar who has read in the multivolume annotated Saudi edition, concludes that, once the modern footnotes and other apparatus have been set aside, all the writings of Ibn ʿAbd al-Waḥhab amount to little more than similar short collections of *aḥadith* accompanied by notes so spare that they seem to have been added by a beginning student.[9] This sort of scholarship must have

[8] Collected recently in a monumental annotated edition of several large volumes by the Wahhabi Muslim scholars of Saudi Arabia, *Mu'allafat al-Shaikh al-Imam Muḥammad ibn Abd al-Waḥhab* (Riyadh: Jamiat al-Imam Muḥammad bin Saud al-Islamiyah, 1398H ff), the works of Ibn ʿAbd al-Waḥhab still betray their original spareness, for which one volume would probably have been enough. Hamid Algar provides English translations for a few of these in an appendix to his *Wahhabism: A Critical Essay*.

[9] Hamid Algar, *Wahhabism: A Critical Essay*, 2002, pp. 13–16. Natana DeLong-Bas is more respectful of al-Waḥhab's spareness, attributing it to the new (and, in a sense, Enlightened) eighteenth-century approaches to ḥadith study; but, sensibly, she makes no attempt to present Ibn ʿAbd

made it easier for Ibn ʿAbd al-Waḥhab to take an overwhelmingly negative attitude toward both ecstatic and popular Islamic practice when he had begun writing about *shari'ah* after his return to Arabia.

This cannot have been much before 1740, the year his father died. Muḥammad ibn ʿAbd al-Waḥhab had ended his *hijra* and returned (probably from Syria) to Arabia, to the village of Huraymila, the village in the province of Nejd to which his jurist father had gone after they had both been thrown out of their hometown of al-ʿUyayna for contumacy and schism. Discouraged from preaching, he busied himself writing the *Book of Unicity* which expanded the definitions not only of *shirk* (idolatry, or associating created things with God) and *bida* (anything novel), but also of *kufir* (unbelief in general). He had been contentious before his Medina studies, but he was now so sure of his orthodoxy that he began to take on the village.

On his father's death in 1740, the son, still unmarried, had succeeded to his father's legal office and begun to preach what he had learned, which was wholesale reform of belief and practice according to his own theological plan. He had begun with the Qur'anic injunction to confine all sex to marriage, a stricture which some of the townspeople of Huraymila had taken rather badly—they had tried to kill him—and he had prudently fled.[10] Back at his hometown of al-ʿUyaynah, he had concluded his first pact with a politician, the *emir* (commander or warlord) of al-ʿUyayna, a man named ʿUthman ibn Hamid ibn Mu'ammar. Ibn ʿAbd al-Waḥhab would offer his services as the emir's *imam*, religious leader of the *ummah* (muslim community) and adviser on God's law (shari'ah), if Ibn Mu'ammar would be Ibn ʿAbd al-Waḥhab's emir and command the ummah in jihad. To seal the bargain, the emir would marry his daughter to the imam, ending Ibn ʿAbd al-Waḥhab's long (and presumably Qur'anically celibate) bachelorhood. He was 35. No one has reported whether any experience close to ecstasy followed Ibn ʿAbd al-Waḥhab's wedding (as the former monk, Martin Luther, had reported following his own).

Ibn ʿAbd al-Waḥhab had then proceeded to cement his position as imam with three deeds that were remembered by his followers as exemplary. The first was to cut down a tree, one of a grove of trees which the Uyaynese were in the habit of invoking for blessings and on which they hung offerings. In the view of the new imam, the trees were being honored to the point of veneration and even worship, inspiring idolatry or *shirk*, the greatest sin in Islam. Therefore, they had to be destroyed as the Prophet had destroyed the idols of the Ka'aba in Mecca. Ibn ʿAbd

al-Waḥhab as a thinker ranking with his younger contemporary, Muḥammad al-Shawkani (1760–1834) of neighboring Yemen (Bernard Haykel's exemplar), much less with the great philosophers and theologians of Islam's first millennium, from Abu Hanifa and Ibn Sina to al-Ghazali, Averroës and Ibn ʿArabī. (DeLong-Bas, *Wahhabi Islam*, 2004, pp. 10–11, 46–47, 51–53). Michael Crawford's new short introduction, *Ibn Abd al-Wahhab* (Oxford, UK: Oneworld, Makers of the Muslim World, 2014), is precise and well-informed, and makes much the same judgment.

[10] This detail I find only in Charles Allen, *God's Terrorists, The Wahhabi Cult and the Hidden Roots of Modern Jihad* (Cambridge: Da Capo Press, 2006), p51. The rest of al-Waḥhab's early biography can be found very well sourced in Hammadi Redissi, *Une histoire du wahhabisme* (2007), pp51–60.

al-Waḥhab sent out his followers, who cut down all but the most venerated, which the imam himself came later and finished off. (There is a ḥadith which condemns the destruction of trees when fighting infidels[11] but this ḥadith does not appear in the arguments about the sacred tree of al-ʿUyaynah.)

Ibn al-Waḥhab's second exemplary deed was to tear down the monument over the local tomb of Zayd ibn al-Khattab, a well known and universally respected Companion of the Prophet, the brother of the world-conquering third Caliph of Islam, ʿUmar ibn al-Khattab, and claimed as an ancestor by the early "Zaydi" imams of Yemen. Again the reason given was idolatry, *shirk*. People were visiting and venerating the tomb, in much the same way as Luther's contemporaries had visited and venerated the bones of saints. The Prophet of Islam had long been quoted in a ḥadith ordering the destruction of venerated tombs, and the Prophet's own grave in Medina had survived many generations without a tomb monument, a combination of authorities which brooked no dissent. Ibn ʿAbd al-Waḥhab tore down Zayd's monument with his own hands as the local beneficiaries of the pilgrim trade watched in anger. Emir Ibn Muʿammar stood by with an armed force to make sure no one interfered.

The third exemplary deed was aimed not at *shirk* but at the somewhat more ordinary sin of adultery, or *zina'*, one of the four for which, muslim jurists had long agreed, the *aḥadith* prescribed the death penalty. For adultery by a woman, a ḥadith followed the Torah and specified stoning to death. The sinner in this case was a woman who, much to the surprise of commentators then and now, came of her own free will to confess her adultery to no less an authority than Imam Muḥammad ibn ʿAbd al-Waḥhab himself. The imam, we are told, did not order the immediate stoning that the law allowed. He did not even call in her male relatives to discipline her (which would then have been considered an act of leniency). Instead he cautioned her, told her to go and sin no more, and sent her home. Was she ignorant of the law; did she not know the penalty; or was she too crazy to understand the risk of death? The imam held a sanity inquiry, which found the woman entirely lucid. He summoned her to another hearing, and asked if she were being raped. She said she wasn't, and that she intended to keep on committing *zina'*. Again she sinned, and again she confessed. On the third occasion, Imam al-Waḥhab, heeded the *ulama*, or local islamic sages, and "reluctantly" ordered the woman stoned to death.[12]

What do we learn from this about the religion of Muḥammad ibn ʿAbd al-Waḥhab? Possibly that he was not quite the medieval misogynist of western caricature. Indeed, several of his compendiums of *aḥadith* take up the subject of women, including one, *Kitab al-Nikah* (The Book of Marriage), which is devoted

[11] Abu al-Walid Muḥammad Ibn Muḥammad Ibn Rushd (Averroës), *Bidayat al-Mujtahid wa-Nihayat al-Muqtasid* [The beginning for him who interprets the sources independently and the end of him who wishes to limit himself], ca 1167 CE, in Rudolph Peters, ed., *Jihad in Classical and Modern Islam* (Princeton, NJ: Markus Wiener, 2nd ed., 2005), p36. Averroës notes that although the ḥadith says that Muḥammad allowed the destruction of trees in *jihad*, the first caliph, Abu Bakr, forbade it. Thus, the founder of the Maliki school of *fiqh* allows the destruction of trees (but not animals) in *jihad*, while the founder of the Shafiʿi *fiqh* does not.

[12] The whole odd story is put into English in DeLong-Bas, *Wahhabi Islam*, p27–29.

exclusively to the subject; and the gist of all of them is what the times would call considerably less hostile to the independence of women than many other books on muslim law.[13]

For the many Westerners of today who are tempted to consider this nameless woman a hero, I can offer only a few Western contemporaries of Ibn ʿAbd al-Waḥhab who could have agreed, none of them female, on a list which must be headed by that late-coming Enlightenment *philosophe*, the Marquis de Sade. For those many Westerners who consider stoning (recommended in the Hebrew Bible) to be obsolete, impractical, barbaric, cruel and revolting, one may cite in their favor one of the leading lights of the European Enlightenment, Cesare Beccaría (1738–1794), whose great brief against judicial torture and cruelty[14] now lies at the headwaters of more than two centuries of liberal reform of Western criminal justice. Unfortunately there seems to have been nobody like Beccaría in Ibn ʿAbd al-Waḥhab's Dar al-Islam. The regional *ulama*, for example, had pressed for the stoning, thinking Ibn ʿAbd al-Waḥhab too patient, and then when it was over, criticized the imam for leading a militant local popular opposition to legal precedent (*taqlid*) and therefore to them.[15] Ibn ʿAbd al-Waḥhab's response to this criticism was the same as ever, an appeal from the *taqlid* to the Qur'an and the *aḥadith* on which *taqlid* had originally been based, in addition to the discretion, recommended anew by contemporary judicial reformers, for imams of Ibn ʿAbd al-Waḥhab's high quality and conviction to use their own judgment (*ijtihad*) in drawing legal conclusions from them, with or without legal precedent. In fewer words, where the Qur'an is silent, Sunnah (Tradition) absolutely requires stoning women for adultery.

From here Muḥammad ibn ʿAbd al-Waḥhab might have gone from strength to strength, but he had run into trouble over his basic relationship to power. One of the neighboring lords, Sulayman ibn Muḥammad, technically a vassal of Ibn ʿAbd al-Waḥhab's emir, Ibn Mu'ammar, had applied to the emir to have Ibn ʿAbd al-Waḥhab killed for endangering the established order. Should Ibn Mu'ammar refuse, lord Sulayman had promised to withhold payment of taxes owed to the emir on his very large holdings. The emir had asked his imam what to do. Ibn ʿAbd al-Waḥhab had told him, refuse; it was a test of faith—but if this was a test, Ibn Mu'ammar had not passed it. He had tried instead to compromise by shunning the imam while sparing his life. Unappeased, Lord Sulayman had kept up the pressure until Ibn Mu'ammar had finally told Ibn ʿAbd al-Waḥhab to go away.

---

13 The books are, in addition to *Kitab al-Nikah* [The Book of Marriage], *Kitab al-Tawhid* [The Book of God's Unity] *Kitab al-Jihad* [The Book of Jihad] *Kitab Kashf al-Shubhat* [The Book of Detecting Doubt], and *Risalah fi al-radd ala al-Rafidah* [Treatise on the Rejection by the Rafidah (Shiʿa rejectionists)]. They are analyzed by DeLong-Bas in *Wahhabi Islam*, chapter 4, p27–29, and pp84–88.

14 Beccaria published *Of Crimes and Punishments* in Italy in 1764 and non-scholars should find it entirely readable in this century (though it might prove unsettling to Professor of Law John Yoo or U.S. District Judge William J. Haynes II, who invoked expediency to write legal justifications for the reintroduction of torture into the U.S. justice system after 2001).

15 DeLong-Bas, *Wahhabi Islam*, p29.

For his second *hijra* from Uyaynah, Muḥammad ibn ʿAbd al-Waḥhab went north to al-Dirʿiyah, and his momentous encounter with Muḥammad Ibn al-Saʻud, an emir who would prove to him to be a considerable improvement on Ibn Muʻammar. Within two years of the agreement between them, in 1746, Ibn ʿAbd al-Waḥhab had officially proclaimed jihad against all who "refuse to share his vision of Unity [*tawhid*]", and begun sending out war parties (*ghazu*).[16] He was soon riding at the side of Ibn al-Saʻud at the head of what he called "the army of God." Their army, "victorious […] in argument and language, just as they are victorious by the sword and by the spear,"[17] was winning all the arguments, putting down Muslim heretics in their corner of central Arabia, destroying tombs and other objects of *shirk* (idolatry), killing enemies, taking booty, conquering territory and collecting enough taxes to make the enlarging Saudi state a paying proposition.

According to a sympathetic scholar, Natana DeLong-Bas, the only place in his writings where Ibn ʿAbd al-Waḥhab calls anyone *kafir* (unbeliever), or anything *shirk* (idolatry, polytheism), except with reference to Allah, is in *Kitab Kashf al-Shubhat* (The Book of Debate with Idolaters) where he condemns anyone who puts the Prophet Muḥammad in a place lower than the last and greatest of the prophets.[18] There is, however, no question that from 1746 on, the Wahhab-Saud duumvirate fought to exclude large numbers of self-identified Muslims from the ummah or community of Islam, to define them as kafir—unbeliever—and kill them.[19]

For Ibn ʿAbd al-Waḥhab the goal of the joint project was to subdue any behavior tending to idolatry and unbelief, especially the mystical and ecstatic practices of the Ṣufi and the hagiology and mahdism of the Shiʿa. Among these, he included any intercessory praying to dead "friends of God," or venerating them, or visiting or praying at their tombs, or participating in feasts and offerings commemorating them—extending even to celebrations of the Prophet's own birthday. He physically attacked funerary monuments, especially those with domes, all depiction of God's

[16] Allen, *God's Terrorists*, p54–55.

[17] Muḥammad ibn ʿAbd al-Waḥhab, *Kitab Kashf al-Shubhat* [The Book of Detecting Doubt], in *Mu'allafat al-Shaikh al-Imam Muḥammad Ibn Abd al-Wahhab*, v1, Riyadh: Jamiat al-Imam Muḥammad bin Saud al-Islamiyah, 1398H, p160, translated in DeLong-Bas, *Wahhabi Islam*, p199. DeLong-Bas argues, not very convincingly, that this "army," "victorious […] in argument and language, just as they are victorious by the sword and by the spear," refers primarily to nonviolent preachers.

[18] ibn ʿAbd al-Waḥhab, *Kitab Kashf al-Shubhat* [The Book of Detecting Doubt] in *Mu'allafat al-Shaikh al-Imam Muḥammad Ibn Abd al-Wahhab*, v1, p161–162, in DeLong-Bas, *Wahhabi Islam*, p45n10, p300.

[19] ʻAbd al-Waḥhab's method in his writings on Islamic *fiqh* (law), is to assert a chain of equivalencies until he has established a warrant to use violence on anyone who deviates from the simplest, most rigorous, and most exclusive statement of faith. Glossing the verse, al-Anfal 8:39 of the *Qur'an*: "And fight them until there is no more *fitnah* ["civil strife" or "heresy," but the root meaning is "testing"] and the religion (the worship) exclusively is for Allāh," Ibn abd al-Waḥhab himself wrote, "And Al-Fitnah [heresy] is *shirk* [polytheism]. The Exalted branded the people of *shirk* with *kufir* [apostasy] in an amount of verses that cannot be counted. So *takfīr* [excommunication] must be declared upon them. This is a necessity of *Lā ilāha illā Allāh* [There is no god but God]" (Muḥammad ibn abd al-Waḥhab, "Risālah Aslu Dīn Al-Islām wa Qā'idatuhu" tr., www.Al-Aqeedah.com, @ http://www.saaid.net/kutob/122.pdf, 14 Aug 2014, p. 7).

creatures, including humans, any using or wearing of talismans, the smoking of tobacco or hashish, dancing, playing music, fortunetelling, colorful decoration, silk clothing, shaving beards, wearing robes that do not show the ankle, and using beads (like the rosary) for repeating the 99 names of God.[20] Ibn ʿAbd al-Waḥhab called his followers *muwaḥhidun* (believers in the oneness of God), but his form of Islam was eventually (and idolatrously) dubbed Waḥhabyya by its enemies. Such enemies became ever more numerous, as all tribes who did not convert to Waḥhabyya when offered the choice found themselves automatically defined as *meshrekin* or *mushrikin* (heretics) who could be killed. The muwaḥhidun eventually formed the habit of offering this choice three times, consistent with a ḥadith of the Prophet, and refusal to convert would be followed by immediate and often indiscriminate massacre.

For Emir Muḥammad ibn Sa'ud the most important goal of the joint project seems to have been to unify the Arab tribes by conquest and set up a military state. In lieu of the basic muslim tithe (*zakkat*) he imposed "a religious tax at the rate of one Spanish dollar for every five camels and every forty sheep" and founded a religious police force, the *mutawihin*.[21] When, in 1766, Ibn ʿAbd al-Waḥhab's emir was assassinated at prayer (as had happened to the last three of the four original Just Caliphs) and was succeeded by his son ʿAbd al-Aziz ibn Sa'ud, firearms began to replace spears and scimitars. Muḥammad ibn ʿAbd al-Waḥhab, who was the new emir's father-in-law, soon issued a royal decree (*firman*) to each warrior praying immediate admission to heaven if he died in battle and thus became a martyr. Martyr—*shahid*—was an honor pioneered by the Shiʿa after their epic defeat at Karbala, and understandably subject to Sunni criticism as a species of idolatry; but Ibn ʿAbd al-Waḥhab (like Ibn Taymiyyah before him) seems not to have taken that point.[22]

In the banner year of 1773 C.E., Muḥammad ibn ʿAbd al-Waḥhab and ʿAbd al-Aziz ibn Saud's muwaḥhidun took the town of Riyadh, a town north of al-Uyaynah and al-Dirʿiyah, which was both larger and more strategically placed than either. (Restored after being destroyed by an anti-Waḥhabi Muslim army, it is the capital of the Kingdom of Saudi Arabia today.) Following the victory, in the same year, the seventy-year-old Muḥammad ibn ʿAbd al-Waḥhab resigned his post as imam. His replacement was no less than the new emir, ʿAbd al-Aziz ibn Sa'ud, who now took over leadership of the *ulema*. There seems no way we can know if conversions declined after this promotion but the conquests were hardly interrupted (Figs. 9.3 and 9.4).

---

[20] Allen, *God's Terrorists*, p56. His sources are contemporary European observers (with the attendant biases). The earliest is the German Carsten Niebuhr, sent by the Danish king to reconnoiter Arabia in 1761 (*Description de l'Arabie*, tr., Mourier, Amsterdam: S. Baalde, 1774). Another is Louis de Corancez. A French consul (L. A. *** [Louis Antoine-Olivier de Corancez], *Histoire des Wahabis depuis leur origine jusqu'à la fin de 1809*, Paris: Crapelet, 1810; new edition edited by Hammadi Redissi, Beirut: al-Bouraq («Ètudes» #58), 2015). Another is the Swiss John Lewis Burckhardt, who visited in 1816 and was published in English in 1831 (*Notes on the true History of the Bedouins and Wahabys sect of Islam*, London: Henry Colburn and Richard Bentley, 1831).

[21] Allen, *God's Terrorists*, p54.

[22] Allen, *God's Terrorists*, p59.

Fig. 9.3 Palace of the Saud emirs in ad'Dir'iyah (الدرعية), capital of the Emirate of Dir'iyah, the first Saudi state 1744–1818 CE. (Photo by Petrovic-Njegos at English Wikipedia, CC BY 2.5, https://commons.wikimedia.org/w/index.php?curid=6443234)

Fig. 9.4 Riyadh ("Gardens"), on the Nejd plateau, Saudi Arabia, made capital of the second Saudi Kingdom in 1825 and the third Saudi Kingdom, in 1932. Now the 38th most populous city in Asia. (Photo by lawepw, Public Domain, https://commons.wikimedia.org/w/index.php?curid=66470045)

Muḥammad ibn ʿAbd al-Waḥhab of Najd finally died in 1792 at the venerable age of 89.[23] He would not see the Saudi massacre at Karbala (Iraq) or its conquest

[23] The date of 1792 is given by Redissi (2007), by DeLong-Bas (2004) and by Allen (2006). Julian Baldick (*Mystical Islam*, 1989) gives 1787, but despite the scholarly depth of his book, this date is not convincing. Hamid Algar's date, 1766, given in the chronological appendix to *Wahhabi Islam*

and purging of Mecca and Medina in the next century. Surviving him were his 20 widows and 18 children, who with their descendants were called the *Ahl al-Shaikh* (Family of the Shaikh). They are still called that. Indeed, for more than two centuries their senior male member has been, with few interruptions, the mufti (chief judge) of the Saudi ulema.

Like the Fatimid caliph, Ibn Yasin, the Almoravid emirs (who ruled Morocco and conquered Spain in the eleventh century), Ibn Tumart and his Almohads (who ruled the same empire in the twelfth) and Ibn Taymiyyah, who tried in vain to fight the Mongols in the thirteenth and fourteenth, Muḥammad ibn ʿAbd al-Waḥhab was a would-be Ṣufi mystic who turned Sunni jihadist, killing fellow Muslims in order to propagate his narrow understanding of Islam. At no time does he ever seem to have called for vision or ecstasy, or even a change of heart, but only for obedience and enforcement of the letter of the law.

Al-Waḥhab was a provincial and not much of a scholar, but he cannot be considered apart from the very rich culture of Dar-al-Islam. He was not the only high-profile renewer/reformer (*mujtahid*) in the eighteenth century House of Islam—not even the only one in Arabia in the vicinity of the Holy Cities. Al-Waḥhab's intellectual contemporaries included two highly respected judges who issued their opinions in Yemen south of the Saudi lands in Arabia. They were al-Ṣanʿani (Muḥammad Ibn Ismāʿīl al-Amīr al-Ṣanʿānī, 1688–1769), and al-Shawkani (Muḥammad Ibn ʿAlī al-Shawkānī, 1759–1834). Both al-Ṣanʿani and al-Shawkani, like al-Waḥhab, were admirers of ibn Taymiyyah, the jurist/theologian who had proclaimed the Jihad Fatwa five centuries before, and both favored individual independence in legal thinking (*ijtihad*) and were accordingly willing to question blind trust in precedent (*taqlid*). Unlike the provincial al-Waḥhab, however, both were judges in a venerable dynastic state, the imamate of Sanaa, with a syncretic Muslim tradition called Zaydi.[24] Also unlike al-Waḥhab, both were major thinkers in almost all areas of Islamic learning, al-Shawkani, for example, having written some 150 books. Most strikingly, both al-Ṣanʿani and al-Shawkani repeatedly argued against the automatic condemnation of Ṣufi practices, like the veneration of "saints" at their tombs, as *shirk*—polytheistic practice punishable by death—and they argued in general against what Americans might call the legal "originalism." No, said these reformers, the authority of later generations of Muslims was not inferior to that of the Salafin, not even the Companions of the Prophet. Al-Waḥhab, on the contrary, was a Salafist, meaning that he thought the authority of the late-coming successors was inferior.[25]

(2002), is even less plausible and is probably the mislabeled date of the death of al-Waḥhab's first emir, Muḥammad ibn Sa'ud.

[24] Zaydism or Zaydiyyah is named after an early south Arabian Shiʿah imam. (The tradition was in the news after 2016 under the name Houthi.) The Sunni legal tradition most compatible with Zaydiyyah is Hanafi, and it was Yemeni Islam, reformist in the eighteenth century, that syncretized them.

[25] The rehabilitation (at least in English) of the work of al-Waḥhab's intellectual contemporaries began with Bernard Haykel in his *Revival and Reform in Islam: The Legacy of Muḥammad al-Shawkani* (Cambridge Studies in Islamic Civilization), Cambridge: Cambridge U.P., 2003) and has

Among the students at Medina at about the same time (1730–1731 CE) as young Muḥammad Ibn ʿAbd al-Waḥhab was another future Salafist named Ahmad ibn ʿAbd ar-Rahim al-Dahlawi who would become known as Shah Waliullah.[26] He had come across the Indian Ocean on the centuries-old Hajj route from Muslim north India to the holy cities of Islam, to study in Medina where the Prophet was buried. The two men may even have met there. We do not know, but what we do know is that they came eventually to several of the same fateful conclusions about Islam.

Shah Waliullah al-Dahlawi (1703–1762), the celebrated reform preacher of eighteenth-century India (Waliullah means "Friend-of-God" and Dahlavi "from Delhi"), was the same age as Ibn ʿAbd al-Waḥhab (and likewise of John Wesley and Jonathan Edwards) and we know that the two students at the contemporary Islamic learning centers of Medina in 1732, then in their late 20s, had for a while the same teacher, Muḥammad Ḥayyā al-Sindī ("the Indian") a Naqshabandi Ṣufi and jurist who was an admirer of his fellow Naqshabandi, Ibn Taymiyyah, the thirteenth-century author of the Jihad Fatwa. Al-Sindī, in turn, had been a student of Ibrahim al-Kurani,[27] and al-Kurani was the teacher who taught Ḥadith to Shah Waliullah and introduced him to the ideas of Ibn Taymiyyah. At the time, Waliullah was prolific in Ṣufi mystic visions; he describes forty-seven of them, experienced during his trip, in one of the better-known of his many writings, *Emanations (Spiritual Visions) of Mecca and Medina*.[28] We also know that Shah Waliullah, despite being a Ṣufi, became himself an admirer of Ibn Taymiyyah, and a salafist reactionary, and that on his return to India in 1733, his thinking began to inspire a particularly militant and

---

recently been continued with a new view and erudite scholarship by Ahmed S. Dallal in *Islam without Europe* (University of North Carolina Press. Kindle Edition, 2018). A less prescriptive way of evaluating the Sunnah may not quite qualify as Enlightenment, but one must agree with Dallal that it is misleading to date the "modernization" of the Islamic world from Napoleon's invasion of Egypt at the very end of the eighteenth Western century, as Christopher de Bellaigue does in his *The Islamic Enlightenment: The Struggle Between Faith and Reason, 1798 to Modern Times*, (Liveright Kindle Edition, 2017) because it identifies modernization too readily with Westernization, and thus unhistorically brands the twelfth Muslim century as intellectually static or backward. It also distracts the historians' attention from what looks very much like a zenith of un-religious scientific achievement that Dar al-Islam reached in the third through the fifth Muslim centuries, before al-Ghazali's retreat, in an era (the ninth through the eleventh Christian centuries) during which the West still acknowledges it was Medieval, if not Dark.

[26] The full name, with added honorifics, transliterated, can be Qutb al-Din Ahmad ibn ʿAbd al-Rahim Wali Allah al-Dahlawi or al-Hafidh Imam Hujjatul Allah Shah Ahmad ibn ʿAbd ar-Rahim Wali Allah al-Dahlawi. "Qutb al-Din" means "Pillar of the Faith." "Wali Allah al-Dahlawi" means "Friend of God from Delhi."

[27] Waliullah also included among his Medina teachers, abu Tahir al-Kurdi al-Madani, Wafd Allah al-Makki, and Taj al-Din al-Qali. (According to G. N. Jalbani, *Life of Shah Wali Allah*, Kitab Bhavan, 2006, in a since expurgated article, "Shah Waliullah," *Wikipedia*, 20 Jul 2013, based on Waliullah's own Arabic memoirs, *Al-Irshad ila-Muhimmat-I-Ilm-al-Isnad*, but I have not been able to determine their connections to ʿAbd al-Waḥhab and Ibn Taymiyyah.

[28] The Arabic title is *Fuyud al-haramayn*. Waliullah's Ṣufi writings also include *Altaaful Quds* (in Persian) on esoteric principles of mysticism, and *Al Intibah fi Salaasil ul Auliaullah* (also in Persian) which is brief introductions and histories of various Ṣufi orders and *silsila*s. Neither has struck readers as accounts of Shah Waliullah's own experience of Naqshbandi Sufism.

exclusivist form of Islam in his home country.[29] The self-proclaimed north Indian *mahdi*, Sayed Muḥammad of Jaunpur, had already set a precedent for "reformist jihad" around 1500, and he had been followed by Ahmad Sirhindi, the anti-Shiʿa, anti-*bid'a* Ṣufi shaikh who had refused to kowtow (physically) in 1619 to the Mughal Emperor Jahangir, son of the great Akbar. That refusal was said to have helped Sirhindi to persuade Jahangir to repeal his father's toleration laws: the toleration laws, still celebrated today, which had made Akbar's reign over Hindus and Muslims and Sikhs so brilliant, and which had brought a generation of peace to India's often hostile religious communities.[30]

In India, too, therefore, we can see the same disillusion with Ṣufi mystic piety and the resort to moralism, legalism and jihad against what is termed in Arabic *bida* and *shirk* (the Byzantine Christian Greeks would have used the word *heresy*). Like Sirhindi, Waliullah, who greatly admired Sirhindi, came himself from a line of Ṣufis of the Naqshabandi *tariq*, which included his father, Shah Abdur Rahim, a teacher and administrator of Madrassa Rahimia, the school north of Delhi, where Waliullah himself taught in succession to his father from the time he was about 17 until he went to Medina in 1732. The Madrassa Rahimia set a goal of reconciling "Muslim philosophers (the Ṣufis and the Mutakallim) and the Muslim Jurists (*faqih*)" and in time produced not only Waliullah but a line of political dissidents and *mujahidin* (jihadists) including a son, grandson and great-grandson of Waliullah. For Shah Waliullah Muslim reform took the form of *Da'wah* and *Tableegh* (Islamic propagation) of spiritual revival through a Sufism of reductive austerity, stripped of *bida* and all other threats to the unity of Allah within Islam, including, it seems clear, ecstatic contact with the godhead. It was bleached of the colors of serenely polytheist popular Hinduism, but it would hopefully still have appeal for the largely illiterate masses.[31]

Though acknowledged to be at least partly Ṣufi, it seems to have been thoroughly purged of false claims—or any claims—to mysticism. It seems to some minds that the mystic, or ecstatic experience leaves boundaries blurred, and the oneness of

---

[29] Charles Allen, "The Hidden Roots of Wahhabism in British India," *World Policy Journal: Reconsiderations* XXII:2, Summer 2005 @ http://worldpolicy.org/journal/articles/wpj05-2/allen.html. The full name of Shah Waliullah's teacher is Shaikh Abu Tahir Muḥammad ibn Ibrahim al-Kurani al-Madani of Kurdistan, and the source for his education is Waliullah's own memoirs, *Al-Irshad ila-Muhimmat-I-Ilm-al-Isnad* (the Arabic is still untranslated into English) and *Al-Juz' al-Latif fi Tarjamat al-Abd al-Za'if* (the Persian has been translated into Urdu by Muḥammad Ayyub Qadiri and published in the journal *al-Rahim*, vol. II. no. 5. October, 1964, pp. 18–26.).

[30] Or so goes the legend passed on by Sirhindi's disciples in intolerance, which is belied by Jahangir's law (Twelve Accession Edicts), by Jahangir's Memoirs, and by Jahangir's order to intern Sirhindi for a year in far-off Gwalior until he modified his views of heresy and tolerance. (Irfan M. Habib, "The Political Role of Shaikh Ahmad Sirhindi and Shah Waliullah," *Proceedings of the Indian History Congress*, Vol. 23, Part 1 (1960), pp. 213–216).

[31] "He supported the well-established tradition of the Sufis in the South Asia, while at the same time condemning external influences and innovations (*bid'a*) in Ṣufi practices, advocating the idea of a pure Islam devoid of such influences on the basis that Muslims should assert an independent identity free from the influence of Hindu polytheists." ("Shah Waliullah," *Wikipedia*, accessed 30 Nov 2008).

Allah and the imperatives of his law vulnerable to compromise. Waliullah's thought drew back from that brink. One might have visions, but there was no alternative, no way to God but by law, tradition, and the rites or prayers which they defined. Not only Hindus, but Shiʿa and Ṣufi Muslims needed to be converted.[32]

In 1761, Waliullah wrote to Shah Abdali, Emir of Afghanistan, inviting him to invade Waliullah's own country, Mughal India, and put down the rising Hindu empire of the Marathas: "We beseech you in the name of Prophet to fight a jihad against the infidels of this region… The invasion of Nadir Shah, who destroyed the Muslims, left the Marathas and Jats secure and prosperous. This resulted in the infidels regaining their strength and in the reduction of Muslim leaders of Delhi to mere puppets."[33] The Emir did invade and the resulting war ended with the Third Battle of Panipat in 1761, the retreat of the Hindus, the seizure and bloody sack of the Mughal capital, Delhi, and a decade more of self-deluded Muslim self-congratulation, of which the only beneficiary would be the British Raj.[34]

Before his death in 1762, Waliullah had written a major book with the telling title of *The Conclusive Argument from God*[35] and had come to believe in conversion by violence, to advocate that deviant Muslims, and Hindus, at least those of the higher castes, should have Islam forced upon them, as children are forced to take salutary

[32] The Shah Waliullah spotlighted by Ahmed Dallal in his *Islam without Europe* (2018), is considerably different, since it all but omits from the *mujtahid*'s extensive work his nearly absolute intolerance of doctrinal or liturgical heterodoxy and his approval of ibn Taymiyyah. An Indian scholar, Mahmood Ahmad Ghazi, frankly acknowledges Waliullah's intolerance and jihadism, in his *Islamic Renaissance in South Asia (1707–1867): The Role of Shah Waliallah and His Successors* (New Delhi, India: Adam Publishers, 2004).

[33] Waliullah's letter to the Emir as quoted from Saiyid Athar Abbas Rizvi, *Shah Wali Allah and his times*, p305, in R. Upadhyay, "Shah Wali Ullah's Political Thought: Still a major obstacle against modernisation of Indian Muslims," *South Asia Analysis Group*, Paper #629 (10/03/2003) @ http://www.southasiaanalysis.org/paper629.

[34] A Mughal poet famously described the sack of Delhi in 1761: "They stole and plundered and obscenely enriched themselves. They laid hands upon women. They waved their swords and snatched away wealth … In every lane there was a reign of terror, and every marketplace was a field of combat … The poor were drained bloodless, while tyrants wallowed in their blood … wherever one looked one saw heads and limbs and torsos." (Mir Taqi Mir, *Zikri-i-Mir: The Autobiography of the Eighteenth-Century Mughal Poet: Mir Muḥammad Tqi Mir (1722–1810)*, tr. C. M. Naim, 2nd pb ed., New Delhi, Oxford U.P., 2005, p85, in Ayesha Jalal, *Partisans of Allah: Jihad in South Asia*, Cambridge, MA: Harvard U.P., 2008, p56).

[35] *The Conclusive Argument from God: Shah Wali Allah of Delhi's* **Hujjat Allāh Al-bāligha**, trans., Marcia K. Hermansen, E. J. Brill, 1996. Book 3 is on politics (*irtifaqat*) and, together with Book 6 on the enforcement of orthodoxy, provides a sophisticated argument for religious autocracy as well as permanent distinctions of rank. Hermansen's commentary on Waliullah's book is in her article: Hermansen, "Shāh Walī Allāh of Delhi's *Ḥujjat Allāh al-Bāligha*: Tension between the Universal and the Particular in an Eighteenth-Century Islamic Theory of Religious Revelation," (*Studia Islamica*, No. 63 (1986), pp. 143–157. Published by: Maisonneuve & Larose @ http://www.jstor.org/stable/1595570. Accessed: 08/09/201 1 17:20, esp. 143. (@ https://archive.org/stream/ShahWaliAllahOfDelhisHujjatAllahAlBalighaByMarciaK.Hermansen/Shah+Wali+Allah+of+Delhi%27s+Hujjat+Allah+Al-Baligha+by+Marcia+K.+Hermansen_djvu.txt.

but bad-tasting medicine. Waliullah ordered Muslim rulers on the equivalent of crusade among Christians, writing:

> Oh Kings! Mala ala urges you to draw your swords and not put them back in their sheaths again until Allah has separated the Muslims from the polytheists and the rebellious Kifirs and the sinners are made absolutely feeble and helpless.[36]

Between this initiative of Shah Waliullah and the invasion of the Punjab by Indian jihadists in 1826, a direct line exists, one that more than one historian has extended through other clashes in north India, the North West Frontier, and the several -stans beyond, through the Indian "Mutiny" against British rule in 1857, to the revolt of the Afghan Taliban against Russian rule in the 1970s, and the continued Afghan resistance to the Americans—and to tolerant Muslims.[37] We know that Waliullah's teaching was followed by a long line of disciples, descendants and Rahimia alumni who followed suit with his legalism and often with his advocacy of violent remedies in the nineteenth century, including Waliullah's son, grandson, and great grandson. These descendants of Waliullah were all Ṣufis like him, but they all attacked any Ṣufi trespass on the oneness of Allah. When the supremely influential center of orthodox Sunni education, the Islamic *madrasa* Dar-ul-Ulum Deoband (The House of the Knowledge of Faith at Deoband), was founded north of Delhi in 1866, Waliullah's legacy was fundamental to it, and the influence of Dar ul-Ulum Deoband was felt until the end of the British Raj in 1947 and continues to be felt today.

What later Muslim writers refer to as Islam's eighteenth-century reform movement reached everywhere in Dar al-Islam, from the far east to the Maghrebine west. It moved not only Ibn ʿAbd al-Waḥhab's Arabs and Shah Waliullah's proto-Pakistanis in the eighteenth century, it inspired completely independent Sunni jihads in North Africa, others in Southeast Asia in the nineteenth, and still others along the Niger in West Africa before the seventeenth century had ended.

The rich and complicated story of legalist and jihadist Islam in West Africa is still not well known in the West. Islam had moved east across Africa over many previous centuries, including the seventh century C.E. when Islam began. It had moved both north and south of the Sahara, less through war in the south than through a combination of commercial trade, wandering preacher-scholars, and bands of displaced nobles. State formation and local wars had raised the stakes until empires formed.

---

[36] Waliullah, quoted in Saiyid Athar Abbas Rizvi, *Shah Wali Allah and his times*, p299, in R. Upadhyay, "Shah Wali Ullah's Political Thought: Still a major obstacle against modernisation of Indian Muslims," South Asia Analysis Group, Paper #629 (10/03/2003) @ http://www.southasiaanalysis.org/paper629.

[37] Most prominent among those historians is the British observer Charles Allen, who tends to establish a fully connected chain of influence on evidence that is mostly European, still often fragmentary, and that can be tendentious. (Neither Allen nor I reads enough Arabic or Farsi or Urdu to correct for this limitation.) See Charles Allen, "The Hidden Roots of Wahhabism in British India," *World Policy Journal: Reconsiderations* XXII:2, Summer 2005 @ http://worldpolicy.org/journal/articles/wpj05-2/allen.html; and Allen, *God's Terrorists, The Wahhabi Cult and the Hidden Roots of Modern Jihad* (Cambridge: Da Capo Press, 2006).

In the eleventh, twelfth and thirteenth centuries the Almoravids and Almohads, Muslim Berber dynasties, had ridden north out of Morocco and Mauretania, invoking jihad and conquering Spain. Islam had been the religion of the Mandinké empire of Mali whose ruler, Mansa Musa I, made the famously gold-drenched hajj to Mecca in the fourteenth century, and it was the religion of Mali's successor empire, Songhai, in the fifteenth and sixteenth centuries. Political fragmentation of West and North Africa after 1600 had not reduced the appeal of the faith, whose only competition there for centuries had been local animisms. Toward the end of the seventeenth century the Fula or Fulbe people of the Senegal River valley, many of them already Muslim, began to move northward and eastward into new territory, and by the 1670s some of them were proclaiming military jihad. We do not know exactly why the idea of jihad emerged among the Fulani and we know less about why it emerged then; but it was the most fundamental political fact in the African Sudan until the partition of Africa by the West in 1886, and looks like it might be again in the new millennium.

The Fula or Fulbe jihads had begun in the 1670s, half a century before ʿAbd al-Waḥhab was born, when (according to almost exclusively oral tradition) a scholar of one of the indigenous Berber peoples, Nasr al-Din, began attacking the in-migrating Arabic-speaking Bani-Hassan using the potent accusations of *shirk* (idolatry) *bida* (innovation) and *kufir* (unbelief). (Nasr al-Din died in 1674 during his otherwise successful third battle against the Bubba tribe and the Beni Hassan.) The scholar Malik Sy raised a jihad in 1698 that took the town of Bundu or Bondu (now in Senegal).[38] In 1725, when al-Waḥhab and Waliullah had yet to make their hajj, another Fula Muslim leader, Karamokho Alfa (born Ibrahima Musa Sambeghu and sometimes called Alfa Ibrahim or Alpha Ibrahima) was elected as the first Almamy, or Imam, of the Muslim jihad state of Futa Jallon,[39] at the capital Timbo (now in Guinea). Imam Karamokho Alfa turned out to be no less a warrior than a scholar and only two years later he was launching jihads against neighboring states in the name of a very Waḥhabi-like "purified" Islam.[40]

By the time Imam Alpha died in 1751, Futa Jalon was the dominant state in sub-Saharan West Africa, leading a confederation of provinces in present-day Guinea, Guinea-Bissau, Senegal and Sierra Leone, all of them ruled by orthodox Sunni Muslim Fulani. Soon after ʿAbd al-Waḥhab and Waliullah, and in the same cause of an Islam purified of innovation and polytheism, there were jihads launched by Sunni Muslims in Libya, Algeria and Morocco in North Africa. As the nineteenth century approached, the spectacular series called the Fulani jihad, or jihads, began, fought once more by the Fula people and their leaders against West African Muslim states they considered pagan or unorthodox.

---

[38] David Robinson, "Revolutions in the Western Sudan," in Levitzion & Pouwels, ed., *The History of Islam in Africa*, p133–34; Michael Gomez, "Bundu in the Eighteenth Century," *The International Journal of African Historical Studies*, 20:1(1987), pp. 61–73.

[39] Also called, in various European transliterations, Fouta Jalon, Fouta Djallon, Fuuta Jaloo or Fuuta Jalo*n*.

[40] "Karamokho Alfa" & "Imamate of Futa Jallon," *Wikipedia*, accessed 17 February, 2017.

The pattern of Ṣufi disillusion, self-exile, and jihad, first established in West Africa, best known in Ibn ʿAbd al-Waḥhab's Arabia, and fundamental to Waliullah's north India, would eventually appear as far to the east as Sumatra and the Philippines, with or without identifiable invocations of ʿAbd al-Waḥhab. The pattern remained a persistent strain in Islam everywhere that Islam had been established. Though never the most popular expression of Islam with the Muslim majority, it has often been the most spectacular, and sometimes even the most potent. It has been, and I think still is, the equivalent in Islam of late dynastic Hasidic orthodoxy in Judaism and Evangelical Protestant "fundamentalism" in twentieth-century Christianity.

Bibliography

'Abd Allah, al-Ṣaliḥ al-'Uthaymin, and Darat Al-Malik 'Abd al-'Azīz. 2009. *Muḥammad ibn 'Abd al-Wahhāb: The Man and His Works*. London: I. B. Tauris.

'Abd el-Kader. 1995. *The Spiritual Writings of Amir 'Abd al-Kader*. Ed. Michel Chodkiewicz. SUNY series in Western Esoteric Traditions. Trans. James Chrestensen and Tom Manning. New York: State University of New York Press.

Abbas, Hassan. 2005. *Pakistan's Drift into Extremism: Allah, the Army, and America's War on Terror*. London: M. E. Sharpe.

ʿAbd al-Waḥhāb, Muḥammad Ibn (See Waḥhab).

Abu Dāhish, ʿAbd Allāh ibn Muḥammad ibn Husayn. 2010. The Rise of Muḥammad ibn ʿAbd al-Wahhāb's Da'wa [Mission] in the Southern Arabian Peninsula, Chapter 8. In *A History of the Arabian Penisula*. Trans. Salma K. Jayyusi, ed. Fahd al-Semmari. London: I.B. Tauris, in association with the King Abdul Aziz Foundation for Research and Archives.

Abu-Amr, Ziad. 1994. *Islamic Fundamentalism in the West Bank and Gaza: Muslim Brotherhood and Islamic Jihad*. Bloomington, IN: Indiana University Press.

Abu-ʿUksa, Wael. 2017. *Freedom in the Arab World: Concepts and Ideologies in Arabic Thought in the Nineteenth Century*. Cambridge: Cambridge University Press.

———. 2019. The Construction of the Concepts "Democracy" and "Republic" in Arabic in the Eastern and Southern Mediterranean, 1798–1878. *Journal of the History of Ideas* 80 (2): 249–270.

Adams, Charles J. 1983. Maududi and the Islamic State. In Esposito, *Voices of Resurgent Islam*. New York: Oxford University Press.

Afary, Janet, and Kevin B. Anderson. 2005. *Foucault and the Iranian Revolution: Gender and the Seductions of Islamism*. Chicago: University of Chicago Press. (Rvw Pankaj Mishra in *New York Review of Books* 52:18(November 17, 2005)).

Ahmad, K. Jamil. 1987. Shah Waliullah. In *Hundred Great Muslims*, Library of Islam. Chicago: Kazi Publications.

Aḥmad, Irfan. 2017. *Religion as Critique: Islamic Critical Thinking from Mecca to the Marketplace*, Islamic Civilization and Muslim Networks series. Chapel Hill: University of North Carolina Press.

Ahmed, Akbar S. 1992. *Postmodernism and Islam: Predicament and Promise*. London: Taylor & Francis.

Ahmed, Hussein, and rvw Gabriel Warburg. 2003. *Islam, Sectarianism and Politics in Sudan since the Mahdiyya*. (London: Hurst). *Journal of Islamic Studies* 16(2005): 386–388. http://jis.oxfordjournals.org/cgi/content/full/16/3/386?etoc.

Ahmed, Rafiuddin. 2008. *Sir Sayyid Aḥmad Khan [1817–1898]*. Oxford, UK: Oneworld.

Ahmed an-Na'im, Abdullah. 2008. *Islam and the Secular State: Negotiating the Future of Shari'a*. Cambridge, MA: Harvard University Press.

Ajayi, J.F.A., and M. Crowder. 1987. *History of West Africa*, Studies in African History. Vol. 2. New York: Addison-Wesley Longman Ltd.

Akkach, Samer. 2007. *'Abd Al-Ghani Al-Nabulusi [1641–1731]: Islam and the Enlightenment.* London: Oneworld Academic.

Al Shehabi, Omar H. 2019. *Contested Modernity Sectarianism and Nationalism in Colonial Bahrain*. London: Oneworld Academic.

al-Azmeh, Aziz. 1993. *Islams and Modernities*. London: Verso.

Albertini, Tamara. 2003. The Seductiveness of Certainty: The Destruction of Islam's Intellectual Legacy by the Fundamentalists. *Philosophy East and West* 53 (4): 455–470.

Algar, Hamid. 2002. *Wahhabism: A Critical Essay*. Oneonta, NY: Islamic Publications International.

Ali, Tariq. 2002. *The Clash of Fundamentalisms: Crusades, Jihads and Modernity*. New York: Verso.

Ali, Kecia. 2006. *Sexual Ethics and Islam: Feminist Reflections on Qurān, Hadith, and Jurisprudence*. Oxford, UK: Oneworld.

Aljunied, Syed Muhd Khairuin. 2019. *Hamka [Haji Abdul Malik bin Abdul Karim Amrullah] and Islam: Cosmopolitan Reform in the Malay World*, Southeast Asia Program Publications. Ithaca, NY: Cornell University Press.

Allen, Charles. 2005. The Hidden Roots of Wahhabism in British India. *World Policy Journal: Reconsiderations* XXII (2) http://worldpolicy.org/journal/articles/wpj05-2/allen.html. American Academy of Religion, 'Study of Islam' section, http://groups.colgate.edu/aarislam/response.htm.

———. 2006. *God's Terrorists, the Wahhabi Cult and the Hidden Roots of Modern Jihad.* Cambridge: Da Capo Press.

al-Sanūsī. 2012. In *Encyclopaedia of Islam, First Edition (1913–1936)*. Ed. M.Th. Houtsma, T.W. Arnold, R. Basset, and R. Hartmann. Leiden: Brill. First published online. Consulted online on 15 Nov 2020. https://doi.org/10.1163/2214-871X_ei1_SIM_5172.

al-Waḥhāb, Muḥammad Ibn ʿAbd (See Waḥhab).

Amin, Qasim (1863–1908). 2005. *The Liberation of Women* [1899]*: Two Documents in the History of Egyptian Feminism*. Cairo: American University in Cairo.

Anon. 1817a. *Lam' al-Shihab fi sirat Muhammad Ibn Abd al-Wahhāb*. Cairo: Éditions Abu Hakima, 1967.

———. 1817b. *Lam' al-Shihab fi sirat Muḥammad Ibn Abd al-Waḥhāb*. Cairo: Éditions Abu Hakima, 1967. (Anonymous contemporary critic of al-Waḥhab).

Ansari, Muḥammad Abdul Haq, and Rashid Rahman. 1986. *Sufism and Shari'ah: A Study of Shaykh Aḥmad Sirhindi's Effort to Reform Sufism*. Leicester: Islamic Foundation.

Appleby, R. Scott, ed. 1996. *Spokesmen for the Despised: Fundamentalist Leaders of the Middle East*. Chicago: University of Chicago Press.

Arberry, A.J., ed. 1969. *Religion in the Middle East: Three Religions in Concord and Conflict*. Vol. I of Judaism and Christianity. Cambridge: Cambridge University Press.

Arjomand, Said Amir, ed. 1984. *From Nationalism to Revolutionary Islam*. New York: Macmillan.

Arkoun, Mohammed, and Robert D. Lee. 2019. *Rethinking Islam: Common Questions, Uncommon Answers*. 1st ed. New York: Routledge. (Rvw by Toby E. Huff, Rethinking Islam and Fundamentalism, *Sociological Forum*, 10 (3) (Sep. 1995), 501–518).

Armour, Rollin, Sr. 2002. *Islam, Christianity, and the West: A Troubled History*. New York: Orbis Books.

Asad, Talal. 2003. *Formations of the Secular: Christianity, Islam, Modernity*. Stanford, CA: Stanford University Press.

Aslan, Reza. 2005. *No God but God: The Origins, Evolution, and Future of Islam*. New York: Random House, 2006.

Atmaja, Dwi S., Mark Woodward, and Richard C. Martin. 1997. *Defenders of Reason in Islam: Mu'tazililism from Medieval School to Modern Symbol: An Exploration of Fundamentalism in Islam from the Ninth Century to the Present*. London: Oneworld Academic.

Averroës (Abu al-Walid Muḥammad Ibn Muḥammad Ibn Rushd). 2005. *Bidayat al-Mujtahid wa-Nihayat al-Muqtasid* [The Beginning for Him who Interprets the Sources Independently and the End of him Who Wishes to Limit Himself, ca 1167 CE]. In *Jihad in Classical and Modern Islam*, ed. Rudolph Peters. 2nd ed. Princeton, NJ: Markus Wiener.
Axworthy, Michael. 2008. *Empire of the Mind: A History of Iran*. New York: Basic Books.
Aydin, Cemil. 2017. *The Idea of the Muslim World: A Global Intellectual History*. Cambridge, MA: Harvard University Press.
Ayubi, Nazih. 1991. *Political Islam: Religion and Politics in the Arab World*. London: Routledge. Rvw by Toby E. Huff, Rethinking Islam and Fundamentalism, *Sociological Forum*, 10 (3) (Sep. 1995), 501–518).
Baldick, Julian. 1989. *Mystical Islam: An Introduction to Sufism*. London: I. B. Tauris. New York: New York University Press.
Baron, Beth. 2014. *The Orphan Scandal: Christian Missionaries and the Rise of the Muslim Brotherhood*. Stanford, CA: Stanford University Press.
Bellaigue, Christopher de. 2017. *The Islamic Enlightenment: The Struggle Between Faith and Reason, 1798 to Modern Times*. Liveright, Kindle ed.
Bergesen, Albert J., ed. 2008. *The Sayyid Qutb Reader: Selected Writings on Politics, Religion, and Society*. New York: Routledge.
Berman, Paul. 2003a. *Terror and Liberalism*. New York: Norton. (On Sayyid Qutb).
———. March 2003b. The Philosopher of Islamic Terror. *New York Times Magazine*. (On Sayyid Qutb).
Biegman, Nicolaas H. 2009. *Living Sufism: Sufi Rituals in the Middle East and the Balkans*. Cairo/New York: American University in Cairo Press.
Bin Bishr. 1967–1968. ʿUthman bin ʿAbdullah. *Unwan al-Majd fi tarikh Najd*. Beirut, 1387 AH. (By the contemporary Saudi historian).
Bin Laden, Osama. 2005. *Messages to the World*. Ed. Bruce Lawrence. London: Verso. (bin Laden's statements from 1988–2004).
Blank, Jonah. 2001. *Mullahs on the Mainframe: Islam and Modernity Among the Daudi Bohras*. Chicago: University of Chicago Press. Karachi: Oxford University Press, 2003.
Bonner, Michael. 2006. *Jihad in Islamic History: Doctrines and Practice*. Princeton, NJ: Princeton University Press, Kindle ed.
Bonney, Richard. 2007. *Jihad: From Qu'ran to Bin Laden*. New York: Palgrave Macmillan.
Bostom, Andrew G., ed. 2005. *The Legacy of Jihad: Islamic Holy War and the Fate of Non-Muslims*. Amherst, NY: Prometheus Books.
Bowering, Gerhard, ed. 2015. *Islamic Political Thought, An Introduction*. Princeton, NJ: Princeton University Press, Kindle ed.
Bowering, Gerhard, et al., eds. 2012. *The Princeton Encyclopedia of Islamic Political Thought*. Princeton, NJ: Princeton University Press, Kindle ed.
Brenner, Louis. 1987. Muslim Thought in Eighteenth Century West Africa: The Case of Shaykh Uthman b. Fudi [Dan Fodio]. In *Eighteenth-Century Renewal and Reform in Islam*, ed. N. Levtzion and J.O. Voll. Syracuse, NY: Syracuse University Press.
Brown, Daniel W. 1999. *Rethinking Tradition in Modern Islamic Thought*, Cambridge Middle East Studies Book 5. Cambridge: Cambridge University Press.
Buck-Morss, Susan. 2003. *Thinking Past Terror: Islam and Critical Theory on the Left*. New York: Verso.
Burckhardt, John Lewis. 1831. *Notes on the True History of the Bedouins and Wahabys sect of Islam*. London: Henry Colburn and Richard Bentley.
Burdett, Anita, ed. 2013. *The Expansion of Wahhabi Power in Arabia, 1798–1932*. British Documentary Sources. 8 vols. Cambridge: Cambridge Archive Editions. ISBN: 9781840972702. http://www.cambridge.org/us/academic/subjects/history/middle-east-history/expansion-wahhabi-power-arabia-17981932-british-documentary-sources#YAssoZv98TgvPQT6.99.
Carré, Olivier, and Paul Dumont, eds. 1985. *Radicalismes Islamiques*. 2 vols. Paris: L'Harmattan.

Chattopadhyay, Dilip Kumar. 1977. The Ferazee and Wahabi Movements of Bengal. *Social Scientist* 6 (2): 42–51.
Chayes, Sarah. 2016. *Thieves of State: Why Corruption Threatens Global Security*. New York: W. W. Norton, Kindle ed.
Cimino, Richard. 2005. 'No God in Common': American Evangelical Discourse on Islam After 9/11. *Review of Religious Research* 47 (2): 162–174.
Clancy-Smith, Julia A. 1994. *Rebel and Saint: Muslim Notables, Populist Protest, Colonial Encounters (Algeria and Tunisia, 1800–1904)*, Comparative Studies on Muslim Societies. Vol. 18. Berkeley: University of California Press.
Clarke, Peter B. 1982. *West Africa and Islam: A Study of Religious Development from the 8th to the 20th Century*. London: Hodder Arnold.
Clegg, Claude Andrew, Jr. 1997. *An Original Man: The Life and Times of Elijah Muhammed*. New York: St. Martin's.
Cole, Juan R.I., and Nikki R. Keddie, eds. 1986. *Shi'ism and Social Protest*. New Haven, CT: Yale University Press.
Coll, Steve. 2014. *The Bin Ladens: An Arabian Family in the American Century*. New York: Penguin, Kindle ed.
Cook, Michael. 2001. *Commanding Right and Forbidding Wrong in Islamic Thought*. Cambridge: Cambridge University Press, 2003, 2010.
Cook, David. n.d. Islam and Apocalyptic. http://www.mille.org/scholarship/papers/cookabs.html. (Role of eschatalogy in radical Islamic thought).
Cooke, Miriam, and Bruce B. Lawrence, eds. 2005. *Muslim Networks from Hajj to Hip Hop*, Islamic Civilization and Muslim Networks. Chapel Hill: The University of North Carolina Press.
Corancez, Louis-Alexandre-Olivier de. 1810a. *L'Histoire des wahhabis Depuis leur origine jusqu'à la fin de 1809*. Ed. Hammadi Redissi. Ètudes. Vol. 58. Beirut: al-Bouraq, 2015.
———. 1810b. *History of the Wahhabis (Founders of Saudi Arabia)*. Folios Archive Library. Trans. Eric Tabet. Ithaca Press, 1995.
Corbett, Rosemary R. 2016. *Making Moderate Islam: Sufism, Service, and the "Ground Zero Mosque" Controversy*. Stanford, CA: Stanford University Press.
Crawford, Michael. 2014. *Ibn Abd al-Wahhab*, Makers of the Muslim World. Oxford, UK: Oneworld.
Curtis, Edward E., IV. 2014. *The Call of Bilal: Islam in the African Diaspora*, Islamic Civilization and Muslim Networks. Chapel Hill: The University of North Carolina Press.
Daechsel, Markus. 2006. Scientism and Its Discontents: The Indo-Muslim 'Fascism' of Inayatullah Khan al-Mashriqi. *Modern Intellectual History* 3 (3): 443–472.
Dallal, Ahmad S. 2011. The Origins and Early Development of Islamic Reform. In *The New Cambridge History of Islam*, ed. Robert W. Hefner, vol. 6, 118–120. Cambridge: Cambridge University Press.
———. 2018. *Islam Without Europe: Traditions of Reform in Eighteenth-Century Islamic Thought*. Chapel Hill: University of North Carolina Press.
Dar, B.A. n.d. *Wali Allah: His Life and Times*. http://allamaiqbal.com/publications/journals/review/oct65/1.htm#_edn69.
Darat al-Malik, ʿAbd al'Aziz, and Abd Allah al-Salih 'Uthaymin. 2009. *Muḥammad ibn 'Abd al-Wahhāb: The Man and His Works*. London: I.B. Tauris.
Davidson, Christopher. 2017. *Shadow Wars: The Secret Struggle for the Middle East*. Oxford, UK: Oneworld.
Davis, Eric. 1984. Ideology, Social Class and Islamic Radicalism in Modern Egypt. In *From Nationalism to Revolutionary Islam*, ed. Said Arjomand. Oxford: Macmillan.
De Jong, Frederick. 1987. Mustafa Kamal al-Din al-Bakri (1688–1749): Revival and Reform in the Khalwatiyya Tradition? In *Eighteenth-Century Renewal and Reform in Islam*, ed. N. Levtzion and J.O. Voll. Syracuse, NY: Syracuse University Press.
Dehlvi, Ghulam Rasool. April 2015. Shah Waliullah's Islamic Reformation in 18th Century India: Sufi or Wahhabi? *New Age Islam*. http://www.newageislam.com/ijtihad,-rethinking-islam/

shah-waliullah%E2%80%99s-islamic-reformation-in-18th-century-india%2D%2Dsufi-or-wahhabi?/d/102628.

Dekmejian, R. Hrair. 1985. *Islam in Revolution*. Syracuse, NY: Syracuse University Press.

Delong-Bas, Natana J. 2004. *Wahhabi Islam: From Revival and Reform to Global Jihad*. London: I.B. Tauris. Rvw Laurent Bonnefoy, *Journal of Islamic Studies* 17(2006), 371–372. http://jis.oxfordjournals.org/cgi/content/full/17/3/371?etoc. New York: Oxford University Press, 2004.

———. 2008. *Notable Muslims: Profiles of Muslim Builders of World Civilization & Culture*. Oxford, UK: Oneworld.

Diamond, Larry. 2003. *Islam and Democracy in the Middle East*. Baltimore, MD: Johns Hopkins University Press.

Dragó, F. Sánchez. 1996. Conferencia pronunciada en la Facultad de Filosofía y Letras de la Universidad Complutense de Madrid e incluída en el libro. *El Islám ante el nuevo orden mundial*. VV.AA. Ed. Barbarroja. Madrid. ("The fundamentalist movements of the Muslims are fundamentally a pure movement, a movement to defend their individuality against the uniformity of the market, that *Market* Monotheism that seeks to impose the *American way of life*. tr. Google, quoted in "Sufism in Spain," *Wikipedia*. Accessed 6 Jun 2017).

Eddin, Sufia M. 2006. *Constructing Bangladesh: Religion, Ethnicity, and Language in an Islamic Nation*, Islamic Civilization and Muslim Networks. Chapel Hill: The University of North Carolina Press.

Egerton, Frazer. 2011. *Jihad in the West: The Rise of Militant Salafism*. Cambridge: Cambridge University Press.

Eickelman, Dale, and James Piscatori. 1996. *Muslim Politics*. Princeton, NJ: Princeton University Press.

Einboden, Jeffrey. 2014. *Islam and Romanticism: Muslim Currents From Goethe To Emerson*. London: Oneworld Academic.

El Fadl, Khaled M. Abou. 2001. *And God Knows the Soldiers: The Authoritative and Authoritarian in Islamic Discourses*. Lanham, MD: University Press of America.

———. 2014. *Speaking in God's Name: Islamic Law, Authority, and Women*. Oxford, UK: Oneworld.

El-Ariss, Tarek. 2013. *Trials of Arab Modernity: Literary Affects and the New Political*. New York: Fordham University Press, Kindle ed.

El-Badawi, Emran, and Paula Sanders, eds. 2019. *Communities of the Qur'an: Dialogue, Debate and Diversity in the 21st Century*. Oxford, UK: Oneworld.

Elmarsafy, Ziad. 2009. *The Enlightenment Qur'an: The Politics of Translation and the Construction of Islam*. London: Oneworld Academic.

El-Rouayheb, Khaled. 2015. *Islamic Intellectual History in the Seventeenth Century: Scholarly Currents in the Ottoman Empire and the Maghreb*. Cambridge: Cambridge University Press.

Enayat, Hamid. 1982. *Modern Islamic Political Thought*. Austin: The University of Texas Press.

Ernst, Carl W. 2003. *Following Muhammad: Rethinking Islam in the Contemporary World*, Islamic Civilization and Muslim Networks. Chapel Hill: The University of North Carolina Press, 2004.

Esposito, John L., ed. 1983. *Voices of Resurgent Islam*. New York: Oxford University Press.

———. 1999. *The Islamic Threat: Myth or Reality?* 3rd ed. New York: Oxford University Press.

———. 2002. *Unholy War: Terror in the Name of Islam*. New York: Oxford University Press.

Esposito, John, and François Burgat, eds. 2003. *Modernizing Islam: Religion in the Public Sphere in Europe and the Middle East*. London: C. Hurst.

Esposito, John, and John Voll. 2001. *Makers of Contemporary Islam*. New York: Oxford University Press.

Evanzz, Karl. 1999. *The Messenger: The Rise and Fall of Elijah Muhammed*. New York: Pantheon, 2001.

Fahmy, Khaled. 2008. *Mehmed Ali*, Makers of the Muslim World. Oxford, UK: Oneworld.

Farquhar, Michael. 2016. *Circuits of Faith: Migration, Education, and the Wahhabi Mission*. Stanford, CA: Stanford University Press.

Fathi, Schirin. 2008. *Ali Shariati [1933–1977]*, Makers of the Muslim World. Oxford, UK: Oneworld.

Feener, R. Michael. 2011. *Muslim Legal Thought in Modern Indonesia*. Cambridge: Cambridge University Press.

Feldman, Noah. 2003. *After Jihad: America and the Struggle for Islamic Democracy*. New York: Farrar, Straus & Giroux.

———. 2008. *The Fall and Rise of the Islamic State*. Princeton, NJ: Princeton University Press.

Fierro, Maribel. 2010. *The New Cambridge History of Islam*. Vol. 2 of The Western Islamic World, Eleventh to Eighteenth Centuries. Cambridge: Cambridge University Press.

Flasch, Kurt. 2008. *D'Averroes à Maître Eckhart: Les sources arabes de la mystique allemande*. Conférences Pierre Abelard. Paris: Vrin.

Fry, D.B., ed. 1980. *Sufism and the Islamic Tradition: The Lamahat and Sata'at of Shah Waliullah of Delhi*. Trans. G.N. Jalbani. London: Octagon.

Fuller, Graham E. 2003. *The Future of Political Islam*. New York: Palgrave.

Ghazi, Mahmood Ahmad. 2004. *Islamic Renaissance in South Asia (1707–1867): The Role of Shah Waliallah and His Successors*. New Delhi, India: Adam Publishers.

Gibb, H.A.R. 1947. *Modern Trends in Islam*. Chicago: University of Chicago Press.

Glover, John. 2007. *Sufism and Jihad in Modern Senegal: The Murid Order*, Rochester Studies in African History and the Diaspora. Vol. 32. Rochester, NY: University of Rochester Press.

Gomez, Michael. 1987. Bundu in the Eighteenth Century. *The International Journal of African Historical Studies* 20 (1): 61–73.

Gordon, Stewart. 2007. *When Asia was the World: Traveling Merchants, Scholars, Warriors, and Monks Who Created the "Riches of the East"*. Cambridge: Da Capo Press, Kindle ed.

Green, Nile. 2012. *Sufism: A Global History*, Blackwell Brief Histories of Religion. Malden, MA: Wiley-Blackwell.

Gutman, Roy. 2008. *How We Missed the Story: Osama bin Laden, the Taliban, and the Hijacking of Afghanistan*. United States Institute of Peace.

Habib, Irfan M. 1960. The Political Role of Shaikh Aḥmad Sirhindi and Shah Waliullah. *Proceedings of the Indian History Congress* 23 (Pt 1): 209–223.

Haj, Samira. 2008. *Reconfiguring Islamic Tradition: Reform, Rationality, and Modernity*, Cultural Memory in the Present. Stanford, CA: Stanford University Press. (Wahhab and Abduh).

Hartung, Jan-Peter, and Helmut Reifeld, eds. 2006. *Islamic Education, Diversity and National Identity: Dini Madaris in India Post 9/11*. New Delhi: SAGE.

Hassan, Riaz. 2003. *Faithlines: Muslim Conceptions of Islam and Society*. New York: Oxford University Press.

Haykel, Bernard. 2003. *Revival and Reform in Islam: The Legacy of Muḥammad al-Shawkani*, Cambridge Studies in Islamic Civilization. Cambridge: Cambridge University Press.

Heck, Paul L. 2012. An Early Response to Wahhabism from Morocco: The Politics of Intercession. *Studia Islamica* 107 (2): 235–254. https://www.jstor.org/stable/43577526 (On an essay written 1792–1812 by Muḥammad al-Tayyib Ibn Kiran of Fez, d. 1812).

Hefner, Robert W. 2010. *The New Cambridge History of Islam*. Vol. 6 of Muslims and Modernity: Culture and Society since 1800. Cambridge: Cambridge University Press.

Hegghammer, Thomas. 2010. *Jihad in Saudi Arabia: Violence and Pan-Islamism since 1979*. Cambridge: Cambridge University Press.

———. 2017. *Jihadi Culture: The Art and Social Practices of Militant Islamists*. Cambridge: Cambridge University Press.

Helm, Christine Moss. 1981. *The Cohesion of Saudi Arabia*. London: Croom Helm.

Hermansen, Marcia K. 1986. Shāh Walī Allāh of Delhi's *Ḥujjat Allāh al-Bāligha*: Tension Between the Universal and the Particular in an Eighteenth-Century Islamic Theory of Religious Revelation. *Studia Islamica* 63: 143–157. https://archive.org/stream/ShahWaliAllahOfDelhisHujjatAllahAlBalighaByMarciaK.Hermansen/Shah+Wali+Allah+of+Delhi%27s+Hujjat+Allah+Al-Baligha+by+Marcia+K.+Hermansen_djvu.txt. Accessed 08 Sept 2011.

Heyrman, Christine Leigh. 2015. *American Apostles: When Evangelicals Entered the World of Islam*. New York: Hill & Wang.
Hill, Jonathan N.C. 2010. *Sufism in Northern Nigeria: Force for Counter-Radicalization?* Scotts Valley, CA: CreateSpace Independent Publishing Platform, 2014.
Hiro, Dilip. 1989. *Holy Wars: The Rise of Islamic Fundamentalism*. New York: Routledge.
Hiskett, Mervyn. 1984. *The Development of Islam in West Africa*, Studies in African History. New York: Addison-Wesley Longman.
Hitti, Philip K. 1937. *History of the Arabs*. 10th ed. New York: St. Martin's Publising, 1974.
Hoskin, Andrew. 2017. *Empire of Fear: Inside the Islamic State*. Oxford, UK: Oneworld.
Hourani, Albert H. 1982. *Arabic Thought in the Liberal Age: 1789–1939*. Cambridge: Cambridge University Press, 1983.
Huff, Toby E. 1995. Rethinking Islam and Fundamentalism. Reviewing: *Islam and Postmodernism: Predicament and Promise* by Akbar S. Ahmed; *Rethinking Islam* by Mohammed Arkoun & Robert D. Lee Boulder; *Political Islam: Religion and Politics in the Arab World* by Nazih Ayubi; *Islam and Democracy: Fear of the Modern World* by Fatima Mernissi & Mary Jo Lakeland; *The Failure of Political Islam* by Olivier Roy & Carol Volk. *Sociological Forum* 10 (3): 501–518.
Hunter, W.W. 1871. *Indian Musulmans: Are They Bound in Conscience to Rebel Against the Queen?* London: Trübner & Co.
Ibn ʿAbd al-Waḥhāb, Muḥammad (See Waḥhab).
Imamate of Futa Jallon. 2017. *Wikipedia*. Accessed 17 Feb 2017.
Inayat Khan, Hazrat Pir-o-Murshid. 1914. *A Sufi Message of Spiritual Liberty*. Sufism Series. London, Kindle ed. Orange Sky Project, 2011.
Inayat Khan, Pir Vilayat. 2000. *Awakening: A Sufi Experience*. New York: J.P. Tarcher/Putnam Perigee Reprint.
Iqbal, Muhammad. 1920. *The Secrets of the Self*. Trans. Reynold A. Nicholson. Sufism Series. London, Kindle ed.
———. 1999. *The Reconstruction of Religious Thought in Islam*. Witness-Pioneer. http://www.witness-pioneer.org/vil/Books/MI_RRTI/Default.htm. Last modified: January 11, 2002; Repr. with Introduction by Javed Majeed. Encountering Traditions. Stanford, CA: Stanford University Press, 2013.
Irwin, Robert, ed. 2010. *The New Cambridge History of Islam*. Vol. 4 of Islamic Cultures and Societies to the End of the Eighteenth Century. Cambridge: Cambridge University Press.
Islahi, Zafarul Islam. 2009. Role of Fatawa in the Freedom Movement. http://www.indianmuslims.info/book/export/html/13916.
Jalal, Ayesha. 2009. *Partisans of Allah: Jihad in South Asia*. Cambridge, MA: Harvard University Press.
Jalbani, G.N. 1981. *Life of Shah Wali Allah*. New Delhi: Kitab Bhavan, 2006, 2010.
Juergensmeyer, Mark. 2009. *Global Rebellion: Religious Challenges to the Secular State, from Christian Militias to al Qaeda*. Berkeley: University of California Press.
Kadri, Sadakat. 2012. *Heaven on Earth: A Journey Through Shari'a Law from the Deserts of Ancient Arabia to the Streets of the Modern Muslim World*. New York: Farrar, Straus & Giroux.
Karamokho Alfa. 2017. *Wikipedia*. Accessed 17 Feb 2017.
Kayali, Hasan. 1997. *Arabs and Young Turks: Ottomanism, Arabism, and Islamism in the Ottoman Empire, 1908–1918*. Berkeley: University of California Press.
Kazemi, Farhad. 1984. The Fada'iyan-e Islam: Fanaticism, Politics and Terror. In *From Nationalism to Revolutionary Islam*, ed. Said Amir Arjomand. New York: Palgrave Macmillan.
Keddie, Nikki R. 1968. *An Islamic Response to Imperialism: Political and Religious Writings of Sayyid Jamal al-Din "al-Afghani"*. Berkeley: University of California Press, 2nd ed. 1983.
———. 1972. *Sayyid Jamal al-Din Afghani: A Political Biography*. Berkeley: University of California Press.

———. 1982. Islamic Revival as Third Worldism. In *Le cuisinier et le philosophe: Hommage à Maxime Rodinson*, ed. Jean-Pierre Digard, 275–281. Paris: Maisonneuve et Larose.

———., ed. 1983. *Religion and Politics in Iran*. New Haven, CT: Yale University Press.

———. 1994. The Revolt of Islam, 1700 to 1993: Comparative Considerations and Relations to Imperialism. *Comparative Studies in Society and History* 36 (3): 463–487.

Kedourie, Elie. 2008. *Afghani and Abduh: An Essay on Religious Unbelief and Political Activism in Modern Islam*. London: Routledge.

Kempton, Arthur. 1999. The Lost Tycoons, #1. *New York Review of Books* 46 (9): 68–73. (Elijah Muhammed, Malcolm X & Berry Gordy).

Kepel, Gilles. 1985. *Muslim Extremism in Egypt*. Berkeley: University of California Press.

———. 1994. *The Revenge of God: The Resurgence of Islam, Christianity, and Judaism in the Modern World*. University Park, PA: Penn State University Press.

———. 2000. *Jihad: The Trail of Political Islam* (Paris). Trans. Anthony F. Roberts. Cambridge, NA: Belknap/Harvard University Press, 2002.

———. 2005. *The War for Muslim Minds: Islam and the West*. Cambridge, MA: Harvard University Press.

Kepel, Gilles, and Jean-Pierre Milelli, eds. 2008. *Al Qaeda in Its Own Words*, Trans. from the Arabic Pascale Ghazaleh. Cambridge, MA: Belknap Press/Harvard University Press.

Kerr, Malcolm. 1966. *Islamic Reform: The Political and Legal Theories of Muḥammad Abduh and Rashid Rida*. Berkeley: University of California Press.

Kersten, Carool. 2015a. *Islam in Indonesia: The Contest for Society, Ideas and Values*. New York: Oxford University Press.

———, ed. 2015b. *The Caliphate and Islamic Statehood: Formation, Fragmentation and Modern Interpretations*, Critical Surveys in Islamic Studies. Berlin: Gerlach Press.

———. 2017. *A History of Islam in Indonesia: Unity in Diversity*. New Edinburgh Islamic Surveys. Edinburgh: Edinburgh University Press. New York: Oxford University Press.

Khalidi, Rashid. 2007. *The Iron Cage: The Palestinian Struggle for Statehood*. Oxford, UK: Oneworld.

Khalil, Mohammad Hassan. 2017. *Jihad, Radicalism, and the New Atheism*. Cambridge: Cambridge University Press. (Critique of "New Atheist" discourse of Sam Harris, Ayaan Hirsi Ali, Richard Dawkins, Christopher Hitchens, and Daniel Dennett.).

Khomeini, Imam Ruhollah. 1981. *Islam and Revolution: Writings and Declarations of Imam Khomeini*. Trans. Hamid Algar. Berkeley, CA: Mizan Press.

Kiser, John. 2010. *Commander of the Faithful: The Life and Times of Emir Abd el-Kader: A Story of True Jihad*. New York: Monkfish Book Publishing. Rvw Mark Safranski. http://zenpundit.com/?p=58268.

Knight, Michael Muhammad. 2007. *The Five Percenters: Islam, Hip-hop and the Gods of New York*. Oxford, UK: Oneworld.

Kohlberg, Etan. 1987. Aspects of Akhbari Thought in the Seventeenth and Eighteenth Centuries. In *Eighteenth-Century Renewal and Reform in Islam*, ed. N. Levtzion and J.O. Voll. Syracuse, NY: Syracuse University Press.

Kraemer, Gudrun. 2009. *Hasan al-Banna*, Makers of the Muslim World. Oxford, UK: Oneworld.

Kramer, Martin. 1996. Fundamentalist Islam at Large: The Drive for Power. *Middle East Quarterly*: 37–49.

Küntzel, Matthias. 2007. *Jihad and Jew-Hatred: Islamism, Nazism and the Roots of 9/11*. Trans. from the German by Colin Meade. New York: Telos Press.

Kurzman, Charles, ed. 1998. *Liberal Islam: A Sourcebook*. New York: Oxford University Press.

———, ed. 2002. *Modernist Islam, 1840–1940: A Sourcebook*. New York: Oxford University Press.

Lapidus, Ira M. 1988. *A History of Islamic Societies*. 3rd ed. Cambridge: Cambridge University Press, 2015.

———. 2012. *Islamic Societies to the Nineteenth Century: A Global History*. Cambridge: Cambridge University Press.

Last, Murray. 2010. Reform in West Africa: The Jihad Movements of the Nineteenth Century. In *History of West Africa*, Studies in African History, ed. J.F.A. Ajayi and M. Crowder, vol. 2, 1–29. New York: Addison-Wesley Longman Ltd.
Lawrence, Bruce. 1989. *Defenders of God: The Fundamentalist Revolt Against the Modern Age*. San Francisco: Harper & Row. University of South Carolina Press, 1995.
———. 1998. *Shattering the Myth: Islam Beyond Violence*. Princeton, NJ: Princeton University Press.
———, ed. n.d. *Bin Laden, Messages to the World*. Compiles Osama bin Laden's statements from 1988–2004.
Lefevre, Raphael. 2013. *Ashes of Hama: The Muslim Brotherhood in Syria*. New York: Oxford University Press, Kindle ed.
Levtzion, Nehemia. 1987. The Eighteenth Century: Background to the Islamic Revolutions in West Africa. In *Eighteenth-Century Renewal and Reform in Islam*, ed. N. Levtzion and J.O. Voll. Syracuse, NY: Syracuse University Press.
Levtzion, Nehemia, and Randall L. Pouwels, eds. 2000. *The History of Islam in Africa*. Athens: Ohio University Press.
Levtzion, Nehemia, and John O. Voll, eds. 1987. *Eighteenth-Century Renewal and Reform in Islam*. Syracuse, NY: Syracuse University Press.
Lewis, Bernard. 1990. The Roots of Muslim Rage. *The Atlantic*. Revision of National Endowment for the Humanities 1990 Jefferson Lecture by Princeton Professor emeritus of Near Eastern Studies.
———. 1993. *Islam and the West*. New York: Oxford University Press.
———. 1994. *The Shaping of the Modern Middle East*. New York: Oxford University Press.
Lia, Brynjar. 2008. *Architect of Global Jihad: The Life of al-Qaida Strategist Abu Mus'ab al-Suri*. New York: Columbia University Press.
Lincoln, C. Eric. 1973. *The Black Muslims in America*. Boston: Beacon.
Lotterie, Florence, and Darrin M. McMahon, eds. 2001. *Les lumières européennes dans leur relation avec les autres grandes cultures et religions du XVIIIe siècle*, Études internationales sur le dix-huitième siècle. Vol. 5. Paris: Honoré Champion, 2002.
Louër, Laurence. 2008. *Transnational Shia Politics: Religious and Political Networks in the Gulf*. New York: Columbia University Press/Hurst.
Ludden, David. 2014. *India and South Asia: A Short History*. London: Oneworld.
Mahmood, Fazle. 1972. *A Study of the Life and Works on Shah Wali Allah*. Lahore: n.p.
Malik, Iftikhar H. 2004. Review of Frédéric Grare. *Political Islam in the Indian Subcontinent: The Jamaat-i-Islami*. New Delhi: Manohar: Centre de Sciences Humaines, 2005. In *Journal of Islamic Studies* 15 (3): 393–395. http://www3.oup.co.uk/islamj/hdb/Volume_15/Issue_03/eth320.sgm.abs.html.
Manji, Irshad. 2004. *The Trouble with Islam: A Muslim's Call for Reform in Her Faith*. New York: St. Martin's. (Since retitled *The Trouble with Islam Today*).
Margoliouth, D. S. 2012. Wahhābīya. In *Encyclopaedia of Islam, First Edition (1913–1936)*, ed. M. Th. Houtsma, T.W. Arnold, R. Basset, and R. Hartmann. Leiden: Brill, First published online. Consulted online on 15 Nov 2020. https://doi.org/10.1163/2214-871X_ei1_SIM_5938, 1087.
Marsden, Magnus. 2005. *Living Islam: Muslim Religious Experience in Pakistan's North-West Frontier*. Cambridge: Cambridge University Press.
Martin, B.G. 1976. *Muslim Brotherhoods in Nineteenth-century Africa*, African Studies. Cambridge: Cambridge University Press, 2003.
Martin, Richard C. 1997. *Defenders of Reason in Islam: Mu'tazilism and Rational Theology from Medieval School to Modern Symbol*. London: Oneworld, 2016.
Martin, Richard C., and Abbas Barzegar, eds. 2009. *Islamism: Contested Perspectives on Political Islam*. Stanford, CA: Stanford University Press.
Maududi, Sayyid Abdul al'a. 1932. *Towards Understanding the Quran* (*Risala-e-Diniyat*. Urdu). Trans. Khurshid Ahmad from the text of the sixteenth (revised) edition of the *Risala-e-Diniyat*.

Lahore, Pakistan: University K.I.M. Dawah Centre, 1960. http://www.quranenglish.com/new/Books/01%20Towards%20Understanding%20Islam.pdf.

———. 1950. *Towards Understanding the Quran* (*Tafhim al-Qu'ran*. Urdu, vol. 1, Lahore, Pakistan: Islamic Foundation). Ed., Trans. & abridged Zafar Ishak Ansari. Leicester: University K. The Islamic Foundation, 1988. https://www.kalamullah.com/Books/Towards%20Understanding%20the%20Quran%201.pdf.

———. 1960. *Political Theory of Islam*. Lahore, Pakistan: Islamic Publications. Repr. 1993.

———. 1963. *A Short History of the Revivalist Movements in Islam*. Lahore, Pakistan: n.p.

———. 1967. *Islamic Law and Constitution*. Trans. Khurshid Ahmad. Lahore: Islamic Publications.

———. 2012. *Towards Understanding Islam*. Islamic Circle of North America, Kindle ed.

Mbacké, Khadim, Eric Ross, and John O. Hunwick. 2005. *Sufism and Religious Brotherhoods in Senegal*. Princeton, NJ: Markus Wiener.

McDougall, James. 2006. *History and the Culture of Nationalism in Algeria*. Cambridge: Cambridge University Press, 2007, 2009.

Menchinger, Ethan L. 2016. Free Will, Predestination, and the Fate of the Ottoman Empire. *Journal of the History of Ideas* 77 (3): 445–466. (Lady Mary Wortley Montagu's letter of February, 1718, on hearing that Ottomans were deists.).

Meredith, Martin. 2011. *The Fate of Africa: A History of the Continent Since Independence*. Kindle ed.

———. 2016. *The Fortunes of Africa: A 500-Year History of Wealth, Greed, and Endeavor*. Kindle ed.

Mernissi, Fatema. 1992. Islam and Democracy: Fear of the Modern World. Trans. Mary Jo Lakeland. New York: Perseus, 2002. Rvw Toby E. Huff. 1995. Rethinking Islam and Fundamentalism. *Sociological Forum* 10 (3): 501–518.

Metcalf, Barbara D. 2008. *Maulana Husain*, Makers of the Muslim World. Oxford, UK: Oneworld. (Gandhi's ally, 1879–1957).

———. 2009a. *Husain Ahmad Madani: The Jihad for Islam and India's Freedom*, Makers of the Muslim World. Oxford, UK: Oneworld.

———., ed. 2009b. *Islam in South Asia in Practice*. Princeton, NJ: Princeton University Press, Kindle ed.

Meuleman, Johan, ed. 2002. *Islam in the Era of Globalization: Muslim Attitudes Towards Modernity and Identity*. London: RoutledgeCurzon.

Mir, Mir Taqi. 2005. *Zikri-i-Mir: The Autobiography of the Eighteenth-Century Mughal Poet: Mir Muḥammad Tqi Mir (1722–1810)*. Trans. C.M. Naim. New Delhi: Oxford University Press.

Mishra, Pankaj. 2005. The Misunderstood Muslims. Review of *No God but God: The Origins, Evolution, and Future of Islam* by Reza Aslan and *Foucault and the Iranian Revolution: Gender and the Seductions of Islamism* by Janet Afary and Kevin B. Anderson. *New York Review of Books* 52 (18): 15–18.

———. 2013. *From the Ruins of Empire*. Kindle ed.

Mitchell, Richard P. 1969. *The Society of the Muslim Brothers*. London: Oxford University Press.

Miyakawa, Felicia M. 2005. *Five Percenter Rap: God Hop's Music, Message, and the Black Muslim Mission*. Bloomington: Indiana University Press.

Mohammed, Khaleel. 2018. *Islam and Violence*, Cambridge Elements in Religion and Violence. Cambridge: Cambridge University Press.

Morris, James W, and rvw Zailan Moris. 2003. *Revelation, Intellectual Intuition and Reason in the Philosophy of Mulla Sadra: An Analysis of the al-Hikmah al-Arshiyya*. (London: RoutledgeCurzon). In *Journal of Islamic Studies* 16(2005), 360–362. http://jis.oxfordjournals.org/cgi/content/full/16/3/360?etoc.

Mortimer, Edward. 1982. *Faith and Power: The Politics of Islam*. New York: Vintage Books.

Mottahedeh, Roy. 1996. The Clash of Civilizations: An Islamicist's Critique. *Harvard Middle Eastern and Islamic Review* 2 (2): 1–26.

Moussalli, Ahmad S. 2001. *The Islamic Quest for Democracy, Pluralism, and Human Rights*. Tallahassee: University Press of Florida, 2003.
———. n.d. *Radical Islamic Fundamentalism: The Ideological and Political Discourse of Sayyid Qutb* [1906–1966, chief spokesman for the Muslim Brotherhood in Egypt in the 1950s and 1960s].
Mukherjee, Soumen. 2017. *Ismailism and Islam in Modern South Asia: Community and Identity in the Age of Religious Internationals*. Cambridge: Cambridge University Press.
Musallam, Adnan A. 2005. *From Secularism to Jihad: Sayyid Qutb and the Foundations of Radical Islamism*. Westport, CT: Praeger.
Muztar, Allah Ditta. 1979. *Shah Wali Allah: A Saint Scholar of Muslim India*. Islamabad: n.p.
Na, Abdullahi Ahmed An-Na'im, and 'Abd Allāh Aḥmad Na'īm. 2009. *Islam and the Secular State*. Cambridge, MA: Harvard University Press, Kindle ed.
Nafi, Basheer M. 2006. A Teacher of Ibn 'Abd al-Wahhāb: Muḥammad Ḥayāt al-Sindī and the Revival of Aṣḥāb al-Ḥadīth's Methodology. *Islamic Law and Society* 13 (2): 208–241.
Nasr, Seyyed Vali Reza. 1966. *Mawdudi and the Making of Islamic Revivalism*. New York: Oxford University Press.
———. 1991a. Sufism in the Indian Subcontinent. In *Islamic Spirituality*, ed. Seyyed Hossein Nasr, vol. 2, 239–258. New York: Crossroad.
———, ed. 1991b. *Islamic Spirituality*. New York: Crossroad.
———. 1994. *The Vanguard of the Islamic Revolution: The Jama'at-i Islami of Pakistan*, Comparative Studies on Muslim Societies. Vol. 19. Berkeley: University of California Press.
Nasrin, Taslima Meyebela. 2002. *My Bengali Girlhood: A Memoir of Growing Up Female in a Muslim World*. Trans. Gopa Majumar. New York: Steerforth.
Naumkin, Vitaly V. 2005. *Radical Islam in Central Asia*. Lanham, MD: Rowman and Littlefield.
Niebuhr, Carsten. 1772a. *Beschreibung von Arabien. Aus eigenen Beobachtungen und im Lande selbst gesammleten Nachrichten* (MS begun 1764) Copenhagen. (First European report on Ibn abd al-Wahhab, by the sole survivor of a Danish expedition to Arabia).
———. 1772b. *Description de l'Arabie*. Trans. Mourier. Amsterdam: S. Baalde, 1774.
Nizami, Moin Aḥmad. 2017. *Reform and Renewal in South Asian Islam: The Chishti-Sabris in 18th–19th Century North India*. New York: Oxford University Press.
Norton, Anne. 2013. *On the Muslim Question*, The Public Square. Princeton, NJ: Princeton University Press, Kindle ed. (Enlightenment signaling).
Nusseibeh, Sari. 2017. *The Story of Reason in Islam*. Stanford, CA: Stanford University Press.
O'Fahey, Rex S. 1994. *Enigmatic Saint, Ahmad Ibn Idris* [1760–1837] *and the Idrisi Tradition*. London: C. Hurst and Co. Ltd. Evanston, IL: Northwestern University Press.
Osman, Tarek. 2016. *Islamism: A History of Political Islam from the Fall of the Ottoman Empire to the Rise of Isis*. New Haven, CT: Yale University Press, 2017.
Palmer, Monte, and Princess Palmer. 2005. *At the Heart of Terror: Islam, Jihadists, and America's War on Terrorism*. New York: Rowman & Littlefield.
Pappe, Ilan. 2006. *The Ethnic Cleansing of Palestine*. Oxford, UK: Oneworld, 2007.
———. 2017. *The Biggest Prison on Earth: A History of the Occupied Territories*. Oxford, UK: Oneworld.
Patai, Raphael. 1976. *The Arab Mind*. New York: Scribner's.
Pennel, C.R. 2003. *Morocco: From Empire to Independence*. Oneworld: Oxford, UK.
Peters, Rudolph. 1987. The Battered Dervishes of Bab Zuwayla: A Religious Riot in Eighteenth-Century Cairo. In *Eighteenth-Century Renewal and Reform in Islam*, ed. N. Levtzion and J.O. Voll. Syracuse, NY: Syracuse University Press.
Peters, F.E. 1996a. *The Hajj: The Muslim Pilgrimage to Mecca and the Holy Places*. Princeton, NJ: Princeton University Press.
Peters, Rudolph, ed. 1996b. *Jihad in Classical and Modern Islam: A Reader*. Princeton, NJ: Markus Wiener.

———, ed. 1996c. *Jihad: A History in Documents*. Expanded ed. Princeton, NJ: Markus Wiener, 2005.
Peters, F.E. 2003. *The Monotheists: Jews, Christians, and Muslims in Conflict and Competition*. 2 vols. Princeton, NJ: Princeton University Press.
Peters, Gretchen. 2011. *Seeds of Terror How Drugs, Thugs, and Crime are Reshaping the Afghan War*. Oxford, UK: Oneworld.
Petley, Julian. 2011. *Pointing the Finger: Islam and Muslims in the British Media*. Oxford, UK: Oneworld.
Philliou, Christine M. 2010. *Biography of an Empire: Governing Ottomans in an Age of Revolution*. Berkeley: University of California Press, Kindle ed.
Piscatori, James, ed. 1991. *Islamic Fundamentalisms and the Gulf Crisis*. Chicago: University of Chicago Press.
Qudsi-zadah, Albert. 1970. *Sayyid Jamal al-Din al-Afghani: An Annotated Bibliography*. Leiden: Brill.
Quinn, Charlotte A., and Frederick Quinn. 2003. *Pride, Faith, and Fear: Islam in Sub-Saharan Africa*. New York: Oxford University Press.
Quraishi, Asifa. 2008. Taking Shari'a Seriously. Rvw Noah Feldman. *The Fall and Rise of the Islamic State*. Princeton, NJ: Princeton University Press. In *Constitutional Commentary* 26. University of Minnesota Repository, 2010. https://conservancy.umn.edu/bitstream/handle/11299/170642/26_02_BR_Quraishi.pdf;sequence=1.
Qutb, Sayyid. 2008. *The Sayyid Qutb Reader: Selected Writings on Politics, Religion, and Society*. Ed. Albert J. Bergesen. New York: Routledge.
Radtke, Bernd, John O'Kane, Knut S. Vikor, and Rex S. O'Fahey, eds. 1999. *The Exoteric Ahmad Ibn Idris: A Sufi's Critique of the Madhahib and the Wahhabis: Four Arabic Texts with Translation and Commentary*, Islamic History and Civilization. Leiden: Brill.
Rahman, Fazlur. 1966. *Islam*. 2nd ed. Chicago: University of Chicago Press, 1979.
———. 1982. *Islam and Modernity: Transformation of an Intellectual Tradition*. Chicago: University of Chicago Press.
———. 1999. *Revival and Reform in Islam: A Study of Islamic Fundamentalism*. London: Oneworld Academic.
Rand, Robert. 2006. *Tamerlane's Children: Dispatches from Contemporary Uzbekistan*. Oxford, UK: Oneworld.
Raymond, Jean. 1806. *Mémoire sur l'origine des Wahabys: sur la naissance de leur puissance et sur l'influence dont ils jouissent comme nation*. Paris: Institut Français d'Archéologie Orientale, 1925.
Redissi, Hammadi. 2007. *Une histoire du wahhabisme: Comment l'Islam sectaire est devenu l'Islam*. Paris: Éditions du Seuil (pb Points), 2016.
Redissi, Hammadi, and Louis-Alexandre-Olivier de Corancez, eds. 1810. *L'Histoire des wahhabis Depuis leur origine jusqu'à la fin de 1809*, Ètudes. Vol. 58. Beirut: al-Bouraq, 2015.
Rentz, George. 1969. The Wahhabis. In *Religion in the Middle East: Three Religions in Concord and Conflict*, Islam, ed. A.J. Arberry, vol. II, 270–284. Cambridge: Cambridge University Press.
———. 2004. *The Birth of the Islamic Reform Movement in Saudi Arabia: Muḥammad Ibn Abd Al-Wahhāb (1703/1704–1792) and the Beginnings of Unitarian Empire in Arabia*. London: Arabian Pub.
Rizvi, Saiyid Athar Abbas. 1980. *Shah Wali Allah and his times: A Study of Eighteenth Century Islam, Politics and Society in India*. Canberra, AU: Ma'rifat Publishing House. https://archive.org/details/ShahWaliallahAndHisTimes/mode/2up.
———. 1982. *Shah 'Abd al-'Aziz; Puritanism, Sectarian, Polemics and Jihad*. Canberra, AU: Ma'rifat Publishing House.
———. 2019. Mulla Sadra. In *The Stanford Encyclopedia of Philosophy*, ed. Edward N. Zalta. https://plato.stanford.edu/archives/spr2019/entries/mulla-sadra/.
Robinson, David. 2000. Revolutions in the Western Sudan. In *The History of Islam in Africa*, ed. N. Levtzion and J.O. Pouwels. Athens: Ohio University Press.

Robinson, Francis, ed. 2010. *The New Cambridge History of Islam*. Vol. 5 of *The Islamic World in the Age of Western Dominance*. Cambridge: Cambridge University Press.

Roy, Olivier. 1992. *The Failure of Political Islam*. (Paris). Trans. Carol Volk. Cambridge, MA: Harvard University Press, 1994, 1998. Rvw Toby E. Huff, 1995, Rethinking Islam and Fundamentalism, *Sociological Forum* 10 (3): 501–518.

———. 2002. *L'Islam mondialisé*. Paris: Seuil.

———. 2005. *Globalized Islam: The Search for a New Ummah*. New York: Columbia University Press.

Ruthven, Malise. 1984. *Islam in the World*. New York: Oxford University Press. 2nd ed. revised, 2000; 3rd ed. revised, 2006.

———. 1997. *Islam: A Very Short Introduction*. New York: Oxford University Press. Repr. 2000, Kindle ed. 2012.

———. 2008. The Rise of the Muslim Terrorists. Rvw Sagerman, Singh, Kepel & Milelli, Bergesen, Küntzel, Lia, Feldman, Ahmed an-Na'im, and Gutman. *New York Review of Books* 55 (9) http://www.nybooks.com/articles/21438.

———. 2017. The Islamic Road to the Modern World (Islam & The Enlightenment). *New York Review of Books* 44 (11): 22–25. Notes in reviewing de Bellaigue his use of "Counter-Enlightenment (more usually referred to as Islamism)" (p25).

Schwartz, Stephen. 2003. *The Two Faces of Islam: The House of Sa'ud from Tradition to Terror*. New York: Doubleday.

Shahi, Afshin. 2013. *The Politics of Truth Management in Saudi Arabia*. Oxford: Routledge.

Siddiqi, Mazheruddin. 1982. *Modern Reformist Thought in the Muslim World*. Islamabad: Islamic Research Institute.

Singh, David Emmanuel. n.d. The Independent Madrasas of India: Dar al-'Ulum, Deoband and Nadvat al-'Ulama, Lucknow. www.ocms.ac.uk/docs/madrasas_deoband.pdf+%22Mawlana+Muhammad+%E2%80%98Ali%22+Aligarh&hl=en&ct=clnk&cd=5&gl=us.

Sirriyeh, Elizabeth. 1998. *Sufis and Anti-Sufis: The Defence, Rethinking and Rejection of Sufism in the Modern World*, Routledge Sufi Series. London: RoutledgeCurzon, 2003.

Sivan, Emmanuel. 1985. *Radical Islam: Medieval Theory and Modern Politics*. New Haven, CT: Yale University Press.

Smith, Wilfred Cantwell. 1957. *Islam in Modern History*. Princeton, NJ: Princeton University Press, 2nd ed. Princeton, 1977.

St John, Ronald Bruce. 2017. *Libya from Colony to Revolution*. Oneworld: Oxford, UK.

Steinberg, Jonah. 2011. *Ismaili Modern: Globalization and Identity in a Muslim Community*, Islamic Civilization and Muslim Networks. Chapel Hill: The University of North Carolina Press.

Stephens, Julia. 2018. *Governing Islam: Law, Empire, and Secularism in Modern South Asia*. Cambridge: Cambridge University Press.

Talbi, Mohamed (b. 1921). 1989. Religious Liberty: A Muslim Perspective. *Liberty and Conscience* I (1): 12–20.

Terem, Etty. 2014. *Old Texts, New Practices: Islamic Reform in Modern Morocco*. Stanford, CA: Stanford University Press.

Thomson, Ann. 1997a. Les Lumières et le monde islamique. In *Les Lumières et la solidarité internationale*, ed. Michel Baridon, 101–111. Dijon: Université de Bourgogne.

———. 1997b. Eighteenth-Century Images of the Arab. In *Beyond Pug's Tour: National and Ethnic Stereotyping in Theory and Literary Practice*, DQR Studies in Literature, ed. C.C. Barfoot, vol. 20, 145–157. Amsterdam: Rodopi.

Tibi, Bassam. 1998. *The Challenge of Fundamentalism: Political Islam and the New World Disorder*, Comparative Studies in Religion & Society. Vol. 9. Berkeley: University of California Press.

Titus, M.T. 1959. *Islam in India and Pakistan*. Calcutta: Y.M.C.A. Pub. House.

Triaud, J.-L. 2012. Sanūsiyya. In *Encyclopaedia of Islam, Second Edition*, ed. P. Bearman, Th. Bianquis, C.E. Bosworth, E. van Donzel, and W.P. Heinrichs. Leiden: Brill.. Consulted online on 15 Nov 2020. https://doi.org/10.1163/1573-3912_islam_SIM_6614.

Troeller, Gary. 1976. *The Birth of Saudi Arabia: Britain and the Rise of the House of Sa'ud*. London: Frank Cass Publishers.
Tschannen, Rafiq A., and Bilal Ahmed Tahir. 2020. Wahhabism and the Rise of the Saudis: The Persecuted Become the Persecutors. *The Muslim Times*. https://themuslimtimes.info/2020/10/20/wahhabism-and-the-rise-of-the-saudis-the-persecuted-become-the-persecutors/.
Turabi, Hasan. 1992. Islam, Democracy, the State and the West. *Middle East Policy* 1 (3): 51.
Turner, Colin. 2014. *Islam Without Allah?: The Rise of Religious Externalism in Safavid Iran*. London: Routledge, Kindle ed.
Upadhyay, R. 2003. Shah Wali Ullah's Political Thought: Still a Major Obstacle Against Modernisation of Indian Muslims. *South Asia Analysis Group*, Paper #629. http://www.southasiaanalysis.org/paper629.
Uşakligil, Halid Ziya (1866–1945). 1897. *The Blue and the Black*. Uşakligil's "character Ahmed Cemil is ambivalent about religion in the way that people often are in rapidly secularising societies,"—de Bellaigue. *The Islamic Enlightenment*, 173.
Van Der Lugt, Maria. 2017. The Body of Mahomet: Pierre Bayle on War, Sex, and Islam. *Journal of the History of Ideas* 78 (1): 27–50.
Vissière, Isabelle, and Jean-Louis Vissière. 2000. *Lettres édifiantes et curieuses des jésuites de l'Inde au dix-huitième siècle*, Lire le dix-huitième siècle, 201. Saint-Étienne: Publications de l'Université de Saint-Étienne. Ill. Présentées et annotées par Isabelle et Jean-Louis Vissière. ISBN: 2-86272-189-1.
Viswanathan, Gauri. 1998. *Outside the Fold: Conversion, Modernity, and Belief*. Princeton, NJ: Princeton University Press. (Conversions in Britain and British India).
Voll, John O. 1975. Muḥammad Ḥayyā al-Sindī and Muḥammad ibn 'Abd al-Waḥhab: An Analysis of an Intellectual Group in Eighteenth-Century Madīna. *Bulletin of the School of Oriental and African Studies, University of London* 38 (1): 32–39.
———. 1980. Hadith Scholars and Tariqahs: An Ulema Group. *Journal of Asian and African Studies* 15: 262–267.
———. 1987. Linking Groups in the Networks of Eighteenth-Century Revivalist Scholars: The Mizjaji Family in Yemen. In *Eighteenth-Century Renewal and Reform in Islam*, ed. N. Levtzion and J.O. Voll. Syracuse, NY: Syracuse University Press.
Wadud-Muhsin, Amina. 1992. *Qurān and Woman: Rereading the Sacred Text from a Woman's Perspective*. Kuala Lumpur: Fajar Bakti. New York: Oxford University Press, 1999.
Wahbiyya. 2012. In *Encyclopaedia of Islam, Second Edition*, ed. P. Bearman, Th. Bianquis, C.E. Bosworth, E. van Donzel, W.P. Heinrichs. Leiden: Brill. Consulted online on 15 Nov 2020. https://doi.org/10.1163/1573-3912_islam_DUM_3510.
Waḥhab, Muḥammad ibn 'Abd al. 1398. *Kitab Kashf al-Shubhat* [The Book of Detecting Doubt]. In *Mu'allafat al-Shaikh al-Imam Muḥammad Ibn Abd al-Wahhab*, 160–162. Vol. 1. Riyadh: Jamiat al-Imam Muḥammad bin Saud al-Islamiyah, AH. Trans. DeLong-Bas, *Wahhabi Islam*, 199.
———. 2008. *The Four Principles of Shirk*. Trans. Rasheed Ahmed. South Carolina: CreateSpace Independent Publishing Platform, 2012, Kindle ed.
———. Risalah Aslu Din Al-Islam wa Qa'idatuhu. Trans. www.Al-Aqeedah.com. http://www.saaid.net/kutob/122.pdf. Accessed 14 Aug 2014.
Waliullah Dehlawi. 1925. *Iqd al-Jld ft Bayan Ahkam al-ljtihad wa al-Taqlid* (Arabic). Delhi. (On jurisprudential issues).
———. 1980. *Sufism and the Islamic Tradition: The Lamahat* [Flashes of Lightning] *and Sata'at of Shah Waliullah of Delhi*. Trans. G.N. Jalbani and ed. D.B. Fry. London: Octagon.
——— (Quṭb ad-Dīn Aḥmad Walī Allāh ibn 'Abd ar-Raḥīm al-'Umarī ad-Dihlawī', known as Shah Waliullah Dehlawi, Shaykh al-Islam Imam ul Hind mujaddid, 1703–1752). 1996. *The Conclusive Argument from God* [*Hujjat Allah al-Balighah*]. Part 1, English Trans. Marcia Hermansen. Leiden: E.J. Brill. (Published in the original Arabic, Bareily (India), 1869–1870 and Cairo, 1933. There are other translations in Urdu).

———. n.d. *Fuyud al-Haramayn* (Arabic). Delhi: n.d. (spiritual experiences during his time in Makkah and Madinah).

Warraq, Ibn. 2001. *Why I Am Not a Muslim*. New York: Prometheus Books, 2003.

———. 2003. *Leaving Islam: Apostates Speak Out*. New York: Prometheus Books.

Weismann, Itzchak. 2001. *Taste of Modernity: Sufism, Salafiyya, and Arabism in Late Ottoman Damascus*, Islamic History and Civilization Studies and Texts. Vol. 34. Leiden: Brill. https://archive.org/stream/TasteOfModernitySufismSalafiyyaAndArabismInLateOttomanDamascusByItzchakWeismann/Taste%20of%20Modernity%20-%20Sufism,%20Salafiyya%20and%20Arabism%20in%20Late%20Ottoman%20Damascus%20by%20Itzchak%20Weismann_djvu.txt.

———. 2015. *Abd Al-Rahman Al-Kawakibi: Islamic Reform and Arab Revival*. London: Oneworld Academic.

Wheeler, Brannon. 2006. *Mecca and Eden: Ritual, Relics, and Territory in Islam*. Chicago: University of Chicago Press.

Willis, John Ralph. 1989. *In the Path of Allah: The Passion of Al-Hajj Umar*. London: Routledge, Kindle ed. (A West African Sufi, 1794–1864).

Wood, Simon A. 2012. *Christian Criticisms, Islamic Proofs: Rashid Rida's Modernist Defence of Islam*. London: Oneworld Academic.

Yavuz, M. Hakan. 2009. *Secularism and Muslim Democracy in Turkey*. Cambridge: Cambridge University Press.

Zahid, Farhan. 2014a. Roots of Radical Islamist Ideologies in South Asia. From PhD thesis with same title. Centre Français de Recherche sur le Renseignement, *Tribune Libre* N°40. https://www.cf2r.org/tribune/roots-of-radical-islamist-ideologies-in-south-asia/. (Shah Waliullah and the Wahhabi Movement).

———. 2014b. A Profile of Harkat-Ul-Jihad Islami (Huji), Movement of Islamic Holy Warriors. *Foreign Analysis* 3. https://cf2r.org/foreign/a-profile-of-harkat-ul-jihad-islami-huji-movement-of-islamic-holy-warriors-2/.

Zaman, Muḥammad Qasim. 2007. *Ashraf 'Ali Thanawi: Islam in Modern South Asia*, Makers of the Muslim World. Oxford, UK: Oneworld.

Zarabozo, Jamaal al-Din M. 2003. *The Life, Teachings and Influence of Muḥammad Ibn Abdul-Wahhaab*. The Kingdom of Saudi Arabia: Ministry of Islamic Affairs, Endowments, Dawah and Guidance.

Chapter 10
Conclusion: Ecstasy and the Decay of Ecstasy

Abstract Counter-Enlightenment Piety versus Moralism. Judaism, Christianity and Islam. Defining Religion as the valence of conflicting human values.

The dialectic alternation of ecstasy, piety and moralism lasted long after the eighteenth century in all three Abrahamic religions and remains a feature in the twenty-first. Christians, especially Protestant Christians, found increasing tension between the behavior that God seemed to have commanded to insure their salvation, and the emotional relationship with God, Christ, and their neighbors that conversion seemed to have promised them. In general, despite continual new outbreaks of antinomian conversion, like Pentecostalism, they turned repeatedly to legalism, and usually toward intolerance. The Ḥasidim, too, despite the defeat of the Mithnagdim and antinomian renewals like that of Rabbi Nachman, returned to Torah—the Law—and to legalism. Finally, despite the flourishing of antinomian Ṣufi mysticism in Islam, both Sunni and Shiʿa Islam focused on shariʿah, and even some influential Ṣufi *tariqat* themselves, like Ibn Taymiyyah's Naqshbandiya, began to emphasize the religious law as if it were a counter to piety and to the ecstasies that could lead to its affirmation. Meanwhile, Wahhabism and its avatars throughout the House of Islam continued to condemn the Ṣufis for *shirk*—outrage to monotheism—dividing Muslims from each other, and the House of Islam itself from the House of War.

Religion has not been defeated as the Baron d'Holbach hoped it would back in pre-Revolutionary Paris (or d'Holbach's Revolutionary disciples who worshiped the goddess Reason in Notre Dame). Nor has it quite faded away with the spread of education, security and prosperity, as so many Western thinkers have liked to think since. As Peter Berger, the sociologist of religion, assessed the situation two years before Al Qaeda's attack on the World Trade Center, "The world today, with some exceptions … is as furiously religious as it ever was, and in some places more so than ever."[1] Novelist William H. Gass summed it up a good deal more colorfully

[1] Peter L. Berger (1929–2017), ed. *The Desecularization of the World: Resurgent Religion and World Politics* (Grand Rapids: Eerdmans, 1999), p2. He adds, with the polemical verve of a politically conservative sociologist, "This means that a whole body of literature by historians and social

W. R. Everdell, *The Evangelical Counter-Enlightenment*, Boston Studies in Philosophy, Religion and Public Life 9,
https://doi.org/10.1007/978-3-030-69762-4_10

four years after 9/11: "Nor is the belief—any belief—really dead: druids still frequent the forests, witches stir their kettles, mumbos jumbo, gourds rattle. Beliefs are running wild. Faiths fall, only to reappear as green and fresh as leaves."[2] Stephen Prothero, the historian of religions who published *Religious Literacy: What Every American Needs to Know—and Doesn't* in 2007:

> If there is any general rule to follow regarding the place of religion in modern life, that rule is that God is alive and well and shaking things up in places as disparate as California and Utah, Zimbabwe and Brazil, India and Pakistan, Israel and Tibet.[3]

And in the same year a magisterial philosopher of Western religion, Charles Taylor, concluded:

> Our age is very far from settling into a comfortable unbelief. Although many individuals do so, and more still seem to on the outside, the unrest continues to surface. [...] The secular age is schizophrenic, or better, deeply cross-pressured.[4]

It is true that Western liberal thought has lost much of its patience with religion. It feels embattled. It hoped, I think, that religion would fade away, like slavery or aristocracy, but it hasn't; and these days even slavery and aristocracy can seem to be recovering. Serious atheist thinkers like Sam Harris and Richard Dawkins have begun to insist like the Enlightenment's Baron d'Holbach that the religious "contagion" simply must be cured.[5] Of course, like d'Holbach, they do not see the philosophical point that a conscious commitment to value some things more than others, or behave in certain ways, thought to be "moral," has no more "scientific"

---

scientists loosely labeled 'secularization theory' is essentially mistaken." Before Charles Taylor's *A Secular Age* was published in 2007, prominent in that body of literature would be S. S. Aquaviva, *The Decline of the Sacred in Industrial Society* (*L'Eclissi del Sacro nella Civiltá industriale*, 1961), trans., Patricia Lipscomb (NY: Harper & Row, 1979) and the later work of Berger himself, who had been sympathetic to religious experience at least since his *The Sacred Canopy: Elements of a Sociological Theory of Religion* (Garden City, NY: Doubleday, 1967), and *A Rumor of Angels: Modern Society and the Rediscovery of the Supernatural* (Garden City, NY: Doubleday Anchor, 1969), but who stopped thinking that secularization was inevitable, when he saw Pentecostalism, born among revivalist Protestant Christians in Los Angeles at the beginning of the twentieth century, begin its march to prominence all over what the West once fondly called the Third, the First and the Free Worlds. A year after Berger's *Desecularization of the World*, Rodney Stark inaugurated his project of treating religion as ineradicably human behavior with his *Acts of Faith: Explaining the Human Side of Religion* written with Roger Finke (Berkeley: U. of California Press, 2000).

[2] William H. Gass, "A Forest of Bamboo: The Trouble With Nietzsche," *Harper's*, August, 2005, p88.

[3] Stephen Prothero, *Religious Literacy: What Every American Needs to Know—and Doesn't* (2007), NY: HarperCollins, pb, 2008, p55.

[4] Charles Taylor, *A Secular Age*. (Cambridge, MA: Harvard University Press, 2007), p. 727.

[5] A tactful atheist has recently published a well-informed and sympathetic book on how to understand religion and religious experience that incidentally advises atheists to call off their evangelical campaign to rid the world of religions. Tim Crane, *The Meaning of Belief: Religion from an Atheist's Point of View* (Cambridge, MA: Harvard U. Press, 2017) fails to protect his own belief from the same attack, by following convention and not including atheism among religions.

provability than a religion has, and that indeed, that moral commitment is philosophically almost indistinguishable from religion. Dostoevsky's Ivan Karamazov was only half right when he argued that without God anything is permitted. Those of my students who agree that religion needs to be "cured"; continue to wonder, as I have, how they can avoid making a decision that is essentially a religious one when they commit to an ethical principle: to wit, that religion "should be" cured.

The Jansenist "convulsionaries" who had writhed and prophesied in Paris not long before David Hume came to d'Holbach's salon there were a spectacle that left a permanent memory. Similarly spectacular were the Baptists, Presbyterians and Methodists who did the same just west of Jefferson's Monticello, the missionary Moravians who founded singing communes in Saxony and Carolina, and the Jews who first trembled and danced before the Lord in Międzybóż. They described the same sort of experience as the Muslim Sufis had for centuries, an embodied ecstasy (*wajd*) leading to *fanâ*, the passing away of the self in union with Allah (an experience missed or rejected by Ibn Taymiyyah and Ibn abd al-Wahhab). The experience imposed new values and changed their lives. We may now conclude that the Jansenists and Methodists that Hume observed in his lifetime were not so different, and that Hume well knew that the distinction he made between two ecstatic "false" religions, "Superstition and Enthusiasm," and "true religion" was a specious one.[6]

Religious commitment has, of course, put many teeth on edge in our own time; but the great error of the atheists, in my view, has been to find ultimate commitments like those in all "religious" people, and not to find them in all "non-religious" people like themselves. As Shaftesbury asserted in 1707, "even atheism is not exempt from [enthusiasm]."[7] Moreover, if we can be more precise and think with more care, we may prevent our own religions from developing in the same ways. Given the anthropological argument that all of us have religions, we can also avoid the risk of fighting fire with fire and making things a good deal worse instead of better. Nothing has multiplied the number of proponents of religious intolerance so much as the effort of the modern faith-scorning materialisms to suppress each other, as when secular capitalists go out to crush secular socialists in Palestine and discover that the socialists of Fatah have been superseded by the salafist Muslims of Hamas, not to

[6]Cf. Hume, "Of Superstition and Enthusiasm," in *Essays Moral and Political*, Edinburgh: A. Kincaid 1741, pp141–143. "True religion," (Hume rather disingenuously states, is neither, and corrupted by both.) At the end of his life Hume summed himself up as "a man of mild disposition, of command of temper, of an open, social, and cheerful humour, capable of attachment, but little susceptible of enmity, and of great moderation in all my passions." In Paris he learned of Jansenists, and in Edinburgh, he saw Methodists first hand; but he made no specific attacks on either; rather the contrary. When Rousseau appeared as a refugee on his doorstep in 1765, full of enthusiasm, Hume received him with his usual genial imperturbability and found him a home in England; but within a year, Rousseau had decided he was an enemy.

[7]"there have been *Enthusiastical atheists*. Nor can divine inspiration, by its outward marks, be easily distinguished from it. For inspiration is a real feeling of the Divine Presence, and enthusiasm *a false one*. But the Passion they raise is much alike."—Shaftesbury, "A Letter Concerning Enthusiasm" (Sep, 1707) *Characteristics of Men, Manners, Opinions, Times* (1st edition, 1708), London: Grant Richards, 1900, vol. 1, Sec. 7, p. 37.

mention the capitalists of Israel and the United States upstaged by Haredi (Ultra-Orthodox) Jews or evangelical Christians.

The history of religious change in the nineteenth and twentieth centuries, particularly with respect to Christianity, has again and again been called "secularization," but is this the right way to describe the change? In *A Rumor of Angels: Modern Society and the Rediscovery of the Supernatural* (1969), Peter Berger tried to show that secularization wasn't succeeding; but nearly 50 years later in his stylish polemic *Enlightenment Now!* (2018), Steven Pinker says it's been going great guns, and so much the better, yet is under withering fire and badly needs defending.[8] It's not likely that secularization is what happened between Berger's take and Pinker's.

Max Weber, a German founder of the Sociology of Religion in the 1900s, tried to explain how and why religion was yielding to secularization, starting with his 1904–1905 publication of his classic study, *The Protestant Ethic* (where he first used the iconic word *charisma* to evoke the ascetic selflessness of Zinzendorf's evangelical Moravians).[9] In 1949 Karl Löwith, a German philosopher who had found refuge in America from World War II, published a ground-breaking history of ideas in English, *Meaning in History*, which made it clear that you could not have a philosophy of history without talking about meaning, and that the "meaning" of History was moral, because it could not help invoking time-dependent presuppositions, like the cycles of the pagans, the Providence of the Christians and Providence's secular analogy, Progress. Each of the three makes inescapably ethical assumptions that are indistinguishable from religion and thus (as a Romantic or Counter-Enlightenment thinker would have argued) impossible to establish rationally.[10] His

---

[8] Peter Berger, *A Rumor of Angels* (1969); Stephen Pinker, *Enlightenment Now: The Case for Reason, Science, Humanism, and Progress* (NY: Penguin Viking, 2018). In 1998, in a predecessor to Pinker's book, the New York Academy of Sciences titled volume 775 of their Proceedings *The Flight from Science and Reason*. It presents 42 essays from most of the intellectual disciplines that make up the Academy, expressing the widespread wariness, even fear, of scientists of what they see as the retreat from "Enlightenment" values, including the belief that universal truths and falsehoods can be established by science, and the belief that religion cannot be allowed to contend that any "objective" truth is impossible, in the manner of contemporary postmodernism. Oscar Kenshur's "Doubt, Certainty, Faith, and Ideology," by a professor of Comparative Literature, expressed annoyance at "the "refusal" of "the anti-Enlightenment party … to allow Enlightenment science and reason to escape from the scourge of skeptical doubt [and the party's hearkening] back to a more thoroughgoing skepticism that challenges all knowledge claims." (in Paul R. Gross, Norman Levitt & Martin W. Lewis, eds. *The Flight from Science and Reason, Annals of the New York Academy of Sciences* v. 775, NY: New York Academy of Sciences, 1996, p526).

[9] "Charisma" had appeared a decade before in Rudolph Sohm, *Kirchenrecht* [*Church Law*] (Leipzig: Duncher & Humblot, 1892). Max Weber used it in his *Protestant Ethic and the Spirit of Capitalism* (1904–1905), (tr., Talcott Parsons, NY: Routledge, 2001, p121). For an account of the significant debate on Sohm's term that preceded Max Weber's adoption of it in 1904 and later uses in his *Sociology of Religion* (1922) (tr., Ephraim Fischoff, London: Methuen, 1961, p2) see: David Norman Smith, "Faith, Reason, and Charisma: Rudolf Sohm, Max Weber, and the Theology of Grace," *Sociological Inquiry*, 68:1 pp. 32–60, 1998, p. 37.

[10] Karl Löwith, *Meaning in History: The Theological Implication of the Philosophy of History*, Chicago: U. of Chicago Press, 1949 (tr. into German as *Weltgeschichte und Heilsgeschehen* [World History and the Event of Salvation]).

book has come to initiate a long debate on whether all history might be so fundamentally religious that "secular" history—and secularization—is philosophically impossible.

Another German philosopher, Hans Blumenberg, deepened the debate with a paper titled "Secularisation" in 1962, followed four years later by a big history of ideas, *The Legitimacy of the Modern Age*, which had a similar thesis, but brought considerably more understanding than Pinker has on the relations centuries before the Enlightenment between Western religions and the emerging Renaissance philosophies of nature, or what we now call "science."[11] In the same philosophic tradition, Jürgen Habermas has weighed in on this question several times.[12] Karen Armstrong, in *The Battle for God* (2000), the most comprehensive of her many books on religion, provided a complex intellectual history of the theologies of the three Abrahamics, and the past cultures that envelop them.[13] Armstrong sees religion within the whole matrix of cultures past or present, distant or familiar. Charles Taylor tried to do the same while focusing on the West in his history of the secularization of religion, *A Secular Age* (2007), which might be considered a massive reply to all of them. A more sophisticated intellectual historian, Taylor went back to the eighteenth-century Enlightenment in *A Secular Age* to find the first of a finely drawn series of stages through which religion in the Christian West moved toward secularization, giving secularization itself a faint aura of holiness.[14] And John Ralston Saul wrote a polemic against the amorality of modern technocracy that began by detaching the Enlightenment's exercise of critical reason from any judgment of good or evil. It was, Saul thought, quite different from the quite different

[11] Hans Blumenberg, "'Säkularisation': Kritik einer Kategorie historischer Illegitimität," ["'Secularisation': Critique of a Category of Historical Illegitimacy"] *7th German Philosophy Congress* (1962) repr. in Helmut Kuhn & Franz Wiedemann, eds. *Die Philosophie und die Frage nach dem Fortschritt*, Munich: A. Pustet, 1964; Hans Blumenberg, *The Legitimacy of the Modern Age*, trans., Robert M. Wallace, Cambridge, MA: MIT Press, 1986 (*Die Legitimität der Neuzeit*, Frankfurt: Suhrkamp Verlag, 1966. rev. ed. 1973, 1974, 1976). Cf. *Jnl of the History of Ideas* 80:1(January, 2019).

[12] Jürgen Habermas, *The Philosophical Discourse of Modernity: Twelve Lectures*, 1987, trans., Frederick G. Lawrence from *Der Philosophische Diskurs der Moderne: Zwölf Vorlesungen*, 1985; Habermas, "Faith and Knowledge," tr., Hella Beister & William Rehy, in Eduardo Mendieta, ed., *The Frankfurt School on Religion: Key Writings by the Major Thinkers*, NY: Routledge, 2001; and Habermas, *Between Naturalism and Religion: Philosophical Essays*, trans., Ciaran Cronin, Cambridge, UK: Polity, 2008.

[13] Karen Armstrong, *The Battle for God* (NY: Knopf, 2000). Michael Harrington's 37-year-old *The Politics at God's Funeral: The Spiritual Crisis of Western Civilization* (New York: Henry Holt & Co. 1983), confined to the European-American intellectual tradition, has a more limited depth of field, but Harrington's Christian socialist sympathies gave him a somewhat better understanding of both the Enlightenment and the Counter-Enlightenment.

[14] Charles Taylor, *A Secular Age* (Cambridge, MA: Harvard U. Press, 2007). A further effort is Michael Allen Gillespie's *The Theological Origins of Modernity* (Chicago: U. of Chicago Press, 15 May, 2008).

(and less triumphant) process of adopting and committing to moral values, or even sorting them out.[15]

Anthropologist Talal Asad made a stab in 2003 at studying the modern "secularism" as another religion.[16] Bruce Lawrence had already gone further with a brilliant post-post-modern defense of the equivalency of the abrahamic "fundamentalisms" in *Defenders of God*.[17] With *The Stillborn God* in 2003, Mark Lilla offered a sort of middle way, arguing that "secularization," in the sense that it is usually meant, is not really possible. Both the politics and the religion of a community are human value systems, and thus, as Isaiah Berlin argued, evoking David Hume, both are beyond logical (rationalist) or even scientific (empiricist) justification.[18] That there is no "solution" to either may well imply that neither can be "secularized," in the sense of being reduced to logic, confined to the finite. As Lilla writes, the "urge to connect" religion and politics is "not an atavism," not a regression, but normal.[19] As a consequence here the argument is that secularization of religion is just a sophisticated term for describing change from one religion to another. Any moral system, perhaps especially systems that are held to against what we casually call self-interest, may properly be called a "religion," and if there be persons who hold no system at all against self-interest, they should be assumed to have self-interest as the keystone value of their moral system, which means self-interest should also be identified as a religion. Call it egotism.

---

[15] According to John Ralston Saul, "Voltaire and his friends [...] made the error of thinking that morality and common sense were the natural partners of reason" but it "could quite simply be that reason has nothing to do with democratic freedom or individualism or social justice." (Saul, *Voltaire's Bastards: The Dictatorship of Reason in the West*. (1992) New York: Vintage Books pb, 1993, p34.

[16] According to Talal Asad, "it is common knowledge that religion and the secular are closely linked, both in our thought and in the way they have emerged historically. Any discipline that seeks to understand "religion" must also try to understand its other. [...] because [the secular] is so much part of our modern life, it is not easy to grasp it directly. I think it is best pursued through its shadows, as it were." (Asad. *Formations of the Secular: Christianity, Islam, Modernity*. Stanford, CA: Stanford University Press Kindle ed. 2003). David Sherman put Asad's insight more vividly: "Much as whiteness once held the position among many in North America and Europe of an unremarkable racial category, or even a non-racial category, against which all others were considered remarkable, the secular too often has been taken in academic inquiry as qualitatively neutral, a condition that does not bear mentioning because it is itself unconditioned." (Sherman, "Woolf's Secular Imagery," *Modernism/Modernity* 23:4(2016), pp711–731).

[17] Bruce Lawrence, *Defenders of God: The Fundamentalist Revolt Against the Modern Age*. (Columbia, SC: University of South Carolina Press, 1989, 2nd ed. 1995).

[18] In Hume's words: "The rules of morality, therefore, are not conclusions of our reason." ([David Hume], *Treatise of Human Nature*, London, 1739, Book 3, Part 1, Section 1: Moral Distinctions not deriv'd from Reason, T 457).

[19] Mark Lilla, *The Stillborn God: Religion, Politics and the Modern West* (NY: Knopf, 2007), a book that began as lectures delivered at Oxford University in 2003, the same year that Lilla joined a small platoon of scholars taking another look at Isaiah Berlin and Counter-Enlightenment by publishing "What Is Counter-Enlightenment?" in Joseph Mali & Robert Wokler, eds. *Isaiah Berlin's Counter-Enlightenment, Transactions of the American Philosophical Society*, 93:5(2003), pp1–12.

So what *is* religion, after all? Does it really escape definition, as the infinite in mathematics escapes—by the definition of "definition"? Or is it a simple anthropological category? A cultural phenomenon? A political organization? An individual mental disability? A collective psychological delusion? A socially responsible habit? "The opiate of the people"? "The metaphysics of the masses"?[20] A sublimation of the erotic?[21] A mummer's delight? Is religion a set of special behaviors, as the French term for external religious practice, "*culte*," would suggest, meaning rites and liturgies that can be accurately described by a "neutral" observer? Is it an individual experience, inner, subjective and fundamentally incommunicable, of the immaterial and the infinite? Or is it, as its Latin roots indicate, a social and cultural "re-binding," a guarantee of mutual trust which, being epistemologically closed to one society, must forever remain incomprehensible to members of another? Is there, in short, an idea that is both reasonable and reasonably shareable of what religion *is*.

On his way home from serving in the Thirty Years War, the last and most devastating of the Catholic-Protestant wars in Christian Europe, one veteran, René Descartes, claimed in the first sentence of his famous *Discourse on the Method* (1634) that good sense must be the most evenly distributed of all intellectual qualities, because everyone thinks he has enough of it, and even the most acquisitive seem never to want more of it than they have.

---

[20] "A socially responsible habit" is my attempt to paraphrase David Hume. "Opiate of the people," of course, is from Karl Marx. "Metaphysics of the masses" is from Arthur Schopenhauer, "Religion, A Dialogue," (*Parerga und Paralipomena*, 1851) in *Essays and Aphorisms: The Essays of Arthur Schopenhauer*, trans., T. Bailey Saunders, M.A., Project Gutenberg EBook @ http://www.gutenberg.org/catalog/world/readfile?fk_files=1478212&pageno=1-5.

[21] That religion is a sublimation of the sex drive, or, as Freud would put it, a cathecting of the libido, is of course a lot older than Freud, and is best replied to by William James's delightfully extended footnote to his first Gifford Lecture on the *Varieties of Religious Experience* (given in 1901, only two years after the first publication of Freud's *Interpretation of Dreams*, which James had not read) "It seems to me that few conceptions are less instructive than this re-interpretation of religion as perverted sexuality. [...] the effects are infinitely wider than the alleged causes, and for the most part opposite in nature. It is true that in the vast collection of religious phenomena, some are undisguisedly amatory—e.g., sex-deities and obscene rites in polytheism, and ecstatic feelings of union with the Saviour in a few Christian mystics. But then why not equally call religion an aberration of the digestive function, and prove one's point by the worship of Bacchus and Ceres, or by the ecstatic feelings of some other saints about the Eucharist? [...] Language drawn from eating and drinking is probably as common in religious literature as is language drawn from the sexual life." And if it is argued that "The two main phenomena of religion, namely, melancholy and conversion ... are essentially phenomena of adolescence," because post-pubescents show an increased interest in sex, "One might then as well set up the thesis that the interest in mechanics, physics, chemistry, logic, philosophy, and sociology, which springs up during adolescent years along with that in poetry and religion, is also a perversion of the sexual instinct:—but that would be too absurd." (James. *Writings 1902–1910*: *The Varieties of Religious Experience/Pragmatism/A Pluralistic Universe/The Meaning of Truth/Some Problems of Philosophy/Essays*. ed. Bruce Kuklick, Library of America, 1988, p. 19–20).

> Le bon sens est la chose du monde la mieux partagée, car chacun pense en être si bien pourvu que ceux même qui sont les plus difficiles à contenter en toute autre chose n'ont point coutume d'en désirer plus qu'ils en ont.[22]

If Descartes was not just joking, then religious sensibility must be the most ***un***-evenly distributed of qualities, because so many think that so many others have either too much or too little of it. Some will continue to claim that there is no such thing—that all religious experience is delusion and all reports of it are fraud. Others will accuse only ecstatic or mystical religious experience of being delusion or imposture. The kindest thing many can say of someone who shows signs of being carried away is that he is self-deluded and that those who carry him away should make sure that it is to an accredited sanitarium.

Something akin to this latter view of religion was held by Descartes and his philosophical heirs and successors, who found an intellectual way out of Europe's century-long Protestant-Catholic wars by shifting the faith of thinkers from the actions of the Mass to the axioms of mathematics. This seventeenth-century Age of Reason is where the Western Enlightenment began. Among those heirs of Descartes are to be counted the eighteenth-century political Founders of the United States and nearly all the Framers of its Constitution. Their view, anathema to their modern idolaters in the U.S. Tea Party, had been anticipated in part by many of the great thinkers of medieval Muslim Baghdad and Cordoba, and Jewish thinkers from Maimonides to Moses Mendelssohn. It was also the view—the religion, in fact—of the "enlightened" leaders of opinion in France and of advanced thinkers all over Europe for five or six generations after Descartes. In French they called themselves *philosophes* and their movement, the *Lumières* (Lights, Enlightenment); and they agreed that all revealed religions and all religious organizations must endure skeptical examination. A few philosophes, like d'Holbach, went on to label religious organizations and dogma as "fanaticism," and schemed to "cure" people of religion.[23] Some philosophes refused even the simple label "religion" for their own fundamental beliefs (usually Deism but sometimes atheist materialism or egotism); and by doing so they raised the difficult definitional problem of whether atheism (or for similar reasons Buddhism and Confucianism) can be termed a religion or not. In my own account Confucianism, though it has no formulable theology, is a religion because it postulates a universe that endorses a human morality, a little like the "arc of the moral universe" of the (Baptist) Reverend Martin Luther King that "bends toward justice."

Facing the definitional question leads, in turn, to a philosophical question that is even more knotty: Is there a non-religious position, or point of view, from which one may look on and study religions "objectively"? Archimedes is said to have claimed that he could "move the earth" if he could have a lever long enough and

---

22 Another way of translating the first sentence of Descartes' *Discours de la méthode*: "everyone thinks he is so well endowed with it that even those who are hardest to please in everything else are not in the habit of wanting more of it than they have."

23 Alan Charles Kors, *D'Holbach's Coterie: An Enlightenment in Paris*. Princeton, NJ: Princeton University Press, 1976.

"one firm place on which to stand." The philosophes, like so many moderns, thought that they had found a place to stand; but they were mistaken, and religion's Archimedean point has proved far harder to find than the Earth's. Just as a meta-mathematics implying the axioms of arithmetic is itself a mathematics, so any meta-ethics must itself be an ethics, and (returning to our attempted definition) if it results in the assertion of values (that is, if it is practiced), then it is a religion.

Human beings—animals unique in having some foreknowledge of their own end—have a lust for meaning seemingly no less avid than the lust for air, water, food, shelter, intimacy, offspring and company. We are not only hard-wired to risk our lives for these ends, we have the software, too, in the form of philosophical and ethical questions raised inevitably in human minds by the fact of our mortality.[24] We cannot answer those questions satisfactorily without the complete knowledge of infinity denied to us not only by our biology, but also by science, mathematics and philosophy; and so we habitually proceed into our various futures on faith: the beliefs and assumptions, and "true" stories, which, without being either provable or disprovable, give us what we think will be a better chance at a meaning transcending death. In certain moods, feeling that those unprovables are under threat, we will not only fight to uphold them, but kill and—even more curiously—die to uphold them. The genes for fight or flight, social reciprocity, self-defense, and altruism, preserved for their species-survival value, are turned into values by conscious, thinking humans, and intensified and brought to a focus by religions or ethical philosophies; but those "instincts" are often at odds, and their effects are contradictory, so they are also *ipso facto* thwarted and questioned by religions.[25] This result is clear even when

---

[24] As Judith Shulevitz put it, in her review of a memoir by a Harvard Professor of Hebrew who became aware of his transcendance in the face of death: "Too many pundits, anthropologists and evolutionary biologists fail to imagine their way into the rich, elusive mental condition called 'believing in God' or 'being religious.' They dismiss it as a neurosis, a superstition or a mistake."—Shulevitz, "Time and Possibilities," Review of James L. Kugel, *In the Valley of the Shadow* (NY: Free Press, 2011) *New York Times*, February 11, 2011.

[25] Oren Harman, *The Price of Altruism: George Price and the Search for the Origins of Kindness* (Norton, 2010) has the story of this exceptionally important debate in evolutionary biology that was renewed by W. D. Hamilton (1936–2000), "The Genetical Evolution of Social Behavior," 1 & 2, *Journal of Theoretical Biology* 7(1964), p1–52, which mathematically described "inclusive fitness" (which includes that of kin), and "nepotistic altruism." The term "kin selection" at gene level is usually attributed to John Maynard Smith (1920–2004) because of a letter Smith sent to *Nature* after he had refereed and delayed the publication of Hamilton's paper. Two years later came the antithesis: George C. Williams (1926–2010) published a refutation of Hamilton in *Adaptation and Natural Selection: A Critique of Some Current Evolutionary Thought* (1966). Williams thought he had proved that individuals—not groups—are selected for, and thus that altruism genes can have no survival value. In 1968, after reading Hamilton's original paper, George R. Price (1922–1975) reestablished the natural selection of altruism by discovering an equation with two terms, (1) for covariance of a gene's presence in an individual and the number of the individual's progeny, and (2) for the gene's likelihood of transmission. It worked for finite groups of related individuals, allowing for negative relatedness, explained group selection, and reopened the possibility that altruistic behavior might have evolved in humans. Price published it in his article, "Selection and Covariance," in *Nature* (August 1, 1970). The kin selection/social behavior debate culminated in John Maynard Smith, *Evolution and the Theory of Games* (1982), which used game theory to

other religions and ethics are loudest in condemning them, and perhaps it can explain why the anticlerical Enlightenment *philosophe* Voltaire concluded (to be echoed later by the anticlerical, theist, and revolutionary Robespierre) that "if God did not exist, He would have to be invented."[26]

The intellectual children of the Enlightenment are partial to the idea that morals are a product of human "nature," but it remains an open question whether any moral principle is "natural." Do any of them arise entirely out of the nature of the human animal rather than being imposed on individual humans by their own conscious choices and the choices of others? The pursuit of nourishment is no doubt a natural imperative, but that imperative cannot explain why so many human communities have institutionalized fasting and why almost all have thought it improper to kill and eat each other, as fish do.[27] Sex is obviously a natural drive; but humans who lack the drive, or whose communities forbid its expression, continue to exist and to pass on, if not their genes, at least their memes. Some "deep ecologists" today view human reproduction as immoral but their idea remains alive. The Shakers of the eighteenth century had no reproductive success whatever and have consequently become extinct in the twenty-first century; but they have had, and continue to have, a moral effect on many who were never Shakers or bound by their principle of celibacy (like a Jewish couple I know who met at a Shaker summer camp.) Death, too, is clearly natural; but that does not prevent virtually all human communities from

describe a biological equivalent of Nash Equilibrium, the Evolutionarily Stable Strategy (ESS), which (it has since been argued) accounts for many "self-sacrificing" social behaviors, including those among humans that we often call religious. Price's subsequent despair at having proved that Christian self-sacrifice was a mere artifact of biological selection instead of an ethical commitment, followed by his conversion to evangelical protestant Christianity, a life of voluntary poverty, and his ultimate suicide, seem not to have made Price's science more acceptable to biologists like Richard Dawkins, nor has it greatly enhanced his reputation among scientists who do not share Dawkins's antipathy to theism. One can imagine how Price might have reacted, pre- or post-conversion, to the fairly recent studies, including those of Kent Kiehl (note 30, below), which try to locate empathy and generosity in the neurophysiology of the brain.

[26] "Si Dieu n'existait pas, il faudrait l'inventer." Voltaire, *Epitre à l'auteur du livre des trois imposteurs*, 1769 (*Oeuvres*, ed., Moland, v10, p. 403, one of five times this alexandrine verse was written by Voltaire, *Voltaire électronique*, cited by J. Patrick Lee, C18-L, 10 Jan 2002). Robespierre, the Enlightenment revolutionary, repeated it without acknowledgement on 8 November, 1793, replying to atheist speeches by Hébert and Momoro at the Jacobin Club: "Atheism is aristocratic […] the idea of a great Being who watches over oppressed innocence, and which punishes triumphant crime, is wholly popular […] If God did not exist, He would have to be invented." (in Robespierre, *Oeuvres complètes*, ed., Marc Bouloiseau, 1967, v10, p. 196, my translation.)

[27] In fact, cannibalism turns out to be the rule, rather than the exception, for hundreds and possibly thousands of species, not just fish; and the exception, and in one or two cases the rule, for humans of many different cultures and subcultures, whether civilized or uncivilized, comfortable or *in extremis*, according to Bill Schutt, *Cannibalism: A Perfectly Natural History*, Chapel Hill, NC: Algonquin Books of Chapel Hill, 2017. Jonathan Swift wrote enduringly in 1729 about the moral ambiguity of eating people in *A Modest Proposal For preventing the Children of Poor People From being a Burthen to Their Parents or Country, and For making them Beneficial to the Publick.* (Swift, I expect will be adopted into the English Enlightenment when the English can finally agree that there was one.)

regretting it, and most human communities from actively trying to delay it, or to prevent it—or to believe that life does not end with it.

Violence is equally natural; but so is non-violence. Religious wars have long been called the worst of human violence; but it is an error to fix on religion as the cause of violence. The relation is more subtle. An English Catholic conservative, G. K. Chesterton, put it exceptionally well:

> Bigotry may be called the appalling frenzy of the indifferent. This frenzy of the indifferent is in truth a terrible thing; it has made all monstrous and widely pervading persecutions. In this degree it was not the people who cared who ever persecuted; the people who cared were not sufficiently numerous. It was the people who did not care who filled the world with fire and oppression. It was the hands of the indifferent that lit the faggots; it was the hands of the indifferent that turned the rack. There have come some persecutions out of the pain of a passionate certainty; but these produced, not bigotry, but fanaticism—a very different and a somewhat admirable thing. Bigotry in the main has always been the pervading omnipotence of those who do not care crushing out those who care in darkness and blood. [...] it is precisely because an ideal is necessary to man that the man without ideals is in permanent danger of fanaticism.[28]

Many religions, in fact, have tried to devalue violence, to forbid all violence on principle—religious principle—and some have succeeded, at least for a time, like the Christian Anabaptists (the Amish) and the Jains. In fact it is precisely these moral principles and ethical propositions, multiple, diverse and contradictory as they must be, that cause the adherents of different religions to label each other "good" or "evil"; and these days it is more often the contradictory ethics than it is the mutually incredible theologies, which motivate religious adherents to consider killing each other. That religion is a cause of religious war is historically obvious. That religion also *ends* religious war may be less evident, but it is no less true, even when it is a change in religion that brings about the end.

In fact the opinion is growing, not just among historians but among biologists and anthropologists, that even if it were possible to cure the "sacred disease," the result would not be an increase, but a reduction, instead, in the Darwinian survivability (including long-term reproductive success) of that vast majority of human

---

[28] G. K. Chesterton, *Heretics*, London: John Lane, 3rd ed., 1905, p296, Chapter XX: "Concluding Remarks on the Importance of Orthodoxy" @ http://en.wikiquote.org/wiki/G.K._Chesterton. An elegantly worded version of this insight of Chesterton's: "Frantic orthodoxy is never rooted in faith but in doubt. It is when we are not sure that we are doubly sure," has been attributed to Reinhold Niebuhr by DeWitte Talmadge Holland (*America in Controversy*, W.C. Brown, 1973, p296), but I have not been able to track it down to him. What Niebuhr did write was, "Extreme orthodoxy betrays by its very frenzy that the poison of scepticism has entered the soul of the church; for men insist most vehemently upon their certainties when their hold upon them has been shaken. Frantic orthodoxy is a method for obscuring doubt." in *Does Civilization Need Religion? A Study in the Social Resources and Limitations of Religion in Modern Life* (NY: Macmillan, 1927), pp2–3. Chesterton was a Catholic controversialist. Reinhold Niebuhr was, of course, the celebrated American Protestant Christian thinker who helped found and formulate Cold War liberalism; but when *Does Civilization Need Religion?* was published, he was a Lutheran pastor in Detroit, Michigan, editing the "modernist" *Christian Century*, and opposing American Fundamentalism in the shadow of the 1925 Scopes trial.

communities that now profess or practice religions.[29] Neuroscientists are arguing that millennia of hominid survival have given natural selection a chance to install "religious software" permanently in the brain.[30] Human creative imagination even installed something similar in a fictional species, the ever-rational Vulcans of *Star Trek*, to increase their evolutionary fitness. And beyond the biological, there is the sheer intellectual usefulness of the deviants among us humans, as seen a century ago by Marcel Proust: "Everything great that we know we owe to neurotics [*nerveux*]. It is they and none else who have founded our religions and composed our masterpieces."[31] Ethics and religion are not entirely natural, and they aren't very logical either. The whole philosophy of Nietzsche, is built on this insight that Good and Evil are neither natural nor universal. The philosopher Ludwig Wittgenstein echoed Hume in his first book composed during the First World War, "Hence also there can be no ethical propositions," and thus "it is clear that ethics cannot be expressed," or put into words. "Ethics is transcendental."[32] In the twenty-first century, Western thinkers, wise with the new evolutionary neuropsychology, have been reduced to describing ethical commitments in Darwinian terms as "naturally net fitness-enhancing."

Natural explanations of religion are not enough. There are ideological ones that are just as important, and at least a few concerns that all the things we call

---

[29] A well-informed introduction to this line of thinking is Pascal Boyer, *Religion Explained: Evolutionary Origins of Religious Thought* (NY: Basic Books, 2001). An approach from the philosophic end was taken by James Rachels in *Created from Animals: The Moral Implications of Darwinism* (NY: Oxford U. Press, 1990). At root is a key debate in evolutionary biology—the "fitness" of generosity. Efforts to locate altruism in the brain itself, like Kent Kiehl's studies on brain structures that seem to account for the lower empathy of psychopaths, including "A cognitive neuroscience perspective on psychopathy: Evidence for paralimbic system dysfunction," (*Psychiatry Research*, 142(2006), pp. 107–128). Oren Harman, *The Price of Altruism*. (note 26 above) provides a history of the scientific effort, begun by Darwin and consummated by the tragic success of Price, to assign a Darwinian survival value to altruism.

[30] The hypothesis of a self-transcendence-boosting version of the gene VMAT2 as a genetic basis for religious belief is laid out in Dean H. Hamer, *The God Gene: How Faith is Hardwired into our Genes*, (NY: Anchor, 2005), but fellow neuroscientists like Carl Zimmer find Hamer's evidence too thin. Sally Satel and Scott Lilienfeld (*Brainwashed: The Seductive Appeal of Mindless Neuroscience*, NY: Basic Books, June 4, 2013) find the brain's structure and operation still too complex to pinpoint how this gene, or any gene for emotional experience, is expressed neurophysiologically, or indeed how the experiences themselves are produced. But the larger hypothesis remains promising.

[31] Marcel Proust, *A la recherché du temps perdu*, vol. 7, *Le côté de Guermantes*, II, Paris: Gallimard, 1921, p228. This insight of Proust (a self-described neurotic/*nerveux*) seems to have caught the eye of at least one anglophone author, Gilbert Seldes, who quoted it on the last page of his 1928 book on nineteenth-century U.S. evangelical religious radicals, *The Stammering Century*, chapter 26, new edition, ed., Greil Marcus (NY: New York Review Books, 2012), p411.

[32] Wittgenstein, *Tractatus Logico-Philosophicus* (1922) 6.42. One source of Wittgenstein's thinking was Leo Tolstoy's *The Gospel in Brief*, written in 1881, which Wittgenstein bought by chance just as he was called up for World War One, and which he carried and touted throughout his service. See: Bill Schardt and David Large, "Wittgenstein, Tolstoy and *The Gospel in Brief*," in *The Philosopher*, Volume LXXXIX @ http://atschool.eduweb.co.uk/cite/staff/philosopher/witty.htm.

"religions" have in common. All survivable religions must be seen by their adherents to provide, for both individuals and communities, answers to three hopelessly unscientific philosophical questions: the great ontological question of identity (Who am I?), the great ethical question of purpose (What am I doing here and why should I be doing it?), and the great ethical question of duty (What should I do for, or about, the others?). This is why the Protestant Christian thinker, Paul Tillich, identified God as "ultimate concern," and why it's no wonder so many people take religion so seriously.

Besides these few general ideas that all the things we call "religions" consider, a religion is not primarily a set of beliefs about a god or gods, as Jews, Muslims and Christians usually assume and anticlericals, especially atheists, continue to insist. Thus, I would argue, every doctrinal definition is too narrow to capture the phenomenon. Functional definitions are potentially broad enough, but philosophically fiendish. As John Herman Randall wrote fifty years ago, "The attempt to define the function of religion is notoriously complex and difficult; it has never been satisfactorily carried out."[33]

Thinkers who still try, like Ann Taves, often appeal to two books, also centered on experience, that are now more than a century old. One is *The Varieties of Religious Experience*, the Gifford Lectures, given in Edinburgh in 1901 by a nominal Christian, Harvard's new psychology professor William James.[34] It famously focuses in a self-consciously scientific manner on experience rather than doctrine. The other, *The Elementary Forms of the Religious Life* (1912) by James's contemporary, the pioneering French sociologist (and secular Jew) Émile Durkheim, who set aside the existing definitions of religion as assertions about the supernatural, or about mystery, or about divinity, and then reduced religion to two basic categories of social "phenomena [...] beliefs and rites" which divide everything in a community's experience into two absolutely distinguishable categories, "*profane* and *sacred*."[35] Durkheim's definition can still surprise a modern reader:

> The general conclusion of the chapters to follow is that religion is an eminently social thing. Religious representations are collective representations that express collective realities; rites are ways of acting that are born only in the midst of assembled groups and whose purpose is to evoke, maintain, or recreate certain mental states of those groups.[36]

---

[33] John Herman Randall, Jr., *The Role of Knowledge in Western Religion*, (1955–1956, Boston: Starr King Press, 1958), p101.

[34] William James, *Varieties of Religious Experience* (1902) in James. *Writings 1902–1910*. ed. Bruce Kuklick, Library of America, 1988.

[35] Émile Durkheim, *The Elementary Forms of the Religious Life* (*Les formes élémentaires de la vie religieuse: Le système totémique en Australie*, Paris: Alcan, 1912), trans., Karen E. Fields, NY: Free Press, 1995, p34.

[36] Durkheim, *Elementary Forms*, 1995, p9. Durkheim cast his net broadly, in the modern way: "Fundamentally, then, there are no religions that are false. All are true after their own fashion: All fulfill given conditions of human existence, though in different ways." (*Elementary Forms*, 1995, p2).

As a definition, however, it works reasonably well, even if "profane and sacred" remain hard to define. Considered anthropologically—Durkheim's examples were from anthropologists' reports of Aboriginal Australians—it matters little whether a religion has a theology or not, because what matters most (and has the only chance of being, philosophically speaking, "objective") is what people in a community experience together, and what they actually *do* as a result.

Conventional wisdom has it that Enlightenment values will end our mortal religious conflicts. Here we have considered how the Enlightenment, which many have come to assume is the first act of what we call the "modernization" of Western Civilization (but which has occurred in other cultures, too) produced its own antithesis in its own time, an antithesis that has persisted until the present day in all three Abrahamic religions.[37] Since the mobilization of the "Moral Majority" in the United States in the 1970s, or (if you like) since 1910 when the publication of the Protestant pamphlet-essays on doctrine called *The Fundamentals* began, Americans have understood that "modernity" has its adversaries, even in America, and that these adversaries organize themselves often—perhaps most often—around churches ("evangelical" Protestant or "traditional" Catholic), "conservative" political factions, Salafist imamates, and "Orthodox" or "Haredi" rabbinates.

Since the newest wave of atheist controversialists is almost unanimous in its definition of its adversary, it makes unavoidable the question of whether "religion" is what the atheists say it is. They have, it seems, rarely examined other definitions of religion. But there is no shortage of such definitions; they have been proliferating in colorful varieties in the West since the eighteenth century. Today academic departments of Religion, Religious Studies, and even Theology, not to mention Philosophy of Religion, Philosophy in general, Sociology, and Anthropology, often seem to be putting much of their effort into trying to find a definition ecumenical enough to please every professor, with results that have not always been that promising; but Rodney Stark, a sociologist by training, has written and applied a plausible theory of religion based on transactional ethics that can make even religious wars fit modern value systems.[38]

---

[37] "Modern," the word we use so glibly, was rarely used in the Enlightenment, and "modernize" not at all.

[38] Rodney Stark's multivolume ethics-before-piety reinterpretation of the world history of religions seems to have begun with the book he wrote with C[harles] Y[oung] Glock, published as *American Piety: The Nature of Religious Commitment*. (Berkeley: University of California Press, 1968). He wrote a later philosophical presentation with Wiliam Sims Bainbridge, published as *A Theory of Religion*. (New Brunswick, NJ: Rutgers University Press, 1996). A series of engaging narrative histories followed and found a wide audience. The latest one on the Abrahamic triad is *One True God: Historical Consequences of Monotheism*. (Princeton, NJ: Princeton University Press, 2001; pb, 2003).

In her masterly review of the bidding over this large literature, *Religious Experience Reconsidered*,[39] Ann Taves focuses on definitions based on mental experience—philosophers would call it "phenomenology"—and she singles out dozens of efforts both old and new, beginning with Friedrich Schleiermacher's "feeling of absolute dependence," William James's "feelings, acts, and experiences of individual men in their solitude" and Émile Durkheim's "unified system of beliefs and practices relative to sacred things … set apart and forbidden,"[40] onward to the anti-essentialist (sometimes deconstructionist) phenomenological definitions of late twentieth-century scholars like Robert Scharf, Jeppe Jensen, Russell McCutcheon, Timothy Fitzgerald, and the magisterial Jonathan Z. Smith.[41] The more materialist efforts, still ongoing, of medical and psychological anthropologists remain relevant

[39] Ann Taves, *Religious Experience Reconsidered: A Building-Block Approach to the Study of Religion and Other Special Things*, Princeton, NJ: Princeton University Press. Kindle Edition, 2009-09-28, location 176–229.

[40] Friedrich Schleiermacher, *The Christian Faith* (*Glaubenslehre*, 1821) (*Theology of Schleiermacher: A Condensed Presentation of His Chief Work,* "The Christian Faith" trans., Christian Classics Ethereal Library (CCEL)), p122; William James, *Varieties of Religious Experience* (1902) in *Writings 1902–1910*. ed. Bruce Kuklick, Library of America, 1988, p36; Émile Durkheim, *The Elementary Forms of the Religious Life*, NY: Free Press, 1995, p44. James and Durkheim belong to a period of notable resurgence of sympathetic academic interest in religion on the part of Western intellectuals at the beginning of the twentieth century, as does Evelyn Underhill's English classic, *Mysticism: The Nature and Development of Spiritual Consciousness*, 1911 (Oxford: Oneworld, 1999), republished as the Depression began in 1930, and again at the height of World War II in 1944. We might add the books of Quaker historian-activist Rufus Jones, beginning with *Studies in Mystical Religion*, (London, 1909, Kindle ed., 2017), and those of Jewish philosopher Martin Buber, like *Ekstatische Konfessionen* (Jena, 1909, translated by Esther Cameron as *Ecstatic Confessions*. ed. Paul Mendes-Flohr, Syracuse, NY: Syracuse University Press, 1996). In England this interest can be traced forward to C. S. Lewis and the Inklings, and beyond. As of 2019, the definitive history of Christian mysticism is the seven-volume *Presence of God: a History of Western Christian Mysticism*. Herder & Herder, 1994–2018, by Bernard McGinn.

[41] Taves cites Robert H. Sharf, "Experience," in Mark C. Taylor, ed., *Critical Terms for religious studies* (Chicago: U. of Chicago Press, 1998), Willi Braun & Russell T. McCutcheon, eds. *Guide to the Study of Religion* (London & NY: Cassell, 2000), Timothy Fitzgerald, "Experience," in Braun & McCutcheon, eds. *Guide to the Study of Religion*, and Jeppe Sinding Jensen, *The study of religion in a new key: Theoretical and philosophical soundings in the comparative and general study of religion* (Aarhus: Aarhus University Press, 2003). It is Jonathan Z. Smith's definition of "Religion" in Braun and McCutcheon's *Guide*, that sums up Smith's long career as the dean of the religious phenomenologists. I might add that the older phenomenological approach to the existence of the divine, avoiding supernatural or minimizing non-material explanations in the manner of Enlightenment thinkers, may be found in a quite recent paper by Kai-man Kwan, "The Argument from Religious Experience" in *The Blackwell Companion to Natural Theology* (eds. William Lane Craig & J. P. Moreland, NY: Wiley-Blackwell, 2009, 2012), pp498–552.

but supplementary,[42] as does Taves's own definition based on the way humans "ascribe" special status to anything or any phenomenon.[43]

Philosophers have been gravitating more recently to the phenomenological and empirical (experiential) accounts of religion.[44] Taves has not picked up all the

---

[42] For an account of a series of neurobiological experiments tending to prove that "mystical" experiences are reflected in the brain, there is Andrew B. Newberg, *Why God Won't Go Away: Brain Science and the Biology of Belief* (NY: Free Press?, 2001, pb, NY: Ballantine, 2002). Taves cites Tanya M. Luhrmann, "Yearning for God: Trance as a culturally specific practice and its implications for understanding dissociative disorders," *Jnl of Trauma and Dissociation.* Special Issue: *Dissociation in Culture* 5:2 (2004), p101–129; Luhrmann, "The art of hearing God: Absorption, dissociation, and contemporary American spirituality," *Spiritus* 5:2(2005), p133–157); Michele Stephen, "The self, the sacred other, and the religious imagination," in G. Herdt & M. Stephen, eds. *The Religious imagination in New Guinea* (New Brunswick, NJ: Rutgers University Press, 1989); Courtney Bender, *Worlds of Experience: Contemporary Spirituality and the American religious imagination* (Chicago U. of Chicago Press, 2008); Nina P. Azari, "Religious experience as thinking that feels like something: A philosophical-theological reflection on recent neuroscientific study of religious experience." *Dissertation Abstracts International Section A: Humanities and Social Sciences*, vol. 65:2A(2004), 565; Kenneth R, Livingston, "Religious practice, brain, and belief," *Journal of Cognition and Culture* 5:1–2(2005), p75–117; and "self-identified neurotheologians" Eugene G. D'Aquili & Andrew B. Newberg, whose *The Mystical Mind: Probing the biology of religious experience* (Minneapolis: Fortress Press, 1999) was published almost exactly a century after William James's *Varieties of Religious Experience* pioneered the empirical approach to religion. This is promising, even when you keep in mind the rest of William James's long first footnote to Lecture #1 of the *Varieties* (1901): "the too simple-minded system of thought [called] medical materialism finishes up Saint Paul by calling his vision on the road to Damascus a discharging lesion of the occipital cortex, he being an epileptic. It snuffs out Saint Teresa as an hysteric, Saint Francis of Assisi as an hereditary degenerate. George Fox's discontent with the shams of his age, and his pining for spiritual veracity, it treats as a symptom of a disordered colon. Carlyle's organ-tones of misery it accounts for by a gastro-duodenal catarrh. All such mental overtensions, it says, are, when you come to the bottom of the matter, mere affairs of diathesis (auto-intoxications most probably), due to the perverted action of various glands which physiology will yet discover. And medical materialism then thinks that the spiritual authority of all such personages is successfully undermined." James. *Writings 1902–1910.* Library of America, 1988, p. 19n1.

A more sophisticated medical materialism, however, has recently been extended to the phenomenology of ethics, and includes the studies of Kent Kiehl (note 29, above) and Brick Johnstone (an early example is Johnstone, Bodling, Cohen, Christ, & Wegrzyn, "Right parietal lobe-related 'selflessness' as the neuropsychological basis of spiritual transcendence," *International Journal for the Psychology of Religion.* accessed at @ http://www.tandfonline.com/action/doSearch?AllField=Right+parietal+lobe-related+%E2%80%9Cselflessness%E2%80%9D on 30 May, 2012. Rodney Stark's work (Stark, with C. Y. Glock, *American Piety: The Nature of Religious Commitment.* 1968) advances compatible views, but the most sophisticated attempt so far, I think, to account biologically for ethics (and by extension for what I call the "religious commitment" to values) is what Jesse Graham, Jonathan Haidt, Sena Koleva, Matt Motyl, Ravi Iyer, Sean P. Wojcik, and Peter H. Ditto dub "Moral Foundations Theory," summarized in their article, "Moral Foundations Theory: The Pragmatic Validity of Moral Pluralism," (Chapter 2 in Patricia Devine & Ashby Plant, eds. *Advances in Experimental Social Psychology*, vol. 47, Burlington: Academic Press, 2013, pp. 55–130 (made available to me in an online preprint.)

[43] Taves, *Religious Experience Reconsidered*, Kindle Edition, 2009-09-28, location 187.

[44] For example, Robert C. Fuller ("Spirituality in the Flesh: The Role of Discrete Emotions in Religious Life," *Journal of the American Academy of Religion* 2007 75(1):25–51; doi:https://doi.

philosophical arguments, like those of C. D. Broad, that tend to validate her own experiential premise.[45] Perhaps Taves was encouraged, post-publication, by the notably militant atheist Sam Harris coming around to "experiences" (though he would not call them "religious") in a book that begins with what he calls "experiences of self-transcendence." Harris writes that when he was a sixteen-year-old naïve materialist, he was baffled by the reports of others who had had such experiences when they were alone in the Colorado wilderness. Later Harris had an experience himself, "feeling boundless love for one of my best friends" after taking the drug MDMA (marketed, as it happens, under the name Ecstasy).[46]

Ecstatic experiences have indeed been subject to serious scientific investigation, much of it beginning at the turn of this century with Eugene D'Aquili and radiologist Andrew Newberg's scans of meditating monks and nuns.[47] Professor Massimo Pigliucci, a materialist, indeed asserts that religious experience can be entirely accounted for by neurophysiology:

> There has been a lot of talk about the neurological basis of religious experiences lately, with both secular and mystical interpretations of the available results. It turns out that it is now possible to actually replicate mystical experiences with a variety of methods, even under strict laboratory conditions. Does this mean that mysticism is nothing but a byproduct of a brain that malfunctions under unusual circumstances (exposure to drugs, sensory deprivation, brain damage)? Or is there a "god module" in the brain that allows us to perceive an alternative reality? In this talk I will argue for the former and show why science may be about to dismantle the ultimate retreat of anti-materialists, not that that will convince any of them, of course.[48]

---

org/10.1093/jaarel/lfl064), and Sami Pohlson (*Pragmatic Pluralism and the Problem of God*, NY: Fordham University Press, 2016?).

[45] C. D. Broad, "Arguments for The Existence of God," II, in *Journal of Theological Studies*, 40(1939): pp156–167 (reprinted in Broad, *Religion, Philosophy and Psychical Research* (1953), London: Routledge, 2000). Broad's empiricist epistemology dismissed what he called "naïve realism," and rehabilitated the illusory and hallucinatory as genuine experience that it would be "unreasonable" to dismiss as fraudulent.

[46] Sam Harris, *Waking Up: A Guide to Spirituality Without Religion* (2014) @ https://www.samharris.org/podcast/item/chapter-one. Harris goes on to write that in his book, he "will use spiritual, mystical, contemplative, and transcendent without further apology. [...] Nothing in this book needs to be accepted on faith. Although my focus is on human subjectivity—I am, after all, talking about the nature of experience itself—all my assertions can be tested in the laboratory of your own life." (Yes, one thinks, but tested by whom? Logically, only those who (a) have had such experiences and (b) recognize them in Harris's, may apply the test.)

[47] Newberg, & D'Aquili, *Why God Won't Go Away* (2001). More recent studies led by Brick Johnstone back up Newberg and D'Aquili, finding evidence for selflessness in brain scans, for example: Brick Johnstone, Daniel Cohen, Kelly Konopacki & Christopher Ghan, "Selflessness as a Foundation of Spiritual Transcendence: Perspectives From the Neurosciences and Religious Studies," *The International Journal for the Psychology of Religion* 26:4(2016), pp. 287–303, Published online: 11 Mar 2016 @ https://www.tandfonline.com/doi/abs/10.1080/10508619.2015.1118328. Philosophers of religion (Nelson Pike), industrial engineers (Aaron C. T. Smith), psychologists (Normand Laurendeau) primatologists (C. Robert Cloninger), and theologians (Paul and Cathleen Shrier, and Deepak Chopra) have all picked up the idea.

[48] Massimo Pigliucci, preview to his talk to the Secular Humanists of the Lowcountry in Charleston, South Carolina, in *The Separationist* (September 2002) Newsletter of SHL @ http://life.bio.sun-

But it does not matter so much that mystical experiences may prove to be genetically or physiologically analyzable, or physiologically inducible under laboratory conditions (although one would think that experiences beginning in the '60s had already established physiological inducibility).[49] It is not the mystical experience itself, but the effect of the experience on the behavior of the experimenter, and in particular on his or her values and morals, and the morals of their followers. The experience so often gives rise (immediately or over generations) to the moral convictions that we call "religious," and prompts the explanations that we also call "religious." (Religious dogmatism, legalism or "moralism" is what we should call the most common result of the unpredictable replicability of such experiences.) I would not object to calling those religious explanations "rationalizations" of experience, except that it seems evident to me that such a term would deeply disconcert, if not offend, thinkers like Pigliucci who believe that all "religions" must be theist and that atheisms are barred from inclusion among religions.

Efforts by philosophers to deal with religion have not all been strictly phenomenological. The whole idea of religion can seem self-contradictory, when maverick philosophers continue to point out that logic itself forbids—or rather precludes—the cure for faith that d'Holbach hoped for. As American philosopher George Santayana put it a century ago, "Any attempt to speak without speaking any particular language is not more hopeless than the attempt to have a religion that shall be no religion in particular."[50] Just as it is impossible to develop a meta-mathematics to prove the axioms of geometry (or arithmetic), and as a different choice of axioms can give rise to a completely different (but no less logically consistent) geometry, so there is no meta-ethical knowledge by which we can prove or disprove an ethic, and *a fortiori*, no meta-religious knowledge by which we can prove or disprove a religion. Western philosophers repeatedly rediscovered this truth. Immanuel Kant, at the height of the Enlightenment, wrote two of his books to make it clear. Any investigator who tries to prove or disprove a religion (or an ethics) must assume or assert

---

ysb.edu/~massimo/lectures/mystical-experiences.pdf. Less reductive approaches by philosophers to the question of mystical experience as a neuropsychological phenomenon include Nelson Pike's *Mystic Union: An Essay in the Phenomenology of Mysticism* (Cornell Studies in the Philosophy of Religion. Ithaca, NY: Cornell University Press, 1992).

[49] Among the best written accounts of such experiments is one of the first, Aldous Huxley's *The Doors of Perception* (NY: Harper/London: Chatto & Windus, 1954) about a "trip" that the aging novelist took in 1953 after ingesting peyote (mescaline) at his home in California, which became a bible for the 1960s counterculture (and whose title, borrowed from William Blake, was repurposed by Jim Morrison for his 1960s band). More recent is the late Dr. Oliver Sacks's "Altered States: Self-experiments in chemistry," *The New Yorker*, 27 August, 2012, pp40–47, by a scientist who considered only neural, as opposed to religious, explanations. Another is Michael Pollan's *How to Change Your Mind: What the New Science of Psychedelics Teaches Us About Consciousness, Dying, Addiction, Depression, and Transcendence*, NY: Penguin Press, 2018). Pollan has also published a short essay "How Does a Writer Put a Drug Trip Into Words?" (*NYTimes Book Review*, 24 December, 2018) describing one of the experiences in the book that he had after ingesting the chemical 5-MeO-DMT by smoking the venom of the Sonoran Desert toad.

[50] George Santayana (1863–1952), *The Life of Reason: The Phases of Human Progress*, v3, *Reason in Religion*, 1905, in Clifford Geertz, *The Interpretation of Cultures*, 1973, p87.

something that looks very much like yet another religion. And this religion will be (possibly in every case) the religion of the investigator.

The religion of such a "modern" investigator may or may not be atheism; but whatever it is it will likely say little about God or the absence of gods, and have no doctrines about what Socrates called the activities of supernatural beings. Most likely it will be about ethics—the valuation, or the right and wrong of actions. In the old-fashioned backward-reasoning language of Jean-Jacques Rousseau: "No religion upon earth can dispense with the sacred obligations of morality."[51] For yet another canonical Western writer, Leo Tolstoy, who had powerful effects on both Wittgenstein and Gandhi, there could be no "unsimulated" ethics without roots in religion, dogmatic or not:

> The attempts to found a morality independent of religion are like the actions of children when, wishing to move a plant which pleases them, they tear off the root which does not please and seems unnecessary to them, and plant it in the earth without the root. Without religious foundation there can be no true, unsimulated morality, as without a root there can be no true plant. And so in reply to your two questions, I say religion is man's conception of his relation to the infinite universe, and to its source. And morality is the ever-present guide of life proceeding only from this relation.[52]

This is because whether religions have an elaborate theology (like Judaism or Christianity or Hinduism), or an anti-theology (like Materialism), or have no doctrines at all about a god (like Confucianism or Buddhism or Nationalism), all religions imply an ethics, demand life commitments and erect, endorse and enshrine moral principles—moral principles, often incompatible, that the eighteenth-century West came to call "natural," but aren't.

It thus seems to me that scholars of the Philosophy of Religion like Frederick Ferré and Philip Pecorino have gotten closest to what we mean by "religion" by starting with ethics, equating ethics to human values, and defining religion as the valence or attractive strength that we find in those often contradictory values, or attach to them, explaining our experience and justifying our behavior. As Ferré puts it in his introductory textbook: "Religion is a way of valuing that is most comprehensively and intensively experienced." Pecorino later quoted and intensified Ferré

---

[51] "Qu'il n'y a point de religion qui dispense des devoirs de la morale." Rousseau, "Profession de foi du Vicaire Savoyard" in *Émile* (1761) Livre IV, in *Œuvres complètes*, Tome IV, Paris: Gallimard/Pléiade, 1969, p. 632, translation, Harvard Classics Vol 34, p315. In 1682, a much earlier Enlightenment figure, Pierre Bayle, first raised the converse question of whether a society of atheists would be able to have morality. His answer—that it would—launched what became one of the strongest of the Enlightenment's arguments against religion. (Pierre Bayle, *Pensées diverses sur la comète* [Thoughts on the Comet] (Rotterdam, 1682) ed., A. Prat, Paris: Société nouvelle de librairie et d'édition, 1911–1912, vol. 2, p103).

[52] Tolstoy, "Religion and Morality" in *Contemporary Review* (1894) translated by Vladimir Tchertkoff on Wikisource @ https://en.wikisource.org/wiki/Pamphlets_(Tolstoy)/Religion_and_Morality.

by defining "Religion" as "the most intensive and comprehensive method of valuing that is experienced by humankind."[53]

Extrapolating religion from ethics, rather than the other way around, as Ferré, Pecorino and others have done, is becoming more persuasive. If that move is convincing, we may consider a religion to be the set of ultimately unprovable beliefs we assert, through the stories we tell, the rituals we practice, and the experiences we go through, in order to justify what we value—justify what we choose to do, and how we choose to do it. The beliefs, stories and rituals provide answers to the question that occurs to every thinking person: why we consider—or why we should consider—our acts to be "right" or "wrong," good or evil, or indeed "appropriate" or "inappropriate." They are upheld by learned social behavior—what anthropologists know as "culture"—and conscious or unconscious social sanction, in the same way as our languages. They are shared by any society, large or small, through dissent as well as assent. But they are also upheld by individual commitment, by a faith that those values are "good" (which is not otherwise knowable). Such beliefs issue in behavior, and human behavior is something that can be known and studied in ways that allay the misgivings of scientists.

People who think that religion requires a god or gods will not be sufficiently wary of their very human tendency to alter their behavior by committing to moral principles. Self-identified secular "moderns" will assume that their morals are good and that their commitments to those morals are justified, precisely because they themselves are NOT "religious." In *Enlightenment Now!*, Steven Pinker argues that "resisting entropy and enhancing human flourishing" are the only right principles for human action, but he resists recognizing them as values defined by humans like himself, which are valued religiously by many humans like himself, but not valued so highly, I regret, by all humans, since those values are not, as Enlightenment thinkers would so much have preferred, "self-evident."[54] Conversely they will too often find the contrary morals and commitments of "religious" people to be "evil" and unjustified, simply because "religious people" are, by their definition, theists.

It seems that because the unreligious find the beliefs and doctrines of "religious" people to be contrary to fact—unnatural or illogical or both—the unreligious must find that the moral choices of "religious" people are less justified and less reasonable than their own. But there is a problem with this analysis, the fact that no moral

---

[53] Frederick Ferré, *Basic Modern Philosophy of Religion*, NY: Scribner, 1967. Philip A. Pecorino, *Philosophy of Religion* (Online Textbook, 2002): Chap 10 ("A Definition of Religion"), Section 4 ("The Definition") @ http://www.qcc.cuny.edu/SocialSciences/ppecorino/PHIL_of_RELIGION_TEXT/CHAPTER_10_DEFINITION/The-Definition-of-Religion.htm. (Professor Pecorino's is one of the first online textbooks.)

[54] Steven Pinker, *Enlightenment Now! The Case for Reason, Science, Humanism and Progress* (NY: Viking Penguin, 2018), p. 32. Pinker occasionally adds what he thinks of as human flourishing's complement, "reducing suffering" (p. 30). He must mean the suffering of humans, though animals, we know, suffer too, often to nourish us in our flourishing. No doubt we can reduce both, but there is a case for the positive value of human suffering, a case that adherents of the world's earlier religions have not been the only ones to make.

system is truly "reasonable."[55] Judgments of good and evil are not contrary to fact. Nor are they factual. All of them have repeatedly proved to be full of contradictions, and though the motivations for some, and perhaps most behaviors are clearly natural, built into our nervous system below the level of consciousness, there are no natural moral systems because the natural motivations contradict each other, like "fight or flight," and "justice or peace." The point was made by no less a Modern atheist than Albert Einstein:

> It seems to me that the idea of a personal God is an anthropological concept which I cannot take seriously. I feel also not able to imagine some will or goal outside the human sphere. [...] I believe that we have to content ourselves with our imperfect knowledge and understanding and treat values and moral obligations as a purely human problem—the most important of all human problems.[56]

The daunting truth is that, as philosophers in Western and other modern cultures have known for centuries, ethical choices, of "good" and "evil," "right" and "wrong," are impossible to "prove." Unless, of course, they are proved supernaturally, by assuming or invoking an axiomatic source, perhaps somewhere in infinity, a standard of standards, a judge whose judgments are superior to nature, including human nature.

Science can routinely expect to find truths that are universal, despite being provisional; but to the universalism that science expects, ethics can only aspire. Notions of right and wrong cannot reach it. Science can devise an atom bomb, and an Einstein can explain, forty years before it does, the science by which the bomb will work; but only people can say whether it is right or wrong to do so. Not only are the assertions of ethics always provisional, they are always sanctioned by a particular human community and its culture.[57] Ethics assert, but cannot prove, their relevance to any other community partly because they cannot demonstrate that they have, or do not have, exceptions (cannibalism, for example—or abortion). They therefore appeal to the universal; and most religions can be seen, no matter how hard Immanuel Kant tried to get around it, as that appeal to the universal that strives to justify any system of values or ethics. The Enlightenment's effort to make morals as universal as mathematics paralleled its effort to save (through Deism) the universality of theistic religion. Theistic religions with supreme universal gods, or better yet, like the Abrahamics, a single supreme universal god, have an easier time asserting a claim

---

[55] That a commitment to ethical principles is a matter of unjustified and non-rational faith is the central disturbing message of Alasdair MacIntyre's fundamental text in philosophical ethics, *After Virtue* (London: Duckworth, 1981; 2nd ed., Notre Dame, IN, Notre Dame U. Press, 1984).

[56] Einstein, in Max Jammer, *Einstein and Religion: Physics and Theology*, 1995.

[57] Here is Isaiah Berlin again, channeling Herder, one of the founders of his Counter-Enlightenment (or, as Berlin was still calling it in 1965, "Romanticism"): If Herder is right [...] if the Greek ideal and the Indian ideal are totally incompatible, which he not merely confessed but emphasized with a kind of joy [...] then the notion of a final answer to the question of how to live becomes absolutely meaningless. It can mean nothing at all, because all the answers are, presumably, incompatible with one another." *The Roots of Romanticism*: (2nd Edition, Princeton: Princeton U. Press, pb, 2001), p76.

to make the same maxims and regulations for everybody; but as the Counter-Enlightenment thinkers validated religious feeling, they were less alert to the risk of drawing back on cultural universalism, including morality—and religion.

This insight about the ineffability of ethics and values is David Hume's, but, like the rest of Hume's first great book, it was ignored. It took the Romantics to take it to heart, together with other thinkers of the West's Counter-Enlightenment, writers from Hamann, Herder and Schiller to Staël, Blake, Coleridge, Mary Shelley and even the peremptory Emerson, individualists and communitarians alike. The Romantics followed the evangelical pioneers in Europe and America, and those pioneers built the Counter-Enlightenment. They turned the inflexible Protestant (and Catholic) doctrinal orthodoxies that had hardened over a century of wars with each other not into a dry mathesis, but into what they called a "heart" religion, open to emotion and to the extraordinary emotional experience of the ecstatic and the mystical vision, and they took that experience to the general population. Instead of taking refuge in mathematics and logic like Descartes and the other great seventeenth-century European thinkers who heralded the Enlightenment, the evangelicals, like the Romantics, largely accepted the deep paradoxes of human nature, the contradictions in the relationship of morality to motivation and feeling; and the evangelicals revived their old religion on the grounds of ecstatic experience.

We can see much the same development among the east European Hasidic Jews, and we can see it much earlier in the Islamic world from the eighth and ninth centuries, where Ṣufi mysticism arose at the same time as algebra, cosmology and rational medicine, to the eleventh and twelfth centuries where the exact sciences conceded to Sufism in the thought of al-Ghazali and Ibn Taymiyyah.

From the moment of experiencing conviction of sin and the mercy of the Christian God, to the moment in Christian or Ṣufi mystic practice, or in Hasidic prayer, when the self seems to shrink to nothing and become one with Allah or Elohim or God, and even to the less transcendental moment of abstinence in Twelve-Step programs, these peak experiences evoke—or better, inspire—"the most intensive and comprehensive method of valuing that is experienced by humankind"—religion, as Pecorino defines it.

Of course, such moments are not the only reasons for the embrace of values. It is universally admitted, even by those who have been born "again" that being born the first time subjects every human being, helpless at birth, to a religious and moral education. Willy-nilly, life presents choices. This happens whether or not an ecstatic experience occurs, and it does not preclude the child's adoption of moral commitments simply because they are modeled and/or reinforced by the child's nurture. The rituals and ceremonies of communities, vast or intimate, cultures or subcultures, can also, as Durkheim argued, be a decisive influence on the ways by which humans become moral, believers in right and wrong, and concomitantly believers in religions.

Moral or religious "conversion" may also occur suddenly under the influence of charismatic leaders, or impressment by a community, with or without the individual experience of ecstasy; but the most sudden and consequential moral conversions almost always occur as a result of ecstatic experiences like those in late eighteenth-century Virginia. Ecstatic experiences also historically have the capacity to change the commitments made by community pressure or by family nurture; and it is less clear that nurture, or even a tumultuous adolescence, can do the same.

On the other hand, it is clearly in the West that an elite suspicion of conversion, and contempt for religious ecstasy, has probably been most evident. Chinese civilization, whose mainstream religious tradition, ethical but nominally godless, seems at first to make little room for either ecstasy or conversion; but it actually provides less evidence of this disdain for them so characteristic of the modern West.

It also seems clear that the eighteenth century—the era when the West was undergoing the cultural changes that have since given it hegemony over the globe—was precisely the era when the Western elites' disdain for religious ecstasy was getting its start. Already before 1700, "enthusiasm," a sixteenth-century Englishing of the Greek word for "possession by a god," had been adapted to refer to the irrational state of mind of those who were gripped by religion instead of freed by "philosophy." In 1683 John Locke added to his Enlightenment-founding masterpiece, then still in manuscript, on the philosophical basis of knowing, a chapter titled "Enthusiasm," which he defined as

> a third ground of assent, which with some men has the same authority, and is as confidently relied on as either faith or reason; I mean enthusiasm: which, laying by reason, would set up revelation without it. Whereby in effect it takes away both reason and revelation, and substitutes in the room of them the ungrounded fancies of a man's own brain, and assumes them for a foundation both of opinion and conduct.[58]

Although "the Passion they raise is much alike," wrote John Locke's student, the 3rd Earl of Shaftesbury, as he reached for a faith-saving distinction in 1707, "inspiration is a real feeling of the Divine Presence, and Enthusiasm a false one."[59] Later in the eighteenth century the enlightened French would apply the word "fanatisme"

---

[58] John Locke, *Essay Concerning Human Understanding* (1689) Book 4, Chapter 19, §3, ed. Peter H. Nidditch, Oxford: Clarendon Press, 1975.

[59] Anthony Ashley Cooper, 3rd Earl of Shaftesbury, "A Letter Concerning Enthusiasm" (Sep, 1707) *Characteristics of Men, Manners, Opinions, Times* (1st edition, 1708), London: Grant Richards, 1900, vol. 1, Sec. 7, p. 37. Jonathan Swift's earliest acerbic takeoff on "enthusiasm" as "madness" had already made an appearance in "Digression" IX of his *Tale of a Tub* in 1704, the same year as the poetic praise of it by one John Dennis; but Shaftesbury's take on "enthusiasm" in 1707 probably reflected what he heard about the refugee Protestant "French Prophets" who arrived in London late in 1706 claiming sudden divine inspiration, and organized a millennial, pre-Pentecostal sect that called up the still unquiet ghosts of the Puritan Revolution. By 1709, when Richard Kingston, published *Enthusiastik Imposters, No Divinely inspir'd Prophets, the second part* (London, 1709) the Prophets had made some specific prophecies that were not fulfilled and had passed their moment, but the English disdain for "enthusiasm" remained until the Romantic nineteenth century. Four years after Shaftesbury, Joseph Addison wrote a *Spectator* essay that took "religious enthusiasm" as a general problem, recommending that it be replaced by "devotion," and asserting that "The two great errors into which a mistaken devotion may betray us, are, enthusiasm and superstition." (*Spectator* #201, Oct 20, 1711). David Hume, a devoted young reader of Addison, came to a similar view, substituting "true religion" for "devotion" as the preservative against both "superstition" and "enthusiasm" (Hume, "Of Superstition and Enthusiasm," in *Essays Moral and Political*, Edinburgh: A. Kincaid 1741, pp141–152 @ https://books.google.bg/books?id=IHQPAAAAQAAJ

to Catholic churchmen. ("Fanatic," yet another antique word, in this case Roman, means someone possessed by a god—or, as we say for short in the United States, a "fan.")[60]

Of course, most of thinkers of the rising Enlightenment believed in their own moralities as the evangelicals did, and believed their own morality was and should be universal. They also believed that although a commitment to most moralities was a good thing, a moral thing in itself; only those religions were to be tolerated if the morality they promulgated did not contradict their own. And as if that did not require faith enough, most of them believed, with Immanuel Kant, that moral commitment was rational, dictated by the laws of nature if not by logic. From "natural law," "natural religion" would naturally follow—"natural religion" then meaning (in the Christian West) either stand-alone Deism or the prerequisite for divine revelation.

The Counter-Enlightenment, Evangelicals, Jansenists, Ḥasidim, Ṣufis, and Romantics, changed that paradigm. Moral commitment was indeed a good thing, but a moral commitment was by no means rational. Commitments to logically opposed moral codes, might be equally good simply because they were commitments. No community could survive the absence of all moral commitment. The unnaturalness of religion, further, was part of its strength, since "human nature" had long been known to be ridden with moral contradictions. In any case, so the Counter-Enlightened maintained, trust and respect should be given to the irrational sources of both belief and ethics.

Thus a Counter-Enlightenment, led by ecstatics and evangelicals (and Romantics) in all three Abrahamic religions, re-legitimized mysticism and inspiration at the same time the rational Enlightenment was arising to attack them, a contrary movement that turned on its head David Hume's demonstration that all ethics were necessarily unreasonable, and made it a powerful argument for the old religions.

The disagreement about how the more sober-minded faithful should treat co-religionists who report ecstasies—and vice-versa—continues to this day in all three Abrahamic religions: Judaism, Christianity and Islam, not to mention their fundamentalist variants and their "New Age" competitors; but it was in the seventeenth and especially in the eighteenth centuries that the issue was joined between both kinds of believers, on the one hand, by those whose moral (religious) commitment was cemented by ecstatic enlightening experiences, their own or reported, and by those children of the new Enlightenment who came to believe that no ecstatic

&dq=inauthor%3A%22David%20Hume%22&hl=bg&pg=PR1#v=onepage&q=whimsy&f=false).

[60] Shaftesbury, "A Letter Concerning Enthusiasm" (Sep, 1707) *Characteristics of Men, Manners, Opinions, Times*, London: Grant Richards, 1900, vol. 1, Sec. 7, p. 37–38. Shaftesbury moves easily in the same paragraph from the Greek-derived term, *Enthusiasm*, to the Roman, *Fanaticism*: "For when the Mind is taken up in Vision, and fixes its view either on any real Object, or mere Specter of Divinity; when it sees, or thinks it sees any thing prodigious, and more than human; its Horror, Delight, Confusion, Fear, Admiration, or whatever Passion belongs to it, or is uppermost on this occasion, will have something vast, *immane*, and (as Painters say) *beyond Life*. And this is what gave occasion to the name of *Fanaticism*, as it was us'd by the Antients in its original Sense, for an Apparition transporting the Mind."

experience could be trusted, that no rapture could be rational, and that no appeal to divine revelation could possibly overrule the "natural law."

This inquiry into how Zinzendorf, Edwards, Wesley, the Baal Shem, Rousseau, ʿAbd al-Wahhab, and all three of their Abrahamic religions engendered evangelical movements that developed in step with what historians now call the Counter-Enlightenment is a historical one. It does not prove the existence of God or gods nor does it prove their nonexistence. It need not be read as an attack on any religion, including the atheistic religions. Religion may not be curable, but like so many confusing things about our species it has a chance of being better understood.

Bibliography

Adamson, Sophia, Ralph Metzner, and Padma Catell. 1985. *Through the Gateway of the Heart: Accounts of Experiences with MDMA and Other Empathogenic Substances*. 2nd ed. San Francisco: Four Trees Publications. Solarium Press, 2013.

Allport, G.W., and J.M. Ross. 1967. Personal Religious Orientation and Prejudice. *Journal of Personality and Social Psychology* 5: 432–443.

Altieri, Charles. 2004. *The Particulars of Rapture: An Aesthetics of the Affects*. Ithaca, NY: Cornell University Press.

Anderson, Allan. 2001. *African Reformation: African Initiated Christianity in the Twentieth Century*. Trenton, NJ: Africa World Press.

Andrews, Edward D. 1953. *The People Called Shakers*. New York: Oxford University Press.

Aquaviva, S.S. 1961. *The Decline of the Sacred in Industrial Society* [L'Eclissi del Sacro nella Civiltá industriale]. Trans. Patricia Lipscomb. New York: Harper & Row, 1979.

Argyle, Michael. 2000. *Psychology and Religion: An Introduction*. New York: Routledge.

Armstrong, Karen. 2000. *The Battle for God*. New York: Knopf.

Asad, Talal. 2003. *Formations of the Secular: Christianity, Islam, Modernity*. Stanford, CA: Stanford University Press Kindle ed.

Azari, Nina P. 2004. Religious Experience as Thinking that Feels Like Something: A Philosophical-Theological Reflection on Recent Neuroscientific Study of Religious Experience. *Dissertation Abstracts International Section A: Humanities and Social Sciences* 65 (2A): 565.

Azari, Nina P., Rüdiger J. Seitz, and Matthias Franz. 2009. Value Judgments and Self-Control of Action: The Role of the Medial Frontal Cortex. *Brain Research Reviews* 60 (2): 368–378. https://doi.org/10.1016/j.brainresrev.2009.02.003.

Bartz, J.D. 2009. Theistic Existential Psychotherapy. *Psychology of Religion and Spirituality* 1 (2): 69–80. https://doi.org/10.1037/a0014895.

Bayle, Pierre. 1682. *Pensées diverses sur la comète* [Thoughts on the Comet] (Rotterdam), ed. A. Prat. Paris: Société nouvelle de librairie et d'édition, 1911–1912.

Bender, Courtney. 2008. *Worlds of Experience: Contemporary Spirituality and the American Religious Imagination*. Chicago: University of Chicago Press.

Berger, Peter L. 1967. *The Sacred Canopy: Elements of a Sociological Theory of Religion*. Garden City, NY: Doubleday.

———. 1969. *A Rumor of Angels: Modern Society and the Rediscovery of the Supernatural*. Garden City, NY: Doubleday Anchor.

———., ed. 1999. *The Desecularization of the World: Resurgent Religion and World Politics*. Grand Rapids: Eerdmans.

Berlin, Isaiah. 1965. *The Roots of Romanticism*. "Sources of Romantic Thought" Mellon Lectures, ed. Henry Hardy. Princeton, NJ: Princeton University Press, 1999, 2001, 2nd ed. 2013.

Blumberg, Lynn. June 2014. What Happens to the Brain During Spiritual Experiences?: The Field of Neurotheology Uses Science to Try to Understand Religion, and Vice Versa. *The Atlantic*. https://www.theatlantic.com/health/archive/2014/06/what-happens-to-brains-during-spiritual-experiences/361882/.
Blumenberg, Hans. 1962. *'Säkularisation': Kritik einer Kategorie historischer Illegitimität* ['Secularisation': Critique of a Category of Historical Illegitimacy]. 7th German Philosophy Congress. Repr. Die Philosophie und die Frage nach dem Fortschritt, ed. Helmut Kuhn, and Franz Wiedemann. Munich: A. Pustet, 1964.
———. 1966. *The Legitimacy of the Modern Age* [Die Legitimität der Neuzeit. Frankfurt]. Trans. Robert M. Wallace. Cambridge, MA: MIT Press, 1986.
Boyer, Pascal. 2001. *Religion Explained: Evolutionary Origins of Religious Thought*. New York: Basic Books.
Braun, Willi, and Russell T. McCutcheon, eds. 2000a. *Guide to the Study of Religion*. London & New York: Cassell.
———, eds. 2000b. *Guide to the Study of Religion*. Continuum. Repr. 2006, 2007, 2009.
———, eds. 2018. *Reading J. Z. Smith: Interviews & Essay*. New York: Oxford University Press.
Broad, C.D. 1939. Arguments for the Existence of God II. *Journal of Theological Studies* 40: 156–167. (Repr. in Broad. *Religion, Philosophy and Psychical Research* (1953). London: Routledge, 2000).
———. 1953. *Religion, Philosophy and Psychical Research*. London: Routledge, 2000.
Brown, David H. 2003. *Santeria Enthroned: Art, Ritual, and Innovation in an Afro-Cuban Religion*. Chicago: University of Chicago Press.
Buber, Martin. 1909. *Ekstatische Konfessionen* (Jena). Trans. Esther Cameron as *Ecstatic Confessions*, ed. Paul Mendes-Flohr. Syracuse, NY: Syracuse University Press, 1996.
Bultmann, Rudolf K. 1953. *Kerygma and Myth: A Theological Debate*. London: SPCK.
———. 1957. *History and Eschatology: The Presence of Eternity*. (1954–1955 Gifford Lectures). Edinburgh: University Press. Waco, TX: Baylor University Press, 2019.
Burns, Elizabeth. 2019. *Continental Philosophy of Religion*. Cambridge: Cambridge University Press.
Butler, Melvin L. 2002. 'Nou Kwe nan Sentespri' (We Believe in the Holy Spirit): Music, Ecstasy, and Identity in Haitian Pentecostal Worship. *Black Music Research Journal* 22 (1): 85–125.
Chappel, James G. 2019. Democracy Without God. Rvw Martin Hägglund. In *This Life: Secular Faith and Spiritual Freedom*. New York: Pantheon, Boston Review.
Chesterton, G.K. 1905. *Heretics*. 3rd ed. London: John Lane.
Cox, Harvey Gallagher. 1995. *Fire from Heaven: The Rise of Pentecostal Spirituality and the Reshaping of Religion in the Twenty-First Century*. Reading, MA: Addison-Wesley.
Coyne, Jerry A. 2015. *Faith vs. Fact. Why Science and Religion Are Incompatible*.
Crane, Tim. 2017. *The Meaning of Belief: Religion from an Atheist's Point of View*. Cambridge, MA: Harvard University Press.
D'Aquili, Eugene G., and Andrew B. Newberg. 1999. *The Mystical Mind: Probing the Biology of Religious Experience*. Minneapolis: Fortress Press. Cambridge: International Society for Science and Religion, 2007. ("'self-identified neurotheologians.'").
Daechsel, Markus. 2006. Scientism and Its Discontents: The Indo-Muslim 'Fascism' of Inayatullah Khan al-Mashriqi. *Modern Intellectual History* 3 (3): 443–472.
Davie, Grace. 2007. *The Sociology of Religion*. New Delhi: Sage Publications/Pine Forge Press.
Davis, Caroline Franks. 2004. *The Evidential Force of Religious Experience*. Ohio: Ohio University Press.
Dawkins, Richard. 2006. *The God Delusion*. Boston: Houghton Mifflin.
de Graffenreid, Julie, and Zoe Knox, eds. 2019. *Voices of the Voiceless: Religion, Communism, and the Keston Archive*. Waco, TX: Baylor University Press.
De Waal, Cornelis. 2006. Having an Idea of Matter: A Peircean Refutation of Berkeleyan Immaterialism. *Journal of the History of Ideas* 67 (2): 291–314.
Dennett, Daniel, and rvw Dawkins. 2006a. The God Delusion. *Free Inquiry* 27 (1).

———. 2006b. *Breaking the Spell*. New York: Penguin Group.
Derby, Lauren. 2008. Imperial Secrets: Vampires and Nationhood in Puerto Rico. *The Religion of Fools? Superstition Past and Present; Past & Present* 199 (Supplement 3): 290–312. http://past.oxfordjournals.org/content/vol199/suppl_3/index.dtl?etoc.
Dimond, Sydney George. 1926. *The Psychology of the Methodist Revival*. London: Humphrey Milford.
———. 1932. *The Psychology of Methodism*. London: Epworth Press.
Dorrien, Guy. 2020. *In a Post-Hegelian Spirit: Philosophical Theology as Entangled Discontent*. Waco, TX: Baylor University Press.
Durkheim, Émile. 1912. *The Elementary Forms of the Religious Life* [Les formes élémentaires de la vie religieuse: Le système totémique en Australie. Paris: Alcan]. Trans. Karen E. Fields. New York: Free Press, 1995.
Eagleton, Terry, and rvw Dawkins. 2006. The God Delusion. *The London Review of Books*.
Earman, John. 2003. *Hume's Abject Failure: The Argument Against Miracles*. Oxford: Oxford University Press.
Edinger, Edward F. (1923–1998). 1972. *Ego and Archtype: Individuation and the Religious Function of the Psyche*. New York: C. G. Jung Foundation.
Edwards, P. 1972. *The Encyclopedia of Philosophy*. Vol. 7, 1–27. New York: Macmillan.
Edwards, Paul. 2009. *God and the Philosophers*. Amherst, NY: Prometheus.
Ehrenreich, Barbara. 2006. *Dancing in the Streets: A History of Collective Joy*. New York: Metropolitan Books. New York: Henry Holt, 2007.
Eliade, Mircea. 1978–1985. *History of Religious Ideas*. 3 vols. Chicago: University of Chicago Press.
———. 1987. *The Encyclopedia of Religion*. Vol. 12, 159–165. New York: Macmillan.
Emden, Christian J. 2006. Toward a Critical Historicism: History and Politics in Nietzsche's Second 'Untimely Meditation'. *Modern Intellectual History* 3 (1): 1–31.
Erikson, Erik. 1958. *Young Man Luther: A Study in Psychoanalysis and History*. New York: W.W. Norton.
———. 1959. *Identity and the Life Cycle: Selected Papers*. New York: International Universities Press.
Ferguson, R. Brian. 2018. Why We Fight: A Close Look at the Archaeological Record Suggest War May Not Be in Our Nature After All. *Scientific American* 319 (3): 76–81.
Ferré, Frederick. 1967. *Basic Modern Philosophy of Religion*. New York: Scribner.
Fitzgerald, Timothy. 2000. Experience. In *Guide to the Study of Religion*, ed. W. Braun and R.T. McCutcheon. London & New York: Cassell.
Foley, Duncan K. 2006. *Adam's Fallacy: A Guide to Economic Theology*. Cambridge, MA: Harvard University Press.
Frank, J.D. 1973. *Persuasion and Healing: A Comparative Study of Psychotherapy*. New York: Schocken Books.
Frobenius, Leo. 1913. *The Voice of Africa: Being an Account of the Travels of the German Inner African Exploration Expedition in the Years 1910–1912*. Trans. Rudolf Blind. London: Hutchinson & Co.
Fromm, Eric. 1950. *Psychoanalysis and Religion*. New Haven, CT: Yale University Press.
Fuller, Robert C. 2007. Spirituality in the Flesh: The Role of Discrete Emotions in Religious Life. *Journal of the American Academy of Religion* 75 (1): 25–51.
Ganje-Fling, M.A., and P.R. McCarthy. 1991. A Comparative Analysis of Spiritual Direction and Psychotherapy. *Journal of Psychology and Theology* 19 (1): 103–117. (Psychology of religion).
Gans, Herbert J. 1994. Symbolic Ethnicity and Symbolic Religiosity: Towards a Comparison of Ethnic and Religious Acculturation. *Ethnic and Racial Studies* 17: 577–592.
Gass, William H. 2005. A Forest of Bamboo: The Trouble with Nietzsche. *Harper's*: 88ff.
Geertz, Clifford. 1973. *The Interpretation of Cultures*. New York: Basic Books, 3rd ed. 2017.
Geertz, Armin W. Feb 2011. When Cognitive Scientists Become Religious, Science is in Trouble: On Neurotheology from a Philosophy of Science Perspective. *Religion*. Published Online.

Gelfand, Michele. 2018. *Rule Makers, Rule Breakers: How Tight and Loose Cultures Wire Our World*. New York: Scribner.

Geschiere, Peter. 2008. Witchcraft and the State: Cameroon and South Africa: Ambiguities of 'Reality' and 'Superstition'. *The Religion of Fools? Superstition Past and Present; Past & Present* 199 (Supplement 3): 313–335. http://past.oxfordjournals.org/content/vol199/suppl_3/index.dtl?etoc.

Gillespie, Michael Allen. 2008. *The Theological Origins of Modernity*. Chicago: University of Chicago Press.

Glazier, Stephen D., ed. 2001. *Encyclopedia of African and African-American Religions*. New York: Routledge.

Glossop, Ronald J. 1967. The Nature of Hume's Ethics. *Philosophy and Phenomenological Research* 27: 527–536.

Goldberg, David W. Feb 2011. d'aquili and Newberg's Neurotheology: A Hermeneutical Problem with Their Neurological Solution. *Religion*. Published Online.

Goldstein, Jan E. 1998. Enthusiasm or Imagination? Eighteenth-Century Smear Words in Comparative National Context. In *Enthusiasm and Enlightenment in Europe, 1650–1850*, ed. Lawrence E. Klein and Anthony J. La Vopa. (also published in *Huntington Library Quarterly*, 60(1997): 1–2, 29–49).

———. 2005. Hysteria Complicated by Ecstasy: The Case of Nanette Leroux. Princeton. In *The Post-Revolutionary Self: Politics and Psyche in France, 1750–1850*. Cambridge, MA: Harvard University Press.

———. 2010. *Hysteria Complicated by Ecstasy: The Case of Nanette Leroux*. Princeton, NJ: Princeton University Press.

Gould, Stephen Jay. 1999. *Rocks of Ages: Science and Religion in the Fullness of Life*. (Twin NOMA nonoverlapping *magisteria*).

Graham, Jesse, Jonathan Haidt, Sena Koleva, Matt Motyl, Ravi Iyer, Sean P. Wojcik, and Peter H. Ditto. 2020. Moral Foundations Theory: The Pragmatic Validity of Moral Pluralism, Chapter 2. In *Advances in Experimental Social Psychology*, vol. 47. Amsterdam: Elsevier. (online preprint).

Gray, John. 2003. *Straw Dogs: Thoughts on Humans and Other Animals*. London: Granta Books. (Augustinian depravity).

———. 2018. *Seven Types of Atheism*. London: Allen Lane. New York: Farrar, Straus and Giroux, 2018.

Green, T.H. (1836–1882). 1884. *Prolegomena to Ethics*. Oxford: Clarendon Press.

Green, Ronald M. 1978. *Religious Reason: The Rational and Moral Basis of Religious Belief*. New York: Oxford University Press.

———. 1988. *Religion and Moral Reason: A New Method for Comparative Study*. New York: Oxford University Press.

Gregory, Brad S. 2006. The Other Confessional History: On Secular Bias in the Study of Religion. *History and Theory* 45: 132–149.

———. 2008. Back to the Future: A Response to Robert Orsi, 'Abundant History': A Forum. *Historically Speaking*: 20–22.

Gross, Paul R., Norman Levitt, and Martin W. Lewis, eds. 1996. *The Flight from Science and Reason*, Annals of the New York Academy of Sciences. Vol. 775. New York: New York Academy of Sciences.

Habermas, Jürgen. 1987. *The Philosophical Discourse of Modernity: Twelve Lectures*. Trans. Frederick G. Lawrence from *Der Philosophische Diskurs der Moderne: Zwölf Vorlesungen*, 1985.

———. 2001. Faith and Knowledge.," Trans. Hella Beister, and William Rehy. In *The Frankfurt School on Religion: Key Writings by the Major Thinkers*, ed. Eduardo Mendieta. New York: Routledge.

———. 2008. *Between Naturalism and Religion: Philosophical Essays*, Trans. Ciaran Cronin. Cambridge, UK: Polity.

Hägglund, Martin. 2019. *This Life: Secular Faith and Spiritual Freedom*. New York: Pantheon.
Hall, G.S. 1904. *Adolescence: Its Psychology and Its Relations to Physiology, Anthropology, Sociology, Sex, Crime, Religion, and Education*. 2 vols. New York: Appleton.
Hamer, Dean H. 2004. *The God Gene: How Faith is Hardwired into Our Genes*. New York: Doubleday Anchor, 2005. Rvw Carl Zimmer, *Scientific American*, October, 2004.
Hamilton, W.D. 1964. The Genetical Evolution of Social Behavior 1 & 2. *Journal of Theoretical Biology* 7: 1–52, "inclusive fitness" and "nepotistic altruism".
Hardwick, Rev. John Charles. 1938. *Totalitarianism. What It Really Means*. (Pamphlet). London.
Hardy, Alister Clavering. 1965. *The Living Stream: A Restatement of Evolution Theory and Its Relation to the Spirit of Man*, Gifford Lectures 1963–1964. New York: Harper and Row, Collins, 1965.
———. 1966. *The Divine Flame: An Essay Towards a Natural History of Religion; The Second of Two Series of Gifford Lectures on Science, Natural History and Religion Delivered in the University of Aberdeen, During the Session 1964–1965*. New York: Collins. The Religious Experience Research Unit, Manchester College, 1978.
———. 1976. *The Biology of God: A Scientist's Study of Man the Religious Animal*. London: Jonathan Cape.
———. 1979. *The Spiritual Nature of Man: A Study of Contemporary Religious Experience*. New York: Oxford University Press.
Harman, Oren. 2010. *The Price of Altruism: George Price and the Search for the Origins of Kindness*. New York: Norton.
Harrington, Michael. 1983. *The Politics at God's Funeral: The Spiritual Crisis of Western Civilization*. New York: Henry Holt & Co.
Harris, Sam. 2014. *Waking Up: A Guide to Spirituality Without Religion*. https://www.samharris.org/podcast/item/chapter-one.
Hastings, Derek. 2010. *Catholicism & the Roots of Nazism: Religious Identity & National Socialism*. New York: Oxford University Press.
Hauser, Marc D. 2006. *Moral Minds*. New York: HarperCollins.
Hay, D. 1994. "The Biology of God": What is the Current Status of Hardy's Hypothesis? *International Journal for the Psychology of Religion* 4 (1): 1–23.
Heidegger, Martin. 2004. *The Phenomenology of Religious Life*. Trans. Fritsch & Gosetti. Bloomington: Indiana University Press.
Helminiak, Daniel A., Louis Hoffman, and Eric Dodson. 2009. A Critique of the "Theistic Psychology" Movement as Exemplified in Bartz's "Theistic Existential Psychotherapy". *The Humanistic Psychologist*. Published Online 29 May 2012.
Henry, Michel. 2003. *I Am the Truth: Toward a Philosophy of Christianity*. Stanford, CA: Stanford University Press.
Herdt, G., and M. Stephen, eds. 1989. *The Religious imagination in New Guinea*. New Brunswick, NJ: Rutgers University Press.
Herskovits, Melville. 1941. *The Myth of the Negro Past*. Repr. ed. Boston: Beacon Press, 1990.
Hick, John. 2013. *The Fifth Dimension: An Exploration of the Spiritual Realm*. Oxford, UK: Oneworld.
Hinman, Joseph. 2014. *The Trace of God: A Rational Warrant for Belief*. Colorado Springs, CO: GrandViaduct.
Hoge, Dean R., and Thomas P. O'Connor. 2004. Denominational Identity from Age Sixteen to Age Thirty-Eight. *Sociology of Religion* 65 (1): 77–85.
Hoge, D., and G. Petrillo. 1978. Development of Religious Thinking in Adolescence: A Test of Goldman's Theories. *Journal for the Scientific Study of Religion* 17: 139–154.
Holland, DeWitte Talmadge. 1973. *America in Controversy*, 296. Dubuque: W.C. Brown.
Hollywood, Amy. 2001. *Sensible Ecstasy: Mysticism, Sexual Difference, and the Demands of History*. Chicago: University of Chicago Press.
Horgan, John. 2003. *Rational Mysticism: Dispatches from the Border Between Science and Spirituality*. Boston: Houghton Mifflin.

Hume, David. 1739. *Treatise of Human Nature*. (London). In *The Complete Works of David Hume: An Enquiry Concerning Human Understanding, A Treatise of Human Nature, The History of England, The Natural History of Religion, Essays, Personal Correspondence*. Kindle ed. 2020.

———. 1741. Of Superstition and Enthusiasm. In *Essays, Moral, Political and Literary*, ed. Eugene F. Miller, 73–79. Indianapolis, IN: Liberty Classics, 1985.

Hutton, Ronald. 2001. *Shamans: Siberian Spirituality and the Western Tradition*. London/New York: Hambledon and London.

Huxley, Aldous. 1954. *The Doors of Perception*. New York: Harper. London: Chatto & Windus.

Inzlicht, Michael, Alexa M. Tullett, and Marie Good. February 2012. The Need to Believe: A Neuroscience Account of Religion as a Motivated Process. *Religion, Brain & Behavior*. Published Online.

Jackle, C. 1973. What's Psychotherapy: What's Pastoral? *Journal of Pastoral Care* 27 (3): 174–177.

James, William. 1896. The Will to Believe: An Address to the Philosophical Clubs of Yale and Brown Universities. *The New World* 5: 327–347. In James, *Writings* 1878–1899, 457–479.

———. 1902. *Varieties of Religious Experience*. Cambridge, MA: Harvard University Press, 1985.

———. 1988. The Will to Believe: An Address to the Philosophical Clubs of Yale. In *Writings 1902–1910: The Varieties of Religious Experience/Pragmatism/A Pluralistic Universe/The Meaning of Truth/Some Problems of Philosophy/Essays*, ed. Bruce Kuklick. New York: Library of America.

———. 1992. *Writings 1878–1899: Psychology: Briefer Course/The Will to Believe/Talks to Teachers and to Students/Essays*. Ed. Gerald E. Myers. New York: Library of America.

Jammer, Max. 1999. *Einstein and Religion: Physics and Theology*. Princeton, NJ: Princeton University Press.

Jaspers, Karl, and Rudolf Bultmann. 1958. *Myth and Christianity: An Inquiry into the Possibility of Religion Without Myth*. New York: Noonday Press.

Jay, Martin. 2006. *Songs of Experience: Modern American and European Variations on a Universal Theme*. Berkeley: University of California Press.

Jeffrey, Anne. 2019. In *God and Morality*, ed. Elements in the Philosophy of Religion. Cambridge: Cambridge University Press.

Jenkins, Philip. 2002. *The Next Christendom: The Coming of Global Christianity*. Oxford: Oxford University Press.

Jennings, Timothy R. 2013. *The God-Shaped Brain: How Changing Your View of God Transforms Your Life*. Downers Grove, IL: InterVarsity Press. (Kindle ed., 2013).

Jensen, Jeppe Sinding. 2003. *The Study of Religion in a New Key: Theoretical and Philosophical Soundings in the Comparative and General Study of Religion*. Aarhus: Aarhus University Press.

Johnson, Carina L. 2006. Idolatrous Cultures and the Practice of Religion. *Journal of the History of Ideas* 67 (4): 597–622.

Johnstone, Brick, Daniel Cohen, Kelly Konopacki, and Christopher Ghan. 2016. Selflessness as a Foundation of Spiritual Transcendence: Perspectives from the Neurosciences and Religious Studies. *The International Journal for the Psychology of Religion* 26 (4): 287–303. https://doi.org/10.1080/10508619.2015.1118328.

Johnstone, Brick, Greyson Holliday, and Daniel Cohen. 2016c. Heightened Religiosity and Epilepsy: Evidence for Religious-Specific Neuropsychological Processes. *Mental Health, Religion & Culture* 19 (7): 704–712.

Johnstone, Brick, Robin Hanks, Braj Bhushan, Daniel Cohen, Jarett Roseberry, and Dong Pil Yoon. 2017. Selflessness As A Universal Neuropsychological Foundation Of Spiritual Transcendence: Validation With Christian, Hindu, And Muslim Traditions. *Mental Health, Religion & Culture* 20 (2): 175–187. Received 15 Mar 2017, Accepted 17 May 2017, Published online 20 Jul 2017.

Johnstone, Brick, Angela Bodling, Dan Cohen, Shawn E. Christ, and Andrew Wegrzyn. Right Parietal Lobe-Related 'Selflessness' as the Neuropsychological Basis of Spiritual Transcendence. *International Journal for the Psychology of Religion*. http://www.tandfonline.com. Accessed 30 May 2012. http://www.tandfonline.com/action/doSearch?AllField=Right+parietal+lobe-related+%E2%80%9Cselflessness%E2%80%9D.

Johnstone, Brick, Stacey Bayan, Laura Gutierrez, David Lardizabal, Sean Lanigar, Dong Pil Yoon, and Katherine Judd. Neuropsychological Correlates of Forgiveness. *Religion, Brain & Behavior*: 24–35.

Jones, Rufus M. 1909. *Studies in Mystical Religion*. London: Macmillan, Kindle ed., 2017.

———. 1914. *Spiritual Reformers in the 16th and 17th Centuries*. Boston: Beacon, 1959.

Jones, W.E. 1998. Religious Conversion, Self-Deception, and Pascal's Wager. *Journal of the History of Philosophy* 36 (2): 167–188.

Jones, James W. 2015. *Can Science Explain Religion?: The Cognitive Science Debate*. New York: Oxford University Press.

Jorjorian, A.D. 1972. Reflections Upon and Definitions of Pastoral Counseling. *Pastoral Psychology* 23 (224): 7–15.

Juergensmeyer, Mark, ed. 2006. *Thinking Globally About Religion: The Oxford Handbook of Global Religions*. New York: Oxford University Press, Online Sep 2009.

———, ed. 2017. *Terror in the Mind of God: The Global Rise of Religious Violence*. 4th ed. Berkeley and Los Angeles: University of California Press.

Jung, C.G. 1938. *Psychology and Religion*. New Haven, CT: Yale University Press.

———. 1948. A Psychological Approach to the Dogma of the Trinity. In *Psychology and Religion: West and East*, ed. R.F.C. Hull. Princeton, NJ: Princeton University Press.

———. 1957. The Undiscovered Self. In *Civilization in Transition*, ed. R.F.C. Hull. Princeton, NJ: Princeton University Press.

———. 1971. Stages of Life. In *The Portable Jung*, ed. J. Campbell. New York: Penguin Books.

Kakar, S. 1982. *Shamans, Mystics and Doctors: A Psychological Inquiry into India and its Healing Traditions*. Boston: Beacon Press.

Kenny, Anthony. 2007. Presidential Lecture. *Philosophy* 82 (321): 381–397.

Key, Alex S. 2008. *The Third Basic Instinct: How Religion Doesn't Get You*. AlexSKey.com.

Kiehl, Kent A. 2006. A Cognitive Neuroscience Perspective on Psychopathy: Evidence for Paralimbic System Dysfunction. *Psychiatry Research* 142: 107–128.

Kiev, A. 1964. *Magic, Faith and Healing*. New York: Free Press.

Kirkland, Dennis. 2008. *Mormons and Muslims: A Case of Matching Fingerprints*, Mormons and Muslims Are More Alike Than You Might Think. Penerbit: Xulon Press.

Klemm, W.R. 2017. Accommodating Religion to Modern Neuroscience. *Mental Health, Religion & Culture* 20 (1): 1–19.

Kneale, Matthew. 2015. *An Atheist's History of Belief: Understanding Our Most Extraordinary Invention*. Berkeley, CA: Counterpoint.

Konner, Melvin. 1982. *The Tangled Wing: Biological Constraints on the Human Spirit*. New York: Holt, 2nd ed. 2002, 2003.

———. 2019. *Believers: Faith in Human Nature*. Rvw Elaine Pagels, NYTBR.

Kors, Alan Charles. 1976. *D'Holbach's Coterie: An Enlightenment in Paris*. Princeton, NJ: Princeton University Press.

Kramer, Fritz W. 1985. Empathy—Reflections on the History of Ethnology in Pre-Fascist Germany: Herder, Creuzer, Bastian, Bachofen, and Frobenius. *Dialectical Anthropology (Historical Archive)* 9 (1–4): 337–347.

Kripal, Jeffrey J. 2001. *Roads of Excess, Palaces of Wisdom: Eroticism and Reflexivity in the Study of Mysticism*. Chicago: University of Chicago Press.

Kselman, Thomas. 2008. How Abundant is 'Abundant History'?, "'Abundant History': A Forum". *Historically Speaking*: 16–18.

Kugel, James L. 2011. *In the Valley of the Shadow: On the Foundations of Religious Belief*. New York: Free Press.

Kuklick, Bruce. 1985. *Churchmen and Philosophers: From Jonathan Edwards to John Dewey*. New Haven, CT: Yale University Press.

Kurtz, Angela Astoria. 2009. God, not Caesar: Revisiting National Socialism as 'Political Religion'. *History of European Ideas* 35: 236–252.

Kwan, Kai-man. The Argument from Religious Experience. In *The Blackwell Companion to Natural Theology*. Malden, MA: Blackwell.

Lambek, Michael. 1982. *Human Spirits: A Cultural Account of Trance in Mayotte* [Comoro Archipelago]. Cambridge: Cambridge University Press.

Landmann, M. 1976. Critiques of Reason from Weber to Bloch. *Telos* 29: 187–198.

Lattin, Don. 2010. *The Harvard Psychedelic Club: How Timothy Leary, Ram Dass, Huston Smith and Andrew Weil Killed the Fifties and Ushered in a New Age for America*. New York: HarperCollins.

Laughlin, Charles D., John McManus, and Eugene G. D'Aquili. 1990. *Brain, Symbol, and Experience: Towards a Neurophenomenology of Human Consciousness*. Boston: New Science Library, Shambhala pb June 16, 1990.

Laurendeau, Normand M. 2013. Christian Mysticism and Science: The Psychological Dimension. *Theology and Science*. Published Online.

Lawrence, Bruce. 1989. *Defenders of God: The Fundamentalist Revolt Against the Modern Age*. Columbia, SC: University of South Carolina Press, 2nd ed. 1995.

Leithart, Peter J. 2014. *Gratitude: An Intellectual History*. Waco, TX: Baylor University Press, 2018.

Leuba, J.H. 1912. *The Psychological Study of Religion: Its Origin, Function, and Future*. New York: Macmillan.

———. 1916. *The Belief in God and Immortality*. Boston: Sherman, French.

Levitt, Norman. 2007. What a Friend We Have in Dawkins. *eSkeptic*.

Lewis, Ioan M. 1971. *Ecstatic Religion: A Study of Shamanism and Spirit Possession*. Penguin. 3rd ed. New York: Routledge, 2003.

Lilla, Mark. "What is Counter-Enlightenment?" in Joseph Mali & Robert Wokler, eds. Isaiah Berlin's Counter-Enlightenment, Transactions of the American Philosophical Society, 93:5(2003), pp 1–12.

———. 2007. *The Stillborn God: Religion, Politics and the Modern West*. New York: Knopf.

Linz, Juan. 1996. The Religious Use of Politics and/or the Political Use of Religion. In *Totalitarianism and Political Religion*. Vol. 1 of Concepts for the Comparison of Dictatorships, ed. H. Maier. Trans. J. Bruhn. New York: Dover Publications, 2004. ("Political religion" as a solecism, since politics is by definition un-transcendental).

Livingston, Kenneth R. 2005. Religious Practice, Brain, and Belief. *Journal of Cognition and Culture* 5 (1–2): 75–117. ("self-identified neurotheologians").

Lloyd, Vincent W. 2011. *The Problem with Grace: Reconfiguring Political Theology*. Stanford, CA: Stanford University Press.

Locke, John. 1689. Essay Concerning Human Understanding. Ed. Peter H. Nidditch, Oxford: Clarendon Press, 1975.

Loveland, J. 2001. Buffon, the Certainty of Sunrise, and the Probabilistic Reductio Ad Absurdum. *Archive for History of Exact Sciences* 55 (5): 465–477.

Löwith, Karl. 1949. *Meaning in History: The Theological Implication of the Philosophy of History*. Chicago: University of Chicago Press. Later translated into German titled *Weltgeschichte und Heilsgeschehen* [World History and the Event of Salvation].

Luckmann, Thomas. 1967. *The Invisible Religion*. New York: Macmillan.

Luhmann, Niklas. 2013. *A Systems Theory of Religion*, Cultural Memory in the Present. Ed. André Kieserling and Trans. David A. Brenner with Adrian Hermann. Stanford, CA: Stanford University Press.

Luhrmann, Tanya M. 2004. Yearning for God: Trance as a Culturally Specific Practice and Its Implications for Understanding Dissociative Disorders. *Journal of Trauma and Dissociation. Special Issue: Dissociation in Culture* 5 (2): 101–129.

———. 2005. The Art of Hearing God: Absorption, Dissociation, and Contemporary American Spirituality. *Spiritus* 5 (2): 133–157.

———. 2012. *When God Talks Back: Understanding the American Evangelical Relationship with God*. New York: Knopf.

Luhrmann. 2014. Book Symposium: Tanya Luhrmann's *When God Talks Back. Religion, Brain & Behavior* 4 (1): 65–72. https://doi.org/10.1080/2153599X.2013.768536.
Lustick, Ian S. 1988. *For Land and the Lord: Jewish Fundamentalism in Israel.* New York: Council on Foreign Relations.
Maalouf, Amin. 2001. *In the Name of Identity: Violence and the Need to Belong*. Trans. Barbara Bray. New York: Arcade Publishing, 2002.
MacCormack, Sabine. 2006. Gods, Demons, and Idols in the Andes. *Journal of the History of Ideas* 67 (4): 623–648.
MacDonald, Michael. 1981. *Mystical Bedlam: Madness, Anxiety, and Healing in Seventeenth-Century England.* New York: Cambridge University Press.
MacIntyre, Alasdair. 1981. *After Virtue*. London: Duckworth. 2nd ed. Notre Dame, IN: Notre Dame University Press, 1984.
Mack, Phyllis. 1993. *Visionary Women: Ecstatic Prophecy in Seventeenth-Century England.* Berkeley: University of California Press.
———. 1999. Die Prophetin als Mutter: Antoinette Bourignon. In *Im Zeichen der Krise. Im Europa des 17. Jahrhunderts*, ed. Hartmut Lehmann and A.C. Trepp. Göttingen: Vandenhoeck & Ruprecht.
Malebranche, Nicholas. 1680. *Traité de la nature et de la grâce* [Treatise on Nature and Grace (1695)]. Trans. with intro. and notes by Patrick Riley. Oxford: Clarendon Press, 1992.
Mali, Joseph, and Robert Wokler, eds. 2003. Isaiah Berlin's Counter-Enlightenment. *Transactions of the American Philosophical Society* 93 (5): 1–196.
Malony, H. 1991. *Newton. Psychology of Religion: Personalities, Problems, Possibilities*. Grand Rapids, MI: Baker Pub Group.
Marcuse, Herbert. 1955. *Eros and Civilization: A Philosophical Inquiry into Freud.* Boston: Beacon Press, 2nd ed. 1966, 1974.
Marsden, George M. 1977. Fundamentalism as an American Phenomenon: A Comparison with British Evangelicalism. *Church History* 46.
———. 1991. *Understanding Fundamentalism and Evangelicalism.* Grand Rapids, MI: Eerdman's, 1998.
———. 2001. *Religion and American Culture*. 2nd ed. San Diego: Harcourt College Publishers.
Martin, David. 1993. *Tongues of Fire: The Explosion of Protestantism in Latin America*. Oxford, UK & Cambridge, MA: Blackwell.
Martin, Luther H. 2002. Marcel Gauchet: The Disenchantment of the World. In *Review Symposium in Method & Theory in the Study of Religion*, vol. 14, 114–120. Leiden: Koninklijke Brill NV.
Marty, Martin R., and R. Scott Appleby, eds. 1995. *Fundamentalisms Comprehended*, The Fundamentalism Project. Vol. 5. Chicago: University of Chicago Press, 2004.
Matossian, Mary Kilbourne. 1989. Great Awakening or Great Sickening. In *Poisons of the Past: Molds, Epidemics and History*. New Haven, CT: Yale University Press.
Maza, Sarah. 2004. Stephen Greenblatt, New Historicism, and Cultural History, or, What We Talk About When We Talk About Interdisciplinarity. *Modern Intellectual History* I (2): 249–265.
McCutcheon, Russell T. 2001. *Critics Not Caretakers: Redescribing the Public Study of Religion*. New York: State University of New York Press.
McFetridge, Grant. 2004. *Peak States of Consciousness: Theory and Applications*. Vol. 1 of *Breakthrough Techniques for Exceptional Quality of Life*. Institute for the Study of Peak States Press.
———. 2008. *Peak States of Consciousness: Theory and Applications*. Vol. 2 of Acquiring Extraordinary Spiritual and Shamanic States. Institute for the Study of Peak States Press.
McGinn, Bernard, ed. 1987. *Encyclopedia of Apocalypticism*. New York: Continuum.
———. 1994–2018. Presence of God: A History of Western Christian Mysticism. 7 vols. Herder & Herder, New York.
McGinn, Bernard, and Moshe Idel, eds. 1996. *Mystical Union in Judaism, Christianity, and Islam: An Ecumenical Dialogue*. New York: Continuum International.
McKenzie, J.G. 1940. *Psychology, Psychotherapy and Evangelicalism*. New York: Routledge, 2018.

McKenzie, Alan T. 1990. *Certain, Lively Episodes: The Articulation of Passion in Eighteenth-Century Prose*. Athens: University of Georgia Press.
McLoughlin, William G. 1961. Pietism and the American Character. *American Quarterly* 13.
———. 1967. *Isaac Backus and the American Pietist Tradition*. Boston: Little, Brown, 1970.
———. 1978. *Revivals, Awakenings, and Reform: An Essay on Religion and Social Change in America, 1607–1977*, Chicago History of American Religion. Chicago: University of Chicago Press, 1980.
McNamara, Patrick. 2010. *The Neuroscience of Religious Experience*. Cambridge: Cambridge University Press.
McNeill, William H. 1997. *Keeping Together in Time: Dance and Drill in Human History*. Cambridge, MA: Harvard University Press.
Michael, Mark. 2008. *Hysterical Men: The Hidden Mystery of Male Nervous Illness*. Cambridge, MA: Harvard University Press.
Miles, Jack. 2019. *Religion As We Know It: An Origin Story*. (Rvw Elaine Pagels, NYTBR, 1 Dec 2019).
Miller, Peter N. 2006. History of Religion Becomes Ethnology: Some Evidence from Peiresc's Africa. *Journal of the History of Ideas* 67 (4): 675–696.
Moser, Paul K. 2013. *The Severity of God: Religion and Philosophy Reconceived*. Cambridge: Cambridge University Press.
Mumford, M.A. Snell, and M. Hein. 1993. Varieties of Religious Experience: Continuity and Change in Religious Involvement. *Journal of Personality* 61: 289–293.
Murphy, Larry G., J. Gordon Melton, and Gary L. West, eds. 1993. *Encyclopedia of African-American Religions*, Religion and Society series. Vol. 2. New York: Routedge/Berkshire Publishing Group.
Murrell, Nathaniel Samuel. 2010. *Afro-Caribbean Religions: An Introduction to Their Historical, Cultural, and Sacred Traditions*. Philadelphia: Temple University Press.
Nagel, Thomas. 2006. Review of Dawkins. In *The New Republic*. (By "as much an outsider to religion" as Dawkins).
Ndjio, Basile. 2008. Mokoagne moni: Sorcery and New Forms of Wealth in Cameroon. *The Religion of Fools? Superstition Past and Present; Past & Present* 199 (Supplement 3): 271–289. http://past.oxfordjournals.org/content/vol199/suppl_3/index.dtl?etoc.
Nelson, James B. 1992. *The Intimate Connections: Male Sexuality, Masculine Spirituality*. London: SPCK.
Nelson, Robert H. 2003. *Economics as Religion: From Samuelson to Chicago and Beyond*. University Park, PA: Penn State University Press.
Nelson, James B., and Sandra P. Longfellow, eds. 1994. *Sexuality and the Sacred: Sources for Theological Reflection*. Louisville, KY: Westminster/John Knox Press.
Newberg, Andrew B., and Mark Robert Waldman. 2009. *How God Changes Your Brain: Breakthrough Findings from a Leading Neuroscientist*. New York: Ballantine Books.
Newberg, Andrew. 2013. *Principles of Neurotheology*, Ashgate Science and Religion Series. New York: Ashgate.
———. 2014. *The Metaphysical Mind: Probing the Biology of Philosophical Thought*. San Bernardino, CA: CreateSpace. (Kindle ed. 2014).
———. 2015. *God and the Brain: The Physiology of Spiritual Experience*. Original recording by Sounds True, Oct 7.
Newberg, Andrew B., and Eugene D'Aquili. Why God Won't Go Away: Brain Science and the Biology of Belief. New York: Free Press, 2001. New York: Ballantine, 2002. Kindle ed. 2008.
Newberg, Andrew B., and Mark Robert Waldman. 2006a. *Born to Believe: God, Science, and the Origin of Ordinary and Extraordinary Beliefs*. New York: Free Press. Atria Books reprint, 2006.
———. 2006b. *Why We Believe What We Believe: Uncovering Our Biological Need for Meaning, Spirituality, and Truth*. New York: Free Press.
———. 2016. *How Enlightenment Changes Your Brain: The New Science of Transformation*. New York: Penguin/Random House, Kindle ed.

Nichols, Aidan. 1991. *A Grammar of Consent: The Existence of God in Christian Tradition*. Notre Dame, IN: University of Notre Dame Press.

Niebuhr, Reinhold. 1927. *Does Civilization Need Religion? A Study in the Social Resources and Limitations of Religion in Modern Life*. New York: Macmillan Co.

———. 1932. *Moral Man and Immoral Society: A Study of Ethics and Politics*. New York: Charles Scribner's Sons.

———. 1935. *An Interpretation of Christian Ethics*. New York: Harper & Brothers. New York: Meridian, 1956.

———. 1937. *Beyond Tragedy: Essays on the Christian Interpretation of History*. New York: Scribner's.

———. 1941. *The Nature and Destiny of Man: A Christian Interpretation*. Vol. 1 of Human Nature. New York: Charles Scribner's Sons. Vol. 2 of Human Destiny. New York: Scribner's, 1943.

———. 1944. *The Children of Light and the Children of Darkness: A Vindication of Democracy and a Critique of Its Traditional Defense*. New York: Scribner's.

———. 1949. *Faith and History: A Comparison of Christian and Modern Views of History*. New York: Scribner's.

———. 1952. *The Irony of American History*. New York: Scribner's.

———. 1955. *The Self and the Dramas of History*. New York: Scribner's.

———. 1958. *Pious and Secular America*. New York: Scribner's.

Niewûhner, F., and Yves Labbé, eds. 1997. *Petit dictionnaire des philosophes de la religion*. Belgium: Brepols.

Orr, H. Allen. 2007. A Mission to Convert. (Rvw Dawkins, Wolpert, Roughgarden). *NY Review of Books* 54 (1). www.nybooks.com/articles/19775.

Orsi, Robert A. 2004. *Between Heaven and Earth: The Religious Worlds People Make and the Scholars Who Study Them*. Princeton, NJ: Princeton University Press.

———. 2008a. Abundant History: Marian Apparitions as Alternative Modernity, "'Abundant History': A Forum". *Historically Speaking*: 12–16.

———. 2008b. A Response to the Commentary on 'Abundant History', "'Abundant History': A Forum". *Historically Speaking*: 25–26.

Pals, Daniel L. 2000. 12: Intellect. In *Guide to the Study of Religion*, ed. Willi Braun and Russell T. McCutcheon. New York: Continuum, Repr. 2006, 2007, 2009.

Pecorino, Philip A. 2002. *Philosophy of Religion* (Online Textbook): Chap 10 ("A Definition of Religion"), Section 4 ("The Definition"). http://www.qcc.cuny.edu/SocialSciences/ppecorino/PHIL_of_RELIGION_TEXT/CHAPTER_10_DEFINITION/The-Definition-of-Religion.htm.

Pigliucci, Massimo. 2002. Talk to the Secular Humanists of the Lowcountry in Charleston, South Carolina. *The Separationist*. Newsletter of SHL. http://life.bio.sunysb.edu/~massimo/lectures/mystical-experiences.pdf.

Pike, Nelson. 1992. *Mystic Union: An Essay in the Phenomenology of Mysticism*, Cornell Studies in the Philosophy of Religion. Ithaca, NY: Cornell University Press.

Pinker, Stephen. 2018. *Enlightenment Now: The Case for Reason, Science, Humanism, and Progress*. New York: Penguin Viking.

Poewe, Karla, ed. 1994. *Charismatic Christianity as a Global Culture*. Columbia, SC: University of South Carolina Press.

Pohlson, Sami. 2016. *Pragmatic Pluralism and the Problem of God*. New York: Fordham University Press.

Polkinghorne, John. 1984. *The Quantum World*, Princeton Science Library. Princeton, NJ: Princeton University Press, 1986.

———. 1998. *Belief in God in an Age of Science*, Dwight Harrington Terry Foundation Lectures. New Haven, CT: Yale University Press.

———. 2010. *A Polkinghorne Reader*. Ed. Thomas Jay Lord. West Conshohocken, PA: Templeton Press.

Pollan, Michael. 2018a. *How to Change Your Mind: What the New Science of Psychedelics Teaches Us About Consciousness, Dying, Addiction, Depression, and Transcendence*. New York: Penguin Press.

———. December 2018b. How Does a Writer Put a Drug Trip Into Words? *New York Times Book Review*.
Preus, J. Samuel, ed. 1987. *Explaining Religion: Criticism and Theory from Bodin to Freud*. New Haven, CT: Yale University Press. Bodin, Cherbury, Fontenelle, Vico, Hume, Comte, Tylor, Durkheim, Freud.
Price, George R. August 1970. Selection and Covariance. *Nature*.
Prince, R., and C. Savage. 1972. Mystical States and the Concept of Regression. In *The Highest State of Consciousness*, ed. John White. Garden City, NY: Doubleday Anchor.
Prothero, Stephen. 2008. *Religious Literacy: What Every American Needs to Know—and Doesn't*. New York: HarperCollins.
Proudfoot, Wayne. 1987. *Religious Experience*. Berkeley: University of California Press.
———, ed. 2004. *William James and a Science of Religions: Reexperiencing the Varieties of Religious Experience*. New York: Columbia University Press.
Proust, Marcel. *A la recherché du temps perdu*, Le côté de Guermantes II. Vol. 7. Paris: Gallimard.
Ptacin, Mira. 2019. *THE IN-BETWEENS: The Spiritualists, Mediums, and Legends of Camp Etna*. New York: Liveright Publishing.
Rachels, James. 1990. *Created from Animals: The Moral Implications of Darwinism*. New York: Oxford University Press.
Randall, John Herman, Jr. 1958. *The Role of Knowledge in Western Religion (1955–1956)*. Boston: Starr King Press.
Rawls, John. 2000. *Lectures on the History of Moral Philosophy*. Cambridge, MA: Harvard University Press.
Regan, C.H.N. Malony, and B. Beit-Hallahmi. 1980. Psychologists and Religion: Professional Factors and Personal Belief. *Review of Religious Research* 21: 208–217.
Renz, Karl. 2005. *The Myth of Enlightenment: Seeing Through the Illusion of Separation*. Agoura Hills, CA: Inner Directions Foundation.
Reynolds, Anthony. 2005. Romantic Ignorance the Hope of Nonknowledge. *Angelaki: Journal of Theoretical Humanities* 10 (3): 15–25.
Rieff, Philip. 2007. *Charisma: The Gift of Grace, and How It Has Been Taken Away From Us*. New York: Pantheon Books.
Robespierre. 1967. *Oeuvres de Maximilien Robespierre*. Vol. 10 of *Discours, 5e partie, 27 juillet 1793–27 juillet 1794*, ed. Marc Bouloiseau et al. Paris: Société des Études robespierristes.
Rorty, Richard, and Gianni Vattimo. 2004. *The Future of Religion*. Il futuro della Religione. Solidarità, carità. Ironia. Garzanti Libri. Ed. Santiago Zabala. New York: Columbia University Press, 2005.
Rosenthal, Judy. 1998. *Possession, Ecstasy, and the Law in Ewe Voodoo*. Charlottesville: University of Virginia Press.
Roughgarden, Joan. 2007. *Evolution and Christian Faith: Reflections of an Evolutionary Biologist*. New York: Island.
Rousseau, Jean-Jacques. 1761a. *Émile*. Œuvres complètes, Tome IV. Paris: Gallimard/Pléiade, 1969.
———. 1761b. *Émile*. Trans. Harvard Classics. Vol 34.
Rubiés, Joan-Pau. 2006. Theology, Ethnography, and the Historicization of Idolatry. *Journal of the History of Ideas* 67 (4): 571–596.
Sacks, Oliver. August 2012. Altered States: Self-Experiments in Chemistry. *The New Yorker*.
Santayana, George. 1905. The Life of Reason: The Phases of Human Progress, Vol. 3 of 5 of Reason in Religion. London: Prometheus, 1998.
Sasson, Diane. 1983. *The Shaker Spiritual Narrative*. Knoxville: University of Tennessee Press.
Satel, Sally, and Scott Lilienfeld. 2013. *Brainwashed: The Seductive Appeal of Mindless Neuroscience*. New York: Basic Books. (Versus Andrew Newberg).
Saul, John Ralston. 1992. *Voltaire's Bastards: The Dictatorship of Reason in the West*. New York: Vintage Books, 1993.
Schardt, Bill, and David Large. Wittgenstein, Tolstoy and The Gospel in Brief. *The Philosopher* LXXXIX. http://atschool.eduweb.co.uk/cite/staff/philosopher/witty.htm.

Scherer, Matthew. 2015. *Beyond Church and State: Democracy, Secularism, and Conversion*. Cambridge: Cambridge University Press.
Schering, Ernst. 1982. Pietismus und die Renaissance der Mystik. Pierre Poiret als Interpret und Wegbereiter der romanischen Mystik in Deutschland. In *Pietismus-Herrentum-Erweckungsbewegung*. Cologne.
Schleiermacher, Friedrich. 1821. *Theology of Schleiermacher: A Condensed Presentation of His Chief Work*. The Christian Faith [*Glaubenslehre*]. Translated Christian Classics Ethereal Library (CCEL).
Schopenhauer, Arthur. 1851. Religion, A Dialogue [*Parerga und Paralipomena*]. In *Essays and Aphorisms: The Essays of Arthur Schopenhauer*. Trans. T. Bailey Saunders, M.A., Project Gutenberg EBook. http://www.gutenberg.org/catalog/world/readfile?fk_files=1478212&pageno=1-5.
Schreiner, Susan. 2010. *Are You Alone Wise? The Search for Certainty in the Early Modern Era*, Oxford Studies in Historical Theology. New York: Oxford University Press.
Schutt, Bill. 2017. *Cannibalism: A Perfectly Natural History*. Chapel Hill, NC: Algonquin Books of Chapel Hill.
Scott, David. 1999. An Obscure Miracle of Connection. In *Refashioning Futures: Criticism after Postcoloniality*, 106–127. Princeton, NJ: Princeton University Press.
Seldes, Gilbert. 1928. *The Stammering Century*. New edition, Ed. Greil Marcus. New York: New York Review Books, 2012.
Semmel, Bernard. 1971. The Halévy Thesis. *Encounter* 37 (1): 44–56.
———. 1974. *The Methodist Revolution*. London: Heinemann.
Semple, Robert A. 1810. *History of the Rise and Progress of Baptists in Virginia*. Richmond, VA: John O'Lynch. (Revised ed. Richmond: Pitt and Dickinson, 1894).
Shafranske, E.P. 1996. *Religion and the Clinical Practice of Psychology*, Psychology of religion. Washington, DC: American Psychological Association.
Shafranske, E.P., and H.N. Malony. 1990. Clinical Psychologists: Religious and Spiritual Orientations and their Practice of Psychotherapy. *Psychotherapy* 27: 72–78.
Shaftesbury, Anthony Ashley Cooper, 3rd Earl of (1671–1713). 1707. A Letter Concerning Enthusiasm. In *Characteristics of Men, Manners, Opinions, Times*, 1708. vol. 1, London: Grant Richards, 1900.
Shah, Timothy Samuel, and Jack Friedman. 2018. *Homo Religiosus?: Exploring the Roots of Religion and Religious Freedom in Human Experience*, Cambridge Studies in Religion, Philosophy, and Society. Cambridge: Cambridge University Press.
Sharf, Robert H. 1998. Experience. In *Critical Terms for Religious Studies*, ed. M.C. Taylor. Chicago: University of Chicago Press.
Sharma, Arvind. 2015. *To the Things Themselves: Essays on the Discourse and Practice of Phenomenology of Religion*. Berlin: De Gruyter.
Shaw, Jane. 2008. Abundant History: Protestantism and Alternative Modernities, "'Abundant History': A Forum". *Historically Speaking*: 18–20.
Sherman, David. 2016. Woolf's Secular Imagery. *Modernism/Modernity* 23 (4): 711–731.
Shermer, Michael. August 2015a. The Meaning of Life in a Formula. *Scientific American*: 86.
———. 2015b. *The Moral Arc: How Science Makes Us Better People*. New York: St. Martin's Griffin, 2016.
———. 2017. *Heavens on Earth: The Scientific Search for the Afterlife, Immortality, and Utopia*. New York: Henry Holt & Company.
———. January 2019. The Case for Scientific Humanism. *Scientific American*.
Shostak, Marjorie. 1982. *Nisa: The Life and Words of a!Kung Woman*. Cambridge, MA: Harvard University Press, 1989.
Shrier, Paul, and Cahleen Shrier. 2008. Empathy: Mirror Neurons, Pauline Theology, and the Meaning of Care. *Journal of Pastoral Theology* 18 (1): 25–43.
Shulevitz, Judith. 2011. Time and Possibilities. Rvw James L. Kugel. In *In the Valley of the Shadow*. New York: Free Press. *New York Times*, February 2011.

Shweder, R. 1990. *Thinking Through Cultures*. New York: Cambridge University Press.
Sicard, abbé. 1895. *A la recherche d'une religion civile*. Paris, 1976.
Silk, Mark. 2004. Numa Pompilius and the Idea of Civil Religion in the West. *Journal of the American Academy of Religion* 72 (4).
Simpson, George Eaton. 1962. *The Shango Cult in Nigeria and Trinidad*. onlinelibrary.wiley.com/doi/10.1525/aa.1962.64.6.02a00050/pdf.
———. 1965. *The Shango Cult in Trinidad*. Rio Piedras: University of Puerto Rico, Inst. of Caribbean Studies.
———. 1970. *Religious Cults of the Caribbean: Trinidad, Jamaica, and Haiti*. 2nd ed. Rio Piedras: University of Puerto Rico Press.
———. 1978. *Black Religion in the New World*. New York: Columbia University Press.
Smith, Wilfred Cantwell. 1979. *Faith and Belief: The Difference Between Them*. Princeton, NJ: Princeton University Press. Repr. Boston: Oneworld Publications, 1998.
Smith, John Maynard. 1982. *Evolution and the Theory of Games*. Cambridge: Cambridge University Press.
Smith, Jonathan Z. 1978. *Map is not Territory: Studies in the History of Religions*. Brill Academic Pub. Chicago: University of Chicago Press, 1993.
Smith, J.Z., ed. 1995. *The Harper-Collins Dictionary of Religion*. San Francisco: HarperSanFrancisco. (Psychology of religion).
Smith, David Norman. 1998a. Faith, Reason, and Charisma: Rudolf Sohm, Max Weber, and the Theology of Grace. *Sociological Inquiry* 68 (1): 32–60.
Smith, Jonathan Z. 1998b. Religion. In *Critical Terms for Religious Studies.*, ed. Mark C. Taylor, 2nd ed. Chicago: University of Chicago Press.
———. 1998c. Religion, Religions, Religious. In *Critical Terms for Religious Studies*, ed. Mark C. Taylor, 269–284. Chicago and London: University of Chicago Press.
———. 2000. 3: Classification. In *Guide to the Study of Religion*, ed. Willi Braun and Russell T. McCutcheon. New York: Continuum. Repr. 2006, 2007, 2009.
Smith, Daniel B. 2007. *Muses, Madmen, and Prophets. Rethinking the History, Science, and Meaning of Auditory Hallucination*. New York: The Penguin Press.
Smith, Aaron C.T. 2008a. The Neuroscience of Spiritual Experience in Organizations. *Journal of Management, Spirituality & Religion* 5 (1): 3–28.
Smith, S.A. 2008b. Introduction. *The Religion of Fools? Superstition Past and Present; Past & Present* 199 (Supplement 3): 7–55. http://past.oxfordjournals.org/content/vol199/suppl_3/index.dtl?etoc.
———, ed. 2008c. *The Religion of Fools? Superstition Past and Present*; *Past & Present*. 199 (Supplement 3). http://past.oxfordjournals.org/content/vol199/suppl_3/index.dtl?etoc.
Sohm, Rudolph. 1892. *Kirchenrecht [Church Law]*. Leipzig: Duncher & Humblot.
Solomon, Sheldon, Jeff Greenberg, and Tim Pyszczynski. 2016. *The Worm at the Core: On the Role of Death in Life*. New York: Penguin.
Srinivas, Tulasi. 2010. *Winged Faith: Rethinking Globalization and Religious Pluralism Through the Sathya Sai Movement*. New York: Columbia University Press.
Starbuck, E.D. 1899. *Psychology of Religion*. New York: Scribner's.
Stark, Rodney. 2001. *One True God: Historical Consequences of Monotheism*. Princeton, NJ: Princeton University Press, 2003.
———. 2005. *The Victory of Reason: How Christianity Led to Freedom, Capitalism, and Western Success*. New York: Random House.
Stark, Rodney, and Wiliam Sims Bainbridge. 1996. *A Theory of Religion*. New Brunswick, NJ: Rutgers University Press.
———. 2013. *Religion, Deviance, and Social Control*. New York: Routledge.
Stark, Rodney, and Roger Finke. 2000. *Acts of Faith: Explaining the Human Side of Religion*. Berkeley: University of California Press. (Using rational choice theory, cost-benefit modeling).
Stark, Rodney, and C[harles] Y[oung] Glock. 1968. *American Piety: The Nature of Religious Commitment*. Berkeley: University of California Press.

Steigmann-Gall, Richard. 2003. *The Holy Reich: Nazi Conceptions of Christianity, 1919–1945*. New York: Cambridge University Press.

Stenger, Victor J. 2007. *God, The Failed Hypothesis: How Science Shows That God Does Not Exist*. New York: Prometheus Books.

Stephen, Michele. 1989. The Self, the Sacred Other, and the Religious Imagination. In *The Religious Imagination in New Guinea*, ed. G. Herdt and M. Stephen. New Brunswick, NJ: Rutgers University Press.

Sterk, Andrea, and Nina Caputo, eds. 2014. *Faithful Narratives: Historians, Religion, and the Challenge of Objectivity*. Ithaca, NY: Cornell University Press.

Strawn, Brad D., and Warren S. Brown. 2014. Living with Evangelical Paradoxes. *Religion, Brain & Behavior* 4 (1): 49–90. In "Book Symposium: Tanya Luhrmann's *When God Talks Back*," *Religion, Brain & Behavior* 4:1(2014), 65–72. Published online: 01 May 2013.

Strozier, Charles. 1994. *Apocalypse: On the Psychology of Fundamentalism in America*. Boston: Beacon Press.

Sullivan, Winnifred. 1995. *Paying the Words Extra: Religious Discourse in the Supreme Court of the United States*. Cambridge: Center for the Study of World Religions.

Sussman, Robert W., and C. Robert Cloninger. 2011. *Origins of Altruism and Cooperation*: 36 (*Developments in Primatology: Progress and Prospects*). Washington University Conference, March, 2009. Springer, Kindle ed., 2011.

Swatos, William H., Jr., ed. 1998. *Encyclopedia of Religion and Society*. London: Sage Publications/ Rowman & Littlefield. (Online Hartford Institute for Religion Research, Hartford Seminary, http://hirr.hartsem.edu/ency/).

———. 1998. Mysticism. In *Encyclopedia of Religion and Society, Anthropology of Religion*. Walnut Creek, CA: AltaMira. http://hirr.hartsem.edu/ency/Mysticism.htm.

Swift, Jonathan. 1729. *A Modest Proposal for Preventing the Children of Poor People from Being a Burthen to Their Parents or Country, and for Making Them Beneficial to the Publick*. 3rd ed. Dublin & London: Weaver Bickerton, 1730.

Swinburne, Richard. 1996. *The Existence of God*. New York: Oxford University Press. 2nd ed. of *Is there a God?* Oxford University Press, 2004.

Tashjian, Victoria B., and rvw Toyin Falola. 2004. Ghana in Africa and the World: Essays in Honor of Adu Boahen. *African Studies Review* 47 (2): 168–171.

Taves, Ann, ed. 1989. *Religion and Domestic Violence in Early New England: The Memoirs of Abigail Abbot Bailey*. Bloomington: Indiana University Press.

———, ed. 1999. *Fits, Trances, & Visions: Experiencing Religion and Explaining Experience from Wesley to James*. Princeton, NJ: Princeton University Press.

———, ed. 2009. *Religious Experience Reconsidered: A Building-Block Approach to the Study of Religion and Other Special Things*. Princeton, NJ: Princeton University Press. Kindle ed.

Taylor, Charles. 1989. *Sources of the Self: The Making of the Modern Identity*. Cambridge, MA: Harvard University Press, 1992. (Enlightenment values in public institutions, Romantic ones in private).

Taylor, Charles. 2007. *A Secular Age*. Cambridge, MA: Harvard University Press.

———. 2011. Why We Need a Radical Redefinition of Secularism. In *The Power of Religion in the Public Sphere*, ed. Eduardo Mendieta and Jonathan Vanantwerpen, 34–59. New York: Columbia University Press.

Taylor, Mark C., ed. 1998. *Critical Terms for Religious Studies*. 2nd ed. Chicago: University of Chicago Press.

Taylor, Eugene. 1999a. *Shadow Culture: Psychology and Spirituality*. Washington, DC: Counterpoint.

Taylor, Mark C. 1999b. *About Religion: Economies of Faith in Virtual Culture*. Chicago: University of Chicago Press.

Thiselton, Anthony. 2002. *A Concise Encyclopedia of the Philosophy of Religion*. Oxford, UK: Oneworld.

Thun, Nils. 1948. *The Behmenists and the Philadelphians: A Contribution to the Study of English Mysticism in the 17th and 18th Centuries*. Uppsala: Almquist & Wiksells.

Tolentino, Jia. May 2019. Losing Religion and Finding Ecstasy in Houston: Christianity Formed My Deepest Instincts, and I have Been Walking Away from it for Half My Life. *The New Yorker*. https://www.newyorker.com/magazine/2019/05/27/losing-religion-and-finding-ecstasy-in-houston.

Tolstoy, Leo. 1881. *The Gospel in Brief*. Trans. Aylmer Maude at http://www.fredsakademiet.dk/library/gospel.pdf.

———. 1893. *The Kingdom of God is Within You; or Christianity not as a Mystical Teaching but as a New Conception of Life* [*Tsárstvo Bózhiye vnutrí vas*]. (1st published edition in French). English Trans. Mrs Aline Delano (New York, 1894). In *Tolstoy on Civil Disobedience and Non-Violence*, ed. New York: Bergman, 1967; New York: Signet NAL, 1968. Trans. Constance Garnett. New York: Cassell, 1894. https://www.gutenberg.org/ebooks/4602.

———. 1894. Religion and Morality. *Contemporary Review*. Trans. Vladimir Tchertkoff on Wikisource https://en.wikisource.org/wiki/Pamphlets_(Tolstoy)/Religion_and_Morality.

Tomasello, Michael. 2016. *A Natural History of Human Morality*. Cambridge, MA: Harvard University Press.

———. 2018. The Origins of Morality: How We Learned to Put Our Fate in One Another's Hands. *Scientific American* 319 (3): 70–75.

Torrey, E.F. 1986. *Witchdoctors and Psychiatrists*. New York: Harper and Row.

Turner, V. 1969. *The Ritual Process*. Ithaca, NY: Cornell University Press.

Underhill, Evelyn. 1911. *Mysticism: The Nature and Development of Spiritual Consciousness*.

van der Leeuw, Gerardus. 1963. *Religion in Essence and Manifestation - A Study in Phenomenology*. 2 vols. New York: Harper & Row Torchbook. Repr. Princeton University Press, 1986.

Van der Meer, Philip R., and Robert P. Swierenga, eds. 1990. *Belief and Behavior: Essays in the New Religious History*. New Brunswick: Rutgers University Press.

Vermeil, Edmond. 1939. Pourquoi une religion nationale en Allemagne? *Revue de Métaphysique et de Morale* 46 (1): 65–88. ("Religion politique").

Veysey, Laurence. 1978. *The Communal Experience: Anarchist & Mystical Communities in Twentieth-Century America*. Chicago: University of Chicago Press, Phoenix pb edition with a new Preface. (*The Communal Experience: Anarchist & Mystical Counter-Cultures in America*. New York: Harper, 1973. Includes "The Ferrer Colony," "Vedanta Monasteries" and "New Mexico, 1971").

Voegelin, Eric. 1938. The Political Religions. In *Collected Works*, ed. Manfred Henningsen, vol. 5. Columbia, MO: University of Missouri Press, 2000.

von Stuckrad, Kocku. January 2013. Secular Religion: A Discourse–Historical Approach to Religion in Contemporary Western Europe. *Journal of Contemporary Religion*.

Vovelle, Michel. 1988. *La Revolution contre l'Église: De la Raison à l'Être Suprème*. Paris: Éditions Complexes.

Waldman, Mark Robert & Chris Manning. NeuroWisdom: The New Brain Science of Money, Happiness, and Success. Kindle eBook, 2017.

Wallace, Anthony F.C. 1966. *Religion: An Anthropological View*. New York: Random House.

———. 1970. *The Death and Rebirth of the Seneca*. New York: Knopf.

Wallin, J.E. Wallace, and rvw J.G. McKenzie. 1942. Psychology, Psychotherapy and Evangelicalism. *The American Journal of Psychology* 55 (2): 304–304.

Walter, E.V. 1959. Power, Civilization and the Psychology of Conscience. *American Political Science Review* 53 (3).

———. 2006. *Pascal's Fire: Scientific Faith and Religious Understanding*. Oxford, UK: Oneworld.

———. 2013. *Morality, Autonomy, and God*. Oxford, UK: Oneworld.

Ward, Keith. 2007. *The Case for Religion*. Oxford, UK: Oneworld.

Weber, Max. 1922. *Sociology of Religion*. Trans. Ephraim Fischoff, 1961. Beacon Press. 2nd ed. 1993.

———. 1968. *Max Weber on Charisma and Institution Building: Selected Papers*. Chicago: University of Chicago Press.
Weber, Eugene. 1999. *Apocalypses: Prophecies, Cults, and Millennial Beliefs Through the Ages*. Cambridge: Harvard University Press.
Weber, Max. 2001. *The Protestant Ethic and the Spirit of Capitalism (1904–1905)*. Trans. Talcott Parsons. New York: Routledge.
Weishampel, J.F., Sr. 1858. *The Testimony of a Hundred Witnesses: Or, The Instrumentalities by Which Sinners Are Brought To Embrace the Religion of Jesus Christ. From Christians of Different Denominations*. Compiled Elder J. F. Weishampel, Sen. Baltimore: J. F. Weishampel Jr.
Weiss, Ellen. 1987. *City in the Woods: The Life and Design of an American Camp Meeting on Martha's Vineyard*. New York: Oxford University Press.
Wenger, Tisa. 2009. *We Have a Religion: The 1920s Pueblo Indian Dance Controversy and American Religious Freedom*. Chapel Hill: University of North Carolina Press.
Wexler, Bruce E. 2007. *Brain and Culture: Neurobiology, Ideology, and Social Change*. Cambridge, MA: MIT Press.
White, John, ed. 1972. *The Highest State of Consciousness*. Garden City, NY: Doubleday Anchor. White Crow Books, 2012.
Wildman, Wesley J. 2014. *Religious and Spiritual Experiences*. Cambridge: Cambridge University Press.
Williams, George C. 1966. *Adaptation and Natural Selection: A Critique of Some Current Evolutionary Thought*. Princeton, NJ: Princeton University Press, 1996.
Wittgenstein, Ludwig. 1922. *Tractatus Logico-Philosophicus*. Trans. C.K. Ogden. EBook #5740, Project Gutenberg, 2010.
Wolpert, Lewis. 2007. *Six Impossible Things Before Breakfast: The Evolutionary Origins of Belief*. New York: Norton.
Wood, James, and rvw Sam Harris. December 2006. Letter to a Christian Nation. *The New Republic*.
Wright, Robert. 1994. *The Moral Animal: Why We Are the Way We Are: The New Science of Evolutionary Psychology*. New York: Vintage, 1995.
Yalom, I.D. 1980. *Existential Psychotherapy*. New York: Basic Books.
Yandell, Ketih E. 1994. *The Epistemology of Religious Experience*. Cambridge: Cambridge University Press.
Yandell, Keith E. 1995. *The Epistemology of Religious Experience*. Cambridge: Cambridge University Press.
Yong, Amos. 2004. The Holy Spirit and the World Religions: On the Christian Discernment of Spirit(s) 'After' Buddhism. *Buddhist-Christian Studies* 24: 191–207.
Young, Jason R. 2011. *Rituals of Resistance: African Atlantic Religion in Kongo and the Lowcountry South in the Era of Slavery*. Baton Rouge, LA: Louisiana State University Press.
Ziolkowski, Theodore. 2007. *Modes of Faith: Secular Surrogates for Lost Religious Belief*. Chicago: University of Chicago Press.
Žižek, Slavoj. 2000. *The Fragile Absolute—or, Why is the Christian Legacy Worth Fighting for?* New York: Verso.

Index

W. R. Everdell, *The Evangelical Counter-Enlightenment*, Boston Studies in Philosophy, Religion and Public Life 9,
https://doi.org/10.1007/978-3-030-69762-4

T

Z